The UN anc

Through an … ng international territorial administration, … ekeeping, the implementation of sanctions and the provision of humanitarian aid – Guglielmo Verdirame shows that the powers exercised by the UN carry a serious risk of human rights abuse. The International Law Commission has codified and developed the law of institutional responsibility, but, while indispensable, these principles and rules cannot on their own ensure compliance and accountability. The 'liberty deficit' of the UN, and of other international organisations, remains an urgent legal and political problem. Some solutions may be available; indeed, recent state and institutional practice offers interesting examples in this respect. But at a fundamental level we need to ask whether the power shift from states to international organisations really advances liberty.

GUGLIELMO VERDIRAME is Professor of International Law at the Department of War Studies and the School of Law at King's College London. Before taking on this position, he was a Lecturer at the University of Cambridge and Fellow of the Lauterpacht Centre for International Law. His main areas of research and teaching are public international law, and legal and political philosophy. He is a barrister at 20 Essex Street chambers, London.

CAMBRIDGE STUDIES IN INTERNATIONAL AND COMPARATIVE LAW

Established in 1946, this series produces high quality scholarship in the fields of public and private international law and comparative law. Although these are distinct legal sub-disciplines, developments since 1946 confirm their interrelation.

Comparative law is increasingly used as a tool in the making of law at national, regional and international levels. Private international law is now often affected by international conventions, and the issues faced by classical conflicts rules are frequently dealt with by substantive harmonisation of law under international auspices. Mixed international arbitrations, especially those involving state economic activity, raise mixed questions of public and private international law, while in many fields (such as the protection of human rights and democratic standards, investment guarantees and international criminal law) international and national systems interact. National constitutional arrangements relating to 'foreign affairs', and to the implementation of international norms, are a focus of attention.

The Board welcomes works of a theoretical or interdisciplinary character, and those focusing on the new approaches to international or comparative law or conflicts of law. Studies of particular institutions or problems are equally welcome, as are translations of the best work published in other languages.

A list of books in the series can be found at the end of this volume.

The UN and Human Rights

Who Guards the Guardians?

Guglielmo Verdirame

CAMBRIDGE
UNIVERSITY PRESS

CAMBRIDGE UNIVERSITY PRESS
Cambridge, New York, Melbourne, Madrid, Cape Town,
Singapore, São Paulo, Delhi, Mexico City

Cambridge University Press
The Edinburgh Building, Cambridge CB2 8RU, UK

Published in the United States of America by Cambridge University Press, New York

www.cambridge.org
Information on this title: www.cambridge.org/9781107617476

First published 2011
First paperback edition 2013

A catalogue record for this publication is available from the British Library

Library of Congress Cataloguing in Publication Data
Verdirame, Guglielmo.
The UN and human rights : who guards the guardians? / Guglielmo Verdirame.
p. cm. – (Cambridge studies in international and comparative law ; 82)
Includes bibliographical references and index.
ISBN 978-0-521-84190-0 (hardback)
1. United Nations. 2. Human rights. I. Title. II. Series.
K3240.V4695 2011
341.498–dc22 2011014118

ISBN 978-1-107-61747-6 Paperback

For Nina

Contents

Foreword

The framers of the Charter of the United Nations 'decided to create an organisation to ensure respect for fundamental human rights, establish conditions under which justice and the rule of law could be maintained, and "promote social progress and better standards of life in larger freedom"'.[1] But in setting out these lofty ideals they could not have foreseen the wide range of tasks the organisation would be called upon to undertake by its member states and the challenges these would present for it to act consistently with its own expressed moral values. By the end of the first decade of the twenty-first century these have evolved to include peacekeeping, peacebuilding and peace enforcement; field operations; *de jure* exercise of legislative, executive and judicial power through the administration of territory (for a relatively short period as in Timor-Leste or for nearly a decade as in Kosovo); *de facto* exercise of powers in refugee camps; sanctioning behaviour deemed to threaten international peace and security; and delivery of relief or humanitarian assistance in multiple forms and places. None of these undertakings can be performed through following a template; rather the demands of each vary according to place and context, the mandate and the persons involved. There is today a paradox: on the one hand there has been 'declining public confidence'[2] in the organisation while on the other ever more complex and dangerous mandates have been assigned to it.

Alongside the expansion in the nature and functions of international organisations has been another, interrelated, story, that of

[1] Report of the Secretary General, 'In Larger Freedom: Towards Development, Security and Human Rights for All', UN Doc A/59/2005, 21 March 2005, para. 13.
[2] *Ibid.*

the growth of human rights law and procedures. Through the work first of its Commission on Human Rights and more recently that of the Human Rights Council, the UN has created a significant edifice for the protection of human rights and fundamental freedoms. Today UN member states are bound by a plethora of human rights standards and are answerable to a number of mechanisms for failure to comply with those obligations. However, these two stories sit somewhat uneasily together: the UN has too often fallen short in ensuring high standards of respect for fundamental human rights and the rule of law from its own personnel, thereby undermining trust in the institution in the very persons it has been mandated to serve.

These are the themes examined in this book. Professor Verdirame analyses the ways in which the UN (and other international organisations) may be factually responsible for the commission of human rights abuses and the gap between such actions and their accountability. Unlike many international lawyers Professor Verdirame's starting point is that of empirical observation: the witnessing of violations of human rights in refugee camps under the administration and control of UNHCR and the realisation of their not infrequent occurrence. His concern is how those responsible for such abuses as collective punishment of vulnerable inmates can be held accountable. There is of course a vast literature on the UN, describing the ways in which it has responded to its changing place in international relations, including from international lawyers. However, many such studies have focused on a single facet of its work (for example peacekeeping or territorial administration) or a specific mandate (such as that in Rwanda or the former Yugoslavia). More extensive legal discussion has concentrated on its normative functions. In contrast Professor Verdirame provides a detailed account of the organisation's human rights obligations and shortcomings across a broad range of its activities.

Although Professor Verdirame questions the scholarly tradition of non-polemic and dispassionate writing, his work is fully scholarly in the sense of being well researched and based in both institutional practice and legal doctrine. He does not condemn international institutions but accepts the reality that the nature of their work means that they exercise direct power over individuals who are not part of the organisation and who are thus exposed to the risk of human rights violations from this source. What he does ask is that the weakening of state authority through the expansion of international organisations (both numerically and functionally) is not unequivocally accepted as beneficial for human rights protection. Like states, international organisations can and do act abusively, but the development of (albeit limited) avenues of redress for victims of state human rights abuse have not yet been extended in the case of international organisations. Those who have had their human rights violated by UN peacekeeping forces, in UNHCR refugee camps, or by UN bodies bringing relief to afflicted areas remain unlikely to obtain any form of just satisfaction. Professor Verdirame reflects on the various administrative, quasi-judicial and judicial controls that are beginning to be introduced, and sees merit in particular in the legal construct of 'equivalent' protection. Nevertheless he concludes that it remains the case that the liberal democratic state offers the best means for the advancement of human rights. In light of the work of the International Law Commission on the responsibility of international organisations and recent case law, including that of the European Court of Human Rights, I welcome this book as a timely and challenging study of the relationship between states, international organisations and individuals and of the importance of accountability in the international arena, whoever the wrongdoer.

Christine Chinkin
LSE, 2011

Acknowledgements

Two people have shaped my thinking about the topic of this book: Barbara Harrell-Bond and Christine Chinkin. Barbara Harrell-Bond, whom I met while still an LLM student, directed me towards the study of human rights and refugee law. She made it possible for me to embark upon field research on refugees in East Africa for the Refugee Studies Centre at the University of Oxford. As a lawyer fresh from university and with hardly any social sciences training, I had the opportunity to learn how to conduct socio-legal research by working alongside a formidable anthropologist and to observe international organisations in action. Her self-abnegation in the commitment to the cause of refugees and human rights set a standard of moral aspiration, inadequate though it often made me feel. On my return from East Africa, I began a doctorate at the LSE under the supervision of Christine Chinkin, writing a thesis on the accountability of the UN for human rights violations. She, more than anyone else, helped me in the transition to the world of legal scholarship. The discussions we had as part of the supervisions, and those we have had since as colleagues and friends, invigorated me intellectually and charged me with renewed enthusiasm.

I began to think of international organisations as perpetrators of human rights violations during fieldwork in East Africa. If so many refugees had not had the patience to share with me some of their most private and traumatic experiences, I would have remained ignorant. I am grateful to the Ford Foundation, and its then human rights officer in Nairobi, Marguerite Garling, for funding that research, as well as to the colleagues with whom I worked, in particular Hannah Garry and Zachary Lomo. The findings of that research have been published in

Rights in Exile: Janus-Faced Humanitarianism, but Chapter 6 of this book still draws significantly from it.

Before moving to Cambridge, I spent three years as a junior research fellow at Merton College, Oxford. Junior research fellowships are dream jobs for a young academic, and Merton and Oxford offered the best possible intellectual environment. I am indebted to many in Oxford, but especially to Vaughan Lowe and Larry Siedentop: Vaughan for guiding me in my early years as a legal academic and for representing, in his unique effortless and self-effacing way, a model of clarity and intellectual rigour, combining adherence to principles and rules with a measure of healthy incredulity; and Larry for reigniting an interest in political philosophy and the history of ideas that had been left dormant for too long.

In Cambridge, James Crawford has been a great academic mentor. On many occasions I benefited from his legendary promptness at responding to requests for advice and for comments on drafts. No matter how clear I made it that I appreciated how busy he was and I really did not wish to impose on him, within twenty-four hours at most, a reply, which combined clarity, brevity and helpfulness, would arrive.

I have discussed aspects of this book with a great number of other colleagues over the years. With pre-emptive apologies to anyone I may leave out – a forgetfulness that I blame on the frantic pace that characterises the final weeks of work on a book – I would like to mention: the examiners of my PhD thesis, Nigel White and Patricia Tuitt; Mindy Chen-Wishart and Guy Goodwin-Gill in Oxford; Sir Elihu Lauterpacht and Amanda Perreau-Saussine in Cambridge; Jim Cavallaro, Ryan Goodman and Mindy Roseman at Harvard; Katja Peshke who provided me with useful material on Bosnia.

Offering the same pre-emptive apology as above, I should also thank the following people who at various stages provided me with research assistance: Nimrod Avigal; Tomas Furlong; Jessie Hohmann; Rurik Jutting; Rob Miles; Qudsi Rasheed; and Henry Warwick. I am especially indebted to Sean Aughey, Ishaani Shrivastava and Michal Jorek whose help over the last few months was crucial.

On a personal note I should say that this was a very difficult book to complete. *Rights in Exile* and various personal vicissitudes delayed its writing. I would like to thank Nienke van Schaverbeke, Richard Woodham and especially Finola O'Sullivan at Cambridge University Press, not least for their patience.

The people who deserve my deepest gratitude are, in England, friends who have become like family, in particular the late Cornell Adams and Henry Newman; and, in Italy, my mother, my father, my brother and my niece. It is to my mother and my niece that this book is dedicated.

Abbreviations

AC	Appeal Cases
Admin. LR	Administrative Law Reports (Canada)
AFDI	*Annuaire Français de Droit International*
AJIL	*American Journal of International Law*
All ER	All England Law Reports
AOI	Arab Organisation for Industrialisation
Austral. YBIL	*Australian Year Book of International Law*
BSTDB	Black Sea Trade and Development Bank
BverfGE	Bundesverfassungsgericht (Federal Constitutional Court)
BYBIL	*British Year Book of International Law*
CARE	Co-operative for Assistance and Relief Everywhere
CDTs	Conduct and Discipline Units
CDU	(United Nations) Conduct Disciplinary Unit
CEDAW	Convention for the Elimination of All Forms of Discrimination Against Women
CMLR	*Common Market Law Reports*
CMRS	Center for Migration and Refugee Studies
CNRT	National Council of East Timorese Resistance
Com. Int.	Comunitá Internazionale
CTS	Consolidated Treaty Series
DFID	Department for International Development
DHA	Department of Humanitarian Affairs
DLR	*Dominion Law Reports*
DPKO	(United Nations) Department of Peacekeeping Operations
EBRD	European Bank for Reconstruction and Development
EC	European Community

ECJ	European Court of Justice
ECHR	European Convention for the Protection of Human Rights and Fundamental Freedoms
ECOSOC	Economic and Social Council
ECR	European Court Reports
ECtHR	European Court of Human Rights
EEC	European Economic Community
EFSF	European Financial Stability Facility
EHRLR	*European Human Rights Law Review*
EHRR	European Human Rights Reports
EJIL	*European Journal of International Law*
ELR	*European Law Review*
EPAU	Evaluation and Policy Analysis Unit
ESA	European Space Agency
EU	European Union
EUFOR	European Union Force
EULEX	European Union Rule of Law Mission in Kosovo
F.2d	Federal Reporter (Second Series)
F.3d	Federal Reporter (Third Series)
FAO	Food and Agriculture Organisation
FIDA	International Federation of Women Lawyers
FMR	Forced Migration Review (formerly Refugee Participation Network)
FRY	Federal Republic of Yugoslavia
F. Supp.	Federal Supplement
GA	General Assembly
GYBIL	*German Year Book of International Law*
Harv. HR J.	*Harvard Human Rights Journal*
Harv. Int. L. J.	*Harvard International Law Journal*
HRC	Human Rights Committee
Hum. Rts. Q.	*Human Rights Quarterly*
IBRD	International Bank for Reconstruction and Development
ICAO	International Civil Aviation Organisation
ICC	International Criminal Court
ICCPR	International Covenant on Civil and Political Rights
ICESCR	International Covenant on Economic, Social and Cultural Rights
ICJ	International Court of Justice
ICJ Reports	Reports of the International Court of Justice

ICLQ	*International and Comparative Law Quarterly*
ICRC	International Committee of the Red Cross
IDA	International Development Association
IDPs	Internally displaced persons
IFOR	Implementation Force
IGAD	Inter-Governmental Authority on Development
IIC	Independent Inquiry Commission
IJRL	*International Journal of Refugee Law*
ILA	International Law Association
ILC	International Law Commission
ILM	International Legal Materials
ILO	International Labour Organisation
ILOAT	International Labour Organisation Administrative Tribunal
ILR	*International Law Reports*
IMCO	Intergovernmental Maritime Consultative Organisation
IMF	International Monetary Fund
Indian J. Int. L.	*Indian Journal of International Law*
Int. Aff.	*International Affairs*
INTERFET	International Force for East Timor
Int. Org.	*International Organization*
Int. Rev. R.C.	*International Review of the Red Cross*
IPTF	International Police Task Force
IRO	International Refugee Organization
ITC	International Tin Council
J. Ref. St.	*Journal of Refugee Studies*
KFOR	Kosovo Force
KLA	Kosovo Liberation Army
Leiden J. Int. L.	*Leiden Journal of International Law*
LNTS	League of Nations Treaty Series
LWF	Lutheran World Federation
MICAH	International Civilian Support Mission in Haiti
Mich. J.Int.L.	*Michigan Journal of International Law*
MIPONUH	United Nations Civilian Police Mission in Haiti
MINURCA	United Nations Mission in the Central African Republic
MINURCAT	United Nations Mission in the Central African Republic and Chad

MINUSTAH	United Nations Stabilisation Mission in Haiti
MONUSCO	United Nations Organisation Stabilisation Mission in the Democratic Republic of Congo
MOU	Memorandum/a of Understanding
MSF	Médecins sans Frontières
NATO	North Atlantic Treaty Organisation
NDF	Nordic Development Fund
NGO	Non-governmental organisation
NIB	Nordic Investment Bank
N.Y.S.	New York Supplement
OAU	Organisation of African Unity
OIOS	Office of Internal Oversight Services
OLS	Operation Lifeline Sudan
ONUC	United Nations Operation in Congo
ONUMOZ	United Nations Operation in Mozambique
OSCE	Organisation for Security and Co-operation in Europe
RC	*Recueil des Cours de l' Academie de Droit International*
RGDIP	*Révue Générale de Droit International Public*
Riv. It. Dir. Int.	*Rivista Italiana di Diritto Internazionale*
SC	Security Council
SEA/VAM	Sexual Exploitation and Abuse Victim Assessment Mechanism
SFOR	Stabilisation Force in Bosnia and Herzegovina
SGBV	Sex- or gender-based violence
SIU	Special Investigation Unit
SOFAs	Status of Force Agreements
SPLA	Sudan People's Liberation Army
UDHR	Universal Declaration of Human Rights
UK	United Kingdom
UKTS	United Kingdom Treaty Series
UN	United Nations
UNAMET	United Nations Mission in East Timor
UNAMID	United Nations Mission in Darfur
UNAMIR	United Nations Assistant Mission for Rwanda
UNAMSIL	United Nations Mission in Sierra Leone
UNAVEM	United Nations Angola Verification Mission
UNAVEM III	United Nations Angola Verification Mission III
UNDP	United Nations Development Programme
UNEF	United Nations Emergency Force

UNESCO	United Nations Educational Scientific and Cultural Organisation
UNHCR	United Nations High Commissioner for Refugees
UNICEF	United Nations Children's Fund
UNIDO	United Nations Industrial Development Organisation
UNIFIL	United Nations Interim Force in Lebanon
UNITAF	Unified Task Force
UN Jur. YB	*United Nations Juridical Yearbook*
UNMEE	United Nations Mission in Ethiopia and Eritrea
UNMIBH	United Nations Mission in Bosnia and Herzegovina
UNMIH	United Nations Mission in Haiti
UNMIK	United Nations Mission in Kosovo
UNMIS	United Nations Mission in Sudan
UNMISET	United Nations Mission of Support in East Timor
UNMIT	United Nations Integrated Mission in Timor-Leste
UNMOGIP	United Nations Military Observer Group in India and Pakistan
UNOCHA	United Nations Office for the Co-ordination of Humanitarian Affairs
UNOMSIL	United Nations Observer Mission in Sierra Leone
UNOPS	United Nations Office for Project Services
UNOSOM	United Nations Operation in Somalia
UNOSOM II	United Nations Operation in Somalia II
UNOTIL	United Nations Office in Timor Leste
UNPROFOR	United Nations Protection Force
UNRRA	United Nations Relief and Rehabilitation Administration
UNRWA	United Nations Relief and Works Agency for Palestine Refugees in the Middle East
UNSMIH	United Nations Support Mission in Haiti
UNTAC	United Nations Transitional Authority in Cambodia
UNTAES	United Nations Transitional Administration in Eastern Slavonia, Baranja and Western Sirmium
UNTAET	United Nations Temporary Administration in East Timor
UNTAG	United Nations Transitional Assistance Group
UNTEA	United Nations Temporary Administration in West Irian
UNTMIH	United Nations Transition Mission in Haiti
UNTS	United Nations Treaty Series

UNTSO	United Nations Truce Supervision Organisation
US	United States of America
U.S.	United States Supreme Court Reports
USCS	United States Code Service
USSR	Union of Soviet Socialist Republics
USTS	United States Treaty Series
Virg. J. Int. L.	*Virginia Journal of International Law*
WFP	World Food Programme
WHO	World Health Organisation
WTO	World Trade Organisation
Yale H. R. Dev. L. J.	*Yale Human Rights and Development Law Journal*
Yale J. Int. L.	*Yale Journal of International Law*
Yale L. J.	*Yale Law Journal*
YBILC	*Year Book of the International Law Commission*
YB Int. Humanit. L.	*Year Book of International Humanitarian Law*

Table of cases (international)

AD HOC ARBITRATION

COMMITTEE AGAINST TORTURE

EUROPEAN COMMISSION OF HUMAN RIGHTS

EUROPEAN COURT OF HUMAN RIGHTS

EUROPEAN COURT OF JUSTICE

HUMAN RIGHTS COMMITTEE

A v. Australia, Communication No. 560/1993. 295
Sayadi and Vinck v. Belgium, Communication No. 1472/2006. 305–306, 314, 317, 375, 382, 384

INTERNATIONAL COURT OF JUSTICE

Accordance with International Law of the Unilateral Declaration of Independence in Respect of Kosovo, Advisory Opinion, 22 July 2010). 71, 74, 84, 96–97, 259–260, 262
Aegean Sea Continental Shelf (Greece v. Turkey), Order, ICJ Reports (1976) 3.
Aegean Sea Continental Shelf (Greece v. Turkey), Judgment, ICJ Reports (1978) 3. 189 fn 172, 347
Applicability of Article VI, Section 22 of the Convention on the Privileges and Immunities of the United Nations, Advisory Opinion, ICJ Reports (1989) 177. 100, 355–357
Application of the Convention on the Prevention and Punishment of the Crime of Genocide (Bosnia and Herzegovina v. Serbia and Montenegro), Judgment, 26 February 2007). 222
Application of the Convention on the Prevention and Punishment of the Crime of Genocide (Bosnia and Herzegovina v. Yugoslavia), Order, ICJ Reports (1993) 325. 129, 346
Application of the Convention on the Prevention and Punishment of the Crime of Genocide (Bosnia and Herzegovina v. Yugoslavia), Judgment (Preliminary Objections), ICJ Reports (1996) 595. 346
Application for Review of Judgment 333 of the United Nations Administrative Tribunal, Advisory Opinion, ICJ Reports (1987) 18. 323
Armed Activities on the Territory of the Congo (Democratic Republic of Congo v. Uganda), Judgment, ICJ Reports (2005) 168. 172, 327
Border and Transborder Armed Actions (Nicaragua v. Honduras), ICJ Reports (1998) 69. 88
Certain Expenses of the United Nations, Advisory Opinion, ICJ Reports (1962) 151. 63, 66–67, 69, 76, 81, 208, 235, 323–324, 341 fn 82
Certain Phosphate Lands in Nauru (Nauru v. Australia), Judgment (Preliminary Objections), ICJ Reports (1992) 240. 61–62
Constitution of the Maritime Safety Committee of the Intergovernmental Maritime Consultative Organisation, Advisory Opinion, ICJ Reports (1960) 150. 347–348
Corfu Channel Case (UK v. Albania), Judgment (Merits), ICJ Reports (1949) 4. 157

INTERNATIONAL CRIMINAL TRIBUNAL FOR THE FORMER YUGOSLAVIA

PERMANENT COURT OF INTERNATIONAL JUSTICE

WTO

OTHER

Table of cases (national)

CANADA

GERMANY

ITALY

KOSOVO

THE NETHERLANDS

SWITZERLAND

UNITED KINGDOM

A Company Ltd v. Republic of X, High Court, Queen's Bench Division (Commercial Court), 87 ILR 412, [1990] 2 Lloyd's Rep 520. 357
Buron v. Denman, High Court of Admiralty, Parry (ed.) VI *British International Law Cases* (1965) 385. 43
Her Majesty's Treasury v. Mohammed al-Ghabra, R (on the application of Hani El Sayed Sabaei Youssef) [2010] UKSC 2. 350
Her Majesty's Treasury v. Mohammed Jabar Ahmed and others [2010] UKSC 2. 350, 373–375
J.H. Rayner (Mincing Lane) Ltd v. Department of Trade and Industry and Others, House of Lords, [1990] 2 AC 418; High Court, 77 ILR 56; Court of Appeal, 80 ILR 49. 62, 130, 133
Le Louis, High Court of Admiralty (1817), in Parry (ed.), III *British International Law Cases* (1965) 691. 42, 43
Liversidge v. Anderson [1942] A.C. 206. 373
Maclaine Watson v. Department of Trade and Industry, House of Lords, (1990) 29 ILM 670. 130, 133
The Moorcock (1889) 14 PD 64. 79
Nissan v. Attorney General, High Court [1967] 2 All ER 200; Court of Appeal [1968] 1 QB 286; House of Lords [1970] AC 179. 114
R (on the application of Al-Jedda) (FC) (Appellant) v. Secretary of State for Defence (Respondent), [2007] UKHL 58; [2008] 1 AC 332. 104, 113–115, 220, 317, 350, 372–375
R v. Bow Street Stipendiary Magistrate, ex parte Pinochet Ugarte (No. 3), House of Lords, [1999] 2 All ER 97.
R (on the application of Faisal Attiyah Nassar Al-Saadoon, Khalaf Hussain Mufdhi v. Secretary of State for Defence [2009] EWCA Civ 7. 104, 376
R (Limbuela) v. Secretary of State for the Home Department [2006] 1 AC 106. 287
R v. Secretary of State for the Home Department, Ex parte Simms [2000] AC 115. 374
San Juan Nepomuceno, High Court of Admiralty (1824), 1 Hag. Adm. 265, Parry (ed.) III *British International Law Cases* (1965) 711. 43
Westland Helicopters v. Arab Organisation for Industrialisation (AOI), Judgment of the Swiss Federal Court, 19 July 1988, 80 ILR 652; 18 *Revue de l' arbitrage* (1989) 525. 130

UNITED STATES OF AMERICA

Abdi Hosh Ashkir et al. v. United Nations, US District Court for the District of Columbia, Civ. No. 97–2266 (TFH). 352

Table of legal instruments

Treaties are listed in alphabetical order, UN documents in chronological order.

TREATIES

Additional Articles to the Definitive Treaty of Peace and Amity between Austria, Great Britain, Portugal, Prussia, Russia, Sweden and France, Vienna, 30 May 1814; 63 CTS (1814–15) 193.

African Charter on Human and Peoples' Rights, Banjul, 27 June 1981; 21 ILM 58.

Agreement between Great Britain and Muscat for the Termination of the Export of Slaves ('Hammerton Treaty'), 2 October 1845; 99 CTS (1845–46) 27.

Agreement concerning West New Guinea (West Irian) (Indonesia-Netherlands), New York, 15 August 1962; reproduced in 57 AJIL (1963) 493.

Agreement concerning the Nordic Development Fund, 3 November 1988.

Agreement establishing the European Bank for Reconstruction and Development, 29 May 1990.

Agreement establishing the Inter-Governmental Authority on Development, 21 March 1996.

Agreement establishing the Nordic Investment Bank, 1 January 2005.

Agreement for the Prosecution and Punishment of the Major War Criminals of the European Axis, London, 8 August 1945; 82 UNTS 280.

Agreement on CAB International, 4 September 1987.

Agreement on a Comprehensive Political Settlement in Cambodia, Paris, 23 October 1991; 31 ILM 183.

Agreement on the Implementation of Principles Governing the Protection and Provision of Humanitarian Assistance to War-Affected Civilian Populations, between the Government of Sudan, the Sudan Peoples' Liberation Movement (SPLM) and the UN-Operation Lifeline Sudan (OLS), Geneva, 15 December 1999.

Agreement Relating to the Legal Status, Facilities, Privileges, and Immunities of the United Nations Organisation in the Congo, 27 November 1961, 414 UNTS 229.

Border Environment Cooperation Commission – North American Development Bank Charter, amended 6 August 2004.

Charter of the United Nations, San Francisco, 26 June 1945.

Constitution of the Food and Agriculture Organization of the United Nations, Quebec, 16 October 1945, (1946–47) *UN Yearbook* 693; 12 USTS 980.

Constitution of the International Labour Organisation, Part XIII of the Treaty of Peace Between the United States of America, the British Empire, France, Italy, and Japan and Poland, Versailles, 28 June 1919; 225 CTS 188.

Constitution of the World Health Organization, New York, 22 July 1946; 14 UNTS 185.

Convention against Torture and Other Cruel, Inhuman or Degrading Treatment or Punishment, New York, 10 December 1984; 24 ILM 535.

Convention for the Amelioration of the Condition of the Wounded in Armies in the Field, Geneva, 22 August 1864; 129 CTS 361.

Convention for the Elimination of All Forms of Discrimination Against Women, New York, 18 December 1979; 19 ILM 33.

Convention for the Prevention and Punishment of the Crime of Genocide, New York, 9 December 1948; 78 UNTS 277.

Convention on the High Seas, Geneva, 27 April 1958; 450 UNTS 11.

Convention on the Law of the Sea, Montego Bay, 10 December 1982; UN Doc. A/CONF.62/122.

Convention on the Law of Treaties, Vienna, 23 May 1969; 1155 UNTS 331.

Convention on the Law of Treaties between States and International Organisations or between International Organisations, Vienna, 21 March 1986; 25 ILM 543.

Convention on the Privileges and Immunities of the Specialised Agencies of the United Nations, New York, 21 November 1947; 33 UNTS 261.

Convention on the Privileges and Immunities of the United Nations, New York, 13 February 1946; 1 UNTS 15.

Convention on the Rights of the Child, New York, 20 November 1989; 1577 UNTS 3.

Convention on the Safety of United Nations and Associated Personnel, New York, 9 December 1994; GA Res. 49/59.

Convention Relating to the Status of Refugees, Geneva, 28 July 1951; 189 UNTS 137; and Protocol to the Convention relating to the Status of Refugees, Geneva, 31 January 1967; 606 UNTS 267.

Declaration of the Eight Courts Relative to the Abolition of the Slave Trade, Vienna, 8 February 1815; Martens NR-T-II 432.

Declaration of the Eight European Courts on the Abolition of the Slave Trade, 8 February 1815, annexed as Act XV to the 1815 General Treaty of Vienna Congress, 63 CTS 473.

Draft Convention on Expediting the Delivery of Emergency Relief (1984), drafted by the UN Disaster Relief Co-ordinator, UN Doc. A/39/267/Add. 2-E/1984/96/Add.2.

Energy Charter Treaty, Lisbon, 17 December 1994; 2080 UNTS 95.

Engagement between Great Britain and King Fanatoro and the Chiefs of Cape Mount (West Africa), 2 January 1846; 99 CTS (1845–46) 272.

Establishing Agreement of the Black Sea Trade and Development Bank, 30 June 1994.

European Convention for the Protection of Human Rights and Fundamental Freedoms, Rome, 4 November 1950; 213 UNTS 221; Protocol I, Paris, 20 March 1952; Protocol XI, Strasbourg, 11 May 1994.

Exchange of Letters Constituting an Agreement Between the United Nations and Belgium Relating to the Settlement of Claims Filed Against the United Nations in the Congo by Belgian Nationals, 20 February 1965; (1965) UN Jur. YB 39.

Exchange of Letters Constituting an Agreement Between the United Nations and Greece Relating to the Settlement of Claims Filed Against the United Nations in the Congo by Greek Nationals, 20 June 1966; 563 UNTS 3.

Exchange of Letters Constituting an Agreement Between the United Nations and Italy Relating to the Settlement of Claims Filed Against the United Nations in the Congo by Italian Nationals, 18 January 1967; 588 UNTS 197.

Exchange of Letters Constituting an Agreement Between the United Nations and Switzerland Relating to the Settlement of Claims Filed Against the United Nations in the Congo by Swiss Nationals, 3 June 1966; 564 UNTS 193.

Final Act of the Congress of Vienna, Vienna, 9 June 1815; 64 CTS (1815) 492.

General Act of the Brussels Conference on the African Slave Trade, Brussels, 2 July 1890; 173 CTS (1890).

General Framework Agreement for Peace in Bosnia and Herzegovina ('Dayton Peace Agreement'), Paris, 14 December 1995; 35 ILM 75.

Geneva Convention (I) for the Amelioration of the Condition of the Wounded and Sick in Armed Forces in the Field, Geneva, 12 August 1949; 75 UNTS 31.

Geneva Convention (II) for the Amelioration of the Condition of the Wounded, Sick and Shipwrecked Members of the Armed Forces at Sea, Geneva, 12 August 1949; 75 UNTS 85.

Geneva Convention (III) Relative to the Treatment of Prisoners of War, Geneva, 12 August 1949; 75 UNTS 135.

Geneva Convention (IV) Relative to the Protection of Civilians in Time of War, Geneva, 12 August 1949; 75 UNTS 287.

Hague Convention (V) Respecting the Rights and Duties of Neutral Powers and Persons in Case of War on Land, The Hague, 18 October 1907; 1 Bevans 654.

Instrument for the Amendment of the Constitution of the International Labour Organization (ILO Constitution), Montreal, 9 October 1946; 15 UNTS 35.

International Convention for the Elimination of All Forms of Racial Discrimination, New York, 21 December 1965; 660 UNTS 195.

International Covenant on Civil and Political Rights (and Optional Protocol to the International Covenant on Civil and Political Rights), New York, 16 December 1966; 999 UNTS 171.

International Covenant and Economic, Social and Cultural Rights, New York, 16 December 1966; 999 UNTS 3.

Marrakesh Agreement establishing the World Trade Organisation, 15 April 1994; 1867 UNTS 3.

Memorandum of Understanding between the United Nations and Afghanistan, Kabul, May 1998.

Organisation of African Unity: Convention on the Specific Aspects of Refugee Problems in Africa, Addis Ababa, 10 September 1969; 1000 UNTS 46.

Protocol I Additional to the Geneva Conventions of 12 August 1949, and Relating to the Protection of Victims of International Armed Conflict, Geneva, 8 June 1977; 1125 UNTS 3.

Protocol II Additional to the Geneva Conventions of 12 August 1949, and Relating to the Protection of Victims of Non-International Armed Conflicts, Geneva, 8 June 1977; 1125 UNTS 609.

Slavery Convention, Geneva, 25 September 1926, 60 LNTS 253; as modified by the Protocol of 7 December 1953; 212 UNTS 17.

Statute of the International Criminal Court, Rome, 17 July 1998; 37 ILM 999.

Treaties between Great Britain and the Chiefs of Sano and Moricaryah, Malaghea, Fouricane and Benira (West Africa), 20, 23 and 28 May 1845; 98 CTS (1845) 205.

Treaty Establishing the European Community (Amsterdam Consolidated Version), 10 November 1997, C 340 *Official Journal of the EC*.

Treaty for the Suppression of the African Slave Trade, London, 20 December 1841; 92 CTS (1841–32) 437.

Treaty of Peace Between the United States of America, the British Empire, France, Italy, and Japan and Poland, Versailles, 28 June 1919; 225 CTS 188; *ibid.*: Agreement Between the United States of America, Belgium, the British Empire and France, of the One Part, and Germany of the Other Part, with Regard to Military Occupation of the Territories of Rhine.

Treaty on Principles Governing the Activities of States in the Exploration and Use of Outer Space, including the Moon and Other Celestial Bodies (1966), GA Res. 2222 (XXI), 19 December 1966.

Treaty on the Functioning of the European Union, 9 May 2008, C 115/47 *Official Journal of the European Union*.

United Nations Convention on the Law of the Sea, Montego Bay, 30 April 1982; 1833 UNTS 3.

Universal Declaration of Human Rights, GA Res. 217A (III), 10 December 1948.

Universal Postal Convention, Stockholm, 28 August 1924; 40 LNTS 43.

UN DOCUMENTS

Economic and Social Council

Resolutions: Res. 1984/37; Res. 1995/56; Res. 1996/31; Res. 1998/9.

Committee on Non-Governmental Organizations (1998) 'Report of the Economic and Social Council', UN Doc. A/53/3.

Committee on Non-Governmental Organizations, 'NGO Committee Recommends Suspension of Consultative Status for "Reporters Without Borders"', Press Release, 20 May 2009.

(1998) 'Report of the Special Rapporteur on Torture', UN Doc. E/CN.4/1998/38.

(1998) 'Report of the Special Rapporteur on Extra-judicial and Summary Executions', UN Doc. E/CN.4/1998/68/Add. 1.

(1999) General Comment 12, 'The right to adequate food (Art. 11)', UN Doc. E/C.12/1999/5.

(1999) 'Report to the Economic and Social Council by Special Rapporteur on Human Rights Violations in Afghanistan', UN Doc. E/CN.4/1999/40.

(2000) 'Report on the First and Second Parts of its 2000 Session', UN Doc. E/2000/88 (Part II).

ECOSOC/6379 NGO/662, Press Release, 23 January 2009.

ECOSOC/6380 NGO/663, Press Release, 26 January 2009.

General Assembly

Resolutions: Res. 57 (I), Res. 74 (I), Res. 181 (II), Res. 1001 (ES-I), Res. 217A (III), Res. 302 (IV), Res. 428 (V), Res. 1166 (XII), Res. 1438 (XIV), Res. 1714 (XVI), Res. 2029 (XX), Res. 2152 (XXI), Res. 2625 (XXV), Res. 31/192, Res. 43/131, Res. 43/173, Res. 44/25, Res. 45/100, Res. 45/111, Res. 46/182, Res. 48/218B, Res. 49/59, Res. 50/8, Res. 51/108, Res. 51/194, Res. 51/195, Res. 51/967, Res. 52/12 B, Res. 52/145, Res. 52/211, Res. 52/247, Res. 53/1, Res. 53/35, Res. 53/164, Res. 53/165, Res. 54/143, Res. 54/193, Res. 54/244, Res. 55/2 (Millennium Development Goals), Res. 55/174, Res. 60/1 (World Summit Outcome), Res. 60/25, Res. 61/267B, Res. 61/494, Res. 62/262, Res. 62/149, Res. 63/3, Res. 63/168, Res. 63/295, Res. 63/308.

(2009) 'Manual on Policies and Procedures Concerning the Reimbursement and Control of Contingent-Owned Equipment of Troop/Police Contributors Participating in Peacekeeping Missions (COE Manual)', UN Doc. A/C.5/63/18.

(2009) 'Statement on behalf of the Nordic Countries by H.E. Ambassador Thomas Winkler', 64th Session, Sixth Committee, 26 October.

International Law Commission

(1964) Third Report on the Law of Treaties, UN Doc. A/CN.4/167, Vol. II.

(1996) Draft Articles on Diplomatic Protection provisionally adopted by the International Law Commission on First Reading, ILC Report (1996), UN Doc. A/51/10, Chapter III.

(1996) Report on the Work of its Forty-Eighth Session, UN Doc. A/51/10.

(1998) Draft Articles on State Responsibility provisionally adopted by the Drafting Committee (Part One, chapters I and II), UN Doc. A/CN.4/L.569.

(1998) Report on the Work of its Fiftieth Session, UN Doc. A/53/10.

(1999) Draft Articles on State Responsibility provisionally adopted by the Drafting Committee (Part One, chapters III-V), UN Doc. A/CN.4/L.574.

(2000) Report on the Work of the Fifty-second Session, UN Doc. A/55/10.

(2001) Draft Articles on State Responsibility Provisionally Adopted by the Drafting Committee on Second Reading, UN Doc. A/CN.4/L.602.

(2002) Report on the Work of the Fifty-fourth Session, UN Doc. A/57/10.

(2003) Report on the Work of the Fifty-fifth Session, UN Doc. A/58/10.

(2004) Report on the Work of the Fifty-sixth Session, UN Doc. A/59/10.

(2004) Responsibility of international organisations: Comments and observations received from Governments and international organisations, 56th Session of the ILC, UN Doc. A/CN.4/545.

(2005) Report on the Work of the Fifty-seventh Session, UN Doc. A/60/10.

(2005) Responsibility of international organisations: Comments and observations received from Governments and international organisations, 57th Session of the ILC, UN Doc. A/CN.4/556.

(2006) Report on the Work of the Fifty-eighth Session, UN Doc. A/61/10.

(2007) Responsibility of international organisations: Comments and observations received from Governments and international organisations, 59th Session of the ILC, UN Doc. A/CN.4/582.

(2008) Report on the Work of the Sixtieth Session, UN Doc. A/63/10.

(2008) Preliminary Report on the Protection of Persons in the Event of Disasters by the Special Rapporteur, 60th Session of the ILC, UN Doc. A/CN.4/598.

(2009) Second Report on the Protection of Persons in the Event of Disasters by the Special Rapporteur, 61st Session of the ILC, UN Doc. A/CN.4/615.

(2009) Report on the Work of the Sixty-first Session, UN Doc. A/64/10.

Secretary General

(1990) Model Status-of-Force-Agreement, UN Doc. A/45/594.
(1991) Model Agreement between the United Nations and Member States contributing personnel and equipment to United Nations peace-keeping operations, UN Doc. A/46/185.
(1992) An Agenda for Peace, UN Doc. A/47/277–S/24111.
(1994) Report on the UN Assistance Mission to Rwanda, UN Doc. S/1994/470.
(1994) Report on Rwanda, UN Doc. S/1994/565.
(1994) Report on the United Nations Mission in Haiti, 15 July 1994, UN Doc. S/1994/828.
(1995) Supplement to an Agenda for Peace, UN Doc. A/50/60, S/1995/1.
(1996) Promotion and Protection of the Rights of Children: Impact of armed conflict on children, UN Doc. A/51/306.
(1996) Report on Administrative and Budgetary Aspects of the Financing of United Nations Peacekeeping Operations, UN Doc. A/51/389, also reproduced in 37 ILM 700.
(1997) Letter to the President of the Security Council of 1 May 1997, UN Doc. S/1997/347.
(1997) Reform on the procedures for determining reimbursement to Member States for contingent-owned equipment, UN Doc. A/51/967.
(1997) Report to the General Assembly on Enhancing the Internal Oversight Mechanisms in Operational Funds and Programmes, UN Doc. A/51/801.
(1997) Report on the Situation in Afghanistan, UN Doc. S/1997/482.
(1997) Report on the Situation in Afghanistan, UN Doc. S/1997/719.
(1997) Report on the Situation in Afghanistan, UN Doc. S/1997/894.
(1997) Letter of the Italian Representative to the Secretary General on the situation in Albania, UN Doc. S/1997/258, reproduced in 52 Com. Int. (1997) 6.
(1998) Report on the Situation in Africa, UN Doc. S/1998/318.
(1998) First Report on the UN Observer Mission in Sierra Leone, UN Doc. S/1998/750.
(1998) Report on the Situation in Afghanistan and its Implications for International Peace and Security, UN Doc. S/1998/222.
(1998) Report on Afghanistan, UN Doc. S/1998/532.
(1998) Report on Afghanistan, UN Doc. S/1998/913.
(1998) Report on protection for humanitarian assistance to refugees and others in conflict situations, UN Doc. S/1998/883.
(1999) Letter to President of the Security Council, UN Doc. S/1999/339.

(1999) Report on the Fall of Srebrenica, UN Doc. A/54/549.
(1999) Report on the Situation in Afghanistan and its Implications for International Peace and Security, UN Doc. S/1999/362.
(1999) Report on the UN Interim Administration Mission to Kosovo, UN Doc. S/1999/779.
(1999) Report on the Situation in East Timor, UN Doc. S/1999/1024.
(1999) The Fall of Srebenica, UN Doc. A/54/549.
(1999) Report on the Situation in Afghanistan and its Implications for International Peace and Security, UN Doc. S/1999/362.
(1999) Report on the Situation in Afghanistan, UN Doc. S/1999/698.
(1999) Report on the United Nations Interim Administration in Kosovo' UN Doc. S/1999/987.
(1999) Report on Afghanistan, UN Doc. S/1999/994.
(1999) Report of the Secretary-General Pursuant to Paragraph 10 of Security Council Resolution 1244 (1999), UN Doc. S/1999/672.
(1999) Observance by the United Nations Forces of International Humanitarian Law, Bulletin of the Secretary General. UN Doc. ST/SGB/1999/13.
(2000) Report on the Situation in Afghanistan and its Implications for International Peace and Security, UN Doc. S/2000/581.
(2000) Report on the Situation in Afghanistan and its Implications for International Peace and Security, UN Doc. S/2000/875.
(2000) Report on the Situation in Afghanistan and its Implications for International Peace and Security, UN Doc. S/2000/1106.
(2000) Rules and procedures to be applied for the investigation functions performed by the Office of Internal Oversight Services, UN Doc. A/55/469.
(2000) Secretary General Press Release, UN Doc. SG/SM/7338, 24 March 2000.
(2000) Speech of Secretary-General Kofi Annan addressing the Security Council at its 4120th Meeting to deliver his Report on the situation between Iraq-Kuwait (UN Doc. S/2000/208), 24 March 2004.
(2000) We the peoples: The Role of the United Nations in the 21st Century, UN Doc. A/54/2000.
(2001) Report of the Secretary-General pursuant to paragraph 5 of resolution 1330 (2000), UN Doc. S/2001/186.
(2001) Report on the Activities of the Office of Internal Oversight Services, UN Doc. A/55/826.
(2001) Road Map Towards the Implementation of the United Nations Millennium Declaration of 6 September 2001, UN Doc. A/56/326.

(2003) Secretary-General's Bulletin: Special measures for protection from sexual exploitation and sexual abuse, 9 October 2003, UN Doc. ST/SGB/2003/13.
(2004) Note by the Secretary General, UN General Assembly, 2 December 2004, UN Doc. A/59/565.
(2005) Twentieth report of the Secretary General on the United Nations Organization Mission in the Democratic Republic of the Congo, UN Doc. S/2005/832.
(2005) In Larger Freedom: Towards Development, Security and Human Rights for all, UN Doc. A/59/2005.
(2006) Letter dated 15 June 2006 from the Secretary-General Kofi Annan to the President of the Security Council, UN Doc. S/PV.5474.
(2007) Letter dated 26 March 2007 from the Secretary-General addressed to the President of the Security Council, UN Doc. S/2007/168 (annexing the 'Main provisions of the Comprehensive Proposal for the Kosovo Status Settlement').
(2007) Protection of Persons in the Event of Disasters, Memorandum by the Secretariat, UN Doc. A/CN.4/590.
(2007) Report of the Special Committee on Peace-keeping Operations and its Working Group on the 2007 resumed session, UN Doc. A/61/19 (Part III).
(2008) Report of the Secretary General on the United Nations Interim Administration Mission in Kosovo, UN Doc. S/2008/354.
(2008) Report of the Secretary General on the United Nations Interim Administration Mission in Kosovo, UN Doc. S/2008/692.
(2008) Speech at an event on 'Responsible Sovereignty: International Cooperation for a Changed World', 15 July, UN Doc. SG/SM/11701.
(2008) Report on The United Nations Interim Administration Mission in Kosovo, UN Doc. S/2008/458.
(2009) Implementing the Responsibility to Protect, UN Doc. A/63/677.
(2009) Report of the Secretary General on the United Nations Interim Administration Mission in Kosovo, UN Doc. S/2009/149.
(2009) Report of the Secretary-General: Special measures for protection from sexual exploitation and sexual abuse, 17 February 2009, UN Doc. A/63/720.
(2009) Report of The United Nations Interim Administration Mission in Kosovo, UN Doc. S/2009/300.
(2009) Twenty-seventh report of the Secretary-General on the United Nations Organization Mission in the Democratic Republic of the Congo, UN Doc. S/2009/160.

(2009) Report of the Secretary General on the United Nations Interim Administration Mission in Kosovo, UN Doc. S/2009/497.
(2009) Report of the Secretary General to the General Assembly on the Financing of UN Peacekeeping Operations, UN Doc. A/60/696.
(2010) Report of the Secretary General on Kosovo to the Security Council, UN Doc. S/2010/5.

Security Council

On Afghanistan: Res. 1076 (1996), Res. 1193 (1998), Res. 1214 (1998), Res. 1267 (1999), Res. 1333 (2000).
On Albania: Res. 1101 (1997), Res. 1173 (1998).
On al-Qaida and the Taliban: Res. 1390 (2002).
On Angola: Res. 864 (1993).
On Bosnia and Herzegovina: Res. 819 (1993), Res. 1031 (1995), Res. 1035 (1995), Res. 1088 (1996), Res. 1103 (1997), Res. 1144 (1997), Res. 1184 (1998), Res. 1575 (2004).
On Burundi: Res. 1072 (1996).
On Cambodia: Res. 668 (1990), Res. 718 (1991), Res. 792 (1992).
On the Central African Republic: Res. 1159 (1998).
On Chad: Res. 1923 (2010).
On children and armed conflict: Res. 1882 (2009).
On the Democratic Republic of Congo: Res. 1565 (2004), Res. 1246 (1999), Res. 1257 (1999), Res. 1493 (2003), Res. 1856 (2008).
On Eastern Slavonia: Res. 1037 (1996).
On East Timor: Res. 1264 (1999), Res. 1272 (1999), Res. 1410 (2002), Res. 1473 (2003), Res. 1480 (2003), Res. 1543 (2004), Res. 1573 (2004), Res. 1599 (2005), Res. 1677 (2006), Res. 1690 (2006), Res. 1703 (2006), Res. 1704 (2006), Res. 1867 (2008), Res. 1912 (2010).
On Eritrea and Ethiopia: Res. 1298 (2000).
On general issues relating to sanctions: Res. 1730 (2006).
On the Great Lakes region: Res. 1050 (1996), Res. 1234 (1999), Res. 1258 (1999).
On Guinea-Bissau: Res. 1233 (1999).
On Haiti: Res. 841 (1993), Res. 867 (1993), Res. 940 (1994), Res. 975 (1995), Res. 1048 (1996), Res. 1063 (1996), Res. 1123 (1997), Res. 1141 (1997), Res. 54/193 (2000–2001), Res. 1542 (2004).
On the implementation of the report of the Panel on United Nations Peace Operations (S/2000/809): Res. 1327 (2000).
On Iran: Res. 1737 (2006).

On Iraq: Res. 660 (1990), Res. 661 (1990), Res. 662 (1990), Res. 665 (1990), Res. 666 (1990), Res. 670 (1990), Res. 688 (1991), Res. 706 (1991), Res. 712 (1991), Res. 986 (1995).
On Liberia: Res. 788 (1992), Res. 1343 (2001).
On Libya: Res. 748 (1992).
On Kosovo: Res. 1160 (1998), Res. 1199 (1998), Res. 1203 (1998), Res. 1244 (1999); Res. 1312 (2000).
On the non-proliferation of weapons of mass destruction: Res. 1540 (2004).
On North Korea: Res. 1718 (2006).
On the manipulation of the Oil for Food programme: 1538 (2004).
On the Palestine Question: Res. 50 (1948).
On the protection of civilians in armed conflict: Res. 1674 (2006), Res. 1894 (2009).
On refugee camps and humanitarian crises in Africa: Res. 1208 (1998), Res. 1265 (1999).
On the responsibility to protect: Res. 1674 (2006), Res. 1894 (2009).
On Rwanda: Res. 918 (1994).
On Sierra Leone: Res. 1132 (1997), Res. 1181 (1998), Res. 1231 (1999), Res. 1260 (1999), Res. 1270 (1999), Res. 1289 (2000), Res. 1299 (2000), Res. 1306 (2000), Res. 1313 (2000).
On Somalia: Res. 733 (1992), Res. 794 (1992), Res. 814 (1993).
On South Africa: Res. 418 (1977); Res. 421 (1977).
On Southern Rhodesia: Res. 232 (1966), Res. 253 (1968), Res. 277 (1970), Res. 409 (1977).
On Sudan: Res. 1044 (1996), Res. 1054 (1996), Res. 1070 (1996); Res. 1706 (2006); Res. 1769 (2007) on Darfur.
On terrorism: Res. 1373 (2001), Res. 1452 (2002), Res. 1617 (2005), Res. 1730 (2006), Res. 1735 (2006), Res. 1822 (2008), Res. 1904 (2009).
On Trieste: Res. 16 (1947).
On Yugoslavia: Res. 713 (1991), Res. 721 (1991).
On Western Sahara: Res. 1198 (1998).
On women and peace and security: Res. 1325 (2000), Res. 1820 (2008), Res. 1888 (2009).
(1983) Provisional Rules of Procedure of the Security Council, UN Doc. S/96/Rev.7.
(1996) Memorandum of Understanding Between the Secretariat of the United Nations and the Government of Iraq on the Implementation of Security Council Resolution 986 (1995), UN Doc. S/1996/356.

(1997) Letter of the Albanian Government to the Security Council, UN Doc. S/1997/259, reproduced in Com. Int. (1997) 6.
(1999) Letter of the President of the Security Council to the Secretary General, UN Doc. S/1999/340.
(2000) Report of the Security Council Mission Visit to the Democratic Republic of Congo, UN Doc. S/2000/416.
(2000) Report of the Security Council Mission to East Timor and Indonesia, UN Doc. S/2000/1105.
(2000) Report of the Security Council Special Mission Visit to Eritrea and Ethiopia, UN Doc. S/2000/413.
(2000) Report of the Security Council Mission on the Implementation of Security Council Resolution 1244 (1999), UN Doc. S/2000/363.
(2000) Report of the Security Council Mission to Sierra Leone, UN Doc. S/2000/992.
(2000) Statement by the President of the Security Council, UN Doc. S/PRST/2000/20.
(2001) Report of the Panel of Experts on the Illegal Exploitation of Natural Resources and Other Forms of Wealth of the Democratic Republic of the Congo, UN Doc. S/2001/357.
(2002) Report of the Security Council Mission to Kosovo and Belgrade, Federal Republic of Yugoslavia, UN Doc. S/2002/1376.
(2003) Statement of the President of the Security Council, UN Doc. S/PRST/2003/26.
(2005) Report of the Security Council mission to Central Africa, 4 to 11 November 2005, UN Doc. S/2005/716.
(2005) A comprehensive strategy to eliminate future sexual exploitation and abuse in United Nations peacekeeping operations, UN Doc. A/59/710.
(2006) Comprehensive report prepared pursuant to GA Res. 59/296 on sexual exploitation and sexual abuse, including policy development, implementation and full justification of proposed capacity on personnel conduct issues, UN Doc. A/60/862.
(2006) Report of the Security Council mission on the electoral process in the Democratic Republic of the Congo, UN Doc. S/2006/434.
(2006) Statement of the President of the Security Council, UN Doc. S/PRST/2006/28.
(2007) Report of the Secretary-General pursuant to paragraph 8 of resolution 1698 (2006) concerning the Democratic Republic of Congo (on the prevention of exploitation of natural resources), UN Doc. S/2007/68.

(2008) United Nations Comprehensive Strategy on Assistance and Support to Victims of Sexual Exploitation and Abuse by United Nations Staff and Related Personnel, UN Doc. A/RES/62/214.
(2008) Report of the Security Council Mission to Afghanistan, 21 to 28 November 2008, UN Doc. S/2008/782.
(2008) Report of the Security Council Mission to Djibouti (on Somalia), the Sudan, Chad, the Democratic Republic of the Congo and Côte d'Ivoire, 31 May to 10 June 2008, UN Doc. S/2008/460.
(2008) Report on The United Nations Interim Administration Mission in Kosovo, UN Doc. S/2008/458.
(2008) Report on Children and Armed Conflict in the DRC, UN Doc. S/2008/693.
(2009) Report of the Security Council Mission to Haiti (11 to 14 March 2009), UN Doc. S/2009/175.
(2009) Security Council Cross-Cutting Report No.1: Children and Armed Conflict, 15 April 2009.
(2010) Approved resources for peacekeeping operations for the period from 1 July 2009 to 30 June 2010, UN Doc. A/C.5/64/15.

Other

Commission of Inquiry on Rwanda (1999) 'Report of the Independent Inquiry into the Actions of the United Nations during the 1994 Genocide in Rwanda', UN Doc. S/1999/1257.
Commission of Inquiry on Somalia (1994) 'Report of the Commission of Inquiry established pursuant to Security Council Resolution 885 (1993) to investigate armed attacks on UNOSOM II personnel which led to casualties among them'.
Committee on Economic, Social and Cultural Rights, General Comment 12 (Art. 11), UN Doc. E/C.12/1999/5.
Committee on the Rights of the Child, 'Concluding Observations on Iraq 26/10/1998', UN Doc. CRC/C/15/Add.94.
Department of Humanitarian Affairs (1996) 'Afghanistan Weekly Update No. 191', 6 November.
Department of Humanitarian Affairs (1997) 'Report of the DHA Mission to Afghanistan', 15 June.
Department of Peace-keeping Operations (2003) 'Directives for Disciplinary Matters Involving Military Members of National Contingents', UN Doc. DPKO/MD/03/00993.

Department of Peace-keeping Operations (2003) 'Directives on Sexual Harassment in United Nations Peace-keeping and other Field Missions', UN Doc. DPKO/DSHCPO/2003/002.

Department of Peace-keeping Operations (2010) 'United Nations Peacekeeping Operations: Background Notes, 28 February 2010'.

Department of Peace-keeping Operations – Lessons Learnt Unit (1995), 'The Comprehensive Report on Lessons Learned from United Nations Operation in Somalia (UNOSOM), April 1992 – March 1995'.

Department of Peace-keeping Operations and Department of Field Operations (2008) 'UN Peace-keeping Operations: Principles and Guidelines: "Capstone Doctrine"'.

Department of Political Affairs (1992) Repertoire of the Practice of the Security Council. Supplement 1981–1984, UN Doc. ST/PSCA/1/Add. 9; and (2000) Supplement 1985–1988, UN Doc. ST/DPA/1/Add. 10.

Human Rights Commission Res. 1998/70, UN Doc. E/CN.4/Res/1998/70.

Human Rights Commission Res. 1999/9, UN Doc. E/CN.4/Res/1999/9.

Human Rights Committee (1984), General Comment 14 (Art. 6), UN Doc. HRI\GEN\1\Rev.1.

Human Rights Committee (1986), General Comment 15, UN Doc. HRI\GEN\1\Rev.1.

Human Rights Committee (1997), 'Concluding Observations of the Human Rights Committee: Iraq. 19/11/1997', UN Doc. CCPR/C/79/Add/84.

Inter-Agency Gender Mission to Afghanistan, 'Report of the Mission to Afghanistan 12–24 Nov. 1997' (available through the Division for the Advancement of Women).

Kosovo Human Rights Advisory Panel, Annual Report 2008.

Office of Internal Oversight Services (1997) 'Report on Audit and Investigation of the International Criminal Tribunal for Rwanda', UN Doc. A/51/789.

Office of Internal Oversight Services (1998), 'Report of the Office of Internal Oversight Services for the Period between 1 July 1997 and 30 June 1998', 23 September 1998, UN Doc. A/53/428.

Office of Internal Oversight Services (1999), 'Report on the Investigation into Allegations of Theft of Funds by a Staff Member of the United Nations Conference on Trade and Development', UN Doc. A/53/811.

Office of Internal Oversight Services (2001) 'Report for the Period from July 1 1999 to June 30 2000', UN Doc. A/55/436.

Office of Internal Oversight Services (2008) 'Review of Results-Based Management at the United Nations', 22 September 2008, UN Doc. A/63/268.

Office of Legal Affairs (1962) 'Note to the Under-Secretary for Special Political Affairs and the Under-Secretary for General Assembly Affairs on the Legal Policy concerning the Detention by the UN of Mercenaries', UN Jur. YB (1962) 241.

Office of Legal Affairs (1992) 'Letter to the President of the ICRC on the Question of the Application of the 1949 Geneva Conventions', 17 September, UN Jur. YB (1992) 431.

Office of Legal Affairs (1994) 'Question of Juridical Personality and Legal Capacity in Relation to United Nations Agencies, Programmes and Funds' UN Jur. YB (1994) 478.

Report of the Special Committee on Peace-keeping Operations (1995) 'Comprehensive Review of the Whole Question of Peace-keeping Operations in All their Aspects', UN Doc. A/50/230.

Review Panel on UN Peace Operations (2000) 'Report of the Panel on United Nations Peace Operations' ("Brahimi Report"), UN Doc. A/55/305, S/2000/809.

Sub-commission on Prevention of Discrimination and Protection of Minorities Res. 1998/17.

UNHCR, Road to Refugee 2: Into the Sahara (online documentary).

UNHCR – Kakuma Sub-Office (1994) Letter from the Senior Protection Officer, James Lynch, to Assefa Teferi Woldekidan, 19 July (on file with the author, and UNHCR ref. KEN/NRB/PT/94/IC/0794).

UNHCR – Kakuma Sub-Office (1996), Memorandum from the Officer-in-Charge to Refugees Working for NGOs in Kakuma, 4 April (on file with the author).

UNHCR – Kakuma Sub-Office (undated) Protection document prepared by the Protection Assistant, 'Implementing Protection'.

UNHCR – Executive Committee of the High Commissioner's Programme (1997) 'Memoranda of Understanding', UN Doc. EC/47/SC/CRP.51.

UNHCR – Executive Committee of the High Commissioner's Programme (2000) 'Organization Oversight and Performance Review Framework', UN Doc. EC/50/SC/INF.6.

UNHCR Policy Development and Evaluation Service, 'UNHCR's Evaluation Policy', 1 September 2002 (available from www.unhcr.org/3d99a0f74.html).

UNHCR Policy Development and Evaluation Service, 'The use of cash grants in UNHCR voluntary repatriation operations: Report of a "lessons learned" workshop', 30 September 2008, PDES/2008/09.

UNHCR Policy Development and Evaluation Service, 'Evaluation of UNHCR's efforts to prevent and respond to sexual and gender-based violence in situations of forced displacement', 6 October 2008, PDES/2008/08.

UNICEF (1994), *Children of War Wandering Alone in Southern Sudan*. Written by J. Zutt, New York: UNICEF.

UNICEF (1996), *Impact of Armed Conflict on Children*, Written by Graça Machel, 26 August 1996, UN Doc. A/51/306.

UNICEF CF/DOC/PR/1999/29, Press Release, 12 August 1999.

UNICEF (in collaboration with the Ministry of Health of Iraq), 'Iraq Child and Maternal Mortality Survey 1999', July 1999.

UNMIK Administrative Direction No. 2009/1.

UNMIK Emergency Decree No. 1999/1, UN Doc. UNMIK/ED/1999/1.

UNMIK Regulations: 1999/1, 1999/8, 1999/18, 1999/22, 1999/24, 2000/1, 2000/6, 2000/15, 2000/24, 2000/38, 2000/44, 2000/45, 2000/47, 2000/59, 2001/4, 2001/9, 2005/52, 2005/53, 2006/06, 2006/12.

UNMIK 'Note Verbale to a Permanent Mission to the UN Regarding the Legal Personality and Treaty-Making Power of UNMIK', UN Jur. YB (2004) 351.

UNMIT Human Rights and Transitional Justice Section, 'Report on Human Rights Developments in Timor-Leste August 2006 – August 2007' (available from http://unmit.unmissions.org/LinkClick.aspx?fileticket=pylFCrJl59g%3d&tabid=826&mid=884).

UN OCHA Integrated Regional Information Network for Central and Eastern Africa (IRIN-CEA), Weekly Round-up 68, 20 April 2001.

Unpublished letter of 3 February 2004 by the United Nations Legal Counsel to the Director of the Codification Division, quoted in ILC Report (2004).

UN Sub-Commission on the Promotion and Protection of Human Rights, 'Humanitarian situation of the Iraqi population', UN Doc. E/CN.4/Sub.2/2000/L.32.

UNTAET Regulations: 1999/1, 1999/2, 1999/3, 2000/11, 2000/14, 2000/15, 2000/16, 2000/24, 2000/30, 2001/2.

World Food Programme (1998) 'Strategic Framework for the UN in Afghanistan of 12 September 1998'.

World Health Assembly Res. 46 (40), 14 May 1993.

Peacekeeping

(1986) Memorandum of the Office of Legal Affairs, UN Jur. YB 300.
(2005) Agreement between Burundi and the United Nations concerning the Status of the United Nations Operation in Burundi, signed at Bujumbura, 17 June 2005 (and entered into force on the same date), UN Jur. YB 25.

Other international documents

Burma Centrum Nederland, 'Transcript of the Press Conference of Sadako Ogata, UN High Commissioner for Refugees', The Hague, 1 September 1998.
Council of Europe Recommendation 1824 (2008).
Council of Europe Resolution 1597 (2008).
European Commission for Democracy through Law (Venice Commission), *Opinion on the Constitutional Situation in Bosnia and Herzegovina and the Powers of the High Representative*, adopted at 62nd plenary session (11–12 March 2005).
European Commission for Democracy through Law (Venice Commission), *Opinion no. 326/2004 on a Possible Solution to the Issue of Decertification of Police Officers in Bosnia and Herzegovina*, 24 October 2005.
FAO Conference Res. 1/61.
General Regulations of the World Food Programme.
High-Level Panel on Threats, Challenges and Change (2004), 'A More Secure World, Our Shared Responsibility', UN Doc. 1/59/656.
High Representative for Bosnia and Herzegovina, Decision of 23 March 2007: 'Order on the Implementation of the Decision of the Constitutional Court of Bosnia and Herzegovina in the Appeal of Milorad Bilbija et al. 23 March 2007 AP-953/05'.
Human Rights Advisory Panel, 'Annual Report 2008' (available from www.unmikonline.org/human_rights/documents/annual_report2008.pdf).
IBRD Res. 93–10; IDA Res. 93–6, 'The World Bank Inspection Panel', 22 September 1993.
ICRC Press Release of 15 May 1996 (96/19).
ICRC Statutes of 24 June 1998 (in 324 Int. Rev. R.C. 1998).
Independent Inquiry Committee into the United Nations Oil-for-Food Programme, 'Management of the Oil-for-Food Programme', 7 September 2005, Vol. I at 4 (available from www.iic-offp.org/Mgmt_Report.htm).

International Monetary Fund Executive Board Decision No. 12864 (02/102), 'Guidelines on Conditionality', 25 September 2002.

International Monetary Fund Policy, Development and Review Department, 'Review of the 2002 Conditionality Guidelines', 3 March 2005.

Letter to the President of the ICRC (1992), 'Questions on the Application of the 1949 Geneva Conventions for the Protection of War Victims and Their Additional Protocols in Peacekeeping Operations of the United Nations', UN Jur. YB 430.

Letters dated 23 June 2008 from the Permanent Representative of Switzerland to the United Nations addressed to the President of the General Assembly and the President of the Security Council, attaching discussion paper 'Improving the Implementation of Sanctions Regimes Through Ensuring "Fair and Clear Procedures"', UN Doc. A/62/891-S/2008/428.

Ombudsman Institution in Kosovo (2001), 'First Annual Report'.

Ombudsman Institution in Kosovo (2002), 'Second Annual Report'.

Oral Statements of Serbia in the advisory proceedings before the ICJ concerning the question of accordance with international law of the Unilateral Declaration of Independence in respect of Kosovo, 1 December 2009.

Panel on the Humanitarian Situation in Iraq (1999), 'Report of the Second Panel Established Pursuant to the Note by the President of the Security Council of 30 January 1999 (S/1999/100), concerning the current humanitarian situation in Iraq', UN Doc. S/1999/356, annex II.

'Rambouillet Accords: Interim Agreement for Peace and Self-Government in Kosovo', 18 March 1999, annexed to UN Doc. S/1999/648.

Statement of Principles signed by KFOR and the KLA, September 1999.

World Bank Inspection Panel, *China: Western Poverty Reduction Project Investigation Report* (Report of 28 April 2000).

World Bank Inspection Panel, *Ecuador: Mining Development and Environmental Control Technical Assistance Project* (Report of 16 May 2000).

Written Statement of Serbia in the advisory proceedings before the ICJ concerning the question of accordance with international law of the 'Unilateral Declaration of Independence in respect of Kosovo'.

UNHCR Statute annexed to GA Res. 428(V), 14 December 1950.

NATIONAL AND REGIONAL LEGISLATION AND OTHER STATE PRACTICE

Bosnia and Herzegovina

Constitution of Bosnia and Herzegovina (Annex 4 of the Dayton Peace Agreement, 14 December 1995; 35 ILM 75).
Law on State Border Service of Bosnia and Herzegovina, Official Gazette of Bosnia and Herzegovina 2/2000, 26 January 2000.

EU/EEC

Council Decision 2010/322/CFSP of 8 June 2010.
Council Joint Action 2008/124/CFSP of 4 February 2008.
Council Joint Action 2009/445/CFSP of 9 June 2009.
Council Regulation (EC) No 44/2001 of 22 December 2000 on jurisdiction and the recognition and enforcement of judgments in civil and commercial matters.

Germany

Constitution of Germany.

Italy

Constitution of Italy.

Kosovo

Constitution of Kosovo.
Unilateral Declaration of Independence, 17 February 2008.

South Africa

Constitution of South Africa.

United Kingdom

International Development Committee (House of Commons), 'Kosovo: The Humanitarian Crisis', 15 May 1999, Third Report – Session 1998–99 (HC 422).
International Development Committee (House of Commons), 'Mozambique: Report and Proceedings of the Committee, Minutes of Evidence and Appendices', 3 May 2000, Fifth Report – Session 1999–00 (HC 326).

International Development Committee (House of Commons), 'After Seattle – The World Trade Organisation and Developing Countries', 29 November 2000, Tenth Report – Session 1999–00 (HC 227).
International Development Committee (House of Commons), 'First Special Report', 24 January 2001 (HC 82).
International Development Committee (House of Commons), 'DFID and the World Bank', 5 March 2008, Sixth Report – Session 2007–08 – Volume I: Report, together with formal minutes (HC 67–1).
International Development Committee (House of Commons), 'The World Food Programme and Global Food Security', 15 July 2008, Tenth Report – Session 2007–08 – Volume I: Report, together with formal minutes (HC 493-I).
Letter of the Earl of Aberdeen to Mr Everett, 20 December 1841, XXX *British and Foreign State Papers* (1841–42) 1178.
Letter of Mr Stevenson to Viscount Palmerston, 27 February 1841, XXX *British and Foreign State Papers* (1841–42) 1137.
Letter of Viscount Palmerston to Mr Stevenson, 27 August 1841, XXX *British and Foreign State Papers* (1841–42) 1152.
Slave Trade Abolition Act 1807.
United Nations Act 1946.

United States

Act to prohibit United States contributions to the United Nations for the purpose of paying or reimbursing the legal expenses of United Nations Officers or Employees charged with malfeasance, and for other purposes, HR 1072 (referred to House Committee on Foreign Relations on 13 February 2009).
Executive Order 10422 (1953), 22 USCS §287.
Foreign Sovereign Immunities Act 1976, 28 USCS §1602.
House of Representatives Committee on Foreign Affairs, Committee Oversight Plan, International Security/UN/Peacekeeping/General for the 111th Congress, 28 January 2009.
House of Representatives Committee on Foreign Affairs hearing on 'United Nations Peacekeeping Operations: An Underfunded International Mandate – the Role of the United States', 2 April 2008, Serial No. 110–161.
International Organizations Immunities Act 1945, 22 USCS §288a.

Restatement (Third) of Foreign Relations Law of the United States.
United Nations Reform Act 1999, 113 Stat. 1501.
United Nations Reform Act of 2005, HR 2745, 109th Cong.
United Nations Transparency, Accountability, and Reform Act of 2009, HR 557 111th Cong.

Introduction

Three categories of questions arise in a study of the accountability of the United Nations (UN) for violations of human rights. The first category is factual and empirical: does the UN violate human rights? If so, how? Which of its activities pose a greater risk of such violations? The second category comprises doctrinal questions: is the UN bound by international human rights law? What legal consequences follow from the breach by the UN of a rule of international human rights law? How can its obligations be enforced and compliance with them improved? The third category of questions is philosophical: how should we ideally limit the *power* of international organisations? Is the power shift from states to international organisations, and the weakening of the state that follows from it, a good thing?

The focus of this book is on the doctrinal questions. I do address some empirical and factual questions but not comprehensively. As for the philosophical ones, for the most part I limit myself to identifying them and stressing their importance.

The main factual argument is that there are at least four categories of UN operations – the provision of humanitarian assistance; peacekeeping; international administration; and the implementation of sanctions – in which the powers of the UN are so extensive that violations of human rights can result, and have resulted, directly from their exercise. To demonstrate this proposition, I draw, at least in part, on the findings of my own empirical research – particularly in relation to the administration of refugee camps.

The main doctrinal arguments are, first, that the UN is bound by international human rights law and international humanitarian law; secondly that, although some confusion persists about particular aspects of the application of the law of institutional responsibility (for example in relation to attribution), the legal framework governing the responsibility of international organisations is sufficiently clear, and that there is consequently no general or systemic doctrinal constraint on the application of secondary rules of responsibility to international institutions; and thirdly that inadequacies in the legal enforcement of and compliance with human rights produce both a 'liberty deficit' and an 'accountability deficit'. The doctrine of equivalent protection, first developed by the German Constitutional Court and now adopted by international human rights courts, is a welcome attempt to address these two deficits judicially. But it is not enough. Political and administrative solutions must also be found.

As I hinted above, in this book I do not articulate a full position on the philosophical questions relating to the phenomenon of UN power over individuals, but I am certainly not proceeding on the assumption that the UN, and international organisations in general, are inherently good, and that a power shift from states to international organisations is always a positive development. My sketch for an argument on the philosophical issues is that there is a twofold relationship between the state and the principle of liberty (or human rights) that international organisations cannot reproduce or replace: first, the state *embodies* the idea of collective liberty which contemporary international law articulates through the principle of self-determination; secondly, the state *enables* individual liberty by providing the best political space within which it can be exercised and safeguarded.

Origins of this project

I decided to write on the accountability of the UN for violations of human rights in the late 1990s, when I was conducting fieldwork on refugees in East Africa. One of the most disquieting findings to emerge from that research was that many of the violations of human rights inflicted on refugees resulted from the conduct of the Office of the United Nations High Commissioner for Refugees (UNHCR) and of humanitarian non-governmental organisations (NGOs). During one of my first visits to a refugee camp, in north-western Kenya in 1997, I found evidence of the imposition of collective punishment on its entire population on two separate occasions. Refugees, whose survival depended almost entirely on food aid, were subjected to the punitive suspension of food distribution after some had staged a protest against the UNHCR. I, like most people, viewed the UNHCR and NGOs as protectors of human rights. The discovery of their power over individuals came as a surprise.

In the course of subsequent fieldwork in Kenya, Tanzania, Uganda, Sierra Leone and Liberia, I confirmed that what had happened in that camp was not an isolated incident and that human rights violations in refugee camps are endemic.

Until not so long ago the proposition that the UN can violate human rights would have been dismissed as merely academic – where the word academic is given the meaning philistines like to give it, that is 'scholarly to the point of being unaware of the outside world'.[1] Yet, far from being an academic invention, the phenomenon of UN abuse of human rights is real. Why has it been neglected and played down for so long? One reason is distance from the situations where the power of international organisations manifests itself: armed conflicts, post-conflict situations and refugee camps are trodden by only a few academics outside the departments of social anthropology and development studies. It is not a coincidence that the first to observe the phenomenon of UN power in humanitarian crises were anthropologists and journalists.[2]

My disappointment with the failure of most international law scholarship to observe the UN critically seems to be shared by José Alvarez. He observes that 'international lawyers have not examined their institutional creations closely enough. The literature on IOs [international organisations] and their impact on law is replete with half-truths, some derived from the continuing hold of legal positivism and others inspired by international lawyers' idealistic aspirations for multilateral institutions.'[3]

Another reason, for the paucity of critiques of the UN may be the intellectual hostility to the state and to the idea of sovereignty that grew in the aftermath of the Second World War. For many, international organisations are allies in the struggle against the state, which they see as a hotbed of nationalism, intolerance and conflict. To expose the failures and shortcomings of international organisations is – they fear – to play into the hands of states. To put it in the words used by a former Secretary General to hush criticism about the

1 *Oxford English Dictionary*.

2 E.g. B. E. Harrell-Bond, *Imposing Aid* (Oxford University Press, 1986) and W. Shawcross, *The Quality of Mercy: Cambodia, Holocaust and Modern Conscience* (London: André Deutsch, 1984).

3 J. E. Alvarez, *International Organisations as Law-Makers* (Oxford University Press, 2005), 586.

organisation: 'Everything you say will be used against this organization by the enemies of the United Nations.'[4]

There is something paradoxical about the anti-statist international lawyer – how can one be *for* international law but *against* its makers? Albeit counter-intuitive, anti-statism is a widespread attitude in the field of international law today – often a habit of the mind rather than a properly conceived ideology. The attack on the state does however have a fully respectable philosophical pedigree: from Rousseau's *Second Discourse*[5] via Bakunin's *Statism and Anarchy*[6] to the various references to the abolition of the state interspersed in Marx's work (for example in *German Ideology*[7]). The post-war reaction against the nation state is exemplified by Cassirer's *The Myth of the State*.[8]

The predominant conception of international organisations is that they exist to find solutions to problems that cannot be adequately addressed by states on their own. Seen in this perspective, international organisations are another face of the rise of technocracy. But technocracy breeds bureaucratic power and shuns external control. This predominant managerial and technocratic conception of international organisation has also shored up the 'assumption that international organisations are, necessarily, a good thing, an assumption which often takes the place of argument'.[9] All in all, it is hardly surprising that this theoretical approach to international organisations 'has singularly failed to keep organisations in check'.[10]

Ideas about international organisations have somewhat evolved in recent years. Their conduct has now begun to attract some serious critical scrutiny, including by academics. Few would dispute today that there are circumstances where international institutions, and the UN in particular, possess sufficient direct power over individuals to interfere with fundamental rights. International lawyers embraced these

[4] S. Hazzard, 'Reflections. Breaking Faith-I', *The New Yorker*, 25 September 1989, 63 at 63.

[5] J. J. Rousseau, 'Discourse on the Origin and Foundations of Inequality Among Men', in V. Gourevitch (ed.), *Rousseau: The Discourses and other early political writings* (Cambridge University Press, 1997), 111ff.

[6] M. A. Bakunin, 'Statism and Anarchy', in M. Shatz (ed.), *Cambridge Texts in the History of Political Thought* (Cambridge University Press, 2000).

[7] K. Marx, 'The German Ideology', in J. O'Malley (ed.), *Marx: Early Political Writings* (Cambridge University Press, 1994), 119ff.

[8] E. Cassirer, *The Myth of the State* (New Haven: Yale University Press, 1946).

[9] J. Klabbers, *An Introduction to International Institutional Law* (Cambridge University Press, 2002) 37.

[10] J. Klabbers, 'Two Concepts of International Organisations', 2 *International Organisations Law Review* (2005) 277 at 289.

developments somewhat belatedly, but the claim that the UN may be a perpetrator of human rights abuses would no longer shock most of them.[11] This awareness has, however, neither allayed uncertainty about the relevant international legal framework, nor remedied problems about the accountability of the UN. Moreover, it is still true that the focus of systematic attention by international lawyers is on the normative dimension of international organisations rather than on their operational side. Notable contributions to the study of the former have appeared in recent years,[12] but there is still a paucity of works on the latter.

My first reaction to the discovery of the other face of international organisations was that the field of international law suffered from a dearth of empirical observation. We had to grasp the phenomenon of human rights violations by international organisations first, in order to be able later to approach critically the legal issues pertaining to their accountability. The book that Barbara Harrell-Bond and I wrote, *Rights in Exile: Janus-Faced Humanitarianism* (2004), sought to fill this gap of empirical knowledge by offering an exposé of the violations of the human rights of refugees. The intellectual and sometimes emotional resistance to the idea that the UN could be committing human rights violations would – we believed – give way in the face of findings based on extensive fieldwork.

We thus set out to produce a scholarly – rather than journalistic or 'trade' – exposé, thinking that, although a scholarly exposé might not have the immediate (but often short-lived) impact of a newspaper or an NGO report, it stood a better chance of contributing to a lasting shift of perceptions about the reality of refugee assistance among academics, international and national civil servants, and activists – the key players who over time help mould the discourse and the agenda of international refugee policy. We adopted the Holmesian 'Experience is the

[11] Among the first to analyse the UN's own human rights problems were: F. Mégret and F. Hoffmann, 'The UN as a Human Rights Violator?' 25 Hum. Rts. Q. (2003), 314; A. Reinisch, 'Securing the Accountability of International Organisations', 7 *Global Governance* (2001), 131; R. Wilde, '*Quis Custodiet Ipsos Custodes*?: Why and How UNHCR Governance of "Development" Refugee Camps Should be Subject to International Human Rights Law', 1 Yale H. R. Dev. L. J. (1998), 107. See also: G. Verdirame, 'Human Rights and Refugees: The Case of Kenya', 12 J. Ref. St. (1999), 54.

[12] In addition to Alvarez, *supra* note 3, see also A. Boyle and C. Chinkin, *The Making of International Law* (Oxford University Press, 2006), esp. at 108ff.

life of the law' as a motto for the book (and, more generally, for that particular phase of my research).

While generally well-received, some thought *Rights in Exile* too polemical. Indeed, parts of it probably were, in line with our denunciatory intent. But is an outright rejection of polemics in academic writing not too constraining? Read Bentham's *Anarchical Fallacies*[13] or Burke's *Reflections on the Revolution in France*[14] to get a sense of the sometimes fiercely polemical tone of past intellectual discourse. Ultimately it is predilection for caution and fear of boldness – neither a virtue – that dictate that scholarly writing must never be polemical.

Rights in Exile did not purport to offer a doctrinal analysis of the law, focusing instead on the dynamics of the violations of the human rights of refugees by both host states and the UNHCR. In my doctoral thesis, I set out to develop such a doctrinal analysis critically. In the following years, my thinking about the phenomenon of international organisation began to move in a more theoretical direction. In addition to the doctrinal challenges, I also saw a dearth of philosophical thinking as a constraint on our discussions of international organisations. The reality of international organisation has in many respects outpaced our thinking about it: the *phenomenon* has grown faster than the *noumenon*. Something similar happened to international human rights law. In *On Human Rights*, Jim Griffin argues there are discrepancies between the philosophy of human rights and international human rights law, with the latter expanding at a steady pace often on the basis of 'nearly criterionless claims about human rights'.[15] Paraphrasing what Alexander Herzen said about the English and liberty,[16] it could be said that the international human rights movement invented international human rights law without having any theories about it.

The study of international organisations, and the field of international law in general, are in my view overdue for a philosophical reflection on the primary questions. We must think about what purposes international institutions serve; how they should be controlled; how to structure the relationship between liberty and human rights, on the one hand, and power of the state and of non-state actors, on

[13] J. Bentham, 'Anarchical Fallacies', in J. Bowring (ed.), *The Works of Jeremy Bentham* (1843), Vol. 2, 489.
[14] E. Burke, *Reflections on the Revolution in France* [1790] (London: Penguin Classics, 1986).
[15] J. Griffin, *On Human Rights* (Oxford University Press, 2008), 192.
[16] See T. Stoppard, *The Coast of Utopia Part III: Salvage* (London: Faber and Faber, 2002).

the other hand; and, more fundamentally, about the impact that these developments have on liberty. We have *few* theories on all of the above and, if those we have are of little practical use, '[t]he fault is that there is *not enough* theory'.[17]

This book does not, however, generally address this need for 'more theory' that I have come to regard as central. Tempted as I am to forfeit the Holmesian pragmatist motto ('Experience is the life of the law'), the limits of which I have explored elsewhere,[18] for an overtly (polemically?) anti-Holmesian one ('Ideas are the life of the law'), this is not yet the book in which to do so.

'Experience is the life of the law' and 'Ideas are the life of the law' are not statements that stand in necessary contradiction. Law needs experience and ideas, the real and the abstract, the actual and the normative. Mottoes aside, however, pragmatism did nourish such an aversion to ideas, abstraction and even rules. Combined with its reductionist notion of the truth as 'what works best', this aversion makes Philip Allott's description of pragmatism as an 'unphilosophy' entirely appropriate.[19]

A superb distillation of anti-pragmatism is this passage from Keynes's *General Theory*:

'Practical men, who believe themselves to be quite exempt from any intellectual influences, are usually the slaves of some defunct economist. Madmen in authority, who hear voices in the air, are distilling their frenzy from some academic scribbler of a few years back. I am sure that the power of vested interests is vastly exaggerated compared with the gradual encroachment of ideas. Not, indeed, immediately, but after a certain interval; for in the field of economic and political philosophy there are not many who are influenced by new theories after they are twenty-five or thirty years of age, so that the ideas which civil servants and politicians and even agitators apply to current events are not likely to be the newest. But, soon or late, it is ideas, not vested interests, which are dangerous for good or evil.'[20]

17 I. Kant, 'On the Common Saying: "This May be True in Theory but it does not Apply in Practice"', in M. J. Gregor (ed.), *The Cambridge Edition of the Works of Immanuel Kant in Translation: Practical Philosophy* (Cambridge University Press, 1999), 273.

18 G. Verdirame, '"The Divided West": International Lawyers in Europe and America', 18(3) EJIL (2007), 553.

19 See P. Allott, *Towards the International Rule of Law: Essays in Integrated Constitutional Theory* (London: Cameron May, 2005), 470, fn. 17; see also my article, 'The Divided West', *supra* note 18, esp. at 558–67.

20 J. M. Keynes, *The General Theory of Employment, Interest and Money* (London: Palgrave Macmillan, 1936), 383.

Scope and content

Categorising the variety of operations undertaken by the UN and by its agencies is not an easy task. The development of an operational practice that is not always consistent with institutional mandates complicates matters.

The category of UN operations with which international lawyers have traditionally been familiar is peacekeeping. Peacekeeping operations have evolved beyond the sheer monitoring of a border zone or of military activities within a territory with a view to preventing conflict. They have become, especially since the 1980s, 'multifunctional'. This move towards multifunctional peacekeeping has not been accompanied by more pervasive regulation.

UN agencies have also mounted large field operations outside the framework of peacekeeping – for example the administration of refugee camps and the provision of relief assistance. A specific legal framework for these operations is not normally found in resolutions of the Security Council or the General Assembly. When they do intervene, these organs usually limit themselves to short statements, which commend the work of the UN agencies on the ground, or condemn actions of government or insurgents, particularly those that interfere with the delivery of relief or when they endanger the lives of humanitarian personnel. The paucity of regulation coming from the political organs of the UN has ensured significant operational autonomy, but has also undermined accountability.

In a review of peacekeeping in the 1990s, the then Secretary-General adopted a categorisation of UN interventions in the peacekeeping area that is conceptual rather than legal, and casts little light on the regulation of these various types of operations. He identified six types of intervention: preventive diplomacy and peacemaking; traditional peacekeeping; post-conflict peace-building; disarmament; sanctions; and enforcement action. Of these actions, the first three would require the consent of the affected state(s), while the last three would normally all be undertaken under Chapter VII of the Charter (disarmament can be undertaken either as a consensual operation or as part of an enforcement action). Most of these operations are established under Chapter VI or VII, but, as acknowledged by the Secretary General, some operations are carried out entirely outside the umbrella of the Security Council. This can pose some problems, as '[t]he more difficult situation is when post-conflict (or preventive) peace-building activities are seen to be necessary in a country where the United

Nations does not already have a peacemaking or peace-keeping mandate. Who then will identify the need for such measures and propose them to the Government? If the measures are exclusively in the economic, social and humanitarian fields, they are likely to fall within the purview of the resident coordinator. He or she could recommend them to the Government.' The thematic approach identified by the Secretary General is not entirely satisfactory, but it is preferable to seeking to classify UN operations according to their formal legal basis under the Charter, since institutional practice has developed considerably and for many, if not most, UN operations the only plausible legal basis is an implied power.

In deciding which UN activities would be the focus of this book, the key criterion has been the presence of a significant measure of direct power over individuals other than employees of the organisation. It is this direct power that carries the greatest risk of human rights abuses. The following four categories of UN operations have been selected on this basis: the provision of relief assistance; the international administration of territory; peacekeeping missions; and sanctions. The authorisation to use force under Chapter VII of the Charter is not included in this analysis, although it does raise issues of compliance with both human rights and international humanitarian law. Given the mechanism of delegation, however, wrongful acts committed in the course of those operations would not normally be committed directly by the UN through its institutional bureaucracy. This is not to say that the legal responsibility of the UN is, in principle, excluded in cases of authorisation to use force. As for the treatment of employees, this wasn't included in the book not because their human rights cannot potentially be violated by the UN, but because the focus is on individuals outside the organisations.

Both the World Bank and the International Monetary Fund (IMF) have been accused of adopting policies and running projects in breach of human rights, particularly in developing countries. However, the impact of their activities on individuals, albeit significant, is not normally direct but mediated through the state in receipt of assistance. Indeed, it is the state that implements the fiscal or monetary decisions on which a particular IMF loan is conditional, or builds the particular infrastructural project for which the World Bank made a grant available. Moreover, although as specialised agencies they are closely linked to the UN, the World Bank and the IMF are not part of the UN *stricto sensu*.

The book begins with an analysis, in Chapter 1, of key concepts and definitions. In Chapter 2, I deal with the human rights obligations of the UN – an area which has not so far received the attention it deserves, as most doctrinal work has concentrated on the rights side of the legal personality of international organisations rather than on their obligations. Chapter 3 focuses on the law of responsibility of international organisations on which the ILC has now produced a complete set of draft articles.[21]

With Chapter 4 begins the detailed analysis of UN operations in which issues of compliance with human rights arise. Chapter 4 also looks into the provision of humanitarian assistance by the UN, discussing the general international legal framework applicable to relief operations and examining the violations of human rights in the course of such operations through a case study – the UN humanitarian operations in Afghanistan in the 1990s. The second part of this chapter draws on my 2001 article in the *Human Rights Quarterly*. Chapter 5 deals with peacekeeping operations, in respect of which obligations under international humanitarian law must be considered in addition to human rights. Chapter 6 examines the assumption of administrative powers by the UN, distinguishing between *de jure* and *de facto* international administrations, with refugee camps as the main case study of the latter. Much of the recent case law on international institutional activities and human rights has arisen in relation to the implementation of sanctions regimes imposed by the Security Council – the topic of Chapter 7.

Chapter 8 analyses mechanisms for holding the UN accountable when it violates human rights. Their effectiveness is assessed both in the light of existing practice and on the basis of their hypothetical application to some of the situations examined in the previous chapters. The role of courts, both domestic and international human rights ones, is examined, with a special focus on one of the most interesting and potentially very significant legal constructs to have been developed in recent decades: the doctrine of equivalent protection. The implications of this doctrine for the concept of sovereignty and the international legal order are briefly explored.

My conclusions, and in particular my endorsement of the doctrine of equivalent protection, may be regarded as statist – an epithet to

[21] See ILC, Report on the Work of the Sixty-first Session (2009), UN Doc. A/64/10, paras. 31ff.

which I no longer instinctively object. It does seem to me incontrovertible that, from the point of view of the advancement of human rights, there is at present no better alternative to the liberal democratic state. States are sometimes the worst enemies of liberty, but they enable it in a way and to an extent unmatched by any international organisation. Without the enabling function of the state, without this necessary political condition, the idea that human rights could thrive abstracted from any political and historical substratum is a pious illusion.

Post-scriptum on the politics of footnoting

I have an aversion to lengthy footnotes that aim to impress or terrify the reader with a list of references sometimes as comprehensive as a bibliography. I am one of those who would like footnote inflation in academia to be reversed as resolutely as grade inflation.[22] In my view, a reference should do no more than point the reader to the source or sources for a particular assertion or argument where such sources were relied upon and must thus be acknowledged. Providing a small bibliography for each assertion and argument has the unfortunate consequence of promoting an attitude of intellectual caution: nothing bold is put forward unless accompanied by a reassuringly meaty footnote.

Throughout this book, I will try to limit the use of footnotes to references and citations. Minor digressions and long quotations will be in the main text but in smaller font and single-spaced.

[22] For an analysis of footnote and citation behaviour, see J. Bensman, 'The Aesthetics and Politics of Footnoting', 1(3) *Politics, Culture and Society* (1988) 443.

1 Concepts and definitions

Introduction

A number of concepts and ideas central to the argument of this book require some exploration at the outset. First, there is no agreed legal definition of international organisation, although working definitions have been adopted in specific instruments. There is also a tendency in the legal literature to disregard the operational dimension of international organisations, and of the UN in particular, probably because the expansion in operational activities has not followed a predetermined plan. In a book such as this, both of these aspects of international organisations – their definition and the history of their operational expansion – require attention.

Secondly, the autonomy of international organisations is often treated as a useful fiction, that is a statement of fact that bears little or no relation to reality but serves a function. The utility of the fiction of autonomy is, in particular, that it buttresses the legal personality of international organisations. The view that autonomy is a fiction colours perceptions of international organisations, but is it still correct? Do we really need to suspend disbelief in order to regard international organisations as autonomous? Rather, could their autonomy not be, at least in respect of some of their activities, a social fact?

Thirdly, international human rights law provides normative terms of reference for one of the main arguments of this book – the proposition that international organisations violate human rights. I do not aim to offer a comprehensive account of this body of law here. There is, however, an argument that is worth investigating: the discrepancy between international human rights law (now almost entirely unhinged from its roots in constitutional law) and the philosophical foundations of human rights. Could this gap between ideas and practice have an impact on the human rights related work of international organisations?

Fourthly, the idea of humanitarianism provides a moral underpinning to most of the UN activities examined in this book - peacekeeping operations, international administrations, the provision of relief and development assistance. A short historical excursus into the origins of modern humanitarianism will reveal themes that have not lost their relevance and tensions that persist.

Fifthly, the term accountability is often deployed in criticisms of international organisations; yet it does not benefit from the same clarity of its cognate ideas - as responsibility and liability.

By way of introduction, and occasional digression, this chapter will explore these five areas.

International organisations

The foundations of the law of international organisations were laid down in the period before the Second World War. The main concern at the time was to secure the presence of these fledgling actors in an international arena completely dominated by states. It was, for example, considered necessary to preserve international institutions from the jurisdiction of national courts by bestowing immunity upon them. Later, and in a manner consistent with these concerns, international organisations were also shielded from being sued by states in international courts. The view that international organisations are at the mercy of powerful states and always at risk of being bullied by them remains dominant today.

Since the end of the Second World War, international institutions, both under the UN umbrella and outside of it, have grown in number and undertaken an ever wider range of operational activities - a process of expansion that has often been dysfunctional. The practice of various organisations shows that the powers that they actually exercise normally go beyond the terms of their original mandates; and that their modus operandi often results from an informal normative framework comprising policy statements, internal guidelines, and operational codes and practices. Meanwhile, key aspects of the legal regime governing the activities of international organisations have not undergone a process of change or reconsideration. In most respects, the legal regulation of the activities of international institutions lags behind developments in institutional practice, and does not always offer prompt solutions to new problems and challenges.

Definition of international organisations

In its work on responsibility the ILC chose not to follow the definition of international organisation in the Vienna Convention on the Law of Treaties between States and International Organisations or between International Organisations.[1] The Convention defines the term 'international organisation' as an 'intergovernmental organisation' (Article 2(1)(i)) – a definition which, for all its succinct simplicity, seems of little use except insofar as it excludes some types of international organisations, namely those established by states through organs other than their governments, and those which include as members entities other than states.[2]

For its work on the responsibility of international organisations, the ILC opted instead for a broader definition in the following terms: 'an organisation established by a treaty or other instrument governed by international law and possessing its own international legal personality. International organisations may include as members, in addition to States, other entities.'[3] This definition, which has been generally met with favour by states,[4] includes organisations created by virtue of 'instruments, such as resolutions adopted by the General Assembly of the United Nations or by a conference of States',[5] as well as those with non-state actors among their members. Both definitions – the one in the Vienna Convention and the more recent one in the Draft Articles on Responsibility of International Organisations – are only for the purposes of the instruments in which they appear. They do not seek to capture or create an international legal definition of general validity.

[1] Convention on the Law of Treaties between States and International Organisations or between International Organisations, Vienna, 21 March 1986, 25 ILM 543.

[2] This reading of the definition in the Vienna Convention is shared by the International Law Commission (ILC, Report on the Work of the Fifty-fifth Session (2003), UN Doc. A/58/10, Commentary to draft article 2, at 38–9).

[3] Article 2, Draft Articles on the Responsibility of International Organisations (ILC, Report on the Work of the Sixty-first Session (2009), UN Doc. A/64/10 at 20).

[4] States have generally favoured these changes regarding them as consistent with 'current reality' (G. Gaja, 'Seventh Report on Responsibility of International Organisations by the Special Rapporteur', 61st Session of the ILC (2009) UN Doc. A/CN.4/610 at 4).

[5] ILC Report, *supra* note 2 at 40.

Attempts at definitions of general validity are found in the academic literature. Schermers and Blokker, for example, emphasise the public nature of international organisations as a crucial element distinguishing them from non-governmental organisations. The other elements in their proposed definition are: that the organisation has come into existence by international agreement; that it has at least one organ with a will of its own; and that it is established under international law.[6]

A particular definitional problem concerns operational programmes created by organs of the UN, such as the United Nations Children's Fund (UNICEF), UNHCR, the United Nations Relief and Works Agency (UNRWA), the United Nations Development Programme (UNDP) and the World Food Programme (WFP).[7] The activities of these programmes often have a direct impact on large numbers of individuals, and the potential for human rights violations in the course of their operations is accordingly significant. Should they be considered independent international organisations, or simply activities of the parent organisation, that is the UN? There is no clear answer to this question on the basis of the ILC definition. While these programmes clearly satisfy the first criterion in that definition (i.e. they are created by an instrument governed by international law), whether they possess separate legal personality depends, to a significant extent, on whether they are recognised in the first place as separate and autonomous entities.[8]

This problem may be dismissed as merely descriptive, but the characterisation of an entity as international organisation has normative consequences, most importantly on its treaty-making power and its responsibility. Little guidance can be derived from the Charter, which treats specialised agencies as self-standing organisations and makes

[6] H. G. Schermers and N. M. Blokker, *International Institutional Law* (4th edn., Dordrecht: Martinus Nijhoff, 2003), 30. See also the analysis of the debate on the definition of international organisations in Alvarez, *International Organisations as Law-Makers* at 4ff., and in J. Klabbers, *An Introduction to International Institutional Law* (Cambridge University Press, 2002), 6ff.

[7] UNDP: GA Res. 2029 (XX), 22 November 1965; UNHCR: GA Res. 428 (V), 14 December 1950; UNICEF: GA Res. 57 (I), 11 December 1946. An interesting case is that of the UN Industrial Development Organisation (UNIDO) which was initially established as a subsidiary organ of the General Assembly and was later transformed into a specialised agency (P. Bretton, 'La transformation de l' ONUDI en institution spécialisée', 25 AFDI (1979) 567). In the humanitarian field, another important organisation established as a subsidiary organ by the General Assembly (GA Res. 302 (IV), 8 December 1949) is UNRWA.

[8] See Chapter 2.

provision for the relationship between the UN and specialised agencies at Article 63, but is silent on operational programmes.

The Charter prescribes two conditions for specialised agencies: the constituent instrument must be a treaty, and the agencies must have 'wide international responsibilities, as defined in their basic instruments, in economic, social, cultural, educational, health and related fields' (Art. 57, I). Their relationship with the UN is governed by a relationship agreement which spells out the terms of the co-ordinative and recommendatory role of the UN pursuant to Articles 58 and 63 of the Charter. While there is almost universal agreement on the proposition that specialised agencies have international legal personality, it is argued by some that their legal personality, in contrast with that of the UN, is not opposable to non-member states.[9]

There is certainly no prerequisite that institutions in the UN family should adopt the form of the specialised agencies in order to be self-standing organisations; the question of the legal nature of operational programmes does not, in other words, find an answer in their *not* being specialised agencies. This negative element of the nature of operational programmes is only useful insofar as it indicates that the relationship between the operational programme and the UN is not going to be governed by the Charter model of the specialised agency, but, rather, by the specific terms of the act, normally a resolution of the General Assembly, which established the programme.

Two general factors are of paramount importance in addressing the question of the legal nature of operational programmes. First, there can be no doubt about the significance of their activities, which often have a greater and more direct impact on individuals than the activities of specialised agencies. Secondly, it must be borne in mind that, their subaltern legal status notwithstanding, these programmes tend to act independently of the parent organ that created them. Put in other terms: they are autonomous. Such autonomy is not normally provided for in the resolutions that established the operational programme, with the exception of UNIDO which was initially created as a subsidiary organ and only later converted into a specialised agency and which, already as an operational programme, was empowered to

[9] W. Meng, 'Article 57', in B. Simma (ed.), *The Charter of the United Nations: A Commentary* (2nd edn., Oxford University Press, 2002), 944 at 950. On the notion that the personality of the UN should be non-opposable, see Judge Kryzov's diss. op. in *Reparation for Injuries Suffered in the Service of the United Nations*, Advisory Opinion, ICJ Reports (1949), 174 at 218–19; this view was rejected by the majority of the Court (at 185).

'function as an autonomous organisation within the United Nations' under the terms of its mandate.[10] In most other cases, the autonomy of the operational programme is a reality rather than a precept. White has indeed noted that, while specialised agencies have a reporting obligation to the Economic and Social Council, operational programmes have often become rivals of the Council.[11] It would almost appear, in light of these considerations, that operational programmes are international organisations, trapped in an ill-suited institutional form that bears little relation to the reality of their activities, as well as to their autonomy and modus operandi.

These factors must be brought to bear on the determination of the legal nature of operational programmes. A programme that has complete control over its activities, like most of those examined in this book, should be treated as a discrete legal person, not least because this is 'essential in order to enable the subsidiary bodies to discharge their mandates, as well as to protect the parent organisations from liability resulting from the activities of their subsidiaries'.[12] Indeed, responsibility, and the resulting reputational damage, should be ascribed to the actual institution that committed the wrongful acts so that the group of officials that make up that institution, and decide and implement its activities, are associated with it.

To regard an operational programme as an independent international organisation is not to absolve the UN, as the parent organ, of its political and legal responsibility in the event of a wrongful act. Due to the nature of its relationship with the operational programmes, the UN would normally bear at least some responsibility for any UNHCR or UNDP activity, whereas the same cannot be said about specialised agencies.

Prerequisites for the lawful establishment of an operational programme are that a UN principal organ has acted in accordance with the Charter in establishing it, and that the parent organ exercises some control over its

[10] GA Res. 2152 (XXI), 17 November 1966.

[11] N. White, *Keeping the Peace: The United Nations and the Maintenance of International Peace and Security* (Manchester University Press, 1997), 146.

[12] 'Question of Juridical Personality and Legal Capacity in Relation to United Nations Agencies, Programmes and Funds', *UN Juridical Yearbook* (1994), 478 at 479. This view was somewhat nebulously qualified by the subsequent statement that legal capacity and legal personality are different and that subsidiary agencies 'thus cannot perform international acts or incur international obligations, except as expressly authorised by their parent bodies' (at 480).

subsidiary.[13] In particular, the parent organ retains the power to revise, and even to revoke, the mandates of the subsidiary agencies.[14] The WFP is a special case in that it has two parent organs, the UN General Assembly and the Food and Agricultural Organisation (FAO).

The authority and control of parent organs does not contradict the autonomy of operational programmes. In the *Effect of Awards* case, the International Court of Justice (ICJ) even accepted that in principle the decisions of the UN Administrative Tribunal – a subsidiary organ of the General Assembly – can bind the General Assembly itself, as long as the General Assembly had intended to confer these powers on the Tribunal;[15] that, put in other words, the General Assembly as parent organ could establish a subsidiary body that was independent in its decision-making and even able to bind the General Assembly itself.

The degree of autonomy that operational programmes concretely possess depends on the terms of their mandates, but also on institutional practice. In particular, the creation of a professional civil service and the process of bureaucratisation have contributed to buttressing their autonomy. With time these programmes have developed distinct institutional identities and organisational ethoi, while inter-agency competition often characterises their interactions with one another.[16] The size of their staff, their budget, the range and importance of their operations have often overtaken those of the putatively more autonomous specialised agencies.[17] The field offices of UNHCR or UNICEF, with

[13] D. Sarooshi, 'The Legal Framework Governing United Nations Subsidiary Organs', LXVII BYBIL (1996) 413 at 416. Sarooshi adds that the subsidiary organ has to have such a degree of independence from the parent organ as to warrant its 'separateness' as an entity from the parent organ. This, however, seems to be a corollary of creation, rather than a condition of lawfulness.

[14] For example, UNHCR's mandate is renewed by the General Assembly every five years and has been modified and expanded in the course of the years (G. S. Goodwin-Gill, *The Refugee in International Law* (3rd edn., Oxford: Clarendon Press, 2007), 428, footnote 40, and 481ff.).

[15] *Effect of Awards of Compensation Made by the UN Administrative Tribunal*, Advisory Opinion, ICJ Reports (1954), 60–1.

[16] M. Barnett and M. Finnemore, 'The Politics, Power and Pathologies of International Organizations', 53 Int. Org. (1999), 699 at 704ff.

[17] This was already noted by J. Dagory, 'Les rapports entre les institutions spécialisées et l' organisation des Nations Unies', 73 RGDIP (1969), 286 at 291. UNHCR had 6,650 staff members and a budget of US$2 billion in 2009 (www.unhcr.org.uk/about-us/history-of-unhcr.html). FAO, on the other hand, which is a specialised agency, had 3,600 members of staff and a biennial budget of US$2.2 billion in 2010–11 (www.fao.org/VA/Employ.htm and www.fao.org/about/strategic-planning/en). WFP's budget was larger than one of its parent bodies, FAO (US$4 billion in 2009, www.wfp.org/about/donors/wfp-donors/2009).

their display of agency flags, photographs of the head of the institution, and various gadgets and posters bearing the institutional logo, illustrate these developments. Operational programmes, like other international organisations, have thus grown more powerful as a result of the concurrent affirmation of 'the legitimacy of the rational-legal authority they embody' and of 'control over technical expertise and information'.[18]

An important difference between specialised agencies and operational programmes remains that the latter rely principally on voluntary contributions from states to finance their operations and are therefore potentially more susceptible to pressure from donor countries.[19] It would be wrong to conclude, however, that operational programmes are more easily manoeuvrable by states; on the contrary, it may often be easier for them to evade the political control of states. In fact, whereas the plenary organs of specialised agencies include representatives of member states and are entrusted with a function of control and general policy-making, operational programmes are not normally subject to forms of direct control by member states. Their conduct is subject only to indirect scrutiny by states through the parent organ, usually the General Assembly, or the Economic and Social Council. The General Assembly tends to discharge its functions of control over operational programmes in a manner that can be described, at best as cursory, at worst as entirely negligent. For example, with respect to UNHCR, Goodwin-Gill has observed that its resolutions are 'rarely consistent in their language, and their rationale, too, is often hidden'.[20] He has underscored that these resolutions have an 'after the event' nature and end up simply rubber-stamping changes in institutional practice and competence that have already occurred. His conclusion is that the General Assembly seems to have 'established subsidiary organs that act as specialised agencies without having that qualification'.[21]

History of international organisations

The League and its predecessors

The precursors of international organisations were the Public International Unions. First established in the second half of the nineteenth century, they included the International Telegraph Union (1865),

[18] Barnett and Finnemore, *supra* note 16, at 707.

[19] See D. Williams, *The Specialised Agencies and the UN: The System in Crisis* (London: C. Hurst, 1987) 43.

[20] Goodwin-Gill, *supra* note 14 at 11 and 15, footnote 61.

[21] Dagory, *supra* note 17 at 291.

the Universal Postal Union (1874) and the International Railway Congress Association (1884). By 1914 their number had grown and there were Public International Unions dealing with such different matters as communication, infrastructure, trade, intellectual property, labour, agriculture, public order, relief, health, education, and even inter-state conflicts.[22]

Commentators of the period coined the term 'international administrative law' to describe the body of treaty law that emerged from the establishment of the Public International Unions.[23] Already at that time, the rise of the Unions was often explained in functionalist terms, as a consequence of the development and expansion of national public administrations since 'the vast majority of the interests which are the objects of public administration have evolved and have by now become group interests in the community of civilised states and, as such, [have become] international interests';[24] the Unions were also seen as advancing the commercial interests of states.[25] Such functionalist approaches would, with time, lead to a re-definition of national sovereignty. As observed by Reinsch, the view that 'everything must be avoided which would constitute a derogation of the complete rights of sovereignty' had already been abandoned in the pre-1914 period.[26]

With some foresight, he also observed:

'The number and extent of the international activities already entered upon are surprising. It is not so much the case that nations have given up certain parts of their sovereign powers to international administrative organs, as that they have, while fully reserving their independence, actually found it desirable, and in fact necessary, regularly and permanently to co-operate with other nations in the matter of administering economic and cultural interests. Without legal derogation to the sovereignty of individual states, an international de facto and convention jurisdiction and administrative procedure is thus growing up, which bids fair to become one of the controlling elements in the future political relations of the world.'[27]

[22] See C. N. Murphy, *International Organisation and Industrial Change. Global Governance Since 1850* (Cambridge: Polity Press, 1994) 47–8.

[23] U. Borsi, 'Carattere ed oggetto del diritto amministrativo internazionale', 12 Riv. It. Dir. Int. (1912), 368; N. L. Hill, *International Administration* (London: McGraw-Hill, 1931); P. S. Reinsch, 'International Administrative Law and National Sovereignty', 3 AJIL (1909) 1; P. S. Reinsch, *Public International Unions: Their Work and Organisation. A Study in International Administrative Law* (London: Publication for the World Peace Foundation, 1911); W. Schucking, 'L'organisation internationale', 15 RGDIP (1908) 15.

[24] Ullman's *Völkerrecht* cited in Schucking, *supra* note 23, at 15, footnote 1.

[25] Hill, *supra* note 23, at 14–16.

[26] Reinsch (1909), *supra* note 23 at 10.

[27] *Ibid.* at 14.

The constituent instruments of the Unions were treaties normally adopted after a diplomatic conference convened by public or, in some cases, private initiative.[28] Membership of the Unions was open to all states, with the obvious exception of those Unions that operated in a geographically defined area. Unions had permanent organs, normally a Commission, performing executive functions, and a 'legislative' body, the Congress or Conference.

Unanimity was normally required for decisions.[29] An important distinction in the Unions' law was between the convention and the *règlement*, the former indicating the fundamental law, always treaty-based, that constituted and regulated the functioning of the Unions, the latter referring to resolutions adopted by their organs. Changes to the conventions always required the presence of 'diplomatic representatives', while changes in the *règlement* 'may be made by technical delegates'.[30] At the outset, the Unions worked with the governments of the country where their headquarters were based, and in some cases, their head offices were in the national ministry most closely associated with their work. Even the Unions that had separate offices – like the Labour Office, the predecessor of the International Labour Organisation (ILO) – operated in close conjunction with the host government, under whose supervision and direction they had been placed.

It was not long before the view emerged that Public International Unions had to be regarded as discrete legal persons. The Commission, appointed by the Director of the International Agricultural Institute in 1914 to investigate 'the questions concerning the legal status'[31] of that Institute, concluded that the states parties to the 1905 Convention which had created the Institute were obliged to accord domestic legal recognition to it. Such obligation was not explicitly provided for under that Convention, but – according to the Commission – it was implied. On this analysis, the 1905 Convention had established '54 different legal entities, all identical, except for their different nationality'.[32] This conclusion was not shared by Fusinato, a member of the Permanent Court of Arbitration. He argued instead that the Institute 'must be considered as a real international legal entity, composed of the state parties

[28] *Ibid.* at 20. [29] *Ibid.* at 29; Hill, *supra* note 23 at 6.

[30] Reinsch (1909), *supra* note 23 at 30.

[31] G. Fusinato, *Avis sur les questions touchants la personalité juridique de l' Institut International d' Agriculture* (Rome: Imprimerie de l' Institut Internationale de l' Agriculture, 1914) 3.

[32] *Ibid.* at 5.

to the 1905 Convention, and recognised as such in the territory of those states'.[33] He also added that the law applicable to the Institute should be that deriving from the 'personal statute of the Institute (as resulting from the 1905 Convention and from the following *règlements*)'.[34] The Fusinato view prevailed over time and international organisations were recognised as international legal persons.

Other principles of international institutional law were crystallised around this period. For example, the principle emerged that 'the members of these international Commissions are not called to defend the interests of their own country, but act – with all the freedom of their conscience – for the benefit of the union of countries which they represent'.[35] Initially, the staff of Public International Unions, unlike those of subsequent organisations, were almost exclusively nationals of the country in which the Union had its headquarters; the Swiss government, for instance, reserved most of the positions in the Unions it hosted for its own citizens.[36] Although, with the exception of the European Danube Commission, immunities or privileges were not normally bestowed upon the Unions and their officials in the pre-1914 period, this changed with the League of Nations whose Covenant granted immunity to its officials (Article 7, 4).[37]

The League of Nations was the first international organisation that could claim to be global in terms of competence. Its responsibilities included the peaceful settlement of disputes, the promotion of welfare, free communication and disarmament. The Covenant of the League may have fallen short of cosmopolitan aspirations, but it still managed to embrace 'a wide range of interests, somewhat greater in extent than a casual reading of the Covenant would intimate'.[38]

The League established auxiliary organs to deal with economic and social questions, including the first international programme for refugees, with the appointment of Fridtjof Nansen as High Commissioner for Russian Refugees in 1921. Although mainly limited to Europe, the League's involvement with refugees and other displaced persons soon expanded beyond assistance to Russian refugees. Unlike the approach

[33] *Ibid.* at 8. [34] *Ibid.* [35] Schucking, *supra* note 23 at 15.

[36] Reinsch (1909), *supra* note 23 at 33.

[37] L. F. L, Oppenheim, *International Law* (2nd edn., London: Longmans, Green and Co., 1912), 516. On the evolution of the law on the immunities of international organisations see J. L. Kunz, 'Privileges and Immunities of International Organisations', 41 AJIL (1947), 828 esp. at 857–9, and W. Jenks, *International Immunities* (London: Stevens, 1961).

[38] Hill, *supra* note 23 at 79.

that dominates refugee assistance today – centred on the provision of emergency relief and on the pursuit of repatriation as the preferred solution to the refugee problem – the League's work for refugees aimed mainly at securing their legal status in countries of asylum and at finding a durable solution, for the most part through local integration. The League encouraged repatriation in the case of Russian refugees, but in the end 'only a fraction of the total number of refugees returned to their homeland'.[39] The League played a pivotal role through the High Commissioner in the settlements of Asia Minor Greeks expelled from Turkey as part of the Greco-Turkish population exchange, of ethnic Bulgarians in Bulgaria, and of Armenian refugees in Syria.[40] After 1933 an ad hoc High Commissioner was appointed to deal with German refugees. The first High Commissioner for Jewish Refugees, James McDonald, resigned after two years publicly denouncing the German Reich for its persecution of Jews and advocating a more proactive role of the League.[41]

Another area in which the work of the League was seminal was the economic restructuring of war-affected countries. For example, a committee was established in 1921 to propose a scheme for the economic reconstruction of Austria. A Commissioner General, appointed by the Council of the League and residing in Vienna, advised the Austrian government on financial matters. His consent was necessary to release money that formed part of the credits granted to Austria. As a result of the recommendations of the committee and of the work of the Commissioner, important policies were implemented such as the downsizing of the civil service.[42] On other occasions in the 1920s, the League assumed some measure of administrative control in relation to economic reconstruction with the consent of the affected country (e.g. in Hungary, Bulgaria and Greece).[43] In the case of Bulgaria, the work of the Commissioner of the League was mainly related to refugees and the Commissioner's approval was necessary for the implementation of plans of assistance to refugees that required external resources.[44]

The ILO deserves a special mention, because it became the main specialised organisation within the circle of the League, its budget

[39] C. Skran, *Refugees in Inter-War Europe* (Oxford: Clarendon Press, 1995) 149.
[40] *Exchange of Greek and Turkish Populations*, Advisory Opinion, (1925) PCIJ Series B, No. 10.
[41] Skran, *supra* note 39 at 230ff. [42] Hill, *supra* note 23 at 84–8. [43] *Ibid.*
[44] See Skran, *supra* note 39 at 167ff.

nearly a third of that of the League's.[45] The initial mandate of the ILO was quite limited, but, pioneering a trend that would characterise other international institutions, the ILO soon undertook functions that 'went well beyond the modest task assigned to it by article 396 in Part XIII of the Versailles Treaty'.[46] The ILO's modus operandi, which became typical of a certain type of multilateral action, involved standard-setting, gathering and dissemination of information, and, to a more limited extent, monitoring. The ILO did undertake an operational role on various occasions, but its operative functions were quite narrowly conceived and consisted mainly of the provision of technical cooperation to countries engaged in economic or legal reforms affecting the labour market.[47]

The functional and operational expansion of the League could not have taken place without its large body of professional international civil servants. The existence of a professionalised civil service facilitated the development of an institutional ethos and an organisational identity, which with time became important factors in shaping institutional practice. The League's building, with its modern architecture, was a centrepiece for many career-minded and glamour-searching individuals, and for scores of dyed-in-the-wool socialites that rotated around them; this world was brilliantly portrayed in Albert Cohen's riveting *Belle du Seigneur*, a mordant literary indictment of international careerism.[48]

The Covenant extended diplomatic privileges and immunities to 'officials of the League when engaged on the business of the League' (Article 7, 4), in order to protect them from pressure from states and to guarantee the independence of the organisation. Before then, the grant of immunity to officials of international organisations had been rare.[49] The Covenant did not grant jurisdictional immunity to the League as a legal person, but it did make provision for privileges such as the inviolability of 'buildings and other property occupied by the League or its officials' (Article 7, 5). Furthermore, in 1926 the League reached an agreement with the Swiss government that essentially guaranteed

[45] Hill, *supra* note 23 at 113.

[46] V. Y. Ghebali, *The International Labour Organisation: A Case-Study on the Evolution of UN Specialised Agencies* (Dordrecht: Martinus Nijhoff, 1988) 13.

[47] *Ibid.* at 242ff. [48] A. Cohen, *Belle du Seigneur* (Paris: Gallimard, 1968).

[49] Kunz, *supra* note 37.

the organisation's immunity from lawsuits in Switzerland. This regulation of the immunity of the League was seminal: the immunity of the organisation and of its officials, subject to the functionalist approach,[50] is still a central principle of international institutional law, embodied in the UN Charter and in two Conventions.[51]

International institutional law was consolidated in the interwar period. The primary concern remained to secure the presence of international institutions in a state-dominated world. The experience of the League of Nations, and of the wide array of institutions, committees and other organs associated with it, moulded archetypical forms of multilateral action that are still in place today, and prompted an intense debate on 'international government', as part of which proposals that would be deemed daring even today were made and given serious consideration.[52] Although the operational activities of the League never matched those developed by the UN, the question of accountability was raised in the context of international administration, an area where the League did take on significant responsibilities. The League was severely criticised for the way it administered the territories of Saarland and Danzig for which it was responsible under the peace settlement. In particular, in the Saarland, where its powers were extensive, the League was accused of oppressing the German population and of acquiescing in the French policy of 'gallicisation' of the Saarland.[53]

Towards the 1930s the reform of the League was on the agenda, but the predominant concern was related to the League's failures in the maintenance of peace rather than to its performance in other areas. The outbreak of the war in 1939 cut short this debate.

[50] For the view that the UN Charter, by introducing the functional necessity doctrine, actually 'marked an historical shift towards the diminution of international immunities', see C. H. Brower, 'International Immunities: Some Dissident Views on the Role of Municipal Courts', 41 Virg. J. Int. L. (2000) 1 at 20.

[51] Convention on the Privileges and Immunities of the United Nations (1946) 1 UNTS 15; Convention on the Privileges and Immunities of the Specialised Agencies (1947) 33 UNTS 261.

[52] M. D. Dubin, 'Transgovernmental Processes in the League of Nations', 37 Int. Org. (1983), 469.

[53] W. H. Dawson, *The Saar Territory: Its History, Population, Industry and Government by the League of Nations* (publisher not indicated, 1934), 18ff.; Hill, *supra* note 23 at 96–9; R. Jones and S. S. Sherman, *The League of Nations: From Idea to Reality* (London: I. Pitman, 1927) 164.

The UN

Within a few years of its establishment the UN found itself entangled in cold war politics. The admission of European states that had fallen under the sphere of influence of one or the other bloc and the intervention in Korea were deeply divisive issues that risked paralysing the organisation, but, these challenges notwithstanding, the process of international organisation was not halted by the cold war.[54]

Most of the main institutional actors under the UN umbrella that continue to have a significant operational dimension today were in place by 1951. Some specialised agencies were created in the aftermath of the Bretton Woods Conference in July 1944 – the World Bank and the IMF. Others, like the FAO, the World Health Organisation (WHO) and United Nations Educational, Scientific and Cultural Organisation (UNESCO), were established as new organisations in the 1940s; the ILO survived the dissolution of the League, although its Constitution was amended so that it could, among other things, become a specialised agency of the UN. A number of important operational programmes, like UNICEF, UNRWA and UNHCR, had also come to existence by 1950. The late-comers were the WFP and UNDP – the former established in 1961 and the latter in 1965.

An important distinction for institutions under the UN umbrella is between specialised agencies and operational programmes. Specialised agencies are established by treaty and are in all respects self-standing organisations. Operational programmes are normally established by a resolution of the General Assembly and are subsidiary organs of the UN. As already mentioned above, despite their apparent lack of autonomy, the operational programmes act independently of their parent organ and perform a wide range of operational activities that have a direct impact on individuals.

The UN's first large-scale operation not involving the use of force was the provision of relief assistance in post-war Europe. The UN Relief and Rehabilitation Administration (UNRRA) coordinated activities for the relief and repatriation of those who had been displaced by the war in Europe, and organised the repatriation of about seven million persons

[54] With a rather vivid simile, Philip Allott writes that after the Second World War '*intergovernmental organizations* multiplied like flies on rotting meat' (*Eunomia* (2nd edn., Oxford University Press, 2001) xiii).

in a few years.[55] The UN did not, however, play a significant role in the humanitarian crisis that followed the partition between India and Pakistan, during which fourteen million people are believed to have crossed the border in one or the other direction – to date the largest recorded instance of forced migration. UNRRA was dismantled in June 1947, when the International Refugee Organization (IRO) was established to deal with the two million refugees for whom repatriation was not an option. The IRO became a very large operational agency, with a staff of nearly 3,000 persons at the peak of its activities and a fleet of forty ships.[56] The IRO was eventually liquidated in 1951, when the Office of the UNHCR was created. With most of the work for European refugees from the war completed in the 1950s, UNHCR remained a relatively small organisation for the first two decades of its existence: in 1971 its staff still numbered only 350,[57] but in the late 1970s, following the refugee crisis in South East Asia, its expenditure more than tripled. The trend continued in the 1980s and 1990s, although a funding crisis hit the organisation in the second half of the 1990s.[58] The other main international institution responsible for refugees – UNRWA – was created in 1949, and began to act as an operational agency quite early on, focusing on the provision of housing and education. In some respects, UNRWA resembled the office of the League's High Commissioner for Refugees more than UNHCR, not least because of the prominent role that refugees played in its administration.[59] This exposed UNRWA to accusations of being 'politicised' and of having espoused the Palestinian national cause rather than adhering strictly to the humanitarian terms of its mandate.[60]

Although certainly stifled by the confrontational climate of the cold war, on at least two occasions in the 1960s the UN succeeded in mounting large-scale complex operations that included elements of peacekeeping, humanitarian assistance and territorial administration. The

[55] L. Holborn, *Refugees: A Problem of Our Time* (Metuchen (NJ): Scarecrow Press, 1975) Vol. I, 26. See also G. Loescher, *UNHCR and World Politics: A Perilous Path* (Oxford University Press, 2001).

[56] Holborn, *supra* note 55 at 30–3.

[57] *Ibid*. Vol. II, 1399.

[58] UNHCR, *The State of the World's Refugees* (Oxford University Press, 2000) 166–7; Loescher, *supra* note 55 at 105ff.

[59] See also L. Takkenberg, *The Status of Palestinian Refugees in International Law* (Oxford: Clarendon Press, 1998).

[60] For example, A. Perlmutter, 'Patrons in the Babylonian Captivity of Clients: UNRWA and World Politics', 25 Int. Org. (1971) 306.

most important of these operations was the UN Operation in Congo (ONUC) in 1960–4. ONUC was primarily a peacekeeping operation,[61] but, in addition to its 20,000 troops, it also employed a staff of some 3,000 for its civilian component and performed important administrative functions. Various UN agencies also operated in Congo: for instance, UNHCR and the ILO ran a joint programme in Kivu province which had been affected by the arrival of thousands of Rwandan Tutsi refugees after 1959, and UNESCO administered its then largest educational programme. The other prominent UN operation in this period was the UN Temporary Administration (UNTEA) in West Irian (West New Guinea) in 1962–3. Albeit smaller in size than ONUC, UNTEA exercised effective control over territory, maintaining security and public order, organising the civil service and the judiciary, and building infrastructure.

As mentioned, the Charter strengthened the provisions in the League's Covenant on the immunity of the organisation and on the independence of international civil servants. Indeed, Article 105 of the Charter confers 'such privileges and immunities as are necessary for the fulfilment of its purposes' on the Organisation and on its officials. Article 100 affirms the independence of civil servants from governments or 'from any other authority external to the Organisation', while Article 101 provides that 'the paramount consideration in the employment of the staff and in the determination of the conditions of service shall be the necessity of securing the highest standard of efficiency, competence, and integrity'.

The principle of the independence of the civil service was flouted already in the early history of the UN. The first Secretary General accepted the fact that various member states screened their nationals before they could take up a position with the UN. In the case of the USSR and other countries in the eastern bloc, such screening was largely conducted behind the scenes. The US, on the other hand, entrusted an official body – the International Organizations Employees Loyalty Board – with this task. Far from contesting the legitimacy of this step, the Secretary General entered into 'a written secret agreement with the US Department of State whereby … applicants for and incumbents in UN Secretariat positions were "screened", without their

[61] ONUC's operational modalities blur the distinction between peacekeeping and enforcement action (White, *supra* note 11, at 260–1). See also R. Higgins, *United Nations Peace-keeping 1946–1967: Documents and Commentary* (1969–1981) Vol. III: Africa. In recent practice, this blurring has occurred even more distinctly (C. D. Gray, *International Law and the Use of Force* (3rd edn., Oxford University Press, 2008), 263).

knowledge, by US agents'.[62] In the early 1950s, a number of US nationals working for the UN even appeared before the US Senate's Committee on Anti-American Activities, and some of them lost their jobs. Some employees brought their cases to the UN Administrative Tribunal and received monetary compensation. The UN Administrative Tribunal had actually ordered reinstatement, but the Secretary General found that it was 'impossible or inadvisable' to reinstate, granting compensation in lieu of reinstatement.[63] The dismissal of these employees formed the basis for the award of damages that then led to the Advisory Opinion of the ICJ in *Effect of Awards*.[64] Other US employees brought a similar case against the Director General of UNESCO who did not renew their contracts after they refused to appear before the International Organizations Employees Loyalty Board of the US Civil Service. In informing them of his decision, the Director General of UNESCO wrote: 'I cannot accept your conduct as being consistent with the high standards of integrity which are required of those employed by the Organization.' Judicial bodies, however, opposed this clear breach of the principle that the international civil service should be independent: the Administrative Tribunal of the ILO found in favour of the employees, and the ICJ recognised both the competence of the Administrative Tribunal to hear their complaints and the validity of its decision.[65]

The actions of the Secretary General of the UN and the Director General of UNESCO at the time violated the Charter. Although the victims were awarded compensation, no other remedial steps were taken, and such overt interference with the independence of the international civil service continued unabated for many years. It was only in 1986, when the US courts finally deliberated on this matter, that the work of the International Organizations Employee Loyalty Board was terminated. The District Court for the Eastern District of Pennsylvania held that Executive Order 10422, with which President Eisenhower had established the Board in 1953, was unconstitutional in that it violated the First Amendment rights of free speech and free association.[66]

[62] Hazzard, 'Reflections. Breaking Faith-I', at 63.

[63] See M. Cohen, 'The United Nations Secretariat – Some Constitutional and Administrative Developments', 49 AJIL (1955) 295 at 307.

[64] *Effect of Awards* case, *supra* note 65 at 47.

[65] *Judgment of the Administrative Tribunal of the International Labour Organisation upon Complaints Made against the United Nations Educational, Scientific and Cultural Organisation*, Advisory Opinion, ICJ Reports (1956) 77.

[66] *Hinton v. Devine*, 633 F. Supp. 1023. See also M. A. Roy, 'US Loyalty Program for Certain UN Employees Declared Unconstitutional', 80 AJIL (1986) 984.

Although the District Court did not concern itself with the violation of the Charter, its decision indirectly put an end to such violation, after years of acquiescence and complicity on the part of the very organs of the UN entrusted with ensuring the respect of the Charter. To those who made accusations of connivance with practices that infringed the Charter, the then Secretary General responded with an argument 'that would henceforth be used by UN senior officials to deflect inquiry into malfunction and malpractice at the organization: "Everything you say will be used against this organization by the enemies of the United Nations".'[67]

Given the tendency towards bureaucratisation,[68] and on account of the close connection between operational practice and institutional culture, these 'original sins' played an important and much-neglected role in the development of the fledgling international civil service and in shaping its ethos. In the short term, '[t]he number of international employees who, in a steady draining, left the United Nations system during its first decade because of intimidation, indignation or disillusion may be estimated at several hundred. Some were encouraged to resign with special payments, sixty others were removed as part of an "efficiency survey", carried out in 1952, whose records were immediately destroyed.'[69]

Despite these constraints on the independence of the civil service, the UN continued to expand and to undertake an ever-greater operational role, a process that accelerated between the late 1960s and the 1980s when the UN provided humanitarian relief in various conflicts – in Biafra, Ogaden, Bangladesh, Indochina and Sudan among other places. This process gained further momentum after the end of the cold war, once it became easier to reach the necessary political consensus to mount complex humanitarian operations as well as peace-support ones.

The history of UNHCR illustrates some of the idiosyncrasies at play in this process of operational expansion. Until at least the mid-1970s UNHCR was small compared with its size today. It had been operational in a field sense on a few occasions, for example in Congo in 1960. The core of UNHCR's mandate as defined in its statute[70] was supposed to be implemented through protection activities, i.e. activities that aimed at ensuring that refugees could find an adequate replacement

[67] Hazzard, *supra* note 63 at 63.
[68] Barnett and Finnemore, *supra* note 16 at 699.
[69] Hazzard, *supra* note 63 at 68.
[70] GA Res. 428 (V), 14 December 1950.

for the diplomatic protection denied to them by their countries of nationality. As a result, within UNHCR the Division of International Protection 'dominated a rigid hierarchy'.[71] Another advantage offered by this focus on the legal work of the organisation and on its protection activities was that the organisation could be shielded from the 'politically charged atmosphere of the United Nations'.[72]

With the refugee crisis in Indochina in the 1970s, UNHCR became a predominantly operational organisation, in charge of so-called care and maintenance programmes to assist refugees. The focus on protection in UNHCR's mandate was progressively eroded; 'responsibility and accountability to mandate fell by the wayside, to the extent that many organisational units today appear institutionally incapable of relating their performance and activities to the mandate of UNHCR as a whole'.[73] In addition, UNHCR became more reluctant to challenge states since it was by now closely cooperating with them in the management of refugee camps and settlements, and in the provision of relief assistance. As has been observed, 'the pursuit of protection activities necessarily results in a tension between state and individual, and between states and the international agency charged with that responsibility. UNHCR cannot expect always to please all sides, but the art is to stay close to principles, not to throw them overboard in an excess of "realistic" cohabitation.'[74]

The number of empirical studies of the operational practice of international institutions has grown over the last two decades, although the misconceived assumption that the operational dimension of the UN is marginal is still found in the legal literature.[75] The fundamental fact of the growing *power* of international institutions is beginning to receive attention, but the legal and policy implications of these developments have not yet been taken on board fully by scholars, not to mention international organisations themselves. One reason for this slow response may be the resilience of the belief that 'any increase

[71] G. S. Goodwin-Gill, 'Refugee Identity and Protection's Fading Prospect', in F. Nicholson and P. Twomey (eds.), *Refugee Rights and Realities* (Cambridge University Press, 1999) 220 at 235.

[72] *Ibid.* at 224.

[73] *Ibid.* at 235. See also: Loescher, *supra* note 55, 363–4; G. Verdirame and B. E. Harrell-Bond, *Rights in Exile: Janus-Faced Humanitarianism* (Oxford: Berghahn Books, 2005) 291–6.

[74] E.g. B. Conforti, *The Law and Practice of the United Nations* (3rd edn., Leiden: Martinus Nijhoff, 2005) 249.

[75] *Ibid.*

in international organisation is a triumph of idealism over realism, that more is always better, and that cooperation is *ispo facto* better than conflict ... And the unspoken assumption, of course, is that international officials are selfless dedicated missionaries with only the best interests of the world community at heart.'[76]

The concept of autonomy and international organisations

It is commonplace to regard international institutions as controlled by powerful states and subservient to their interests. This view is normally associated with the scepticism of realists about the ability of norms to influence the conduct of states and about the effectiveness on the international plane of international actors other than states.[77] Without delving into the extensive debate on realism and on the different schools of thought in international relations, it is at least worth mentioning that various historical and empirical studies are now casting critical light on this notion.[78]

An excellent account of various schools of thought on international organisation is in Alvarez's *International Organisations as Law-Makers* at 17–57. These schools of thought are, for the most part, linked to one of the various denominations in which the field of international relations and political science is divided in the US academe. As I have argued elsewhere,[79] despite the appearance of great diversity of opinion, a set of basic assumptions runs through most of these approaches to international relations and political science.

Among the most significant recent contributions to the study of international organisations are those of scholars who have demonstrated the importance of bureaucratic elements and organisational culture in international organisations. In particular, 'drawing on long-standing Weberian arguments about bureaucracy and sociological institutionalist approaches to organizational behavior', Michael Barnett and Martha

[76] S. Strange, *The Retreat of the State. The Diffusion of Power in the World Economy* (Cambridge University Press, 1996) 162.

[77] Klabbers, *supra* note 6.

[78] See, for example, A. Klotz, *Norms in International Relations: The Struggle against Apartheid* (Ithaca (NY): Cornell University Press, 1995), and T. Risse, S. C. Ropp and K. Sikkink (eds.), *The Power of Human Rights: International Norms and Domestic Change* (Cambridge University Press, 1999), especially Risse's and Sikkink's Introduction, 'The socialisation of international human rights norms into domestic practices' at 1.

[79] See my article '"The Divided West": American and European International Lawyers', 18 EJIL (2007).

Finnemore have argued that 'the rational-legal authority that international organizations embody gives them power independent of the states that created them and channels that power in particular directions'.[80] Moreover, while accepting that states may place constraints of various types on international organisations, 'the notion that they are passive mechanisms with no independent agendas of their own was not borne out by any detailed empirical study of an international organization that we have found'.[81] Studies of UNHCR have shown that, while this organisation was 'born with little autonomy and few prospects for expansion ... [it] was able to capitalize on world events and use its authority to greatly expand both the groups of people it assisted and the kinds of assistance it could give'.[82] The case studies in Chapters 4 and 5 of this book, as well as my own research for *Rights in Exile*, lend further support to these findings, as they discuss various instances in which the UN and its operational programmes acted autonomously, sometimes even in disregard of the will of the political organs of the organisation.

But what does autonomy mean in this context? An autonomous institution is one that possesses a will distinct from that of its member states and can act independently of them. But distinct will does not necessarily entail the power 'to take decisions binding its membership by a mere majority of its members'.[83] To impose the requirement that autonomy be predicated on power, understood in the Hohfeldian sense of the ability to change the legal position of others, is to set the bar too high. In the case of neither individuals nor states is evidence of Hohfeldian power over others normally required as proof of their autonomy (or, to employ the terms typically used in relation to individuals, of their agency or freewill).

Conceptualising international organisations as entities whose autonomy is not a mere legal postulate but a social and political fact radically changes perceptions about them. In particular, it causes us to reconsider the assumption that the power international organisations may occasionally wield over individuals is really another manifestation of

[80] Barnett and Finnemore, *supra* note 16, at 699. See also M. Barnett and F. Finnemore, 'The Power of Liberal International Organizations', in M. Barnett and R. Duvall (eds.), *Power in Global Governance* (Cambridge University Press, 2005) 169.

[81] Barnett and Finnemore, *supra* note 16 at 705.

[82] M. Barnett and F. Finnemore, *Rules for the World: International Organisations in Global Politics* (New York: Cornell University Press, 2004) 73 and also 118–20.

[83] Klabbers, *supra* note 6 at 55.

state power through other means. It also casts doubt on the justificatory arguments, frequently resorted to by international organisations, that simplistically place the blame for anything that goes wrong on member states. True, it would be certainly unwise to move to the opposite extreme and conclude that the UN and other international institutions have developed the unfettered ability to act entirely autonomously and to resist all attempts by the states to influence their conduct, but it makes little sense to continue to perceive international organisations as forces for good faced with the constant risk of being engulfed by state leviathans bent on pursuing nothing but their own selfish interests.

Such starry-eyed views of the UN are exemplified in the following passage from a classic work in the field:

'Anyone who cares about the future of the developing countries can only hope for a massive increase in the number of operational activities of the United Nations. In fact, if technical assistance and aid come from a universal organization such as the United Nations, if, in other words, the flow of capital coming from wealthy countries and intended for poor countries is "filtered" by such an Organization, the assistance becomes neutral in that it is freed from political, or even military, conditioning. Unfortunately, precisely owing to these characteristics, the operational activities of the United Nations represent only a modest fraction of the over-all volume of international assistance, most of which is still covered by *direct* aid and by contributions granted on a bilateral or multilateral scale. In other words, the multiplication, inexplicable under various aspects, of United Nations organs intended for operational functions has unfortunately not been matched, owing to the lack of funds, by real and effective action for development. Since this is the present situation, it is impossible to agree with those observers who hold that the United Nations is being transformed into a large operational agency. In fact, the Organization is and remains, as it was conceived of at San Francisco, an entity whose powers are predominantly normative, an entity intended not to act, but to dictate rules to the States.'[84]

International human rights law

One of the central propositions advanced in this book is that the UN has at times violated human rights in the course of its operations. The normative terms of reference for this proposition are those set in international human rights law; I take this body of law as a given

[84] See *supra* note 75 at 249; emphasis in original.

for the purposes of my argument. Occasionally I do use the term liberty instead of human rights. When I do so, I am not suggesting that this term provides an accurate conceptual synthesis of international human rights law as it is today; on the contrary, my view is that international human rights law today has moved away from any reasoned concept of liberty. Rather, I use the term liberty to stress that a particular act or omission violates not only human rights in the positive law sense, but also a more profound idea of liberty.[85]

International human rights law has been accused of lacking philosophical coherence; there is, to use Jim Griffin's words, a 'discrepancy between philosophy and international law'.[86] It is true that legislation, whether domestic or international, is seldom a pure reflection of the ideas that preceded it; at the very least, those ideas will have been mediated through the prism of social, political and economic interests. But the gap between the idea and the phenomenon is even wider in the case of international human rights law, characterised by an almost boundless and ever-expanding catalogue of claims recognised as human rights including many rights of uncertain scope and content, and even 'manifesto rights' (the right to peace or the right to development) with no discernible, let alone actionable, legal content. Joseph Raz, who has probably been more sympathetic to international human rights law than most contemporary legal philosophers, agrees that, while 'human rights enjoy a rational justification', they are not 'grounded in a fundamental moral concern but depend on the contingencies of the current system of international relations'.[87] If the best case that can be made for human rights is that they are the offspring of international politics, it is not one that carries great moral force.

In fairness, Raz's theory of human rights is not limited to this argument. The mainstay of his position is that international human rights 'normally derive from three layers of argument': first an individual interest that is elevated to the level of moral right; secondly the duty of the state to promote the interest in question; and thirdly the acceptance of the limitation of sovereignty in respect of such interest and duty. Even so, it is difficult to see how such 'layers

[85] On the relationship between the idea of liberty and human rights see G. De Ruggiero, *Storia del Liberalismo Europeo* (Milan: Feltrinelli, 1959) 335ff.

[86] Griffin, *On Human Rights* (2008) 191ff.

[87] J. Raz, 'Human Rights Without Foundations', in S. Besson and J. Tasioulas (eds.), *The Philosophy of International Law* (Oxford University Press, 2010) 321 at 336.

of argument' are sufficient to produce a theory of human rights that is not merely descriptive.

From the 'unphilosophy' of international human rights law derive some important features. International human rights are disembodied and abstracted from any political or historical reality. Indeed, international human rights law in many ways epitomises the idea of abstracted right which Hegel in the *Philosophy of Right* and Marx in his essay *On the Jewish Question* criticised – a fact which has not escaped the attention of contemporary Marxist scholars.[88]

While the 'unphilosophy' of international human rights law and its abstracted and depoliticised nature have no bearing on legal determinations of breaches, they are relevant to the kind of human rights culture that has put down roots in international organisations: the clear-headed liberalism – right or wrong as it might be – that defines constitutional human rights in the most advanced liberal democracies has been replaced by a deep ideological confusion. This confusion is fuelled by the ever-lengthening catalogue of human rights, and by the dilution of their normativity through the notion that human rights have become 'grammar' or a 'language'.[89] It is true, as David Kennedy once wrote, that international human rights law may have become part of the problem, but, as I have argued elsewhere, it is difficult to see how the deconstructionism and rule-scepticism on which postmodernist approaches are premised can be part of any solution.[90]

Humanitarianism

Humanitarianism escapes easy definitions. As a set of ethical principles, a mindset, an emotional disposition or an intellectual tradition,

[88] B. Bowring, *The Degradation of the International Legal Order* (New York: Routledge-Cavendish, 2008) 119ff.

[89] See, for example, S. Marks and A. Clapham, *International Human Rights Lexicon* (2nd edn., Oxford University Press, 2005), viii, citing E. Said, *Reflections on Exile* (Cambridge, MA: Harvard University Press, 2001) 430.

[90] See D. Kennedy, 'The International Human Rights Movement: Part of the Problem?', 15 *Harvard Human Rights Journal* (2001) 99; Verdirame, 'The Divided West' at 553. On rule-scepticism as a defining element of American legal pragmatism (and its epigones such as the Critical Legal Studies movement), see H. L. A. Hart, 'American Jurisprudence through English Eyes: The Nightmare and the Noble Dream', 11 *Georgia Law Review* (1977) 969.

humanitarianism is relevant to a study of the UN because many UN programmes, particular those that have a direct impact on individuals, are justified on such humanitarian grounds as the alleviation of suffering.

Since the 1980s humanitarianism has come under severe criticism, initially by social scientists, whose studies of the operational reality of the world of relief and aid cast doubt on the ethical claims of humanitarianism, but now also by journalists, philosophers and legal scholars.[91] Critics of humanitarianism have questioned the assumptions of modern humanitarianism, challenging the notion that the operational problems experienced by various humanitarian organisations might be merely an example of a good idea that is not being implemented well and raising the possibility that there may be problems with the very idea of humanitarianism itself.

There are three streams of criticism that are particularly relevant to the present enquiry. First, there is the relationship between humanitarianism and power – as Rieff puts it, humanitarianism's 'history of functioning as an adjunct to imperial domination'.[92] This is illustrated by the historical excursus on the origins of modern day international humanitarianism in the battle to end the slave trade. Secondly, there is the tendency to fetishise organisational mandates as part of the 'infatuation with and reliance upon the law' of modern humanitarianism[93] – a problematic trend particularly in light of the inclusion in the mandates of the principles of neutrality and impartiality. Thirdly, there is the relationship between humanitarianism and human rights.

The struggle to end the slave trade and the origins of modern international humanitarianism

British efforts to assert a general right to search and seizure of vessels

Commonly heralded as the starting point of the process of international organisation,[94] the Congress of Vienna in 1815 also witnessed

[91] Among the pioneers in the field were: Harrell-Bond, *Imposing Aid* and Shawcross, *The Quality of Mercy*. See also A. De Waal, *Famine Crimes: Politics and the Disaster Relief Industry in Africa* (Oxford: James Currey, 1997) and D. Rieff, *A Bed for the Night: Humanitarianism in Crisis* (New York: Simon & Schuster, 2002). The most prominent critique by a legal scholar is D. Kennedy, *The Dark Sides of Virtue: Re-assessing International Humanitarianism* (New Jersey: Princeton University Press, 2004).

[92] Rieff, *supra* note 91 at 76. [93] *Ibid.*

[94] D. Armstrong, *The Rise of International Organisation. A Short History* (London: Macmillan, 1982); C. Archer, *International Organizations* (2nd edn., London: Routledge, 1992) 6–7.

the adoption of the Declaration of the Eight Courts Relative to the Abolition of the Slave Trade, largely as a result of British pressure, that condemned the slave trade.[95]

The Declaration was later incorporated in the Final Act of the Congress of Vienna and, as such, became part of the treaty that formed the basis for the European order following the Napoleonic wars.[96] However, the wording of the declaration was carefully calibrated in order to avoid the creation of an obligation to abolish the slave trade.

For example, the Declaration provided that:

'considering the universal abolition of the Slave Trade as a measure particularly worthy of their attention, conformable to the spirit of the times, and to the generous principles of their august Sovereigns, they are animated with the sincere desire of concurring in the most prompt and effectual execution of this measure, by all the means at their disposal, and of acting in the employment of these means, with all the zeal and perseverance which is due to so great and noble a cause.'

The Declaration also explained that 'however honourable their [the Sovereigns'] views, they cannot be attained without due regard to the interests, the habits, and even the prejudices of their subject'.

Despite an earlier success with the inclusion of an abolitionist clause in a treaty with France, Britain's hopes of securing a legally binding international commitment to end the slave trade,[97] and to establish a common international maritime policy for the suppression of this practice, did not thus materialise in Vienna.

That the abolition of the slave trade had reached such a high position on Britain's foreign policy agenda as to prompt its leaders to raise it in Vienna was due to the strength of the abolitionist movement in Britain. Normally inspired by religion, but also including in their midst private individuals and secular associations that had been influenced by the

[95] Declaration of the Eight Courts Relative to the Abolition of the Slave Trade, 8 February 1815, in W. G. Grewe (ed.), *Fontes Historiae Juris Gentium* (Berlin: Walter de Gruyter, 1992), Vol. 3/1, 376 and in Martens, NR, T, II, 432. Also: Declaration of Eight European Courts on the Abolition of the Slave Trade, 8 February 1815, annexed as Act XV to the 1815 General Treaty of Vienna Congress, 63 CTS 473.

[96] Article 118, No. 15 of the Final Act of the Congress of Vienna, 9 June 1815, 64 CTS (1815) 492. The Final Act was signed by Great Britain, Austria, France, Portugal, Prussia, Russia, Spain and Sweden-Norway.

[97] Additional Articles to the Definitive Treaty of Peace and Amity between Austria, Great Britain, Portugal, Prussia, Russia, Sweden and France, 30 May 1814, 63 CTS (1814–15) 193.

ideas of the Enlightenment, the abolitionists developed a network of support across Britain that became one of the most effective ways of promoting social change at first in Britain and then throughout the world. Through assiduous campaigning beginning in the 1780s, the abolitionists obtained a landmark victory with the adoption in 1807 of the Slave Trade Abolition Act.[98] The abolitionists were one of the first examples of a 'civil society' movement propounding a humanitarian cause.[99] It found in Britain a naturally fertile soil owing to the strong economy and sizeable middle class, and to the traditional respect for free speech. However, even the array of legal scholars, politicians and socialites involved in the abolitionist movement, progressive though they undoubtedly were by the standards of their day, were not always the champions of human equality as we would intend it today. Indeed, 'the emancipationists wished to free the slave within the minimum decency which humanity required, but they insisted on European guardianship ... As a result, the primary goal was the creation of societies that, in the words of French premier Georges Clemenceau, "complied with certain principles of government" to be determined by Europeans.'[100] Humanists – or humanitarians as we would say today – for the most part accepted the premise of European guardianship as a 'sacred trust of civilisation'.

It is important to avoid romanticising 'civil society' as a force that pushes for change from the grassroots level and defies established power. As argued by Gramsci,[101] civil society movements are historically a political expression of the elite and are normally respectful of the underlying balance of power in a society. In the case of the British anti-slavery movement, the religious ideals of Protestant reformists played a crucial role. The British elites were prepared to embrace the abolition of the slave trade as part of a package of religious

[98] The first European country to abolish the slave trade officially was Denmark in 1802, even though slavery was still lawfully practised in some of her colonies for another decade (S. Daget, 'The Abolition of the Slave Trade', in J. F. Ade Ajayi (ed.), *General History of Africa. Africa in the XIX Century Until the 1880s* (Oxford: Heinemann, 1989) 64). Britain had been among the most important slave-trading nations in the eighteenth century after the Peace Treaty of Utrecht in 1713 had secured her monopoly of the trade to Latin America.

[99] D. B. Davis, *The Problem of Slavery in the Age of Revolution: 1770–1823* (New York: Ithaca: Cornell University Press, 1975) 68.

[100] S. N'zatioula Grovogui, *Sovereigns, Quasi Sovereigns, and Africans. Race and Self-Determination Under International Law* (Minneapolis: University of Minnesota Press, 1996) 79.

[101] A. Gramsci, *Quaderni dal Carcere* (V. Gerrantana (ed.), 2nd edn., Torino: Einaudi, 1975–1977) 40–1, 1222–4, 1235–7, 1249–50, 1603 and 2010–11.

reforms that aimed at rescuing Britain from evil. In this respect, their association with the Jacobins and with Thomas Paine in the 1790s has been regarded as a tactical error as it undermined their credentials in the eyes of part of their domestic constituency.[102]

In the years that followed the Congress of Vienna, Britain continued to pursue diplomatic efforts to canvass enough international support in favour of a common international maritime policy against the slave trade, but without success.[103] At the heart of the British policy lay the right to visit, search and seize vessels suspected of transporting slaves. The other European powers, wary of British naval supremacy, feared that the international legal acceptance of the right of seizure would consolidate the policing role of the British Navy.

Another strategy adopted by Britain in this period was to include a provision on the abolition of the slave trade in treaties concluded with other countries for different purposes, such as commercial agreements.[104] By doing so, Britain often managed to establish the right of search and seizure bilaterally.[105] For instance, the Hammerton Treaty of 2 October 1845 between Britain and the Sultan of Muscat allowed the Royal Navy to search, seize and confiscate vessels belonging to the subjects of the Sultan suspected of transporting slaves, providing in the preamble that the Sultan agreed to the end of the slave trade 'in deference to the wishes of Her Majesty and of the British nation, and in furtherance of the dictates of humanity'.[106] Abolitionist clauses were also included in some of the agreements between Britain and various African chiefdoms during the British colonial expansion in that continent.[107] Throughout the nineteenth century Britain also made

[102] See C. D. Kaufmann and R. A. Pape, 'Explaining Costly International Moral Action: Britain's Sixty-year Campaign Against the Atlantic Slave Trade', 53 Int. Org. (1999) 631 at 662.

[103] Davis, *supra* note 100 at 35.

[104] J. Martinez, 'Anti-Slavery Courts and the Dawn of International Human Rights Law', 117 Yale L. J. (2007–2008) 550 at 569.

[105] R. Howell, *The Royal Navy and the Slave Trade* (London: Croom Helm, 1987), 9. For a complete list of the treaties that contained a clause on the abolition of the slave trade signed by Britain until 1850, see also R. Phillimore, *Commentaries upon International Law* (3rd edn., London: Butterworths, 1879) 420–1.

[106] Article 3, Agreement between Great Britain and Muscat for the Termination of the Export of Slaves ('Hammerton Treaty'), 2 October 1845, 99 CTS (1845–46) 27.

[107] See for instance: Engagement between Great Britain and King Fanatoro and the Chiefs of Cape Mount (West Africa), 2 January 1846, 99 CTS (1845–46) 272; Treaties between Great Britain and the Chiefs of Sano and Moricaryah, Malaghea,

recognition of newly independent states in Latin America conditional upon their total renunciation of the slave trade.

However important, this state practice was not alone sufficient to establish a generally binding international standard against the slave trade, at least so long as the main European powers did not join in. Throughout the nineteenth century, Britain continued to stop foreign vessels on the Atlantic Ocean, particularly along the West African coast, generally incurring the protest of the states concerned. In the 1840s, the British Navy, officially authorised by Parliament, searched Portuguese and Brazilian ships unilaterally. In the case of Brazil, the British intervention was particularly aggressive, and involved the burning of ships of slave traders in Brazilian territorial waters and harbours. This nearly led to a war with Brazil, averted when Brazil finally capitulated and ratified a treaty giving British ships a right of search and visit.[108] Over time, however, European powers began to change attitude and bilateral treaties were concluded with Britain establishing a system of international courts for the suppression of the slave trade. These treaties, having been long forgotten, are now the object of attention by legal historians who have come to regard them as 'the first international human rights courts … They were made up of judges from different countries. They sat on a permanent, continuing basis, and they applied international law.'[109]

Far from being consistent, British practice was traversed by the tension between unilateral enforcement and the pursuit of international cooperation through law and diplomacy. The British were more prepared to coerce comparatively less powerful states like Portugal, Brazil or Cuba, than the US or France. Indeed, in official dealings with US and French officials, Britain for the most part did not claim a right to search and seize vessels belonging to countries with which there was no agreement to this effect, although this may be an indication of that discrepancy between stated practice and actual practice which characterised both British and US policy in this area: the US, where the slave trade – but not

Fouricane and Benira (West Africa), 20, 23 and 28 May 1845, 98 CTS (1845) 205. These agreements normally contained provisions on free trade and access of British goods to local markets, as well as other provisions constituting the seeds of the colonial system of 'indirect rule' (M. Mamdani, *Citizen and Subject: Contemporary Africa and the Legacy of Late Colonialism* (Kampala: Fountain; London: James Currey, 1996) 17).

108 Kaufmann and Pape, *supra* note 103 98 at 659.

109 Martinez, *supra* note 105 at 552.

slavery – had been banned in 1793, was aware of the fact that vessels flying the American flag were engaging in the trade but did not take any step to suppress it; Britain, on the other hand, while maintaining that it was not searching vessels under foreign flags unless there was a treaty authorising the British fleet to do so, nonetheless continued to police the seas, especially off the West African coast.[110] There were times, however, when Britain did argue that her warships were entitled to examine the papers of foreign vessels and, if necessary, to board the ship.[111] Other countries, like the US for instance, categorically denied that the British fleet had such a right, and, perhaps not so surprisingly, Britain herself vehemently denied the existence of such a right when Haiti, having banned the slave trade, began to stop and search foreign vessels.[112]

In the still numerous cases in which the British Navy sought and seized vessels of countries with which there was no agreement, Britain was acting in contravention of the international law in force at the time. In these cases, Britain would usually deny having searched or seized the vessels in question – thereby implicitly confirming the legal validity of the principle that there was no general right to stop and search – although its practice would also refer to principles of 'humanity and universal morality' at a time in which the natural law tradition was still very strong.[113]

Courts and the slave trade

Courts maintained a cautious attitude when dealing with cases of foreign ships seized on the high seas by the Royal Navy for slave trading. An illustration is the landmark judgment of the High Court of Admiralty in the *Le Louis* case, which reversed the decision of the vice-admiralty court that had condemned a French ship for engaging in the slave trade.[114] In his judgment, Sir William Scott explained that

[110] See, for instance, letter from the Earl of Aberdeen to Mr Everett, 20 December 1841, XXX British and Foreign State Papers (1841–42) 1178.

[111] Letter of Viscount Palmerston to Mr Stevenson, 27 August 1841, XXX British and Foreign State Papers (1841–42) 1152.

[112] Letter of Mr Stevenson to Viscount Palmerston, 27 February 1841, XXX British and Foreign State Papers (1841–42) 1137.

[113] See for instance J. Noyes 'Christianity and Late XIX Century British Theories of International Law' in M. W. Janis (ed.), *The Influence of Religion on the Development of International Law* (Dordrecht: Martinus Nijhoff, 1991).

[114] *Le Louis*, High Court of Admiralty (1817) in C. Parry (ed.), *British International Law Cases* (1965), Vol. III at 691.

there was no right of search in time of peace and that the slave trade could not be equated to piracy and treated as another crime *jure gentium*. Unlike pirates, slave traders did not, in his view, engage in the 'act of freebooters, enemies of the human race, renouncing every country, and ravaging every country in its coasts and vessels indiscriminately, and thereby creating an universal terror and alarm'.[115] Slave traders were 'persons confining their transactions (reprehensible as they may be) to particular countries, without exciting the slightest apprehension in others'.[116] The different treatment reserved under the law of nations to pirates is indeed revealing. Pirates were 'enemies of the human race' (*hostes humani generis*) because they disrupted the international public order by interfering with the safety of navigation and with commerce, but slave traders, who certainly caused much greater suffering, were not treated as *hostes humani generis*.

In the *Le Louis* case, the High Court of Admiralty rejected the argument that the right of visit and search derived from the need to enforce Britain's own navigation laws by checking the nationality of a ship to ensure that she was not disguising her true flag. Considerable weight was given to the fact that a significant number of countries were still practising slavery and that Britain could not impose its will on them. The High Court of Admiralty upheld this precedent in subsequent decisions.[117]

In an important passage, the Court explained:

> 'To press forward to a great principle by breaking through every other great principle that stands in the way of its establishment; to force the way to the liberation of Africa by trampling on the independence of other states in Europe; in short, to procure an eminent good by means that are unlawful is as little consonant to private morality as to public justice.'[118]

Some courts were, however, prepared to push the boundaries. For example, the 1822 case *United States v. The Schooner La Jeune Eugenie*[119] concerned a French vessel which was carrying slaves and had been seized by an American warship on the coast of Africa. The French

[115] *Ibid*. at 705. [116] *Ibid*.

[117] For instance in *San Juan Nepomuceno, Yambi*, (1824) 1 Hag. Adm. 265, in Parry, *supra* note 115 at 711 and in *Buron v. Denman*, in Parry, *supra* note 115, Vol. VI at 385.

[118] *Le Louis*, *supra* note 1145 at 703.

[119] *United States v. The Schooner La Jeune Eugenie*, 26 F. Cas. 832, (2) *Mason's Reports*, 409. The case is also in E. D. Dickinson, *A Selection of Cases and Other Readings on the Law of Nations* (New York: McGraw-Hill, 1929) 13.

consul protested that the American courts had no jurisdiction to hear the case. The Circuit Court stated that the preliminary jurisdictional matter concerned the international legal status of the prohibition of the slave trade. It was held that 'at the present moment the traffic is vindicated by no nation, and is admitted by almost all commercial nations as incurably unjust and inhuman';[120] as a result 'in all cases, where it is not protected by a foreign government, [the courts will have] to deal with it as an offence carrying with it the penalty of confiscation'.[121] The fact that France not only had abolished the slave trade in law but had also ceased to tolerate its practice by her citizens was decisive. The court still deemed it necessary to distinguish this case from other cases in which the slave trade is carried out with the consent of a state.

The Court explained that:

> 'The independence of nations guarantees to each the right of guarding its own honour, and the morals and interests of its own subjects. No one has a right to sit in judgement generally upon the actions of another ... No nation has ever yet pretended to be the *custos morum* of the whole world; and though abstractedly a particular regulation may violate the law of nations, it may sometimes, in the case of nations, be a wrong without a remedy.'[122]

In a later case, in 1841, concerning fugitive slaves from a Spanish colony, the Supreme Court of the United States declared the slave trade an 'atrocious violation of human rights', and held that the US was not under an obligation to return the slaves to the Spanish authorities.[123]

But the most important contribution to the campaign to end the slave trade did not come from domestic courts, but from the mixed courts established under bilateral treaties concluded by Britain with Spain, Portugal and the Netherlands since 1819. Based in Sierra Leone, Cuba, Brazil and Suriname, these courts worked on the basis of the detailed regulations found in annexes to the treaties that have established them.[124] Their effectiveness is demonstrated by data that show that, during their peak years of operation in the 1830s and 1840s, the mixed courts heard cases involving a significant percentage of the total transatlantic slave trade' – as much as nearly 40 per cent of known slave trading voyages in 1835.[125]

[120] *La Jeune Eugenie*, *supra* note 120 at 847. [121] *Ibid.* [122] *Ibid.*
[123] *The United States v. The Libellants and Claimants of the Schooner Amistad*, 40 U.S. 518.
[124] Martinez, *supra* note 105 at 579 and 595.
[125] *Ibid.* at 597–8.

The progressive adoption of multilateral treaty standards

As Britain realised that 'it could not rely on its military power alone, but instead had to utilise that power in conjunction with cooperative legal action to achieve its goals',[126] the practice of concluding bilateral treaties was stepped up and Britain began to promote the adoption of multilateral treaties.

The first major success of this strategy was the Treaty of London for the Suppression of the Slave Trade, adopted in 1841 by five European powers – Great Britain, France, Austria, Prussia and Russia.[127] This treaty established mutual rights of search and visits when there were 'reasonable grounds' for suspecting that a merchant vessel belonging to any of the parties to the treaty was engaged in the slave trade (Article 2). Although this treaty instituted a form of international cooperation for policing the high seas, it did not go as far as establishing universal jurisdiction for the suppression of the slave trade. Proceedings for the confiscation of the vessels could be started only before 'the competent Tribunal of the Country to which she [the vessel] belongs'.[128] At that time only piracy thus met the definition of a crime *jure gentium*, for which universal jurisdiction existed. Whereas slave traders were often referred to as 'pirates' in public statements, their treatment under the international law remained substantially different.

The 1890 Brussels Conference recognised the right to stop vessels under 500 tons in the open sea suspected of trading in slaves, and to examine their papers.[129] Mutual rights of search and visit were

[126] *Ibid.* at 554.

[127] Treaty of London for the Suppression of the African Slave Trade, 20 December 1841 (Martens, T. XII, 170; 92 CTS (1841–42) 437). On 24 February 1848, Belgium acceded to this treaty, but France never ratified it. H. Fischer, 'The Suppression of Slavery in International Law' 3 ICLQ (1950) 28.

[128] Article 10, Treaty of London, *supra* note 127. The principle of the exclusive jurisdiction of the flag state for offences committed on the high seas was still invoked by France in the *Lotus* case (*France v. Turkey*), Judgment, (1927) PCIJ Reports Series A, No. 10. The Court held that there was no principle of customary international law 'in regard to collision cases to the effect that criminal proceedings are exclusively within the jurisdiction of the State whose flag is flown'. See also Fischer, *supra* note 127, at 45.

[129] Article 42, General Act of the Brussels Conference on the African Slave Trade, 2 July 1890, Martens NRG II, XVII, 345; 173 CTS (1890). L. Oppenheim, *International Law* (1st edn., London: Longmans, Green and Co., 1905), Vol. I at 321. All European states, the US, Persia, Turkey, Zanzibar and the Congo Free State signed and ratified the General Act. A. M. Trebilcock, 'Slavery' in R. Bernhardt (ed.), *Encyclopaedia of*

established, but their exercise vis-à-vis vessels belonging to non-state parties was expressly excluded. This provision, which legally was superfluous as it merely confirmed a general principle of treaty law (*pacta tertiis nec nocent nec prosunt*), implicitly recognised that the enforcement of the ban on the slave trade could not yet be considered part of customary international law.[130] The Brussels Conference also established an International Maritime Bureau in Zanzibar to gather information and documentation from all the powers involved in the suppression of the trade.[131] Albeit its powers were limited compared to contemporary international organisations, the Bureau represented one of the first concerted efforts to establish a multilateral institution for a humanitarian purpose. The twinning of multilateralism and humanitarianism was thus inaugurated.

The right to stop and board a ship on the high seas suspected of being involved in the slave trade acquired customary status in the following decades, although, as is often the case with customary law, it is difficult to identify the precise moment in time when the rule crystallised. By the beginning of the twentieth century most commentators in international law still maintained that this right could be exercised only on the basis of a treaty provision.[132]

While before the First World War the attempts to introduce a ban had been limited to the slave trade, after the War slavery per se became illegal with the adoption of the Slavery Convention in 1926.[133] The Final Act of the Berlin Conference had expressly referred to the existence of slavery (Article 42), but had fallen short of prohibiting it. The idea that international law could go as far as limiting the sovereignty of states and impose obligations on the treatment of individuals took some time to be accepted, and, when it finally was, freedom from slavery became the first human right protected under international law. The right of search, visit and seizure of ships engaged in the slave trade also became part of customary international law in the period during the two wars.

Public International Law (Amsterdam: North-Holland Pub. Co., 1985), vol. VIII at 482. Fischer, *supra* note 127 at 49.

130 Article 45, General Act of the Brussels Conference, *supra* note 130.

131 *Ibid.* Chapter V (Arts. 74–80).

132 See L. Oppenheim, *supra* note 37, at 347 and J. Westlake, *International Law* (Cambridge University Press, 1904–1907), 166–7. Sir Robert Phillimore, however, argued that the slave trade was a 'legal as well as a natural crime'. Phillimore, *supra* note 105 at 410.

133 Slavery Convention (1926) 60 LNTS 253.

Any remaining doubt that this was so was dispelled with the adoption of the Geneva Convention on the High Seas in 1958 – which included a provision to this effect and was expressly declaratory of customary international law existing at the time.[134]

The birth of modern humanitarianism

A full account of the origins of modern humanitarianism would require an investigation into the history of a closely related idea, that is the concept of a just humanitarian war – or, to use current terminology, the doctrine of humanitarian intervention. That investigation would take us to Augustine, as far as the intellectual origins of the idea are concerned, and to the Greek struggle for liberation from Ottoman rule, as far as state practice is concerned.[135] But, if one thinks of humanitarianism in a purely non-forcible sense, the campaign to end the slave trade was a defining moment. All the ingredients of international humanitarianism were present in that campaign: the emergence of a body of enlightened public opinion in a leading Western country; the mobilisation of support domestically and internationally; the attempt to bring political and military power to bear on the cause; the tension between unilateralism and multilateralism; and the process of legalisation, first, and institutionalisation, later.

The contrasting interpretations of the anti-slavery movement which have emerged among historians can also cast some light on current debates on humanitarianism.[136] According to one historical interpretation, there were no true humanitarian concerns behind the end to the slave trade: Britain and the abolitionists were moved exclusively by economic interest and, in a Machiavellian way, sought to create a humanitarian discourse to justify their actions.[137] Such scepticism also characterises Foucault's analysis of another great humanitarian campaign of the late eighteenth and early nineteenth centuries and which is also often connected to the rise of the humanitarian conscience: the reform of the penal system that led to the prohibition on torture and

[134] Article 22, Convention on the High Seas (1958) 450 UNTS 11. It was later confirmed by Art. 110, Convention on the Law of the Sea (1982), UN Doc. A/CONF.62/122.

[135] See G. J. Bass, *Freedom's Battle: The Origins of Humanitarian Intervention* (New York: Vintage, 2008).

[136] T. Bender (ed.), *The Anti-slavery Debate. Capitalism and Abolitionism as a Problem in Historical Interpretation* (Berkeley: University of California Press, 1992).

[137] E. Williams, *Capitalism and Slavery* (Chapel Hill: University of North Carolina Press, 1944).

to the rise of detention as the standard form of punishment. Indeed, Foucault argued that, in spite of its avowed humanitarian ethos, the aim of this reform was not 'to punish less, but to punish better; to punish with an attenuated severity perhaps, but in order to punish with more universality and necessity; to insert the power to punish into the social body'.[138]

According to a different school of thought, the abolitionist movement did represent a moment of real growth in our humanitarian conscience: an illustration of the power of sympathy, the process of imaginative identification with the suffering of the other,[139] and of the strengthening of 'our feeling of responsibility for the stranger's suffering'.[140] These interpretations derive support from recent studies by economic historians who have calculated the significant costs born by Britain to suppress the slave trade, believed by some to have been as high as 2 per cent of its annual national income for most of the nineteenth century, which corresponds approximately to the proportion of national income spent annually on defence in many European countries.[141]

Other historians have seen domestic political factors as decisive in determining the British military campaign to end the slave trade. Throughout the first half of the nineteenth century the Protestant Dissenters, who were staunch abolitionists, held the key to the precarious balance of power between the two main parties in Britain, the Tories and the Whigs.[142] Because of their political leverage, the Dissenters could succeed in putting British naval action to stop the trade high on the political agenda in spite of the significant economic costs of abolition first, and of the military campaign to stop the trade later.

One of the lessons of this early example of an international humanitarian action is the connection between power and humanitarianism. Britain monopolised the great humanitarian campaign to end the slave trade in the nineteenth century, although the fact that it proved

138 M. Foucault, *Discipline and Punish: The Birth of the Prison* (Harmondsworth: Penguin, 1979) 82.

139 L. Hunt, *Inventing Human Rights* (New York: W. W. Norman & Company Inc., 2007) 65–6.

140 T. L. Haskell, 'Capitalism and the Origin of Humanitarian Sensibility', in T. Bender (ed.), *The Anti-slavery Debate. Capitalism and Abolitionism as a Problem in Historical Interpretation* (Berkeley: University of California Press, 1992) 128.

141 Martinez, *supra* note 104 at 557.

142 Kaufmann and Pape, *supra* note 103.

very difficult even for Britain, the world's leading super power then, to overcome international resistance to the suppression of the slave trade testifies to the enduring strength of the principles of the freedom of the high seas and of national sovereignty. Today the discourse of humanitarianism is still often associated with the richer and more powerful, the 'givers' in the aid relationship and at the same time those with political and military might.[143] Many realists would see in this a confirmation of the fact that humanitarianism is nothing but a smokescreen for new and perhaps more sophisticated forms of hegemony. Doubtless, it is important to be aware of the hegemonic side of humanitarianism, not only because humanitarians might become the unwitting executioners of a hegemonic strategy, but also, on the positive side, because, learning from the experience of the Dissenters in Britain, they could exploit national political divisions to further a humanitarian agenda. To paraphrase Bernard Kouchner's enthusiastic approval of the war in Kosovo as an example of 'might being on the side of human rights',[144] one could argue that, while there is merit in having might on the side of human rights rather than against them, one should always be aware of the risk that the distance between 'might on the side of human rights' and 'human rights on the side of might' may be a short one.

Whether the abolitionist movement really sealed the birth of a new humanitarian sensibility or not, its historical importance for the later developments of international human rights and humanitarian law and for international organisations can hardly be underestimated. In the wake of the anti-slave trade movement, other humanitarian campaigns were launched in the second half of the nineteenth century. King Leopold's crimes in Congo became a cause célèbre at the turn of the century and a movement of journalists, intellectuals and activists managed to put the brutality of the colonisation of Congo on the agenda.[145] Two Public International Unions were founded to deal with the slave trade and its consequences: the Union for the Suppression of the Slave Trade, originally envisaged in the General Act of the Brussels Conference in 1890, which came to existence in 1912 and was endowed with two international offices, one in Zanzibar and the other one in Brussels attached to the Belgian Foreign Ministry, as it was common at the time for

[143] C. N. Murphy, *International Organisation and Industrial Change*, 48.

[144] See Rieff, *supra* note 91 at 217.

[145] The history of that movement is recounted in A. Hochschild, *King Leopold's Ghost* (London: Macmillan, 1999).

international organisations to operate directly from the office of a ministry of one of the founding members; and the Union for the Suppression of the White Slave Traffic, which came to existence in May 1904.[146] These two Unions became 'the first major global international organisations with a mandate to end abuses of human rights around the world'.[147]

On another front, the founding of the International Committee of the Red Cross (ICRC) in 1863 signalled the growth of humanitarianism in another direction, that is the attempt to humanise the conduct of warfare. Capturing and promoting this humanitarian spirit – 'the spirit of Solferino' – to the point of almost becoming its embodiment, the ICRC played a pivotal role in the development of international humanitarian law. The campaign to end the slave trade had demonstrated what a private movement could achieve in terms of changing state practice and international law. The ICRC took this a step further by directly spearheading the adoption of treaties and becoming actively involved in the international law-making process.[148]

But the contribution of the ICRC was not limited to the development of international law. The ICRC was, and remains, a predominantly operational organisation, whose mandate, ethos and modus operandi have shaped the field of humanitarian assistance especially, but not exclusively, during armed conflict. At the heart of the ICRC model is the principle of neutrality: 'The ICRC is especially concerned *to be perceived* as neutral. The ICRC tries to avoid, or minimise, or balance if possible whatever impact its humanitarian protection may have on the power and status of states and the various factions engaged in power struggles.'[149] The operationalisation of neutrality is however problematic, as discussed in more detail in Chapter 4. One of the most difficult decisions ever taken by the ICRC was not to publicise the evidence it possessed about the extermination of European Jews during the Second World War.[150] The key meeting took place as early as October

[146] Oppenheim, *supra* note 37 at 622. [147] Murphy, *supra* note 144 at 105.

[148] The first humanitarian law treaty to be adopted as a result of an ICRC initiative was the Convention for the Amelioration of the Condition of the Wounded in Armies in the Field (1864) 129 CTS 361.

[149] D. P. Forsythe, *The Humanitarians: The International Committee of the Red Cross* (Cambridge University Press, 2005) 173–4.

[150] C. Moorehead, *Dunant's Dream: War, Switzerland and the History of the Red Cross* (London: Harper Collins, 1998) xxiv–xxxi.

1942. While it would appear that before this meeting the majority of the members of the Committee had been in favour of some public form of condemnation of the concentration camps, in the final vote all but one were persuaded that a public appeal would have been useless or even counter-productive. The fear of being perceived as partisan, and of the consequences that this could have had on the work of the ICRC in Axis-occupied Europe, were the main reasons for their final decision to abstain from any public condemnation of the concentration camps.

Humanitarianism and human rights

The relationship between humanitarianism and human rights is more problematic than would at first appear. To begin with, the hegemony of the idea of human rights has had an impact on the theory and practice of humanitarianism, as evidenced by the proliferation of rights-based approaches to humanitarian assistance.[151] Moreover, the applicability of human rights law to armed conflict – once a disputed contention but now settled law – challenges the speciality of international humanitarian law in a legal sense too.[152]

Points of contact and even overlap between humanitarianism and human rights do exist. Indeed, the history of the campaign to end the slave trade is fascinating also because, contrary to the 'Nuremberg-centric' accounts of the developments of international human rights law,[153] that campaign was both the first international humanitarian campaign and the first international human rights campaign. Within the anti-slave trade movement, one finds precursors of both discourses.

Nevertheless, it is appropriate that these two sets of ideas remain distinct, mainly because humanitarianism and human rights strike a different balance between norm and fact. To impose the balance underlying one on the other can be detrimental to both.[154] Humanitarianism seeks to alleviate suffering. It is a philosophy of damage containment that is built on a sense of pragmatism about brutal facts – some man-made, some not – that destroy the lives of human beings. Human rights

[151] See, for example, the Sphere Project's *Humanitarian Charter and Minimum Standards in Disaster Response* (London, 1998), available at www.sphereproject.org.

[152] See issue 6(2) of the *European Human Rights Law Review*, guest-edited by myself and dealing with Human Rights in War.

[153] Martinez, *supra* note 105 at 632.

[154] I have explored this argument in 'Human Rights in Wartime: A Framework for Analysis', 6 *European Human Rights Law Review* (2008) 689.

are, instead, a more aspirational idea. Certain practices, like slavery or torture, can find no justification either in a human rights or in a humanitarian perspective, but, if one moves to other areas such as free speech or arbitrary detention, the very different balance between norm and fact struck by these two sets of ideas will result in different outcomes. Of course, human rights do not cease in wartime or in the aftermath of a fierce natural disaster. But the illusion that it is *practically* possible to achieve proper respect for human rights – rather than simply to alleviate the damage – in the midst of those events is one that we cultivate at our own peril: for ultimately it will require that the inevitable gap between norm and fact be filled in, either through a dilution of the norm or a denial of the fact.

Accountability

The idea that 'power entails accountability, that is the duty to account'[155] for its exercise has always been a central tenet of liberalism.[156] Demands for accountability have grown following the expansion of the state, and the processes of bureaucratisation and institutionalisation which, as Weber explained, characterise the evolution of rational-legal forms of power in modern societies.[157] Various mechanisms have been developed by modern liberal states to ensure that bureaucracies are subjected to the rule of law, and act as instruments for its promotion without turning into uncontrollable and even oppressive leviathans.

Accountability is a semantically broad concept and one for which it is often difficult to find a corresponding term in other languages.[158] While for some this breadth condemns accountability to vagueness, especially when compared with the notion of responsibility, others consider one of its virtues precisely the fact that 'it allows us to move the conceptual discussion beyond the traditional concept of responsibility

155 ILA Committee on the Accountability of International Organisations, 'Final Report' (Berlin, 2004) 5.

156 On the link between accountability and liberalism, see: D. Oliver, *Government in the United Kingdom: The Search for Accountability, Effectiveness and Citizenship* (Milton Keynes: Open University Press, 1991) 24ff.; and C. Harlow, *Accountability in the European Union* (Oxford University Press, 2002) 6ff.

157 M. Weber, *Wirtschaft und Gesellschaft* (Tübingen: Verlag Von J.C.B. Mohr (Paul Siebeck), 1922). Italian edition: *Economia e Società* (1999, Edizioni di Comunità), vol. I at 207–20.

158 ILA Committee, *supra* note 155 at 5; Harlow, *supra* note 157 at 13ff.

of states or international organisations as the primary accountability mechanism in international law'.[159] When applied to international organisations, the term is sometimes used in the sense of financial accountability, although this is only one aspect of accountability. The International Law Association (ILA) has distinguished three levels of accountability of international organisations: first, the extent to which the organisation is subject to 'forms of internal or external scrutiny and monitoring, irrespective of potential and subsequent liability and/or responsibility'; secondly, 'tortious liability for injurious consequences arising out of acts or omissions not involving a breach of any rule of international and/or institutional law'; thirdly, 'responsibility arising out of acts or omissions which do constitute a breach of a rule of international law and/or institutional law'.[160]

The struggle to make international institutions accountable is relatively novel. It was not until the 1980s that the question of the accountability of international organisations received some belated attention. In the 1990s, in particular, international financial institutions came under intense public scrutiny and accepted the need for certain institutional reforms.[161] Before then, the predominant view was that international institutions had a role to play in ensuring the accountability of states by monitoring their compliance with international law and by setting standards for their conduct (also referred to as 'active accountability'),[162] but the question of the accountability for the way in which international institutions exercised their powers (or 'passive accountability') was overshadowed by the perceived need to secure their work in a state-dominated world.

The greater attention received by the question of accountability of international organisations is the result of a number of factors. First, any unbound exercise of power cannot but stride with the rights culture that gained strength particularly after the fall of the Soviet bloc in the late 1980s, and the spread of liberal democracy, although it is

159 D. Curtin and A. Nollkaemer, 'Conceptualising Accountability in International and European Law', XXXVI *Netherlands Yearbook of International Law* (2005) 3 at 9.

160 ILA Committee, *supra* note 156. See also I. Dekker, 'Making Sense of Accountability in International Institutional Law', XXXVI *Netherlands Yearbook of International Law* (2005) 83.

161 See, for example, J. A. Fox and D. L. Brown (eds.), *The Struggle for Accountability: The World Bank, NGOs and Grassroots Movements* (Cambridge (MA): MIT Press, 1998).

162 International organisations are thus sometimes referred to as having a function of control, see N. Valticos, 'Contrôle', in R. J. Dupuy (ed.), *A Handbook on International Organizations* (2nd edn., Dordrecht: Martinus Nijhoff, 1998) 461.

still not clear at this point whether the political and economic rise of China since the beginning of the new century will offer an ideological alternative to the liberal democratic model. Secondly, scrutiny into the operational performance of international organisations has noticeably increased since the 1980s, leading to the publication of various exposés by journalists and academics.[163] Finally, the management of the UN has been the object of intense political debate in some countries, particularly in the US during the Clinton administrations after the Republicans led by Jesse Helms gained control of Congress.

International organisations are sometimes said to suffer from a democratic deficit and from a legitimacy deficit, and greater accountability is proposed as a solution to these problems. This debate, which has for the most part focused on the European Union (EU),[164] is of only indirect relevance to this book, which deals, instead, with what could be called the liberty deficit of international organisations, and the accountability deficit that follows from it.

[163] See *supra* note 91.

[164] See A. Arnull and D. Wincott (eds.), *Accountability and Legitimacy in the European Union* (Oxford University Press, 2002); and Harlow, *supra* note 157.

2 Human rights obligations of international organisations

Introduction

In the vast literature on international institutional law, discussions of the obligations of international organisations have been sporadic. Some authors have examined the human rights obligations of non-state actors,[1] but these analyses have not normally offered general insight into the creation of obligations for international organisations. The extensive scholarship on the legal personality of international organisations tends to concentrate on their rights and omits to analyse their duties. And, as for the ILC's work on the responsibility of international organisations, this deals with secondary rules and touches on the obligations of international organisations only peripherally. All in all, this area remains largely uncharted.[2]

Any analysis of obligations in international law must begin with a reference to Article 38 of the Statute of the ICJ, which, on its face, deals only with the law to be applied by the Court in deciding disputes between states, but is widely regarded as the most authoritative statement on the sources of international law. In a formal sense, the source of any obligation binding an international organisation will be one of those enumerated in Article 38 – treaty, custom, general principles, judicial decisions or academic writings – but a merely formal approach to this topic will not take us very far. Doubtless, international

[1] E.g. A. Clapham, *Human Rights Obligations of Non-State Actors* (Oxford University Press, 2006).

[2] See C. Eagleton, 'International Organisation and the Law of Responsibility', 76(I) RC (1950) 323 at 385ff. and F. Morgenstern, 'Legality in International Organizations', XLVIII BYBIL (1976–77) 241 at 253.

organisations, like states, will be bound by obligations arising under treaties to which they are parties, but what about constituent instruments? International organisations are not, technically, parties to them. Yet, it is generally accepted that constituent instruments may be a source of international legal obligations for organisations. It is not entirely clear, however, how obligations are to be distilled from such instruments. Furthermore, international organisations have not generally become parties to the multilateral treaties through which much international law-making has taken place in recent decades, especially in the area of human rights. Does this mean that international organisations are not bound by those principles and rules? That they are, in a human rights sense, actors *legibus soluti*?

A solely formal approach to the obligations of international organisations will also fail to provide an answer to the applicability of customary international law to them: are international organisations bound by any rule of customary international law that is relevant to the exercise of their powers? Or is specific evidence of both institutional practice and *opinio juris* required in respect of each customary rule?

As mentioned, these questions do not find an answer in the ILC's project on the responsibility of international organisations, which follows the same distinction between primary and secondary rules adopted in relation to state responsibility. Nevertheless, the ILC has tangentially considered some issues pertaining to the sphere of primary obligations: first, in relation to definitional provisions (in particular Article 2(2) on the 'rules of the organisation'; Article 4 on 'wrongful act'; and Article 9 on 'breach of an international obligation'); and, secondly, in relation to specific primary rules (for example, the rules on complicity) included in the Draft Articles on the Responsibility of International Organisations, as was indeed done for state responsibility, because of their close link to the operation of secondary rules.

There are at least four key issues that must be addressed as part of a general theory on the creation of obligations binding international organisations: the obligatory effects (if any) of international legal personality; the obligations arising under constituent instruments; the obligations arising under acts of the organisation; and the effects for organisations of the obligations of member states.

Overarching the specific question of the application of international human rights law to international organisations are the fundamental values of the international system. The Preamble of the UN Charter offers an indication of what those values might be: security and peace ('to save succeeding generations from the scourge of war'); human rights ('to reaffirm faith in fundamental human rights'); rule of law ('to establish conditions under which justice and the obligations arising from treaties and other sources ... can be maintained'); and quality of life ('to promote social progress and better standards of life in larger freedom'). An international system that allowed international organisations to be unbound by human rights obligations would fail to advance all or some of these values. Nor, to be fair, does anyone seriously put forward the idea that international organisations should be thus unbound. The main challenge for the jurist is thus to find systemically coherent and analytically cogent explanations for the application of international human rights obligations to international organisations.

The meaning of institutional practice

The concept of institutional practice occupies an important position in international institutional law. Institutional practice is relevant to the determination of the extent of implied powers and to the interpretation of the constituent instrument of the organisation. Furthermore, the 'established practice' of the organisation carries 'considerable weight' for the purposes of determining the 'rules of the organisation'; this expression is used in the Vienna Convention on the Law of Treaties and in the Draft Articles on the Responsibility of International Organisations to mean 'the constituent instruments, decisions, resolutions and other acts of the organisation adopted in accordance with those instruments and established practice of the organisation'.[3] Institutional practice may also be relevant to the identification of customary rules binding the organisation.

But what counts as institutional practice? It is important to distinguish three levels of such practice. First, there is the practice of the political organs of the organisation, normally comprising decisions, resolutions and statements. Secondly, there is the institutional practice which emanates from the upper bureaucratic levels of the organisation – heads of division, country representatives and other senior officials – and which comprises a variety of acts such as: public statements; operational decisions; press releases; guidelines and policy statements;

[3] Article 2(1)(j), Vienna Convention on the Law of Treaties between States and International Organisations or between International Organisations (1986), UN Doc. A/Conf.129/15; Art. 2(b), Draft Articles on the Responsibility of International Organisations, ILC Report (2009), UN Doc. A/64/10 and para. 15 of the Commentary.

memoranda of understanding; legal opinions and so on. Thirdly, there is the actual conduct of the organisation.

One should not make the mistake of assuming consistency across these three levels of Institutional practice. Of course, state practice is not always consistent either. The existence of a gap between what states say they do and what they do is well known.[4] But what is peculiar about at least some international institutions, especially the operational programmes of the UN, is that the second level of practice, that is the practice of the bureaucracy, is often more determinative of the actual conduct of the organisation than the first level. The political organs are so far removed from operational decisions that the bureaucracy is often in control – an observation which accords with the empirical studies confirming the bureaucratic nature of international organisations mentioned in the previous chapter. Again, it may be objected that this can happen in states too. After all, when Max Weber developed his theories of bureaucratic power, it was state bureaucracies that he had in mind. The difference however is this: states, especially the most advanced liberal democracies, have a machinery of legal and political accountability, of constitutional checks and balances that ensure that the link between the political level and the operational level is never completely severed and that bureaucratic power is reined in. In international organisations this machinery is either lacking or grossly inadequate. This observation should have a bearing on the normative weight that we attach to institutional practice. The bureaucratic level of institutional practice should not be treated as established for the purposes of determining the rules of the organisation, unless it is also reflected in the practice of the political organs.

International legal personality

Autonomy and personality

A legal person is 'a right-and-duty bearing unit',[5] and legal personality is 'the capacity of being a subject of legal duties and legal rights,

[4] E.g. diss. op. of Judge Read, *Fisheries Case (UK v. Norway)*, ICJ Reports (1951) 116 at 191.

[5] F. W. Maitland, quoted in J. Dewey, 'The Historic Background of Corporate Legal Personality', XXXV Yale L. J. (1926) 655 at 656. In this rare incursion into the legal field, the philosopher John Dewey also argued that 'person signifies what the law makes it signify' (at 655).

of performing legal transactions and of suing and being sued at law'.[6] These apparently uncomplicated definitions disguise the intense jurisprudential debate on the concept of legal personality.[7] In the field of international law, legal personality has come under attack from several fronts – from the New Haven School to feminist jurisprudence.[8] The common thread of these attacks is the supposedly exclusionary effect of this legal construct: who falls outside it and why? Much recent scholarship has, in particular, questioned whether international law should continue to regard as 'non-persons' powerful and important actors such as multinational corporations.[9]

As far as international organisations are concerned, at least since the *Reparation* case, there has been no dispute about them possessing some measure of international legal personality. There is however one theoretical issue, already discussed in Chapter 1, which deserves a few more words here: the autonomy of international organisations.

In essence, autonomy in this context is the 'distinction, in terms of legal powers and purposes, between an organisation and its member states'.[10] Autonomy is both a postulate and an effect of legal personality. In other words, international organisations deserve legal personality by virtue of being distinct from member states, but legal personality also becomes one of the ways in which they can maintain such distinction – not simply in a juridical sense, but also in the more important sense of preserving their separate will. Legal personality is thus a cause, but also a consequence of the *fact* of autonomy. Taking this argument further: there ought to be no personality without some measure of personhood (or, as Klabbers calls it, of 'organisationhood').[11]

This theory – sometimes called the 'distinct will' theory – is not without its sceptics. For example, Brölmann observes that a distinct will is

[6] H. Kelsen, *The Law of the United Nations: A Critical Analysis of its Fundamental Problems* (London: Stevens and Sons, 1950) 329.

[7] On the history of the idea of international legal personality, see J. E. Nijman, *The Concept of International Legal Personality: An Inquiry into the History and Theory of International Law* (The Hague: T. M. C. Asser Press, 2004).

[8] *Ibid*. at 325–34 and 347ff.

[9] See Clapham, *supra* note 1.

[10] I. Brownlie, *Principles of Public International Law* (7th edn., Oxford University Press, 2008) 677.

[11] J. Klabbers, *An Introduction to International Institutional Law* (Cambridge University Press, 2002) 36. Support for the distinct will theory of personality can also be found in the ILC's commentary to Art. 2 of the Draft Articles on the Responsibility of International Organisations (see ILC Report (2009), UN Doc. A/64/10, at 47).

'admittedly of a somewhat metaphysical character, and how it should be identified is not generally elaborated upon by writers'.[12] Klabbers refers to the argument that '[i]n one way, the international organisation is little more than the tool in the hands of the member states, and, viewed from this perspective, the distinct will of the organisation is little more than a legal fiction'.[13] This is in essence the realist idea that, in a substantive rather than formal sense, international organisations should be regarded 'simply as fora for attempting to resolve conflict of national interests, and therefore lacking [in] distinct personality'.[14] The implications of realism for international institutional personality are similar to those of determinism in the sphere of individual responsibility. Realism and determinism maintain that the conduct of, respectively, an international institution and a person is predetermined by factors beyond their volition. Taken to their extreme, these positions are incompatible with the concept of legal personality and the responsibility that follows from it.[15]

It is precisely in order to address this realist challenge that it is important to appreciate that the autonomy of international organisations is a social and political fact. Once it is accepted that international organisations can, and do, operate as discrete institutional agents rather than as the long arm of their most powerful member states; that they are bureaucracies and not simply sounding boards for states; that their true social and political nature is much more than the sum of the wills of their member states, it will become clear that their legal personality is not a mere legal fiction, which, while perhaps convenient or even necessary, bears little relation to reality.

In a legal sense, although the realist preconception is ingrained in argument about international organisations (not least within international organisations themselves), the autonomy of international organisations is normally presumed, rather than based on a case-by-case factual assessment. Such presumption of autonomy characterises the notion of legal personality in other areas of the law too. For example, criminal responsibility can be excluded on grounds of

[12] C. Brölmann, *The Institutional Veil in Public International Law: International Organisations and the Law of Treaties* (Oxford and Portland, Oregon: Hart Publishing, 2007) 21.

[13] *Ibid.* at 12.

[14] N. White, *The Law of International Organisations* (2nd edn., Manchester University Press, 2005) 27.

[15] On determinism and criminal responsibility, see H. L. A. Hart, *Punishment and Responsibility: Essays in the Philosophy of Law* (Oxford: Clarendon Press, 1968) 28ff.

insanity or intoxication, but only after proving those particular situations.[16] On the other hand, psychological or environmental factors that can in practice affect the psycho-social autonomy of an individual do not usually constitute sufficient grounds for departing from the presumption of autonomy for the purposes of criminal responsibility or legal capacity under private law (the doctrine of undue influence in English law can be seen as an equitable attempt to remedy the rigidity of the distinction between capacity and absence of it).

In international institutional law the presumption of autonomy can be overridden in two ways. First, it can be challenged in relation to the commission of a specific act. For example, if it is shown that in a particular situation the will of an international organisation was forced 'giving it no effective choice but to comply with the wishes'[17] of a coercing state or international organisation, international responsibility for the wrongful act will fall on the author of the coercion.[18] Softer, or perhaps more effectively disguised, temporary deprivations of the autonomy of an international organisation – such as those affected through political and economic pressure – that do not attain such a high level will not have consequences for the responsibility of the organisation.

Secondly, the presumption of autonomy can be challenged in a more general sense. If it is shown that the organisation lacks overall autonomy, then its very claim to be a legal person will be adversely affected.[19] An illustration of this type of situation is in the decision of the ICJ in the *Phosphate Lands in Nauru* case, where it was held that the Administering Authority for Nauru 'did not have an international legal personality distinct from those of the States'.[20] The Administering Authority had been established under the Trusteeship over Nauru granted by the UN jointly to Australia, New Zealand and the UK in 1947 following a previous mandate of the League of Nations. The Court

16 A. Ashworth, *Principles of Criminal Law* (6th edn., Oxford University Press, 2009) 210ff.

17 J. Crawford, *The International Law Commission's Articles on State Responsibility: Introduction, Text and Commentaries* (Cambridge University Press, 2002) 156.

18 Article 15, Draft Articles on the Responsibility of International Organisations, ILC Report (2009), UN Doc. A/64/10. See also Chapter 3.

19 J. D'Aspremont, 'The Abuse of Legal Personality of International Organisations and the Responsibility of Member States', 4 *International Organisations Law Review* (2007) 91 at 105.

20 *Case Concerning Certain Phosphate Lands in Nauru (Nauru v. Australia)*, Judgment (Preliminary Objections), ICJ Report (1992) 240 at 258.

observed that the Administrator 'was at all times appointed by the Australian Government and was accordingly under the instructions of that Government' and that his acts 'were subject to confirmation or rejection by the Governor-General of Australia'.[21] Following this line of argument some authors dispute the legal personality of the Northern Atlantic Treaty Organisation (NATO) on the grounds that it is a mere association of states and lacks a distinct will from that of its members,[22] while others have proposed a test of effective and overwhelming control on the part of one or a few member states over the decision-making process of the international organisation to determine whether the organisation should be deprived of its legal personality.[23]

In the course of the International Tin Council litigation, it was argued that the relationship between a state and an international organisation can in some circumstances be described as one of agency.[24] This is a theory that bears little relation to the reality of international organisations; in any event, it does not imply that the organisation is so lacking in autonomy that it should be deprived of its personality, for an agent, even under private law, can still be a legal person in his or her own right.

Understanding autonomy can also help us solve the riddle of the legal personality of UN operational programmes. As explained in Chapter 1, these programmes often enjoy greater decision-making and operational autonomy than specialised agencies. Their constituent instruments, for example the WFP's General Regulations, sometimes expressly recognise that operational programmes possess legal personality.[25] It is widely accepted that, even where such provisions do not feature in the constituent instrument, by virtue of their organisational structure and of the functions they perform, operational programmes possess a degree of international legal personality, albeit derivative from the parent organisation.[26] The mandates of the specialised programmes

[21] *Phosphate Lands in Nauru*, *supra* note 20 at 257.

[22] J. Verhoeven, *Droit International Public* (Bruxelles: De Boek & Larcier, 2001) 613.

[23] D'Aspremont, *supra* note 19.

[24] C. Chinkin, *Third Parties in International Law* (Oxford University Press, 1993) 114–18. *J.H. Rayner (Mincing Lane) Ltd v. Department of Trade and Industry and Others* [1990] 2 AC 418 for the House of Lords' decision, while the decisions of the High Court and of the Court of Appeal are reported respectively at 77 ILR 56 and 80 ILR 49.

[25] GA Res. 1714 (XVI), 19 December 1961, and in FAO Conference Res. 1/61, 24 November 1961.

[26] For example, the General Regulations of WFP state that the 'Programme ... shall, *drawing on* the legal personality of the United Nations, have legal capacity'

spell out the terms of their relationship of subsidiarity with the parent organs of the UN, normally the General Assembly and the Economic and Social Council. For example, UNHCR is mandated to follow 'policy directives' of the General Assembly and of the Economic and Social Council, and can engage in other activities, 'such as repatriation and resettlement, as the General Assembly may determine'.[27] UNICEF, on the other hand, must act 'in accordance with such principles as may be laid down by the Economic and Social Council and its Social Commission'.[28] Rules of treaty interpretation do not apply to the interpretation of these mandates given that they are acts of a UN organ and not treaties 'having certain special characteristics' (such as constituent instruments).[29]

Legal personality in international decisions

The Permanent Court of International Justice discussed the legal personality of international organisations in an advisory opinion on the ILO.[30] But it was in the advisory opinion in the *Reparation* case that institutional legal personality was examined in a systematic fashion, this time by the ICJ and in regard to the UN.[31] The General Assembly had requested an opinion on the capacity of the UN to bring an international claim for damages caused to its employees and to the organisation. The Court found that the UN is endowed with international legal personality, because 'the Organisation was intended to exercise and enjoy, and is in fact exercising and enjoying, functions and

(emphasis added). Some trace the ultimate legal source of their personality to Art. 104 of the Charter conferring personality on the UN (I. Seidl-Hohenveldern and K. Rudolph, 'Article 104', in B. Simma (ed.), *The Charter of the United Nations: A Commentary* (2nd edn., Oxford University Press, 2002) 1302 at 1308). On the personality of UNRWA see W. Dale, 'UNRWA – A Subsidiary Organ of the United Nations', 23 ICLQ (1974) 576. In support of the legal personality of subsidiary organs, see Brownlie, *supra* note 10 at 678. Practice that evidences the international legal personality of subsidiary organs are the bilateral agreements concluded by ad hoc Tribunals with states on the enforcement of sentences (e.g. www.unictr.org/Legal/BilateralAgrements/tabid/99/Default.aspx). A restrictive view of the extent of the legal personality of subsidiary organs is held by M. Hilf and D-E. Khan, 'Article 22', in Simma, *The Charter of the United Nations* 420 at 427.

27 GA Res. 428 (V) at paras. 3 and 9.

28 GA Res. 57(I) at paras. 3(a) and 9.

29 *Certain Expenses of the UN*, Advisory Opinion, ICJ Reports (1962) 151 at 157.

30 *Competence of the International Labour Organisation to Regulate, Incidentally, the Personal Work of the Employers*, Advisory Opinion (1926) PCIJ Reports Series B, No. 13.

31 *Reparation for Injuries Suffered in the Service of the United Nations*, Advisory Opinion, ICJ Reports (1949) 174.

rights which can only be explained on the basis of the possession of a large measure of international personality and the capacity to operate upon an international plane'.[32] The UN is thus 'a subject of international law and capable of possessing international rights and duties, and ... has capacity to maintain its rights by bringing international claims'.[33] The Court then considered whether 'the sum of the international rights of the Organisation comprises the right to bring the kind of international claim described in the Request for this Opinion'.[34] The Court answered this question in the affirmative, having had regard to the 'purposes and functions as specified or implied in its [the UN's] constituent documents and developed in practice'.[35]

According to Bowett, the pronouncement of the ICJ in the *Reparation* case was premised on a circular notion of international legal personality: personality is inductively inferred from the existence of specific rights and duties, while at the same time the capacity of the organisation to bear a particular right or duty is deduced from its international legal personality.[36] International legal personality is thus a flawed concept, with at best an exclusively descriptive validity, and it should be replaced with a case-by-case enquiry to determine if the organisation has a particular right or duty. This also seems to be the view of Elihu Lauterpacht who, commenting on the distinction between powers and personality, asks 'if it is in any event necessary to determine the scope of powers, what function is performed by the concept of personality?'[37]

Rama-Montaldo has given a different reading of the *Reparation* case endeavouring to salvage the concept of international legal personality from the charge of circularity. He has argued that the Court adopted an objective and material approach to the question of personality, first by identifying certain objective structural prerequisites of international legal personality, and secondly by attaching to such personality 'precise legal consequences in regard to the potential activities of

[32] *Ibid*. at 179. [33] *Ibid*. [34] *Ibid*. [35] *Ibid*. at 180.

[36] D. W. Bowett, *The Law of International Institutions* (4th edn., London: Sweet and Maxwell, 1982) 337. Sands and Klein, who have authored the recent editions of Bowett's book, subscribe to the original author's view that legal personality is circular (P. Sands and P. Klein, *Bowett's Law of International Institutions* (6th edn., London: Sweet and Maxwell, 2009) 476).

[37] E. Lauterpacht, 'The Development of the Law of International Organization by the Decisions of International Tribunals', 152 IV RC (1976) 381 at 407.

the organization'.[38] According to Rama-Montaldo, there are rights and duties 'that find their source in personality itself – like … the rights to bring a claim, to negotiate, to conclude a special agreement, protest, request for an inquiry, etc'.[39] Schermers and Blokker describe the Rama-Montaldo position as 'a somewhat different approach',[40] whereas Klabbers, while agreeing that in principle some rights may flow automatically from 'organisationhood', opines that these are 'limited to those of a more or less procedural character'.[41]

The thesis that any international legal person has a minimum of rights and duties that derive directly from personality has some appeal, although it is regrettable that the ICJ did not make the case for it clearly in the *Reparation* case. There is a passage in that opinion where the Court appears to infer the personality of the UN from the 1946 Convention on the Privileges and Immunities of the United Nations,[42] thus justifying Bowett's concerns about the circular nature of the notion of personality.

The practical consequences of these juxtaposed views of international legal personality may not seem at first significant. Certain basic rights of international organisations, such as those alluded to by the Court in the *Reparation* case, can find a sound enough legal basis in the functions and powers vested upon any organisation by its constituent instrument, without need to resort to the notion of rights inherent to personality. But it is on the too often neglected plane of obligations – as will be discussed later – that the notion that personality has a predetermined normative content can make a significant difference.

Despite the disagreement on its predetermined content, every commentator would agree that the legal personality of international organisations is a personality 'with a variable content'.[43] There is no general

[38] M. Rama-Montaldo, 'International Legal Personality and Implied Powers of International Organisations', XLIV BYBIL (1970) 111 at 116. Rama-Montaldo's views are shared by C. F. Amerasinghe, *Principles of the Institutional Law of International Organizations* (2nd edn., Cambridge University Press, 2005) 98–9 and 140–1.

[39] *Ibid*. at 139.

[40] H. G. Schermers and N. M. Blokker, *International Institutional Law* (4th edn., Dordrecht: Martinus Nijhoff, 2003) 989, fn. 13.

[41] Klabbers, *supra* note 11 at 36.

[42] *Reparation*, *supra* note 31 at 179: 'It is difficult to see how such a convention could operate except upon the international plane and as between parties possessing international personality.'

[43] M. Bettati, 'Création et Personalité Juridique des Organisations Internationales', in R. J. Dupuy (ed.), *A Handbook of International Organizations* (2nd edn., Dordrecht: Martinus Nijhoff, 1998) 33 at 53.

principle of equality of international organisations. Their legal personality is also flexible over time, as international institutions often take on new functions in the course of their existence.

Since the *Reparation* case, the ICJ has had a handful of other occasions to consider the legal personality of international organisations, but has not embarked upon any new general analysis of this concept, limiting itself to consider whether a specific function was grounded in the constituent instrument. In *Certain Expenses*, for example, the Court discussed the scope and meaning of the expression 'the expenses of the organisation' in Article 17(2) of the Charter.[44] The Court had to determine the scope of a right of the UN – the right to have expenses covered by member states – to which corresponded a duty of member states. Different states had submitted that they were not under an obligation to cover expenses for the peace-keeping operations in Congo, which, in their view, had not been duly authorised. To address this argument, the Court had to make a preliminary finding on the capacity of the UN to establish the peacekeeping operations in question. In its opinion, the Court recognised a large measure of personality to the UN, holding that the General Assembly had the right to establish peacekeeping operations in spite of the lack of an express provision in the Charter, and that by doing so the Assembly had not 'usurped or impinged upon the prerogatives conferred by the Charter on the Security Council'.[45] The Court rejected the argument that there had been a violation of the Charter in the implementation of the resolution of the Security Council on the operations in Congo, inasmuch as the Secretary General, rather than the Security Council, had determined which states were going to participate in the mission.[46] It was also found that the term 'expenses' did not refer only to 'regular expenses',[47] and that internal irregularities in the establishment of the operations would not change the qualification of the expenditure as 'expenses of the organisation' for the purposes of Article 17(2).[48] In the view of the Court, the ultimate test for determining whether the 'expenses' were 'expenses of the organisation' was 'their relationship to the purposes of the UN' as set forth in Article 1 of the Charter.[49] Since the action in question 'was appropriate for the fulfilment of one of the stated purposes of the United Nations, the presumption is that

[44] *Certain Expenses*, *supra* note 29. [45] *Ibid.* at 177. [46] *Ibid.* at 175.
[47] *Ibid.* at 161. [48] *Ibid.* at 168. [49] *Ibid.* at 167.

such an action is not *ultra vires* the Organisation [sic]', and that, even 'if the action was taken by the wrong organ, it was irregular as a matter of that internal structure [of the organisation], but this would not necessarily mean that the expense incurred was not an expense of the Organisation'.[50]

The much-discussed *Legality of Nuclear Weapons (WHO request)* case arose from a request of the Assembly of the WHO for an opinion on the legality of the use of nuclear weapons in armed conflict.[51] The Court examined the scope of the Charter-based right of the WHO, as a specialised agency of the UN, to request an advisory opinion 'on legal questions arising within the scope of their activities' (Article 96, II). The Court drew a distinction between the effects on health of the use of nuclear weapons, which would come under the competence of the WHO, and the question of the legality of the use of nuclear weapons, which formed the subject matter of the request. The latter, in the Court's view, was not covered by the functions of the WHO as enumerated under Article 2 of its Constitution.[52]

The Court maintained that international institutions 'are governed by the "principle of speciality", that is to say, they are invested by the States which create them with powers, the limits of which are a function of the common interests whose promotion those States entrust to them'.[53] For Lauterpacht the principle of speciality is 'an expression directly derived from French law' which the Court employed without any 'introductory or explanatory comment'.[54] Furthermore, although the implied powers of an organisation were considered by the Court, it was controversially held that the competence of the WHO to address the legality of the use of nuclear weapons could not be grounded by

[50] *Ibid.* at 167–9.

[51] *Legality of the Use by a State of Nuclear Weapons in Armed Conflict* (World Health Organization Request), Advisory Opinion, ICJ Reports (1996) 66, 110 ILR 1. See L. Boisson de Chazournes and P. Sands (eds.), *International Law, the International Court of Justice and Nuclear Weapons* (Cambridge University Press, 1999). See World Health Assembly Res. 46 (40), 14 May 1993.

[52] *Nuclear Weapons – WHO Request, supra* note 51 at 75–6.

[53] *Nuclear Weapons – WHO Request, supra* note 51 at para. 25. The principle of speciality is sometimes traced back to the advisory opinion of the Permanent Court of International Justice in *Jurisdiction of the European Commission of the Danube between Galatz and Braila*, Advisory Opinion (1926), PCIJ Reports Series B, No. 14.

[54] E. Lauterpacht, 'Judicial Review of the Acts of International Organisations', in Boisson de Chazournes and Sands, *supra* note 51 at 98–9.

necessary implication on its constituent instrument.[55] It was found that, as a result of the 'logic of the overall system contemplated by the Charter', the responsibilities of a specialised agency like the WHO could not be construed so widely as to allow them to encroach upon the responsibilities of other parts of the UN system, in particular the exclusive competence of the UN on 'questions concerning the use of force, the regulation of armaments and disarmament'.[56] In his dissenting opinion, Judge Weeramantry was critical of this approach, which, in his view, denied the obvious interrelatedness of health and peace and the fact that health matters do sometimes overlap with concerns about peace and security.[57]

The reasoning of the Court in *Nuclear Weapons (WHO Request)* has been widely criticised, described by some as 'formalistic, oversimplistic, cynical and even logically flawed'.[58] However, this case concerned a particular right of an international organisation (that is the right to seek an advisory opinion from the ICJ), the corresponding obligation of which was incumbent on the Court itself. Moreover, the ICJ also knew that it was going to address the issues raised in the WHO request as a result of the similar request for an advisory opinion by the General Assembly. The opinion of the Court was not in actual fact premised on a narrow approach to international legal personality in general: the Court's approach to the legal personality of the UN is generous but only at the expense of the legal personality of the specialised agencies. The problem with the Court's approach is the principle of speciality. The Court assumed, wrongly, that the rights of the WHO must terminate where the rights of the UN begin, thus leaving no room for co-extensive activities. The reasoning of the Court is at variance with much institutional practice, especially in the humanitarian field where functional overlap is frequent. Functional overlap should not be of concern

[55] Elsewhere the Court used the expression 'necessary intendment' (*Effect of Awards of Compensation Made by the UN Administrative Tribunal*, Advisory Opinion, ICJ Reports (1954) 47 at 56–7).

[56] *Nuclear Weapons – WHO Request, supra* note 51 at para. 26.

[57] *Ibid.* at 133–4, 148 (diss. op. of Judge Weeramantry). See also Judge Koroma's diss. op. at 201ff.

[58] M. Bothe, 'The WHO Request', in Boisson de Chazournes and Sands, *supra* note 51, 103 at 104. See also D. Akande, 'The Competence of International Organisations and the Advisory Jurisdiction of the International Court of Justice', 9 EJIL (1998) 437 at 444 and 447–8. See also V. Leary, 'The WHO Case: Implications for Specialised Agencies', in Boisson des Chazournes and Sands, *supra* note 51 at 127.

unless it is accompanied by contrasting practice, as is the case when a specialised agency or programme acts in a manner that contradicts the practice of other bodies of the UN.

To conclude on this survey of international decisions on legal personality, it may be helpful to focus on certain terms recurrent in decisions and writings on the subject and not always used with the greatest analytical rigour and consistency. In particular, the terms 'functions', 'powers' and 'rights' are used almost interchangeably, as are 'capacity' and 'competence'. The term 'functions' should refer to the activities assigned to an international organisation by its constituent instrument as required for the fulfilment of the purposes of the organisation. As for the terms 'powers' and 'rights', their analytical definition is the topic of much legal philosophy. Without delving into that debate, it is useful to distinguish legal powers in the restrictive Hohfeldian sense from powers in a broad sense. In Hohfeldian terms, a power is the ability to alter legal rights and duties of other persons, or legal relations generally. Used in a broader sense, a power is the generic ability to affect others, but does not entail a change in their legal position.[59] It is correct to say that the Security Council, acting under Chapter VII of the Charter, has powers in the restrictive Hohfeldian sense. But powers in this sense are otherwise rare. Again relying on Hohfeld, one could speak of rights of international organisations only where a correlative duty exists. Thus, for example, the UN possesses the right to have the expenses of the organisation covered by member states – the question at the heart of the *Certain Expenses* case. As for capacity and competence, the need to keep them conceptually distinct was observed in discussions of the ILC.[60] Properly defined, competence is the sum of the functions of an organisation, whereas capacity is the legal ability to bear rights and duties.

Constituent instruments themselves are not immune from terminological confusion. For example, Article 16 of the Constitution of the FAO provides that '[t]he Organization shall have the capacity of a legal person to perform any

[59] This is how Halpin summarises Hart's analysis, which is, in turn, an interpretation of Bentham (see A. Halpin, 'The Concept of a Legal Power', 16 *Oxford Journal of Legal Studies* (1996) 129 at 131). See also H. L. A. Hart, *Essays on Bentham* (Oxford University Press, 1982) 194–219.

[60] P. H. F. Bekker, *The Legal Position of Intergovernmental Organizations* (Dordrecht: Martinus Nijhoff, 1994) 88.

legal act appropriate to its purpose which is not beyond the powers granted to it by this Constitution'. For greater terminological accuracy, this provision should read: 'The Organisation shall have the capacity of a legal person to perform any legal act appropriate to functions which are not beyond the competence granted to it by this Constitution'.

Are there obligations that flow automatically from international legal personality?

Although the ICJ observed in *Reparation* that 'attendant duties and responsibilities' flowed from the 'entrusting of certain functions' to the UN,[61] in practice its decisions have dealt only with rights of international organisations (the ILO, the UN and the WHO). The only oblique reference to a specific obligation in the *Reparation* case is to the duty of the Organisation to remind member states of certain obligations.[62] Such a dearth of judicial decisions on institutional duties should not surprise. UN organs and specialised agencies are much more likely to make use of the advisory jurisdiction of the Court to invoke their rights rather than to request clarifications on their duties.

As far as the handful of mainly indirect references to the obligations of international organisations in the post-*Reparation* case law is concerned, two advisory opinions of the ICJ are worth mentioning: *Effect of Awards*[63] and *Interpretation of Agreement*.[64] In the *Effect of Awards* opinion, the Court justified the establishment of the UN Administrative Tribunal by the General Assembly notwithstanding the absence of an express provision in the Charter in the following terms:

> 'It was inevitable that there would be disputes between the Organization and staff members as to their rights and duties … It would, in the opinion of the Court, hardly be consistent with the expressed aim of the Charter to promote freedom and justice for individuals and with the constant preoccupation of the United Nations Organization to promote this aim that it should afford no judicial or arbitral remedy to its own staff for the settlement of any disputes which may arise between it and them.'[65]

The Court thus inferred the power of the General Assembly to establish the UN Administrative Tribunal from one of the aims of the Charter.

61 *Reparation*, *supra* note 31 at 179. 62 *Ibid.*

63 *Effect of Awards*, *supra* note 55.

64 *Interpretation of the Agreement of March 1951 between the WHO and Egypt*, Advisory Opinion, ICJ Reports (1980) 73.

65 *Effect of Awards*, *supra* note 55 at 57.

The Court did not overtly state that the UN was under an implied duty to provide a remedy to its own staff for the settlement of disputes, but it did assert that failure to provide such remedy would be incompatible with the Charter.

In the *Interpretation of Agreement* case, the ICJ made an explicit, albeit curt, reference to the obligations of international organisations. In an important passage, it explained that 'international organizations are subjects of international law, and, *as such*, are bound by any obligations incumbent upon them *under general rules of international law*, under their constitutions or under international agreements to which they are parties'.[66]

The dictum in the *Interpretation of Agreement* case thus seems to indicate that obligations 'under general rules of international law' flow automatically from the personality of international organisations. But to what does the expression 'general rules of international law' exactly refer? The ICJ has used such an expression – as well as the analogous 'general international law'[67] – without explaining what is meant by them. The most plausible interpretation is that these locutions are shorthand for customary international law of universal or quasi-universal applicability and for general principles of law.

Subjecting international organisations to this body of law, notwithstanding the absence of any evidence of them specifically consenting to each rule of it, is consistent with the approach adopted in the 1950s and 1960s towards newly independent states.[68] Then too the view was taken that the international legal personality that followed from statehood had automatic obligatory consequences in respect at least of general custom. It would, after all, be extremely disruptive for the international system to tolerate the presence of actors that are endowed with legal personality, and thus with the legal capacity to operate upon the international plane, but are exempt from a body of universally or almost universally accepted rules.

[66] *Interpretation of Agreement*, *supra* note 64 at 90, emphasis added. See also Judge El-Erian's Separate Opinion at 168.

[67] See, for example, *Accordance with International Law of the Unilateral Declaration of Independence in Respect of Kosovo*, Advisory Opinion, 22 July 2010 (available at www.icj-cij.org/homepage/pdf/20100722_KOS.pdf) at paras. 79–84.

[68] E.g. R. Jennings and A. Watts (eds.), *Oppenheim's International Law* (9th edn., London: Longman, 1992) 14 and 29.

Support for the view that general international law is binding on international organisations is also found in the jurisprudence of the European Court of Justice (ECJ). In a series of cases, culminating with the decision in *Racke*, the ECJ has found that customary international law binds the EU/EC, and that it also forms part of the Community legal order.[69]

The view that international organisations are bound by customary international law by virtue of their legal personality ensures systemic coherence and is consistent with the analyses of legal personality developed by the ICJ and the ECJ. A fortiori, international organisations are bound by rules of *jus cogens*, as indeed confirmed by Article 53 of the Vienna Convention on Treaties between States and International Organisations and between International Organisations themselves.[70] Nor is there any reason for exempting international institutions from general principles of law recognised by civilised nations.[71] As a result of the effect of custom and general principles, international organisations are bound by an extensive body of legal rules – so much so that one wonders whether it is really true that, as suggested by the ILC, '[f]or an international organisation most obligations are likely to arise from the rules of the organisation'.[72]

Only those rules of customary international law that are relevant to the activities of the international organisation will matter in practice. Subjection to the customary rules of human rights, for example, has very limited relevance for those organisations that do not perform activities that can affect the fundamental rights and liberties of individuals. It is, however, relevant to the UN for the operations discussed in this book.

Redressing the 'rights-bias' of international legal personality

The analysis of the obligations that flow automatically from legal personality can help us advance the debate on the concept of international

[69] Case C-286/90, *Anklagemyndigheden v. Peter Michael Poulsen and Diva Navigation Corp.* [1992] ECR I-6019 at paras. 9–10; Case C-162/96, *A. Racke GmbH and co. v. Hauptzollamt Mainz* [1998] 3 CLMR 219 at para. 45. See P. Eeckhout, *External Relations of the European Union: Legal and Constitutional Foundations* (Oxford University Press, 2004) 324ff. The decision in *Racke* is criticised in A. Arnull *et al.*, *Wyatt and Dashwood's European Union Law* (5th edn., London: Thomson Sweet & Maxwell, 2006) 194–5.

[70] Case T-315/01, *Kadi v. Council and Commission*, at paras. 226–31; Case T-306/01, *Yusuf and Al Barakaat International Foundation v. Council and Commission*, at paras. 277–81.

[71] Brownlie, *supra* note 10 at 688.

[72] See the commentary to Art. 9 in ILC Report (2009), *supra* note 11 at 78.

legal personality. As mentioned, the terms of this debate are defined by two contrasting positions on the question of whether legal personality has a predetermined content: for some it does, for others it does not. What these positions have in common is a rights-bias in the approach to the legal personality of international institutions. The question of the predetermined content of legal personality is assimilated to the question of the rights of international organisations, while the obligatory side of personality is almost completely ignored. Interestingly, the question of the permissive content is actually of less consequence than that of the obligatory content of personality. In fact, the rights that have been said to flow automatically from legal personality are rights for which an express or implied basis in the constituent instrument can always be found. The same cannot be said of obligations based on custom.

To argue that obligations flow automatically from the conferral of international legal personality on international organisations is also consistent with the rationale of the concept of personality. The rights-bias is indeed surprising if one considers that for Leibniz, one of the fathers of the concept of international legal personality, a fundamental purpose of personality was 'to limit the arbitrary use of power … to confirm and capture in a legal notion the ruler's subjection to the law of nations'.[73] A conception of the international legal personality of international organisations that places appropriate emphasis on duties can restore that purpose.

Obligations arising under the constituent instrument

In the *Reparation* case, the ICJ observed that 'rights and duties [of the organisation] will depend upon its purposes and functions as specified or implied in its constituent documents and functions in practice'.[74] Indeed the proposition that an international organisation may be bound by obligations arising under its constituent instrument, notwithstanding the fact that it is not a party to this instrument, is uncontroversial.[75] The real question is how these obligations are identified, and in particular whether obligations can arise by implication, as is the case with rights.

[73] Nijman, *supra* note 7 at 78. [74] *Reparation*, *supra* note 31 at 180.
[75] This argument is developed in detail by Chinkin, *supra* note 24 at 94–6.

Express obligations

Obligations that feature expressly in a constituent instrument should pose no difficulty. Express obligations in constituent instruments are often competence-delimiting. As derivative rather than original entities,[76] international organisations are obliged to respect these limitations on their competence; failure to do so could result in their conduct being ultra vires. The idea that, as long as there is no prohibition, there is no need to demonstrate the existence of a permissive rule – the so-called *Lotus* principle – cannot extend to international organisations. States may be, like Englishmen in the Blackstonian conception of liberty, free to do anything that is not expressly prohibited, but for international organisations there are inherent limits.[77]

As far as human rights obligations are concerned, the direct references to them in the Charter are sufficient to establish a legal basis for their general applicability to the activities of the UN. One of the purposes of the UN, enumerated in Article 1 of the Charter, is indeed to promote and encourage 'respect for human rights and for fundamental freedoms', and Article 2 expressly obliges the UN to act in accordance with certain principles 'in pursuit of the purposes stated in Article 1'. A general obligation to respect human rights arises under the Charter from the combination of these two provisions.

Specific legal obligations connected to the general principles in Article 2 are fleshed out in other provisions of the Charter. For example, Article 55 asserts that the UN shall 'promote' inter alia 'universal respect for, and observance of (*respect effectif*), human rights and fundamental freedoms for all without distinction as to race, sex, language or religion'. On the one hand, the use of the word 'promote' – rather than 'ensure' or 'secure' – indicates a programmatic nature for this obligation, in light of the fact that the UN is not empowered to enforce human rights the world over. On the other hand, 'universal respect'

[76] On this point see the Lisbon Decision of the German Constitutional Court, 2 BvE 2/08, 2 BvE 5/08, 2 BvR 1010/08, 2 BvR 1022/08, 2 BvR 1259/08 and 2 BvR 182/09 (30 June 2009), available at www.bundesverfassungsgericht.de/entscheidungen/es20090630_2bve000208en.html. This decision is examined in Chapter 8.

[77] A criticism of *Lotus*, and of the 'old, tired view of international law' it supposedly expresses, is in para. 2 of the Declaration of Judge Simma in the *Advisory Opinion on Kosovo*, *supra* note 67 (available at www.icj-cij.org/docket/files/141/15993.pdf). See also Koskenniemmi's analysis of the Lotus principle as an expression of the pure fact approach to sovereignty (M. Koskenniemmi, *From Apology to Utopia: The Structure of International Legal Argument* (Cambridge University Press, 2005) 255–8).

and 'observance' are robust terms – and the locution *respect effectif* used in the French text is even more so. The duty to respect and observe human rights in its activities is an implied and indispensable condition for the promotion by the UN of effective compliance with human rights by states. Paraphrasing the aforementioned passage in *Effect of Awards*,[78] it could be said that, since disputes on the fundamental rights of individuals are bound to arise in the course of UN operations, it would hardly be consistent with the expressed aim of the Charter to promote freedom and justice, and with the constant preoccupation of the UN to do the same, if the UN were allowed to act without regard to human rights (and, where relevent, to international humanitarian law).

Other references to human rights are found in Chapter XII of the Charter dealing with the now defunct Trusteeship system, especially at Article 76. Although trust territories no longer exist, it is evident from these provisions that under the Charter this exceptional exercise of governmental authority by the UN was to be accompanied by duties, including the obligation 'to promote the political, economic, social and educational advancement of the inhabitants' of the territory. These standards ought to offer a guide for analogous situations where the UN exercises governmental functions.

Implied obligations

Should there be a doctrine of implied obligations to mirror that of implied powers? If so, what should its tenets be? Before seeking to answer these questions, it is necessary to explore the doctrine of implied powers in some detail.

The Permanent Court of International Justice considered implied powers in its advisory opinion on the *Competence of the ILO*, where it recognised that the ILO had the power to provide an incidental regulation of the work of employers, regardless of the lack of an express reference to employers in its constituent instrument.[79] The Permanent Court explained that this power was consistent with the institutional goal of assuring humane conditions of labour and the protection of workers, and that 'a limitation of the powers of the International Labour Organization, clearly inconsistent with the aim of the scope of Part XIII [of the Treaty establishing the organisation] … would have

[78] *Effect of Awards*, *supra* note 65. [79] *Competence of the ILO*, *supra* note 30.

been expressed in the Treaty itself'.[80] The Court thus seemed to suggest that powers necessary to the fulfilment of institutional purposes can always be implied, unless they are expressly excluded from the constituent instrument.

In the *Reparation* case the ICJ fine-tuned this position by making reference to 'those powers which, though not expressly provided in the Charter, are conferred upon it by necessary implication as being essential to the performance of its duties' (*fonctions* in French). A number of judges dissented from the majority on the question of implied powers, most notably Judge Hackworth. He did not reject the notion of implied powers outright but took the view that '[i]mplied powers flow from a grant of express powers, and are limited to those that are "necessary" to the exercise of powers expressly granted'.[81] Dissenting on the same issue in *Effect of Awards*, Judge Hackworth explained that '[t]he doctrine of implied powers is designed to implement, within reasonable limitations, and not to supplant or vary, expressed powers'.[82]

The disagreement within the ICJ on implied powers is therefore on their scope and on the basis of the implied power: should each implied power be grounded in a specific express power as opined by Judge Hackworth? Or does it suffice that the power can be shown to be necessary to the performance of the functions of the organisation? Or, as the ICJ suggested in *Certain Expenses*, is an implied power presumed to exist whenever the organisation 'takes action which warrants the assertion that it was appropriate for the fulfilment of one of the stated purposes of the United Nations'?[83]

Much depends on how one interprets the term 'necessary'. For some it should be given its literal meaning of 'indispensable' or 'absolutely imperative', for others it should be read in the particular context of implied powers as meaning 'essential' or 'vital'.[84] According to Lauterpacht, the opinions in the *Reparation* and *Effect of Awards* cases suggest that 'necessary' means 'something more than "important" but less than "indispensably requisite"'.[85]

80 *Competence of the ILO*, *supra* note 30 at 18.

81 See diss. op. of Judge Hackworth in *Reparation*, *supra* note 31 at 198.

82 See diss. op. of Judge Hackworth in *Effect of Awards*, *supra* note 55 at 80.

83 *Certain Expenses*, *supra* note 29 at 168.

84 U. Linderfalk, *On the Interpretation of Treaties* (Dordrecht: Springer, 2007) 292.

85 Lauterpacht, *supra* note 37 at 430–2.

Implied powers have also been the object of extensive jurisprudence and scholarly debates in the field of EU/EC law. Of particular importance in this context is the opinion of the ECJ on the EU accession to the European Convention for the Protection of Human Rights and Fundamental Freedoms (ECHR)[86] – a question that is part of the broader issue of the treaty-making power of the EU/EC. Treaty-making is in itself a curious power: through its exercise an international organisation can limit itself on the international plane by entering into binding relations with states or with other international organisations. Human rights treaties, in particular, impose numerous obligations and confer only very few, mainly procedural, rights on parties. The ECJ had to decide whether, in the absence of an express provision in the founding treaties conferring a treaty-making power in the human rights sphere on the EU, the EU possesses such a power in respect of accession to the ECHR. Rather surprisingly, the ECJ ruled that the Community did not have sufficient personality to accede to the ECHR, because accession would entail 'a modification of the system for the protection of human rights in the Community, with equally fundamental institutional implications for the Community and for Members States'; in the Court's view, such changes can be brought about only by way of a Treaty amendment.[87]

Writers' views on the acceptable extent of implied powers differ a great deal. At one extreme, there are those who have theorised 'inherent powers' as a broader conceptual category than implied powers. The doyen of this school of thought was Finn Seyersted who argued that the fact that international organisations exercise territorial and personal jurisdiction to a more limited extent than states is due to a difference of fact between them and states, and not to differences in their inherent legal capacity. In his view, an international organisation can perform any act as long as it is not expressly forbidden by its constituent instrument – a position resulting in an extension of the *Lotus* principle to international organisations.[88] In this perspective, it is

[86] Opinion 2/94 [1996] ECR I-1759. See G. Gaja, 'Opinion 2/94, Accession by the Community to the European Convention for the Protection of Human Rights and Fundamental Freedoms', 33 *Common Market Law Review* (1996) 973. On the implied treaty-making power of UNMIK, see 'Note Verbale to a Permanent Mission to the UN Regarding the Legal Personality and Treaty-Making Power of UNMIK', *UN Juridical Yearbook* (2004) 351–2.

[87] *Ibid.* at para. 34–5. See Eeckout, *supra* note 69 at 82ff.

[88] F. Seyersted, 'International Personality of Intergovernmental Organizations: Do Their Capacities Really Depend upon Their Constitutions?', 4 Indian J. Int. L.

not necessary 'to look for specific provisions in the constitution, or to resort to strained interpretations of texts and intentions, or to look for precedents or other constructions to justify legally the performance by an intergovernmental organisation of a sovereign or international act not specifically authorised in its constitution'.[89] Other supporters for this approach include Nigel White and Alan Dashwood.[90]

At the opposite end of the spectrum of opinion on implied powers is the view that the powers of international organisations should be interpreted restrictively, in accordance with the principles of state sovereignty and with the consensualist bases of the international system. This was traditionally the position associated with the post-war Soviet doctrine of Grigory Tunkin (as opposed to the early Soviet doctrine of Evgeny Pashukanis who, as far as I know, did not deal with these questions),[91] but it has received support from other scholars concerned about the trend to interpret constituent instruments beyond their objective meaning.[92]

In the middle are the supporters of functional necessity, the idea that international organisations 'can reasonably claim such rights and privileges as would enable them to function effectively'.[93] Although conceptually distinct from inherent powers, the functional necessity approach does not produce a substantively different outcome, at least in relation to organisations endowed with broad functions such as the UN or the EU.

Klabbers argues that the scope of implied powers is the litmus test of the autonomy of international organisations. In his view,

(1964) 1 at 20–5. See also, by the same author, *Objective International Personality of Intergovernmental Organisations: Do Their Capacities Really Depend upon Their Constitutions?* (Copenhagen, 1963) and *Common Law of International Organisations* (Leiden-Boston: Martinus Nijhoff Publishers, 2008); the latter is a reprint in one volume of Seyersted's extensive writings on the subject.

[89] Seyersted, Indian J. Int. L., *supra* note 88 at 22.

[90] See N. White, *The Law of International Organisations* (2nd edn., Manchester University Press, 2005) at 87–9 and by the same author 'The UN Charter and Peacekeeping Forces: Constitutional Issues', 3 *International Peacekeeping* (1996) 43; A. Dashwood, 'Implied External Competence of the EC', in M. Koskenniemi (ed.), *International Law Aspects of the European Union* (The Hague: Kluwer Law International, 1998) 113.

[91] See G. I. Tunkin, 'The Legal Nature of the United Nations', 119(III) RC (1966) 1.

[92] R. J. Araujo, 'Objective Meaning of Constituent Instruments and Responsibility of International Organisations', in M. Ragazzi (ed.), *International Responsibility Today: Essays in Memory of Oscar Schachter* (Leiden: Martinus Nijhoff, 2005) 346.

[93] Klabbers, *supra* note 11 at 36–9 and 148–53.

'[i]f an organisation's powers are limited to those powers explicitly granted, then the organisation remains, in effect, merely a vehicle for its members rather than an entity with a distinct will of its own' and the 'very *raison d'être* [of international organisations] comes into question'.[94] It is not, however, clear why the distinct will of an organisation should be predicated on a broad measure of implied powers. If the organisation was endowed with significant powers to begin with, why should the express nature of their conferral make a difference?

Taking a step back from this debate, one can begin by posing a simple question: why do we speak of implied *powers*? At the risk of exhuming the analogy between contract and treaty, it is rather striking that we do not speak instead of implied *terms* – as one would in contract law. Analytically, an implied power is always based on an implied term.[95] This is so whether the test for implication is necessary connection to a specific express term (and power) in the constituent instrument or more generally to a function or even to a purpose of the organisation.

The possibility of implying terms into treaties is not really in dispute.[96] Direct support for it can be found in Article 56(1) of the Vienna Convention on the Law of Treaties, which provides that a right of withdrawal 'may be implied by the nature of the treaty', as well as in the language used by the ICJ itself in the cases considered above (e.g. 'by necessary *implication*').[97]

The implication of terms in constituent instruments has, however, been discussed under the framework of the doctrine of effectiveness (efficacy to contract is, incidentally, one of the general principles applicable to implication in contract law too).[98] The principle of effectiveness has normally been understood as coterminous with the teleological interpretation of treaties, although Fitzmaurice preferred to consider effectiveness as the teleological

94 *Ibid.* at 65. 95 See e.g. Linderfalk, *supra* note 84 at 287ff.

96 Lord McNair, *The Law of Treaties* (Oxford: Clarendon Press, 1961) 437.

97 See also A. Aust, *Modern Treaty Law and Practice* (2nd edn., Cambridge University Press, 2005) 249–50.

98 *The Moorcock* (1889) 14 PD 64 at 68. See the diss. op. of Judges Spender and Fitzmaurice on the dangers of the principle of maximum effect in treaty interpretation in *South West Africa* cases, ICJ Reports (1962) 319 at 511ff; and H. Waldock, 'Third Report on the Law of Treaties', ILC Yearbook (1964), Vol. 2 at para. 29 on the nexus between effectiveness and implication.

principle 'expressed in a more restrained form'.[99] Thirlway suggests that the principle can be distinguished as two 'incarnations of the same idea' – the first one being the rule that all provisions of the treaty 'must be supposed to have been intended to have significance and to be necessary to convey the intended meaning ... and [that] an interpretation that reduces some part of the text to the status of pleonasm, or mere surplusage, is prima facie suspect'; and the second one, the rule that 'the instrument as a whole, and each of its provisions, must be taken to have been intended to achieve some end, and that an interpretation which would make the text ineffective to achieve the object is, once again, prima facie suspect'.[100] Others have argued that, while latitude may be appropriate in relation to the internal functioning of international organisations, greater caution is warranted for implied terms which impact upon the rights and duties of member states.[101]

So, what do we gain by speaking of implication of terms rather than conducting the analysis with the toolbox with which international lawyers are familiar, in particular implied powers and effectiveness? First, there is a problem with the principle of effectiveness. As observed by McRae, 'given its broad conception, and its tendency to deny ... any hard and fast limitations or rules, it [the principle of effectiveness] is equally or more likely to operate quite differently, as a licence to judicial activism or legislation'.[102] Secondly, to speak of implied terms instead of implied powers makes the suggestion that obligations can be implied not so radical after all. Indeed, 'implied term' is a neutral formulation, for a term can give rise to rights or duties (and sometimes to both).

Moreover, despite the efforts described above, the limits of teleological interpretation are not clear, and there is a real risk that,

[99] G. Fitzmaurice, *The Law and Procedure of the International Court of Justice* (1956) at 49. On treaty interpretation and the principle of effectiveness, see also M. Fitzmaurice, 'Dynamic (Evolutive) Interpretation of Treaties: Part I', 21 *Hague Yearbook of International Law* (2009) 101.

[100] H. Thirlway, 'The Law and Procedure of the International Court of Justice 1960–1989', 62(III) BYIL (1991) 44. See also Linderfalk, *supra* note 84 at 290.

[101] See e.g. K. Skubiszewski, 'Implied Powers of International Organisations', in Y. Dinstein and M. Tabory (eds.), *International Law at a Time of Perplexity: Essays in Honour of Shabtai Rosenne* (Dordrecht: Martinus Nijhoff, 1989) 859.

[102] P. McRae, 'The Search for Meaning: Continuing Problems with the Interpretation of Treaties', 33(2) *Victoria University of Wellington Law Review* (2002) at Section II C.

under the guise of effectiveness, an unbridled instrumentalism sets in which justifies every power that is a means to perform a function or to pursue a purpose. A quick look at the breadth and generality of the purposes of the UN will show that such an approach would essentially justify any power. The problem is that, while effectiveness should be one of the principles applicable to implication of terms in constituent instruments, it cannot provide the sole basis for implication, lest we adopt a framework that poses no real limits and only serves to offer *ex post facto* justifications for expansions in powers.

In addition to seemingly – and wrongly – excluding obligations, the other reason for objecting to the terminology of implied powers is the breadth of the term 'powers'. Is it admissible to imply any power, including, in particular, a strong power in the Hohfeldian sense (see the discussion at pp. 69–70)? The doctrine of implied powers does not put limits based on the strength of the power, although it is reasonable to assume that, when the implied power is such that it can affect the legal position of others, the bar for implication should be set higher. In their rightly celebrated joint dissenting opinion in the *South-West Africa* cases, Judges Fitzmaurice and Spender were expressing a similar concern, when they stated that one reason why the 'extensive interpretations' of the key provision in the Mandate (Article 7) put forward by the majority were not justified was 'the unilateral character of that provision' which 'could be invoked against, but not by, the Mandatory'.[103] Having said that, the power held to have been properly implied in one of the leading authorities in this area – the *Effect of Awards* opinion – was in all probability a strong Hohfeldian power.

The analysis above highlights the limits of the existing debate on implied powers, but does not, at first, seem to take us very far on the front of implied obligations. It is however possible to draw some conclusions. To begin with, the term 'implied powers' is something of a misnomer. The question is whether constituent instruments of international organisations can accommodate implied terms. The general answer is that they can, but there is no reason in principle why only terms that confer powers on the organisations should be susceptible to implication. Obligations can be implied too. Furthermore, the limits of implication for terms containing obligations must not be different

[103] Diss. op. of Judges Spender and Fitzmaurice, *supra* note 98 at 513.

from those applicable to the implication of terms conferring powers. If one adopts Judge Hackworth's analysis, the principal such limit is that the implied term must be necessary to the fulfilment of a specific power that is provided for expressly. If one prefers the position of the majority in the *Reparation* and *Effect of Awards* cases, a close connection to a generic function or to an institutional purpose will suffice for implying terms. But there is no reason why the terms that are implied should be only permissive and never obligatory. Nor is there principled basis for justifying a more generous approach to the implication of powers (or rights or functions) than to the implication of duties.

Obligations arising under institutional acts

Some institutional acts can have the effect of binding the organisation on the international plane. First, although the UN Charter does not expressly provide that decisions of the Security Council under Chapter VII are binding on the organisation too, such an obligation can be easily derived by necessary implication from Articles 1 and 2 of the Charter combined with the provisions of Chapter VII. Secondly, institutional acts can contribute to the formation of custom; in such instances, the organisation will be bound by those obligations via customary international law.[104] Thirdly, some institutional acts may have binding effect as unilateral acts on the basis of the principle which was stated by the ICJ in *Nuclear Tests* and which is susceptible to being extended to international organisations.[105]

Outside these categories determining the legal effects of UN institutional acts is quite problematic. In *Certain Expenses*, the ICJ observed that certain resolutions of the General Assembly of the UN are not 'merely hortatory', but have 'dispositive force and effect'.[106] The Court referred to Article 18 of the Charter, which mentions 'decisions' of the General Assembly on 'important questions', including those pertaining

[104] See R. Higgins, *The Development of International Law Through the Political Organs of the United Nations* (London: Oxford University Press for the Royal Institute of International Affairs, 1963).

[105] *Nuclear Tests Cases (Australia v. France; New Zealand v. France)*, ICJ Reports (1974) 253 at paras. 44–6.

[106] *Certain Expenses, supra* note 29 at 163. See also Amerasinghe, *supra* note 38 at 192ff.

to the budget and to membership of the organisation. Article 18 does not expressly refer to resolutions of a general norm-creating character, such as those on human rights, but it seems barely arguable that the very resolutions with which the General Assembly seeks to promote the adoption of binding rules by states should have no force and effect on the UN itself.

Human rights obligations can thus arise under numerous resolutions of the General Assembly, in particular those that heralded the adoption of multilateral human rights treaties.[107] Other resolutions of both the Security Council and the General Assembly, which have addressed human rights issues in specific situations, may equally give rise to human rights obligations.[108] Furthermore, the Universal Declaration of Human Rights – the first resolution of the General Assembly on human rights – provides 'an authoritative guide' to the interpretation of the generic provisions of the Charter on human rights.[109] Article 28 of the Declaration is particularly important, since it provides that 'everyone is entitled to a social and international order in which the rights and freedoms set forth in this Declaration can be fully realised'. Such an international order must be one where, amongst other things, international organisations are bound by those human rights obligations relevant to the powers they exercise.

It is also important to distinguish acts that are merely internal from those that have effects on the international plane. In its project on institutional responsibility, the ILC dealt with the consequences of the demarcation between internal rules and international law, but for very

[107] For example, Convention on the Prevention and Punishment of the Crime of Genocide (1948), 78 UNTS 277; Universal Declaration of Human Rights, GA Res. 217A (III) (1948); International Covenant on Civil and Political Rights (1966), 999 UNTS 171; International Covenant on Economic, Social and Cultural Rights (1966), 993 UNTS 3; Convention on the Elimination of All Forms of Discrimination Against Women (CEDAW) (1979), 19 ILM 33; Convention against Torture and Other Cruel, Inhuman or Degrading Treatment or Punishment, GA Res. 39/46 (1984); Convention on the Rights of the Child, GA Res. 44/25 (1989).

[108] G. Quinn, 'The General Assembly into the 1990s', in P. Alston (ed.), *The United Nations and Human Rights: A Critical Appraisal* (Oxford: Clarendon Press, 1992) 55 at 77. On the protection of women in armed conflict see, e.g., SC Res. 1325 (2000); SC Res. 1820 (2008); and SC Res. 1888 (2009). On the protection of children in armed conflict see, e.g., SC Res. 1612 (2005), GA Res. 63/241 (2009), GA Res. 64/146 (2010), SC Res. 1882 (2009).

[109] Brownlie, *supra* note 10 at 559; Universal Declaration, *supra* note 107.

good reasons preferred not to express a clear-cut view on this issue.[110] The ICJ addressed this question in its opinion on the *Kosovo Case*, moving the boundary in favour of the international law characterisation of acts that might at first appear internal. The Court had to determine whether the regulations adopted on behalf of the UN Mission in Kosovo (UNMIK) by the Special Representative, most notably the Constitutional Framework, were acts 'of an internal law rather than an international law character'.[111] The Court observed that the 'binding force' of the Constitutional Framework derived from the 'binding character of resolution 1244 (1999) and thus from international law',[112] and concluded that the Constitutional Framework did 'form part of the international law' which the Court had to consider and apply.[113]

Institutional acts that have no binding effect on the international plane may still have prescriptive force in an internal or administrative sense.[114] Some standard-setting resolutions of the General Assembly may be in this category: they do not bind the organisation as a matter of international law, but they bind some or all of its organs as a matter of internal law.[115]

The internal prescriptive force of resolutions of the General Assembly is particularly relevant to the activities of operational programmes which are normally constituted as subsidiary organs of the General Assembly.[116] Moreover, under Article 60 of the Charter, 'responsibility for the discharge of the functions' of the UN in the area of international economic and social co-operation 'shall be vested in the General Assembly and, under the authority of the General Assembly,

[110] Article 9(2), Articles on the Responsibility of IOs, and the commentary to Article 9 in ILC Report (2009), UN Doc. A/64/10, at 79. The notion of an internal law of international organisations, first formulated in relation to the UN (L. Focsaneanu, 'Le droit interne de l' Organisation des Nations Unies', 3 *Annuaire Français de Droit International* (1957) 315), is now invoked to explain the peculiarity of organisations such as the EU (e.g. E. Paasivirta and P. J. Kuijper, 'Does One Size Fit All? The European Community and the Responsibility of International Organisations', 36 *Netherlands Yearbook of International Law* (2005) 169).

[111] *Kosovo Advisory Opinion*, *supra* note 67 at para. 88. The Constitutional Framework is UNMIK Regulation No. 2001/9.

[112] *Ibid.* [113] *Ibid.* at para. 93. [114] Higgins, *supra* note 104 at 4.

[115] E.g. GA Res. 45/111 ('Basic Principles for the Treatment of Prisoners'); GA Res. 45/113 ('UN Rules for the Protection of Juveniles Deprived of their Liberty'); GA Res. 45/110 ('UN Standard Minimum Rules for non-Custodial Measures'); GA Res. 40/33 ('UN Standard Minimum Rules for the Administration of Juvenile Justice').

[116] The *Effects of Awards* case was rather peculiar because the Court concluded that the General Assembly was bound by the awards of the Tribunal, which it had established.

in the Economic and Social Council'. In part owing to the failure of the General Assembly to exercise its powers of control and policy direction over operational programmes like UNICEF, UNHCR, UNDP and over UN operations in general, there are only a few resolutions addressed specifically to them and these tend to be unsubstantial in terms of content. Nevertheless, the operational programmes should consider themselves bound, at least as a matter of internal law, by the general terms of the resolutions of the political organs.

Specialised agencies are in a different position. Article 58 of the Charter empowers the UN to 'make recommendations for the co-ordination of the policies and activities of the specialised agencies'. The agreement between the UN and the specialised agencies is meant to flesh out the terms of their relationship. However, the practice of the IMF, the World Bank and the International Civil Aviation Organization (ICAO) suggests that some specialised agencies do not consider themselves bound by the resolutions of the General Assembly, although the Assembly, supported by the Secretariat, traditionally views its powers vis-à-vis the specialised agencies more extensively.[117]

Institutional acts may also emanate from the Secretary General of the UN. The guidelines for UN forces about compliance with international humanitarian law, for example, were adopted as a communication in the Bulletin of the Secretary General.[118] The Bulletin is considered 'binding on members of UN forces in the same way as are all other instructions issued by the Secretary General in his capacity as "commander in chief" of UN operations'.[119] It has, in other words, prescriptive force in an internal sense. Together with the entry into force in 1999 of the Convention on the Safety of UN Personnel, the Bulletin of the Secretary General ought finally to put an end to the

But this conclusion does not contradict the relationship of subsidiarity between the Assembly and the Tribunal, since the power to bind the General Assembly had been vested with the Tribunal by the Assembly itself. See *supra* note 55.

117 Schermers and Blokker, *supra* note 40 at 1073–5; I. Shihata, *The World Bank in a Changing World* (Dordrecht: Martinus Nijhoff, 1991), Vol I, 99ff.; D. Williams, *The Specialised Agencies and the United Nations* (London: C. Hurst, 1987) 160ff.

118 Secretary General, 'Observance by the United Nations Forces of International Humanitarian Law', UN Doc. ST/SGB/1999/13, reprinted in 836 Int. Rev. R. C. (1999) 812.

119 D. Shraga, 'UN Peacekeeping Operations: Applicability of International Humanitarian Law and Responsibility for Operations-Related Damage', 94 AJIL (2000) 406 at 409.

past antinomian practice that denied the applicability of international humanitarian law to UN forces (see Chapter 6).

In the peacekeeping context, rules of engagement are another important category of institutional acts under which obligations may arise. Soldiers and officers on the ground are often more familiar with these rules than with the Security Council mandate for their mission or with the relevant Status of Forces Agreement. Rules of engagement are drafted by the Secretariat, which, while retaining some discretion, has to tailor them to the mandate of the mission as established by the Security Council.

The effects of the human rights obligations of member states

At present, there is no mechanism for automatically ascribing obligations incumbent on member states to international organisations. As a result of an important judicial development closely examined in Chapter 8 – the doctrine of equivalent protection – conduct by an international organisation that breaches human rights obligations of its member states may however have significant repercussions on the responsibility of the member state. The human rights obligations of member states, while devoid of direct legal effects on the organisation, may also have political consequences – and even indirect legal ones – insofar as the doctrine of equivalent protection places an incentive on those states to monitor the conduct of the international organisation in order to minimise the states' risk of incurring responsibility on a derivative basis.

As will be seen in more detail, the case law on the doctrine of equivalent protection is far from settled. Despite the remaining uncertainty, however, under this doctrine the obligation to ensure respect[120] for

[120] See, e.g., Art. 2(1), International Covenant on Civil and Political Rights (ICCPR) (1966), 999 UNTS 171. As has been mentioned above (see text accompanying note 78 *supra*), the obligation to ensure also applies to humanitarian law obligations. See Art. 1 in each of the four Geneva Conventions and in Protocol I: Geneva Convention (I) for the Amelioration of the Condition of the Wounded and Sick in Armed Forces in the Field, Geneva (1949), 75 UNTS 31; Geneva Convention (II) for the Amelioration of the Condition of the Wounded, Sick and Shipwrecked Members of the Armed Forces at Sea (1949), 75 UNTS 85; Geneva Convention (III) Relative to the Treatment of Prisoners of War (1949), 75 UNTS 135; Geneva Convention (IV) Relative to the Protection of Civilians in Time of War, Geneva (1949), 75 UNTS 287; Protocol I Additional to the Geneva Conventions of 1949, and Relating to the Protection of Victims of International Armed Conflict (1977), 1125 UNTS 3.

human rights does not cease when states voluntarily transfer functions to international organisations, and states may, in certain circumstances, incur responsibility for breaches resulting from institutional conduct. States which host UN operations are, in principle, also under an obligation to ensure that the UN, like any other authority in the country, complies with the full spectrum of human rights obligations undertaken by those states. In practice, however, it is quite often the case that the weaker the territorial state, the stronger the UN. In fact, the range of powers that UN agencies assume on the ground tend to be inversely correlated to the strength of national institutions. Internal strife and conflict – most notably in the case of failed states – are precisely the situations in which the need for a multifunctional UN presence is the greatest.

The doctrine of equivalent protection places a significant burden on member states, but where does this doctrine leave the international organisation? In particular, could the state that has incurred responsibility nominally for its own conduct but, to all intents and purposes, for conduct of an international organisation, seek to recover from the latter? There would in all likelihood be no forum to which to bring such a dispute. More fundamentally, at present the law does not offer a cause of action to the state seeking to bring the claim, unless – that is – the conduct in question also causes a breach of some international obligation incumbent on the organisation which the state can action. What the law in its present state does not provide is a general obligation, incumbent on the UN or other international organisations, not to violate rules of international human rights law whenever such violations could cause one or more member states to incur responsibility on a derivative basis and/or under the doctrine of equivalent protection (the two bases are not coextensive).

It could be objected that it is neither practical nor desirable to generically oblige international organisations not to expose member states to responsibility for breaches of human rights obligations, since the human rights obligations of their members vary. However, this challenge could be readily addressed by providing that the UN ought to comply with treaty standards accepted by some but not all of its member states, whenever such compliance is devoid of consequences for other member states – which, at least in the human rights field, would be so in the vast majority of cases. The consequence of this approach would be that the UN would always have to adhere to the highest standard of human rights binding on one or more of its member states, rather than to the lowest common denominator.

Another argument is that an international organisation that puts in place conduct capable of causing a member state to incur responsibility is abusing its rights and acting in breach of good faith. Fitzmaurice proposed that 'the duty of acting in good faith ... [be] enhanced by the fact that not only is there, as a rule, no certainty that an aggrieved foreign State will be able to bring the matter before an international tribunal or other appropriate forum, or obtain the enforcement of any finding given in its favour if it does'. Put in other terms, international law should compensate the absence of a method for asserting the rights of the state against the international organisation by placing a duty on the international organisation to conduct itself on the higher *uberrimae fidei*, rather than simply *bonae fidei*, standard.[121] This argument, attractive though it might be, would be met with the objection that, in the jurisprudence of the ICJ, the principle of good faith is not a source of obligation where none would otherwise exist; it can reinforce, expand or deepen an existing obligation, but it cannot create an altogether new one.[122]

Conclusion

International organisations have resorted to some original legal arguments to resist the application of human rights obligations to their activities. For example, the former General Counsel of the IMF invoked the 'savings clause' in Article 24 of the International Covenant on Economic, Social and Cultural Rights which protects the UN Charter and constitutions of specialised agencies.[123] The focus of the protection enshrined in this 'savings clause', however, is the *impairment* of the relevant constitutive instruments. Its intent is not to exonerate the UN and its specialised agencies from fundamental human rights.

[121] G. Fitzmaurice, 'The Law and Procedure of the International Court of Justice 1954–9 – General Principles and Sources of International Law', 35 BYBIL (1959) 183 at 212 and, in general, at 207–16.

[122] *Case Concerning Border and Transborder Armed Actions (Nicaragua v. Honduras)*, ICJ Reports (1998) 69 at para. 94.

[123] Clapham, *supra* note 1 at 146. See also the equivalent provision in Art. 46 of the ICCPR.

The reality is that much – probably most – human rights law binds the UN and other international organisations already through custom. A general obligation to respect human rights may also be grounded in the Charter, expressly or by necessary implication. Difficulties can arise in relation to particular human rights obligations, which have not received universal or quasi-universal acceptance as custom and which are too specific to be implied in the Charter. An example is the prohibition on the death penalty, which has attained customary status in Europe but not beyond. It would be far-fetched to argue that it arises under the Charter by necessary implication, given the number of states that continue to endorse this practice. The prohibition is, however, contained in resolutions approved by the General Assembly with a significant, albeit certainly not overwhelming, majority.[124] These resolutions must be binding at least on the subsidiary organs of the UN, but do they bind the UN as a whole? Would a Security Council mandated peacekeeping mission, for example, be obliged to respect their terms? The best position is that, in the absence of unanimity, a resolution of a norm-creating character must still have dispositive force on the organisation itself, although this is clearly without prejudice to the legal powers of the Security Council under Chapter VII of the Charter.

The practical effects of the doctrine of equivalent protection should also be taken into account (see Chapter 8). International organisations must give some regard to the potential responsibility of their members. At present it is not possible to put this point any higher, but international organisations can ignore the important judicial development represented by equivalent protection at their own peril: sooner or later, either governments or judges will find ways of holding them to account directly.

Furthermore, although the analysis above has focused on the creation of obligations for international organisations, the legal and political force of human rights must be kept in mind. Liberal democratic governments, courts and, perhaps most importantly of all, public opinion will at some point step in to ensure that power, in its new manifestations, is subject to such limitations as are necessary

[124] See GA Res. 62/149 (2007) adopted by 104 votes to 54 with 29 abstentions; and GA Res. 63/168 (2009) adopted by 106 votes to 46 with 34 abstentions.

to protect liberty. International organisations cannot hope to be immune from the force of human rights-based arguments. As the ECHR found in *Matthews*, these rights cannot be made 'theoretical or illusory' because the face of the power that violates them has changed.[125]

[125] *Denise Matthews v. UK*, Judgment, 18 February 1999, Application No. 24833/94, 28 EHRR 361.

3 International institutional responsibility

Introduction

In 2000 the ILC decided to include the responsibility of international organisations in its programme of work, appointing Professor Giorgio Gaja as Special Rapporteur in 2002.[1] Since then the work of the Commission has proceeded at a steady pace, leading to the adoption of a draft set of articles.

Although the rules on state responsibility offered a starting point and a framework of reference,[2] the ILC was faced with more than a

[1] ILC Report (2000), UN Doc. A/55/10 at para. 729 and ILC Report (2002), UN Doc. A/57/10 at paras. 461–3. On the background to the project on the responsibility of international organisations see G. Gaja, 'First Report on Responsibility of International Organisations' (2003), 55th Session of the ILC, UN Doc. A/CN.4/532 at paras. 3–11. The sixty-six draft articles approved on first reading at the end of its 61st Session, see ILC Report (2009), UN Doc. A/64/10 at paras. 31ff.). In this chapter the draft articles on the responsibility of international organisations are referred to as Draft Articles on Responsibility of International Organisations; articles on the responsibility of states as Articles on State Responsibility.

[2] Gaja, 'First Report', *supra* note 1 at para. 11; Gaja, 'Sixth Report on Responsibility of International Organisations' (2008), 60th Session of the ILC, UN Doc. A/CN.4/597 at para. 5. See also the observations of Trial Chamber II of the International Criminal Tribunal of the FRY in *Prosecutor v. Dragan Nikolic* (Decision on the defence motion challenging the exercise of jurisdiction by the Tribunal), 9 October 2002, Case No. IT-94-2-PT at paras. 61–3. Other important works of secondary literature adopting this general view include: C.F. Amerasinghe, *Principles of the Institutional Law of International Organisations* (2nd edn., Cambridge University Press, 2005) 384ff.; M. H. Arsanjani, 'Claims against International Organizations: *Quis Custodiet Ipsos Custodes*', 7 *Yale Journal of World Public Order* (1981) 131; C. Eagleton, 'International Organisations and the Law of Responsibility', in 76(I) RC (1950) 323 at 323; M. Hirsch, *The Responsibility of International Organisations Toward Third Parties: Some Basic Principles* (Dordrecht: Martinus Nijhoff, 1995) 7–10; P. Klein, 'The Attribution of Acts to International Organizations', in J. Crawford, A. Pellet, S. Olleson and K. Parlett (eds.), *The Law of International Responsibility* (Oxford University Press, 2010) 297 at 296;

few new challenges. Some states observed at the outset that there was 'no customary international law on the responsibility of international organisations'[3] and that institutional practice was often unavailable. The body of case law on international institutional responsibility had traditionally been quite thin, but, shortly before the ILC began its work,[4] domestic and international jurisprudence on international institutional law entered into a phase of rather idiosyncratic expansion, making the codification of international law in this area more of a challenge.

A general problem in the development of these rules concerns the gap between the project on state responsibility and the project on the responsibility of international organisations. Some areas of the law of responsibility not previously addressed in the Articles on State Responsibility – for example, the responsibility of states in connection with the act of an international organisation – have been dealt with by the Commission through its work on institutional responsibility, but others have fallen through the cracks of the two projects. For example, the Articles on State Responsibility deal with countermeasures adopted by a state in response to the internationally wrongful act of another state, while the Draft Articles on the Responsibility of International Organisations cover the adoption of countermeasures by either a state or an international organisation in response to the internationally wrongful act of an international organisation. The adoption of countermeasures by an international organisation in response to the internationally wrongful act of a state is not covered in either

N. Q. Dinh, P. Daillier and A. Pellet, *Droit International Public* (6th edn., Paris: LGDJ, 1999) 756; I. Scobbie, 'International Organizations and International Relations', in R. J. Dupuy (ed.), *A Handbook of International Organizations* (2nd edn., Dordrecht: Martinus Nijhoff, 1998) 831 at 887. See also F. V. Garcia-Amador, 'First Report on State Responsibility by the Special Rapporteur', 8th Session of the ILC, UN Doc. A/CN.4/96, and in (1956, II) YBILC 173 at 189–190.

[3] Observations submitted by Germany, comments and observations received from governments and international organisations, ILC (2005), UN Doc A/Cn.4/556 at 47.

[4] In the ECHR, see *Beer and Regan v. Germany*, Judgment, 18 February 1999, Application No. 28934/95; *Denise Matthews v. UK*, Judgment, 18 February 1999, Application No. 24833/94, 28 EHRR 361; *Case of Bosphorus Hava Yallari Turizm ve Ticaret Anonim Sirketi v. Ireland*, Judgment, 30 June 2005, Application No. 45036/98, *D v. Turkey*, Application No. 24245/03; *Behrami and Behrami v France*, Application No. 71412/01 and *Saramati v France, Germany and Norway*, Application No. 78166/01, Decision on Admissibility. In the ECJ, see Case T-306/01, *Yusuf and Al Barakaat International Foundation v. Council and Commission*, Judgment, 21 September 2005; Case T-315/01 and C-415/05 P, *Kadi v. Council and Commission*; Case T-253/02, *Ayadi v. Council and Commission*.

project. Reopening the state responsibility project to fill in any gaps would be too big a task, and probably not justified by the significance of the problem because interpretation by analogy can help fill in these gaps without great difficulty.

International organisations generally engaged with the work of the Commission, submitting comments and observations. Two broad trends have emerged. First, the EU sought to distinguish itself from other international organisations, often calling for the adoption of special rules. Secondly, some international organisations have been apprehensive about the scope of their responsibility as a result of the approach adopted by the Commission to issues such as attribution and the responsibility of an international organisation in connection to the act of a state. The Special Rapporteur and the Commission have responsed by defending, on the one hand, the adoption of rules of general applicability and, on the other, a principled and purposive approach to responsibility that does not offer international organisations easy deliverance.

Conceptual issues

International institutional responsibility 'comes into operation after it has been decided that a breach of international law has occurred';[5] its main purpose is to identify the consequences that flow from that breach. The underlying concept of responsibility is of responsibility as liability rather than answerability.[6]

Crucially, international institutional responsibility, like state responsibility, focuses on the political entity, rather than the human agents who perpetrated the breach. This feature has exposed the law of international responsibility to what has been described as the individualist challenge, which 'concerns the effects that the imposition of liability has on the interests of the general population of the responsible state. When a state incurs liability, the resulting costs may be borne by the entire citizenry of the state and not its leadership or officials.'[7] These observations would however also apply to public liability in domestic law: the entire citizenry, for example, will bear the costs of the negligence of health professionals employed

[5] J. Crawford and J. Watkins, 'International Responsibility', in S. Besson and J. Tasioulas (eds.), *The Philosophy of International Law* (Oxford University Press, 2010) 283 at 284.
[6] *Ibid.* [7] *Ibid.* at 289.

by the public sector. The individualist challenge is not, in essence, so much a challenge to the idea of a regime of state responsibility under international law, as one to the idea of the state as such; and, in particular, it is a challenge to the idea that the state has *power* to affect the life of its often unwitting population through the various human agents that act in its name. The possibility that responsibility be ascribed to the state under international law is only one manifestation of this power, and generally not the one of greatest consequence.[8]

Is the concept of international institutional responsibility also exposed to the individualist challenge that has been levied against state responsibility? The individualist challenge carries greater moral force when it can be shown that an innocent multitude is likely to suffer from the consequences of the conduct of a few individuals. As discussed below, in certain circumstances the member states of an international organisation may incur derivative responsibility for the wrongful acts of the organisation. The analogy is with shareholders of a company: both member states and shareholders may be faced with the consequences of illegal acts which they did not commit, but this is a risk which was accepted by states upon joining the international organisation, and by shareholders upon purchasing shares in the company. It is true that innocent individuals living in the member states which have incurred derivative responsibility may also be affected. Such a risk cannot be completely ruled out, at least in theory. Nevertheless, given that these consequences would be shared with other member states and that, in any event, the economic consequences of the ascription of responsibility to an international organisation are in absolute terms quite modest, what in practice would be transferred to innocent individuals is negligible.[9]

As is the case with many general propositions about international organisations, the last one also requires an EU qualification. In general terms, the more powerful an organisation, the greater the impact which the ascription

[8] I take Murphy's remark that '[t]he individualist objection reminds us that the state system in international law and practice requires justification' as essentially going in the same direction as my argument above. L. Murphy, 'International Responsibility', in Besson and Tasioulas, *supra* note 5, 299 at 303.

[9] See Murphy's scepticism about counter-arguments to the individualist challenge that rely on the putatively negligible effects of ascriptions of responsibility (Murphy, *supra* note 8 at 302).

of international responsibility to it could have on individuals, although such impact would be mediated through the member states. The point can be illustrated with an example taken from the response of the EU to the euro crisis in the spring of 2010. In May 2010, as the euro was coming under intense pressure in the international financial markets, euro area member states set up the European Financial Stability Facility (EFSF). As explained in the extraordinarily laconic website of the EFSF, this body was entrusted with the 'capacity to issue bonds guaranteed by euro area members for up to €440 billion for on-lending to euro area member states in difficulty, subject to conditions to be negotiated with the European Commission in liaison with the European Central Bank and International Monetary Fund and to be approved by the Eurogroup'.[10] The EFSF was set up as a Luxembourg-registered company 'owned by euro area Member States'.[11] It was not therefore directly owned by the EU. Nevertheless, this must surely be one of the largest ever economic interventions to be administered not by a state, but by a group of states with the assistance of an international organisation. Given the prominent role of the EU Commission in the lending decisions of the EFSF, the EU could in certain circumstances incur derivative liability for the wrongful acts of the EFSF (e.g. under complicity), or even direct responsibility if attribution was established.

It is important to distinguish the international law regime of institutional responsibility from other regimes of institutional responsibility. Such other regimes include national law and the internal law of the organisation. Whether international organisations can incur responsibility under domestic law also depends on their status and immunities under that law. Responsibility under national law arises, in practice, 'either under contracts concluded by international organisations, and to which a national law is applicable or in circumstances where tortious acts are attributable to an organisation irrespective of any contractual link'.[12] The national law will also determine whether the particular responsibility in question is contractual, tortious, restitutionary or criminal.

As for the regime of institutional responsibility under the internal law of the organisation, it requires a further distinction: between a *lex specialis* on international responsibility and a self-standing regime of internal responsibility; or, using the terminology of the ILC in the project on state responsibility, between strong forms of *lex specialis*

10 See www.efsf.europa.eu. 11 *Ibid.*

12 P. Sands and P. Klein, *Bowett's Law of International Institutions* (6th edn., London: Sweet and Maxwell, 2009) 521.

and weaker ones.[13] The difference is one of degree: a special rule on attribution or forms of reparation changes one aspect of the regime of international institutional responsibility but does not replace it entirely, whereas a complete set of special rules will create a separate system. An example, albeit contested, of *lex specialis* in the weak sense is the rule on the attribution to the EU of conduct of member states where they are giving effect to binding acts of the EU. This example, which is examined below, is discussed in the ILC commentary.[14] Another example are the rules on attribution in certain treaties in the field of international humanitarian law – such as Article 3 of the 1907 Hague Convention (IV) and Article 91 of Additional Protocol I – which make the state responsible for 'all acts' committed by persons forming part of the armed forces.[15] Examples of internal regimes of responsibility – or *lex specialis* in the strong sense – are the regime of community tort under Article 340 of the Consolidated EU/EEC Treaty (formerly Article 288(2) of the Treaty Establishing the European Communities),[16] and the regime of liability in employment matters under the UN Administrative Tribunal.[17] The ICJ dealt with the distinction between rules of the organisation that are merely internal and those that have an international law character in its opinion on the *Declaration of Independence of Kosovo*, where it accepted the international law characterisation of acts – in that case regulations adopted by the Special Representative on behalf of UNMIK – that might at first appear

[13] See commentary to Art. 55 of the Articles on State Responsibility, in J. Crawford, *The International Law Commission's Articles on State Responsibility: Introduction, Text and Commentaries* (Cambridge University Press, 2002) 308.

[14] See the ILC commentary on Art. 63, ILC (2009) at 173–5. See also: E. Paasivirta and P. J. Kuijper, 'Does One Size Fit All? The European Community and the Responsibility of International Organisations', 36 *Netherlands Yearbook of International Law* (2005) 169; S. Talmon, 'Responsibility of International Organisations: Does the European Community Require Special Treatment?', in M. Ragazzi (ed.), *International Responsibility Today: Essays in Memory of Oscar Schachter* (Leiden: Martinus Nijhoff, 2005) 405.

[15] See M. Zwanenburg, *Accountability of Peace Support Operations* (Leiden: Martinus Nijhoff, 2005) 84.

[16] The Consolidated Versions of the Treaty on European Union and the Treaty on the Functioning of the European Union, inclusive of the amendments introduced through the Lisbon Treaty, is available at http://register.consilium.europa.eu/pdf/en/08/st06/st06655.en08.pdf. See A. Arnull *et al.*, *Wyatt and Dashwood's European Union Law* (5th edn., London: Thomson Sweet & Maxwell, 2006) 483–96 (references are still to the pre-Lisbon treaties – hence to Art. 288(2)).

[17] See C. F. Amerasinghe, *The Law of the International Civil Service* (2nd edn., Oxford: Clarendon Press, 1994).

internal.[18] Based on this finding of the Court, it may be appropriate to regard internal regimes of responsibility as still possessing some international law character.

Wrongful act and breach

Under the Draft Articles on Responsibility of International Organisations a wrongful act is an action or omission by an international organisation which constitutes a breach of an international obligation.[19] In parallel with the Articles on State Responsibility, a breach of an international obligation is said to occur 'when an act of that organisation is not in conformity with what is required of it by that obligation, regardless of its origin or character'.[20]

An issue that has given rise to intense debate is the inclusion of omissions in the definition of wrongful act. The Special Rapporteur explained that 'omissions are wrongful when an international organisation is required to take some positive action and fails to do so', giving the example of the failure of the UN to prevent genocide in Rwanda.[21] In its comment on the work of the Commission, the IMF maintained that an organisation that fails to take action as a result of the lawful exercise by its member states of their powers should not be responsible for the omission, explaining that '[t]he decision-making processes of international organisations are legal imperatives in their own right' and that an international organisation finds itself in a different position from that of a state.[22] The Special Rapporteur rejected this position, which would essentially have the effect of exempting international organisations from any obligation as long as decisions are taken pursuant to the terms of their constituent instruments.[23]

Another important question is whether the breach of a rule of the organisation should be characterised as an internationally wrongful

[18] *Accordance with International Law of the Unilateral Declaration of Independence in Respect of Kosovo*, Advisory Opinion of 22 July 2010, at para. 88.

[19] Article 4, Draft Articles on Responsibility of International Organisations.

[20] Article 9, Draft Articles on Responsibility of International Organisations (see also Art. 12, Articles on State Responsibility).

[21] G. Gaja, 'Third Report on Responsibility of International Organisations' (2005), 57th Session of the ILC, UN Doc. A/CN.4/553, paras. 8–10.

[22] Comments and Observations received from International Organisations, UN Doc. A/CN.4/582, 6–7.

[23] See, G. Gaja, 'Seventh Report on Responsibility of International Organisations' (2009), 61st Session of the ILC, UN Doc. A/CN.4/610, para. 20.

act. The answer depends on the characterisation of the underlying primary obligation. If it is an international one, its breach will be too; and it will be governed by the rules on the responsibility of international organisations. If the rule is merely internal, its breach will be governed by internal secondary rules.

This question is far from devoid of practical consequences, especially in the context of UN operations. Does a breach of the terms of its mandate by a UN peacekeeping mission, for example, constitute an internationally wrongful act or not? The key issue is the legal nature of the body of rules referred to as the mandate of the operation. If the mandate is a Security Council resolution – for example in the case of peacekeeping operations – the breach would have to be regarded as an internationally wrongful act: it would be odd, to say the least, to treat a resolution of the Security Council as a merely internal act. If the mandate is a resolution of the General Assembly – for example the Statute of UNHCR[24] – the same conclusion would be appropriate. But if the mandate is an internal administrative regulation, the position may well differ. The ILC chose not to express 'a clear-cut view' on this issue and adopted an article to this effect[25] – a position dictated by the consideration that the demarcation of the internal law of the organisation from its international obligations pertains to the sphere of primary rules. As discussed above, however, in the Kosovo opinion the ICJ endorsed the international law characterisation of acts previously treated by some as merely internal.[26]

The EU has maintained that the internal rules of the organisation should be taken into account in determining whether there is a breach of an international obligation in the case of 'mixed agreements', that is treaties to which both the EU and its member states are parties.[27] Reference to the rules of the organisation would permit the identification of the legal person – organisation or member state – that possesses the relevant competence. Some scholars supported the EU's position and advocated the adoption of a special rule to this effect.[28] However, no special rule has been inserted in the articles approved on first

[24] GA Res. 428(V) of 14 December 1950.

[25] Article 9(2), Draft Articles on the Responsibility of International Organisations, and the commentary to Article 9 in ILC Report (2009), *supra* note 1 at 79.

[26] *Supra* note 18.

[27] Comments and Observations received from Governments and International Organisations (2004) UN Doc. A/CN.4/545, 21–4.

[28] E.g. Talmon, *supra* note 14 at 414–20. The text of the article proposed by Talmon is at 420.

reading, although the rule on *lex specialis* adopted by the Commission may have left this possibility open.

Attribution

The ILC has adopted four rules on attribution of conduct to international organisations (Articles 5–8). This is an area where institutional and judicial practices are still far from consolidated, with the attribution of conduct in UN-authorised operations and to the EU giving rise to particular difficulties. Moreover, much of the extant institutional practice relates to private law claims and is not, as such, relevant to the process of identifying rules on the attribution of conduct for the purposes of international responsibility.[29]

The four Articles adopted by the ILC comprise one general and three specific rules. The general rule, found in Article 5, addresses the conduct of organs and agents of the organisation. Article 6 deals with the attribution of the conduct of a state organ placed at the disposal of an international organisation. Article 7 covers the attribution of ultra vires conduct, and Article 8 the attribution of conduct subsequently adopted by an international organisation.

The general rule

The general rule under Article 5(1) is that the conduct of organs or agents in the performance of their functions shall be considered an act of the organisation. Article 5(2) adds that the rules of the organisation apply to the determination of the functions of organs and agents. Article 2(b) defines the rules of the organisation as comprising 'the constituent instruments, decisions, resolutions and other acts of the organization adopted in accordance with those instruments, and established practice of the organization'.[30]

The key terms in Article 5 are 'organs', 'agents' and 'functions'. The definition of the term organ is a straightforward matter. If a person or entity is characterised as an organ by virtue of 'formal organic ties'[31] with the organisation, that characterisation will determine the attribution of the act of the organ to the organisation regardless of the position of the organ in the organisation. There is no provision similar

[29] In this sense, see also Zwanenburg, *supra* note 15 at 98.
[30] See Chapter 2 on the meaning and relevance of established practice (57ff.).
[31] Klein, *supra* note 2 at 298–9.

to Article 4(1) of the Articles on State Responsibility which refers to 'legislative, executive, judicial or other functions' of the organ, given that such a typology does not apply to international organisations.

The term agent is more problematic. According to the Articles, agents include 'officials and other persons or entities through whom the organisation acts'.[32] This definition is based on a passage in the *Reparations* case where it was stated that the word 'agent' must be understood 'in the most liberal sense, that is to say, any person who, whether a paid official or not, and whether permanently employed or not, has been charged by an organ of the organisation with carrying out, or helping to carry out, one of its functions – in short any person through whom it acts'.[33] As the ICJ stated in another decision, also relied upon by the ILC to illustrate the basis of Article 5, '[t]he essence of the matter lies not in their [the agents'] administrative position but in the nature of their mission'.[34] If the person or entities through whom the organisation is acting are, however, organs of a state and are placed at the disposal of the organisation, then Article 6 would apply.

A definition of functions does not feature in Article 5, which simply states that the rules of the organisation 'shall apply to the determination of the functions of its organs and agents', thus leaving 'the possibility open that, in exceptional circumstances, functions may be considered as given to an organ or agent even if this could not be said to be based on the rules of the organisation'.[35] Moreover, as a result of the inclusion of established practice in the determination of the rules of the organisation, '[i]t may be held that, when practice develops in a way that is not consistent with the constituent instrument, the organisation should not necessarily be exempt from responsibility in the case of conduct that stretches beyond the organisation's competence'.[36]

It might be argued that the effect of the definition of the key terms of Article 5 is that conduct can be too easily attributed to international organisations. For example, the conduct of a private subcontractor is

[32] Article 2(c), Draft Articles on the Responsibility of International Organisations.

[33] *Reparation for Injuries Suffered in the Service of the United Nations*, Advisory Opinion ICJ Reports (1949) 174 at 177, and ILC Report (2009), *supra* note 23 at 51–2.

[34] *Applicability of article VI, section 22, of the Convention on the Privileges and Immunities of the United Nations*, Advisory Opinion, ICJ Report (1989) 177.

[35] ILC Report (2009), *supra* note 1 at 61.

[36] G. Gaja, 'Second Report on Responsibility of International Organisations' (2004), 56th Session of the ILC, UN Doc. A/Cn.4/541, para. 24.

attributable to the organisation, if it is shown that the organisation was acting through it. This question has been considered so far mainly in relation to private security companies, with some opining that the ILC rules on attribution are sufficiently broad to allow the attribution of conduct of private military contractors to an international organisation.[37] But there is no reason why the same conclusions should not apply to the attribution of acts of non-governmental organisations subcontracted by an international organisation for the provision of specific services.

The consequences of the attribution of conduct of subcontractors are far-reaching. In many of its operations (peacekeeping, international administration, refugee camps, relief operations) the UN tends to act through other entities, which it subcontracts for a particular function. The acts of these subcontractors are potentially attributable to the UN and could engage its international responsibility. As observed by the Special Rapporteur, the practice of including clauses in contracts between international organisations and private subcontractors stipulating that the subcontractor will not be considered an agent or member of staff of the organisation does not dispose of the question of attribution under international law.[38] Seen from the perspective of advancing UN accountability, the solution adopted by the ILC is fitting. If the IMF, instead, had had its way and the general rule had limited attribution to the conduct of individuals acting in their official capacity, the attribution of a wide range of acts undertaken, for all intents and purposes, in order to perform institutional functions would have been precluded.

Klein applies the criterion of 'effective control' to determine whether a non-governmental organisation is an agent of an international institution.[39] As discussed below, this criterion operates under Article 6 of the Draft Articles on Responsibility of International Organisations in relation to organs of states or organs or agents of international organisations placed at the disposal of another international organisation, neither of which fits the description of a non-governmental organisation (with the exception of a non-governmental organisation that is already an agent of an international institution and is then placed at the disposal of another).

[37] N. White and S. MacLeod, 'EU Operations and Private Military Contractors: Issues of Corporate and Institutional Responsibility', 19 EJIL (2008) 965 at 973–6. See also their other contribution in that issue of the EJIL to the symposium on 'Private Military Contractors and International Law'.

[38] Gaja, 'Seventh Report', *supra* note 23 at para. 23.

[39] See Klein, *supra* note 2 at 300–1.

The question of the legality or propriety of the delegation of functions to a private organisation is a separate matter. The answer depends on the rules of the organisation. In *Meroni v. High Authority*, the ECJ distinguished between the delegation of 'clearly defined executive powers the exercise of which can, therefore, be subject to strict review in the light of objective criteria determined by the delegating authority' and the delegation of 'a discretionary power, implying a wide margin of discretion which may, according to the use which is made of it, make possible the execution of actual economic policy'.[40] In the judgment of the Court, while delegations of the first kind are generally permissible, delegations of the second kind have the effect of replacing 'the choices of the delegator with the choices of the delegate' thereby resulting in 'an actual transfer of responsibility'.[41] The Court held that a 'delegation of the first kind cannot appreciably alter the consequences involved in the exercise of the powers concerned, whereas a delegation of the second kind, since it replaces the choices of the delegator by the choices of the delegate, brings about an actual transfer of responsibility'.[42] Sarooshi suggests that 'for a delegation of discretionary Chapter VII powers to be lawful, the Council must ensure that it retains the right at all times to change the decision of its delegate so that it can exercise effective authority and control over the way in which the delegated powers are being exercised'.[43] Commenting on the *Meroni* case, he adds that 'the actual transfer of responsibility was not in itself the reason why the Court found the purported delegation of powers to be unlawful. The problem was that the High Authority could not under the terms of establishment of the subsidiary organs exercise direct authority and control over them in terms of being able to change their decisions.'[44]

Attribution under the general rule in Article 5 does not entail effective control over conduct, which is the main requirement in Article 6 – the provision that deals with the attribution of the conduct of organs of a state or organs or agents of an international organisation placed at the disposal of another international organisation. There is no inconsistency in this approach. Article 6 attribution can be distinguished from attribution under the general rule because two international legal persons are engaged: the state or international organisation to which the organ belongs, and the international organisation at whose disposal it is placed. In such cases, the requirement of effective control over the conduct severs the link with the first international legal person and establishes the nexus with the second one. Where, however, the external agent does not belong to another international legal

[40] Case 9/56 [1958] ECR 133 at 152. [41] *Ibid.* [42] *Ibid.*
[43] D. Sarooshi, *The United Nations and the Development of Collective Security: the Delegation by the Security Council of its Chapter VII Powers* (Oxford University Press, 2000) 41.
[44] *Ibid.* at 37.

person, there is no other competitor for responsibility under international law, and no reason to adopt a test of effective control in order to determine to which entity the conduct should be properly ascribed. To prove attribution in these cases it will suffice to show that the international organisation is acting through that particular agent – that it is performing its functions, broadly and purposively understood, through the other person or entity.

Attribution under Article 6

The rule that gives rise to the greatest difficulties concerns the attribution of the conduct of an organ of a state placed at the disposal of an international organisation. Organs lent by states to international organisations include, most notably, military contingents assigned to UN peacekeeping operations. Article 6 of the Draft Articles on the Responsibility of International Organisations adopts the test of effective control to determine the attribution of conduct in these circumstances. As extensively shown by the Special Rapporteur, this test is grounded in institutional and state practice, as well as academic writings.[45]

Effective control does not mean exclusive control.[46] Even where the state still possesses a measure of control over the organ, the international organisation may still be responsible for the specific conduct it controlled. Peacekeeping missions are a case in point: sending states normally retain some control over their troops, as evidenced, for example, by the continuing applicability of national martial laws and codes of military discipline, but this does not preclude, in principle, the attribution of specific conduct effectively controlled by the UN.[47]

There is a clear distinction, at least conceptually, between organs placed at the disposal of an organisation in terms of Article 6 and agents through whom the organisation acts in terms of Articles 2(c) and 5. Unlike an agent, an organ retains a link with the lending state. Should that link be completely severed, the organ would become an agent of the organisation insofar as the international organisation is acting through it. But, as long as there is still a link between the organ and the state, the question of attribution should be determined by reference to the criterion of effective control under Article 6.

[45] Gaja, 'Second Report', *supra* note 36 at paras. 29–49. See also Hirsch, *supra* note 2 at 64ff.

[46] See Gaja, 'Second Report', *supra* note 36 at para. 40.

[47] Commentary to Art. 6, Draft Articles on the Responsibility of International Organisations, ILC Report (2009), *supra* note 1 at 64–6.

Despite the conceptual clarity of this distinction, a grey area exists in practice. For example, is a military or public administration expert seconded to an international organisation an agent through whom the international organisation is acting or an organ placed at its disposal? Some states have argued that such a person could only be an agent, on the grounds, presumably, that the degree of control by the lending state is insufficient.[48] Indeed, if the person in question has lost the attributes of an organ of the lending state, this position is correct, but whether secondment has had this effect or not can only be assessed by examining all the facts and circumstances. In its work on state responsibility, the ILC explained that '[t]he reference to a "State organ" covers all the individual or collective entities which make up the organisation of the state and act on its behalf'.[49] Based on this definition, a key issue is thus whether the expert in question ceased to act on behalf of the lending state upon being seconded to the international organisation. The fact that the sending state can re-call the expert at any time is important, although probably not determinative since it can be construed as an enduring power of the lending state to reactivate the link with its organ rather than as conclusive evidence that the expert continues to act on behalf of the state.

ECtHR case law on attribution

Attribution of organs of a state placed at the disposal of an international organisation has been at the heart of a number of important decisions of the European Court of Human Rights (ECtHR) and of English courts under the Human Rights Act 1998.[50] The factual pattern in many of these cases is similar: a complaint is brought against a state party to the Convention (or, in the case of domestic litigation in England, against a public authority) alleging a breach of a Convention right; the breach is believed to arise from conduct that is in some measure international (for example because it involves an international organisation or because it occurs abroad, or both); the respondent objects to the jurisdiction of the court on the grounds that the breach is not attributable to it.

[48] See the Statement on behalf of the Nordic Countries by H.E. Ambassador Thomas Winkler, 64th Session of the General Assembly, Sixth Committee, 26 October 2009.

[49] Crawford, *supra* note 13 at 94.

[50] In the ECtHR, see *Matthews*; *Behrami* and *Saramati*; and *Bosphorus supra* note 4. In English courts, see *R (on the application of Al-Jedda) (FC) (Appellant) v. Secretary of State for Defence (Respondent)* [2007] UKHL 58; *R (on the application of Faisal Attiyah Nassar Al-Saadoon, Khalaf Hussain Mufdhi v. Secretary of State for Defence* [2009] EWCA Civ 7.

The ECtHR considered questions of attribution as part of its application of Article 1 of the Convention which obliges state parties to 'secure to everyone within their jurisdiction the rights and freedoms' guaranteed under the Convention. The jurisdictional assessments under Article 1 are of three types: *ratione personae*, i.e. whether the conduct is attributable to the state; *ratione loci*, i.e. whether the conduct occurred within the territorial jurisdiction of the state; and *ratione materiae*, i.e. whether the conduct is within the subject matter of the Convention.

Discerning a coherent set of principles on attribution in the ECtHR case law is no easy task. Not only are these decisions often difficult to reconcile with one another, their internal logic is sometimes deficient. One of the main problems has been the failure to make jurisdictional determinations with the necessary rigour.

The first of these Strasbourg authorities on attribution, *Matthews v. UK*, arose from a complaint by a resident of Gibraltar against a breach of her right to free elections under Article 3 of Protocol I resulting from EC legislation that excluded residents of Gibraltar from participation in the elections to the European Parliament. The Court held that the UK was 'responsible under Article 1 of the Convention for securing the rights guaranteed by Article 3 of Protocol No. 1 in Gibraltar regardless of whether the elections were purely domestic or European',[51] but did not tackle the question of attribution.

The key passages in the Court's judgment read as follows:

'30. The Court notes that the parties do not dispute that Article 3 of Protocol No. 1 applies in Gibraltar ... There is therefore clearly territorial "jurisdiction" within the meaning of Article 1 of the Convention.

31. The Court must nevertheless consider whether, notwithstanding the nature of the elections to the European Parliament as an organ of the EC, the United Kingdom can be held responsible under Article 1 of the Convention for the absence of elections to the European Parliament in Gibraltar, that is, whether the United Kingdom is required to "secure" elections to the European Parliament notwithstanding the Community character of those elections.

32. The Court observes that acts of the EC as such cannot be challenged before the Court because the EC is not a Contracting Party. The Convention does not exclude the transfer of competences to international organisations provided that Convention rights continue to be "secured". Member States' responsibility therefore continues even after such a transfer.

[51] *Matthews*, *supra* note 4 at para. 35.

33. In the present case, the alleged violation of the Convention flows from an annex to the 1976 Act, entered into by the United Kingdom, together with the extension to the European Parliament's competences brought about by the Maastricht Treaty. The Council Decision and the 1976 Act (see paragraph 18 above), and the Maastricht Treaty, with its changes to the EEC Treaty, all constituted international instruments which were freely entered into by the United Kingdom. Indeed, the 1976 Act cannot be challenged before the European Court of Justice for the very reason that it is not a "normal" act of the Community, but is a treaty within the Community legal order. The Maastricht Treaty, too, is not an act of the Community, but a treaty by which a revision of the EEC Treaty was brought about. The United Kingdom, together with all the other parties to the Maastricht Treaty, is responsible *ratione materiae* under Article 1 of the Convention and, in particular, under Article 3 of Protocol No. 1, for the consequences of that Treaty.

34. In determining to what extent the United Kingdom is responsible for "securing" the rights in Article 3 of Protocol No. 1 in respect of elections to the European Parliament in Gibraltar, the Court recalls that the Convention is intended to guarantee rights that are not theoretical or illusory, but practical and effective (see, for example, the above-mentioned United Communist Party of Turkey and Others judgment, pp. 18–19, § 33). It is uncontested that legislation emanating from the legislative process of the European Community affects the population of Gibraltar in the same way as legislation which enters the domestic legal order exclusively via the House of Assembly. To this extent, there is no difference between European and domestic legislation, and no reason why the United Kingdom should not be required to "secure" the rights in Article 3 of Protocol No. 1 in respect of European legislation, in the same way as those rights are required to be "secured" in respect of purely domestic legislation. In particular, the suggestion that the United Kingdom may not have effective control over the state of affairs complained of cannot affect the position, as the United Kingdom's responsibility derives from its having entered into treaty commitments subsequent to the applicability of Article 3 of Protocol No. 1 to Gibraltar, namely the Maastricht Treaty taken together with its obligations under the Council Decision and the 1976 Act.'[52]

While the conclusion of the Court on the jurisdiction *ratione loci* is incontrovertible, the rest of its reasoning confuses three separate issues: the scope of the primary obligation (that is the obligation under Article 1 to secure the rights and freedoms of the Convention); jurisdiction *ratione materiae*; and jurisdiction *ratione personae*. The Court states, correctly, that it would have no jurisdiction over acts of the EC, but the legal basis it offers for asserting jurisdiction in the present case would appear to be broad enough to justify jurisdiction in respect of the acts

[52] *Ibid.* at paras. 30–4.

of any international organisation to which competences have been transferred by a state party to the Convention, as long as no equivalent protection is offered by the transferee organisation.[53] Central to the Court's finding was the observation that the conduct causing the breach of the Convention right could not be challenged before the ECJ. In proceedings before the Commission, a number of commissioners had already regarded this factor as capable of distinguishing *Matthews* from similar precedents.[54]

The leading pre-*Matthews* precedent is *M & Co. v. Germany*.[55] In its submissions to the Court, the UK government had argued that 'to engage the responsibility of any State under the Convention, that State must have a power of effective control over the act complained of'.[56] The argument of the UK government essentially relied on the principle that responsibility should ensue only if, and to the extent that, the state has effective control over the conduct. Lack of effective control would thus preclude the attribution of the act in question to the state. As discussed above, the Court rejected this argument.

An important ECtHR decision on effective control and attribution is *Loizidou v. Turkey*.[57] It was held that 'the responsibility of a Contracting Party could also arise when as a consequence of military action – whether lawful or unlawful – it exercises effective control of an area outside its national territory'.[58] However, no issue of attribution of conduct to an international organisation arose in *Loizidou*, which deals exclusively with issues of state responsibility.

The judgment of the Court in *Matthews* does seem to be premised on the notion that the act which is the immediate cause of the breach is attributable to the EC rather than the UK, while the decision to transfer competences to the EC, enabling the EU in the first place to adopt the act, is attributable to the UK. This is probably the sense of the Court's remarks on effective control over the act.[59]

In the *Bosphorus* case, the applicant was a Turkish airline which had leased aircraft from the Yugoslav Airlines after the entry into force of the UN sanctions against the Federal Republic of Yugoslavia.[60] Acting pursuant to EC legislation implementing the relevant Security Council resolutions, the Irish authorities impounded one of the leased aircraft

[53] See Chapter 8 for an analysis of the doctrine of equivalent protection.
[54] See, in particular, the diss. op. of Mr Schermers.
[55] Decision on Admissibility, 9 February 1990, Application No. 13258/87.
[56] *Ibid.* at para. 26. [57] Judgment, 18 December 1996, Application No. 15318/89.
[58] *Ibid.* at para. 52. [59] *Ibid.* at para. 34. [60] *Bosphorus*, *supra* note 4.

at Dublin airport – an act which according to the applicant company breached its right to property under Article 1 of Protocol I of the ECHR. This case was ostensibly more complex than *Matthews* because the determination of attribution required consideration of the position of three international legal persons: the UN, the EC and the Republic of Ireland. Once again, the Court failed to deal with attribution cogently. In finding in favour of the respondent state, the Court reasoned that the key determination was whether the Irish authorities had exercised any discretion in deciding to impound the aircraft: if the impoundment resulted from an exercise of discretion, the allegation of a breach would have to be considered on its merits; if, on the other hand, the impoundment was a necessary act, the doctrine of equivalent protection would apply and the Court would proceed to an assessment of the quality of human rights protection afforded under the legal system to which competences had been transferred by the state party.[61]

The next stage in the evolution of the ECtHR jurisprudence was the ruling in *Behrami* and *Saramati*,[62] which has attracted considerable and almost exclusively critical commentary.[63] The applicants in *Behrami* complained, under Article 2, of the death of Gadaf Behrami, son of one of the applicants and brother of the other, and of the serious injury suffered by one of them as a result of the explosion of fragments of a cluster bomb dropped during the 1999 Kosovo war. It was alleged that the French Kosovo Force (KFOR) troops knew that there were unexploded devices on the site but failed to remove them. The applicant in *Saramati* complained, under Article 5 alone as well as in conjunction with Article 13 of the Convention, about his extra-judicial detention by KFOR troops between 13 July 2001 and 26 January 2002, and, under Article 6, about the lack of access to courts.

[61] *Ibid.* at paras. 143–57. [62] *Behrami* and *Saramati*, *supra* note 4.

[63] See: P. Klein, 'Responsabilité pour les faits commis dans le cadre d' operations de paix et étendue du pouvoir de contrôle de la Court européenne de droits de l'homme: quelques considérations critiques sur l' arrêt *Behrami et Saramati*', 53 AFDI (2007) 43; M. Milanović and T. Papić, 'As Bad As It Gets: The European Court of Human Rights' Behrami and Saramati Decision and General International Law', 58 ICLQ (2009) 267; P. Palchetti, 'Azioni di forza istituite o autorizzate dalle Nazioni Unite davanti alla Corte europea dei diritti dell' uomo: i casi *Behrami* e *Saramati*', 90 *Rivista di Diritto Internazionale* (2007) 681; A. Sari, 'Jurisdiction and International Responsibility in Peace Support Operations: The *Behrami* and *Saramati* Cases', 8 *Human Rights Law Review* (2008) 151; G. Verdirame, 'Breaches of the European Convention on Human Rights Resulting from the Conduct of International Organisations', 2 *European Human Rights Law Review* (2008) 209.

The respondent states raised jurisdictional objections on both *ratione personae* and *ratione loci* grounds, succeeding on the former. The essence of their objection was that the acts of which the applicants complained were not attributable to the respondent states, and could not thus engage the jurisdiction of the Court.

The Decision of the Grand Chamber sets out the mandates of KFOR and UNMIK, and their legal bases, in detail, beginning with the relevant provisions in the UN Charter, including Chapter VII and Article 103, and proceeding with: the Military Technical Agreement of 9 June 1999 between the Federal Republic of Yugoslavia and KFOR; UN Security Council Resolutions, in particular Resolution 1244 of 10 June 1999; the Agreement of 18 June 1999 on the Russian participation in KFOR; UNMIK Regulation no. 2000/47 on the Status, Privileges and Immunities of KFOR and UNMIK and their Personnel in Kosovo; the KFOR Main Standing Operating Procedures of March 2003; and various documents on detention and de-mining in Kosovo.

On the basis of these instruments the relationship between UNMIK and KFOR was summarised in the following terms:

> 'UNMIK was a subsidiary organ of the UN endowed with all-inclusive legislative and administrative powers in Kosovo including the administration of justice … it was headed by a Special Representative of the Secretary General and reported directly to the UN Security Council via the Secretary General. KFOR was established as an equal presence but with a separate mandate and control structure: it was a NATO led operation authorised by the UN Security Council under unified command and control. There was no formal or hierarchical relationship between the two presences nor was the military in any way accountable to the civil presence.'[64]

Having considered the legal bases for the two contested activities, that is de-mining (*Behrami*) and detention (*Saramati*), the Court concluded that the supervision of de-mining fell within UNMIK's mandate and the issuing of detention orders fell within that of KFOR. The Court then reasoned that both the inaction of UNMIK (its failure to de-mine the land) and the action of KFOR (the order to detain Mr Saramati) were attributable to the UN because of the Chapter VII foundations common to both UNMIK and KFOR.

Attribution to the UN posed a greater difficulty in the case of KFOR than UNMIK: KFOR is an example of the Security Council delegating its

[64] *Behrami, supra* note 4 at para. 118.

powers to member states while UNMIK is a subsidiary organ of the UN. In the Court's analysis, for the acts of KFOR to be attributable to the UN, 'delegation must be sufficiently limited so as to remain compatible with the degree of centralisation of UN Security Council collective security constitutionally necessary under the Charter'.[65] The 'key question' for the Court was 'whether the UN Security Council retained ultimate authority and control so that operational command only was delegated'[66] – a question which it held should be answered affirmatively in the case of KFOR too.

One difficulty remained: distinguishing *Bosphorus*. The Court did so by explaining that in *Bosphorus* 'the impugned act (seizure of the applicant's leased aircraft) had been carried out by the respondent State authorities, on its territory and following a decision by one of its Ministers.[67] The Court did not therefore consider that any question arose as to its competence, notably *ratione personae*, vis-à-vis the respondent State despite the fact that the source of the impugned seizure was an EC Council Regulation which, in turn, applied a UN Security Council Resolution.'[68] In *Behrami* and *Saramati*, instead, the 'the impugned acts and omissions of KFOR and UNMIK' could not 'be attributed to the respondent States and, moreover, did not take place *on the territory of those States* or by virtue of a decision of their authorities'.[69]

This attempt to distinguish *Bosphorus* is unpersuasive. At least as far as the detention order in *Behrami* and *Saramati* is concerned, it is difficult to maintain that the impugned act did not take place 'by virtue of a decision' of French authorities. That decision may have rested on the solid legal foundations of Security Council Resolution 1244, but there is no doubt that a French official at some point *decided* to detain the applicant, a situation not materially different from the decision to seize the aircraft taken by the Irish authorities in *Bosporous* or from the act of the German authorities giving effect to the decision of the ECJ in *M & Co*. The case of *Behrami* and *Saramati* is also not materially dissimilar from the violations of international obligations during the Korean War for which the US had to answer, despite the fact that the military intervention was authorised and monitored by the Security Council and then the General Assembly; nor is it dissimilar to the incident concerning the Chinese embassy in Belgrade, following which

[65] *Id.* at para. 132. [66] *Id.* at para. 133. [67] *Bosphorus*, *supra* note 4 at para. 135.
[68] *Behrami*, *supra* note 4 at para. 151. [69] *Ibid.* at paras. 150–1, emphasis added.

the US, rather than the UN or NATO, offered an *ex gratia* payment to the Chinese authorities.[70]

An important factor, reflected in the decision of the Court, is that in *Behrami* and *Saramati* the challenged act took place outside the territory of the respondent states. While not disputing that its jurisdiction *ratione loci* was engaged, as the acts in question came under the *Bankovic* exceptions to territoriality, the Court refers to territory in passages that have nothing to do with territorial jurisdiction – such as the one just cited above where territory emerges as a factor somehow relevant to attribution. The extra-territoriality of the acts thus appears to have weighed in the thinking of the Court well beyond the determination of the Court's jurisdiction *ratione loci*. A possible explanation is that, faced with the prospect of an expansion in its jurisdiction over the conduct of international organisations as significant as would have resulted from the combined effect of its approach to extra-territoriality and its doctrine of equivalent protection, the Court chose to apply the brakes – perhaps a legitimate policy objective in itself but one that the Court pursued without a coherently reasoned juridical basis.

Special Rapporteur Gaja joined the chorus of academic criticism in one of his reports, observing that 'had the Court applied the criterion of effective control set out by the Commission, it would have reached the different conclusion that the conduct of national contingents allocated to KFOR had to be attributed either to the sending state or to NATO'.[71] Indeed, the Court seemed to assume that effective control is tantamount to ultimate authority and control – a position that finds no support in the commentary of the ILC or in institutional practice.

As with any determination on attribution, however, the analysis of the facts is pivotal. The Court may have done itself a disfavour by providing an incomplete summary of the facts and of the submissions of respondent states. For instance, the Norwegian government had explained that a new Commander of KFOR was appointed every six months by NATO and that, although the commander was a Norwegian national at the time of some of the relevant facts, '[i]n all operational matters no national military chain of command existed between Norwegian authorities and him' and that the 'Norwegian authorities were in no position to instruct … [him] … nor could he or she deviate

[70] Klein, *supra* note 2 at 302. [71] Gaja, 'Seventh Report', *supra* note 23 at para. 26.

from NATO orders or policies'.[72] In oral submissions this point was made even more forcefully: 'the applicants in fact claimed that they were within the jurisdiction of the respondent States because of the coincidental nationality of KFOR personnel. If one follows this astonishing proposition, States contributing troops to a peacekeeping operations could have jurisdiction because of the nationality of force commanders or engineer units.'[73] An argument of international public policy, which should have deserved greater attention, was also advanced in support of the position of the respondent states: if conduct can be attributed to states on the basis of a generalised presumption that coincidental nationality entails sufficiently effective control, 'a person would fall in and out of the Court's jurisdiction, depending on coincidental circumstances, resulting in temporary applicability with unclear duration of different regional instruments, with random and unpredictable consequences' and 'this would require States to interfere in the operations, contrary to the requirements of unified command and control'.[74]

But notwithstanding the possibility that a proper analysis of the facts of the case might have justified the conclusion of the ECtHR, its reasoning remains flawed. The Court's principal failure in *Behrami* was to focus on the wrong question (whether the impugned acts and omissions could be attributed to the UN), and ignore the right one (whether they could be attributed to the respondent states).[75] Having determined that the acts and omissions were attributable to the UN, it concluded that it had no jurisdiction *ratione personae*. The premise of this finding is that attribution to the international organisation excludes attribution to the state: put in other terms, that dual attribution is not possible. This is the central mistaken assumption in the *Behrami* reasoning, on which its passages on effective control hinge. Given that the situations in which dual or multiple attribution can arise are far from rare, the *Behrami* doctrine can be particularly detrimental to the accountability of states (directly) and international organisations (indirectly) for violations of human rights. The ECtHR has indeed already followed *Behrami*

[72] Observations of the Government of Norway concerning admissibility in *Saramati v. France, Germany v. Norway.*

[73] Verbatim Record of the hearing held on 15 November 2006 in the cases of *Behrami and Behrami v. France and Saramati v. France, Germany and Norway*, at 13 (Submissions of Mr Fife, Agent for Norway).

[74] *Ibid.* at 15 (Submissions of Mr Fife).

[75] See *Behrami* and *Saramati*, *supra* note 4 at paras. 128–41.

in a number of cases dealing with the international missions in Kosovo and Bosnia and Herzegovina.[76]

If the Court had, instead, begun by considering whether there was attribution to the respondent states, it would have applied Article 5 of the Articles of State Responsibility. The main issue would have been whether the French and Norwegian individuals accused of those violations remained organs of France and Norway. Instead, the Court approached a case concerning state responsibility ignoring entirely the rules on state responsibility, and assuming that the answer could be derived, *a contrario*, from the application of the rules on the responsibility of international organisations.

In other cases, the ECtHR avoided dealing with the question of attribution *ratione personae* by dismissing the application on some other ground. In *Senator Lines*, where a decision of the European Court of First Instance was challenged by a German company for breaching the right to a fair trial, the Court held that the applicant did not satisfy the victim requirement in the Convention.[77] The decision of the Court in *Emesa Sugar* is even more telling.[78] A company had brought proceedings in Strasbourg against every member state of the EU, alleging that it had suffered a breach of its right to a fair trial by being deprived of the possibility to respond to the Opinion of the Advocate General in proceedings before the ECJ. The Court declared the application inadmissible because the summary injunction proceedings that had preceded the referral to the ECJ did not concern 'civil rights and obligations' within the meaning of Article 6 of the Convention. The Court did not even address the objection to its jurisdiction *ratione personae* raised by the respondent states, although, analytically, that objection ought to have been considered before the assessment of the well-foundedness of the claim under Article 6.

National case law on attribution

National courts have also grappled with questions of attribution in UN operations. In the case of *Al-Jedda*, concerning the detention without trial in Iraq of a British citizen on suspicions of terrorism,[79] the British

[76] *Kasumaj v. Greece*, Application No. 6974/05, and *Gajic v. Germany*, Application No. 31446/02, both cases concerning the occupation of private property by KFOR troops; *Beric and others v. Bosnia and Herzegovina*, Application No. 36357/04 and others, paras. 28–30, concerning the removal from public and political-party positions of certain individuals.

[77] *Senator Lines v. Austria and fourteen other member states of the EU*, Application No. 56672/00.

[78] *Emesa Sugar N.V. v. The Netherlands*, Application No. 62023/00.

[79] *Al-Jedda*, *supra* note 50.

government relied on *Behrami* and *Saramati* for its argument that the detention of Al-Jedda was attributable to the UN rather than Britain by reason of the Security Council resolutions adopted after the invasion of Iraq, in particular resolution 1546 of 2004. The House of Lords rejected the analogy between Iraq and Kosovo, which would have had the consequence of making the UN responsible for torture or illegal detentions in Iraq – an absurd outcome particularly in light of the history of the intervention in Iraq. The House of Lords rightly held that '[it] cannot realistically be said that UN and UK forces were under the effective command and control of the UN, or that UK forces were under such command and control when they detained the appellant'.[80] The existence of a UN Security Council authorisation in Iraq at the relevant time did, however, have elements in common with the authorisation effected through Security Council resolution 1244 in relation to Kosovo. Lord Brown, who admitted to having great difficulty with the question of attribution, concluded that the only basis for distinguishing Iraq from Kosovo was the lack of 'ultimate authority and control' by the UN in Iraq, a term that, he underscored, is 'somewhat elusive'.[81]

In the end, the *Al-Jedda* appeal failed on a separate and even more troubling point: the effect of Article 103 of the UN Charter and the acceptance by the House of Lords of the view that Article 103 can act as a trump card, albeit with certain qualifications. This aspect of *Al-Jedda* is discussed in Chapter 8 (372ff.).

Before *Al-Jedda*, the leading English authority on the question of attribution of conduct in UN operations was *Nissan v. AG*.[82] The case was brought by a British subject who ran a hotel in Nicosia which British troops occupied while on a peacekeeping mission established initially under a treaty between Britain and Cyprus and subsequently brought under a UN resolution. The Court of Appeal found that the Crown was liable for the acts of British troops committed before they came under a UN mandate.

Lord Denning observed:

'They were under the command of the United Nations commander. They flew the United Nations flag. They wore the berets and arm-flashes to denote that they were no longer the soldiers of the Queen, but the soldiers of the United Nations. They were acting as agents for the United Nations, which is a

[80] *Ibid.* at paras. 22–4. [81] *Ibid.* at para. 148.
[82] The judgments of the High Court, Court of Appeal and House of Lords are reported respectively in [1967] 2 All ER 200; [1968] 1 QB 286; [1970] AC 179.

sovereign body corporate. Their actions thenceforward were not to be justified by virtue of the royal prerogative of the Crown of England. They were to be justified only by virtue of the United Nations. I do not think the Crown can be expected to pay compensation thereafter. It must be paid by the United Nations themselves or perhaps by the Cyprus Government who agreed to provide all necessary premises. At any rate, it is not payable by the British Crown.'[83]

The House of Lords decided, instead, that the liability of the Crown extended to the period of the UN mandate. Lord Pearce reasoned that the Court of Appeal had misunderstood 'the relevant regulations, which do not justify the view that the British troops were no longer soldiers of Her Majesty or that the Secretary-General of the United Nations was responsible for them', adding that this was 'a misunderstanding of what the United Nations are and what are its operations. It is a legal personality created by treaty but not a sovereign state. It is an instrument of the collective policy of a number of states whose sovereignty it uses ... U.N.O. is not a sovereign but only an organization, an instrument of collective security.'[84] The House of Lords examined the Regulations for the UN Force in Cyprus closely and adopted, in all but name, an effective control test that led their Lordships to the above conclusion.

In a case brought nearly forty years later in the Netherlands, the District Court of The Hague reached a different conclusion about the conduct of Dutch peacekeepers in Srebrenica.[85] The Court held that, since the Dutch contingent was part of the UN Protection Force in Bosnia (UNPROFOR), their acts and omissions in relation to the massacre of Srebrenica 'should be attributed strictly, as a matter of principle, to the United Nations', explaining that 'participation in a UN peacekeeping operation on the basis of chapter VII of the Charter implies that the "operational command and control" over the troops made available is transferred to the UN', although such 'transfer does not include, or at least not necessarily, the personnel matters of the troops and the material logistics of the deployed

[83] [1967] 1 QB 286 at 341. [84] [1970] AC 179 at 198.

[85] The District Court of The Hague issued two decisions on the Srebrenica massacre within a short time of each other, the first one focusing on attribution (*M. M-M, D.M and A.M (Mustafic) and H.N. (Hasan Nuhanovic) v. The Netherlands*, Case No. 265615/HA ZA 06-1671, Judgment, 10 September 2008) and the second one on immunity (*Foundation Mothers of Srebrenica v. The Netherlands and the UN*, Case No. 295247/HA ZA 07-2973, Judgment in the incidental proceedings of 10 July 2008). Both decisions were reported in LV *Netherlands International Law Review* (2008) 425.

detachment, nor the decision about whether or not to retreat'.[86] The Oberlandsgericht of Vienna reached a similar conclusion in *N.K. v. Austria*, a case concerning damage to property allegedly caused by a member of the Austrian contingent in the UN Disengagement Observer Force established under Security Council resolution 350 of 1974 and entrusted with the supervision of the ceasefire between Israeli and Syrian forces.[87]

Dual or multiple attribution

The ECtHR's central mistake in *Behrami* was, as mentioned, to assume that the application of the effective control test in Article 6 must result in the identification of only one responsible entity, that there is, in other words, no room for dual and/or multiple attribution – views which find support neither in the work of the ILC nor among academic writers.[88] The Commission, in particular, emphasised that the article 'only provides positive criteria of attribution',[89] but not a criterion of non-attribution to the state the organ of which has been placed at the disposal of the international organisation. This point could have been made more clearly in Article 6, for example by specifying that Article 6 is without prejudice to the attribution of conduct to the state on the basis of the rules of state responsibility. In any event, the reports and commentaries leave little room for any ambiguity on this question.

It is however true that, while accepting the possibility of dual or multiple attribution in principle, the ILC appears to have failed to appreciate its practical significance, stating, instead, that 'it may

[86] Case 265615, *ibid.* at paras. 4.8 and 4.11 (LV *Netherlands International Law Review* (2008) 425 at 450–1).

[87] 77 ILR 470. See also Zwanenburg, *supra* note 15 at 93–6.

[88] See Gaja, 'Second Report', *supra* note 36 at para. 6, and ILC Report (2004), UN Doc. A/59/10, at 101; Hirsch, *supra* note 2 at 65ff and Committee on Accountability of International Organisations of the International Law Association, *Report of the Seventh Conference*, New Delhi (2002) 797; K. M. Larsen, 'Attribution of Conduct in Peace Operations: The "Ultimate Authority and Control" Test', 19 EJIL (2008) 509 at 517; Klein, *supra* note 2 at 307; F. Messineo, who characterises the exclusion of dual attribution as a 'misconception' in 'The House of Lords in *Al-Jedda* and Public International Law: Attribution of Conduct to UN-Authorised Forces and the Power of the Security Council to Displace Human Rights', LVI *Netherlands International Law Review* (2009) 35 at 40.

[89] ILC Report (2004), *ibid.* at 102 and ILC Report (2009), *supra* note 1 at 58.

not frequently occur in practice'.[90] Yet, in his report, the Special Rapporteur had discussed the 1999 NATO-led Kosovo campaign as an example of an operation where conduct would have often been susceptible to dual or multiple attribution. Other examples include the international intervention in the former Yugoslavia in 1993–94 under Security Council resolution 836 of 1993, which permitted member states, acting nationally or through regional organisations, to 'take, under the authority of the Security Council and subject to close coordination with the Secretary-General and UNPROFOR, all necessary measures, through the use of air power, in and around the safe areas ... to support UNPROFOR in the performance of its mandate'. Under that resolution a system of dual authorisation was in place, with the consequence that acts were potentially attributable to both NATO and the UN, and probably also to individual member states of NATO.

Outside peacekeeping and peace enforcement, dual or multiple attribution also arises more frequently than is assumed. The facts in the case of *D v. Turkey* illustrate a situation typical of arrangements that exist in the field of refugee assistance and are discussed in detail in Chapter 6.[91] The application was brought to the ECtHR by an Iranian couple who had been sentenced to 100 lashes each for having engaged in pre-marital sex. They had applied for refugee status at the local offices of the UNHCR, as Turkey is one of many countries where refugee status determination, in principle a state-run administrative procedure, is entirely handled by the UNHCR.[92] In November 2006 their application for refugee status was rejected with a 'barely reasoned decision by UNHCR', which had also produced a statement dismissing the severity of the penalty inflicted in Iran and alleging that it would have in practice involved 'the symbolic application of the sentence bearing in mind the individual's state of health'.[93] The applicants succeeded in their case against Turkey and, although the ECtHR could not have ruled on the responsibility of UNHCR, its analysis of the facts indicates that, insofar as the 'barely reasoned' rejection and subsequent statements constituted violations

[90] ILC Report (2004), *ibid.* at 101 and now also in the introductory commentary on Chapter II, ILC Report (2009), *supra* note 1 at 56.

[91] *D v. Turkey, supra* note 4. See Verdirame, *supra* note 63 at 209–13.

[92] See Chapter 6 below.

[93] *D v. Turkey, supra* note 4 at paras. 21 and 28.

of the Convention, they may have been subject to attribution to both UNHCR and Turkey.

In some cases, the entities to which the same act is potentially attributable are both or all international organisations. As discussed (see Chapter 1 at 14ff.), permanent subsidiary programmes established by the General Assembly of the UN – such as UNHCR, UNDP and UNICEF – meet the definition of an international organisation adopted by the ILC in its work on responsibility. They are, as such, within the scope of the Articles on the Responsibility of International Organisations and can, in particular, be subject to the obligation to make reparation for wrongful acts.[94] These wrongful acts may also be attributable to the UN, as parent body of the operational programmes. The UN could invoke the provisions, found in the constituent instruments of some operational programmes,[95] that exclude its liability for claims arising in the context of the operations of the programme. But it is possible that such exclusions of liability would be regarded as in breach of the human right to a remedy, where, for example, a subsidiary programme saddled with large claims is financially disabled by the parent organ to meet its obligations.

When the other entity to which the act is simultaneously attributable is a non-governmental organisation or a private company, the issue of dual attribution is complicated by the limited nature of the regime of international responsibility for corporations and non-governmental organisations.[96]

The EU question

In its observations to the ILC, the EU maintained that it deserves special treatment in at least two respects: in a vertical sense in relation to acts undertaken by member states to implement EU law; in a horizontal sense in relation to acts connected to treaties to which both the EU and member states are parties (the so-called mixed agreements).[97] The horizontal dimension is relevant to the question of the breach of

[94] E. Lauterpacht, 'The Legal Effect of Illegal Acts of International Organisations', in R. Y. Jennings (ed.), *Essays in Honour of Lord McNair* (London: Stevens, 1965) 88 at 89.

[95] E.g. Statute of UNHCR annexed to GA Res. 428(V), 14 December 1950, at sec. 20.

[96] *Supra* note 37, and accompanying text, and A. Lindblom, 'The Responsibility of Other Entities: Non-Governmental Organisations', and C. Tomuschat, 'The Responsibility of Other Entities: Private Individuals', in Crawford *et al.*, *supra* note 2 at 318 and 343.

[97] Comments and Observations received from Governments and International Organisations (2004), *supra* note 27 at 18–25.

an international organisation discussed above; the vertical dimension pertains to attribution.

The EU proposed the adoption of a special rule on attribution to prescribe the attribution of the conduct of an organ of a member state implementing the binding act of the EU. This proposal has found some support among scholars. It has been argued, for example, that the general rule on attribution of conduct views international organisations 'very much as a traditional "organic body", reflecting a classical image of a legal person that acts via its own organs and agents', and neglecting the fact that a regional economic integration organisation, such as the European Union, 'acts largely in a "disembodied" manner, not only through its organs or agents in the traditional sense of these words, but also through the national authorities of its Member States'.[98]

The view that attribution through the existing articles is inappropriate in the case of the EU rests on two arguments. The first one is, as just discussed, that the EU belongs to the special genus of 'regional economic integration organisations', which are recognised by third party states as possessing the public powers conferred on them by the member states. Evidence of such third party recognition is the treaty practice whereby certain organisations and their members enter declarations of competences to indicate to other parties how competences are allocated between member states and the organisation on matters covered by the treaty.[99] The second argument is that there should be no attribution to the state where the state is implementing a binding act of the organisation because it has no discretion or control.[100]

Special Rapporteur Gaja rejected the proposal that a special rule of attribution should be devised for the EU and EU-like institutions, noting that, while this proposal may find some support in WTO jurisprudence, it had been turned down by the ECtHR and the ECJ.[101] The Special Rapporteur's preferred solution for dealing with the 'EU

[98] See, e.g., Paasivirta and Kuijper, *supra* note 14 at 213.

[99] *Ibid.* at 204–12. See Art. 1 of Annex IX to the UN Convention on the Law of the Sea; Art. 1(2) and (3) of the Energy Charter Treaty (1994) 2080 UNTS 95; and the Marrakesh Agreement establishing the World Trade Organisation (1994) 1867 UNTS 3.

[100] See Talmon, *supra* note 14 at 421.

[101] Gaja, 'Seventh Report', *supra* note 23 at paras. 32–3. The WTO case is *European Communities – Protection of Trademarks and Geographical Indication for Agricultural Products and Foodstuffs*, Report of 15 March 2005 (WT/DS174/R) at para. 7.725; the

question' was the notion of responsibility without attribution, that is the idea that an international organisation may, in certain circumstances, be responsible on the international plane for conduct that is attributable not to it but to a state.[102] This idea has not been met with great favour, and does not appear in the ILC commentaries to the articles.

In his *Seventh Report*, the Special Rapporteur discussed coercion as an example of responsibility without attribution. The rule on coercion adopted by the ILC (Article 15 of the Draft Articles on the Responsibility of International Organisations) mirrors the one previously adopted by the Commission in relation to state responsibility (Article 18 of the Articles on State Responsibility). Under this rule, an international organisation guilty of coercion bears responsibility for the act of the state or other international organisation it coerced, provided the act would be wrongful (but for the coercion) and the coercing organisation does so with knowledge of the circumstances. To use the words of the ILC in its commentary on state responsibility, it is in general true that instances of derivative responsibility, such as complicity or coercion, 'may seem to blur the distinction maintained in the articles between the primary or substantive obligations of the State and its secondary obligations of responsibility'; moreover, 'the idea of the implication of one State in the conduct of another is analogous to problems of attribution'.[103] It does not follow, however, that the combination of primary and secondary rules typical of derivative responsibility, needs to be viewed as the basis for a broader concept of responsibility without attribution.

On the current draft of the Articles – absent, that is, both the notion of responsibility without attribution and the proposal advanced by the EU – attribution of the conduct of an organ of a state implementing an act of an international organisation is possible through at least two routes: the organ of the state can be treated either as an 'agent of the organisation' under Article 5 or as an organ placed at the disposal of the organisation under Article 6. While the Article 5 route has been the object of much attention, the Article 6 route has not.[104]

ECtHR one is *Bosphorus* and the ECJ one is *Kadi*, *supra* note 4 – both discussed *supra* note 1 and accompanying text.

102 Gaja, 'Second Report', *supra* note 36 at paras. 11–13.

103 Crawford, *supra* note 13 at 146–7.

104 Neither Paasivirta and Kuijper, nor Talmon devote attention to the Art. 6 route, and most of the examples of Art. 6 attribution in the Special Rapporteur's and in the Commission's reports are taken from peace support missions.

The commentary to the Articles on State Responsibility explains that the organ placed at the disposal of the receiving state must be 'acting with the consent, under the authority of and for the purposes of the receiving State' and that 'in performing the functions entrusted to it by the beneficiary State, the organ must also act in conjunction with the machinery of that State and under its exclusive direction and control, rather than on instructions from the sending State'.[105] The commentary mentions the Judicial Committee of the Privy Council as an example of a state placing an organ at the disposal of another.[106] The Articles on State Responsibility, however, adopt a test for determining attribution of conduct of organs placed at the disposal of other states, which was judged ill-suited to international organisations. The test under state responsibility is that the organ be acting 'in the exercise of the governmental authority of the state', but international organisations 'only rarely exercise that type of authority'.[107]

Would it be plausible to maintain that the EU has effective control, within the meaning of Article 6 of the Draft Articles on the Responsibility of International Organisations, over the adoption of a statutory instrument by a Secretary of State implementing the terms of an EU directive?[108] Or that it has effective control over a national court applying EU law? When the EU act which is being implemented is binding, the proposition that the national implementing authority has no effective control over it is far from far-fetched. As for the application by national courts of EU law, one way of looking at this relationship is, indeed, to regard national courts as Community law courts whenever they are mandated to apply EU law.[109] The EU would probably have no difficulty with these positions, but member states may resist a solution based on the idea that, in a wide range of circumstances, they have no direction and control over executive and judicial organs.

Attribution via Articles 5 or 6 does not, however, address the two arguments advanced by the advocates of a special rule on attribution for the EU and EU-like institutions. Even if their views are not

[105] Crawford, *supra* note 13 at 103. [106] *Ibid*. at 105.

[107] Gaja, 'Second Report', *supra* note 36 at para. 47.

[108] See Talmon, *supra* note 14 at 414.

[109] See J. Temple Lang, 'The Duties of National Courts under Community Constitutional Law', 22 *European Law Review* (1997) 3; Lord Slynn of Hadley, 'What is a European Community Law Judge?', 52 *Cambridge Law Journal* (1993) 234.

sufficiently grounded in the current state of the law, as the Special Rapporteur argues, might they have a good point in a *lex ferenda* sense? Doubtless, the EU is a distinctive international organisation endowed with significant public powers, and treaty practice in many areas has had to adapt to the expansion in its competences, but it is not the only international organisation on which states have conferred public powers. Another example is the conferral of enormous public powers in the area of international peace and security to the UN (also keeping in mind that powers do not come much more 'public' than war and peace). Nor is the close connection between the EU and member states in the implementation of binding acts of the EU a unique phenomenon, although the frequency and extent of it are unparalleled; binding acts of the Security Council are also implemented by national authorities.

As for concerns about dual attribution, the advantage of the current articles is that they neither exclude nor impose it. The creation of a special rule that would automatically place an entire category of acts and omissions of state organs outside the realm of state responsibility should not be taken lightly. States have not, after all, expressly consented to such a rule.

The ILC solved the question of the special position of the EU by adopting Article 63 on *lex specialis* which provides that the draft articles do not apply where there are 'special rules of international law, including rules of the organisation applicable to the relations between the international organisation and its members'. The commentary notes the particular importance that rules of the organisation are likely to play; for example, they may affect the consequences of a breach of international law by that organisation where the injured party is a member state or another international organisation.[110]

Attribution of conduct in the international administration of territory

Attribution can pose particular problems in the international administration of territory because a number of different international legal persons are normally involved. International organisations will include the UN and sometimes a regional organisation such as NATO. In some cases, such as Kosovo at least until the Declaration of Independence of 17 February 2008, a state has nominal sovereignty but does not display any of the attributes of sovereignty. In other cases, such as Bosnia, the state exercises sovereign functions alongside an international administration.

[110] *Supra* note 14 at 175.

Under the rules on state responsibility, acts of persons or entities exercising elements of governmental authority are attributed to the state if the person or entity was empowered by the law of the state to exercise such authority, provided that the person or entity was acting in that capacity in the particular instance (Article 5).[111] But what if the entity exercising elements of governmental authority is another international legal person? Although Article 5 was drafted with para-statal entities primarily in mind,[112] there is no reason why it ought not to apply, in principle, to an international legal entity exercising elements of governmental authority. For example, in the many countries where governments delegate the process of refugee status determination or the administration of refugee camps to the UNHCR, the conduct of UNHCR in the exercise of those functions may also be attributed directly to the state (as well as to UNHCR itself). The difference between this example and the position of the High Representative in Bosnia or the UN administration in Kosovo is that the power to exercise governmental authority was not conferred on the latter entities by the law of the state, but by, respectively, a treaty and a resolution of the Security Council. The state should bear responsibility for the entities which its law empowered, but not for those which were empowered otherwise. Thus, while the international nature of the person or entity exercising elements of governmental authority has no bearing on the question of attribution under Article 5 of the Articles on State Responsibility, the international source of the authority does.

In *Sejdić and Finci v Bosnia*, the applicants challenged the provisions in the Bosnian Constitution which made them ineligible to stand for election to the House of Peoples and to the President on the ground of their Roma and Jewish origin. Although the Constitution of Bosnia and Herzegovina is an annex to the Dayton Peace Agreement, the ECtHR still considered that Bosnia could be held responsible for those provisions because '[t]he power to amend it [the Constitution] was, however, vested in the Parliamentary Assembly of Bosnia and Herzegovina, which is clearly a domestic body' and because 'the powers of the international administrator for Bosnia and Herzegovina (the High Representative) do not extend to the State Constitution'.[113]

In the cases that are described in Chapter 6 as *de facto* control of territory, an important question is whether it can be said that the law

[111] Article 5, Articles on State Responsibility.
[112] Crawford, *supra* note 13 at 101.
[113] At para. 30, Applications Nos. 27996/06 and 34836/06.

of the state truly 'empowered' the international organisation to exercise governmental functions. As will be discussed there, the *de facto* terminology does not signify absence of a legal basis under domestic law for the exercise of administrative functions, but, rather, absence of an international legal mandate to take over the administration of a particular territory. In some of the examples of *de facto* exercise of governmental functions by the UN, the law of the land may empower an international organisation to perform certain functions – for example, where a ministerial decree specifically designates certain areas of the country for refugee settlement and identifies UNHCR as the organisation responsible for their management.

In cases of both de facto and de jure administration of territory Article 5 of the Articles on State Responsibility can thus permit the *direct* attribution of the wrongful act of the organisation to the state. This should not be confused with those instances of derivative responsibility which may be relevant to international administration – in particular complicity[114] and the responsibility of a state that seeks to avoid compliance with one of its international obligations.[115] In terms of the allocation of responsibility between the international administration and the state, actual exercise of sovereignty should be of paramount importance in line with a general criterion of effectiveness.

Effectiveness is a general concept in international law relevant, for example, to territorial disputes (e.g. *Frontier Dispute (Burkina Faso v. Mali)*).[116] In the context of state responsibility, effectiveness generally means effective control over the specific conduct (as discussed, for example, in relation to Article 6 of the Draft Articles on Responsibility of International Organisations).

While in most cases of international administration, there will be a role for both the international organisation and the state, there are cases in which one of the two is wholly excluded from the administration. The administration of Kosovo is an example of a sovereign state – Serbia, at least until the Declaration of Independence – possessing a 'sovereignty shorn of the last vestige of power'.[117] In *Legal Consequences for States of the Continued Presence of South Africa in Namibia*, the ICJ dealt with a situation that was almost the

[114] Article 57, Draft Articles on Responsibility of International Organisations.

[115] Article 60, Draft Articles on Responsibility of International Organisations.

[116] Judgment, ICJ Reports (1986) 554 at 586–7. See also E. Milano, *Unlawful Territorial Situations in International Law: Reconciling Effectiveness, Legality and Legitimacy* (Leiden: Brill, 2006) Ch. 2.

[117] *Lighthouses in Crete and Samos (France v. Greece)* (1937) PCIJ Reports Series A/B, No. 71 at 127 (diss. op. of Judge Hudson). In the *Lighthouses in Crete and Samos* case, the hollow sovereign was the Ottoman Sultan.

reverse: South Africa had continued to exercise effective control in Namibia in spite of the termination of its mandate, that is of its title to administer Namibia. Regardless of the lack of any title to territory South Africa continued to exercise rights connected to sovereignty, albeit unlawfully.

Attribution of ultra vires conduct

Under the rule in Article 7, the ultra vires conduct of an organ or agent is attributable to the organisation, provided that the organ or agent acted 'in that capacity'. This rule is analogous to the one found in Article 7 of the Articles on State Responsibility and the words 'in that capacity' serve an equally important purpose as in the context of state responsibility: by requiring 'a close link between the *ultra vires* conduct and the organ's or agent's functions' they exclude purely private conduct.[118]

Ultra vires conduct results in two separate internationally wrongful acts whenever it breaches both a rule of the organisation that possesses an international law character and another rule of international law. This situation can arise only in relation to international organisations, because the internal rules of the state do not have an international law characterisation. As discussed however (see pp. 97–98), not all breaches of the rules of the organisation will result in internationally wrongful acts and thus not all ultra vires conduct will have this dual dimension.

Human rights violations will often include both dimensions. For example, UNHCR's refugee encampment policy, which is examined below in Chapter 6, constitutes a violation of both the rules of the organisation and of human rights obligations. Assuming that it is true that this practice emanates from an official policy of UNHCR, rather than from the decisions of 'bogus' local officials contravening instructions, it also signals a systemic problem of excess of authority with important practical consequences on the plane of compliance and accountability. The imposition of collective punishment on the entire population of a refugee camp is a clear example of ultra vires conduct, because the officials who adopted the measure were acting in excess of authority or in contravention of instructions.

Another important question relates to the attribution of off-duty conduct. Many of the cases in which peacekeepers have been accused

[118] Commentary to Article 7 in ILC Report (2009), *supra* note 1 at 71, and Klein, *supra* note 2.

of sexual violence and exploitation arose from such conduct. In its Commentary to Article 7, the ILC refers to a 1986 memorandum of the Office of Legal Affairs of the UN concerning claims involving off-duty acts which stated that 'the Organisation has no legal or financial liability for death, injury or damage resulting from such acts ... We consider the primary factor in determining an "off-duty" situation to be whether the member of a peace-keeping mission was acting in a non-official/non-operational capacity when the incident occurred and not whether he/she was in military or civilian attire at the time of the incident or whether the incident occurred inside or outside the area of operation.'[119]

This position, which the ILC endorses,[120] is correct in principle, but necessitates some caveats. First, the UN may bear no responsibility *under international law* for the off-duty conduct of peacekeepers, but the responsibility in tort of an organisation is a separate matter which is not necessarily governed by international law, as agreements concluded by the UN with states hosting peacekeeping missions confirm.[121] Bringing a tort claim against the organisation would pose many difficulties, from the identification of the proper law to jurisdiction (including the question of immunity). Nevertheless, it is not possible to exclude a priori the tortious responsibility of the organisation, not least because such a determination can only be made by reference to a specific body of national tort law and not in the abstract.

Secondly, where the off-duty conduct of the peacekeepers is not isolated but widespread or even systemic, the UN may still bear responsibility for omissions if they caused a breach of its positive obligations under human rights law, international humanitarian law or both.

Thirdly, the policy reason that is offered to justify the fact that the scope for attributing off-duty conduct is more limited in peacekeeping operations than under some provisions of the *jus in bello* is not entirely

[119] 'Liability of the UN for Claims Involving Off-Duty Acts of Members of Peacekeeping Forces – Determination of "Off-Duty" Versus "On-Duty" Status', UN Jur. YB (1986) 300, also cited in the commentary to Art. 7, ILC Report (2009), *supra* note 1, at 73–4. The importance of this distinction was also stressed by the UN Secretariat in 2004 UN Jur. YB (2004) 323).

[120] In support of this position, see also Zwanenburg, *supra* note 15 at 106 and 127.

[121] See, e.g., Articles 54–55 of the Agreement between Burundi and the United Nations concerning the Status of the United Nations Operation in Burundi, *signed at* Bujumbura, 17 June 2005 (and *entered into force* on the same date), UN Jur. YB (2005) 25.

convincing. The reason is that the 'UN commander is in command but does not have disciplinary powers in the same sense as national commanders'.[122] This is in essence an argument about the degree of command control which may be true in most cases but not all. Where this is not the case, the UN should follow the more demanding *lex specialis* on attribution under Article 91 of Additional Protocol I of the Geneva Conventions or Article 3 of The Hague Convention (IV) of 1907 referred to above (see p. 96). UN peacekeeping missions that have agreed to ensure full respect for the principles and rules of the Geneva Conventions and the Additional Protocols should be presumed to have also accepted the *lex specialis* on attribution at Article 91 of Additional Protocol I.[123]

Derivative responsibility

The Draft Articles on the Responsibility of International Organisations deal with two categories of derivative responsibility: the responsibility of the international organisation in connection with the act of a state or another international organisation (Articles 13–18), and the responsibility of the state in connection with the act of an international organisation (Articles 57–62). Some heads of derivative responsibility – complicity (Articles 13 and 57), direction and control (Articles 14 and 58), and coercion (Article 15 and 59) – are analogous to the state responsibility ones; others address situations which arise only in relation to international institutions and for which novel solutions had to be devised.

Responsibility of the international organisation in connection with the act of a state or another international organisation

Article 16 provides that in certain circumstances an international organisation may incur responsibility for acts committed by states pursuant to one of its decisions, authorisations or recommendations. The general conditions for such responsibility to arise are that the act would be internationally wrongful if committed by the organisation and that it would circumvent one of its international obligations. In addition, in the case of non-binding acts (i.e. authorisations and recommendations), causation must be proven, i.e. it must be shown that

[122] Zwanenburg, *supra* note 15 at 106.
[123] See, e.g., Article 6 of the Burundi-UN Agreement, *supra* note 121.

the state or international organisation committed the wrongful act 'because of that authorisation or recommendation'. In the words of the Commission, the purpose of this rule is to cover the possibility that the organisation may 'try to influence its members in order to achieve through them a result that the organisation could not lawfully achieve directly'.[124]

The development of a kind of doctrine of 'undue influence' in international institutional law is to be welcomed. Given the varied nature of the activities of international organisations and of their interactions with states, it is also entirely appropriate that this category of derivative responsibility should not be limited to acts that are binding on member states, but also extend to non-binding ones. The objection that a mere recommendation should not expose the organisation to responsibility is addressed by the requirement of causation. Proof of causation will require 'a contextual analysis of the role that the authorisation or recommendation actually plays in determining the conduct of the member state or international organisation'.[125]

Most of the acts addressed by international organisations to states are non-binding, and probably only a small percentage of these non-binding acts has the potential to engage the derivative responsibility of the organisation. There has to be some power imbalance in the relationship between the organisation and the state (or, indeed, between the organisation and another organisation) that leaves the state little choice but to act pursuant to the recommendation. Examples may include a set of socio-economic policy reforms, recommended by an international financial institution to a state at risk of financial default, which violate human rights; or the rejection of an entirely well-founded claim for refugee status by a UNHCR official and the consequent deportation of the applicant to his country of origin in breach of the prohibition on *non-refoulement*.[126]

Could the UN ever incur responsibility on this basis for acts committed by member states pursuant to a resolution of the Security Council? The 'without prejudice' provision in respect of the UN Charter in Article 66 of the Draft Articles on the Responsibility of International Organisations precludes this possibility at least in respect of those resolutions that engage the obligation of member states to accept and

[124] Commentary to Article 16, ILC Report (2009), *supra* note 1 at 88.
[125] *Ibid.* at 91. [126] See *D v. Turkey*, *supra* note 4.

carry out the decisions of the Security Council pursuant to Article 25 of the Charter. In a separate opinion to an Order in the *Bosnia Genocide* case, Judge Lauterpacht had raised the troubling idea that the arms embargo imposed on Bosnia could make members of the UN 'accessories to genocide'.[127] Because of Article 66, the Draft Articles cannot be relied upon in support of the view that either the derivative responsibility of the organisation or the accessory responsibility of the member state could be established.

Jurisdictional issues often arise when cases of derivative responsibility are brought before treaty-based organs. As explained by the Special Rapporteur, lack of jurisdiction *ratione personae* prevented both the ECtHR and the Human Rights Committee (HRC) from examining the position of international organisations in a number of cases involving their derivative responsibility (and potentially also their direct responsibility).[128]

Responsibility of the state in connection with the act of an international organisation

Rules not modelled on state responsibility and specific to international institutional responsibility are those on the responsibility of a member state seeking to avoid compliance (Article 60), and on the responsibility of a member state for the wrongful acts of the organisation (Article 61).

Responsibility of the state seeking to avoid compliance

There is some conceptual overlap between this head of derivative responsibility and the doctrine of equivalent protection, discussed in Chapter 8. The formulation originally proposed by the Special Rapporteur amounted to a statement of that doctrine. It provided that the state could incur responsibility if it circumvented one of its obligations by transferring a competence that relates to the performance of that obligation to an international organisation.[129] In spite of a generally positive response to the inclusion of a version of the doctrine of equivalent protection in the Articles, some states and international

[127] *Application of the Convention on the Prevention and Punishment of the Crime of Genocide (Bosnia and Herzegovina v. Yugoslavia)*, Provisional Measures, Order of 13 September 1993, ICJ Reports (1993) 325 at 441 (sep. op. of Judge Lauterpacht).

[128] Gaja, 'Third Report', *supra* note 21 at para. 33.

[129] See Article 28 in the ICL Report (2008), UN Doc. A/63/10.

organisations expressed apprehension about the breadth of this head of responsibility for states. The Special Rapporteur acceded to calls for a narrowing of this basis of responsibility, adding, in an amended draft, subjective elements which, while falling short of a bad faith requirement, amount to an 'assessment of intent'.[130] The result is that, under the latest version of Article 60 approved by the ILC, in order to establish the derivative responsibility of the state under this rule, it must be shown that the state is seeking to avoid complying with one of its obligations; that it is taking advantage of the fact that the organisation has competence; and that it is prompting the organisation to commit the act that gives rise to its derivative responsibility.

Responsibility of member states

Academic literature on this topic is vast, much of it originating from litigation on the Arab Organisation for Industrialisation (AOI) and on the International Tin Council (ITC).[131] In a seminal work which preceded the project of the ILC, Moshe Hirsch found support in existing academic literature for seven regimes of responsibility for member states: limited responsibility; concurrent responsibility; secondary responsibility; indirect responsibility; responsibility in accordance with the parties' intention; responsibility of the members according to

[130] Gaja, 'Seventh Report', *supra* note 23 at paras. 77ff and 82.

[131] On the AOI see *Westland Helicopters v. Arab Organisation for Industrialisation* (AOI), Interim Award of 5 April 1984, 80 ILR 600; the judgment of the Swiss Federal Court of 19 July 1988, 80 ILR 652 and 18 *Revue de l' arbitrage* (1989) 525. On the *International Tin Council* see *J.H. Rayner Ltd v. Department of Trade and Industry* [1990] 2 AC 418 for the House of Lords' decision, while the decisions of the High Court and of the Court of Appeal are reported respectively at 77 ILR 56 and 80 ILR 48; see also Case 241/87, *Maclaine Watson and Co. Ltd v. Council of the EC and Commission of the EC*, 96 ILR 201. Among the academic commentaries on these cases, see in particular C. F. Amerasinghe, 'Liability to Third Parties of Member States of International Organizations: Practice, Principle and Judicial Precedent', 85 AJIL (1991) 259 and R. Sadurska and C. Chinkin, 'The Collapse of the International Tin Council: A Case of State Responsibility?' 30 VJIL (1989–1990) 845.

Without purporting to reproduce the references to the extensive secondary literature on this topic, which the Special Rapporteur reviewed in his Fourth Report (see G. Gaja, 'Fourth Report on Responsibility of International Organisations' (2006), 58th Session of the ILC, UN Doc. A/CN.4/564), I only refer readers to the following works, all antecedent to the work of the ILC, which examined this question in particular detail: Amerasinghe, *Principles*, *supra* note 2 at 407ff.; H. G. Schermers and N. M. Blokker, *International Institutional Law* (4th edn., Dordrecht: Martinus Nijhoff, 2003) 1007ff.; Hirsch, *supra* note 2 at 149ff.; M. Harwig, *Die Haftung der Mitgliedstaaten für Internationale Organisationen* (Berlin: Springer, 1993).

their obligations towards the organisations; and responsibility according to the functions and objects of the organisation.[132] He concluded that 'the overwhelming majority of writers are of the opinion that the members of international organisations bear some responsibility toward third parties for wrongful acts committed by the organisation' and that 'international customary law rejects the principle of concurrent responsibility'.[133]

Hirsch also put forward the proposal, *de lege ferenda*, that a distinction be made between voluntary and non-voluntary injured parties, on the basis that the former consented to a degree of risk while the latter did not.[134] The effect of this distinction is that persons injured by the acts or omissions of an international organisation who 'do not have the reasonable capability to envisage the loss and adopt the necessary measures to reduce the risk and cover themselves in advance' would benefit from a higher measure of protection, including, most importantly, the right to recover from member states where the international organisation fails to provide an adequate remedy.[135] The approach advocated by Hirsch would assist persons seeking to bring human rights claims for the conduct of international organisations, since, as non-voluntary injured parties, they could always benefit from the additional protection.

There are, however, problems with the Hirsch proposal. First, the distinction between voluntary and non-voluntary injured parties is problematic. Does it make sense, for example, in relation to alleged victims of human rights violations? It could be argued that a resident of Eastern Congo can reasonably foresee that, unless he seeks refuge abroad, there is a very serious risk that he may suffer a violation of one or more of his fundamental human rights at some point in time. Does this make him a voluntary injured party in the event of such a violation? The answer must be negative: the foreseeability of a human rights violation should never be construed as a form of constructive consent to it. Nor should a victim's right to a remedy be affected by this consideration. Secondly, it is difficult to see why the beliefs or attributes of the injured party should determine the basis for responsibility.

To what extent should one approach the question of the responsibility of members states on the basis of an analogy with corporations?

[132] Hirsch, *supra* note 2 at 137–72.
[133] *Ibid.* at 146–7. [134] *Ibid.* at 163–9. [135] *Ibid.* at 166.

The tendency has been to place significant reliance on this analogy, although some have criticised it.[136] The corporate analogy is normally premised on the corporation being a limited liability one. In reality, the company law of every country recognises and regulates more than one type of company, and the nature and extent of shareholders' liability varies accordingly. There is, conceptually, no difficulty with the notion that a juridical person has a personality that is entirely distinct from that of its members or shareholders, even though they can be still liable for its debts. Thus, contrary to the position of some authors, a regime of subsidiary responsibility of member states entails neither a denial of the legal personality of the organisation nor (for what it is worth) a rejection of the corporate analogy.[137]

Article 61 of the Draft Articles on the Responsibility of International Organisations is based on the notion that member states are not generally responsible for the internationally wrongful acts of an international organisation. The policy reasons advanced by the Special Rapporteur in support of his approach are, first, that it would not be fair to make states responsible for conduct with which they have no link beyond the relationship of membership with the organisation that put that conduct in place; and, secondly, that there is a risk that international organisations would be exposed to the continuous interference of member states concerned about their potential liability.[138] While both these concerns are justified, it is true, as shown throughout this book, that, far from a risk of excessive interference, the problem is often that member states abdicate their supervisory functions over UN operations.

The Special Rapporteur also relied on judicial precedents, in particular the judgments in the ITC litigation which did reject the notion that member states are liable for the debts incurred by international organisations. In *J. H. Rayner (Mincing Lane) Ltd v. Department of Trade and Industry and Others*, the creditors of the ITC brought an action against the UK government to recover their losses. The plaintiffs argued, inter

[136] H. G. Schermers, 'Liability of International Organisations', 1 *Leiden Journal of International Law* (1988) 3 at 6–9.

[137] See the authors cited by Gaja, 'Fourth Report', Add. 2, *supra* note 132 at 10 at footnote 162, in particular Hartwig, *supra* note 132 at 290ff.

[138] Gaja, *supra* note 132 at 12–13, also citing R. Higgins, 'The Legal Consequences for Member States of Non-Fulfilment by International Organisations of their Obligations toward Third Parties: Provisional Report', 66-I *Annuaire de l' Institut de Droit International* (1995) 373 at 393.

alia, that member states of the ITC carried secondary liability for the debts of the organisation, and that the organisation had acted as the members' agent.[139] The High Court's decision to dismiss the claim was affirmed by the Court of Appeal and the House of Lords. The English courts were at pains to avoid two possible results: (a) the direct recognition of the international legal personality of the ITC without incorporation, on the one hand; and (b) the concurrent responsibility of member states, on the other. Since (a) would have led to the sole responsibility of member states – a highly undesirable outcome in their eyes – the courts resorted to the convoluted fiction of the 'body corporate' to recognise that the ITC was a legal person and thus bore responsibility for its debts. It is important to bear in mind that the conclusion in the ITC cases that there is no 'plausible evidence' of the existence of a rule of joint and several liability of member states under international law[140] was reached in the context of financial claims and in respect of a sectorial international institution. The near universal membership of the UN would make the application of a regime of secondary or concurrent responsibility of member states even less viable and appropriate.

In the scheme of Article 61 and, more generally, of the derivative responsibility of states for acts of international organisations, there are exceptions to the general principle that member states are not responsible for the acts of an international organisation. First, member states may incur responsibility through any of the other instances of derivative responsibility – that is, complicity, direction and control, coercion and responsibility to seek to avoid compliance. Secondly, the member state incurs responsibility if it has accepted responsibility for a particular act (Article 61(1)(a)). Thirdly, the member state that 'has led the injured party to rely on its responsibility' may also incur responsibility (Article 61(1)(b)). Fourthly, a *lex specialis* in the constituent instrument or another treaty may be applicable. For example, Article VI of the Outer Space Treaty creates a regime of concurrent responsibility for international organisations and member states that

139 *J. H. Rayner, supra* note 132. While liability based on agency 'may theoretically be a proper basis for the direct liability of members of an international organization, it must be recognised that proof of such agency is not easy' (see Amerasinghe, *supra* note 2 at 420).

140 *Maclaine Watson v. Department of Trade and Industry* (1990) 29 ILM 670 at 675 (per Lord Templeman).

are also parties to the treaty.[141] By contrast, some constituent instruments expressly exclude the liability of member states.

In a 1991 study, Amerasinghe identified numerous provisions excluding liability in the constituent instruments of international organisations.[142] That list need not be reproduced here, but owing to the passage of time some additions must be made. The constituent instruments of the Black Sea Trade and Development Bank (BSTDB) and the European Bank for Reconstruction and Development (EBRD) contain a widely drafted general limitation on members' liability that, 'no member, by reason of its membership, shall be liable for the obligations of the Bank'.[143] Similarly, Article 15 of the International Coffee Agreement 2007 provides that no member of the International Coffee Organization 'shall be responsible by reason of its membership of the Organization for any liability arising from borrowing or lending by any other Member or entity with such projects'. Furthermore, Article 22(2) states that '[a] Member's liability is limited to the extent of its obligations regarding contribution specifically provided for in this Agreement', adding that '[t]hird parties dealing with the Organization shall be deemed to have notice of the provisions of this Agreement regarding the liabilities of Members'. The constituent instrument of the North American Development Bank contains a differently crafted exclusion of liability to the effect of expressly limiting the liability of the parties on capital shares to the unpaid portion of their issue price while providing that upon suspension or termination, '[t]he liability arising from their subscriptions to the capital stock of the Bank shall continue until all direct and contingent obligations have been discharged'.[144] Other provisions, found in the constituent instruments of the CAB International, Inter-Governmental Authority on Development (IGAD), Nordic Development Fund (NDF) and Nordic Investment Bank (NIB), contain no limitation on liability but provide for the continuing liability of members upon withdrawal or termination of the organisation for obligations towards the organisation incurred prior to the date of withdrawal or termination.[145]

[141] Treaty on Principles Governing the Activities of States in the Exploration and Use of Outer Space, including the Moon and Other Celestial Bodies (1966), GA Res 2222 (XXI), 19 December 1966.

[142] Amerasinghe 'Liability', *supra* note 132 at 270–1 and footnotes 47–53.

[143] Article 7(3), Establishing Agreement of the BSTDB, 30 June 1994; Article 5(7) Agreement Establishing the EBRD, 29 May 1990.

[144] Article II, section 2(c) and Article VIII, section 3, BECC-NADB Charter, amended 6 August 2004.

[145] Article XIV, Agreement on CAB International, 4 September 1987; Article 22(b), Agreement Establishing the IGAD, 21 March 1996; Article 17, Agreement Concerning the NDF, 3 November 1988; Article 18, Agreement Establishing the NIB, 1 January 2005 and Article 18 of the Statutes of the NIB, 1 January 2005.

Article 61 is a secondary rule and does not override the positive obligations of member states under international human rights law. These may include the obligation to ensure that international organisations of which they are members do not contravene human rights. Although neither membership of the organisation nor involvement in the decision leading to the violative conduct have been accepted as sufficient to establish control of an international organisation, a failure to exercise due diligence with regard to the conduct of an institution may suffice to hold its member states responsible.[146] However, in this context it is not the wrongful conduct of an international organisation that will be attributed to its member states; rather, it is the states' failure to exercise due care that results in their responsibility of member states.[147]

Complicity

The rules on complicity are found in Article 13 for complicity of the international organisation in connection with an act of a state, and in Article 57 for the complicity of the state in connection with an act of an international organisation.

These two provisions reproduce, *mutatis mutandis*, the corresponding provision in the Articles on State Responsibility (Article 16). Each comprises three crucial elements: the conduct capable of resulting in complicity has to 'aid or assist' the state or international organisation that has principal responsibility; the complicitous organisation must have acted 'with knowledge of the circumstances of the internationally wrongful act'; and the act would be wrongful if committed by the complicitous organisation. The ILC proceeded on the basis that there was no general reason 'to distinguish the case of an international organisation aiding or assisting a state or another international organisation from that of a state aiding or assisting another state'[148] – an approach which was for the most part met with approval.

In its comments on Article 13, the IMF expressed fundamental disagreement with the 'blanket application' of Article 16 of the Articles on State Responsibility, but did not propose an alternative formulation. It also pre-emptively rebutted the argument that the financial assistance it provides could amount to aiding or assisting because

[146] Klein, *supra* note 2 at 309ff. [147] *Ibid.*
[148] ILC Report (2005), UN Doc. A/60/10 at 93.

'[n]either IMF itself, nor the provision of financial assistance by IMF, is capable of precluding such [wrongful] conduct or contributing significantly to it'.[149] The first of these points is misplaced: the power to preclude the wrongful conduct is never considered a prerequisite for aiding or abetting. On the second point, the IMF observed that '[g]iven the fungible nature of financial assistance' references to aiding or assisting in the case of financial assistance 'can only mean assistance that is earmarked for the wrongful conduct', and that it 'cannot contribute significantly to such conduct because IMF financing is not targeted to particular conduct'.[150] Put in terms of Articles 13 and 57, the argument is that the requirement of knowledge of the circumstances is satisfied only where assistance is specifically targeted to the wrongful conduct. However, this argument is unpersuasive. The fact that assistance is fungible, and that its use or destination can be altered by the recipient state, does not automatically imply that the IMF, or other donors, have no knowledge of the circumstances. It may be reasonable to presume that the donor had no knowledge of the circumstances, where the wrongful act took place after the assistance was diverted from an agreed and expressly stated purpose.

The concrete meaning of 'aiding or assisting' will depend on the wrongful act in question and will often involve complex factual and evidential assessments.[151] Examples of aiding or assisting by international organisations may be the provision of humanitarian assistance to Afghanistan under the Taliban, or to Ethiopia under the Derg.[152] As mentioned before, one consequence of the expansion of positive obligations in the human rights sphere is that the responsibility of the accessory, state or international organisation may often be direct.

[149] Comments and Observations received from International Organisations (2007) UN Doc. A/CN.4/582 at 10.

[150] *Ibid.*

[151] A. Reinisch, 'Aid or Assistance and Direction and Control between States and International Organisations in the Commission of Internationally Wrongful Acts' (unpublished paper).

[152] On Afghanistan see below, Chapter 5. On the use of Band Aid money, see the report by the Africa Editor of the BBC World Service, Martin Plaut, 'Ethiopia Famine Aid "Spent on Weapons"', broadcast on 3 March 2010 (http://news.bbc.co.uk/1/hi/world/africa/8535189.stm). See also the CIA document 'Ethiopia: Political and Security Impact of the Drought', 4 January 1985, released under the Freedom of Information Act and available through www.foia.cia.gov (or, more simply, through the hyperlink on the BBC page).

Circumstances precluding wrongfulness

Articles 19 to 26 are closely modelled on the corresponding articles on State Responsibility,[153] since 'there would be little reason for holding that circumstances precluding wrongfulness of the conduct of States could not be relevant also for international organisations'.[154] The defences of consent (Article 19), self-defence (Article 20), *force majeure* (Article 22), distress (Article 23), necessity (Article 24), and compliance with peremptory norms (Article 25) are nearly identical to the equivalent articles on State Responsibility, although their application to international institutions will give rise to specific challenges and require some adjustments.

Self-defence, for example, 'is likely to be relevant for precluding wrongfulness only of acts of a small number of organisations, such as those administering a territory or deploying an armed force', and the 'self' in self-defence is sometimes to be understood as the particular mission.[155] As for necessity, 'as a matter of policy, [it] should not be invocable by international organisations as widely as by States'.[156]

Force majeure, which relates to the 'occurrence of an irresistible force or an unforeseeable event, beyond the control of the organization',[157] has been invoked by international organisations in several cases.[158] Financial distress might, in certain circumstances, amount to *force majeure*.[159]

Distress is applicable in theory to international organisations although, as the ILC Commentary notes, there are no known cases of the defence actually being invoked.[160] Although there is no practice on distress in cases of international institutional responsibility, it is

[153] ILC Report (2009), *supra* note 1 at 93–4. [154] *Ibid.* at 96.

[155] ILC Report (2006), UN Doc. A/61/10, at 266; the Special Rapporteur specifically mentions that the invocation of self-defence is not limited to the UN since '[s]ome other organisations deploy military forces or are involved in the administration of territory' (Gaja, *supra* note 132 at para. 18). A memorandum of the Legal Bureau of the Canadian Department of Foreign Affairs and International Trade stated that 'self defence could well include the defence of the safe areas and the civilian population in those areas', where 'self-defence' is used in the sense of the 'defence of the mission' (ILC Report (2009), *supra* note 1 at 96).

[156] ILC Report (2009), *supra* note 1 at 105.

[157] Article 23, Draft Articles on the Responsibility of International Organisations.

[158] ILC Report (2009), *supra* note 1 at 101, citing Judgment No. 24 of the Administrative Tribunal of the OAS, *Torres et al. v. Secretary General of the Organization of American States*.

[159] Gaja, 'Fourth Report', *supra* note 132 at 11.

[160] ILC Report (2009), *supra* note 1 at 102.

conceivable that a UN official might be forced to commit a wrongful act because there is 'no other reasonable way' to save his life or the lives of other persons who are 'in a special relationship of protection with the author of the wrongful act'.[161] It is however difficult to conceive of situations where distress could be invoked to justify the breach of a human rights obligation.

A question of more than mere theoretical significance is whether peacekeeping missions can invoke distress to justify a breach of their mandate in order to protect the life of persons entrusted in their care. An example is that of the UNAMIR during the 1994 genocide in Rwanda. Thousands of civilians sought refuge in UN compounds and other buildings under 'UN protection', which were besieged by the Interahamwe militia. When Belgian peacekeepers stationed at the École Technique Officielle withdrew, thousands were slaughtered. Although the mandate and the rules of engagement probably allowed UNAMIR to take appropriate action to defend civilians, the Department of Peacekeeping Operations (DPKO) insisted on a very narrow interpretation, precluding the full use of even the limited means at UNAMIR's disposal.[162] Had such interpretations been correct, could UNAMIR nonetheless have invoked distress to justify undertaking action not expressly allowed under the terms of its mandate in order to save the lives of people entrusted in its care? As long as no peremptory norm of international law was violated through such action, the answer must be affirmative. The emerging doctrine of responsibility to protect would, in certain circumstances, appear to support such humanitarian assistance by an international institution.[163]

As indicated by Special Rapporteur Gaja, necessity is 'probably the most controversial circumstance precluding wrongfulness'.[164] Article 24 adds an important requirement to those found in the corresponding rule on state responsibility (Article 25): the essential protected interest must be an essential interest of the international community as a whole insofar as the organisation has, in accordance with

161 S. Szurek, 'Circumstances Precluding Wrongfulness in the ILC Articles on State Responsibility: Distress', in Crawford *et al.* (eds.), *supra* note 2 at 418 and 489.

162 R. Dallaire, *Shake Hands with the Devil: the Failure of Humanity in Rwanda* (Canada: Random House, 2003) 233. For a full account of what happened at the school, see Human Rights Watch/Fédération Internationale des Ligues des Droits de l'Homme *Leave None to Tell the Story: Genocide in Rwanda* (New York, 1999); African Rights, *Rwanda: Death, Despair, Defiance* (2nd edn., London, 1995) 1113ff.

163 *Supra* note 162.

164 Gaja, 'Fourth Report', *supra* note 132 at 13.

international law, the function to protect that interest. The ILC viewed this position as the middle way between 'the view of those who favour placing international organisations on the same level as States and the opinion of those who would totally rule out the invocability of necessity by international organisations'.[165]

Content of responsibility

Part III (Articles 27–41) of the Draft Articles on the Responsibility of International Organisations deals with the content of international responsibility, comprising chapters on general principles, on reparation and on serious breaches. It closely follows the corresponding part in the Articles on State Responsibility, except for a few areas where the rules on state responsibility could not be imported without adjustment.

One such area is the role of internal rules for the organisation that seeks to justify its failure to comply with obligations related to the content of its responsibility (Article 31). The Articles on State Responsibility include two rules which are meant 'to give effect for the purposes of State responsibility to the general principle that a State may not rely on its internal law as a justification for its failure to comply with its international obligations':[166] the first one is Article 3 which asserts the irrelevance of the characterisation of an act as lawful under national law for the purposes of its characterisation under international law; the second one is Article 32 which asserts the irrelevance of internal law for the state seeking to justify its failure to comply with obligations on the content of state responsibility.

There is no equivalent to Article 3 in the Draft Articles on the Responsibility of International Organisations, because the internal rules/international rules dualism does not work for international organisations: many rules of the organisation are not simply relevant to international law, they *are* international law. But it is still necessary to prevent an international organisation from relying on an internal rule to escape its responsibility, because, if such a comprehensive escape route existed, an international organisation would only have to pass a resolution to absolve itself from the consequences of its internationally wrongful acts. The purpose of Article 31 is precisely to foreclose such a get-out by providing that an organisation cannot rely on its internal

[165] ILC Report (2009), *supra* note 1 at 105.

[166] Crawford, *supra* note 13 at 207.

rules as a justification for failing to comply with obligations deriving from the content of its responsibility. Internal rules dealing specifically with the responsibility of the organisation towards its members are excluded from this general rule (Article 31,2).

Another issue requiring a different solution from what is available under the rules on state responsibility is the role of members of the responsible organisation. Articles 39 provides that they have a duty to take, in accordance with the rules of the organisation, all appropriate measures in order to provide the organisation with the means for effectively fulfilling its obligations to make full reparation for the injury caused by the internationally wrongful act. This rule applies to both states and organisations which are members of an international organisation.

The approach to serious breaches of obligations under peremptory norms closely reflects what already exists under state responsibility. Under Article 41 states and international organisations are obliged to cooperate to bring an end, through lawful means, to any serious breach by an international organisation of a peremptory rule. It is right that Article 41 should be addressed to states as well as international organisations, but an asymmetry remains: the obligations of international organisations in respect of serious breaches committed by states are not covered by either set of articles on international responsibility given that Article 41 in the Articles on State Responsibility refers only to serious breaches by states and Article 41 in the Draft Articles on the Responsibility of International Organisations only to serious breaches by international organisations. Nevertheless, it is beyond dispute that the duty to cooperate also applies to international organisations in relation to serious breaches committed by states, bearing in mind, however, that the commentary to Article 41 specifies that this provision 'is not designed to vest international organisations with functions that are alien to their respective mandates'.[167] Member states of the organisation responsible for the serious breach are not singled out in Article 41 as coming under a heightened duty to cooperate, but this duty is 'particularly significant when States are in a position to make a significant contribution in order to achieve the intended result'.[168]

[167] ILC Report (2009), *supra* note 1 at 127.

[168] G. Gaja, 'Fifth Report on Responsibility of International Organisations' (2007), 59th Session of the ILC, UN Doc. A/CN.4/583 at para. 58.

Implementation of responsibility

The draft articles on the implementation of the responsibility of an international organisation are divided into two chapters: invocation and countermeasures. They generally follow the corresponding provisions in the Articles on State Responsibility.

The ILC chose to extend the rule on the exhaustion of local remedies to international organisations, although, as acknowledged in the commentary to Article 44,[169] academic opinion on this issue is divided. The main argument against the applicability of this rule to international organisations is that international organisations do not offer means of local redress,[170] and that they 'do not have jurisdictional rights or powers over individuals in the same way that States have' since they 'do not have developed judicial systems, apart from their own internal systems ... for settling disputes with their staff members'.[171]

In any event, the rule on the exhaustion of remedies reproduces the language used in the state responsibility project, and is limited in effect to any available and effective remedy provided by the organisation. While it is arguable that international organisations often provide available and effective remedies to employees through such bodies as the UN Administrative Tribunal, the same is not true for third parties who suffer injury in peacekeeping operations or in situations of *de facto* control over territory such as refugee camps.

International human rights courts and tribunals have interpreted the rule on the exhaustion of local remedies in a purposive manner emphasising the concrete effectiveness and substantive availability of the remedy in question.[172] This interpretation is also appropriate in relation to international human rights claims brought against international organisations. Given that, as the following chapters show, individuals who allege that an international organisation has violated their human rights have hardly any recourse to effective internal mechanisms, satisfying the requirement that local remedies be exhausted should pose no difficulty.

[169] *Ibid.* at 136. [170] Eagleton, *supra* note 2 at 395.

[171] Amerasinghe, *supra* note 2 at 486. Amerasinghe justifies his conclusion also on the basis of an analysis of the *Reparation* case (*ibid.* at 484). Wellens is among those authors who have taken the view that the rule on the exhaustion of local remedies should, in principle, apply to international organisations (K. Wellens, *Remedies against International Organisations* (Cambridge University Press, 2002) 66–8).

[172] See D. Shelton, *Remedies in International Human Rights Law* (2nd edn., Oxford University Press, 2005) 124–5, 141, 142–3 and R. Pisillo Mazzeschi, *Esaurimento dei ricorsi interni e diritti umani* (Turin: Giappichelli Editore, 2004).

Particularly relevant to human rights is the rule on the invocation of responsibility by a state or an international organisation other than an injured one (Article 48). Under this rule, the non-injured party – state or international organisation – is entitled to invoke the responsibility of an international organisation if the obligation is owed to a group of states or international organisations that includes the one invoking responsibility, and if such obligation is established for the protection of a collective interest of the group. The protection of human rights is an example of such collective interests.

A non-injured state or international organisation is also entitled to invoke the responsibility of an international organisation in respect of *erga omnes* obligations, but invocation by a non-injured international organisation is subject to the additional condition that the function of the organisation must include the safeguarding of the interest of the international community underlying the *erga omnes* obligation. The invocation cannot, in other words, be ultra vires. Practice in this area is scant, although there is some EU practice in the analogous area of the invocation of the responsibility of states for breaches of *erga omnes* obligations.[173]

The law on countermeasures necessitated a few adjustments from the state responsibility project. First, a further limit was introduced to the effect of requiring injured states or international organisations adopting countermeasures to do so, as far as possible, in such a way as to limit their effects on the exercise by the responsible international organisation of its functions (Article 50(4)). Secondly, a special rule was inserted to deal with countermeasures by members of an international organisation, whose entitlement to adopt countermeasures is subject to two further conditions: that the countermeasures are not in breach of the rules of the organisation and that no other appropriate means are available for inducing compliance (Article 51).

Conclusion

Judicial practice on the principles and rules of institutional responsibility is still rather scant – certainly so in comparison with state

[173] See ILC Report (2009), *supra* note 1 at 145. P. Palchetti, 'Reactions by the European Union to Breaches of Erga Omnes Obligations', in E. Cannizzaro (ed.), *The European Union as an Actor in International Relations* (The Hague: Kluwer Law International, 2002) 219ff.

responsibility. In particular, issues related to the content and invocation of responsibility have seldom been the object of judicial decisions. On attribution, instead, there have been a number of often conflicting decisions. With a rather curious logic, courts, the ECtHR especially, have considered the attribution of certain acts to international organisations not in order to decide on the responsibility of those organisations but in order to determine questions of attribution of conduct to states.

Navigating around these difficulties and uncertainties, the ILC has developed a set of rules on the responsibility of international organisations which represent an important milestone in the promotion of the accountability of international organisations. One has to be realistic, however, about what the law on responsibility can and cannot achieve: accountability is much harder to advance in the absence of a clear set of principles and rules consequential upon the commission of an internationally wrongful act, yet the law on responsibility cannot on its own ensure accountability. It creates a framework for dealing with an international organisation responsible for a breach of an international obligation, but it does not solve the problem of enforcement of the international obligations of international organisations.

4 UN relief and development operations

Introduction

Relief operations aim to provide emergency humanitarian assistance to people affected by natural or man-made disasters, while development operations pursue the more long-term goal of improving social and economic conditions in developing countries. The principal providers of emergency humanitarian assistance are the UNHCR, UNICEF and the WFP, as well as myriads of local and international NGOs; the principal international institutional actors in the development sphere are UNDP and international financial institutions such as the World Bank and the IMF.[1]

Long-term development aid is often given on a bilateral basis, although many donor states choose to donate to an international organisation or an NGO which operates in the territory of the intended recipient rather than directly to the state.

Despite the importance of aid operations, no international aid law has emerged. In 2008 the ILC embarked upon a project on the protection of persons in the events of disasters which is expected to clarify some of the relevant legal issues.[2] In the meantime, it is possible to make some general observations on the legal framework applicable to UN aid

[1] On UNDP see M. Darrow and L. Arbour, 'The Pillar of Glass: Human Rights in the Development Operations of the United Nations', 103 AJIL (2009) 446.

[2] See E. Valencia-Ospina, 'Preliminary report on the protection of persons in the event of disasters by the Special Rapporteur', 60th Session of the ILC, 5 May 2008, UN Doc. A/CN.4/598 ('First Report'); Valencia-Ospina, 'Second report on the protection of persons in the event of disasters by the Special Rapporteur', 61st Session of the ILC, 7 May 2009, UN Doc. A/CN.4/615 ('Second Report'). The definition of disaster provisionally adopted by the ILC excludes armed conflict (Draft Article 2 in the Second Report).

operations. First, insofar as it can be shown that international organisations involved in relief and development operations are subject to human rights obligations, those obligations, together with other relevant institutional duties, will be part of the legal framework of their operations. Secondly, the provision of humanitarian assistance in armed conflict is subject to special rules.[3] Thirdly, the General Assembly and the Security Council of the UN have often referred to the provision of aid by subsidiary programmes of the UN in their resolutions. Although such references are seldom so extensive as to provide a comprehensive legal framework, they are part of the law applicable to specific operations. Fourthly, where aid is given in the form of financial assistance, the terms of the loan agreement will govern the relationship between donor organisation and recipient state.

Loans are not normally used by the UN, while they are the main form of assistance offered by the IMF. The practice of the IMF is to receive from a country wishing to borrow a Letter of Intent and/or a Memorandum of Economic and Financial Policy stipulating policy measures the country will undertake in return for access to Fund's resources. These documents are supposedly 'prepared by the [country's] authorities, with the cooperation and assistance of the Fund staff'.[4] However, the IMF acknowledges that country 'authorities generally do not write the first draft of the letter of intent'.[5] In contrast, the financial arrangement constitutes a unilateral decision of the Executive Board. It is the IMF, drawing on the policy documents, that sets the conditions for financing and determines whether those conditions are met.[6] Consequently, the legal basis for the binding nature of conditions lies in the Executive Board's decision rather than the policy documents.

There is no internationally agreed definition of development aid or humanitarian relief assistance.[7] Non-binding attempts at definitions

[3] See Art. 23, Geneva Convention (IV) Relative to the Protection of Civilians in Time of War (1949), 75 UNTS 287; Art. 70, Protocol I Additional to the Geneva Conventions of 1949, and Relating to the Protection of Victims of International Armed Conflict (1977), 1125 UNTS 3; Art. 18(2), Protocol II Additional to the Geneva Conventions of 12 August 1949, and Relating to the Protection of Victims of Non-International Armed Conflicts (1977), 1125 UNTS 609 (hereinafter Protocol I or II to the Geneva Conventions); Art. 8(2)(b)(iii) and (e)(iii) of the ICC.

[4] IMF Executive Board Decision No. 12864 (02/102), 'Guidelines on Conditionality', 25 September 2002.

[5] IMF Policy, Development and Review Department, 'Review of the 2002 Conditionality Guidelines', 3 March 2005.

[6] R. Leckow, 'Conditionality in the Developments in the International Monetary Fund', 3 *Current Developments in Monetary and Financial Law* (2005) 53 at 58.

[7] See P. Daillier, M. Forteau, N. Q. Dinh, A. Pellet, *Droit International Public* (8th edn., Librairie Générale de Droit et de Jurisprudence, 2009).

include the 2003 resolution of the Institut de Droit Interational where humanitarian assistance was defined as 'all acts, activities and the human and material resources for the provision of goods and services of an exclusively humanitarian character, indispensable for the survival and the fulfilment of the essential needs of the victims of disaster'.[8] The proposed Draft Convention on Expediting the Delivery of Emergency Relief is purposefully vague on the question of definition, stating in a circular manner that 'emergency assistance' means 'the relief consignments and services of an exclusively humanitarian and non-political character provided to meet the needs of those affected by disasters'.[9] Nor is a definition of humanitarian assistance found in the treaties on the law of armed conflict, although they contain numerous examples of assistance that is to be regarded as 'humanitarian', including not only food relief and medical services, but also educational services and the facilitation of religious worship.[10]

The principles of neutrality and impartiality, originally developed in the context of the law of armed conflict, are now relevant to all relief operations, whether in the midst of an armed conflict or outside one. They thus require consideration. The relationship between these principles and human rights is not always straightforward. Indeed, too strict an adherence to neutrality and impartiality has sometimes been seen as a contributing factor to human rights violations.

All these issues are examined in the first part of this chapter, together with other legal aspects of the provision of humanitarian assistance. The second part of the chapter is devoted to a case study of the UN relief and development operations in Afghanistan. This case shows, first, that the UN violated the principle of non-discrimination and, secondly, that such a violation arose as a result of decisions taken by the bureaucracy of the organisation. By contrast, the resolutions of

[8] Article I(1), Resolution on Humanitarian Assistance adopted by the Sixteeenth Commission in Bruges, 2 September 2003.

[9] Draft Convention on Expediting the Delivery of Emergency Relief (1984), drafted by the UN Disaster Relief Co-ordinator, UN Doc. A/39/267/Add. 2-E/1984/96/Add.2 reproduced in Annex H in Kalshoven, *infra* note 14 at 248.

[10] For example: Art. 24, Geneva Convention (I) for the Amelioration of the Condition of the Wounded and Sick in Armed Forces in the Field (1949), 75 UNTS 31; Arts. 25–28, Geneva Convention (III) Relative to the Treatment of Prisoners of War (1949), 75 UNTS 135; Arts. 23, 55, 108, Geneva Convention (IV) Relative to the Protection of Civilians in Time of War (1949), 75 UNTS 287 (hereinafter Geneva Convention I, III or IV); Art. 69(1), Protocol I to the Geneva Conventions; Art. 18(2), Protocol II to the Geneva Conventions.

the political organs of the UN generally conformed to principle. How could both the legal principles and the political organs of the UN be flouted so blatantly? Bureaucracies, international ones included, know how to resist the application of rules and the will of their political masters. In the case of the UN, the bureaucratic practice can end up being more 'effective' – that is more capable of determining institutional conduct – than 'hard law' (including rules of *jus cogens*, as is arguably the case with the principle of non-discrimination), in spite of the hierarchical superiority and greater normative strength of the latter. This case study also illustrates how the relationship between human rights standards and humanitarianism can become strained.

Debates on the effectiveness and the morality of aid are also relevant to the broader context of this chapter.[11] These debates, which are not explored in detail here, have a bearing on the legal dimension because they shape its aspirational side, as expressed for example by the development of the responsibility to protect and the adoption of policy statements such as the Millennium Development Goals. At least as important are debates on the militarisation and privatisation of aid. Militarisation can transform the humanitarian operation into a forcible intervention with important consequences for its legality. The trend towards militarisation of aid, especially of relief in conflict situations, appears to be endorsed by large sectors of the UN humanitarian bureaucracy, and the practice of the organisation is beginning to reflect this.[12] Privatisation through the subcontracting of services to NGOs and companies poses a series of problems for the application and enforcement of international law, because some principles

[11] See, for example, W. Easterly, *The White Man's Burden: Why the West's Efforts to Aid the Rest Have Done So Much Harm and So Little Good* (Oxford University Press, 2006). The debate on effectiveness has not been limited to academic economists. Policy experts and journalists have also contributed to it. A thoughtful example of one such contribution is L. Polman, *War Games: The Story of Aid and War in Modern Times* (London: Viking, 2010). As for the debate on morality, see P. Singer, *The Life You Can Save: Acting Now to End World Poverty* (New York: Random House, 2009) and Thomas Nagel's review essay 'What Peter Singer Wants of You', LVII (5) *New York Review of Books* (2010) 24.

[12] See, for instance, SC Res. 1208 (1998) on the situation in refugee camps in Africa, in which the Council expressed its support 'for the inclusion in the United Nations Stand-by Arrangements of military and police units and personnel trained for humanitarian operations, as well as related equipment' (at para. 11). In favour of this trend is A. Donini, 'Asserting Humanitarianism in Peace-Maintenance', 4 *Global Governance* (1998) 81.

of international law only apply to states.[13] Privatisation also raises the questions of attribution of conduct which have been discussed in Chapter 3.

International law and humanitarian assistance

Uncertainty on the international law governing humanitarian assistance persists. One reason for this uncertainty is the situation-specific and fluid nature of state and institutional practice. Another reason is that different legal regimes can apply to humanitarian operations: international humanitarian, human rights, refugee and UN law – and to a lesser extent environmental law – are all part of the normative framework. International humanitarian law instruments contain various provisions on the delivery of humanitarian assistance in the context of an armed conflict. Human rights law is especially important as it accords protection to such rights as non-discrimination, the right to life and economic and social rights, all of which contribute to determining the scope of any such legal entitlement to humanitarian assistance as may exist.[14] International refugee law constitutes an important framework for the provision of humanitarian assistance to persons that come under one of the refugee definitions.[15] Furthermore, a process of fertilisation from the refugee area into the broader area of humanitarian relief has taken place, because refugees have traditionally been one of the main recipient groups of humanitarian assistance[16] and UNHCR has emerged as a leading operational actor in the

[13] D. Schindler gives the example of the principle of non-intervention, 'Humanitarian Assistance, Humanitarian Interference and International Law', in R. J. Macdonald (ed.), *Essays in Honour of Wang Tieya* (Dordrecht: Kluwer, 1994) 689 at 701. See also M. J. Domestici-Met, 'Aspects Juridiques Récents de l'Assistance Humanitaire', 35 AFDI (1989) 117; M. Bothe, 'Relief Actions: The Position of the Recipient State', in F. Kalshoven (ed.), *Assisting the Victims of Armed Conflict and Other Disasters* (Dordrecht: Martinus Nijhoff Publishers, 1989) 91 at 95–6; P. Macalister-Smith, 'Rights and Duties of the Agencies Involved in Providing Humanitarian Assistance and their Personnel in Armed Conflict', in Kalshoven, *ibid.*, at 99.

[14] On the right to receive humanitarian assistance, see references at note 55.

[15] Convention relating to the Status of Refugees (1951), 189 UNTS 137, and the Protocol to the Convention relating to the Status of Refugees (1967), 606 UNTS 267 (the 1951 Convention as modified by the Protocol will be hereinafter referred to as '1951 Refugee Convention'); Organisation of African Unity: 1969 Convention on the Specific Aspects of Refugee Problems in Africa (1969), 1000 UNTS 46 (hereinafter the OAU Refugee Convention).

[16] C. Skran, *Refugees in Inter-War Europe* (Oxford: Clarendon Press, 1995); B. E. Harrell-Bond, *Imposing Aid* (Oxford University Press, 1986) and, by the same author, 'The

humanitarian sphere. Another important category of displaced persons who are often beneficiaries of humanitarian assistance are internally displaced persons (IDPs). While the experience of displacement is common both to refugees and to IDPs, they are legally distinct groups. In particular, there is no specific treaty regime for IDPs as there is for refugees. Their status as IDPs is regulated by general international law, including most importantly human rights law, but increasingly also by an extensive body of soft law.[17] Interestingly, the provision of material assistance to IDPs is often carried out by the same institutions responsible for assisting refugees – in particular UNHCR.[18] Finally, the law of international organisation constitutes another source of legal regulation of humanitarian operations, shaped, in this area more than in most others, by implied powers and evolving institutional practice.[19]

Any agreement between an international organisation and a state concerning a programme of humanitarian assistance also constitutes a source of legal regulation for the provision of that assistance. In practice, there are numerous examples of humanitarian operations carried out in the absence of any specific agreement with the government concerned, or with agreements that are very basic. In some situations there is no government in effective control with which an agreement can be concluded. In addition, a state of regulatory uncertainty is sometimes perceived as advantageous, because it ensures a 'free hand' in the conduct of the humanitarian operation.[20]

Experience of Refugees as Recipients of Aid', in A. Ager (ed.), *Refugees: Perspectives on the Experience of Forced Migration* (London: Pinter, 1998) 136.

[17] G. S. Goodwin-Gill, *The Refugee in International Law* (3rd edn., Oxford: Clarendon Press, 2007) 481–8.

[18] On IDPs see: R. Cohen and F. Deng, *Masses in Flight: The Global Crisis of International Displacement* (Washington DC: The Brookings Institution, 1998); W. Kälin, 'Guiding Principles on Internal Displacement, Annotations' (Revised Edition), 38 *Studies in Transnational Legal Policy* (2008) 1; R. Cohen, 'The Guiding Principles on Internal Displacement: An Innovation in International Standard Setting', 10 *Global Governance* (2004) 459; S. T. E. Kleine-Ahlbrandt, *The Protection Gap in the International Protection of Internally Displaced Persons: the Case of Rwanda* (2nd edn., Geneva: Graduate Institute of International Studies, 2004); T. Weiss and D. Korn, *Internal Displacement – Conceptualization and its Consequences* (New York: Routledge, 2006).

[19] For instance on the evolution of the UNHCR mandate see Goodwin-Gill, *supra* note 18, at 8–18.

[20] Human Rights Watch, 'Failing the Internally Displaced. The UNDP Displaced Persons Program in Kenya' (New York, 1997) at 89–90.

Financial constraints are also a consideration. In its correspondence with Human Rights Watch, UNDP explained its failure to reach a 'formal agreement' with the government of Kenya in part 'because of the difficulty in reaching agreement with the Government' but also because of 'the uncertainty over funding that made it impossible for UNDP to enter into specific commitments that would have allowed it to call for reciprocal formal commitments from the Government'.[21]

Finally, an agreement may at times be deemed detrimental to the implementation of assistance programmes in those parts of the country that are under the effective control of insurgents.

In this respect, the practice developed by UNICEF's Operation Lifeline Sudan in the 1990s for the delivery of assistance to the civil war-ridden southern parts of the country is noteworthy. Central to such practice were tripartite agreements between the government, UNICEF, and representatives of the insurgents – the Sudan People's Liberation Army. Exporting this model to other situations may not be so easy due to the likely reluctance of governments to enter into agreements with insurgents in their territory.

As a result of the conflation of legal regimes, there are only a few examples of humanitarian assistance – such as that provided to prisoners of war – which are regulated by the clear-cut resort to one of the legal regimes and to its specific provisions and rules. The vast majority of humanitarian emergencies are, instead, characterised by elements that could warrant at least partial recourse to one or more of these regimes. In addition, there is a degree of conceptual fluidity with notions, categories and principles moving across these various legal regimes. For instance, the role of private actors, the problem of accountability of humanitarian agencies and the question of enforcement cut across the permeable boundaries between these legal regimes.

In order to determine the law that is applicable to the provision of humanitarian assistance in a given situation, a thorough analysis of the factual context is necessary. Some elements are of particular importance. To begin with, there is the cause of the humanitarian crisis – be it an international armed conflict, an internal armed conflict, a natural disaster or, more generally, government policies that constitute gross violation of human rights obligation. The place of delivery of the assistance must also be considered: is the assistance distributed

[21] *Ibid.* at 89 and 149.

in the country where the humanitarian emergency originates or is it delivered to persons who have crossed an international border? In addition, the consent of the government to the humanitarian operation is a material element for determining the question of the legality of the operation. Finally, the legal status of the beneficiaries has to be taken into account: everyone is entitled to respect for his or her human rights, but some categories of persons (for example refugees and prisoners of war) are entitled to the specific protection granted to them under special instruments and provisions.

The Responsibility to Protect

Questions pertaining to the legality of the use of force do not normally arise in development operations, but they may do so in relief operations. The Francophone legal literature distinguishes between *intervention humanitaire* and *intervention d'humanité*, that is: the non-forcible provision of humanitarian assistance (save for the deployment of such security forces as may be necessary to protect the safety of humanitarian personnel) from the doctrine of humanitarian intervention *stricto sensu*, namely the use of force on humanitarian grounds.[22] An intervention humanitaire may escalate into an intervention d'humanité if force is used on such a scale as to engage the international law principles on the use of force.

The concept of Responsibility to Protect emerged as an attempt to breathe fresh air into these notions, and to approach humanitarian crises from what purported to be a new angle. Its development goes back to the aftermath of NATO's controversial military intervention in Kosovo in 1999. In response to a call from the then UN Secretary General, Kofi Annan, for consensus on humanitarian intervention, the government of Canada, together with a group of major foundations, established the International Commission on Intervention and State Sovereignty. In their 2001 report *The Responsibility to Protect*, this International Commission set out the principle that, while the state remains responsible for the protection of its people, when the 'population is suffering serious harm, as a result of internal war, insurgency, repression or state failure, and the state in question is unwilling or unable to halt or avert it, the principle of non-intervention yields to the

[22] E. Spiry, 'Interventions Humanitaires et Interventions d'Humanité: La Pratique Française face au Droit International', 102 RGDIP (1998) 407; M. Bettati, 'Un Droit d'Ingerence?', 95 RGDIP (1991) 639.

international responsibility to protect'.[23] The report suggested three pillars for protection: to *prevent*, by addressing the causes of internal conflicts; to *react*, by using political, economic and military sanctions before turning to Security Council authorised military intervention; and to *rebuild*, by establishing good governance. Secretary General Kofi Annan considered the Responsibility to Protect a new mechanism to ensure the accountability of states to their citizens and to each other.[24]

The Responsibility to Protect was adopted at the 2005 World Summit,[25] with the proviso that it should not extend beyond four situations: genocide, war crimes, ethnic cleansing and crimes against humanity. UN Secretary General Ban Ki-Moon has argued that expanding the principle to cover other calamities 'would undermine the 2005 consensus and stretch the concept beyond recognition or operational utility',[26] since 'today, the responsibility to protect is a concept, not yet a policy; an aspiration, not yet a reality'.[27] On 28 April 2006, the Security Council unanimously adopted Resolution 1674 on the Protection of Civilians in Armed Conflict, which reaffirmed the provisions of the World Summit Outcome Document.[28]

In 2009 Secretary General Ban Ki-Moon adopted a report on the implementation of the Responsibility to Protect,[29] based on a three-pillar analysis. The first pillar of the Responsibility to Protect is the

[23] See International Commission on Intervention and State Sovereignty, *The Responsibility to Protect: Report of the International Commission on Intervention and Sovereignty* (Ottawa: International Development Centre, 2001) XI.

[24] UN Secretary-General Kofi Annan, 'In Larger Freedom: Towards Development, Security and Human Rights for all', UN Doc. A/59/2005, 21 March 2005. See: C. Stahn, 'Responsibility to Protect: Political Rhetoric or Emerging Legal Norm', 101(1) AJIL (2007) 99; G. Molier, 'Humanitarian Intervention and the Responsibility to Protect After 9/11', 53 *Netherlands Journal of International Law* (2006) 37; L. Boisson de Chazournes, 'Responsibility to Protect: Reflecting Solidarity', in R. Wolfrum and C. Kojima (eds.), *Solidarity; A Structural Principle of International Law* (Heidelberg: Springer, 2010) 93.

[25] '2005 World Summit Outcome', GA Res. 60/1 (2005).

[26] UN Secretary-General Ban Ki-Moon's speech at an event on 'Responsible Sovereignty: International Cooperation for a Changed World', in Berlin, 15 July 2008, UN Doc. SG/SM/11071.

[27] Notes by the Secretary General, UN General Assembly, 2 December 2004, UN Doc. A/59/565.

[28] SC Res. 1674 (2006), para. 4.

[29] Report of UN Secretary General Ban Ki-Moon, 'Implementing the Responsibility to Protect', 2009 (UN Doc. A/63/677). On 7 October 2009, the General Assembly adopted

responsibility of the state itself. The second pillar focuses on the responsibility of the international community, which may intervene subject to the consent of the state. When the sovereign authority is 'weak, divided or uncertain about how to proceed, lacks the capacity to protect its population effectively, or faces an armed opposition that is threatening or committing crimes and violations relating to the responsibility to protect, measures under pillar two could play a critical role'.[30] Assistance under the second pillar would include aiding disadvantaged groups in a way that 'enhances equality and social justice, raises their education levels and increases their opportunities for meaningful political participation'.[31] The third pillar addresses responsibility to take collective action through the Security Council by non-forcible measures, such as a reference to the International Criminal Court or the adoption of diplomatic sanctions. Recourse to forcible measures is the last resort.

Despite the great resonance it had, the notion of the Responsibility to Protect has not changed the law on humanitarian intervention. Nor has it changed the principles governing multilateral and unilateral relief operations when no force is used. As a legal doctrine the Responsibility to Protect does little more than re-state well-established principles. As an aspirational statement, it is too cautious and vague.

Another example of aspirational soft law is the Millennium Development Goals, which have a bearing on the area of development rather than relief. There are eight major development goals including in poverty, hunger, education and health contained in the Millennium Declaration, which was adopted by 189 nations and signed by 147 heads of state and governments during the UN Millennium Summit in September 2000.[32]

The consent of the host state

The project on the Responsibility to Protect reaffirms the requirement of the consent of the host state to relief operations. But is this requirement really part of the law? The *Nicaragua* decision is the starting point for answering this question, as it is still the only case in which

resolution 63/308, reaffirming the principle, taking note of the Secretary General's implementation report and debates held on the 23, 24 and 28 July and deciding to continue consideration of the topic.

[30] *Ibid*. at para. 29. [31] *Ibid*. at para. 43. [32] UN Doc. A/Res/55/2.

the International Court of Justice considered the legal aspects of the provision of humanitarian assistance in armed conflict.

The Court found that the United States had violated the customary law prohibition of the threat or use of force, and the principle of non-intervention in the affairs of another state.[33] In particular, it held that the 'support given by the United States, up to the end of September 1984, to the military and paramilitary activities of the *contras* in Nicaragua, by financial support, training, supply of weapons, intelligence and logistic support'[34] was in breach of the principle of non-intervention. As regards US support to the *contras* after October 1984, the Court took into account the decision of the Congress on that date to allocate funds to the *contras* only for 'humanitarian assistance'.[35] Under US legislation, 'humanitarian assistance' was defined as 'the provision of food, clothing, medicine, and other humanitarian assistance, and it does not include the provision of weapons, weapons systems, ammunition, or other equipment, vehicles, or material which can be used to inflict serious bodily harm or death'.[36] Nicaragua had alleged that the US had actually continued to help the *contras* even after October 1984 by providing intelligence information. The Court found that it did not have clear evidence on this claim and decided to 'limit itself to a declaration as to how the law applies in this respect'.[37]

The Court observed that:

'... there can be no doubt that the provision of strictly humanitarian aid to persons or forces in another country, whatever their political affiliations or objectives, cannot be regarded as unlawful intervention, or as in any other way contrary to international law ...

... if the provision of humanitarian assistance is to escape condemnation as an intervention in the internal affairs, not only must it be limited to the purposes hallowed in the practice of the International Committee of the Red Cross (ICRC), namely "to prevent and alleviate human suffering" and "to protect life and health and to ensure respect for the human being", it must also, and above all, be given without discrimination to all in need.'[38]

The characteristics of humanitarian assistance are more specifically defined as those 'indicated in the first and second of the fundamental principles declared by the Twentieth International Conference of the

[33] *Case Concerning Military and Paramilitary Activities in and Against Nicaragua (Nicaragua v. United States of America)*, ICJ Reports 14 (1986), at para. 292.

[34] *Ibid.* at para. 242. [35] *Ibid.* [36] *Ibid.* at para. 243. [37] *Ibid.*

[38] *Ibid.* at paras. 242–3.

Red Cross, that is: the prevention and alleviation of human suffering wherever it may be found; the protection of life and health; the ensurance of respect for the human being; and the promotion of mutual understanding, friendship, co-operation and lasting peace amongst all peoples'.[39] These purposes appear vague at a closer examination. The last principle in particular seems to broaden the spectrum of activities designated as 'humanitarian' beyond the proper meaning of this term.

The Court characterised the conflict between the *contras* and the government of Nicaragua as an armed conflict not of an international character, but added that the actions of the US in and against Nicaragua fell under the legal rules relating to international conflicts. However, since 'the minimum rules applicable to international and to non-international conflicts are identical', the Court did not think it necessary 'to address the question whether those actions must be looked at in the context of the rules which operate for the one or for the other category of conflict'.[40] The legal basis for the Court's statement on the principles governing the provision of humanitarian assistance in armed conflict was therefore Common Article 3.

On the basis of the *Nicaragua* analysis, *Oppenheim's International Law* summarises the legal position on the provision of humanitarian assistance as follows:

> '... the objection [based on the principles of non-intervention and on the prohibition on the use of force] to humanitarian intervention does not apply to humanitarian assistance to those in need in another state; even in a situation of conflict within a state, humanitarian assistance will not constitute intervention, so long as it is given (or perhaps is at least available) without discrimination between the parties to the conflict.'[41]

Compared with the *Nicaragua* decision, the position emerging from the body of UN law on this matter – and more specifically the resolutions of the General Assembly on humanitarian questions – seems cautious. For example, the General Assembly has asserted that, in delivering humanitarian assistance, 'the sovereignty, territorial integrity and national unity of states must be fully respected in accordance with the Charter of the United Nations' and that, as a consequence, 'humanitarian assistance should be provided with the consent of the affected country and in principle on the basis of an appeal by the

[39] *Ibid.* [40] *Ibid.* at para. 219.

[41] R. Jennings and A. Watts, *Oppenheim's International Law* (9th edn., London: Longman, 1992) 444.

affected country'.[42] Hence, the possibility of delivering humanitarian assistance without the consent of the interested state has been ruled out by the General Assembly, at least as long as this assistance comes from states or governmental organisations – a position which, insofar as it also applies to armed conflict, contrasts with the Court's decision in *Nicaragua*.

Similarly, with regard to Responsibility to Protect, SC Res. 1674 (2006) and SC Res. 1894 (2009) on the protection of civilians in armed conflict, both reaffirm the purposes and principles of the UN Charter including territorial integrity and sovereignty of all states. Moreover, while SC Res. 1706 (2006), expanding UNMIS's mandate to cover deployment into Darfur, referred to the World Summit Outcome and to SC Res 1674, it also affirmed the territorial integrity of Sudan and invited the Sudanese government's consent. By contrast, SC Res. 1769 (2007), authorising under Chapter VII the deployment of a joint UN–AU force (UNAMID) to Darfur, referred to neither Responsibility to Protect nor the World Summit Outcome and again reaffirmed the territorial integrity of Sudan.

Was the Court right in saying that humanitarian assistance provided without the consent of the state in the context of an armed conflict cannot be regarded as contrary to international law? Or does the insistence of the General Assembly on the consent of the affected state express the lowest common denominator that states have agreed to? At first, the normative strength of the General Assembly resolutions may appear quite strong, particularly in light of the fact that these resolutions were passed with near unanimity.

The Court's decision on the question of the normative status of General Assembly resolutions has a more cautious nuance in *Legality of the Threat or Use of Nuclear Weapons*[43] than in *Nicaragua*.[44] In the *Nuclear Weapons* case the Court

[42] GA Res. 46/182, 19 December 1991; GA Res. 43/131, 8 December 1988; GA Res. 45/100, 29 January 1991; GA Res. 51/194, 10 February 1997. See also the Agreed Conclusion 1998/1 in the Report of the Economic and Social Council for the Year 1998, Chapter VII 'Humanitarian Affairs Segment' (UN Doc. A/53/3). In addition, one of the most cited documents of international law of the 'new world order' era, a report submitted by the Secretary General to the General Assembly in 1992 (GA, Report of the SG on the Work of the Organisation, *An Agenda for Peace. Preventive Diplomacy, Peace-making and Peace-keeping*, UN Doc. A/47/277 – S/24111, 17 June 1992) affirms that 'the UN will need to respect the sovereignty of the State … and humanitarian assistance must be provided in accordance with the principles of humanity, neutrality, and impartiality' (at 12–13).

[43] *Legality of the Threat or Use of Nuclear Weapons* (GA Request), Advisory Opinion, ICJ Reports (1996) 226, (hereinafter '*Nuclear Weapons*') at para. 70ff.

[44] *Nicaragua*, *supra* note 34 at paras. 99–100.

concluded that the resolutions on nuclear weapons had often been adopted 'with substantial numbers of negative votes and abstentions' and that they fell short of 'establishing the existence of an *opinio juris* on the illegality of the use of such weapons'.[45]

The pronouncement of the Court, on the other hand, appears weaker not only because of the lack of a doctrine of *stare decisis* in international law, but also because the Court did not really explain the reasons for its conclusion. Instead, it resorted to a well-established rhetorical device for eluding controversial issues: to pretend that no such controversy exists asserting that 'there was no doubt' on the view it was taking. In actual fact the doubts are still significant.

Nevertheless, the Court's conclusion can find a strong basis in the terms of Article 1 of the Geneva Conventions which oblige state parties 'to ensure respect' for the Conventions 'in all circumstances'. The effect of this provision, combined with others that confer a right to humanitarian assistance on various categories of individuals in armed conflict,[46] is that, notwithstanding their rights under the principle of non-intervention, states may be under an obligation to allow the consignment of relief supplies in certain circumstances. Although the Court did not refer to Article 1 of the Geneva Conventions in the passages on humanitarian assistance, it had emphasised the importance of this provision in the section that preceded those passages dedicated to the analysis of the applicable law.[47] In the context of a humanitarian crisis during an armed conflict, a state's obligation to ensure respect for the Geneva Conventions may entail the duty to grant access to providers of humanitarian assistance. In particular, when the humanitarian crisis is such as to engage those 'elementary considerations of humanity'[48] which the Court had highlighted in a previous case and which are the linchpin of Common Article 3, the obligation to ensure respect is, surely, at its highest.

45 *Nuclear Weapons*, *supra* note 44 at para. 71.

46 The categories are: aliens in the territory of a party to the conflict (Art. 38(1), Geneva IV); population in an occupied territory (Art. 59, Geneva IV; Art. 70, Protocol I; Art. 18(2), Protocol II); and protected persons in occupied territories (Art. 62, Geneva IV). Schindler, *supra* note 14 at 689–701. Bothe, *supra* note 14 at 91.

47 *Nicaragua*, *supra* note 34 at para. 220.

48 *Corfu Channel Case (UK v. Albania)*, Judgment (Merits), ICJ Reports (1949) 4 at 22. 'Elementary considerations of humanity' were the basis for the finding in that case that Albania had been under an obligation to notify other states of the existence of a minefield in its territorial sea. The Martens Clause also contains a similar reference to 'principles of humanity and dictates of public conscience' (e.g. Art. 1(2), Protocol I).

The strongest counter-argument to this analysis is Article 18 of Protocol II, which provides that, in the event of 'undue hardship owing to a lack of supplies' essential for the survival of the civilian population, 'relief actions for the civilian population which are of an exclusively humanitarian and impartial nature and which are conducted without any adverse distinction shall be undertaken *subject to the consent of the High Contracting Party concerned*' (emphasis added).[49] Protocol II is meant to advance the protection of victims of non-international armed conflict, but, in this respect at least, its terms are less progressive than those of Common Article 3 as interpreted by the International Court of Justice in *Nicaragua*.

Outside an armed conflict, the terms of the argument about the requirement of consent are different. As the ILC Special Rapporteur on the Protection of Persons in the Event of Disasters observed, however, the position 'may be evolving towards greater recognition of a positive duty on affected States to request assistance, at least where the domestic response capacity is overwhelmed by a disaster'.[50] A duty to request assistance is not tantamount to a duty to grant access, although it could be argued that, where the state breaches its duty by failing to request assistance, a non-forcible humanitarian operation may be a permissible countermeasure.

The position on the requirement of consent from the host state to a relief operation can be summarised as follows:

1. In the context of an international armed conflict, the provision of humanitarian assistance without the consent of the affected state is not in breach of international law – and, in particular, of the principle of non-intervention – so long as it is 'truly' humanitarian in nature (i.e. having regard to the nature, purpose and modalities of the assistance that is provided).
2. In the context of a non-international armed conflict, the consent of the affected state to the provision of external humanitarian assistance may be required under Article 18, Protocol II to the Geneva Conventions, although the International Court of Justice in *Nicaragua* may have taken a different view.
3. In the vast range of situations in which humanitarian crises occur outside an armed conflict, both natural and man-made disasters, things are less clear. Developments in the area of humanitarian

[49] See also Art. 3(2) of Protocol II which stresses that 'nothing in this Protocol shall be invoked as a justification for intervening, directly or indirectly, for any reason whatever, in the armed conflict or in the internal or external affairs' of the state.

[50] Memorandum by the Secretariat, 'Protection of Persons in the Event of Disasters' (2007) UN Doc. A/CN.4/590, para. 57.

> intervention are to be watched closely. Indeed, if it is true, as some authors argue, that international law is evolving towards the recognition of a right of humanitarian intervention,[51] this should lead a fortiori to the recognition of the right to mount a humanitarian operation that does not involve the use of force in the absence of the consent of the territorial state. It would also follow that this right could be exercised by a state unilaterally or collectively through international institutions.

On this analysis, therefore, the type of disaster determines the extent of the duties of the affected state and, in particular, the question of consent. According to the Institut de Droit International, across these different situations a minimum common denominator exists. Its resolution on humanitarian assistance provides that in all disasters '[a]ffected states are under the obligation not arbitrarily and unjustifiably to reject a *bona fide* offer exclusively intended to provide humanitarian assistance or to refuse access to the victims'.[52]

Whether the UN has the same rights and obligations as states in this area is a different question. It is conceivable, for example, that the *Nicaragua* rule be limited to states, and that for UN relief operations, even in the context of an international armed conflict, the consent of the host state be an absolute requirement. It is not immediately clear, however, what the basis for such a distinction would be, and it was quite appropriate for the Institut de Droit International to refer to duties of 'the assisting State or organisation' in respect of humanitarian assistance.[53] Whatever the rights and obligations of the UN in an ordinary situation, it is beyond dispute that a decision of the Security Council under Chapter VII can dispose of the requirement of consent.

At times, however, the Security Council prefers to reiterate the principle that a particular intervention is subject to the consent of the host state (e.g. SC Res. 1706 (2006) on the situation in Sudan authorising the deployment of peacekeeping troops to Darfur and inviting the consent of the government).

A right to humanitarian assistance?

As discussed, various categories of individuals have a right to humanitarian assistance in an armed conflict.[54] Outside an armed conflict the

[51] See C. Greenwood, 'Humanitarian Intervention: The Case of Kosovo', 10 *Finnish Yearbook of International Law* (1999) 141 at 161–71, and A. Cassese, '*Ex Iniuria Ius Oritur*: Are we Moving towards the International Legitimation of Forcible Humanitarian Counter-measures in the World Community?', 10 EJIL (1999) 23.

[52] Article VIII(1), *supra* note 8. [53] *Ibid.* Art. V(3–4). [54] See *supra* note 47.

1951 Refugee Convention provides that refugees lawfully staying in a country should be accorded 'the same treatment with respect to public relief and assistance as … nationals' (Article 23). The Convention on the Rights of the Child obliges states to 'take appropriate measures to ensure' that a refugee child or a child asylum-seeker 'shall … receive appropriate protection and humanitarian assistance' (Article 22). Proposals for a general right to receive humanitarian assistance do not seem to have gone far.[55]

The First Report of the ILC in 2007 noted members' discussion and disagreement on a right to humanitarian assistance.[56] Some members, concerned about sovereignty and non-intervention, opposed the existence of a right that implies a duty on the affected state to accept assistance;[57] others supported the right, presumably belonging to other states or NGOs, to provide assistance coupled with an obligation, incumbent on the affected state, to seek assistance where necessary.[58] Some members noted that victims have, individually, a right to humanitarian assistance, as this is implicit in international humanitarian law and international human rights law, but that such a right is typically exercised collectively.[59]

In spite of the absence of a general provision to this effect it can be argued that the right to receive humanitarian assistance derives from the protection afforded to such fundamental rights as the right to life, the right to an adequate standard of living, including adequate food, clothing and housing, the right to be free from hunger, the right to the enjoyment of the highest attainable standard of physical and mental health.[60] If such a right does exist as a matter of international human rights law, states not only have a duty to provide humanitarian

[55] See Valencia-Ospina, First Report, *supra* note 2 at paras. 54–5. See also: M. J. Domestici-Met, 'Propos sur le droit à l'assistance', in M. Bettati, M. J. Domestici-Met and G. J. Tanja (eds.), *Law in Humanitarian Crises*, Vol. II: *Access to Victims: Right to Intervene or Right to Receive Humanitarian Assistance?* (Luxembourg: Office for Official Publications of the European Union, 1995) 125; Domestici-Met, *supra* note 14 at 122–3; R. J. Dupuy, 'L'assistance humanitaire comme droit de l'homme contre la souveraineté de l'Etat' in Kalshoven, *supra* note 14, 27.

[56] ILC, 'First Report', *supra* note 2 at paras. 241–6. [57] *Ibid.* at para. 242.

[58] *Ibid.* at para. 243. [59] *Ibid.* at para. 245.

[60] Special Rapporteur Valencia-Ospina suggested that a right to humanitarian assistance may be implicit in human rights law (First Report, *supra* note 2 at para. 54). Article 6, International Covenant on Civil and Political Rights (1966), 999 UNTS 171 and Arts. 11–12, International Covenant and Economic, Social and Cultural Rights (1966), 999 UNTS 3 have been invoked in support of this proposition. On the social dimension of the right to life and the positive obligations of states under it, see Human Rights Committee, General Comment 14 (Art. 6).

assistance to their own population, but they might also be under a duty to allow external actors to provide it, if they are not capable of fulfilling their obligation.[61] Article 11 of the International Covenant on Economic, Social and Cultural Rights (ICESCR) lends some support to this view by affirming that in order to implement the fundamental right to be free from hunger state parties will act individually and through international cooperation.[62]

Aside from the question of the basis and scope of the right to humanitarian assistance, a rights-based approach to the protection of victims of disasters finds some support in state practice.[63] What this means in practice is not however always clear.

UN resolutions

The General Assembly has not limited itself to resolutions of a general nature on humanitarian assistance. It has also developed an extensive practice on specific situations.[64] The analysis of this practice of the General Assembly, and also, in the fewer cases in which it intervened, of the Security Council, can cast some light on the international law on humanitarian assistance as has been concretely applied to particular crises. However, these situation-specific resolutions do not offer a cohesive picture. While the vast majority of them laid great emphasis on the importance of the consent of states, in some instances they have mentioned the duty of the state to allow external humanitarian assistance. For example, the General Assembly emphasised the need to secure 'humanitarian access' to the civilian population in Kosovo during the 1999 crisis.[65] Resolutions on the crisis in Sudan stressed the importance of 'the full involvement of the Government of Sudan' in

[61] This argument is developed by Domestici-Met, *supra* note 14 at 122. See also: Draft Principles of International Relief in Natural Disaster Situations in R. J. Hardcastle and A. T. L. Chua, 'Humanitarian Assistance: towards a Right of Access to Victims of Natural Disasters', 325 Int. Rev. R.C. (1998) 589.

[62] Article. 11(2) ICECSR. See also Art. 2(1) of the ICESCR and General Comment 12 (XX Session, 1999) adopted by the Committee on Economic, Social and Cultural Rights (UN Doc. E/C.12/1999/5).

[63] Valencia-Ospina, Second Report, *supra* note 2 at para. 8.

[64] See, for example, GA Res. 57/148, 16 December 2002; GA Res. 57/149, 16 December 2002; GA Res. 59/216, 22 December 2004; GA Res. 29/219, 22 December 2004; GA Res. 60/216, 22 December 2005; GA Res. 61/218, 20 December 2006; GA Res. 62/91, 17 December 2007; GA Res. 62/102, 17 December 2007; GA Res. 63/136, 11 December 2008; GA Res. 63/125, 11 December 2008; GA Res. 64/74, 7 December 2009.

[65] GA Res. 53/164, 25 February 1999, at paras. 10 and 17.

the conduct of the UN's main humanitarian operation there, Operation Lifeline Sudan, reiterating that humanitarian activities 'should operate within the principle of national sovereignty'.[66]

In its resolutions, the Security Council has often called for parties to the conflict to ensure the 'safe and unhindered access for humanitarian organisation to those in need'.[67] In a few cases, the Security Council has included these clauses in resolutions taken under Chapter VII. For instance, it demanded that Iraq 'allow immediate access by international humanitarian organisations to all those in need of assistance in all parts of Iraq and make available all necessary facilities for their operations'.[68]

On occasion, the Council has included a clause in its resolution obliging a state to cooperate with humanitarian agencies, including NGOs. For instance, resolution 687 of 1991 bound Iraq, 'in furtherance of its commitment to facilitate the repatriation of all Kuwaiti and third country nationals', to 'extend all necessary co-operation to the ICRC, providing lists of such persons, facilitating the access of the ICRC to all such persons wherever located or detained and facilitating the search by the ICRC for those Kuwaiti and third country nationals still unaccounted for'. Resolution 1199 of 1998 concerning the situation in Kosovo formulated this obligation in more general terms: the Federal Republic of Yugoslavia was asked to 'facilitate, in agreement with the UNHCR and the International Committee of the Red Cross, the safe return of refugees and displaced persons to their homes'.

In resolution 1244 on Kosovo, acting under Chapter VII the Security Council emphasised that the Federal Republic of Yugoslavia had to allow 'unimpeded access to Kosovo by humanitarian aid organisations and to co-operate with such organisations so as to ensure the fast

[66] GA Res. 53/1, 11 January 1999. Operation Lifeline Sudan was in principle supervised by the General Assembly, which never specified terms of reference.

[67] For the practice until 1990, see B. G. Ramcharan, 'The Security Council and Humanitarian Emergencies', 9 *Netherlands Quarterly of Human Rights* (1991) 19. Examples from more recent practice are: SC Res. 1231 (1999) on Sierra Leone; SC Res. 1233 (1999) on Guinea-Bissau; SC Res. 1234 and 1258 (1999) on the Democratic Republic of Congo; and SC Res. 1265 (1999), which did not deal with a specific situation but was adopted in a response to reports of the Secretary General on the causes of conflict in Africa and on humanitarian assistance (respectively UN Doc. S/1998/318 and UN Doc. S/1998/883).

[68] SC Res. 688 (1991).

and effective delivery of international aid'.[69] With these resolutions the Council has strengthened the already important role assigned by international humanitarian law to NGOs (the ICRC and other 'impartial humanitarian organisations').

A widely recognised milestone in the practice of the Security Council in the field of humanitarian assistance was resolution 794 of 1992 on Somalia, which established Operation Restore Hope. The Council determined that 'the magnitude of the human tragedy caused by the conflict in Somalia, further exacerbated by the obstacles being created to the distribution of humanitarian assistance, constitutes a threat to international peace and security'.[70] The use of force by its members for avowedly humanitarian purposes was allowed by the Council.[71] Somalia is an example of the escalation from a humanitarian operation to a forcible intervention on humanitarian grounds.

The distinction between natural and man-made disasters

The ILC project adopts a definition of disaster that, quite rightly, is not premised on the distinction between natural and man-made disasters.[72] Rather, it draws a distinction between armed conflict and other types of disaster, leaving the former out of the scope of the project. The basis for this distinction is not the intensity of human suffering, but it still rests on solid legal foundations given that armed conflict is subject to a special set of international law principles and rules.

In its resolution on humanitarian assistance, the Institut de Droit International preferred a different approach distinguishing between disasters of natural origin, 'man-made disasters of technological origin' and disasters 'caused by armed conflicts or violence'.[73]

Even outside armed conflicts, the distinction between man-made and natural disasters is unhelpful because '[d]isasters generally arise

[69] SC Res. 1244 (1999). Earlier the Security Council had demanded that the Federal Republic of Yugoslavia 'allow free and unimpeded access to humanitarian organisations and supplies' – SC Res. 1199 (1998).

[70] See also para. 10 of that resolution in which the Council authorised 'the Secretary-General and Member States ... to use all necessary means to establish as soon as possible a secure environment for humanitarian relief operations in Somalia'.

[71] C. M. Pontecorvo, 'Somalia e Nazioni Unite', in P. Picone (ed.), *Interventi delle Nazioni Unite e Diritto Internazionale* (Padova : Cedam, 1995) 201; J. M. Sorel, 'La Somalie et les Nations Unies', 38 AFDI (1992) 61 at 74.

[72] Valencia-Ospina, First Report, *supra* note 2 at paras. 46–9.

[73] Article I(2), *supra* note 7.

from a complex set of factors, making virtually impossible any effort to identify a single sufficient cause'.[74] Nevertheless, the tendency to represent all disasters as 'acts of God' is deep-seated in humanitarian practice, and reflected in much existing soft law on humanitarian assistance. Yet, it has been conclusively shown that there is a nexus between the widespread commission of human rights violations and the occurrence of such apparently 'God-sent' humanitarian emergencies as famines.[75]

Neutrality and impartiality

The resolutions of the General Assembly and of the Security Council, and the decision of the ICJ in *Nicaragua* have one element in common: they view neutrality and impartiality as essential principles of humanitarian assistance.

For instance, GA Res. 46/182, 19 December 1991, which contains an annex on the Guiding Principles of Humanitarian Assistance, asserts that such assistance must be provided in accordance with the principles of 'humanity, impartiality and neutrality'. In *Nicaragua*, the Court had affirmed that the characteristics of humanitarian aid 'were indicated in the first and second of the fundamental principles declared by the Twentieth International Conference of the Red Cross', which included the giving of aid 'without discrimination to all in need in Nicaragua, not merely to the *contras* and their dependents'.[76]

Neutrality and impartiality can be traced to the practice and the Statutes of the ICRC,[77] and have been subsequently absorbed in international humanitarian law instruments. The original 'ethical' rationale for neutrality and impartiality has been at least in part superseded by a more 'pragmatic' rationale. These principles are now seen as an indispensable pre-condition for humanitarian organisations to be allowed access to those who need assistance in a conflict and, perhaps more importantly, for them to ensure the safety of their own staff.

The security of humanitarian personnel has become a real concern given the rise in the numbers of UN and NGO officials killed in situations of conflict: 198 UN aid workers were killed between 1992 and 2000, and this figure would be

[74] Valencia-Ospina, Second Report, *supra* note 2 at para. 49.

[75] A. Sen, *Poverty and Famines: An Essay on Entitlement and Deprivation* (Oxford: Clarendon Press, 1981). See also A. de Waal, *Famine Crimes; Politics and the Disaster Relief Industry in Africa* (Oxford: James Currey, 1997).

[76] *Nicaragua*, *supra* note 34 at para. 243.

[77] See Chapter I.2(d) and I.4 of Statute of ICRC.

much larger if NGO workers were included.[78] Such concerns have been partly addressed with the adoption of the Convention on the Safety of United Nations and Associated Personnel.[79] Under the Statute of the International Criminal Court (Article 8, 2, b), it is a war crime intentionally to direct 'attacks against personnel, installations, material, units or vehicles involved in a humanitarian assistance or peacekeeping mission in accordance with the Charter of the United Nations, as long as they are entitled to the protection given to civilians or civilian objects under the international law of armed conflict'.

When applied to humanitarian action, neutrality and impartiality are complementary terms: 'neutrality' requires an obligation not to take sides in a conflict (a duty 'not to do'), whereas 'impartiality' requires that, 'when it comes to action', humanitarian organisations intervene without giving any preference to any party to the conflict.

This is the analysis of the two terms that is offered by Denise Plattner.[80] Etymologically, 'neutrality' is the quality of an entity that is neither 'male' nor 'feminine' and, by extension, that is 'neither one thing nor the other'. 'Impartiality' is literally the attribute of an entity or person who is 'not party' to a particular question, dispute or contract.

Humanitarian organisations are obliged not to take sides in the conflict, which entails a duty not to declare allegiance or support to, or to make public statements in favour of, any party. Moreover, they are obliged to act without discriminating against any of the parties to the conflict. Neutrality and impartiality also encompass an obligation to determine the beneficiaries of the humanitarian assistance on no grounds other than their need, and the attendant obligation to assist individuals in proportion to such need.[81] This approach is also consistent with the meanings given by the ICRC to the terms 'neutrality' and 'impartiality'.

At the 25th International Conference of the Red Cross in October 1986, it was concluded that humanitarian action ought to make 'no discrimination as to nationality, race, religious beliefs, class or political opinions. It endeavours to relieve the suffering of individuals, being guided solely by their needs, and

78 'The Dangers of Trying to Help', *The Economist*, 10 March 2001.

79 GA Res. 49/59, 9 December 1994.

80 D. Plattner, 'ICRC Neutrality and Neutrality in Humanitarian Assistance', 311 Int. Rev. R.C. (1996) 161 at 165. See, also, M. Weller, 'The Relativity of Humanitarian Neutrality and Impartiality', American Society of International Law - Proceedings of the 91st Annual Conference.

81 J. Pictet, 'Les principes fondamentaux de la Croix-Rouge et la Paix', 746 Int. Rev. R. C. (1984) 79.

to give priority to the most urgent cases of distress'. On neutrality, on the other hand, it was stated that: 'In order to continue to enjoy the confidence of all, the Movement may not take sides in hostilities or engage at any time in controversies of a political, racial, religious or ideological nature.'[82]

Since the 1980s, the practice of humanitarian neutrality and impartiality has come under severe criticism from some NGOs. For example, Médecins sans Frontières (MSF) has argued that 'impartial humanitarian aid distributed without discrimination openly and publicly to both parties is not appropriate if one of the parties does not simply aim at defeating the other, but at exterminating' a population.[83] Numerous experiences in so-called complex humanitarian emergencies confirm these concerns.[84] In Rwanda not only did the UN decide to disengage in the first few weeks of the genocide, it also repeatedly called for a cease-fire in order to allow negotiations between the parties and to facilitate the delivery of humanitarian assistance.[85] As has been correctly remarked, 'calling for a cease-fire is a political act' especially if it occurs in the midst of a genocide.[86] In addition, the Secretary General stressed the fact that the UN had to respect neutrality and support the lawful authorities in the country, although a number of international NGOs had established in early April 1994 that acts of genocide were being perpetrated in Rwanda.[87] Finally, the appearances of neutrality were preserved by misrepresenting the Rwandan genocide as 'calamitous circumstances', 'convulsions', and as the result of a 'frenzy of massacres' and of 'unruly elements responsible for the massacres'[88] – formulae

[82] See also the ICRC Statutes of 24 June 1998 (in 324 Int. Rev. R.C. (1998)) and Plattner, *supra* note 81 at 168.

[83] Domestici-Met, *supra* note 14 at 127.

[84] African Rights, 'Humanitarianism Unbound?', Discussion Paper No. 5 (London, November 1994).

[85] On this, see E. David, 'Aspects juridiques de la responsabilité des différents acteurs dans les évènements du Rwanda (avril–juillet 1994)', Commission d'enquête parlementaire du Sénat concernant les évènements du Rwanda, in Belgian Parliamentary Documents (Doc. Parl.), Sénat, 1997–98, 1–611/13, 6 December 1997, Annexe 6, 6–24.

[86] African Rights, *supra* note 85 at 32.

[87] Secretary General's Report to the SC of 20 April 1994 (UN Doc. S/1994/470). On the Rwandan genocide, see African Rights, *Rwanda: Death, Despair and Defiance* (2nd edn., London, 1995); Human Rights Watch/Federation Internationale des Ligues des Droits de l' Homme (FIDH), *Leave None to Tell the Story: Genocide in Rwanda* (1999) at 625–8. On Rwanda, see the Report of the Independent Commission of Inquiry appointed by the UN (1999).

[88] Human Rights Watch/FIDH, *supra* note 88. See, for example, the report of the Secretary General presented to the Security Council on 13 May 1994, more than one month after the beginning of the genocide (UN Doc. S/1994/565).

which disguised the genocidal nature of the killings. It is one thing to claim neutrality in the face of generic massacres, quite another to do so in the face of genocide. Similarly, as noted by David Keen and Ken Wilson, 'relief organisations have tended to conceptualise famines in terms of food shortages and needs, and accordingly to construct relief operations as logistical exercises. However, effective relief in conflict-related famines depends on understanding the relationship between aid and the dynamics of conflict'.[89]

Weller has observed that, in order to analyse humanitarian neutrality and impartiality, it is necessary to take into account the different legal character of these principles, and the relativity of their content deriving from the context and from the specific regulation of the operation or the organisation.[90] While bearing this in mind, the case that humanitarian neutrality and impartiality can have dramatic unintended consequences remains compelling.[91] A neutral and impartial humanitarian operation will often allow material assistance to end up in the hands of the government or the non-state actor responsible for systematic violations of human rights and humanitarian law. In addition to the diversion of aid to a non-humanitarian purpose, the distribution of aid through the authorities in control of the territory – a requirement frequently imposed by governments and insurgents to grant access to the humanitarian organisations – poses a serious problem where the authorities make aid available on a discriminatory basis. Humanitarian operations can also enhance 'the legitimacy of the controlling authority', be it an insurgent rebel group or the government of the country, regardless of the widespread violations of human rights and humanitarian law that it may be committing.[92] Finally, neutrality and impartiality can improve the strategic and logistical support to parties to the conflict, if 'the military or political objectives of the controlling authority or combatant force coincide with the logistical requirements of the humanitarian operation'.[93] Such support can,

89 D. Keen and K. Wilson, 'Engaging with Violence: A Re-assessment of Relief in Wartime', in J. Macrae and A. Zwi (eds.), *War and Hunger: Rethinking International Responses to Complex Emergencies* (London: Zed Books, 1994) 209.

90 Weller, *supra* note 81.

91 African Rights, *supra* note 85; de Waal, *supra* note 76.

92 *African Rights, supra* note 85 at 5.

93 African Rights, *supra* note 85 at 4. On the use of Band Aid money, see the report by the Africa Editor of the BBC World Service, Martin Plaut, 'Ethiopia Famine Aid "Spent on Weapons"', broadcast on 3 March 2010 (http://news.bbc.co.uk/1/hi/world/africa/8535189.stm). See also the CIA document 'Ethiopia: Political and Security Impact of the Drought', 4 January 1985, released under the Freedom of Information

for example, consist of keeping lines of communication and transport facilities open.

Relief to Ethiopia in the wake of the 1984–85 famine illustrates the problems with neutrality and impartiality. Some of the neediest groups were barely reached by the aid operation as a result of continued manipulation by the Ethiopian government, treated as a partner by humanitarian organisations throughout the crisis. Closing an eye to the crimes committed by the Ethiopian forces in the course of that conflict and not reporting them was an implicit term in the 'gentleman's agreement' between the Ethiopian authorities and the humanitarian organisations.[94]

Albeit normally unintended, these consequences of humanitarian operations cannot be ignored by humanitarian organisations, including the UN.[95] In some circumstances, it may be appropriate to revisit the modus operandi based on neutrality and impartiality and face difficult dilemmas: can humanitarian organisations be neutral and impartial in every situation? Given that humanitarian action can at times assist the authorities that are in control of the territory, should humanitarian organisations renounce their neutrality and impartiality and treat parties to the conflict differently, taking also into account compliance with human rights and humanitarian law?

A principled approach to the tension between extreme humanitarian impartiality and neutrality on the one hand, and respect for human rights on the other, begins with an assessment of the relative strength of the obligations involved. The ICRC, for example, has to abide by its own constitutional requirement to be neutral and impartial. UN agencies and programmes are subject to different constitutional obligations, and for them extreme neutrality and impartiality may not be an option if these principles cannot be reconciled with their other legal obligations. A UN operational agency cannot choose to remain neutral and impartial in the course of a collective action under Chapter VII of the UN Charter, unless expressly authorised by the Security Council.[96] Moreover, because of the applicability of human rights and

Act and available through www.foia.cia.gov (or directly through the hyperlink in the BBC page).

[94] See de Waal, *supra* note 76 at 106–32.

[95] See the discussion on complicity in Chapter 2 (pp. 135ff.).

[96] For example, SC Res. 1333 (2000) expressly exempts humanitarian organisations from the ban on flights into and from Afghanistan as part of the sanctions against the Taliban (at para. 11–12).

humanitarian law to its activities, a UN operation cannot purport to remain neutral and impartial when the authorities of the host state or insurgent groups are committing gross violations of humanitarian law and/or human rights.

While a case could be made that the neutrality of the ICRC in humanitarian action may be justifiable, on account of its unique history and role, the group-think incorporation of this principle in the praxis of other international organisations is unwise. There is a pragmatic case for one organisation to maintain 'access' to the most 'complex' scenarios but there are inherent dangers in most, or even all, international organisations choosing to preserve access by not opposing human rights violations while hiding behind a cloak of 'impartiality'.

An original solution to this clash of values and normative systems is to redefine the principles of neutrality and impartiality in accordance with the evolution of international law. As suggested by Weller, it is hardly conceivable that insistence on compliance with basic rules of international human rights and humanitarian law should still be regarded 'as an un-neutral or partial act'.[97]

The breach of the principle of non-discrimination in the provision of humanitarian assistance to Afghanistan and to Afghan refugees in Pakistan

The history of relief to Afghanistan

The treatment of women was one of the key issues in the Afghan wars of the 1990s: indeed, if 'it would be an exaggeration to say that the war in Afghanistan was fought over the status of women', this 'would not be wholly untrue'.[98] It was against this challenging background that the delivery of humanitarian assistance took place.

In the course of these operations the principle of non-discrimination was violated in three respects. First, the employment of local staff by

[97] Weller, *supra* note 81 at 9.

[98] D. Cammack, 'Gender Relief and Politics During the Afghan War', in D. Indra (ed.), *Engendering Forced Migration* (Oxford: Berghahn Books, 1999) 94 at 95. On the Taliban regime, see also P. Marsden, *The Taliban: War, Religion and the New Order in Afghanistan* (Oxford University Press, 1998) and W. Maley (ed.), *Fundamentalism Re-born? Afghanistan and the Taliban* (London: Hurst and Company, 1998), particularly Nancy Dupree's chapter 'Afghan Women under the Taliban' at 145.

the UN in Afghanistan was often on a discriminatory basis. Following pressure and even intimidation from the Taliban authorities, Afghan women hired as local staff members by the UN were dismissed shortly after the establishment of the new regime. In whichever way responsibility for these practices is allocated between the UN and the Afghan authorities in power at the time, it cannot be overlooked that UN agencies at the very least passively accepted the incorporation of discrimination into their employment policies and practices.

Secondly, the principle of non-discrimination was breached during the provision of humanitarian assistance to Afghan refugees in the camps in Pakistan. In particular, assistance in the form of education and of employment opportunities offered by the UN often neglected women and girls. This can be explained by concerns about the opposition to such programmes by the mujahideen leadership in the camps. At the operational level, in spite of some protest, UNICEF and UNHCR substantially caved in to the mujahideen who controlled many of the refugee camps. This failure to uphold the rights of Afghan refugee women is best illustrated by the comparative data on the education of refugee girls and boys. The level of literacy in those camps was 60% among the refugee boys, but it was as low as 6% among girls aged six to eleven and 3% in the group of girls aged eleven to seventeen.[99] 'Culture' was used as a justification for explaining this failure to uphold the rights of women. This justification is not only untenable legally and morally, but is also empirically flawed: literacy rates in Afghanistan in 1978 were characterised by a much smaller gender imbalance than the imbalance that emerged later in the refugee camps (95% of women were illiterate, as opposed to 92% of men).[100]

Thirdly, the humanitarian assistance by the UN following the Taliban's rise to power in 1996 provides a further example of violations of human rights. The relationship between the Taliban government and aid agencies had been volatile from the outset, mainly because of the frictions which arose as a result of the treatment imposed on women by that government. The UN was heavily involved in Afghanistan under

[99] Total enrolment in 1988 was over 100,000 boys and less than 8,000 girls (figures cited in H. Charlesworth and C. Chinkin, *The Boundaries of International Law. A Feminist Analysis* (Manchester University Press, 2000) at 266, fn. 113).

[100] Cammack, *supra* note 100 at 104.

the Taliban, allocating some $100 million of humanitarian assistance in 1998, about half of the total humanitarian aid to Afghanistan, the rest being provided by NGOs.[101] To an even larger extent than in the camps, the delivery of various forms of humanitarian assistance to women in Afghanistan by the UN was systematically hindered.

Following the 11 September 2001 terrorist attacks, in response to the Taliban's refusal to deliver Osama bin Laden, the US and Allied coalition forces launched Operation Enduring Freedom. The allied forces in cooperation with the anti-Taliban Northern Alliance quickly toppled the Taliban regime in the first phase of the conflict. In December 2001, the UN sponsored the Bonn Conference which agreed a process for political reconstruction and created the Afghan Transitional Authority, led by Hamid Karzai, who subsequently was elected president in December 2004 and was re-elected in November 2009. During this period, the conflict entered a second phase consisting of an ongoing counter-insurgency effort. The provision of humanitarian assistance in post-Taliban Afghanistan still faces challenges, but at least the official government does not practise discrimination on a scale remotely comparable to the Taliban period.

The experience of the UN in Afghanistan, which the rest of this chapter examines, should not be forgotten. The Taliban regime was responsible for more than occasional or even systemic human rights violations. It instituted a system of sexual apartheid, which can be defined as the 'the oppression of individuals, and their exclusion from equal enjoyment of human rights, on the ground that they are women'[102] or, paraphrasing the definition of racial apartheid in the Statute of the International Criminal Court,[103] as a 'regime of systematic oppression and domination' over women. The UN not only failed to prevent sexual apartheid in Afghanistan, it chose to appease the Taliban by not opposing their policies and even incorporating discrimination against women into its humanitarian assistance and local employment practices.

[101] World Food Programme, Strategic Framework for the UN in Afghanistan of 12 Sept. 1998, previously available at www.wfp.org/OP/Countries/afganistan/strat_framework.html, visited 27 March 2001; weblink no longer active.

[102] R. Cook, 'The Elimination of Sexual Apartheid: Prospects for the Fourth World Conference on Women', Issue Paper on World Conferences No. 5, American Society of International Law (1995) at 3.

[103] Statute of the International Criminal Court, 37 ILM 999.

In analysing the UN response, it is important to distinguish three levels of institutional practice. First, there is the practice of the political organs of the UN (the General Assembly, the Security Council and the Secretary General), which should in principle provide the framework for the conduct of the organisation. Secondly, there is the practice of the institutional bureaucracy of the various departments and agencies of the UN, distinct from the practice of the political organs, and expressed in reports, positions and statements of policy bodies, of senior civil servants, and of country or regional representatives. This level of organisational practice will be here referred to as bureaucratic practice. The third level is the operational one or the actual conduct of the UN. This tends to be shaped, as we shall see, by the bureaucracy rather than the political organs of the UN.

In international law it is the practice of the political organs of the UN that normally receives the greatest attention. It is indeed also, and perhaps primarily, through the acts of such organs that international organisations, and the UN in particular, have historically contributed to the development of international law.[104] It is well-established, for example, that evidence of the practice and *opinio juris* of states can be sought by reflection also in the acts of the organs of the international organisations, and of the UN in particular. The bureaucratic practice of the organisation is instead the expression of its more autonomous will. This practice is not, however, endowed with immediate legal consequences on the plane of international law, although it can have evidential weight in international disputes.

For example, in the arbitration between Eritrea and Yemen, Yemen claimed that a hydrocarbon study of the Red Sea region carried out by the World Bank and the UNDP 'constituted recognition of Yemeni title by these international agencies, as well as expert evidence to the same effect', and 'evidence of Ethiopian acquiescence' in the Yemeni title.[105]

Leaving aside the important question of the legal relevance of bureaucratic practice, a singular aspect of this practice is that it can at times

[104] R. Higgins, *The Development of International Law through the Political Organs of the United Nations* (London: Oxford University Press for the Royal Institute of International Affairs, 1963).

[105] *The Eritrea-Yemen Arbitration, Phase I: Territorial Sovereignty and Scope of the Arbitration*, 114 ILR (1999) 1, at paras. 59–60. See also the weight attached to UN evidence in ICJ cases, e.g. *Armed Activities in the Territory of the Congo (Democratic Republic of Congo v. Uganda)*, ICJ Reports (2005) 168 at paras. 58ff.

matter more than the practice of the political organs. It may end up determining the operational behaviour of the organisation, even when it is in contrast with an act or a series of acts of a political organ and with human rights law.[106] Indeed, on the crucial strategic question of the terms of engagement with the Taliban, it was the bureaucracy of the UN that decided what to do, ignoring the pronouncements of the political organs and flouting an established principle of international law. This is a phenomenon of the utmost importance to international law, for it evidences that, contrary to widely held assumptions, an international bureaucracy can at times be sufficiently powerful not only to trump rules but also to ignore the political organs of the organisation.

The practice of the political organs of the UN

In October 1996, a few weeks after the Taliban militias had conquered Kabul, the Security Council adopted resolution 1076. Having expressed concern over 'the continuation and recent intensification of the military confrontation in Afghanistan which have caused civilian casualties and an increase in refugees and displaced persons, and which seriously endanger the stability and peaceful development of the region', the Council called upon 'all Afghan parties immediately to cease all armed hostilities, to renounce the use of force, to put aside their differences and to engage in a political dialogue aimed at achieving national reconciliation and a lasting political settlement of the conflict and establishing a fully representative and broad-based transitional government of national unity'.[107]

The cautious wording of the preamble of this resolution appears to resemble more closely Article 33 rather than Article 39 of the Charter, although authors like Conforti view the request for an immediate ceasefire as a typical provisional measure under Article 40 (Chapter VII).[108] However, other authors, reflecting on the more recent practice of the Council, stress the current tendency to refer explicitly to Chapter VII.[109]

[106] Johan Kaufmann has recognised the importance of the institutional practice and of the acts of senior civil servants for the operational programmes of the United Nations (J. Kaufmann, *United Nations Decision-Making* (Alphen aan den Rijn: Sijthoff & Noordhoff, 1980) 78–9).

[107] SC Res. 1076 (1996).

[108] B. Conforti, *Le Nazioni Unite* (5th edn., Padova: Cedam, 1994) 185.

[109] N. D. White, *Keeping the Peace: The United Nations and the Maintenance of International Peace and Security* (Manchester University Press, 1997) 36–42.

Unlike Conforti, White considers a SC resolution on Armenia's invasion of Azerbaijan in which the Council had requested a ceasefire as taken under Chapter VI and as having only recommendatory value.[110] In the past, the Council did act under Chapter VII without explicitly stating so, most notably in the case of Rhodesia.[111]

Subsequent resolutions of the Council adopted a stronger wording and referred to the 'Afghan conflict ... [as] causing a serious and growing threat to regional and international peace and security'.[112] Finally, in 1999–2000 the Security Council explicitly referred to Chapter VII in two resolutions.[113]

Resolution 1076 mentioned the violations of women's rights, but limited itself to 'denouncing' them.[114] The Council noted that these violations could have 'repercussions' on international relief, but then immediately – and rather contradictorily – proceeded to 'call upon all States and international organisations to extend *all possible* humanitarian assistance to the civilian population of Afghanistan' (emphasis added). It attached no condition on the provision of such assistance. In its following resolutions on Afghanistan, however, the Security Council added that humanitarian assistance must be provided to 'all in need' in Afghanistan. Most importantly, the Council strengthened its call to respect the rights of Afghan women, at first 'urging an end to all discrimination against girls and women and other violations of human rights',[115] and finally demanding an end to such discrimination.[116] These resolutions of the Security Council were adopted unanimously, with the support of Pakistan, Iran and Bahrain among others. When the Security Council finally decided to use its Chapter VII powers, it reiterated its 'deep concern' over the continuing discrimination against women and girls, although the real reason for

110 *Ibid.* at 72.

111 P. Alston, 'The Security Council and Human Rights: Lessons To Be Learned from the Iraq-Kuwait Crisis and its Aftermath', 13 Austral. YBIL (1992) 107 at 146.

112 SC Res. 1193 (1998) and SC Res. 1214 (1998), both of which were adopted unanimously.

113 SC Res. 1267 (1999) and SC Res. 1333 (2000).

114 See SC Res. 1076 (1996) at para. 11, where the Council 'denounces the discrimination against girls and women and other violations of human rights and international humanitarian law in Afghanistan, and notes with deep concern possible repercussions on international relief and reconstruction programmes in Afghanistan'.

115 SC Res. 1193 (1998).

116 SC Res. 1214 (1998).

its intervention was the alleged support of the Taliban to terrorist activities and their refusal to surrender Osama bin Laden to the US. Again, the Council omitted to state clearly that humanitarian assistance would have to be provided without discriminating on grounds of gender.

The General Assembly passed a number of resolutions on the situation in Afghanistan after the Taliban conquest.[117] The most detailed of these resolutions was resolution 52/145,[118] which addressed a list of specific requests to the Afghan authorities. In the part on gender discrimination, the General Assembly spelled out a series of measures that 'all Afghan parties' had to take in order 'bring an end without delay to discrimination on the basis of gender and the deprivation of human rights of women'. Such measures had to ensure:

> '(a) the effective participation of women in civil, cultural, economic, political and social life throughout the country;
> (b) respect for the right of women to work, and their reintegration in employment;
> (c) the right of women and girls to education without discrimination, the reopening of schools and the admission of women and girls to all levels of education;
> (d) respect for the right of women to security of person, and to ensure that those responsible for physical attacks on women are brought to justice;
> (e) respect for freedom of movement of women and their effective access to the facilities necessary to protect their right to the highest attainable standard of physical and mental health;
> (f) equal access of women to health facilities.'[119]

This was an important resolution because it applied the absolute and non-derogable principle of non-discrimination to women in Afghanistan, making no allowances for arguments based on culture.

The non-derogable nature of this principle in time of public emergency has been recognised by state parties to the ICCPR. Article 4 of the Covenant forbids

[117] See GA Res. 51/108, 12 December 1996; GA Res. 51/195, 17 December 1996; GA Res. 52/145, 12 December 1997; GA Res. 52/211, 19 December 1997; GA Res. 53/165, 9 December 1998; GA Res. 55/174, 28 February 2001.

[118] GA Res. 52/145.

[119] GA Res. 52/145 at para. 6. This resolution also urged all Afghan parties to ensure that UN programmes 'are carried out without discrimination against women as participants or as beneficiaries'.

the adoption of emergency measures that 'involve discrimination solely on the ground of race, colour, sex, language, religion or social origin'.[120]

The measures indicated by the General Assembly echo the language of the Convention on the Elimination of All Forms of Discrimination Against Women (CEDAW), which at various points obliges states 'to take all appropriate measures' to eliminate different forms of discrimination.[121] The General Assembly chose to focus on rights – such as the right to work, to education, to health, to freedom of movement and to security of the person – that were at particular risk.

A difference between the practice of the Security Council and that of the General Assembly is that the General Assembly included an appeal to member states and to the broader international community to provide adequate humanitarian assistance 'on a non-discriminatory basis', whereas the Security Council had limited itself to a request that humanitarian assistance be provided to 'all in need'. It may appear to be only a nuance, but reference to the principle of non-discrimination as being legally part of the provision of humanitarian assistance is significant. Overall, it could be said that the General Assembly went a step further than the Security Council in giving due regard to the principle of discrimination in its resolutions.

The Security Council could be criticised for its cautious language, as well as for having failed to adopt more serious measures to deal with discrimination against women in Afghanistan, such as provisional measures or measures not involving the use of armed force under Articles 40 and 41 of the Charter. Crucially, by the late 1990s, the practice of the Security Council in the area of human rights would have supported a more robust stance on the treatment of Afghan women.[122] There were, in fact, a number of precedents where the Security Council had used Chapter VII powers in the face of gross human rights violations. Already during the cold war, the Council had determined that the situations in Rhodesia in the 1960s and 1970s and in South Africa before the end of

[120] On the question of the more general non-derogability of the standard of non-discrimination in treaty relations between states, i.e. on whether this principle is part of *jus cogens*, see H. Charlesworth and C. Chinkin, 'The Gender of Jus Cogens', 15 Hum. Rts. Q. (1993) 63, at 67–70.

[121] See, for example, Art. 3, Convention on the Elimination of All Forms of Discrimination against Women (1979), 19 ILM 33, (hereinafter CEDAW).

[122] Alston, *supra* note 111; S. D. Bailey, 'The Security Council', in P. Alston (ed.), *The United Nations and Human Rights* (Oxford, Clarendon Press, 1992) 304; Ramcharan, *supra* note 68.

apartheid constituted 'a threat to peace'. The basis for these determinations may have been the right of self-determination rather than the principle of non-discrimination, as well as South Africa's 'persistent acts of aggression against its neighbouring States'.[123] But, as argued by Franck, the resolutions of the Security Council on Rhodesia and South Africa were also based on the perception that there was a 'historically demonstrable connection between the proscribed behaviour and a propensity to war'.[124] The 1990–91 resolutions on Iraq – and, in particular, resolution 688[125] – had constituted a watershed in the practice of the Council on matters related to human rights,[126] signalling greater involvement of the Council in human rights and humanitarian matters, often by resort to Chapter VII. In the 1990s the concept of 'threat to the peace' was applied to 'situations of starvation (Somalia), genocide and serious humanitarian crises (Rwanda, Burundi, and Zaire), and civil wars (Liberia and Angola), as well as its most controversial action to restore democracy (Haiti)'.[127] The resolutions on Albania in 1997 and Kosovo in 1998–99 could have afforded the Council further precedential support for a strong Chapter VII-based stance on the treatment of Afghan women.[128]

The situation in Afghanistan differs from these precedents in more than one respect, but an Article 39 determination that the systematic discrimination and persecution of women in Afghanistan threatened the peace would have accorded with the practice of the Security Council. The Council did rather belatedly recognise that the Afghan situation was 'causing a serious and growing threat to regional and international peace and security',[129] but, as the preamble of resolution 1214 clearly shows, it was on the armed conflict in Afghanistan, and not on the discrimination against women, that this determination was based. Later, when Chapter VII measures were adopted,[130] the Council

[123] SC Res. 418 (1977).

[124] T.M. Franck, *Fairness in International Law and Institutions* (Oxford University Press, 1995) 231.

[125] SC Res. 688 (1991). [126] Alston, *supra* note 111 at 116.

[127] White, *supra* note 111 at 59.

[128] On Kosovo see SC Res. 1160, 1199, 1203 and 1244 (1998); SC Res. 1160 (1998) recalled also in SC Res. 1199 (1998), and SC Res. 1203 (1998). On Albania see SC Res. 1101 (1997) and UN Doc. S/1997/258, reproduced in 52 Com. Int. (1997) 6 at 8. China was the only country to abstain in the vote on the resolution on Albania explaining that China has 'never been in favour of the Security Council frequently invoking Chapter VII of the Charter in authorising such actions' (*Ibid.* at 8).

[129] SC Res. 1214 (1998). [130] See *supra* note 115.

again did not use this opportunity to include a more pervasive condemnation of gender discriminatory practices in its resolutions and concurrently to adopt measures specifically targeted at improving the situation of women.

The Security Council does reflect the consensus and, indirectly, value systems of the international community.[131] Discrimination against women is, unfortunately, more widely accepted than other forms of discrimination, and remains acute in most of the fifty-seven member states of the Organisation of the Islamic Conference.[132] It could be argued that the practice of the Council on other types of discrimination, such as for instance discrimination based on religion or language, has also been weaker than its interventions in the case of racial discrimination, and that in any event such interventions were limited to the colonial context and to southern Africa. But it must be emphasised that the persecution against women in Afghanistan was not comparable with most other situations (except for South Africa and Rhodesia), because it was a systemic state-wide regime of discrimination, segregation and humiliation of women.

Human rights law treats the different types of discrimination 'equally', but it is in the area of international criminal law that the gender bias of international law persists. The Charter of the Nuremberg Tribunal[133] only mentioned 'political, racial and religious' grounds of persecution as underlying crimes against humanity, but this was also due to the specific situation that the Charter was addressing (i.e. the particular type of racism and genocide practised by the Nazi regime). The Rome Statute of the International Criminal Court recognises apartheid as a self-standing crime against humanity – Article 7(1)(j). But persecution on various grounds, including gender, can amount to a crime against humanity only in connection with other acts, such as murder, extermination,

[131] On this, see Charlesworth and Chinkin, *supra* note 101.

[132] See also H. Charlesworth, C. Chinkin and S. Wright, 'Feminist Approaches to International Law', 85 AJIL (1991) 613 at 634, who juxtapose the paucity of substantive reservations made to the Convention on the Elimination of All Forms of Racial Discrimination to the plethora of reservations entered by states to CEDAW, as further evidence of this approach; Charlesworth and Chinkin, *supra* note 122 at 68, commenting on the list of human rights norms considered part of *jus cogens* in the *Restatement (Third) of Foreign Relations Law of the United States*; and P. Alston and B. Simma, 'The Sources of Human Rights Law: Custom, Jus Cogens and General Principles', 12 Austral. YBIL (1992) 82 on the bias of *jus cogens*.

[133] Agreement for the Prosecution and Punishment of the Major War Criminals of the European Axis, 8 August 1945, 82 UNTS 280.

enslavement, deportation, imprisonment or other severe deprivation of physical liberty, torture, and different forms of sexual violence – Article 7(1)(h). Hence, institutionalised forms of systematic gender persecution, not consisting of those acts, such as sexual apartheid in Afghanistan, may not constitute a crime against humanity under the definition of the Statute. On the other hand, the Statute has taken a strong stance against sexual violence, in the context of both war crimes and crimes against humanity.[134]

The extent of the discrimination, its systematic character, its consequences especially the loss of life ensuing, for instance, from the lack of access to health facilities, and the central role that the oppression of women has in the ideological discourse of the Taliban government, suggest that the situation in Afghanistan is more comparable to that of apartheid in South Africa than to other examples of discrimination and persecution. In the case of South Africa, the development of the concept of apartheid, the crystallisation of its prohibition, and its criminalisation under international law constituted a very powerful legal and political tool in the struggle against this form of racial discrimination and oppression. But the case of sexual apartheid in Afghanistan was not accompanied by a similarly rubust response.[135]

The Secretary General submitted various reports to the Security Council on the situation in Afghanistan, the first one in March 1997, five months after the Taliban forces had taken over Kabul.[136] The reports of the Secretary General find their legal basis in the power to 'bring to the attention of the Council any matter' which may threaten international peace and stability (Article 99 of the Charter). They can also be prompted by a specific request contained in a resolution of the Security Council, or of the General Assembly.[137] Although the Secretary General is one of the organs of the UN, its reports are in many respects a product of bureaucratic practice, in that it is the staff of the Secretariat and the UN missions in the relevant countries that provide much of the substantive work behind them. In addition to reporting to these

[134] N. E. Erb, 'Gender-based Crimes Under the Draft Statute for the Permanent International Criminal Court', 29 *Columbia Human Rights Law Review* (1998) 401.

[135] This expression is by Judge Higgins (*Nuclear Weapons*, *supra* note 44 at para. 41 (diss. op. of Judge Higgins)).

[136] In 1997, UN Doc. S/1997/482, UN Doc. S/1997/719, UN Doc. S/1997/894. In 1998, UN Doc. S/1998/222, UN Doc. S/1998/532, UN Doc. S/1998/913. In 1999, UN Doc. S/1999/362. In 2000, UN Doc. S/2000/1106, UN Doc. S/2000/875, UN Doc. S/2000/581.

[137] On these reports as an instrument of accountability, see Chapter 8 (323ff.).

organs, the Secretary General also convened meetings of 'concerned countries', at which, however, issues related to women's rights appear to have received limited attention.[138]

The Secretary General's reports throughout 1997, while paying token attention to the violations of women's rights, did not make the link between the provision of humanitarian assistance and a principled stance on the issue of discrimination, and did not propose that the provision of humanitarian assistance be made conditional upon respect for the basic rights of women. In the last two reports of 1998 (UN Doc. S/1998/532, UN Doc. S/1998/913), the situation of women received hardly any attention in the reports of the Secretary General.[139] This may have to do with the fact that in May 1998, the UN had reached the agreement with the Taliban authorities which is discussed below. Later on, attention began to be given again to the situation of women with the report submitted in 2000 presenting some of the 'issues of principle' that affect the UN humanitarian operations in Afghanistan.[140]

The question of discrimination in the UN assistance to Afghanistan had nothing to do with aid conditionality as traditionally understood. Traditional aid conditionality is a way of exerting pressure on states that violate human rights, by making aid dependent upon improvements in their human rights record. In these cases, it is the donor that imposes conditions. In Afghanistan, instead, it was the recipient of aid – the Taliban regime – that imposed a negative human rights condition, by making the continued provision of humanitarian assistance by the UN contingent upon the acceptance of discrimination against women. The rejection of this condition by the UN, even if it led to the suspension of humanitarian assistance whenever, would have been the right response. After all, the UN did not hesitate to suspend humanitarian assistance when the question was the security of UN staff.[141]

To conclude on the practice of the political organs, it must be noted that the Economic and Social Council (ECOSOC) also intervened in the situation in Afghanistan. One of its resolutions is particularly important

138 See, for instance, the letter of the Secretary General to the President of the Security Council of 1 May 1997 (UN Doc. S/1997/347), in which the Secretary General summarised one of these meetings. The question of gross violations of women's rights received only one incidental mention in the ante-penultimate paragraph of the letter: 'All participants voiced their distress at the continued plight of the Afghan people, with special attention drawn to women and girls.'

139 UN Doc. S/1998/532 and UN Doc. S/1998/913.

140 UN Doc. S/2000/1106, at para. 52.

141 UN Doc. S/1998/532, at para. 39.

since the ECOSOC called on the UN, NGOs and donors operating in Afghanistan to formulate and coordinate their programmes 'in such a way as to promote and ensure the participation of women in those programmes, and that women benefit equally with men from such programmes'.[142] In addition to its competence in the area of human rights and, more broadly, international economic and social cooperation (Articles 60 and 62 of the Charter), the ECOSOC also plays an important role by coordinating the work of, making recommendations to, and obtaining information from UN specialised agencies.

Does the ECOSOC in principle have the power to stop the provision of humanitarian assistance by a UN agency? In the case of the specialised agencies, this question can be solved primarily by looking at the specific agreement between the UN and the specialised agency concluded under Articles 57 and 63 of the Charter. In the 1960s the attempts of the General Assembly to stop the World Bank and IMF from assisting Portugal and South Africa were not successful, as the Bank claimed that it was not bound by the resolutions of the General Assembly.[143] At any rate, these considerations may not be so relevant in the context of Afghanistan, where most humanitarian assistance was actually provided by UNHCR and by the WFP, which were established by General Assembly resolutions and act under its authority and, subordinately, under the authority of the ECOSOC.

The other two levels of organisational practice: bureaucratic practice and actual conduct

The response of the political organs can be criticised for having been belated and without real 'teeth'. At least, however, the position taken by the General Assembly in its resolutions was principled, insofar as the principle of non-discrimination was mentioned and recognised in those resolutions. No such recognition of the centrality of this principle can be found in the bureaucratic practice and actual conduct of the UN. On the contrary, the principle of non-discrimination was called into question, undermined, and eventually flouted in order to justify the steady increase of the UN presence in Afghanistan during the Taliban period.

For 1996 around US$124 million were requested by the UN to cover its Afghan operations; in 1997 this figure stood at US$133 million, in 1998 at

[142] ECOSOC Res. 1998/9, 28 July 1998.

[143] See D. Williams, *The Specialised Agencies and the UN: The System in Crisis* (London: C. Hurst, 1987) 160ff.; I. Shihata, *The World Bank in a Changing World*, Vol. I. (Dordrecht: Martinus Nijhoff, 1991) 99ff.

US$157 million and for 1999 a record US$182 million were requested.[144] Inter-agency appeals are launched by the Secretary General, and they are normally followed by a resolution of the General Assembly calling on member states to respond to the appeal.

Before turning to this bureaucratic practice, it is worth considering the response of the UN human rights machinery to the events in Afghanistan in 1990s. Even though Afghanistan is a state party to numerous human rights instruments, the treaty-based human rights organs gave the Afghan situation only scant attention. This is due, at least in part, to the intrinsic limits of the periodic reporting system. Constrained by a timetable set many years in advance, these bodies are normally ill-suited to engineering an emergency response to a human rights crisis. The Charter-based human rights bodies can, instead, react more swiftly. And overall, when confronted with the sexual apartheid instituted by the Taliban in Afghanistan, they did so – especially the Human Rights Commission[145] and the Sub-Commission on Prevention of Discrimination and Protection of Minorities. The language of the resolutions of the Human Rights Commission echoed that of General Assembly resolution 52/145. The Sub-Commission went further than that, acknowledging that humanitarian assistance was provided on a discriminatory basis, calling on states not to 'extend diplomatic recognition' to the Taliban, and urging commercial enterprises 'to refrain from entering into financial agreements' with the Taliban regime until the end of the discrimination against women.[146]

For instance, in resolution 1998/17, the Sub-Commission took note of the 'numerous reports dealing with the unprecedented and extremely difficult situation of women in Kabul and the other parts of Afghanistan controlled by the Taliban, in particular widows who cannot support themselves because they are not permitted to work or to benefit from humanitarian assistance, which is given only to men'.[147]

[144] See www.reliefweb.int/fts/fin98afg.html.

[145] Human Rights Commission Res. 1998/70, 21 April 1998 (UN Doc. E/CN.4/Res/1998/70) and Res. 1999/9, 23 April 1999 (UN Doc. E/CN.4/Res/1999/9).

[146] *Ibid.* On the Sub-Commission's response to allegations of human rights violations, see: A. Eide, 'The Sub-Commission on Prevention of Discrimination and Protection of Minorities', in P. Alston (ed.), *supra* note 124, 211 at 248–52.

[147] Sub-commission Res. 1998/17, 21 August 1998, para. 1

In addition, the Special Rapporteur on human rights violations in Afghanistan, originally appointed in 1984,[148] presented reports to the ECOSOC and, via the Secretary General, to the General Assembly. The situation in Afghanistan was also the object of some attention in the reports submitted by the thematic Special Rapporteurs, for instance by the Special Rapporteur on torture[149] and by the Special Rapporteur on Extra-judicial and Summary Executions.[150]

The bureaucratic practice of the UN was a long way away from that of the human rights bodies. In the autumn of 1996, faced with the introduction of a policy of severe discrimination against women, the UN Office for the Co-ordination of Humanitarian Affairs (UNOCHA) released a policy document containing guidelines on the work of UN agencies in Afghanistan. This early example of institutional practice was characterised by a strict adherence to the fundamental principles governing the work of the UN and the provision of humanitarian assistance, such as the principle of non-discrimination.[151] This response changed radically as a result of a mission of the Department of Humanitarian Affairs (DHA) to Afghanistan in the spring of 1997. The report that resulted from this mission is an important policy document, on which the subsequent operational response of the UN was based. This report is also a good illustration of how institutional practice operates.

The aim of the DHA mission was to devise a common approach for UN agencies vis-à-vis the Taliban authorities. After stating that 'beyond its commitment to the various issues such as gender, the environment and drug control, the dynamic of the UN engagement in Afghanistan relies on a continuum linking the objectives of the UN Charter and internationally recognised human rights, to the practices of the agencies under the constraints of the field',[152] the authors of the report asked whether 'the development of cooperation arrangements with the Taliban are worth the efforts'.[153] Their answer left little room for doubt:

148 ECOSOC Res. 1984/37, 24 May 1984.

149 UN Doc. E/CN.4/1998/38.

150 UN Doc. E/CN.4/1998/68/Add. 1.

151 UN Department of Humanitarian Affairs, *Afghanistan Weekly Update No. 191*, 6 November 1996.

152 UN Department of Humanitarian Affairs, *Report of the DHA Mission to Afghanistan*, 15 June 1997, Introduction.

153 DHA Report, *supra* note 154, at 4.3.

'In our view, the UN system has no real choice. It has to invest reasonable efforts into promoting a substantive dialogue with the Taliban simply to manage the existing gap between their vision of Afghan society, and the international standards to be respected. Furthermore, one should acknowledge the Taliban's impact on the political landscape of Afghanistan, restructuring Afghan society on Islamic tenets and modelling a new identity for Afghanistan.'[154]

According to this report, dialogue with the Taliban had to proceed 'in a constructive, rather than confrontational mode, to avoid harsh response from the Taliban. Pressures must be maintained on the Taliban to allow, and participate in, constructive experiments in education and the role of women in society'.[155] The UN and humanitarian agencies had three options. One option was the 'principle-centred' approach, which would aim at 'making assistance conditional upon changes of policies that are in conflict with the UN Charter and internationally recognised norms and principles'. Another option was the 'tip-toe' approach: 'attempting pragmatic experiments on the ground hoping for the development of a practical arrangement with the Taliban authorities'. And finally there was the 'community empowerment' approach, that is 'developing community capacity to act as counterparts to the UN agencies, in the margin of the authorities wherever possible'.[156] According to the DHA Report, only a combination of these approaches could ensure the success of the UN involvement. But in reality not much of the 'principled-centred' approach made it through to the final recommendations of the report. In particular, it was recommended that 'practical and realistic' objectives for a common position of the UN agencies on gender be identified, and that a 'UN team composed of male and female expatriates should ... elaborate a set of practical objectives for UN agencies to sensitise the authorities on the implications of their policies'.

The reference to 'practical and realistic objectives' must be put in the intellectual context of modern humanitarianism and its deep ambivalence towards human rights. The language of human rights may be present and even pervasive in reports and speeches, but humanitarian action often resists the practical implications of rights;[157] obligations

[154] *Ibid.* [155] *Ibid.*

[156] DHA Report, *supra* note 154 at Executive Summary.

[157] B. Harrell-Bond, *Imposing Aid* (Oxford University Press, 1986) and, by the same author, 'Humanitarianism in a Strait-Jacket', 84 (334) *African Affairs* (1985) 3. See also: African Rights, *supra* note 85.

and legal standards are perceived as 'academic',[158] as emanating from an 'abstract, and sometimes dogmatic environment, centred on the principles'.[159] In line with these notions, the DHA mission formulated recommendations that contravened the principles to which it had earlier paid homage.

For instance, the Strategic Framework for the UN in Afghanistan stated that '*the overarching goal of the United Nations in Afghanistan* is to facilitate the transition from a state of internal conflict to a just and sustainable peace through mutually reinforcing political and assistance initiatives' (emphasis in the text). Having formulated the main goal of the UN action in this fashion, the same document explained that compliance with the principle of non-discrimination in the provision of humanitarian assistance could not be practically attained in the short term.[160] The Special Rapporteur on Human Rights echoed the pragmatic approach, commenting that there is a need for the UN to adopt a 'practical and workable policy' on discrimination against women and girls.[161]

Some institutions did adopt a principled stance on the sexual apartheid imposed by the Taliban regime. In the early months of the Taliban rule over parts of Afghanistan, both UNICEF and the WFP had decided to suspend the delivery of assistance, respectively education and food, when they realised that such assistance could not be provided on a non-discriminatory basis.[162] WFP however believed that its position was undermined 'by the increased food assistance of other organisations, such as the ICRC, that took over some of its programmes'.[163] Doubtless, the failure of all humanitarian organisations active in Afghanistan to agree on a principled approach strengthened the hand of the Taliban regime, which could adopt a divide-and-rule strategy while persevering in its oppressive practices.

[158] N. Morris, 'Protection Dilemmas and UNHCR's Response: A Personal View from within UNHCR', 9 IJRL (1997) 492 at 494. My own criticism to this view is in G. Verdirame, 'Human Rights and Refugees: The Case of Kenya', 12 J. Ref. St. (1999) 54 at 75–6.

[159] DHA Report, *supra* note 154 at Introduction.

[160] *Supra* note 103.

[161] Special Rapporteur for Human Rights, ECOSOC Res. 1998/9, UN ESCOR, 44th plen. mtg., 28 July 1998. In this report, the Rapporteur believed to have also 'observed some relaxation of the restrictions imposed on the rights of women, as a few women doctors and nurses were seen at work in a hospital attending to female patients (at para. 21)'.

[162] See also: Marsden, *supra* note 100 at 110–11 and 115. Among NGOs, Save the Children Fund (UK) and MSF took similar stances.

[163] DHA Report, *supra* note 154 at 3.4.1.

Another important example of institutional practice is the report of the inter-agency mission on gender, which took place in November 1997 and was led by Angela King, UN Special Adviser on Gender Issues and Advancement of Women.[164] This report was very critical of the lack of gender awareness and sensitivity in the UN system, especially the fact that 'despite the attention paid to discrimination against women, and lip service to their importance in rehabilitation and development assistance, most programmes and projects ignore women at all stages of their design and implementation'.[165] While reaffirming the need for a principled approach to the question of humanitarian assistance to Afghanistan, the gender mission recommended the adoption of the 'field-oriented application' as 'the most fruitful way to implement the principle-centred approach'.[166] The field-oriented application was defined as a method of applying principles 'within the context of a practical, people-centred approach to assistance', in which equality is seen as a 'process' to be interpreted also on the basis of 'circumstances and the creative implementation of assistance programmes'.[167] The gender mission, thus, rejected the strict application of the principle-centred approach – characterised by the suspension of any assistance programme for which equal participation and benefit between men and women was prevented by the intervention of the local authorities – on two grounds. First, it was concluded that such strict application would contravene the resolutions of the Security Council and of the General Assembly on Afghanistan, which had not explicitly allowed conditionality of assistance. Secondly, it was argued that the suspension of programmes, as a result of strict conditionality, would not benefit the Afghan population and, especially, the most 'vulnerable' groups, including many women.

Both the inter-agency gender and the DHA missions opted for the continuation of humanitarian operations in Afghanistan. To the extent that it allowed the suspension of humanitarian assistance in certain circumstances, the report of the gender mission was more respectful of principles and rules than the DHA report. However, it still deemed a pure application of principle both unfeasible and counter-productive. Unfeasible it probably was, but was it really counter-productive? The

[164] Report of the Inter-Agency Gender Mission to Afghanistan, 12–24 November 1997, available at www.un.org/womenwatch/afghanistan/documents/1997_IGMreport.pdf.

[165] *Ibid.* at para. 50. [166] *Ibid.* at para. 19. [167] *Ibid.* at para. 18.

interpretation given by the gender mission to the resolutions of the political organs as preventing conditionality was also misplaced, because, as observed before, this was not a case of conditionality. The argument based on the counter-productivity of the strict application of principles only considered some of the short-term consequences of the suspension of assistance, but overlooked long-term ones such as: the legitimation of Afghan authorities by continued collaboration; the facilitation of their gender policies by allowing discrimination against women to be incorporated in the provision of UN humanitarian assistance; and the inevitable loss of credibility of the UN as a promoter and advocate of respect for women's rights.

These reports shaped the actual conduct of the UN vis-à-vis the gender policies of the Afghan authorities. They prepared the ground, in an institutional and intellectual sense, for the Memorandum of Understanding between the Islamic Emirate of Afghanistan and the United Nations, signed in May 1998. This agreement contained twenty-three provisions that deal both with the privileges, immunities and obligations of the UN staff, and with aspects of the humanitarian operations of the UN.

The Memorandum gives token endorsement to the principle-centred approach by asserting that both Afghanistan and the UN 'jointly commit that men and women shall have the right to education and health care and necessary development activities, based on international standards and in accordance with Islamic rules and Afghan culture' (Article 12). But the main substantive provision was Article 13 which provided: 'The Authorities and the UN will make efforts to increase the participation of men and women in health, education – especially health education – and food security. Both parties acknowledge the economic difficulties and the specific cultural traditions that make this goal challenging. As a result, women's access to and participation in health and education will need to be *gradual*' (emphasis added).

This provision is a paralogism. After the initial statement of principle, which is in itself abridged by the significant omission of words like 'equality' and 'equal', Article 13 affirms the existence of two obstacles ('economic difficulties and specific cultural traditions') towards the realisation of this principle. It, then, goes on to conclude that women's access and participation will need to be gradual. However, 'economic difficulties' is a smokescreen, as available economic resources can in principle be distributed equally among men and women. The use of 'cultural traditions', on the other hand, serves an important legitimising function both for the Afghan authorities in justifying their sexual apartheid, and for the UN in justifying its role in Afghanistan. Underlying 'specific cultural traditions' there is a mis-representation of culture as an 'essentialist and homogenous body'.[168] This representation of culture as a singular immutable monolith conceals the frequent coexistence of different, even conflicting, interpretations of fundamental norms within a culture, as well as the fact that the prevalence of one interpretation over the other is contingent upon changeable internal and external factors.

Even in regard to the treatment of UN women employees, the Memorandum allowed discrimination. The Afghan authorities were not prepared to treat 'female Muslim staff' of the UN like other UN staff, in particular on the question of their freedom of movement. According to the Taliban's interpretation of the sharia, Muslim women have to be accompanied by a *mahram* (a male member of the family, usually the husband, father or brother). Under Article 11 of the Memorandum, the possibility to treat Muslim women employees of the UN differently was implicitly recognised. Indeed, Afghanistan obliged itself only 'to be ready to discuss with religious scholars from Islamic countries the movement of international female Muslim staff of the UN who are not accompanied by Mahram [sic] in order to reach a solution in accordance with Sharia'.

In his first report to the Security Council after the conclusion of this agreement, the Secretary General summarised its contents as follows: 'The agreement lays out codes of conduct for both the United Nations and local authorities, sets up a mechanism for joint collaboration and resolution of problems and deals in a preliminary way with gender issues. As a result of the agreement, the United Nations decided, on 28 May, to lift the suspension of its programme in southern and south-western Afghanistan. The United Nations and other humanitarian organizations look forward to improved understanding by the Taliban of their responsibilities towards humanitarian personnel to enable needed assistance to reach their own people.'[169] This summary avoided discussing the most controversial aspects of the Memorandum and did not enable

[168] N. Yuval-Davis, *Gender and Nation* (London: Sage, 1997) 38.

[169] UN Doc. S/1998/532, at para. 40; this report was presented to the council on 19 June 1998.

the Security Council to exercise its functions of oversight and control over the UN mission in Afghanistan.

Various humanitarian NGOs working in Afghanistan criticised the Memorandum. But these criticisms were normally articulated in terms of policy rather than law.

MSF was expelled from Afghanistan in July 1998, partly as a result of its tougher stance on non-discrimination. In a press release on the day of its expulsion, MSF voiced its criticism of the agreement between the UN and the Taliban: 'This accord left such principles as non-discrimination wide open to interpretation. The failure of the UN to take a stronger position is disappointing. The memorandum considerably weakened the position of NGOs, which found themselves on the front line of having to defend humanitarian principles abandoned by the UN.'[170]

What is the legal nature and what are the effects of the 1998 Memorandum? Treaties between international organisations and states are governed, *mutatis mutandis*, by the law that applies to treaties between states.[171] No specific form is requested for the valid conclusion of a treaty,[172] and, thus, in order to determine if the Memorandum constitutes a treaty, or is of a legally non-binding nature, primary regard must be given to the real intention of the parties. The legally binding nature of the Memorandum of Understanding between the UN and

170 MSF, press release of 21 July 1998.

171 Jennings and Watts, *supra* note 42 at 1220. The Vienna Convention on the Treaties between States and International Organisations or between International Organisations (1986), 25 ILM 543, not yet in force (hereinafter the 'Vienna Convention on Treaties between States and International Organisations'), was based on the Draft Articles prepared by the International Law Commission, but has not yet entered into force. See also: G. Gaja, 'A "New" Vienna Convention on Treaties between States and International Organisations and between International Organisations: A Critical Commentary', 58 BYBIL (1987) 235; F. Morgenstern, 'The Convention on the Law of Treaties between States and International Organisations or between International Organisations', in Y. Dinstein (ed.), *International Law at a Time of Perplexity. Essays in Honour of Shabtai Rosenne* (Dordrecht: Martinus Nijhoff, 1989) 435.

172 From the notorious 'Ihlen Declaration' – *Legal Status of Eastern Greenland (Denmark v. Norway)*, (1924) PCIJ Reports Series A/B, No. 53 – to the joint communiqué at the end of a meeting between two Prime Ministers – *Aegean Sea Continental Shelf (Greece v. Turkey)*, Judgment, ICJ Reports (1978) 3 – to the so-called Doha Minutes – the object of the *Qatar v. Bahrain* case, ICJ Reports (1995) 6, international law knows of numerous examples of agreements that were concluded very informally and that still constituted treaties.

the Afghan government is evident from its wording, its object, and, most importantly, the clear intention of the parties. As far as the UN is concerned, its intention to enter into a legally binding agreement governed by international law is also manifest in the above-mentioned report of the Secretary General to the Security Council that treated this Memorandum as a treaty.

In the Advisory Opinion on the *Interpretation of Agreement of 25 March 1951 between the WHO and Egypt*, the Court considered various agreements concluded by Egypt and the WHO between 1949 and 1951, including one that carried the nomenclature of Memorandum. While these documents could be 'regarded as distinct agreements or as separate parts of one transaction', there was no doubt that they established a 'contractual legal regime' between the parties.[173]

The power of the UN to enter into treaties with the states where it operates is uncontroversial. Framework agreements for the provision of humanitarian assistance are normally concluded with the host state both by the UN as a whole and by its agencies and programmes separately. Another example of treaties between the UN and host state in the framework of an intervention of a different nature are the Status of Force Agreements and Memoranda of Agreement, providing the legal framework for a peacekeeping operation (as discussed in Chapter 6).[174]

As far as its validity is concerned, the Memorandum of Agreement between the UN and Afghanistan constitutes a *rara avis* for international lawyers: to the extent that it allows discrimination against women to be incorporated in the provision of humanitarian assistance, the Memorandum may have been void for conflicting with a peremptory norm of international law (*jus cogens*). The *jus cogens* nature of the principle of non-discrimination has been asserted by different authors, and can be based on various arguments, including the non-derogable nature accorded to non-discrimination in human rights instruments, analogy with racial discrimination and the fundamental nature of the standard of non-discrimination as a principle underpinning human rights.[175]

[173] *Interpretation of Agreement of 25 March 1951 between the WHO and Egypt*, Advisory Opinion, ICJ Reports (1980) 73 at 92.

[174] On the Status of Force Agreements, see A. Carlevaris, 'Recenti Sviluppi nella Prassi degli Status of Force Agreements per le Operazioni di Peace-Keeping delle Nazioni Unite', 53 Com. Int. (1998) 667.

[175] See Charlesworth and Chinkin, *supra* note 122, who also refer to other authors who accept than non-discrimination is part of *jus cogens*, and Alston, Simma, *supra* note 134.

In particular, if it is agreed that *jus cogens* entails at least *some* human rights, it is difficult to imagine how gender discrimination – and, indeed, any type of discrimination – could not be part of it. The imposition of gender barriers on access to health can cause loss of life. To the extent that such practices are endorsed by the Memorandum, this treaty also violated the human right to life which, according to some, also has peremptory status.[176] One can add that, in signing the Memorandum the UN disregarded the resolutions of the General Assembly and of the Security Council, which, as we have seen, were demanding an end 'without delay' to discrimination against women in Afghanistan, but the consequences of the failure to comply with these resolutions are far from clear both internally and in relation to third parties.

Article 46 of the Vienna Convention on Treaties between States and International Organisations, states that 'an international organisation may not invoke the fact that its consent to be bound by a treaty has been expressed in violation of the rules of the organisation regarding competence to conclude treaties as invalidating its consent unless that violation was manifest and concerned a rule of fundamental importance'.

In any event, at the very least, the principle of non-discrimination is part of customary law and, as such, it binds the UN.

Humanitarian assistance continued to be provided within the framework laid in the Memorandum until the Taliban were ousted from power in 2001.[177]

Conclusion

The case of Afghanistan exemplifies the dilemmas associated with the delivery of humanitarian assistance. Should the provision of humanitarian assistance have been suspended, given that continuing it required a compromise on such a fundamental standard as the principle of non-discrimination? Operationalising human rights in the provision of humanitarian assistance in extreme situations is bound to be an arduous process. However, allowing discrimination against women to

[176] B. G. Ramcharan, 'The Concept and Dimension of the Right to Life', in B. G. Ramcharan (ed.), *The Right to Life in International Law* (Dordrecht: Martinus Nijhoff, 1985) 1 at 14–15.

[177] As an example of more recent institutional practice confirming this approach see the Strategic Framework, *supra* note 103.

be incorporated in the humanitarian assistance hollows out the word humanitarian and disregards one of the goals of the UN. Principles and standards may be dismissed as 'almost academic in deciding action' in extreme cases,[178] 'abstract and ideal',[179] but if internationally agreed legal principles and standards are irrelevant in 'extreme cases' to offer guidance, what is their use?

In addition to their presumed ineffectuality, two more arguments are deployed to justify the UN's failure to comply with fundamental standards during humanitarian operations. First, it is argued that the humanitarian imperative to save lives at times imposes the sacrifice of other important principles. In legal terms, this argument can be articulated as distress or necessity.[180] However, distress could not be relied upon in the case of Afghanistan, because it is evident that the breach of the principle of non-discrimination was not the only way 'of saving the author's life or the lives of other persons entrusted to the author's care'. Nor would necessity preclude the wrongfulness of the act in this case, since the provision of humanitarian assistance in a discriminatory manner was not 'the only means for the organisation to safeguard against a grave and imminent peril an essential interest of the international community as a whole'. However, the inclusion of gender discrimination in UN programmes to appease the Taliban cannot be the only means to safeguard any such essential interest, not least because the elimination of gender discrimination is itself an essential interest of the international community. It would defeat the logic of necessity to allow one essential interest to be reduced to mere instrument for the promotion of another.

If, in a legal sense, this argument does not travel very far, it may have some traction in a utilitarian framework. A utilitarian might justify the position of the UN with the argument that there was an overall increase in utility since the lives of many were saved, and the welfare of many more improved as a result of the continued provision of humanitarian assistance. In reality, a calculus of utility is even more improbable in this case than in others, but suffice it to say that this justification of the position of the UN could probably be defeated on its own utilitarian terms by the consideration that the sexual apartheid,

[178] See *supra* note 160.

[179] K. L. Cain, 'The Rape of Dinah: Human Rights, Civil War in Liberia and Evil Triumphant, 21 Hum. Rts. Q. (1999) 265 at 297.

[180] Articles 23–26, ILC Draft Articles on the Responsibility of International Organisations.

which the UN buttressed through its intervention, affected the lives and welfare of at least half the population. Moreover, such 'utilitarianism of rights'[181] disguises the longer-term consequences of the inclusion of discrimination in the provision of humanitarian assistance by the UN, and is based on an oversimplification of the process of humanitarian assistance, conveniently de-contextualised and portrayed as the quick act of saving lives in the immediacy of danger. This is evident in Afghanistan, where the policy of engagement failed, as the situation of women showed no improvement and the victims of the Taliban regime only grew in number.

Myron Weiner sought to develop an approach to the ethical dilemmas of humanitarianism that purports to be neo-Aristotelian:[182] one that is not merely deductive and refuses the 'tyranny of principles',[183] opting instead for solutions that are flexible and circumstantial including both deductive and inductive elements, and are based on adaptable maxims rather than immutable axioms.[184] Aristotelian ethics was based on the concept of 'practical wisdom' (*phronesis*), which, unlike 'scientific knowledge' (*episteme*), does not involve universals. However, for the reasons discussed above, there was little or no wisdom, practical or theoretical, in the UN policy towards the Taliban.

The other justificatory argument, which is also echoed in the Memorandum between the UN and Afghanistan, is that of respect for local culture. This argument rests on the fictitious juxtaposition between the heterenomy of human rights norms and the autonomy of local traditions and cultures. Supporting the autonomy of cultures is presented as intrinsically valuable and as the right moral choice.

The emotive appeal of culture could hardly be estimated. Susan Sontag famously summarised Leni Riefenstahl's work on the Nubas as a 'lament for

[181] See Robert Nozick's definition of a 'utilitarian of rights' as one whose 'goal is … to minimise the weighted amount of the violation of rights in the society … even through means that themselves violate people's rights', in R. Nozick, *Anarchy, State and Utopia* (Oxford: Basil Blackwell, 1974) 30.

[182] M. Weiner, 'The Clash of Norms: Dilemmas in Refugee Policies', Paper presented at the Conference on the Growth of Forced Migration, hosted by the Refugee Studies Programme at Wadham College, University of Oxford, 25–27 March 1998.

[183] A. R. Jonsen and S. Toulmin, *The Abuse of Casuistry* (Berkeley: University of California Press, 1988) 5.

[184] See A. C. Macintyre, *Whose Justice? Whose Rationality?* (London: Duckworth, 1988) 92. On the 're-discovery' of Aristotelianism in the ethical sphere, which in part results from Gadamer's hermeneutics – H. G. Gadamer, *Truth and Method* (2nd edn., London: Sheed and Ward, 1989) – see C. A. Viano, *Teorie etiche contemporanee* (Turin: Bollati Boringhieri, 1990).

vanishing primitives'.[185] Sontag argues that the rehabilitation of Riefenstahl since the 1960s as a result of her work on the Nuba is in part due to the continuing appeal exercised 'by the primitivist ideal'; hers is 'a portrait of a people subsisting in a pure harmony with their environment, untouched by "civilisation"'.[186] Such 'laments for vanishing primitives' indeed underlie many defence of cultural identities, simplistically construed, against the perceived aggression of external forces.

However, far from being 'culturally neutral' intruders respectful of different traditions, international institutions in Afghanistan did, wilfully or not, intervened in the local culture lending, through their policy of cooperation and engagement with the Taliban, their support to one interpretation against the other. Their 'deliberate oversimplification of complex cultural meaning and multiplicity of voices obliterates the social fact that the women who were studying and teaching at Kabul University [pre-Taliban] – where they constituted the majority of students and staff – were as much part of Afghan culture as the groups who were at the same time advocating different values'.[187]

How is it possible that the UN could develop a practice that ran contrary not only to international legal standards, but also to the position expressed by its two most powerful political organs? A thorough answer to this question would require an empirical study of the functioning of the UN, focusing on decision-making processes. In the case of Afghanistan, the bureaucratic practice of the organisation, consisting of mission reports and policy statements, played a central role in determining the final terms on which the UN continued its engagement in that country. The reasons for this are manifold. There is no clear and independent monitoring machinery to ensure respect of the relevant principles, as well as decisions and policies laid down by these two organs. Both the General Assembly and the Security Council rely on the Secretary General to keep them updated with developments on the ground – an inappropriate arrangement because the Secretariat is obviously at the heart of the institutional/bureaucratic structure of the organisation. Crucially, the reaction of the political organs of the UN and their efficacy depend on consensus: racial

[185] S. Sontag, 'Fascinating Fascism', collected in S. Sontag *Under the Sign of Saturn* (New York: Anchor Books Doubleday, 1991) 86.

[186] *Ibid.*

[187] G. Verdirame, 'Testing the Effectiveness of International Norms: UN Humanitarian Assistance and Sexual Apartheid in Afghanistan', 23 Hum. Rts Q. (2001) 733 at 766.

discrimination is condemned both legally and politically but gender discrimination does not benefit from the same wide condemnation. Finally, an institutional culture has emerged within the UN that, in the name of an ill-conceived pragmatism, has reduced human rights to empty slogans rather than principles governing actions.

See, for instance, Sadako Ogata's comments on forced labour in the context of UNHCR's much criticised repatriation of the Rohingyas to Burma: 'Forced labour is an old tradition, it is something like a taxation, the poorer you are, the more often you are called in. I am not saying it is good or bad ...' Asked if forced labour does not constitute a human rights violation, she replied: 'It depends on how you define forced labour and how you define human rights violation. I think it has to be understood practically in the context of your community and their tradition, and then the limited choice these people have.'[188]

The essence of human rights is to put constraints on the exercise of power, but power is still mainly identified as the power of the state. Those on whom constraints are placed are likely to express uneasiness, often in the hope to be able to act 'boundlessly'. The development of an institutional culture hostile to principle has accompanied the organisational growth of the UN with its undertaking of operational missions on an ever larger scale. That a cosmopolitan and international bureaucracy can end up being in practice less progressive on such a crucial issue as that of gender discrimination than bodies composed of representatives of states is a deeply troubling fact.

[188] Transcript by Burma Centrum Nederland of the Press Conference of Sadako Ogata, UN High Commissioner for Refugees, The Hague, 1 September 1998.

5 UN peacekeeping operations

Introduction

Devoid of a clear textual foundation in the UN Charter, the phenomenon of peacekeeping operations originated as a practical response to the failure of the system of collective security as originally envisaged by the founders.[1] Since the first UN peacekeeping mission – the UN Truce Supervision Organization (UNTSO) established in 1948 to supervise the cessation of hostilities between Israel and neighbouring Arab states[2] – a total of sixty-three peacekeeping operations have been deployed around the world.[3] In 2005–10 alone, new peacekeeping missions were established in Sudan (UNMIS), East Timor (UNMIT), Darfur (UNAMID), Chad (MINURCAT) and the Democratic Republic of Congo (MONUSCO). By 2010 the UN managed seventeen operations comprising more than 117,000 military, police and civilian personnel across five continents.[4]

Peacekeeping has evolved over time to meet changing political situations and demands. At their inception during the cold war, peacekeeping operations performed a predominantly stabilising role through the military supervision of inter-state ceasefires and limited peace agreements, mostly in the Middle East. Under what is commonly known as the 'traditional interposition model', the majority of the fifteen operations established before 1989 were based on an unarmed or lightly armed military observer presence. With the exception of the intervention in Korea

[1] The literature on peacekeeping is vast. A bibliography prepared by the UN Department of Peacekeeping Operations is available at www.un.org/depts/dhl/pkeep.htm#W.

[2] SC Res. 50 (29 May 1948).

[3] See www.un.org/en/peacekeeping.

[4] See UN DPKO, 'United Nations Peacekeeping Operations: Background Notes' (28 February 2010), available at www.un.org/en/peacekeeping/bnote.htm.

in 1950, which was in any event an example of peace enforcement rather than peacekeeping, these operations were undertaken with the consent of the host state(s).[5] Obliged not to use force except in self-defence and with very little control over territory, such missions gave rise to little potential for abuse of the rights of individuals.

UN peacekeeping progressed into a new phase after the end of the cold war. Operations established since 1989 have often been multifunctional, part of the implementation of negotiated intra-state political settlements. These 'integrated mission model' operations included a mobile military force and a strong civilian component. Peacekeepers often assumed a wide range of new tasks and responsibilities, such as disarmament, police training and supervision, election monitoring, resettlement of refugees and human rights monitoring. The first of such operations is considered to be the UN Transition Assistance Group (UNTAG), which was deployed in Namibia in 1989.[6] An important feature of the mandates of this second generation of peacekeeping has been the exercise of governmental functions which, as will be discussed in Chapter 6, have in some cases come very close to forms of international administration of territory.

The changes in the nature of peacekeeping since the end of the cold war have led to a blurring of the distinction between peacekeeping and peace enforcement, particularly following the interventions in Somalia and in the former Yugoslavia.[7] In the same period the Security Council developed the practice of delegating the use of force to member states through the mechanism of authorisation, first employed for Operation Desert Storm in 1990.

Some UN interventions have involved a combination of traditional peacekeeping, peacekeeping for enforcement purposes, multifunctional peacekeeping, as well as the delegation of the power to use force to member states or a regional organisation. In some cases, a peacekeeping mission evolved in response to changes in the situation on the ground. For example, the mission in Sierra Leone started in 1998 as a small and unarmed observer operation in support of the peace agreement (UNOMSIL). Upon violation of that agreement, the

[5] N. White, *Keeping the Peace: The United Nations and the Maintenance of International Peace and Security* (Manchester University Press, 1993) 202; C. Gray, *International Law and the Use of Force* (3rd edn., Oxford University Press, 2008) 298–302.

[6] See, for example, N. J. Schrijver, 'Introducing Second Generation Peace-keeping: the case of Namibia', 6 *African Journal of International and Comparative Law* (1994) 1.

[7] Gray, *supra* note 5 at 281ff.

Security Council authorised the deployment of over 17,000 troops empowered to act against hostile elements.[8]

But the shift to robust peacekeeping is not without problems. In particular, borderline mandates – those that are ambiguous on the crucial question of the use of force – have often produced confusion, uncertainty, and sometimes prolonged and frustrating discussions between the operational and the political command of the mission.[9] At least equally problematic are interventions that combine a UN peacekeeping force with a Chapter VII authorisation to states, each one deployed under its own mandate and entirely or partially outside the structure of the other. The main examples of such 'co-habitation' of mandates in the 1990s were the UN Assistance Mission in Rwanda (UNAMIR) and the intervention of French troops under Operation Turquoise in 1994, and the United Nations Protection force (UNPROFOR) and NATO in the former Yugoslavia.

Since the end of the cold war there have been two main attempts to reform UN peacekeeping. The first one was the Brahimi Report, which was written in the aftermath of the failures of the collective security system in Somalia, Rwanda and in the former Yugoslavia in the 1990s. The Report contained a wide range of proposals for reform and insisted, among other things, on the need to adopt mandates that are 'clear, credible and achievable' – a recommendation which the Security Council itself endorsed.[10] Implementation of the Brahimi Report has not been easy, not least because some of its recommendations entailed a structural reform of the UN system beyond peacekeeping.[11]

The second major attempt to re-model peacekeeping was Peace Operations 2010, which was launched by the Secretary General in 2006 and culminated in the adoption of the 'Capstone Doctrine'.[12]

[8] On UNOMSIL see SC Res. 1181 (1998). On UNAMSIL see SC Res. 1270 (1999), and SC Res. 1289 (2000) – the latter adopted under Chapter VII of the Charter.

[9] On the problems the ambiguous mandate created for the UN peacekeeping mission in Rwanda (UNAMIR) during the genocide, see R. Dallaire, *Shake Hands with the Devil: The Failure of Humanity in Rwanda* (Canada, Random House, 2004) 233ff.

[10] General Assembly and Security Council, 'Report of the Panel on United Nations Peace Operations ("Brahimi Report")', 21 August 2000, UN Doc. A/55/305, S/2000/809 at paras. 56ff.; SC Res. 1327 (2000).

[11] See Gray, *supra* note 5 at 307ff. and by the same author 'Peacekeeping after the *Brahimi Report*: Is there a Crisis of Credibility for the UN', 6 *Journal of Conflict and Security Law* (2001) 267.

[12] Report of the Secretary General to the General Assembly on the Financing of UN Peacekeeping Operations, UN Doc. A/60/696; Department of Peacekeeping Operations and Department of Field Support, *UN Peacekeeping Operations: Principles and Guidelines: 'Capstone Doctrine'* (2008).

The centrepiece of the Doctrine is 'an alteration of the basic principle that peacekeeping forces should not use force except in self-defence. Instead it calls for "restraint in use of force"'.[13] The difference between peace enforcement and robust peacekeeping under this Doctrine is that '[w]hile robust peacekeeping involves the use of force at the tactical level with the consent of the host authorities and/or the main parties to the conflict, peace enforcement may involve the use of force at the strategic or international level, which is normally prohibited for Member States under Article 2(4) of the Charter unless authorised by the Security Council'.[14] As emphasised by Gray, however, this distinction is not without its difficulties.[15]

The question of command and control

All components of a peacekeeping operation fall under the operational authority of the head of mission. Traditionally this was the force commander, who answered to the Secretary General. With the expansion of peacekeeping into larger civilian roles, however, the practice has been to appoint a Special Representative of the Secretary General with authority over both the civilian and military elements of the mission.[16] This is in order to enhance the overall effectiveness of the mission and to avoid the kind of tensions between the military and civilian components that plagued operations such as UNAMIR during the Rwandan genocide. The presence of a head of mission does not necessarily mean that the mission is under UN command.[17] The actual level of command and control conferred upon the UN may vary in accordance with the terms contained in the participating host state agreement and/or memorandum of understanding with the contributing state.

The diversity of command and control structures raises the question of attribution. In peacekeeping operations, the position of the UN Legal Counsel is that '[a]s a subsidiary organ of the United Nations, an act of a peacekeeping force is, in principle, imputable to the Organisation, and if committed in violation of an international obligation entails the international responsibility of the Organisation

[13] Gray, *supra* note 5 at 324. [14] Capstone Doctrine, *supra* note 12 at 19.
[15] Gray, *supra* note 5. [16] *Ibid.* at 68.
[17] D. Bowett, *UN Forces: A Legal Study of United Nations Practice* (London: Stevens, 1966) at 68.

and its liability in compensation'.[18] The Secretary General maintained that, in such cases, the UN is entitled to 'seek recovery from the State of nationality' – a position endorsed by the General Assembly.[19] In addition to the right to recover, it is appropriate in some circumstances for the UN and the sending state to share responsibility in the first place.

As explained in Chapter 3 (103ff.), the rule of attribution relevant to peacekeeping is Article 6 of the Draft Articles on the Responsibility of International Organisations.[20] The key test for determining attribution of conduct in peacekeeping operations is effective control. Without reiterating the analysis of the various problems to which the application of Article 6 can give rise and which the rapidly expanding case law on this question (in particular the ECtHR decision in *Behrami and Saramati*)[21] has exacerbated, it is useful to remember that in applying the test of effective control to peacekeeping operations one must avoid the mistake made by the District Court of The Hague. It was held by this Court that, since the Dutch contingent in Srebrenica was part of UNPROFOR, its acts and omissions in relation to the massacre of Srebrenica 'should be attributed strictly, as a matter of principle, to the United Nations', because 'participation in a UN peacekeeping operation on the basis of chapter VII of the Charter implies that the "operational command and control" over the troops made available is transferred to the UN'.[22]

In theory, it may be true that peacekeeping operations, particularly those under Chapter VII, 'imply' that the UN has operational command and control. In practice, however, this is not always the case, mainly because states are reluctant to completely relinquish

[18] Unpublished letter of 3 February 2004 by the United Nations Legal Counsel to the Director of the Codification Division, quoted in ILC Report (2004), UN Doc. A/59/10 at 112.

[19] Report of the Secretary General on 'Administrative and Budgetary Aspects of the Financing of United Nations Peacekeeping Operations', 20 September 1996, UN Doc. A/51/389 (reproduced in 37 ILM 700) at para. 42, and GA Res. 52/247, 17 July 1998.

[20] The text of the Draft Articles on the Responsibility of International Organisations is at ILC Report (2009), UN Doc. A/64/10.

[21] *Behrami and Behrami v. France*, Application no. 71412/01 and *Saramati v. France, Germany and Norway*, Application no. 78166/01, Decision on Admissibility.

[22] *M. M-M, D.M and A.M (Mustafic) and H.N. (Hasan Nuhanovic) v. The Netherlands*, Case No. 265615/HA ZA 06-1671, Judgment of 10 September 2008, at paras. 4.8 and 4.11 (at 450–451 in the *Netherlands International Law Review*).

control of their troops. Troops often take orders from their national officers or, at the very least, choose not to follow an order that is opposed by their national commander, even if it emanates from an officer who is more senior in terms of the hierarchy of the mission. For example, in the case of the second UN Operation in Somalia (UNOSOM II), the Commission of Inquiry found that '[t]he Force Commander of UNOSOM II was not in effective control of several national contingents which, in varying degrees, persisted in seeking orders from their home authorities before executing orders of the Forces Command. Many major operations undertaken under the United Nations flag ... were totally outside the command and control of the United Nations'.[23]

The Capstone Doctrine has sought to cast light on authority, command and control in UN peacekeeping missions by distinguishing three levels: a strategic level with the Security Council at the top, followed by the Secretary General (with the assistance of the UN Secretariat) and by the head of mission; an operational level with the head of mission at the top, followed by the top staff of the mission and the component heads; and a tactical level with the components' heads at the top, followed by the civilian, military and police units. This analysis does not, however, show the crucial interplay between states, in particular troop-contributing states, and the UN – a *de facto* 'contamination' of the UN command and control structure affecting each of the levels identified by the Capstone Doctrine. The result is that there can be no hard and fast rule on command and control of UN peacekeeping missions, and each instance of conduct can be attributed only on the basis of a careful examination of the facts, including an assessment of command and control structures both as conceived and as implemented.

Even where it has no effective control over conduct, the UN is not exonerated from responsibility. It can in fact still incur responsibility on a derivative basis. The most likely categories of derivative responsibility to be engaged in peacekeeping missions are complicity under Article 13 of the Draft Articles, and the responsibility of the international organisation for acts committed by states pursuant to one of its decisions, authorisations or recommendations under Article 16 – both discussed in Chapter 3 (135–136 and 127–129, respectively).

[23] Report of the Commission of Inquiry on Somalia, UN Doc. S/1994/653, paras. 243–4, cited in commentary to Article 6 in ILC (2009), *supra* note 20.

Applicable law

Principles and rules of general applicability

Obligations deriving from customary rules of international human rights law and international humanitarian law

As argued in Chapter 2, the conferral of international legal personality on the UN has obligatory consequences. In particular, the UN is bound to respect customary international law, including customary rules of international human rights law and international humanitarian law. Even where the mandate of the peacekeeping mission is silent, therefore, it is possible to ascribe the bulk of human rights and humanitarian obligations to the UN through this route. Saving clauses in the Convention on the Safety of United Nations and Associated Personnel and in the model SOFA lend some support, *a contrario*, to the applicability of these obligations to peacekeeping missions.[24] In order to ensure that these obligations are given the respect and attention they deserve at the operational level, however, their express inclusion in the mandate is still advisable.[25]

It has been correctly observed that human rights and international humanitarian law may continue to bind sending states. In theory, if each national component of the peacekeeping mission is bound by these obligations, the mission as a whole will be bound – at least in a practical if not strictly legal sense.[26] This proposition must however be subject to two qualifications. First, in order to engage the direct responsibility of the sending state for a breach of one of those obligations, it will be necessary to establish attribution of the relevant conduct to the state – a point which emphasises, once again, the importance of developing a correct approach to Article 6 of the Draft Articles on the Responsibility of International Organisations.

[24] See Art. 2(2) of the Convention on the Safety of United Nations and Associated Personnel (1994), 2051 UNTS 363, adopted by the General Assembly in GA Res. 49/59 of 9 December 1994. This Convention came into force on 15 January 1999 and, as at 25 August 2010, has been ratified by eighty-nine states (the most recent ratification coming from Saudi Arabia on 22 March 2010). See C. Bourloyannis-Vrailas, 'The Convention on the Safety of United Nations and Associated Personnel', 44 *International and Comparative Law Quarterly* (1995) 560 at 583; O. Engdahl, *Protection of Personnel in Peace Operations: The Role of the 'Safety Convention' against the Background of General International Law* (2007).

[25] B. E. Klappe, 'International Peace Operations', in D. Fleck (ed.), *The Handbook of International Humanitarian Law* (2nd edn., Oxford University Press, 2008) 635 at 644.

[26] *Ibid.*

Sending states have an incentive to ensure that their national contingents respect human rights and humanitarian obligations in order to avoid findings of responsibility. This incentive is, however, removed if courts proceed on the assumption that the UN has effective control over conduct in all peacekeeping missions and that dual attribution is not a possibility, since the effect of these assumptions will be to preclude attribution of conduct to states and thus to protect states from direct responsibility. Secondly, the extraterritorial application of international human rights law is subject to greater restrictions than that of the law of armed conflict.[27] The plentiful litigation in domestic and international human rights courts in connection to armed conflicts in the 1990s and 2000s shows that human rights law is much more likely to provide a cause of action to these claims than the law of armed conflict. But, in order to succeed, claimants must be able to establish jurisdiction *rat-i-one loci*.

Resolutions of the Security Council

In a departure from its traditional approach based on conflict-specific resolutions, the Security Council has attempted to lay down general rules on armed conflict, adopting a series of resolutions that deal with women, children, and civilians in armed conflict.

A milestone was Security Council resolution 1325 (2000). It covered three main areas. First, it emphasised women's role in preventing and resolving conflict, recognising their capacity as peacebuilders, rather than treating them merely as potential victims of violence. It urged states to ensure that women be involved in decision-making and the prevention, management and resolution of conflicts, and that their presence in field-based operations be expanded, especially among military observers, civilian police, human rights and humanitarian personnel. Secondly, the resolution recognised the need for protection of women, particularly from sexual violence, and stressed the obligation of states to prosecute those responsible for such violence, as well as the need to exclude, where feasible, violent crimes against women from amnesty provisions. Thirdly, the resolution called for the adoption of a 'gender perspective', including gender-sensitive training of personnel on the rights and particular needs of women. States were urged to

[27] G. Verdirame, 'Human Rights in Wartime: A Framework for Analysis', 6 *European Human Rights Law Review* (2008) 689.

increase their financial, technical and logistical support for such training. In two follow-up resolutions, the Security Council reiterated and amplified these recommendations.[28]

With resolution 1612 (2005), the Security Council requested the Secretary General to implement without delay a monitoring and reporting mechanism on the recruitment and use of child soldiers by parties to an armed conflict. This reporting mechanism requires the collection of information on recruitment, as well as on other violations and abuses committed against children affected by armed conflict.[29]

Resolution 1674 (2006) dealt with the protection of civilians in armed conflict. It reaffirmed the above resolutions and condemned all sexual and other violence committed against civilians. It also undertook to ensure that peace support operations employ all feasible measures to prevent such violence and to address its impact where it has taken place.

The 1999 Bulletin of the Secretary General on the Observance by UN Forces of International Humanitarian Law

Debate concerning the applicability of international humanitarian law to peacekeeping operations first arose during the intervention in Korea. On that occasion, as on others subsequently, the UN declared its generic commitment to international humanitarian law in principle, but argued that it was not actually bound by humanitarian law obligations because it was not a party to the relevant treaties. The position of the UN Office of Legal Affairs was 'that the United Nations is not substantively in a position to become a party to the 1949 Conventions' on the grounds that, as an international organisation, it did not possess the powers required to fulfil certain obligations.[30]

[28] SC Res. 1820 (2008) and 1888 (2009).

[29] Security Council Cross-Cutting Report No. 1, 'Children and Armed Conflict' (15 April 2009). See also SC Res. 1882 (2009).

[30] UN Office of Legal Affairs, 'Possible Accession of Intergovernmental Organisations to the Geneva Conventions for the Protection of War Victims', *UN Juridical Yearbook* (1972) 153. For an analytical summary of the main UN documents that preceded the Secretary General's Bulletin, see B. Oswald, H. Durham and A. Bates, *Documents on the Law of UN Peace Operations* (Oxford University Press, 2010) 198. See also H. P Gasser, 'Die Anwendbarkeit des Humanitären Völkerrechts auf militärische Operationen der Vereinten Nationen', 5 *Revue Suisse de Droit International et de Droit Européen* (1994) 443 at 462; C. Greenwood, 'International Humanitarian Law and United Nations Military Operations', 1 Yearbook Int. Humanit. L. (1998) 3; UK Ministry of Defence, *The Manual of the Law of Armed Conflict* (Oxford University Press, 2004) 378–80.

With the expansion of robust peacekeeping and peace enforcement in the 1990s, this position became untenable. At first, the UN sought to address the problem by including specific provisions on respect for the 'principles and spirit' of the Geneva Conventions in SOFAs concluded with host countries. Ironically, the first such SOFA seems to have been the one concluded by UNAMIR in 1993 a few months before the Rwandan genocide – probably the greatest failure of UN peacekeeping of all times.[31] In 1995 the UN Special Committee on Peacekeeping Operations requested the Secretary General to 'complete the elaboration of a code of conduct for United Nations peace-keeping personnel, consistent with applicable International Humanitarian Law'.[32] A group of experts convened by the ICRC worked with the UN Secretariat to develop a set of core humanitarian law principles applicable in UN peacekeeping operations.[33]

This work led to the Bulletin on the Observance by United Nations Forces of International Humanitarian Law issued by the Secretary General in August 1999.[34] Bulletins of the Secretary General are administrative issuances, which are generally accepted by the UN Administrative Tribunal 'as interpreting the Staff Regulations and Staff Rules, or they are recognised as valuable additional regulatory instruments in the application of the Staff Regulations and Rules'.[35] The Bulletin was also promulgated to comply with the Secretary General's obligation, contained in post-1993 SOFAs, to acquaint members of UN operations with the principles and rules of humanitarian law.[36] In this respect, the Bulletin serves primarily as an educational

[31] See Art. 7, UNAMIR SOFA; para. 7(a), UNPROFOR SOFA; para. 7(a), UNIFIL SOFA; para. 6(a), UNAVEM III SOFA.

[32] Report of the Special Committee on Peacekeeping Operations, UN Doc. A/50/230, para. 73.

[33] See ICRC Press Release 96/19, 15 May 1996.

[34] Other instruments include: 'We Are United Nations Peacekeeping Personnel', published as Annex H to the 2007 Model Memorandum of Understanding (MOU), providing, inter alia, that forces will comply with the Secretary General's Bulletin on humanitarian law and the applicable portions of the UDHR 'as the fundamental basis of our standards' (Annex H in UN Doc. A/61/19 (Part III), reprinted in Oswald *et al.*, *supra* note 30 at 381); Directives for Disciplinary Matters Involving Military Members of National Contingents (UN Doc. DPKO/MD/03/00993, extracts in Oswald *et al.*, *supra* note 30 at 387).

[35] W. Münch and W. Göttelmann, 'Article 101', in B. Simma (ed.), *The Charter of the United Nations: A Commentary* (2nd edn., Oxford University Press, 2002) 1252 at 1260.

[36] D. Shraga, 'UN Peacekeeping Operations: Applicability of International Humanitarian Law and Responsibility for Operations-Releated Damage', 94 AJIL (2000) 406 at 407. See also Section 3 of the Bulletin.

tool in disseminating information concerning applicable rules of humanitarian law.[37]

The 1999 Bulletin, which affirmed the applicability of 'fundamental principles and rules of international humanitarian law' in enforcement actions and 'in peacekeeping operations when the use of force is permitted in self-defence',[38] was not meant to fill in a vacuum in the legal basis for the application of international humanitarian law to the UN; nor should it be regarded as a codification of customary rules, 'but rather [as] a summary of what were considered the most important rules in the context of peace support operations'.[39]

The Bulletin consists of ten sections comprising thirty-four articles. The provisions apply to UN forces in situations of armed conflict who are, or may be, actively engaged as combatants 'to the extent and for the duration of their engagement' (Section 1) – a qualification which appears to imply that the status of an operation's personnel as party or non-party to an armed conflict may vary intermittently and which has, quite rightly, been described as 'unfortunate' and likely to engender 'confusion'.[40]

The Bulletin requires that SOFAs concluded by the UN include an undertaking to ensure that the members of the operation act 'with full respect for the principles and rules of the general conventions applicable to the conduct of military personnel', while specifying that such principles and rules are applicable even in the absence of a SOFA. The formula 'principles and rules' of humanitarian law replaces the softer 'principles and spirit' formulation, which had been used previously and which had suggested that the UN did not consider itself 'necessarily constrained by the customary international law provisions of the Conventions and Protocols as the lowest common denominator by which all national contingents would otherwise be bound'.[41]

As far as the specific substantive standards incorporated in the Bulletin are concerned, Section 2 explains that the provisions 'do not constitute an exhaustive list of principles and rules of humanitarian law binding

[37] M. Zwanenburg, *Accountability of Peace Support Operations* (Leiden: Martinus Nijhoff, 2005) 174.

[38] Secretary General, 'Bulletin on the Observance by the United Nations Forces of International Humanitarian Law', UN Doc. ST/SGB/1999/13, reprinted in 38 ILM (1999) 1656; extract in Oswald *et al.*, *supra* note 30 at 201ff. See also Report of Secretary General, 'Road Map Towards the Implementation of the United Nations Millennium Declaration of 6 September 2001', UN Doc. A/56/326, para. 19.

[39] Zwanenburg, *supra* note 37 at 176. [40] *Ibid.* at 190.

[41] Shraga, *supra* note 36 at 408. See paras. 6(a) in: MINURCA SOFA; UNAMSIL SOFA; UNMISET SOFA; and UNMEE-Ethiopia SOFA.

upon military personnel and do not prejudice the application' of other rules of humanitarian law or relevant national laws. Incorporated standards include the protection of the civilian population, means and methods of combat, treatment of civilians and persons *hors de combat*, treatment of detained persons, protection of the wounded and the sick, and medical and relief personnel. This does not amount to the entire body of the law of armed conflict, but only to a summary of some of its provisions. Nothing, for example, is said on the applicability of the law of belligerent occupation to peacekeeping operations.[42] The Bulletin also provides that military personnel are subject to the jurisdiction of their national state's courts in respect of any violations of humanitarian law – a stipulation that is consistent with state and institutional practice evidenced in SOFAs and agreements with troop-contributing states, and does not preclude prosecution before the International Criminal Court (ICC).

Internal rules on sexual abuse and sexual exploitation

In response to allegations of sexual abuse and exploitation published at the beginning of 2005, the UN adopted various internal rules. The most important document in this respect is the Secretary General's Bulletin on Special Measures for Protection from Sexual Exploitation and Sexual Abuse.[43] The Bulletin defines sexual exploitation as 'any actual or attempted abuse of a position of vulnerability, differential power, or trust, for sexual purposes, including, but not limited to, profiting monetarily, socially or politically from sexual exploitation of another' person, while sexual abuse is defined as 'actual or threatened physical intrusion of a sexual nature, whether by force or under unequal or coercive conditions' (Section 1).[44]

As with other examples of administrative self-regulation, enforcement is far from ideal. The Bulletin does require peacekeeping missions to have a staff officer who is the confidential focal point for receiving information and complaints (Section 4(3)). The head of mission is also

[42] On this point see A. Faite, 'Multinational Forces Acting Pursuant to a Mandate of the United Nations: Specific Issues on the Applicability of International Humanitarian Law', 11 *Journal of International Peacekeeping* (2007) 143 at 148–56.

[43] See UN Doc. ST/SGB/2003/13, reprinted in Oswald *et al.*, *supra* note 30 at 435. See also Directive on Sexual Harassment in United Nations Peacekeeping and Other Field Missions for Military Members of National Contingents, Military Observers and Civilian Police Officers (UN Doc. DPKO/CPD/DSHCPO/2003/002, also in Oswald *et al.*, *ibid.* at 418ff.).

[44] UN Doc. ST/SGB/2003/13, *ibid.* at 435.

required to take 'appropriate action in cases where there is reason to believe' that any stipulated standard has been violated (Section 4(2)). In such cases, the head of mission is under a duty to start disciplinary proceedings in terms of the Directives for Disciplinary Matters. As confirmed by these Directives, however, military members of national contingents assigned to a UN peacekeeping force 'shall be subject to the exclusive jurisdiction of their respective participating States in respect of any criminal offences that may be committed by them in the mission area', although they are 'subject to the jurisdiction of the host country/territory in respect of any disputes/claims of a civil nature not related to the performance of their official functions' (Section V).

These jurisdictional limits exacerbate the already serious imbalance of power that inevitably exists in the relationship between a civilian population and an international armed force. The UN rules are not entirely oblivious to this imbalance of power, but what is not fully appreciated is that a more credible enforcement mechanism would go a long way towards alleviating it. Under the existing system, instead, a victim of abuse or exploitation is expected to file a complaint with the very office where the alleged perpetrator is based. She has no effective recourse to the criminal law, often the only process that can give some assurance to victims of serious crimes. Although the possibility of a criminal trial in the country of origin of the peacekeeper does exist, the prospect of a trial in a distant and foreign country is unlikely to give a victim any sense of safety or justice.

Mission-specific obligations

The mandate

A peacekeeping operation is normally established by resolution of the Security Council. The old debate about the powers of the General Assembly in this field, which was at the heart of the *Certain Expenses* case,[45] has lost relevance given that the General Assembly no longer exercises any such power.

As discussed, one of the challenges for the Security Council is to prepare mandates that, while 'clear, credible and achievable',[46] are broad enough 'to cover evolving scenarios'.[47] Flexibility should not, however, become a carte blanche in the form of a mandate that is so open-textured as to leave the operational level completely in control.

[45] *Certain Expenses of the UN*, Advisory Opinion, ICJ Reports (1962) 151.

[46] See *supra* note 10. [47] Klappe, *supra* note 25 at 650.

In principle, if the situation on the ground does change completely, the Security Council should respond by revising the terms of the mandate. The political failure of the Security Council to act promptly in the face of such changes has led to some of the worst failures in the history of UN peacekeeping, most notably during the Rwandan genocide.

A key question to be addressed in the mandate is on the use of force by the peacekeeping mission. The mandate must be sufficiently clear on this point as to allow the adoption of Rules of Engagement that can be implemented by the troops on the ground.[48] The Capstone Doctrine seeks to crystallise the shift towards robust peacekeeping by adopting, as a basic foundation of UN peacekeeping, the principle of 'non-use of force except in self-defence and defence of the mandate' in place of the narrower exception of pure self-defence relied upon in the past.[49] This more purposive approach to the use of force inevitably has repercussions on the other two cornerstones of peacekeeping, that is impartiality and consent. It is nonetheless believed to be better tailored to the challenges that UN forces have to face.[50]

The Capstone Doctrine explains:

'The environments into which United Nations peacekeeping operations are deployed are often characterized by the presence of militias, criminal gangs, and other spoilers who may actively seek to undermine the peace process or pose a threat to the civilian population. In such situations, the Security Council has given United Nations peacekeeping operations "robust" mandates authorizing them to "use all necessary means" to deter forceful attempts to disrupt the political process, protect civilians under imminent threat of physical attack, and/or assist the national authorities in maintaining law and order. By proactively using force in defense of their mandates, these United Nations peacekeeping operations have succeeded in improving the security situation and creating an environment conducive to longer-term peacebuilding in the countries where they are deployed.'[51]

SOFAs

Given the consensual nature of most peacekeeping operations, the SOFAs concluded with host countries constitute an important source of obligations. One of the purposes of SOFAs is to enable peacekeeping

[48] *Ibid.* at 655ff. [49] Capstone Doctrine, *supra* note 12 at 31.

[50] On impartiality and consent see *ibid.* On impartiality, see V. Shyla, 'Impartiality in United Nations Peace-Keeping', 9 *Leiden Journal of International Law* (1996) 63 (dealing with the tensions between impartiality and the use of force at 82–3).

[51] Capstone Doctrine, *supra* note 12 at 34.

missions to function without undue interference. SOFAs normally enumerate the specific freedoms, privileges, duties and immunities attaching to the mission and its members which the host state obliges itself to uphold. Although bilateral in nature, SOFAs embody a careful tripartite balance between the competing interests of the UN, the host state and participating states. As Bowett notes, SOFAs 'represent compromises and shifts between the law of visiting forces on the one hand and the law of international privileges and immunities on the other, against the background of functional necessity'.[52]

In principle a SOFA is concluded for every peacekeeping operation. In practice this has not always been possible, for example where, as in Somalia, there was no effective government. Additionally, it is not uncommon for a SOFA to be concluded after the deployment of the operation with retroactive effect.[53] Aside from specific exceptions relating to immunity and the settlement of disputes, a SOFA generally takes effect from the date of signature and remains in force until the departure of the last element of the UN operation.[54]

In 1990 the Secretary General prepared a UN Model SOFA based upon 'established practice and drawing extensively upon earlier and current agreements'.[55] The model is intended to serve as a basis for drafting individual agreements adapted to the needs of particular operations.[56] The Model SOFA emphasises the exclusively impartial nature of the operation which the host state is under an obligation to respect. The operation and its members are obliged to refrain from any action or activity which is incompatible with the nature of their duties or inconsistent with the agreement (para. 6), and, more specifically, to 'respect all local laws and regulations' – a particularly important provision as it creates a further route through which human rights obligations might

[52] Bowett, *supra* note 17 at 434.

[53] For example, United Nations Operation in the Congo (ONUC) 1960 where negotiations on a SOFA were postponed due to internal disturbances. An agreement was concluded in November 1961 and deemed to have taken effect from the time of deployment (414 UNTS 229). the August 2000 SOFA on KFOR and UNMIK was deemed to have entered into force on 10 June 1999 (Regulation No. 2000/47, s. 11).

[54] Report of the Secretary General, 'Model Status-of-Forces Agreement for Peace-keeping Operations' (9 October 1990), UN Doc. A/45/594, at paras. 59–60.

[55] *Ibid.* The model is found as an Annex to the report, also reprinted in Oswald *et al.*, *supra* note 30 at 39.

[56] *Ibid.* at para. 1. On Model SOFAs and customary international law, see Zwanenburg, *supra* note 37 at 36.

bind both the mission as a discrete legal entity, and, insofar as relevant, its members acting in official capacity.

The Model SOFA prescribes the application of the 1946 Convention on the Privileges and Immunities of the UN to the peacekeeping operation. As a subsidiary organ of the UN, the operation enjoys the status, privileges and immunities of the UN (para. 15). Privileges and immunities also attach to members of the operation, including the special representative or force commander (para. 4). Further protection under Article II of the 1946 Convention extends to the property, funds and assets of participating states used in connection with the operation (para. 5). Ultimate responsibility for the implementation and fulfilment of the privileges, immunities and rights provided for by the SOFA lies with the host government (para. 57). The level of immunity accorded to a member of a peacekeeping force depends on the category of personnel to which he belongs.[57] It has further been suggested that in certain circumstances some members of peacekeeping forces may also benefit from the sovereign immunity of the sending state.[58]

The Model SOFA distinguishes between various types of members in allocating privileges and immunities. First, high-ranking officials including the special representative, the force commander and the head of the civilian police enjoy the privileges and immunities of diplomatic envoys under international law in accordance with Sections 19 and 27 of the 1946 Convention (para. 24). Secondly, members of the UN Secretariat assigned to the civilian component are treated as UN officials entitled to the privileges and immunities under Article V and laissez-passer holders in accordance with Article VII of the 1946 Convention (para. 25). Thirdly, military observers, civilian police and civilian personnel are normally considered as experts on mission enjoying such privileges and immunities as are necessary for the independent exercise of their functions in accordance with Article VI of the 1946 Convention (para. 26). Fourthly, military personnel of national contingents benefit from the privileges and immunities specifically provided for under the SOFA (para. 27). Lastly, locally recruited members

[57] F. J. Hampson and A. Kihara-Hunt, 'The Accountability of Personnel Associated with Peacekeeping Operations', in C. Aoi, C. de Coning and R Thakur (eds.), *Unintended Consequences of Peacekeeping Operations* (New York: United Nations University Press, 2007) 195.

[58] *Ibid.* at 199.

generally enjoy immunities concerning official acts in accordance with Section 18(a) of the 1946 Convention (para. 28).

Responsibility for the maintenance of discipline and good order among members of the operation vests with the special representative or force commander. The military police are given powers of arrest over military members, since the UN cannot exercise executive power over members of national contingents. Arrested individuals must be transferred to their contingent commander for appropriate action (para. 41). Other persons found on the operation's premises may also be arrested and shall be delivered immediately to the nearest appropriate government official (*ibid.*).

The careful compromise between host state, UN and participating state interests is perhaps seen most clearly in the provisions governing jurisdiction. A general rule is that all members of the operation are immune from the legal process of the host state in respect of words spoken or written and all acts performed in their official capacity (*ibid.*). This immunity continues after such persons cease to be members of, or employed by, the operation (para. 46). Nevertheless, the host state and the operation are obliged to cooperate in the investigation of any offences in respect of which either or both have an interest (para. 44). Where the host government suspects that a member of the operation has committed a criminal offence, it should immediately inform the special representative or force commander and present all available evidence (para. 47). The jurisdictional arrangements differ depending on the status of the member in question. Where the accused is a member of the civilian component or a civilian member of a military component, the special representative or force commander will conduct any necessary supplementary inquiry and then seek to decide in conjunction with the host government whether criminal proceedings should be instituted. Failing agreement with the host state on how to proceed, a tribunal of three arbitrators will be appointed to resolve the matter (para. 47(a)). In contrast, where the accused person is a military member of the military component, it is an established principle that the appropriate participating state exercises exclusive jurisdiction (para. 47(b)).

Quite crucially, in contrast with the position of other personnel, the Secretary General has no right to waive immunity in relation to such personnel whose immunities derive from the SOFA itself rather than the General Convention (para. 27). That right remains with the state of nationality of the peacekeeper. The Secretary General, however, undertakes to obtain assurances regarding participating states' willingness to exercise criminal jurisdiction over members of their national contingents (para. 48). The Model SOFA already envisaged that such assurances could be contained in a memorandum of understanding. The Model Agreement with troop-contributing states, discussed below, does indeed contain such a provision at Article 7(22)–(23). As explored in more detail later in this chapter, a failure by the participating state to exercise domestic criminal jurisdiction with regard to certain crimes may result in the assumption of jurisdiction by the ICC over those crimes.

Where civil proceedings are initiated against any member of a peacekeeping mission in the courts of the host state, the host state shall notify the special representative or force commander immediately, who shall certify whether or not the proceeding is related to the member's official duties. If the proceedings relate to official duties, they must be discontinued immediately. By contrast, if they relate to off-duty conduct, they may continue.

The Model SOFA lacks any reference to the applicability of international humanitarian law. In 1992 the UN Secretariat stated that it was in the process of developing a formula on humanitarian law to be inserted into future SOFAs.[59] As discussed above, a number of SOFAs do in fact include references to humanitarian law.[60]

The Model MOU with contributing states

The conditions under which a troop-contributing state is willing to participate in an operation are generally recorded in an agreement or MOU with the UN. In 1991 the Secretary General prepared a draft Model MOU, which was rewritten in 1997 and modified again in 2007.[61] The Model MOU is intended to serve as a basis for drafting individual agreements with troop-contributing states.

[59] Letter to the President of the ICRC, 'Question on the Application of the 1949 Geneva Conventions for the Protection of War Victims and Their Additional Protocols in Peacekeeping Operations of the United Nations', UN Jur. YB (1992) 430.

[60] See *supra* note 31 and note 41.

[61] UN Doc. A/46/185, 23 May 1991; UN Doc. A/51/967 of 27 August 1997; GA Res 61/267B; UN Doc. A/61/494 (3 October 2006); 'Memorandum of understanding between the United Nations and [participating State] contributing resources to [the United Nations Peacekeeping Operation]', in *Manual on Policies and Procedures Concerning the Reimbursement and Control of Contingent-Owned Equipment of Troop/Police Contributors Participating in Peacekeeping Missions (COE Manual)*, UN Doc. A/C.5/63/18 at 161.

The purpose of the Model MOU is to establish the administrative, logistic and financial terms and conditions govern the contribution of personnel, equipment, and services and to specify standards of conduct (Article 3). Annex H to the Model MOU, entitled 'We Are United Nations Peacekeepers', incorporates various standards of conduct. The state is under an obligation to ensure that all the members it contributes comply with these standards and receive the necessary training for their understanding and observance (Article 7(2)–(4)).

Under the Model MOU, responsibility for conducting investigations on allegations of misconduct and for maintaining discipline among national contingents lies upon the relevant contributing state (Article 7(5)–(21)). The Model MOU reaffirms the principle that military members are subject to the exclusive jurisdiction of their respective state but also contains an undertaking of the state to exercise that jurisdiction with respect to crimes or offences committed by members of their contingents. Where an investigation finds that suspicions of misconduct are well founded, the government shall forward the case on to its appropriate authorities for due action.

Articles 9 and 10 of the Model MOU govern the UN's liability for third party claims. These provisions distinguish between claims arising from the acts of the state's personnel or from equipment in the performance of operations under the MOU (for which the UN will be responsible) and those arising from gross negligence or wilful misconduct of the contributing state's personnel (for which that state shall be liable). The UN may be held responsible for such grossly negligent or wilful misconduct but it is entitled to an indemnity from the contributing state in such circumstances.[62] Similarly, the UN has a right to reimbursement for any damage occurring from 'off duty' acts performed outside the operation's functions as provided for in the Model Agreement.

Scope for abuse

Peacekeeping missions have on a number of occasions been found responsible for the conduct of members who, abusing their unique

[62] Article 10. See also G. Gaja, 'Second Report on Responsibility of International Organisations by the Special Rapporteur', 56th Session of the ILC, UN Doc. A/CN.4/541, at 21; UN Secretariat, 'Responsibility of International Organisations: Comments and Observations Received from International Organisations', UN Doc. A/CN.4/545 (25 June 2004), at 18.

position of trust and authority vis-à-vis the local population, committed a variety of human rights violations. The types of violations which have given rise to the greatest concerns have involved sexual abuse and exploitation, torture and arbitrary detentions, and, in Rwanda and in the former Yugoslavia, the failure to prevent genocide.

Sexual abuse and exploitation

A series of reports in the early 2000s published evidence of sexual abuse and exploitation by aid workers and peacekeepers. In particular, media reports in 2004 revealed a pattern of sexual abuse and exploitation in the United Nations Organisation Mission in the DRC (MONUC).[63] Most of the allegations were that peacekeepers were paying for and engaging in sex with women and girls younger than 18. By July 2004, sixty-eight such allegations against MONUC personnel were reported, including the rape of minors and babies, child pornography and organised sex shows. By early 2005, at least seven of these cases of sexual exploitation and abuse were confirmed, and it was proven that children had been used for sex. Payment was reported to range from two eggs to $5 per encounter. Victims included abandoned orphans, who were often illiterate.[64] In only a few instances were those allegations followed by trials in the courts of the peacekeepers' sending states.[65]

This was not the first time that cases of sexual abuse and violence by peacekeepers were reported. Indeed, Graça Machel's seminal report on children in armed conflict had already noted the rise in cases of child prostitution in the areas where UN troops were deployed.[66] Even before her report was released, Ernst Schade brought into light the existence

[63] *The Independent* (London), 25 May 2004, 'Cover story: Sex and death in the heart of Africa', Kate Holt and Sarah Hughes; *The Independent* (London) 12 July 2004, 'Will Congo's women ever have justice?', Kate Holt; *The Times* (London) December 2004, 'Sex scandal in Congo threatens to engulf UN's peacekeepers', Jonathan Clayton and James Bone; *The Independent* (London), 11 February 2005, 'Annan backs tough action to stop Congo Sex abuse', Anne Penketh. As for West Africa, see UNHCR and Save the Children–UK, 'Sexual Violence and Exploitation: The Experience of Refugee Children in Guinea, Liberia and Sierra Leone' (February 2002) available at www.savethechildren.org.uk/en/docs/sexual_violence_and_exploitation.pdf.

[64] UN News Centre, 7 January 2005, 'Peacekeepers' sexual abuse of local girls continuing in DR of Congo, UN finds'.

[65] Human Rights Watch, 'Seeking Justice: The Prosecution of Sexual Violence in the Congo', Vol. 17(1A), 7 March 2005, available at www.hrw.org/en/reports/2005/03/06/seeking-justice-0.

[66] UNICEF, *Impact of Armed Conflict on Children* (1996), UN Doc. A/51/306 at para. 98.

of such abuses during the United Nations Operation in Mozambique (ONUMOZ).[67] Schade described how ONUMOZ staff recruited girls aged as young as twelve into prostitution and employed street children as procurers. He also noted that some members of the operation engaged minors for pornographic activities and live public sex performances with participation from ONUMOZ personnel. According to his report, ONUMOZ staff used official UN vehicles and were dressed in UN uniforms when collecting girls from school. The main individuals implicated in these practices were repatriated following an investigation though, again, it is unknown whether all of those involved were prosecuted for their conduct upon their return. However, judging by the attitudes of the contingent superiors who first reprimanded and then repatriated one military doctor for writing about the sexual abuse by the peacekeeping personnel, it does not seem that prosecution or simply disciplinary proceedings were pursued with the necessary vigour.

The scandals at the start of the first decade of the new millennium were the first ones to receive extensive media attention prompting a response from both the UN and the aid community. An inquiry, launched by the UN's Office of Internal Oversight Services (OIOS), confirmed the frequency of sexual contact between peacekeepers and locals, and twenty specific case reports were compiled.[68] The report cited the discovery of used condoms littering the perimeter of military camps and guard posts.[69] The Secretary General requested Prince Zeid Hussein, Jordan's Ambassador to the UN, to investigate allegations, to undertake a comprehensive review of UN measures on the sexual abuse and to make recommendations on how to address this problem.[70]

The recommendations of the report included the application of all rules in the 2003 Bulletin to all categories of peacekeeping personnel (at 15–18), as well as the dissemination among personnel of the Bulletin, the Code of Personal Conduct for Blue Helmets, and the UN code for peacekeepers (at 26). In terms of improving compliance and

[67] E. Schade, 'Report on experiences with regard to the United Nations peace-keeping forces in Mozambique' (Norway: Redd Barna, 1995).

[68] Office of Internal Oversight Services, 'Investigation into allegations of sexual exploitation and abuse in the UN Organisation Mission in the DRC', 5 January 2005, UN Doc. A/59/661; GA Res. 57/306.

[69] *The Guardian* (London) 25 March 2005, 'Report reveals shame of UN peacekeepers: Sexual abuse by soldiers "must be punished"', Owen Bowcott.

[70] Secretary General, 'Comprehensive review of the whole question of peacekeeping operations in all their aspects', UN Doc. A/59/710, 24 March 2005.

accountability, the report recommended the establishment of a permanent professional investigative capacity to investigate complex cases of serious misconduct, including sexual misconduct, and the participation of an expert in military law from a relevant troop-contributing country as a member of any investigation in order to improve the prospect of prosecution in the home state (at 32–33). The idea of holding on-site court prosecution by troop-contributing countries so as to facilitate access to witnesses and evidence was also put forward (at 35–36).

The report also recommended that perpetrators should be held financially accountable for harm caused to victims (at 94). Given that members of UN forces can be subject to the civil jurisdiction of the host country for non-official acts, this may prove an effective route for ensuring greater protection of victims, as well as for preventing abuses through deterrence, provided that claims are actually brought and judgments executed. The effectiveness of the civil route will, however, depend on the existence in the host country of a judicial system that can operate credibly, fairly and efficiently. The fact that this is not available in most places where peacekeeping missions are deployed should not preclude recourse to this route in those situations where it might be available, for example in Kosovo. There the UN ought to encourage victims to come forward and bring civil claims, and to support the local justice system in dealing with them.

Two important internal mechanisms are the OIOS and the Conduct and Discipline Unit (CDU). The OIOS, which authored the report discussed above, was established in 1994 to increase the strength of internal oversight. It is empowered to conduct internal investigations but does not have criminal jurisdiction over any personnel; it can recommend disciplinary and administrative actions including the payment of repatriations and banning of personnel. The contributing state retains exclusive disciplinary and criminal jurisdiction. As discussed, the state is in principle obliged to cooperate with the UN and report on the outcome of any investigation and any action taken.[71] The CDU, established under the Department of Field Support in 2007, can to send field missions to address misconduct by operation personnel by providing preventative training. In addition, in cooperation with

[71] In July 2008, the Department of Field Support launched the Misconduct Tracking System (MTS), a global database and confidential tracking system for all allegations of misconduct.

the host state, the CDU has developed various confidential reporting mechanisms to encourage the submission of complaints. Victims, for example, may use the Sexual Exploitation and Abuse Victim Assistance Mechanism (SEA/VAM),[72] and receive assistance, including information on how to pursue claims against the alleged perpetrators.

It would be unfair to blame the UN entirely for sexual abuse and exploitation during peacekeeping missions. Peacekeeping missions operate during armed conflict or in post-conflict situations, both 'enabling environments for abuse;[73] the promotion of respect for liberty, personal integrity and security is bound to face enormous challenges in those circumstances. Even if the UN wanted to strengthen criminal law enforcement, it would be met with opposition from states. In terms of hard sanctions, the only one presently available to the UN is the repatriation of the peacekeeper at the end of a disciplinary hearing. Reports from the field suggest that in a few cases repatriation has been ordered.[74]

Right to life, freedom from torture and arbitrary detentions

Violations of the right to life, of the prohibition on torture and cruel, inhuman and degrading treatment or punishment, and of the right to liberty and security have been reported on numerous occasions during peacekeeping operations. Michael Kelly noted a significant incidence of such abuses in the context of operations in states disrupted by a prolonged and particularly brutal internal conflict where the system for the administration of justice has almost completely failed.[75]

In Somalia, for example, the failure to put in place an adequate system for dealing with detainees accused of committing crimes plagued the operation from the outset. The command of the UN-mandated Unified Task Force (UNITAF) determined that 'Article 5' tribunals would not

[72] UN Comprehensive Strategy on Assistance and Support to Victims of Sexual Exploitation and Abuse by United Nations Staff and Related Personnel (2007).

[73] *Ibid.* at 51.

[74] For example, in Liberia, V. Kent, 'Protecting Civilians from UN Peacekeepers and Humanitarian Workers: Sexual Exploitation and Abuse', in C. Aoi, C. de Coning and R. Thakur (eds.), *Unintended Consequences of Peacekeeping Operations* (New York: United Nations University Press, 2007) 44 at 58.

[75] M. Kelly, 'Transitional Justice in Peace Operations: Shaping the Twilight Zone in Somalia and East Timor', 4 *Yearbook of International Humanitarian Law* (2001) 213.

be constituted as they would be inappropriate for dealing with simple criminal offenders or with those accussed of attacking members of UNITAF forces.[76] Due to uncertainty over the application of the laws of occupation to the situation in Somalia, it was also decided that no local tribunals would be convened by UNITAF. Attempts to reconvene the local judicial organs from members of the indigenous population also proved ineffective.

For Kelly the absence of a judicial system in Somalia during the UNITAF's mandate was 'the cancer at the heart of the mission that eventually killed it'.[77] Although UNITAF's rules of engagement permitted detention of civilians, there was no judicial system for trying suspects. Long-term imprisonment eventually ceased largely due to the need to alleviate overcrowding in detention facilities. Members of UNITAF soon began to see no purpose in arresting those responsible for crimes such as mass murder or robbery as, eventually, they would be either forced to release them or hand them over to the village elders who were powerless. There were no means of bringing even those Somalis who killed members of the UNITAF forces to trial. These factors led not only to a loss of morale amongst the troops, but also to their loss of credibility with the local community. Attacks on peacekeeping forces continued with almost complete impunity. With tension, frustration and disillusionment rising, some members of UNITAF either resolved that the only way forward was to administer 'rough justice' or they simply snapped under pressure and employed disproportionate force. In many cases, detention without charge and denial of access to legal representation were reported.[78] But graver allegations were also made, including the extra-judicial execution of detainees,[79] and the application of lethal force in cases of theft.[80] On one occasion after a security breach in the Canadian compound, one Somali was alleged to have

[76] Article 5, Geneva Convention (III) Relative to the Treatment of Prisoners of War (1949) 75 UNTS 135.

[77] Kelly, *supra* note 75 at 251.

[78] *The Guardian*, 25 September 1993, 'UN Forces Deny Somali Detainees Legal Rights', Mark Huband, at 14; *Washington Post*, 7 November 1993, 'Somalis' Imprisonment Poses Questions about U.N. Role', Keith Richburg at A45.

[79] *Washington Post*, 3 July 1997, 'Canadian Panel Blames Brass For Army Misdeeds in Somalia; Violence Linked to "Leadership Failures"', Howard Schneider at A22.

[80] *The Economist*, 5 July 1997, 'Somalia: Good Intentions Turned to Shame', at 48; *The Observer*, 22 June 1997, 'Military Disgrace: Child Roasted on the Peacekeepers' Pyre', Jennifer Gould, at 6.

been tortured and beaten to death,[81] while other peacekeepers were accused of firing upon civilians in the streets indiscriminately.[82] These reports attracted particular attention since some of the more shocking atrocities were caught on camera.[83] The case of Somalia illustrates not only that there is enormous potential for abuse by members of peacekeeping forces, it also shows that, when the rule of law issues are not addressed prompty, in addition to the increase in crime, another consequence will be the collapse in the standards of conduct amongst peacekeepers.[84]

UN peacekeepers in the former Yugoslavia were also accused of unlawful detentions and other violations of human rights and international humanitarian law, although not on a scale comparable with Somalia. Some of these complaints reached the European Court of Human Rights – for example the *Behrami* and *Saramati* cases discussed at length in Chapter 3 in the context of attribution. The cases of arbitrary detention and torture of which coalition forces in Iraq and Afghanistan have been accused were instead in the context of a UN-authorised mission rather than a peacekeeping one. In *Al-Jedda*,[85] the argument was made that even in those cases conduct should be attributed to the UN rather than to states, but this argument was, correctly, rejected by the House of Lords. Less correctly, however, the House of Lords held that the UN Security Council has the power to authorise states to detain individuals on a standard that is lower than the human rights one.

The treatment of detainees is an area which has attracted considerable attention especially since the September 11 attacks on the World Trade Center. Trends have emerged in state practice that may have with time repercussions over detention policies in peacekeeping missions. Interestingly, the convergence of criminal and military detention models that has been noted in state practice since September 11 mirrors the convergence of the human rights and international humanitarian law models of detention that is embodied in the adoption of international

[81] *The Economist*, *ibid.*; *The Observer*, *ibid.*

[82] *The Observer*, *ibid.*; *The Guardian*, supra note 78 at 6.

[83] *The Observer*, *ibid.*; *The Financial Times*, 14 June 1997, 'Italy to Probe Torture Claims', Robert Graham at 2.

[84] Kelly, *supra* note 75 at 213.

[85] *R (on the application of Al-Jedda) (FC) (Appellant) v. Secretary of State for Defence (Respondent)* [2007] UKHL 58.

instruments of 'soft law' such as the UN declarations on basic principles governing detention.[86]

Failure to prevent genocide

Events in Rwanda and Bosnia compelled a re-examination of the performance of peacekeeping in the face of the most horrible crimes. In 1994 the UNAMIR operation in Rwanda failed to prevent the massacre of about 800,000 Tutsis and moderate Hutus. The following year, in July 1995, a 400-strong Dutch protection force, part of UNPROFOR mission in Yugoslavia, failed to protect the Bosniak population seeking refuge in the Srebrenica enclave, a designated 'safe area' since 1993,[87] and was also accused of forcibly expelling refugees who were within the precinct of the military base in Srebrenica.[88] The Army of the Republika Srpska massacred more than 8,000 Bosnian men and boys, and ethnically cleansed the area deporting about 20,000 women and children. In 1999 the Secretary General endorsed two reports which criticised the conduct of the UN and of its member states in Rwanda and Bosnia.[89]

The failure of the peacekeepers in Rwanda and Bosnia cannot be entirely attributed to shortcomings in the mandate and in the rules of engagement under which they were operating. Both the mandate and the rules would have permitted the use of force in defence of the civilian population in each case, but the order to use force was never given. In Rwanda, after the genocide began, the political and strategic command of UNAMIR in New York that the mission should follow rules of engagement narrower than the ones that had

[86] The literature on detention after September 11 is vast. The convergence trend has been examined by R. Charney and J. Goldsmith, 'Terrorism and the Convergence of Criminal and Military Detention Models', 60 *Stanford Law Review* (2008) 1079. The UN declarations on detentions are: GA Res. 43/173 ('Body of Principles for the Protection of All Persons under Any Form of Detention or Imprisonment') and GA Res. 45/111 ('Basic Principles for the Treatment of Prisoners').

[87] See SC Res. 819 (16 April 1993) designating Srebrenica a safe area.

[88] 2008 *Nuhanovic* case before Hague Court – court found UN, not NL responsible for Dutchbat's actions. *H.N. v. the Netherlands*, District Court of the Hague, 10 September 2008, 265615/HA ZA 06-1671 (Neth.)

[89] Report of the Secretary General, 'Report on the Fall of Srebrenica' UN Doc. A/54/549 of 15 November 1999; 'Report of the Independent Inquiry into the Actions of the United Nations during the 1994 Genocide in Rwanda', UN Doc. S/1999/1257 of 15 December 1999.

been issued before the genocide and that were still, technically, in force.[90]

Did the UN violate the obligation to prevent genocide in Rwanda and Bosnia? In the *Bosnia Genocide* decision, the ICJ observed that the obligation to prevent genocide is one of conduct rather than result, meaning that the scope of the duty is to 'employ all means reasonably available … so as to prevent genocide so far as possible'.[91] As a corollary, states do not 'incur responsibility simply because the desired result is not achieved; responsibility is however incurred if the State manifestly failed to take all measures to prevent genocide which were within its power, and which might have contributed to preventing the genocide'.[92] In assessing whether a state has discharged its obligation the Court will consider the limits placed upon that state's conduct by international law, but it will be irrelevant to the assessment of responsibility whether the state could not have prevented the commission of genocide even if it reasonably engaged all means at its disposal. The Court further noted that duty to prevent genocide is a positive obligation the breach of which may be effected by an omission. The obligation may be violated even if there had been no certainty that genocide was about to be committed or was already under way. It is enough that there was awareness, or that there should have been awareness, of the serious danger that acts of genocide would be committed.

The obligation to prevent genocide is not expressly incorporated in the mandates of peacekeeping operations, but it still binds the UN and its subsidiary organs by virtue of customary international law. Applying the *ratio* of the *Bosnia Genocide* case to a peacekeeping operation, the mission would incur responsibility if it 'manifestly failed to take all measures to prevent genocide which were within its powers'. As discussed, the Court did refer to limits placed by international law on the discharge of the obligation to prevent, the prohibition on the use of force being the most conspicuous of such limits. In the case of traditional peacekeeping, it may be argued that resort to force to prevent genocide was not possible because of this legal limit. But, in robust peacekeeping, the position is different. Where the mandate and the

[90] See Dallaire, *supra* note 9 at 232ff.

[91] *Case Concerning Application of the Convention on the Prevention and Punishment of the Crime of Genocide (Bosnia and Herzegovina v. Serbia and Montenegro)*, ICJ Judgment of 26 January 2007, at para. 430.

[92] *Ibid.*

rules of engagement of the peacekeeping operation permit resort to force in order to defend the civilian population, but force is, nevertheless, not employed in the face of an imminent or occurring genocide, the peacekeeping mission will have breached the obligation to prevent genocide.

Enforcement of international obligations

When assessing the available mechanisms for enforcement of international obligations against UN peacekeeping forces, one must distinguish between criminal proceedings and claims of a private law character. A distinction must also be drawn between the institutional vicarious liability of the organisation and the individual liability of members of a peacekeeping operation.

Domestic and international criminal law

Members of national contingents of UN peacekeeping forces are subject to the exclusive criminal jurisdiction of the sending state.[93] They may be tried in proceedings conducted by martial or civilian criminal courts depending on the precise constitutional and statutory frameworks of the sending state. As noted above, domestic criminal proceedings are not always pursued by the authorities of troop-contributing countries for offences committed abroad by their troops. However, the sending state may have conferred criminal jurisdiction on an international criminal tribunal or court established by treaty – such as the ICC – or such jurisdiction may exist by virtue of a Security Council resolution. Accordingly, members of a peacekeeping mission may be brought before an international criminal tribunal where their alleged conduct amounts to an offence under international criminal law.

International criminal judicial organs, both of permanent and ad hoc status, are not generally constrained by immunities from criminal proceedings; however, whether this will be the case in a particular situation depends on the exact language used in each tribunal's constituent instrument. Although there is no precedent to speak of as yet, the breadth of the language used in Article 27 of the Rome Statute, for instance, suggests that immunities would not bar criminal proceedings in the ICC against a member of a peacekeeping operation.

[93] Hampson and Kihara-Hunt, *supra* note 57.

The possibility of prosecution before the ICC is complicated by further jurisdictional considerations. First, the ICC functions under the principle of complementarity. It will not try the accused unless it finds that the relevant state is unwilling or unable genuinely to investigate or prosecute him or her for the relevant crime. As provided by the Model SOFA and Model MOU, primary criminal jurisdiction over national members remains with the contributing state. However, in circumstances where the troop-contributing state, for instance, fails to prosecute or conducts a sham trial, the ICC would be in a position to exercise its jurisdiction. Secondly, many states have entered agreements under Article 98 of the Rome Statute pursuant to which the Court may not request the host states to transfer the sending state's troops to the ICC without the consent of the sending state. The US in particular has entered into many such agreements – over one hundred in total – with states both party and not party to the Rome Statute.[94] Although the validity of the scope of Article 98 agreements beyond those individuals who have been 'sent' by the troop-contributing state has been questioned, it is generally accepted that they are otherwise lawful. Notably, however, the model Article 98 agreement deviates from the Model SOFA as it contains no undertaking that the US will investigate and prosecute offences committed by US personnel.

Private third-party claims

Third-party claims against UN peacekeeping operations and their personnel may be based upon one or more of a variety of causes of action. As the Secretary General has emphasised, the most commonly encountered claims concern non-consensual use and occupancy of premises, personal injury and property loss or damage arising from the ordinary operation of the force and as a result of combat operations.[95] By contrast, human rights are relevant only in a handful of claims where the respondent is a state. In any event, as discussed before, there are a number of obstacles to the successful invocation of human rights accountability mechanisms against the UN, including the lack of jurisdiction *ratione personae* over the UN and the extra-territorial application of human rights treaties.

[94] A list of the Article 98 agreements concluded by the US can be found at www.II.georgetown.edu/guides/article_98.cfm.

[95] Report of the Secretary General, 'Administrative and budgetary aspects of the financing of the United Nations peacekeeping operations: financing of the United Nations peacekeeping operations', UN Doc. A/51/389, at para 3.

Although violative conduct of UN peacekeeping forces gives rise to a claim under the host state's national laws, the UN's comprehensive immunity regime constitutes an insuperable bar to proceedings in national courts. Article VIII of the Convention on the Privileges and Immunities of the United Nations requires the Organisation to establish a dispute settlement mechanism in relation to claims of private law character to which the UN is a party. Additionally, where the UN operates within the territory of a host state with its effective authority, it is also the duty of the state to fulfil its human rights obligations and to alleviate the effects of the immunity of the Organisation by working to establish an impartial judicial body. Accordingly, it is now an established practice that any third-party claims settlement process is governed by the applicable SOFA.

As mentioned above, the Standing Claims Commission envisaged in Article 51 of the Model SOFA is yet to be established. Instead, UN-based local claims review boards have been created in almost every peacekeeping operation to settle third-party claims.[96] These review boards, however, are not established as standard procedures at the outset of a peacekeeping operation but later 'when the need arises'.[97] For example, two years after the authorisation of UNMIK and KFOR, neither operation had a functioning claims procedure in operation.[98] The boards are internal bodies composed exclusively of three or more UN staff members. As the Secretary General has stated, the boards leave 'the investigation, processing and final adjudication of the claims entirely in the hands of the Organization'.[99] The review boards act under authority delegated by the UN Controller to examine claims, negotiate with third parties, approve or recommend a settlement amount within a limited financial authority. Their advisory rulings are not made public.[100]

96 Shraga, *supra* note 41 at 409.

97 Report of the Secretary General, 'Administrative and budgetary aspects of the financing of the United Nations peacekeeping operations: financing of the United Nations peacekeeping operations', UN Doc. A/51/389, 20 September 1996, at para. 25.

98 See Ombudsman Institution in Kosovo, First Annual Report (18 July 2001) 11 (available at www.ombudspersonkosovo.org/repository/docs/E6010718a.pdf).

99 'Administrative and budgetary aspects of the financing of the United Nations peacekeeping operations: financing of the United Nations peacekeeping operations', UN Doc. A/51/389, 20 September 1996, para. 20.

100 UN Doc. ST/A1/149/Rev.4, at para. 18. For criticism see Ombudsman Institution in Kosovo, Second Annual Report (10 July 2002) 2 (available at www.ombudspersonkosovo.org/repository/docs/E6020710a.pdf).

In addition to the ad hoc nature of local claims review boards, injured parties face a number of other difficulties.[101] First of all, the form of adjudication adopted by local claims review boards is such that the injured party has little influence on the result. Additionally, the UN has not developed a second judicial instance for settling disputes in the event that a settlement agreement cannot be reached between the injured party and the institution. Moreover, there are inconsistencies in how claims are dealt with as the negotiating position of the injured party often depends on the diplomatic protection provided by the party's state of nationality.[102]

Nevertheless, a considerable body of substantive rules of liability, based on the general principles of domestic law of torts and on the laws of the host states, has been developed by the UN in connection with this practice of settlement of disputes.[103] These rules are said to primarily take legal effect internally, within the institutional hierarchy, as all of the executive organs are legally bound by them. For instance, liability practice shows that effective *de facto* command is the decisive element for allocating responsibility between international organisations and their member states while self-defence and operational necessity are often relied upon by the UN as circumstances excluding responsibility for wrongful conduct.

Limitations on UN liability

The financial liability of the UN with regard to combat-related and ordinary operational activities of peacekeeping missions is limited by rules set out in General Assembly resolution 52/247.[104] In particular, third-party claims are capped at US$50,000, which is only recoverable in relation to pecuniary loss, and have a limitation period of six months. In exceptional circumstances the Secretary General can accept a claim outside of these parameters. Consistently with the balancing of interests and division of responsibility evident in the Model SOFA, these limits are premised on the principle that in consenting to a peacekeeping operation for its own benefit the host state consents to undertake

[101] K. Schmalenbach, 'Third Party Liability of International Organisations: A Study on Claim Settlement in the Course of Military Operations and International Administrations', 10 *International Peacekeeping: The Yearbook of International Peace Operations* (2006) 33.

[102] *Ibid.* [103] *Ibid.*

[104] GA Res. 52/247, 'Third-party liability: temporal and financial limitations', 26 June 1998.

at least some of the ordinary financial risk involved.[105] Further, consistently with the Model MOU, the limits do not apply to claims arising from the gross negligence or wilful misconduct of personnel provided by troop-contributing countries for peacekeeping operations. Where it is established that such personnel acted wilfully, with criminal intent or because of gross negligence, the UN will assume liability whilst retaining a right of indemnity against the troop-contributing state. However, resolution 52/247 exempts the UN from any third-party liability if the peacekeeping personnel whose conduct is in question are found to have acted out of operational necessity.

Operational necessity excludes the liability of the organisation 'for personal injury, illness or death, and for property loss and damage'.[106] Although in some ways analogous to military necessity, operational necessity is a conceptually distinct category. It applies 'where damage results from necessary actions taken by a peacekeeping force in the course of carrying out its operations in pursuance of its mandates'[107] and is an attempt to adapt necessity, as a general circumstance precluding wrongfulness, to the specifics of a UN peacekeeping operation. The concept is broad enough to cover damage which is either intended or foreseen as inevitable. For the defence to arise:

(a) there must be good faith conviction on the part of the commander that such operational necessity exists;
(b) the action must be strictly necessary, and not simply a matter of convenience, leaving the commander with no time to pursue less destructive means;
(c) the action must be pursuant to an operational plan and not a rash individual pursuit;
(d) the damage must be proportional to what is strictly necessary to achieve the operational goal.

The Secretary General, however, stresses that it is 'difficult, if not impossible' to determine what would constitute operational necessity and adds that 'the decision must remain within the discretionary power of the force commander'.[108] Despite the requirement of good faith on the part of the force commander, this emphasis on pre-operation determination of operational necessity by the commander suggests that *ex post* examinations of such determinations are likely to

[105] Shraga, *supra* note 41 at 410. [106] GA Res. 52/247 of 26 June 1998, at para. 5.
[107] Report of the Secretary General, *supra* note 96 at para. 13.
[108] *Ibid*. at para. 14.

be resisted leading thus to the broadening of the scope, and possibly abuse, of the concept.

Quite apart from merely canvassing it as a possible defence, the Model SOFA refers to operational necessity so as to exclude matters covered by this concept from the jurisdiction of claims review boards.[109] This reference does not take into account the exception, found in both the Draft Articles on the Responsibility of International Organisations and the Articles on State Responsibility, to the effect of excluding the defence of necessity when the 'organisation has contributed to the situation of necessity' (Article 24(2)(b)). In any event, operational necessity has been pleaded by international organisations with such frequency that one author has concluded it has now attained the status of general principle of international liability law.[110] At the very least, however, operational necessity, like any other defence, cannot be invoked when the wrongful act constitutes a breach of a *jus cogens* rule. Additionally, resort to operational necessity should be limited to peacekeeping operations and not extended to other operations, such as humanitarian operations and administrations of territory. There is textual support for such a limitation in resolution 52/247 which provides that 'liability is not engaged in relation to ... members of peacekeeping operations' (para. 6). In the context of humanitarian operations and administrations of territory, justificatory arguments are still developed by the UN and other humanitarian agencies, but, as discussed at the end of the previous chapter, they are usually clothed in utilitarian morality rather than based on the legal concept of operational necessity.

Conclusion

As Zacklin notes, 'the clarity of the applicable law and the consistency of its application is an essential pre-requisite to a well managed operation'.[111] Although there exists now more clarity about the law that governs peacekeeping, there remain some difficulties in applying it. These difficulties stem not only from the jurisdictional restrictions of various international criminal and human rights courts and tribunals,

109 *Ibid.* at para. 15. 110 Schmalenbach, *supra* note 100.

111 R. Zacklin, 'United Nations Management of Legal Issues', in J. Howard and B. Oswald (eds.), *The Rule of Law on Peace Operations. A: 'Challenges of Peace Operations' Project Conference* (Melbourne: Asia-Pacific Centre for Military Law, 2002) 118.

but also from the idiosyncrasies of the various legal systems where proceedings are brought against the persons allegedly implicated.

International humanitarian law was not created with peacekeeping in mind.[112] Furthermore, as Greenwood notes, classification of operation types such as 'peacekeeping' and 'peace-enforcement' is of limited assistance in determining the applicability of humanitarian law, which depends on the existence of an armed conflict.[113] The application of international humanitarian law to peacekeeping operations inevitably involves some measure of adaptation. Due to the unique position of trust and authority of the UN peacekeepers, particularly in the most precariously functioning states with vast political vacuums, it is but a truism to point out the enormous potential for abuse by members of national contingents of the UN. Where abuse was committed and reported, there was quite often no adequate punishment of those implicated, the national authorities and the UN preferring to rely upon the panacea of repatriation when not choosing inaction.

[112] *Ibid.* at 156. [113] Greenwood, *supra* note 30 at 11.

6 International administrations

Introduction

It is axiomatic that authorities that exercise effective control over an inhabited territory have the functional capacity – the power, but not the right – to violate human rights. When the UN, which is no exception to this axiom, exercises territorial control, it normally does so on the basis of an express mandate contained in a resolution of the Security Council, in a treaty, or both; but there are also situations, most notably refugee camps, in which the UN controls an inhabited territory in the absence of such an express mandate, that is on a *de facto* basis.

Those in effective control of territory may be assimilated to 'public officials or other persons acting in an official capacity' for the purposes of the definition of torture and other human rights (see Article 1 of the Convention Against Torture and Other Cruel, Inhuman or Degrading Treatment or Punishment). The Committee Against Torture noted that 'for some years Somalia has been without a central government' and that some 'factions operating in Mogadishu … have set up quasi-governmental institutions and are negotiating the establishment of a common administration. It follows then that, *de facto*, those factions exercise certain prerogatives that are comparable to those normally exercised by legitimate governments'.[1] For a narrower view with respect to the risk posed 'by a non-governmental entity', see *GRB v Sweden* (15 May 1998) CAT/C/20/D/083/1997 (at para. 6.5), where the Committee considered the risk of rape or torture from the Shining Path (*Sendero Luminoso*) in Peru) to fall outside of Article 3 of the Convention.

International administrations of territory by a group of states, rather than by an international organisation, were instituted in the nineteenth

[1] See *Elmi v. Australia* (14 May 1999) CAT/C/22/D/120/1998, at paras. 6.5 and 6.7.

century, the leading examples being the Free City of Cracow (1815–46), the City of Shanghai (1845–1944) and the Island of Crete (1897–1909).[2] The administration of the Saarland by the League of Nations after the First World War was the first instance of an international organisation ruling over a territory. The League of Nations also had an administrative role in the City of Danzig under the terms of the Treaty of Versailles, but on a more limited basis than in Saarland. The resident High Commissioner of the League in Danzig acted as court of first instance in disputes between Poland and Danzig, while appeals were considered by the Council of the League, which could in turn request an advisory opinion from the Permanent Court of International Justice.[3] In the aftermath of the Second World War, the UN drew up plans for various international administrations, for example in the Free City of Trieste and in Jerusalem, but none was implemented until the international administration of West New Guinea (West Irian) in 1962–3 following an agreement between Indonesia and the Netherlands.[4] Since the end of the cold war, international administrations have been set up in various places, including Cambodia, Bosnia and Herzegovina, Eastern Slavonia, East Timor and Kosovo.[5]

The lack of a formal act transferring governmental functions to the UNHCR in refugee camps accounts, at least in part, for the scant attention that the legal implications of this particular exercise of administrative functions by an international organisation has received.[6] Given that the type and extent of administrative powers exercised by UNHCR

[2] C. Stahn, *The Law and Practice of International Territorial Administration* (Cambridge University Press, 2008) 6–7.

[3] See for example *Polish Postal Services in Danzig* (1925) PCIJ Reports Series B, No. 11. See also R. Wilde, *International Territorial Administration: How Trusteeship and the Civilizing Mission Never Went Away* (Oxford University Press, 2008) 111–29.

[4] On *West Irian* see Agreement Concerning West New Guinea (West Irian) (Indonesia-Netherlands) (1962), reproduced in 57 AJIL (1963) 493. On *Trieste* see SC Res. 16 (1947). On *Jerusalem* see: GA Res. 181(II) (1947), and R. Lapidoth and M. Hirsch (eds.), *The Jerusalem Question and Its Resolution: Selected Documents* (Dordrecht: Martinus Nijhoff, 1994).

[5] The literature on international administration has grown rapidly in recent years. Leading monographs in the field include those by Carsten Stahn, Bernhard Knoll and Ralph Wilde (Wilde's book contains a reasoned bibliography at the end). See Stahn, *supra* note 2; B. Knoll, *The Legal Status of Territories Subject to Administration by International Organisations* (New York: Cambridge University Press, 2008); and Wilde, *supra* note 3 at 500–73.

[6] See, however, G. Verdirame and B. E. Harrell-Bond, *Rights in Exile: Janus-Faced Humanitarianism* (Oxford: Berghahn Books, 2005).

vary from one refugee camp to another, and that UNHCR's operational reality often bears little relation to its stated practice, a socio-legal method is necessary to examine these *de facto* international administrations. In some cases, governments administer camps in conjunction with UNHCR, but in most situations they play a marginal role, if any at all, in their administration. In addition, UNHCR often subcontracts non-governmental organisations, which share in the administration of camps for the most part in a position of subalternity to UNHCR.[7]

A *de facto* administration is not always ultra vires. On the contrary, it can be intra vires, as long as it is based on an express or implied term in the mandate of the administering organisation. Conversely, the *de jure* character of an international administration does not imply that the administration is, in all its aspects, intra vires. Its constitution in all likelihood is; it certainly is when the constituent instrument is a decision of the Security Council under Chapter VII of the Charter. But the exercise of particular functions may still be ultra vires if the administering organisation has no basis in an express or implied permissive term in its mandate.

Having said that, the *de facto* administration of refugee camps normally represents an international illegality, in that it is inherently incompatible with international human rights law. Since the commission of a systematic breach of human rights law is not within the legal powers of any operational programme of the UN (save for the vexed, but here irrelevant, question of the effect of Article 103 of the UN Charter on human rights obligations), the *de facto* administration of refugee camps must be treated as generally ultra vires.

Definition and typology

Scholars writing on the subject have sought to remedy the lack of a legally agreed definition of international administration by coming up with their own. For example, Stahn defines international administration as the 'exercise of administering authority (executive, legislative or judicial authority) by an international entity for the benefit of a territory that is temporarily placed under international supervision or assistance for a communitarian purpose'.[8] Wilde suggests that an

[7] B. E. Harrell-Bond, *Imposing Aid* (Oxford University Press, 1986) 64ff.; Verdirame and Harrell-Bond, *ibid.* at 312–16.

[8] Stahn, *supra* note 2 at 43–5.

international administration is a 'formally-constituted, locally-based management structure operating with respect to a particular territorial unit, whether a state, a sub-state unit or a non-state territorial entity'.[9]

For present purposes, it is proposed that international administration be defined as the direct or indirect exercise by an international organisation of such public functions (legislative, executive or judicial) as to place the organisation in effective control of the territory. Such a definition, which encompasses both *de jure* international administrations and *de facto* ones, employs the concept of effective control, with which international lawyers are familiar, and avoids references to notions that seem either inapposite in the context of political governance (e.g. 'management structure') or simply vague (e.g. 'communitarian purpose'). The need to include in the definition both *direct* and *indirect* methods of administration is also recognised by Stahn. In cases of indirect administration, 'international or multinational institutions with independent legal personality (e.g. the Office of the High Representative in Bosnia and Herzegovina or the Coalition Provision Authority in Iraq) exercise territorial authority on behalf of or with the approval of an international organisation'.[10]

Judged by the criterion of effective control, it could be argued that the international presence in Bosnia and Herzegovina falls short of the requirements for international administration, since the public powers with which the High Representative is endowed do not at first appear sufficiently broad to reach that threshold. However, the significance of these powers, in particular the power to remove elected officials, places the High Representative in a position of normative hierarchy that entails at least a significant element of effective control. Subject to this caveat, the Office of the High Representative in Bosnia is treated here as an example of international administration.

The element of effective control of a territory distinguishes international administrations from other exercises of administrative functions by international organisations. For example, in the humanitarian operations described in Chapter 5, some public powers may be exercised by international organisations that provide humanitarian assistance, but these powers do not normally amount to territorial control, except in the case of refugee camps which are for this reason treated as international administrations (albeit, as discussed, *de facto* rather than *de jure*).

[9] Wilde, *supra* note 3 at 21. [10] Stahn, supra note 8 at 45.

In general, it is peacekeeping operations with a large-scale humanitarian component that pose a problem of classification, especially where the absence of a properly functioning government creates the opportunity for the UN mission to fill in the power vacuum and exercise public functions beyond the terms of the mandate of the mission. In these circumstances, the dividing line between peacekeeping and international administration can become blurred. An example is the second UN Operation in Somalia (UNOSOM II). On paper its powers were not so extensive as to reach the threshold of territorial effective control, but, in the absence of a functioning Somali government, UNOSOM II found itself in effective control of portions of territory, *de facto* exercising, from time to time, a wide range of governmental functions.[11]

The mandate of UNOSOM II is spelled out at paragraph 4 of SC Res. 814 of 26 March 1993. Under its terms, 'UN entities, offices and specialised agencies' were mandated 'to assist in the re-establishment of Somali police … at the local, regional or national level' and 'to assist in the restoration and maintenance of peace, stability and law and order'. The various peacekeeping missions in Haiti since February 1993 have also involved a measure of administration. Between 1999 and 2005, the UN Mission in Sierra Leone (UNAMSIL) operated primarily as a peacekeeping mission but with a skeletal administration component working alongside the democratically elected government. An important feature of the international intervention in Sierra Leone were the bilateral arrangements between Britain and Sierra Leone, under which British military forces and British civil servants, while not formally part of the UN military and civilian structure, helped with the implementation of the resolutions of the Security Council.[12] Another example of borderline international administration is the UN Transitional Assistance Group in Namibia (UNTAG), which 'was not called upon to provide international administration in the fullest sense', but did play 'a key role in Namibia's transition to

[11] Stahn, *supra* note 2 at 263–4; S. D. Murphy, 'Nation-Building: A Look at Somalia', 3 *Tulane Journal of International and Comparative Law* (1995) 19; C. E. Philipp, 'Somalia – A Very Special Case', 9 *Max Planck Yearbook of UN Law* (2005) 518.

[12] On *Haiti* see SC Res. 867 (1993), 940 (1994) and 975 (1995), 1048 (1996) for the UN Mission in Haiti 1993–6 (UNMIH); SC Res. 1063 (1996) for the UN Support Mission in Haiti 1996–7 (UNSMIH); SC Res. 1123 (1997) for the UN Transition Mission in Haiti 1997 (UNTMIH); SC Res. 1141 (1997) for the UN Civilian Police Mission in Haiti 1997–2000 (MIPONUH); GA Res. 54/193 for the International Civilian Support Mission in Haiti 2000–1 (MICAH); and SC Res. 1542 (2004) for the UN Stabilization Mission in Haiti (MINUSTAH). On *Somalia* (UNOSOM II) see Report of the Secretary General on the United Nations Mission in Haiti, 15 July 1994, UN Doc. S/1994/828. On *Sierra Leone* (UNAMSIL) see SC Res. 1270 (1999); SC Res. 1289 (2000).

independence' and in organising elections which were generally accepted as free and fair.[13]

In its opinion in *Certain Expenses*, the ICJ appeared censorious of the assumption of administrative functions by peacekeeping missions beyond the terms of their mandate. The Court wrote that the UN Emergency Force (UNEF) 'should have no rights other than those necessary for the execution of its function, in co-operation with local authorities. It would be more than an observers' corps, but in no way a military force temporarily controlling the territory in which it is stationed'.[14] However, the ICJ's criticism was in the context of a traditional peacekeeping operation rather than a multifunctional one.

Crucially, effective control over territory is also the key criterion for determining the scope of application *ratione loci* of human rights obligations. Under the settled jurisprudence of both the ICJ and international human rights courts, human rights treaties apply extraterritorially where, in the words of the ECtHR, the state, 'through the effective control of the relevant territory and its inhabitants abroad as a consequence of military occupation or through the consent, invitation or acquiescence of the government of that territory, exercises all or some of the public powers normally to be exercised by [the government of that territory]'.[15] Unlike states, international organisations are not endowed with territory, and the main basis for the jurisdiction *ratione loci* of international human rights treaties is thus inapplicable to them. Where, however, an international organisation exercises effective control over a particular territory, whatever the basis for such control, it should be presumed that the *ratione loci* jurisdiction of international human rights obligations is established in the same way as it would be if a state had been in their position.

In addition to the distinction between *de facto* and *de jure* international administrations, explored above, other distinctions can cast light on the phenomenon of international administration. First, international administrations are different from other forms of internationalised

[13] J. G. Merills, *International Dispute Settlement* (4th edn., Cambridge University Press, 2005) 260.

[14] *Certain Expenses of the United Nations*, Judgment, ICJ Reports (1962) 151 at 171.

[15] *Bankovic and others v. Belgium and others*, Application No. 52207/99, Admissibility Decision of 12 December 2001, para. 80. See G. Verdirame, 'Human Rights in Wartime: A Framework for Analysis', 6 *European Human Rights Law Review* (2008) 689 at 693–8.

governance – such as internationalised states, international territories and internationalised territories.[16] They must also be distinguished from fiduciary administrations of territory under the now virtually defunct Trusteeship system, because the UN did not normally play a significant administrative role in trust and mandated territories (the League however did in Saarland). In principle, direct administration of territory by the UN would have been possible under the UN Trusteeship system, as it is expressly contemplated in Article 81 of the Charter. In practice, the UN never administered trust territories directly and states were always appointed as administering authorities.[17] Whether in a mandate sovereignty lies with the mandatory state or with other entities (e.g. the population living in the mandated territory, the League of Nations or the UN, etc.) is a moot point.[18]

Secondly, it is possible to discern phases in the history of international administration to which different institutional configurations correspond. Stahn has identified four such periods: 'the era of dispute settlement and neutralisation ... which determined the post-war experiments of the League of Nations and the UN after World War II; the phase of the Cold War ... in which territorial administration served mainly as an *ad hoc* device; the time of the revival and systematisation of territorial administration in the 1990s ... under which international administration became a governance technique and a tool to address the root causes of conflict; and more recent practice ... which is characterised by a return to more limited models of administration safeguarding local ownership and self-government'.[19]

Thirdly, international administrations can be distinguished on the basis of the objectives they are meant to pursue. Lack of clarity about these objectives, however, makes this distinction often difficult to draw. In the most general terms, every international administration is set up to facilitate a transition from one order to a new one as part of the management of a conflict or post-conflict situation, particularly where disputes over territory exist. But, as some have rightly

[16] Stahn, *supra* note 2 at 540–2

[17] D. Rauschning, 'Article 81', in B. Simma (ed.), *The Charter of the United Nations: A Commentary* (2nd edn., Oxford University Press, 2002) 1121–3. See J. Crawford, *The Creation of States in International Law* (2nd edn., Oxford University Press, 2006) 565–601.

[18] R. Jennings and A. Watts, *Oppenheim's International Law* (9th edn., London: Longman, 1992) 296, fn. 6.

[19] Stahn, *supra* note 2 at 160.

argued,[20] it is not particularly helpful to explain all international administrations in terms of the single purpose of post-conflict transition and reconstruction. Even at such a level of generality a qualification would be necessary for those cases – Bosnia and Herzegovina for example – where the international administrative component seems to be part of a constitutional arrangement as settled and definitive as many others.

Historically, the administration of Saarland stands out in terms of its objective, since it was part of a strategy of containment of Germany. The economic exploitation by France of the mining resources of the Saar – one of the most controversial aspects of that administration – purportedly aimed to reduce the risk of a rise in German economic and political power, as well as to provide some compensation to France for war damages. Under Article 45 of the Treaty of Versailles, France was granted 'full and absolute possession, with exclusive rights of exploitation' of the coalmines in the Saar Basin '[a]s compensation for the destruction of the coal-mines in the north of France and as part payment toward the total reparation due from Germany for the damage resulting from the war'.

The organisation of elections and referenda is often one of the stated objectives of *de jure* administrations. Both the Saarland and the West New Guinea administrations were entrusted with the organisation of a referendum on the final status of those territories.

The referendum in West New Guinea did take place, but only after the end of the international administration and the transfer of full administrative responsibility to Indonesia (Articles 14–19, Agreement on West New Guinea). While purportedly concluded to uphold West New Guineans' right to self-determination, the terms of this treaty clearly reveal that it was no more than a face-saving instrument for the Netherlands, which had by then accepted Indonesian rule over West New Guinea. Indeed, the people of West New Guinea were given the opportunity to exercise their 'freedom of choice' after the Indonesia authorities had taken over the administration from the UN and were thus in a position to influence, and even manipulate, the results of the plebiscite directly.[21]

The chief objective of the UN Transitional Authority in Cambodia (UNTAC) was also to prepare the country for free and fair democratic elections, although its role was not confined to supervision and monitoring given that UNTAC was empowered to legislate on electoral matters

[20] Wilde, *supra* note 3 at 191ff and 434–8.

[21] P. W. Van der Veur, 'The United Nations in West Irian: A Critique', 18 Int. Org. (1964) 53.

and its mandate thus surpassed those in other 'instances of UN control of elections' such as Namibia, Nicaragua, Haiti and Angola.[22] UNTAET was established after a referendum on independence had taken place and had as its main objective the implementation of the results of that referendum. The case of the UN Mission in Kosovo (UNMIK) is more complicated because the independence which Kosovo eventually proclaimed in 2008 was not an objective of UNMIK under Resolution 1244, albeit a foreseeable development.

The objectives of *de facto* administrations of refugee camps are not easy to ascertain. Even their supporters would be loath to describe them as instrumental to the protection of refugees. To the extent that the administration of refugee camps is an instrument of policy at all, the only objective they may be credited with seeking to pursue (or perhaps blamed for) is the containment of forced migration.

International *de jure* administrations can also be sub-divided on the basis of their constituent instrument: some are established by treaty, some by resolution of the Security Council, and others by a combination of these two instruments. Examples of treaty-based international administrations are the administration of the Saarland by the League of Nations, based, as discussed, on the Treaty of Versailles,[23] and the UN's Temporary Executive Authority (UNTEA) in West New Guinea (Irian) in 1962, based on a treaty between the Netherlands, the former colonial power of West New Guinea, and Indonesia. International administrations constituted by resolution of the Security Council are the UN Transitional Administration in Eastern Slavonia, Baranja and Western Sirmium (UNTAES), UNMIK and the UN Temporary Administration in East Timor (UNTAET).[24] The UN Mission in Bosnia and Herzegovina (UNMIBH) was constituted both by treaty (the Dayton Peace Agreements)[25] and by resolutions 1031 and 1035 (1995) of the Security Council.

The constituent instruments of UNTAC were also a treaty and a resolution of the Security Council.[26] The Security Council did not use its

[22] *Ibid*. at 21. [23] See Art. 49, Treaty of Versailles (1919) 225 CTS 188.

[24] For UNTAES see SC Res. 1037 (1996); for UNMIK see SC Res. 1244 (1999); for UNTAET see SC Res. 1264 and 1272 (1999).

[25] General Framework Agreement for Peace in Bosnia and Herzegovina (hereinafter Dayton Peace Agreement), signed in Paris, 14 December 1995, 35 ILM 75.

[26] Agreement on a Comprehensive Political Settlement in Cambodia of 23 October 1991, 31 ILM 183 (hereinafter Paris Agreements) and S. Ratner, 'The Cambodia Settlement Agreements', 87 AJIL (1993) 1. With Res. 718 (1991), the Security Council then decided to establish an Advance Mission in Cambodia under its authority.

Chapter VII powers on this occasion, since the exercise of administrative powers had been delegated to the UN by the Supreme National Council, 'a *sui generis* entity' – itself created under the Agreement on a Comprehensive Political Settlement – which had been given 'a special status' by the international community 'in both a Security Council resolution and the Comprehensive Political Agreement'.[27] Hence, although the constituent instrument of UNTAC is a treaty, the legal basis for the assumption of governmental functions is a delegation from an autochthonous body. So far UNTAC is the only international administration to assume governmental powers over the entire territory of a member state of the UN.

The legality of international administrations

The manner of constitution of international administrations is distinct from the question of their international legality. A central aspect of this question is whether international organisations can, as a matter of international law, administer territory. The most authoritative proponent of the view that international law precludes the UN from exercising sovereign powers over an entity other than a trust territory was Hans Kelsen;[28] his position was predicated on the postulate that sovereignty pertains exclusively to the state. International administration does not, however, entail a rejection of this postulate, for international administration by its nature is '*non-sovereign* governance'.[29] The claim that the UN exercises governmental functions over a territory and is in effective control of it does not, in other words, equate to a claim of sovereignty, and there is no general rule of international law precluding the UN, or other international organisations, from administering territory on a non-sovereign basis.

The absence of such a rule is a starting point, but it does not entirely dispose of the question of legality. It is indeed important to determine whether the international organisation in question has the power to administer territory under its own constituent instrument. The prevalent interpretation of the UN Charter is, *pace* Kelsen, that the UN 'was intended to possess sufficient personality to exercise jurisdiction

[27] Ratner, *ibid*. at 10.
[28] H. Kelsen, *The Law of the United Nations: A Critical Analysis of its Fundamental Problems* (London: Stevens and Sons, 1950) 651 and 832ff.
[29] Stahn, *supra* note 2 at 410 (emphasis added).

and control over territory',[30] although the relevant resolutions of the Security Council and of the General Assembly cannot be subsumed under any particular provision in the Charter.[31] While international administration in general does not violate the principle of sovereignty in the abstract, it may violate the sovereignty of a state when it is established without its consent. A decision of the Security Council under Chapter VII of the Charter is required to override this difficulty.

The question of the international legality of the *de facto* administration of refugee camps necessitates a different approach. Refugee camps are normally established with the consent of the host state and do not therefore challenge its sovereignty in a legal sense, although they may undermine the authority of the state, insofar as they dispossess it, though nominally with its express consent or acquiescence, of the capacity to govern a portion of the national territory. The main issue of international legality for the administration of refugee camps by international organisations concerns human rights and refugee law. In *de jure* administrations human rights violations *may* occur, but they cannot be said to be inherent to the concept of a *de jure* international administration. They are not, in other words, inevitable. As will be discussed in greater detail below, human rights violations are, instead, inherent to the concept and reality of refugee camps – understood as the protracted 'warehousing' of people.[32] If there is a refugee camp, there will be, inevitably, a human rights violation. Refugee camps are therefore always illegal because they can only be established and maintained in breach of human rights. The only qualification to this argument on the general international illegality of refugee camps is in relation to those camps which constitute a truly short-term emergency response to a refugee crisis and for which a justification under the human rights derogation regime may exist.

The general illegality of refugee camps, from a human rights point of view, shapes the approach to other questions of international legality, in particular whether it is within the legal personality of the designated international administrator – UNHCR in this case – to establish

[30] Stahn, *supra* note 2 at 415. See also I. Brownlie, *Principles of Public International Law* (7th edn., Oxford University Press, 2008) 167; E. Lauterpacht, 'The Contemporary Practice of the UK in the Field of International Law: Survey and Comment', 5 ICLQ (1956) 405 at 411.

[31] Stahn, *supra* note 2 at 423–46.

[32] See the US Committee for Refugees and Migrants campaign against refugee warehousing (www.refugees.org/uploadedFiles/Investigate/Anti_Warehousing/statement.pdf).

and administer refugee camps. If refugee camps represent an inherent violation of human rights, UNHCR cannot, *ipso facto*, have the legal personality to administer them. The references to refugee camps in resolutions of the Security Council and to UNHCR's role in them may give an aura of implausibility to the claim that UNHCR engages in international illegality every time it is involved in the administration of a camp,[33] but they do not fundamentally detract from this argument: they may amount to evidence of lack of knowledge, on the part of the Security Council, about the real nature of refugee camps or perhaps of an endorsement of their existence. It is difficult to see, however, how such references could have the legal effect of curing a substantial illegality.

Violations of human rights in *de jure* international administrations

If one considers human rights violations as a pathology of government, the UN's lack of general experience of government already poses a significant challenge. Furthermore, UN administrations constitute a form of foreign rule, albeit outwardly benign rather than colonial. This characteristic alone could explain why their legitimacy in the eyes of the local population is, at best, limited and transient. In addition to that, underlying international administrations are often the problematic ideas of exporting democracy and of enlightened or purposive despotism. According to David Chandler, the establishment of UN 'protectorates' is underpinned by the notions 'that democracy can be taught or imposed by international bodies on the basis that some "cultures" are not "rational" or "civil" enough to govern themselves', and that 'a transitional lack of sovereignty and the denial of self-government' is necessary in certain situations.[34]

The idea that enlightened despotism is the best form of government in countries not yet ready for liberty has a respectable liberal pedigree, having been first advanced by thinkers like Montesquieu and Voltaire. Since the end of the cold war, the strongest supporters of the idea of exporting democracy have been American conservatives.[35] Breaking ranks with fellow conservative thinkers,

[33] For example, SC Res. 1923 (2010) on UNHCR's role in refugee camps in Chad.

[34] D. Chandler, *Bosnia: Faking Democracy After Dayton* (2nd edn., London: Pluto Press, 2000) 3 and 65. See also, by the same author, *Empire in Denial: The Politics of State-Building* (London: Pluto Press, 2006).

[35] J. Muravshik, *Exporting Democracy: Fulfilling America's Destiny* (Washington D.C.: American Enterprise Institute Press, 1991).

Fukuyama has emphasised the tension between conservative thought and the great social engineering project of exporting democracy.[36] Prominent critical voices in the lively intellectual debate on the pros and cons of exporting democracy that followed the invasion of Iraq include Ignatieff and Simes.[37]

Another general factor that influences the human rights performance of international administrations is the presence of international and national actors with different and sometimes irreconcilable agendas. In Kosovo, for example, the UN civil administration had to work closely with the NATO-led 'security presence', the EU and the OSCE. And as for national actors, they reflected – as expected – the complexity of local politics, and a diversity of claims and interests. When this state of affairs leads to disagreements of a constitutional nature, the solution should be to apply the terms of the mandate – that is resolution 1244 in the case of Kosovo. But this is often easier said than done, not least because the terms of the mandate are at times purposefully nebulous and leave a regulatory space of uncertainty that can be easily filled by the most politically or economically powerful actor.

Understaffing and lack of adequate financial resources may have affected the human rights performance of UN administrations. For example, in Cambodia, scarce funds and insufficient staffing accounted for the inability of the human rights component of UNTAC to have an impact on the exercise of administrative and legislative powers by all the different *de facto* and *de jure* authorities possessing elements of effective control, including UNTAC itself.[38]

The constituent instruments of international administrations make only oblique reference to the applicability of human rights obligations to their activities. The assumption seems to be that human rights violations are committed by others, and that all the UN and other international actors can do is train, supervise or monitor the real addressees of human rights obligations. The existence of a *risk* that UN administrations could, just like any other embodiment of power, breach human

[36] See F. Fukuyama, *After the Neocons: America at the Crossroads* (London: Profile Books, 2006) or, for those who think a whole book by this author too daunting a prospect, 'After Neo-Conservatism', *New York Times (Magazine)*, 19 February 2006.

[37] For example, M. Ignatieff, 'Democratic Providentialism', *New York Times (Magazine)*, 12 December 2004; D. K. Simes, 'America's Imperial Dilemma', 82 *Foreign Affairs* (Nov/Dec 2003) 91.

[38] D. McNamara, 'UN Human Rights Activities in Cambodia: An Evaluation' in A. Henkin (ed.), *Honouring Human Rights* (The Hague: Kluwer Law International, 2000) 47 at 52.

rights is not generally given adequate recognition in the mandates of international administrations; nor is the principle that individuals should have remedies against administrative, judicial or legislative acts of UN authorities that breach their fundamental rights – an absence of *constitutional* awareness which has, inevitably, repercussions on operational practice. The exception is UNTEA, since the Agreement on West New Guinea treated the UN authorities expressly as addressees of certain human rights obligations, such as 'free speech, freedom of movement and of assembly'.[39]

Virtually every international administration has been suspected or accused of violating the rights of the people it governed. In the Saarland the authority of the Governing Commission appointed by the Council of the League of Nations did not cover the exploitation of the most important natural resource in the region, the coalmines, which the Treaty of Versailles had ceded to France 'in full and absolute possession, with exclusive rights of exploitation, unencumbered and free from all debts and charges of any kind' (Article 45). The French also kept troops, which could be used to restore public order.[40] The main charge levied against the League was that it connived at the French policy of exploitation and gallicisation of the Saarland against the will of its people.[41] UNTEA, despite the express human rights obligations to which it was subjected, rubber-stamped the Indonesian takeover of West Irian and was accused of having aided and abetted the commission of a series of wrongful acts, i.e. the suppression of the West Irian inhabitants' right to self-determination[42] as well as their freedom of speech and association, in breach of both the Agreement on West New Guinea, the UN Charter and customary international law.[43] UNTAC failed to assert its control over the civil administration as foreseen by the Agreement on the Political Settlement,[44] but violations of human rights, which continued throughout the UN mandate in Cambodia, were perpetrated primarily by non-state actors and are not attributable

[39] Article XXII of the Indonesia-Netherlands Agreement, *supra* note 4.
[40] A. Allot, *Le Bassin de la Sarre. Organisation politique et administrative* (Paris: Berger-Levrault, 1924) 131.
[41] See F. M. Russell, *The International Government of the Saar* (University of California Press, 1926) and Stahn, *supra* note 2 at 163–73.
[42] See *supra* note 21. On international responsibility for complicity, see Chapter 3 (135ff.).
[43] Van der Veur, *supra* note 21 at 69–71.
[44] M. W. Doyle, *UN Peace-Keeping in Cambodia: UNTAC's Civil Mandate* (London: Lynne Rienner Publishers, 1995) 34.

to UNTAC. Nevertheless, to the extent that they resulted from such institutional and administrative failures of UNTAC as to constitute violations of the positive obligation to ensure some human rights, UNTAC's international legal responsibility might have been engaged. Moreover, there were also some reports about actions in breach of human rights directly committed by UNTAC in the exercise of its administrative and judicial powers. For instance, Doyle reports that the first two prisoners to be detained by UNTAC in its own prison facilities 'were held without habeas corpus and without trial'.[45]

The human rights record of three international administrations – Bosnia and Herzegovina, Kosovo and East Timor – is considered in more detail below.

Bosnia and Herzegovina

The Dayton Peace Agreement[46] created an institutional arrangement for Bosnia and Herzegovina that is unique from the point of view of both constitutional and international law. The key international player to date is the Office of the High Representative whose task is 'to monitor the implementation of the peace settlement' and 'to maintain close contact with the Parties to promote their full compliance with the civilian aspects of the peace settlement'.[47] Other international players are UNMIBH and a NATO-led multinational force, which was known as the Implementation Force (IFOR) in its first year and as the Stabilisation Force (SFOR) until 2005 when it was replaced by a EU-led force (EUFOR).[48] UNMIBH was entrusted with broad functions, but mainly on an assistance basis. The Dayton arrangements were far from perfect even on paper, often resulting in 'overlapping mandates'.[49]

Provisions for the protection of human rights are disseminated through the Dayton Agreement. The first set of such provisions is found in the Constitution of Bosnia – adopted as Annex 4 of the Agreement – in particular Article II and Annex I of the Constitution. Under Article II, the Republic of Bosnia and Herzegovina and its two

[45] *Ibid.* at 47. [46] Dayton Peace Agreement, *supra* note 25.

[47] Article 2, Annex 10, Dayton Peace Agreement, *supra* note 25.

[48] On *IFOR* see Annex 1A to the Dayton Agreements; on *SFOR* see SC Res. 1088 (1996); on *EUFOR* see SC Res. 1575 (2004); on *UMIBH* see SC Res. 1035 (1995), 1088 (1996), 1103 (1997), 1144 (1997), and 1184 (1998).

[49] F. Ni Aolain, 'The Fractured Soul of the Dayton Peace Agreement: A Legal Analysis', 19 Mich. J. Int. L. (1998) 957 at 993.

federal entities (the Federation of Bosnia and Herzegovina and the Republica Srpska) are obliged to 'ensure the highest level of internationally recognised human rights and fundamental freedoms'. Article II also makes the ECHR directly applicable in Bosnia and Herzegovina, and Annex I lists fifteen additional human rights instruments 'to be applied' there. The public bodies obliged to 'apply and conform to the human rights and fundamental freedoms' referred to in Article II are the state itself, as well as all 'courts, agencies, governmental organs, and instrumentalities operated by or within' the federal entities. The second group of Dayton human rights provisions is found in the Agreement on Human Rights and in the Agreement on Refugees and Displaced Persons, adopted as, respectively, Annex 6 and Annex 7 to the Dayton Peace Agreement. Parties to these two Agreements are the Republic of Bosnia and Herzegovina and its two federal entities.

The Dayton Agreement created a similarly complex architecture for the enforcement of human rights. In addition to the Constitutional Court, three bodies established under Annexes 6 and 7 have jurisdiction to apply human rights: the Human Rights Chamber, the Ombudsman, and the Commission for Real Property Claims of Displaced Persons and Refugees. Yet, neither the substantive nor the procedural provisions for the protection of human rights in the Dayton Agreement treated the High Representative, UNMIBH, or IFOR and its successors as addressees of human rights obligations.

With the demise of UNMIBH and the transformation of IFOR into EUFOR, the main international player left in Bosnia and Herzegovina is the office of the High Representative. It, too, was meant to be terminated, but in 2008, only months before the date set for its termination, the Peace Implementation Council decided to prolong its mandate indefinitely. As a result of another institutional change, the same person has acted as both High Representative and EU Special Representative since then.

The most important development affecting the international presence in Bosnia and Herzegovina is the expansion of the powers of the High Representative. Annex X of the Dayton Agreement entrusted the High Representative with a role of oversight and coordination on the implementation of the civilian aspects of the peace settlement, but not with an express legislative function although the provision in Annex X that the High Representative 'is the final authority in theatre regarding the interpretation of this Agreement' could be seen as forming the basis for an activity of authentic interpretation just short of the power to legislate.[50]

The more interventionist role of the High Representative over the years manifested itself in two ways. First, 'whenever a key international policy goal is blocked within one of the institutions, pressure is brought to bear on the offending parties'.[51] This risks producing a vicious circle: the Dayton Peace Agreement created a weak state but set ambitious goals; when these goals are not met, the international community, frustrated about such a failure, intervenes from above and thus ends up weakening the Bosnian state further. Secondly, since the decision of the Peace Implementation Conference in 1997, the powers of the High Representative have included the enactment of legislation 'when the national authorities are unable to reach agreement',[52] and the power to dismiss public officials, including elected ones – 130 such decisions were taken between March 1998 and June 2010.[53]

The expanded powers of the High Representative, normally referred to as 'Bonn powers', have a sound legal basis in international law. As the Constitutional Court of Bosnia itself acknowledged, '[i]n international law, the High Representative ... has power to make binding decisions, and authorities of Bosnia and Herzegovina have an obligation to co-operate with the High Representative by virtue of both the General Framework Agreement for Peace and Security Council resolutions'.[54]

The position may differ under Bosnian constitutional law. Liberal constitutionalism is simply incompatible with the grant of vast unchecked powers on an executive body. As the Helsinki Committee for Human Rights in Bosnia and Herzegovina explains: 'the High Representative is vested with practically limitless powers to make executive decisions, while not assuming responsibilities for the same, nor is there any legal remedy for such decisions. This also limits the rule of law, because

[50] On this see D. M. Cox, 'The Dayton Peace Agreement in Bosnia and Herzegovina: A Study of Implementation Strategies', LXIX BYBIL (1998) 201 at 214.

[51] *Ibid.* at 214.

[52] *Ibid.* at 206. See also European Commission for Democracy through Law (Venice Commission), *Opinion on the Constitutional Situation in Bosnia and Herzegovina and the Powers of the High Representative*, adopted by the Venice Commission at its 62nd plenary session (11–12 March 2005) at paras. 84ff, available at www.venice.coe.int/docs/2005/CDL-AD(2005)004-e.asp.

[53] See www.ohr.int/decisions/removalssdec/archive.asp?m=&yr=2010.

[54] *Decision of the Constitutional Court of Bosnia and Herzegovina in the Appeal of Milorad Bilbija et al, No. AP-953/05* of 8 July 2006 at para. 62.

the independence of the judiciary is not guaranteed in relation to this international institution'.[55]

The powers of the High Representative are prima facie problematic also from the point of view of international human rights law. Possible justifications include the derogation clauses in human rights treaties,[56] and Article 103 of the UN Charter.[57] These justifications operate at the general level and do not exclude the possibility that in particular instances the High Representative, or UNMIBH, violated human rights.

Specific violations of human rights attributed to international administrations have resulted from vetting and certification procedures for police personnel. Administered by both UNMIBH and the High Representative, these procedures breached due process for failing 'to provide the relevant police officers with a public, adversarial, impartial and independent examination of their rights'.[58] Many of the dismissals that followed were declared unlawful on procedural grounds under domestic law by Bosnian courts,[59] but both UNMIBH and the High Representative opposed these decisions, and resisted their implementation; the only action on which they could agree 'was intimidating the Bosnian courts and authorities into doing nothing'.[60]

The most recurrent violations of human rights of which the institutions of the international administration in Bosnia, and the High

[55] Helsinki Committee for Human Rights, 'Report on the Status of Human Rights in Bosnia and Herzegovina: Analysis for the period January–December 2007', Br: 02A-02/2008 at 7.

[56] Venice Commission, *supra* note 52 at para. 86.

[57] See *supra* note 54 at para. 66.

[58] Venice Commission, *Opinion no. 326/2004 on a Possible Solution to the Issue of Decertification of Police Officers in Bosnia and Herzegovina*, 24 October 2005, para. 47. See also Case No. CH/03/12932, *Rusmir Dzaferovic v. the Federation of Bosnia and Herzegovina*, Decision on merits of the Human Rights Commission within the Constitutional Court of Bosnia and Herzegovina of 7 May 2004 at 72.

[59] For example, *Kemal Kobilica* Zenica Municipal Court, P-97/02 (27 February 2003), affirmed Zenica Cantonal Court, Gz.805/03 (1 August 2003); *Fahrudin Derakovic* Zenica Municipal Court, P-639/02 (11 March 2003); *Nasir Vehabovic Zenica* Municipal Court, P-635/02 (11 March 2003) reversed on other grounds, Zenica Cantonal Court, Gz.921/03 (24 September 2003); *Sabahudin Ibrahimagic* Zenica Municipal Court, P-634/02 (18 March 2003) affirmed Zenica Cantonal Court, Gz.945/03 (1 October 2003); *Amir Deljkic* Zenica Municipal Court, P-640/02 (4 March 2003). But cf., e.g., *Amir Basic* Tuzla Municipal Court, P.219/03 (10 September 2002) where the dismissal was upheld.

[60] European Stability Initiative, 'On Mount Olympus: How the UN Violated Human Rights in Bosnia and Herzegovina, and Why Nothing Has Been Done to Correct it', 10 February 2007 at 1 and 18–19.

Representative in particular, have been accused concern democratic rights. A number of challenges have been brought against decisions of the High Representative to remove an elected official from office or to bar a candidate from participating in elections – powers which are 'fundamentally incompatible with the democratic character of the state and the sovereignty of Bosnia and Herzegovina'.[61]

The jurisprudence of the Constitutional Court identifies two possible routes to judicial scrutiny of the High Representative's acts depending on the capacity in which those acts were committed. First, where the High Representative acts in lieu of the domestic legislator, the Court has held that it can review its acts under Article VI(3)(a) of the Constitution, without however examining whether the High Representative was justified in enacting legislation in place of domestic authorities.[62] Secondly, the Court has emphasised that it has competence to review whether any legislation is in conformity with the Constitution, regardless of the nature of the legislator, provided such an assessment is grounded on one of the jurisdictional bases in Article VI(3) of the Constitution.[63]

Article VI(3) of the Constitution provides as follows:

'The Constitutional Court shall uphold this Constitution.

(a) The Constitutional Court shall have exclusive jurisdiction to decide any dispute that arises under this Constitution between the Entities or between Bosnia and Herzegovina and an Entity or Entities, or between institutions of Bosnia and Herzegovina, including but not limited to:

- Whether an Entity's decision to establish a special parallel relationship with a neighbouring state is consistent with this Constitution, including provisions concerning the sovereignty and territorial integrity of Bosnia and Herzegovina.

- Whether any provision of an Entity's constitution or law is consistent with this Constitution.

Disputes may be referred only by a member of the Presidency, by the Chair of the Council of Ministers, by the Chair or a Deputy Chair of either chamber of the Parliamentary Assembly, by one-fourth of the members of either chamber of the Parliamentary Assembly, or by one-fourth of either chamber of a legislature of an Entity.

[61] Venice Commission, *Opinion on the Constitutional Situation in Bosnia and Herzegovina and the Powers of the High Representative*, *supra* note 52 at para. 90.

[62] *Ibid*. Approved in *Eleven Members of the House of Representatives of the Parliamentary Assembly of Bosnia and Herzegovina*, Case No. U-16/00, Decision of 2 February 2001.

[63] *Trideset i cetiri poslanika Narodne skupštine Republike Srpske*, Case No. 25/00, Decision of 23 March 2001, Official Gazette of Bosnia and Herzegovina, No.17/00.

(b) The Constitutional Court shall also have appellate jurisdiction over issues under this Constitution arising out of a judgment of any other court in Bosnia and Herzegovina.

(c) The Constitutional Court shall have jurisdiction over issues referred by any court in Bosnia and Herzegovina concerning whether a law, on whose validity its decision depends, is compatible with this Constitution, with the European Convention for Human Rights and Fundamental Freedoms and its Protocols, or with the laws of Bosnia and Herzegovina; or concerning the existence of or the scope of a general rule of public international law pertinent to the court's decision.'

Attempts to appeal directly to the Court against a decision of the High Representative were initially declared inadmissible under Article VI(3)(b) of the Constitution of Bosnia for two reasons, that a decision of the High Representative is not a court judgment[64] and that it should be challenged in the lower courts first rather than by filing a petition to the Constitutional Court directly.[65]

With the *Bilbija* case, however, the Constitutional Court steered in a different direction.[66] The High Representative had dismissed Mr Bilbija from his position in the Intelligence and Security Agency in Banja Luka and from other public and party positions on the grounds that Mr Bilbija was involved in a movement in the Republika Srpska protecting war crime indictees from justice. The High Representative had also removed Mr Kalinic from his positions as Speaker of the National Assembly of the Republika Srpska and President of the Serb Democratic Party for failing to prevent material support being provided to war crime indictees. These decisions barred both appellants from holding office in any political party unless and until such time as the High Representative gave express authorisation. Their remuneration, status and privileges ceased immediately. The appellants unsuccessfully challenged the decisions, arguing that no evidence of wrongdoing had been produced, and that the High Representative had unduly intervened in the domestic legal order of Bosnia and Herzegovina and violated their constitutional and ECHR rights.

Crucially, Mr Kalinic and Mr Bilbija adopted a different litigation strategy. Mr Kalinic brought his case against the High Representative

[64] *Trideset i cetiri poslanika Narodne skupštine Republike Srpske*, Case No. U-37/01, Decision on admissibility of 2 November 2001.

[65] *S.T.*, Case No. AP-777/04, Decision on admissibility of 29 September 2004.

[66] *Supra* note 54.

himself, while Mr Bilbija's claim was against the Bosnian state for violations of its positive human rights obligations, in particular the obligation to protect the right to an effective remedy since no institutional mechanism to correct a decision of the High Representative was available. Affirming its previous jurisprudence, the Court held Mr Kalinic's claim inadmissible on the ground that it lacked jurisdiction to review the legality of individual decisions of the High Representative. By contrast, the Court found that Mr Bilbija's claim against the state was admissible and gave rise to a substantial question. Having outlined the international function, powers and legitimacy of the High Representative, the Court recalled the concerns of the Venice Commission found that:

> 'the High Representative does not act as an independent court and that there is no possibility of appeal. The High Representative is not an independent judge and he has no democratic legitimacy deriving from the people of the BiH. He pursues a political agenda, agreed by the international community, which serves the best interests of the country and contributes to the realization of the Council of Europe standards. As a matter of principle, it seems unacceptable that decisions directly affecting the rights of individuals taken by a political body are not subject to a fair hearing or at least the minimum of due process and scrutiny by an independent court.'[67]

The Court also held that the state had a positive obligation to protect the constitutional rights of people within its territory, even where it had transferred functions to an international agency, including the obligation to take reasonable steps to secure an effective remedy for people whose rights had been infringed.[68] The Court reasoned that neither the special status of the High Representative nor the sources of authority in the Dayton Agreement and various Security Council resolutions are capable of depriving the appellants of their constitutional rights or preventing positive obligations attaching to the state to protect such rights. The Court accepted the effectiveness of the decision of the High Representative,[69] but rejected the argument that Article 103 of the UN Charter required that constitutional law be set aside when in conflict with a decision of the Security Council under Chapter VII. It explained that Article 103 does not attempt

[67] *Ibid.* at para. 50. [68] *Ibid.* at paras. 53 and 55. [69] *Ibid.* at para. 65.

to determine the effect of conflict between obligations arising under the Charter and the internal legal orders of member states, and that in any event the Court was bound to give precedence to the Constitution.[70] In the view of the Court, the state's obligation in international law 'to cooperate with the High Representative and to act in conformity with decisions of the Security Council cannot determine the constitutional rights of people who are within the jurisdiction of Bosnia and Herzegovina'.[71] Further, the reference in Article II of the Constitution to the highest level of 'internationally recognised human rights' was not to be understood as restricting rights by reference to limitations arising in international law since the Constitution is the source of authority.[72] The Court concluded that there was no effective legal remedy against individual decisions of the High Representative and that the state had failed to take the steps required by its positive obligation to ensure an effective legal remedy under Article 13 of the ECHR. It thus held that the state was in breach of its human rights obligations,[73] and granted declaratory relief.

The *Bilbija* case testifies to the delicate balancing act which courts must perform in Bosnia. They must act as a check and balance on the extreme powers of the High Representative, but they must also avoid taking their review function so far as to render those powers ineffective.

The High Representative responded by issuing an Order, on 23 March 2007,[74] providing that any attempt to establish a domestic authority to review Decisions of the High Representative would undermine the General Framework Agreement[75] and that all domestic challenges would be declared inadmissible in the absence of prior consent from the Representative.[76] The Order provided that no liability could be incurred by the state in respect of any damage or loss resulting from any decision of the High Representative. It also contained an absolute ouster clause declaring all its provisions non-justiciable before domestic courts.[77] The Order was described by the ECtHR as a

[70] *Ibid.* at paras. 65–7. [71] *Ibid.* at para. 68. [72] *Ibid.* [73] *Ibid.* at paras. 72–4.

[74] High Representative Decision of 23 March 2007: 'Order on the Implementation of the Decision of the Constitutional Court of Bosnia and Herzegovina in the Appeal of *Milorad Bilbija et al.* 23 March 2007 AP-953/05'.

[75] *Ibid*, Art.2. [76] *Ibid*, Art. 3. [77] *Ibid*, Art. 4.

'vigorous response ... which took from the impugned decision of the Constitutional Court any practical effect'.[78]

The extensive public powers vested in the High Representative are problematic. International administrations should be temporary institutions, part of a transition to a new order in which the rule of law based on state sovereignty is restored. The powers of the international administration ought normally to decline over time, only exceptionally to remain constant, but never to increase. The expansion in the powers of the main international organ in Bosnia and Herzegovina signals a failure in the process of building local institutions that are practically viable and based on the rule of law and on respect for human rights. Indeed, while it had been originally envisaged that the international community, through its various institutions, would phase itself out, and that functions performed by the international administration would be progressively transferred to the Bosnian state, the opposite seems to have happened. According to David Chandler, the main reason for this regression is that the pursuit of democratisation through international administration included a 'regulatory and dis-empowering content' hidden behind the language of 'rights protection, multi-ethnic governance, open media and civil society building'.[79]

It is, however, important to keep in mind that, although there is a tendency to think of democracy and human rights as complementary ideas, the difficult relationship between them has troubled not a few political theorists, including Mill and Tocqueville.[80] Democracy can degenerate into populism and even seal its own demise when, for example, a political force inimical to democracy wins elections. Entrenched human rights protection is one of the ways in which liberty, and democracy itself, are protected from these risks. Insofar as the removal powers of the High Representative are strictly necessary to the preservation of liberty and democracy in Bosnia and Herzegovina, they may be justifiable in terms of both democratic theory and human

[78] *Beric and others v. Bosnia and Herzegovina*, Admissibility, 16 October 2007, Application Nos. 36357/04, 36360/04, 41705/04, 45190/04, 45578/04, 45579/04, 91/05, 97/05, 100/05, 101/05, 1121/05, 1123/05, 1125/05, 1129/05, 1132/05, 1133/05, 1169/05, 1172/05, 1175/05, 1175/05, 1177/05, 1180/05, 1185/05, 20793/05 and 25496/05, para. 19.

[79] Chandler, *supra* note 34 at 3.

[80] See A. de Tocqueville, 'Democracy in America' Vol. II, in I. Kramnick (ed.), *Democracy in America and Two Essays on America* (London: Penguin, 2003) Part IV, Ch. 6 ('Quelle espèce de despotisme les nations démocratiques ont a craindre'); J. S. Mill, *On Liberty* (Oxford University Press, 1991) Ch. 3.

rights. These powers can also be seen as a way of addressing the weaknesses of the Bosnian demos: if democracy is the rule of the people, when the depth of ethnic divisions is such that the population of the country does not identify itself as a *people*, that rule will be dysfunctional at best, illiberal and dangerous at worst.

Caplan has argued along similar lines that '[a] lack of international accountability at the local level can be justified on the grounds that emergency situations require extraordinary measures that may extend to the temporary suspension of norms of democratic governance'.[81]

The jurisprudence of the ECtHR under Article 3 of Protocol I of the Convention, which obliges state parties to hold free elections, bears testimony to the practical relevance of these questions. In general, the Court has been very sensitive to national experiences, accepting, for example, that the transition from authoritarian to democratic rule and the principle of secularism require a qualification to the right to stand for elections.[82] The Court has not however had an opportunity to apply these principles to Bosnia, because it has generally dismissed Bosnian cases concerning the Bonn powers of the High Representative on jurisdictional grounds. In *Beric* the ECtHR found that decisions of the High Representative removing persons from office are, in principle, attributable to the UN and that Bosnia and Herzegovina could not be held responsible for such removals.[83] Affirming the reasoning in the earlier case of *Behrami*, the Court reiterated that judicial scrutiny of member states' conduct would interfere with the effectiveness of the UN international civil administration of territory.[84] Most recently, in *Kalinic* and *Bilbija* the Court found that the same reasoning extends to prevent challenge to the High Representative's Order of 23 March 2007.

In the *Sejdic and Finci* case however the ECtHR held that the constitutional prohibition on a Romany and a Jew standing for election to the House of Peoples of the Parliamentary Assembly and for the State Presidency amounted to

[81] R. Caplan, 'Who Guards the Guardians? International Accountability in Bosnia', 12 *International Peacekeeping* (2005) 463 at 474.

[82] See *Zdanoka v. Latvia*, Application No. 58278/2000, Judgment of 17 June 2004; *Refah Partisi (Welfare Party) v. Turkey*, Application Nos. 41340/98, 41342/98, 41343/98 and 41344/98, Judgment of 31 July 2001, (2001) 35 EHRR 3, upheld by the Grand Chamber in Judgment of 13 February 2003, (2003) 37 EHRR 1.

[83] *Ibid*. See Chapter 3 on Attribution.

[84] *Beric*, *supra* note 78 at para. 30.

discrimination and to a breach of Article 3 of Protocol I.[85] Unlike the removal of elected officials, the constitutional prohibition was held to be an act attributable to Bosnia and thus capable of engaging the jurisdiction *ratione personae* of the Court. While the *Sejdic* case adds nothing to the analysis of the compatibility of the Bonn powers of the High Representative with human rights, it does show that, even giving due regard to the particular challenges posed by Bosnia, the ECtHR draws the line at overt discrimination – and quite rightly so.

East Timor

There have been five UN missions in East Timor since 1999. The first one, the UN Mission in East Timor (UNAMET), was mandated to organise the referendum on independence.[86] It was succeeded by UNTAET, a fully fledged international administration established by the Security Council under resolution 1272 (1999). UNTAET, which was accompanied by the deployment of an Australia-led multinational force under the terms of resolution 1264 (1999), operated until May 2002 when it was replaced by the UNMISET, which was in turn succeeded by the UN Office in Timor Leste (UNOTIL).[87] UNMISET and UNOTIL were part of a strategy of gradual phasing out of the international presence in East Timor, as the fledgling institutions of the new state found their feet. The establishment of the UN Integrated Mission in Timor Leste (UNMIT) followed the failure of this strategy.

The responsibilities of UNTAET included the establishment of an effective administration, the development of civil and social services, and the coordination and delivery of humanitarian and developmental assistance. In East Timor, unlike Kosovo, it was clear from the outset that the international administration was meant to prepare the territory for independence. Another difference from Kosovo was that, with the withdrawal of the Australia-led multinational force in February 2000, UNTAET took full control of the military and security aspects of the mission.

UNTAET's legislative and executive powers were extensive. A National Consultative Council, later renamed National Council, was instituted 'to provide advice to the Transitional Administrator on all

[85] *Sejdić and Finci v. Bosnia*, Applications Nos. 27996/06 and 34836/06.

[86] SC Res 1246 (1999); SC Res 1257 (1999).

[87] On UNMISET see SC Res 1410 (2002); SC Res 1473 (2003); SC Res 1480 (2003); SC Res 1543 (2004); and SC Res 1573 (2004). On UNOTIL see SC Res 1599 (2005); SC Res 1677 (2006); SC Res 1690 (2006); and SC Res 1703 (2006).

matters related to the exercise of the Transitional Administrator's executive and legislative functions'.[88] A Transitional Judicial Service Commission was also set up to recommend candidates for judicial and prosecutorial offices and to advise on the removal from office of judges.

It was the responsibility of the head of UNTAET, the Special Representative of the Secretary General, to decide on the continued application of 'laws applied in East Timor prior to 25 October 1999 ... insofar as they do not conflict' with human rights standards. Although the protection and promotion of human rights did not feature as one of the responsibilities of UNTAET under resolution 1272, the need to offer training to UNTAET staff in human rights and humanitarian law and the establishment of an independent East Timor human rights institution were expressly mentioned.

If in Kosovo a fundamental challenge was the reform of the judiciary and of the administration in order to entrench respect for human rights, in East Timor these institutions had to be built from scratch. During the brutal occupation to which this territory was subjected for over two decades hundreds of thousands had been killed, and institutions and social structures had collapsed under the iron fist of the military occupation. Poverty, the displacement of thousands, and the activities of the militias are other factors that made the process of institution-building in East Timor one of the most difficult tasks ever to be undertaken by the UN. The Transitional Administrator adopted regulations on the organisation of courts,[89] on the establishment of panels with exclusive jurisdiction over serious criminal offences,[90] on the organisation of the public prosecution service[91] and on rules of criminal procedures[92] in order to break the cycle of impunity and to begin to assert the rule of law.

As in Kosovo, the delegation of powers from UNTAET to the insurrectional movement, the National Council of East Timorese Resistance (CNRT), and to the former guerrilla army, Falintil, raised problems of compliance with human rights. In particular, individuals suspected of collaboration with the Indonesian authorities during the occupation, especially 'members of the country's Muslim, Protestant, and ethnic

[88] Section 1, UNTAET Regulation No. 1999/2; UNMIK Regulation No. 2000/24.
[89] UNTAET Regulation No. 2000/11 amended by Regulation No. 2000/14.
[90] UNTAET Regulation No. 2000/15. [91] UNTAET Regulation No. 2000/16.
[92] UNTAET Regulation No. 2000/30.

Chinese minorities',[93] were often targeted, as were some of the returnees from West Timor after being 'screened' by the CNRT and Falantil. According to Human Rights Watch, 'the U.N. police lacked the capacity and often the will to prevent such abuse'.[94] Individuals responsible for the heinous crimes perpetrated during the Indonesian occupation were not brought to justice.

The strategy of phasing out international institutions suffered a serious setback in April–June 2006, when a political crisis turned violent, threatening the future of the state. The response was an expansion of the UN presence through the establishment of UNMIT in August 2006 with a broad mandate.[95] UNMIT is mandated to support the government in performing various functions, mainly in the area of security, democratic governance, and the organisation and conduct of elections. These powers, while significant, do not place UNMIT in effective control of East Timor, and UNMIT is not therefore a full international administration. It is, however, noteworthy that the UNMIT's mandate has been steadily expanded to include new tasks.[96] Its significance is confirmed by the size of its budget – $205 million for 2009–10.[97] While perhaps not striking in absolute terms, this figure is four times the budget of UNMIK for the same period. Moreover, in a country where the total annual public expenditure is just over $300 million,[98] UNMIT's expenditure is bound to surpass that of any government department in East Timor. A UNMIT police force has also been deployed, and there have been some reports of use of excessive force, of cruel and degrading treatment and of illegal arrests.[99]

Kosovo

The mandate for the international administration in Kosovo was laid down in resolution 1244, adopted by the Security Council under

[93] Human Rights Watch, *World Report 2001* (New York, 2001), also available on the web at www.hrw.org. See also Amnesty International, 'East Timor: UNTAET, Justice and Refugees One Year after the Ballot' (London, 2000).

[94] Human Rights Watch, *ibid.*

[95] SC Res 1704 (2006).

[96] See SC Res. 1802 (2008); 1867 (2009); 1912 (2010).

[97] See Secretary General, 'Approved Resources for Peacekeeping Operations for the Period from 1 July 2009 to 30 June 2010' (2010) UN Doc. A/C.5/64/15, 22 January.

[98] See the East Timor entry in the CIA World Factbook available at www.cia.gov/library/publications/the-world-factbook/geos/tt.html.

[99] UNMIT Human Rights and Transitional Justice Section, 'Report on Human Rights Developments in Timor-Leste August 2006–August 2007', available at http://unmit.unmissions.org/LinkClick.aspx?fileticket=pylFCrJl59g%3d&tabid=826&mid=884, at 21.

Chapter VII after the 1999 NATO bombing campaign. The possibility of establishing an international presence in Kosovo had first been raised, unsuccessfully, at the Rambouillet peace talks.[100] While not technically part of its mandate, the Statement of the Ministerial Meeting of the G8, which preceded resolution 1244, has also been invoked for interpreting controversial aspects of the mandate of the international administration.

A distinctive feature of the Kosovo administration is the coexistence of a civilian component run by the UN (UNMIK) and headed by a Special Representative of the Secretary General, with a security one led by NATO (the Kosovo Force or KFOR). These two components – or 'presences' in the language of resolution 1244 – are mandated to 'operate towards the same goals and in a mutually supportive manner'.[101] KFOR's main responsibilities were the enforcement of the ceasefire, border monitoring, the demilitarisation of the Kosovo Liberation Army (KLA), and the maintenance of public order and safety in order to facilitate the work of the international civil presence and the provision of humanitarian assistance. The 'international civil' presence was responsible for 'performing basic civilian administrative functions', including the promotion of self-government and autonomy, the maintenance of civil law and order through international police forces pending the establishment of a local police force, the protection and promotion of human rights, and the assurance of safe and unimpeded return of refugees and displaced persons. UNMIK was, in particular, entrusted with legislative and executive powers, including the administration of the judiciary.[102]

[100] See 'Rambouillet Accords: Interim Agreement for Peace and Self-Government in Kosovo' annexed to UN Doc. S/1999/648; S. D. Murphy, 'Contemporary Practice of the United States Relating to International Law', 93 AJIL (1999) 628 at 629ff. On the international administration in Kosovo I have found the following works particularly helpful: J. Friedrich, 'UNMIK in Kosovo: Struggling with Uncertainty', 9 *Max Planck Yearbook of United Nations Law* (2005) 225; B. Knoll, 'From Benchmarking to Final Status? Kosovo and the Problem of an International Administration's Open-Ended Mandate', 16 EJIL (2005) 637 Stahn, *supra* note 2 at 308–32; and M. Weller, *Contested Statehood: Kosovo's Struggle for Independence* (Oxford Univeristy Press, 2009) Ch. 11.

[101] SC Res. 1244 (1999).

[102] Report of the Secretary General on the United Nations Interim Administration Mission in Kosovo, 12 July 1999, UN Doc. S/1999/779, and UNMIK Regulation No. 1999/1. See more generally Kosovo Department of Human Rights and Rule of Law, OSCE Mission in Kosovo, *Parallel Structures in Kosovo* (2003), available from www.osce.org/documents/mik/2003/10/698_en.pdf.

Serbian courts continued to operate in parallel to the UNMIK administered judiciary and were 'an expression of Serbia's continuing claim to sovereignty over the province'.[103] Elena Annette Baylis notes that the role of these parallel courts significantly diminished during the period 1999–2005.

Resolution 1244 does not provide for a clear hierarchy between UNMIK and KFOR. It simply requests 'the Secretary General to instruct his Special Representative to co-ordinate closely with the international security presence'. In principle, the Security Council, acting under Chapter VII, could revise the terms of the security presence or even decide its termination, but in practice there is no intermediate body that can assert the higher authority of the Council over KFOR on the ground. The inter-play between civilian and military components is thus left simply to coordination between actors on the ground.

The roles of UNMIK and KFOR have evolved over the years, generally in line with the principle that one of the key objectives of the international mission was to establish and oversee 'the development of provisional democratic self-governing institutions'.[104] The civilian administration remained under the authority of the Special Representative,[105] although in practice different UN agencies and humanitarian NGOs and offices often operated independently of each other.

Humanitarian NGOs 'flooded' Kosovo in the aftermath of the 1999 conflict. For example, several NGOs would often provide the same services to returnees in one region. UNHCR, which coordinated much of the relief effort, especially towards returnees, saw this as a mixed blessing: on the one hand, the availability of resources and services was a much welcome change from other humanitarian emergencies, but, on the other hand, the proliferation of humanitarian actors also resulted in wasteful use of resources, lack of a coordinated policy and 'amateurish' interventions. This is also due to diverse modi operandi, to the often fierce institutional independence of different international institutions, and, occasionally, to internal rivalries. Particularly in the initial phase of an emergency, humanitarian actors play a *de facto* administrative role since they provide essential services, such as shelter, water and sanitation, food aid, education, and decide on the allocation of scarce resources, functions that are in many ways typically 'governmental'. A UNMIK regulation dealing with NGOs was adopted in the first year of the administration.[106]

[103] E. A. Baylis, 'Parallel Courts in Post-Conflict Kosovo', 32 *Yale Journal of International Law* (2007) 1 at 2 and 12–14.

[104] SC Res. 1244 (1999) at para. 10.

[105] *Ibid.* at para. 6.

[106] UNMIK Regulation No. 1999/22.

At first, although Security Council resolution 1244 did not confer an administrative role on the KLA, KLA-appointed administrators acted as 'a *de facto* government',[107] but in May 2000 UNMIK established a Joint Interim Administrative Structure, comprising the Kosovo Transitional Council and the Interim Administrative Council. At the local level, municipal boards were headed by a UNMIK Municipal Administrator[108] until the direct election of municipal assemblies in October 2000. The powers of these Assemblies are set out in an UNMIK regulation, and are subject to the prerogative of the Special Representative of the Secretary General to set aside decisions which violate the applicable law or fail to take sufficient account of minority interests and rights.[109] Early on, UNMIK also assumed a security role through the establishment of the Kosovo Protection Corps, 'a civilian emergency agency' responsible for the provision of disaster response, humanitarian assistance in isolated areas, rebuilding infrastructure and de-mining.[110]

In May 2001, UNMIK adopted the Constitutional Framework,[111] which provided for the establishment of the Assembly of Kosovo, the government of Kosovo and the judicial system. In its advisory opinion in the *Kosovo* case, the ICJ found that their Constitutional Framework is not a merely internal legislative act, but has an international law character.[112] The first elections of the Kosovo Assembly were held on 17 November 2001, and transfer of competences over governmental affairs was completed in December 2003.[113] However, the Special Representative retained various important powers and ultimate authority, including the power to take 'appropriate measures' where the conduct of the provisional institutions conflicts with resolution 1244.

Powers retained by the Special Representative are enumerated in chapter 8 of Regulation 2001/9. The Special Representative's ultimate authority is clarified in chapter 12. An example of the Special Representative exercising this ultimate authority was his rejection of two laws following the attempt by the Assembly to

[107] See Lawyers Committee for Human Rights, 'A Fragile Peace: Laying the Foundations for Justice in Kosovo' (New York, October 1999) Sec. II, a.

[108] UNMIK Regulation No. 2000/1.

[109] UNMIK Regulation No. 2000/45 at paras. 3.1–3.3, 4.1, and 47.2.

[110] Section 1, UNMIK Regulation No. 1999/8.

[111] UNMIK Regulation No. 2001/9.

[112] *Accordance with International Law of the Unilateral Declaration of Independence in Respect of Kosovo*, Advisory Opinion of 22 July 2010, at para. 88.

[113] Responsibilities of the Assembly are enumerated in chapter 5 of Regulation No. 2001/9.

go beyond its mandated powers and not to comply with all the provisions of the Constitutional Framework, particularly with regard to minority interests.[114]

> Among the first challenges facing the international administration of Kosovo was to define the terms of the continuity with the previous legal order. The Secretary General indicated that 'UNMIK will respect the laws of the Federal Republic of Yugoslavia and of the Republic of Serbia insofar as they do not conflict with internationally recognised human rights standards or with regulations issued by the Special Representative [of the Secretary General]'.[115] Indeed, the first regulation adopted by UNMIK provided that 'the laws applicable in the territory of Kosovo prior to 24 March 1999 shall continue to apply in Kosovo insofar as they do not conflict' with internationally recognised human rights standards, with the fulfilment of the mandate under Security Council resolution 1244, and with UNMIK's own regulations.[116] Subsequent regulations have, however, provided that the applicable law is the law in force in Kosovo on 22 March 1989, the date when the autonomy of the province was repealed; the legislation which entered into force thereafter can be applied on condition that the organ required to implement it has determined that it is not discriminatory or otherwise contrary to international human rights standards.[117]

As a result of the abrogation of all legislation introduced after 1989, the applicable criminal law is currently based on the old Kosovo Criminal Code as opposed to the Yugoslav Criminal Code, although the latter makes provision for crimes against humanity and war crimes.[118]

This change was driven by vigorous protests against the continued application of Yugoslav law, the criminal code in particular, which the Kosovar Albanian population viewed as one of the most severe tools of past discrimination.[119] Demanding a return to the law prior to revocation of Kosovo's

[114] See Report of the Security Council Mission to Kosovo and Belgrade, Federal Republic of Yugoslavia, '14–17 December 2002', UN. Doc. S/2002/1376 of 19 December 2002, para 6.

[115] Report of the Secretary General, *supra* note 102 at para. 36.

[116] Section 3, UNMIK Regulation No. 1999/1.

[117] UNMIK Regulation No. 1999/24 (12 December 1999), sec. 1.1 provides that, '[t]he law applicable in Kosovo shall be: a. The regulations promulgated by the Special Representative of the Secretary-General and subsidiary instruments thereunder; and b. The law in force in Kosovo on 22 March 1989.' Further, sec. 3 states that '[t]he present regulation shall be deemed to have entered into force as of 10 June 1999'. See also UNMIK Regulation No. 2000/59.

[118] Lawyers' Committee, *supra* note 107.

[119] M. Kaminski, 'UN Struggles with a Legal Vacuum in Kosovo; Team Improvises in Effort to Build a Civil Structure', *Wall Street Journal*, 4 August 1999, A14.

autonomy status within Serbia, political representatives of the Kosovar Albanian community threatened to cease cooperation with the UN, and newly appointed judges and prosecutors resigned from office.[120] While Regulation 1999/1 provided for international human rights standards, it did not provide guidance on how to reconcile Yugoslav law with those standards. The controversy, threatening to undermine the entire mission, led to the establishment of the Joint Advisory Council for Legislative Matters.

The Declaration of Independence on 17 February 2008 changed the political context, prompting a further reconfiguration of the international administration. On that same day the Assembly also passed legislation in a number of fields assuming legal control and responsibility over areas previously reserved to the Special Representative. In light of the challenge to UNMIK's authority under the new constitution, on 12 June 2008 the Secretary General reported that UNMIK 'will no longer be able to perform effectively the vast majority of its tasks as an interim administration',[121] and will be beginning a process of reorganisation of the international presence in Kosovo.

This process was completed on 1 July 2009.[122] Under the new arrangements the EU has become the key player through its Rule of Law Mission in Kosovo (EULEX) – the 'largest civilian mission ever launched under the Common Security and Defence Policy'.[123] EULEX is under the overall authority of the UN, in accordance with the framework of resolution 1244.[124] A Kosovo Security Force has been established under the supervision of KFOR, while the Kosovo Protection Corps has been terminated. As a result of the transfer of competences to the EU and to local institutions, UNMIK has reduced its side considerably, as evidenced by its budget which was for approximately $47 million, providing for the deployment of 507 personnel, in 2009–10,

[120] See B. Reka, *UNMIK as International Governance in Post-war Kosova: NATO's Intervention, UN Administration and Kosovar Aspirations* (Skopje: Lagos A., 2003) 188–9.

[121] Secretary General, 'Report of the Secretary General on the United Nations Interim Administration in Kosovo', S/2008/354, at para. 17.

[122] Secretary General, 'Report of the Secretary General on the United Nations Interim Administration in Kosovo', S/2009/497, at para. 2.

[123] See www.eulex-kosovo.eu/en/info/whatisEulex.php. On *EULEX* see Joint Action 2008/124/CFSP of 4 February 2008; Council Joint Action 2009/445/CFSP of 9 June 2009; Council Decision 2010/322/CFSP of 8 June 2010. The *Declaration of Independence* is at www.assembly-kosova.org/?krye=news&newsid=1635&lang=en. On the transfer of authority from UNMIK to EULEX, see E. Milano, 'Il trasferimento di funzioni da UNMIK a EULEX in Kosovo', 91 *Rivista Diritto Internazionale* (2008) 967.

[124] Secretary General, 'Report on The United Nations Interim Administration Mission in Kosovo', UN Doc. S/2008/458 at para. 30.

whereas it had been for $198 million, providing for a personnel of 4,911 people, in 2008–09.[125]

On 22 July 2010 the ICJ delivered its advisory opinion on the following question, as requested by the General Assembly of the United Nations: 'Is the unilateral declaration of independence by the Provisional Institutions of Self-Government in Kosovo in accordance with international law?'[126] Serbia advanced various arguments in support of the international illegality of that declaration, some on the incompatibility between the declaration and various aspects of Security Council resolution 1244 (1999), and others on general international law.[127]

The ICJ found that the declaration of independence did not violate international law. The Court determined that it was not necessary to resolve the question of the limits of self-determination and of the right of 'remedial secession' since the absence in international law of a specific prohibition on unilateral declarations alone disposed of the question of the accordance of the declaration with general international law – a conclusion criticised by some as a convenient revival of the *Lotus* principle.[128] The Court also concluded that the authors of the declaration of independence 'did not act as one of the Provisional Institutions of Self-Government within the Constitutional Framework, but rather as persons who acted together in their capacity as representatives of the people of Kosovo outside the framework of the interim administration' – a finding which, in the Court's view, was confirmed by the silence of the Special Representative of the Secretary General in the face of the declaration.[129] The Court found that it 'cannot accept the argument that Security Council resolution 1244 (1999) contains a prohibition, binding on the authors of the declaration of independence, against declaring independence … The language of Security Council resolution 1244 (1999) is at best ambiguous in this regard.'[130]

Most importantly, the Constitutional Framework of 2001 was replaced by a Constitution which entered into force on 15 June 2008. The new Constitution does not mention any role or function for the UN and does not refer to resolution 1244, but under its transitional provisions

[125] GA Res 62/262 (2008) and GA Res 63/295 (2009). On personnel reduction see Secretary General, 'Report of The United Nations Interim Administration Mission in Kosovo', UN Doc. S/2009/300 (10 June 2009), at para, 18.

[126] GA Res. 63/3.

[127] Written Statement of Serbia, Chapters 7–9; Oral Pleadings for Serbia, CR 2009/24 (1 December 2009).

[128] *Accordance with International Law of the Unilateral Declaration of Independence in Respect of Kosovo*, Advisory Opinion, ICJ Reports (2010) at paras. 79–84. See Judge Simma's Declaration (para. 2) for a criticism of the *Lotus* logic underlying the opinion of the majority on this point.

[129] *Ibid*. paras. 108–9. [130] *Ibid*. para. 118.

the Comprehensive Proposal for the Kosovo Status Settlement of 26 March 2007 takes precedence 'over all other legal provisions in Kosovo', including the Constitution.[131] The Constitution also recognises a special role for the International Civilian Representative, whose functions are modelled on those of the High Representative in Bosnia and include acting as 'the final authority in Kosovo regarding interpretation of the civilian aspects' of the Settlement.[132] In particular, under Article 147, '[n]o Republic of Kosovo authority shall have jurisdiction to review, diminish or otherwise restrict the mandate, powers and obligations' of the International Civilian Representative. As in Bosnia, the EU Representative in Kosovo doubles as the International Civilian Representative.

The task of establishing a multi-ethnic judiciary has proven difficult in Kosovo.[133] An Administrative Department of Justice 'responsible for the overall management of matters relating to the judicial system and the correctional service' was established in March 2000.[134] Lay judges are appointed by the Special Representatives upon a recommendation of the Advisory Judicial Commission, which can also hear complaints on their conduct.[135] International judges and prosecutors have been appointed since the beginning of 2000, although the regulation on their appointment and removal does not guarantee their tenure and confers on the Special Representative the power to remove them at his discretion.[136] After the New Provisional Criminal Code and Provisional Criminal Procedure Code of Kosovo entered into force in April 2004, UNMIK established the independent Kosovo Judicial Council which is responsible for the judiciary and the courts[137] and the Kosovo Ministry of Justice.[138] In February 2008, shortly after independence, a memorandum of understanding between UNMIK, the United Nations Office of Project Services (UNOPS) and the EU

[131] Article 143, Kosovo Constitution, available at www.kushtetutakosoves.info. The Comprehensive Proposal is found in an Addendum to the Letter dated 26 March 2007 from the Secretary General to the President of the Security Council, UN Doc. S/2007/168/Add. 1.

[132] Article 2.1 of Annex IX, Comprehensive Proposal, *ibid*.

[133] For example, two of the six Serb judges appointed by UNMIK fled Kosovo before taking office. 'Report of the Secretary General on the United Nations Interim Administration in Kosovo', UN Doc. S/1999/987 at para. 32.

[134] Article 1.2, UNMIK Regulation No. 2000/15.

[135] UNMIK Regulation No. 1999/18.

[136] UNMIK Regulation No. 2000/6.

[137] UNMIK Regulation No. 2005/52.

[138] UNMIK Regulation No. 2005/53.

was concluded under which the vetting and appointment process for Kosovo's judges and prosecutors will commence.

Resolution 1244 placed UNMIK under an obligation to promote and protect human rights. Such an obligation formed the basis for the analysis of the consistency of the antecedent law described above. In terms of substantive human rights protection, the treatment of minorities in Kosovo has posed a significant challenge since the early days of the mission.[139] The response of UNMIK and KFOR to threats and attacks on Serbs and Roma was often 'belated and uneven'.[140] As a result of KLA pressure and of the ethnic bias of the judiciary appointed and salaried by UNMIK, the right to fair trial of accused Serbs has reportedly been violated.[141] According to Amnesty International, delays in bringing detainees before the judicial authority have been frequent, especially in the context of the unrest in Mitrovica in 2000.[142] On at least one occasion, Amnesty International issued an urgent appeal on the prolonged detention without charge of an Albanian activist.[143] The trafficking of persons, especially of women for the purposes of sexual exploitation, has prompted the adoption of a specific regulation by the Special Representative to increase sanctions on human traffickers,[144] but the problem, which the existence of a 'sex market' for the thousands of soldiers stationed in Kosovo has only made worse, remains serious.

Courts do not have jurisdiction over the international bodies, but the Ombudsperson Institution until 2006 and the Human Rights Advisory Panel since then have had such jurisdiction over UNMIK. The Ombudsperson Institution was first established in 2000, but ceased to have any jurisdiction over UNMIK in March 2006.[145] According to Andrew Clapham, the Ombudsperson Institution is one of a number of

[139] See Human Rights Watch, 'Federal Republic of Yugoslavia: Abuses against Serbs and Roma in the New Kosovo' (New York, August 1999) 1, available at www.hrw.org/reports/1999/kosov2.

[140] *Ibid.*

[141] Amnesty International, 'Federal Republic of Yugoslavia (FRY)/Kosovo: Risk of Serious Miscarriage of Justice in Trial of Serbs', Press release of 20 April 2000; Lawyers Committee, *supra* note 107. See also: *The Guardian*, 'Amnesty and UN Staff Accuse Kosovo War Crimes Tribunal of Ethnic Bias', 20 June 2001.

[142] Amnesty International, 'Setting the Standard? UNMIK and KFOR's Response to the Violence in Mitrovica' (London, 2000).

[143] Amnesty International, 'Amnesty International Protests the Unlawful Detention of Afrim Zeqiri', Press release of 12 February 2001.

[144] UNMIK Regulation No. 2001/4.

[145] UNMIK Regulation No. 2000/38 and UNMIK Regulation No. 2006/06.

positive developments in the area of human rights compliance by the UN which 'enforce and apply human rights as such and not simply as guiding principles. Moreover, the UN went beyond the human rights treaty law that was binding on the Federal Republic of Yugoslavia at the time. These accountability mechanisms are part of a unilateral commitment to use human rights law as part of the parameters for governance.'[146] This assessment may be too optimistic. The Ombudsperson Institution was limited by several factors, in particular its lack of jurisdiction over KFOR and the non-binding nature of its findings; and UNMIK's record in accepting and implementing the findings of the Ombudsperson was 'disappointing'.[147]

After the reform of the Ombudsperson Institution, the task of holding UNMIK to account was transferred to the Human Rights Advisory Panel, created through UNMIK legislation in March 2006.[148] The Panel is fully independent of UNMIK and is mandated to examine complaints from any person or group of persons claiming to be the victim of violation by UNMIK of human rights recognised in a number of international conventions.[149] The Panel's findings are of a strictly advisory nature.[150] Jurisdiction extends to the whole territory of Kosovo but is limited to acts occurring not earlier than 23 April 2005 with the exception of continuing violations.[151] The Special Representative effectively possesses absolute discretion in deciding whether to approve requests for the appearance of UNMIK personnel and for the submission of documents; the Special Representative 'shall take into account the interest of justice, the promotion of human rights and the interests of UNMIK and the United Nations as a whole'.[152]

In practice, the majority of complaints invoke a violation of the ECHR and concern property.[153] However, the Panel has examined other rights too, and its first opinion found a violation of the right to life due to the lack of an effective investigation into the killing

[146] A. Clapham, *Human Rights Obligations of Non-State Actors* (Oxford University Press, 2006) 130–1.

[147] Stahn, *supra* note 2 at 622–3.

[148] UNMIK Regulation No. 2006/12; amended by UNMIK Administrative Direction No. 2009/1. On alternatives to the Panel considered by UNMIK, and the drafting history of the Regulation see B. Knoll and R. J. Uhl, 'Too Little, Too Late: the Human Rights Advisory Panel in Kosovo', 7 EHRLR (2007) 534.

[149] UNMIK Regulation No. 2006/12, sec. 1.2.

[150] *Ibid.* at secs. 1.3, 17. [151] *Ibid.* at sec. 1.2. [152] *Ibid.* sec. 15.3.

[153] Human Rights Advisory Panel, Annual Report 2008, available at www.unmikonline.org/human_rights/documents/annual_report2008.pdf at para. 18.

of the complainant's wife.[154] As of 5 January 2010 the Panel had received a total of 482 cases, of which 452 are pending and 30 are closed.[155] Two complaints, in particular, have attracted considerable public attention. One concerned the deaths of two individuals and injuries to others allegedly resulting from the unauthorised and disproportionate use of force by UNMIK in the dispersal of a street demonstration in February 2007;[156] the other concerned the alleged breach of UNMIK's duty of care towards the Roma residents in camps for internally displaced persons where they suffered from severe lead poisoning.[157] Although the first complaint was found to be admissible,[158] the Special Representative subsequently objected that the complainant had failed to exhaust domestic remedies since the case was under ongoing review by an UNMIK Claims Review Board, part of the United Nations Third Party Claims Process. Pending consideration of this issue by the Panel, the Special Representative issued an Administrative Direction which stated that issues of admissibility can be examined at any stage of proceedings and that complaints in such circumstances shall be inadmissible.[159] The complainant's subsequent appeal against the Administrative Direction was held to be inadmissible since the Direction itself formed part of the Panel's governing instruments.[160] As for the lead poisoning complaint, this was held to be in part admissible and the decision on the merit is pending.

EULEX has set up a separate human rights body, the Human Rights Review Panel, to review 'complaints from any person claiming to be the victim of a human rights violation by EULEX KOSOVO in the conduct of its executive mandate'.[161] Described as a 'complementary channel for the overall accountability of EULEX KOSOVO', the Human Rights Review Panel began to hear cases in June 2010.

[154] *Shaip Canhasi v. UNMIK*, Case No. 04/08, Opinion on merits of 12 November 2008.

[155] Secretary General, 'Report of Secretary General on Kosovo to the Security Council S/2010/5, at para. 44.

[156] *Kadri Balaj (on behalf of Mon Balaj), Shaban Xheladini (on behalf of Arben Xheladini), Zenel Zemeli and Mustafa Nerjovaj v. UNMIK*, Case No. 04/07, Decision on admissibility.

[157] *N. M. and Others v. UNMIK*, Case No. 26/08, Decision on admissibility.

[158] *Balaj*, *supra* note 156.

[159] UNMIK Regulation No. 2006/12. Administrative Direction No. 2009/1, sec. 2.

[160] *Kadri Balaj (on behalf of Mon Balaj), Shaban Xheladini (on behalf of Arben Xheladini), Zenel Zemeli and Mustafa Nerjovaj v. UNMIK*, Case No. 320/09, Decision on admissibility of 12 February 2010.

[161] See www.hrrp.eu/mandate.php.

Conclusion: benign autocracies or international leviathans?

What conclusions can be drawn about the human rights performance of international administrations? As explained before, international administrations are ambitious experiments in governance. The advancement of human rights is almost an impossible mission for a foreign institution whose legitimacy in the eyes of the local population can at best rely only on a short-term line of credit. True, respect for human rights and the rule of law will make the international administration more acceptable to the local population, but such respect is a necessary but not sufficient condition for political legitimacy.

Although each administration is different from another,[162] some common trends can be discerned. First, the institutional configuration of most international administrations has changed over the years. The key international actors involved in the administration – the UN, the EU and *ad hoc* international bodies such as the High Representative in Bosnia and the International Civilian Representative in Kosovo – have mutated, and their responsibilities have shrunk at times, grown at others. Subsidiary organs established by the international actors as part of their administration, such as the human rights bodies, have also undergone various transformations. One institutional solution has often succeeded another, but this is more often than not a sign of a fundamental weakness in the process of state- and institution-building.

Secondly, the phasing out of international administrations has proven a rather elusive objective. While Bosnia, Kosovo and East Timor may not be under international rule to the same extent as in the initial periods of these administrations, the international presence there remains vital.

Thirdly, and most importantly in the context of human rights protection, the autocratic element of international administrations seems to be especially resilient. Both the High Representative in Bosnia and Herzegovina, and the International Civilian Representative in Kosovo are endowed with powers that are difficult to reconcile with the basic tenets of liberal democratic constitutionalism. They have both been careful to shield themselves completely from the review of local courts, including on human rights grounds.

One should not read too much into the fact that similar arrangements have not been put in place in East Timor under UNTAET or UNMIT. They may have

[162] For a critical view on the contribution of UNMIK to the development of the protection of human rights in Kosovo see Knoll and Uhl, *supra* note 148 at 547–9.

been simply unnecessary given that East Timorese courts are unlikely to interfere with international institutions.

The autocratic powers of international administrators pose a real dilemma. On the one hand, they are necessary to protect shaky democratic institutions and as yet uncertain guarantees of human rights. On the other, they constitute an affront to democracy and, in some cases, to human rights. Their purpose may make these powers benign, but no autocracy can remain benign for too long. And now that the transience of these powers is all but nominal, their very existence calls into question the long-term viability of these constitutional and legal arrangements. The best case that can be made for them is that, in their absence, the situation would deteriorate.

Moreover, although the idea of an even partial international autocracy is invidious, it is probably preferable to vest such autocratic powers in an international body than in a local one. A local autocrat is indeed more likely to abandon any noble purpose for which it was originally established, and to degenerate into a pure and simple tyrant. International institutions instead operate under a constant and ultimately healthy pressure from both domestic and foreign actors to phase themselves out. The desire of member states of the UN, the EU or NATO to remove problems from their agenda and to see durable solutions acts as a check and balance on the duration and extent of the involvement of these institutions with the administration of territory. Their bureaucrats may develop a vested interest in prolonging their stay, but the governments of member states, especially those that contribute significant resources, do not generally like to have to justify to their constituencies why a mission that was originally meant to last a few years is continuing over a decade later.

Fourthly, the accountability map of international administrations is, on its face, rather elaborate, but not necessarily effective. There is a tendency for each international actor to have its own human rights body, and sometimes more than one. As discussed, for example, EULEX Kosovo has set up a Human Rights Review Panel, which can hear complaints from any person who claims to have suffered a violation of his or her human rights by EULEX, and a Human Rights and Gender Office, which has an advisory and preventative function. In addition to the EULEX institutions, UNMIK has its own human rights body, the Human Rights Advisory Panel, and OSCE its own human rights advisers. Moreover, under the 2008 Constitution, both courts and the Ombudsperson have jurisdiction over human rights. International institutions could have chosen to rely on national human rights structures for their own accountability, instead of establishing parallel ones. They could have done so on the basis of memoranda of understanding to protect some of their immunities and privileges, or they could have set up special chambers within those national institutions operating under different terms. This course of action would have strengthened the local human rights institutions, on which, once the international administration is gone, the task of promoting and protecting human rights will fall.

Violations of human rights in *de facto* international administrations

The administration of refugee camps by UNHCR is one of the main examples of *de facto* international administration, not least judged by the number of people it affects: more than 7 million of the world's refugees are believed to live 'in camps or segregated settlements in situations lasting ten years or more, some for generations'.[163] The encampment of refugees represents one of the most significant affronts to human liberty in our times to have remained almost entirely outside the public gaze, as well as one of the last surviving total institutions premised on the segregation of human beings.[164] In Merrill Smith's powerful summary: '[b]riefly put, condemning people who fled persecution to stagnate in confinement for much of the remainder of their lives is unnecessary, wasteful, hypocritical, counterproductive, unlawful and morally unacceptable'.[165]

Refugee camps are not the only example of *de facto* territorial administration. First, as discussed above, during peacekeeping missions administrative functions not expressly contemplated under the mandate are sometimes exercised. Secondly, as Chiara Giorgetti has shown, in so-called failed states situations, most notably Somalia, the UN has continued to exercise certain functions of government even after the wide-ranging UN missions in that country came to an end.[166] Although

163 Data from US Committee for Refugees, *World Refugee Survey* (2007).

164 Verdirame and Harrell-Bond, *supra* note 6 at 338. On the theory of total institutions see E. Goffman, *Asylums: Essay on the Social Situation of Mental Patients and Other Inmates* (New York: Doubleday Anchor, 1961).

165 Smith, *supra* note 163.

166 C. Giorgetti, *A Principled Approach to State Failure* (Leiden and Boston: Brill, 2010) esp. 23ff.

these functions are not so extensive as to amount to an international administration, they still represent an example of exercise of significant governmental functions by international organisations on a *de facto* basis.

The administrative structure of refugee camps: 'perfect city' representations and dystopian realities

In UNHCR's triptych of a refugee's life, camps are the central panel – flight being the first and repatriation the last. But what is a refugee camp? For the purposes of this chapter, refugee camps are understood as defined by two main characteristics: the restrictions placed on the freedom of movement of refugees and the mode of governance.[167] These characteristics distinguish refugee camps from other types of refugee settlements, such as agricultural settlements. As refugees do not choose to live in camps but are forced to reside there, camps become means of 'warehousing' refugees, marginalising and often segregating them from the host population.[168] Refugee camps are instituted and administered as spaces separate from the legal and social environment of the host state. Although the degree of 'separateness' varies from one camp to the other, parallel systems for settling disputes and for providing health and welfare services are established as a rule in camps. In this sense, the lack of integration of refugees in the host country is not merely a consequence of their encampment, but the very essence and purpose of camps.

> When UNHCR and aid agencies are not present, the integration of refugees into existing local facilities and resources has sometimes occurred spontaneously. Once they become involved, UNHCR and the aid agencies swiftly introduce the 'registration = food aid logic' followed by the establishment of refugee camps.[169]

In many, if not all, refugee camps, the local offices of UNHCR exercise at least some administrative functions. Authority for the exercise

[167] See A. Schmidt, 'Camps versus Settlements', Forced Migration Online Thematic Guide, September 2003, available at www.forcedmigration.org/guides/fmo021. See also R. Black, 'Putting Refugees in Camps', 2 FMR (1998) 4.

[168] See US Committee on Refugees' 'Campaign to End Refugee Warehousing' at www.refugees.org/article.aspx?id=1109&rid=1179&subm=33&area=About%20Refugees&.

[169] See: Harrell-Bond, *supra* note 7; W. van Damme, 'How Liberian and Sierra Leonean Refugees Settled in the Forest Region of Guinea (1990–1996)', 12 J. Ref. St.(1999) 36), and by the same author, 'Do Refugees Belong in Camps? Experiences from Goma and Guinea', 346 *The Lancet* (1995) 360; Verdirame and Harrell-Bond, *supra* note 6.

of these functions is not generally found in the cooperation agreements concluded by UNHCR with the host state, which are intended to govern the terms of UNHCR's presence in the country but seldom do more than repeat guarantees for the organisation and its staff, such as immunity from the jurisdiction of domestic courts.[170] In spite of the lack of express authority, UNHCR exercises wide-ranging administrative and at times even judicial powers on a *de facto* basis in refugee camps.[171]

A web of agreements between UNHCR and other UN agencies also exists. These Memoranda of Understanding (MoUs) regulate cooperation among various UN agencies involved in the same operation. The activities that are 'typically addressed in inter-agency MoUs include joint contingency planning, joint needs assessments, development of standards and guidelines, and sharing of information. Public information aspects and fund-raising issues, which can be of a joint or agency-specific nature, are sometimes also addressed'.[172] The most thorough examination of UNHCR practice in this field is by Marjoleine Zieck.[173]

There is no model of camp administration that is applied by UNHCR to every camp, but socio-legal and anthropological research on refugee camps has consistently attested to certain features in their administration.[174] The type of administration that is set up in a particular camp depends on various factors, including power relations between the humanitarian agencies on the one hand, and the host government and local authorities on the other; the location of the camp and its distance from judicial and other authorities of the host country; the willingness or reluctance of local civil society to become involved in refugee matters; and the attitude of the field offices of the humanitarian agencies, and of UNHCR in particular. Finally, in a situation characterised by the

[170] The model cooperation agreement used by UNHCR is found in M. Zieck, *UNHCR's Worldwide Presence in the Field* (Nijmegen: Wolf Legal Publishers, 2006) Appendix 2.

[171] Verdirame and Harrell-Bond, *supra* note 6 at 31–6, 182–92.

[172] Executive Committee of UNHCR, 'Memoranda of Understanding', UN Doc. EC/47/SC/CRP.51, at paras. 29–30. See also ECOSOC Res. 1995/56.

[173] Zieck *supra* note 170 at 59ff.

[174] Verdirame and Harrell-Bond, *supra* note 6. On the Kenyan camps, see also J. Hyndman, *Geographies of Displacement: Gender, Power and Culture in UNHCR Refugee Camps* (University of British Columbia, PhD Thesis, 1996), now published as *Managing Displacement: Refugees and the Politics of Humanitarianism* (Minneapolis: University of Minnesota Press, 2000); R. Wilde, '*Quis Custodiet Ipsos Custodes?* Why and How UNHCR Governance of "Development" Refugee Camps Should be Subject to International Human Rights Law', 1 Yale H. R. Dev. L. J. (1998) 5.

lack of a formal legal framework for identifying the responsibilities of different actors, personalities also end up playing a very important role.[175] Law, both domestic and international, plays a surprisingly minor role in the assumption and exercise of governmental powers by UNHCR in refugee camps.

As mentioned, UNHCR, together with the NGOs it may subcontract, exercises a wide range of administrative and judicial, or quasi-judicial and semi-judicial, powers. UNHCR's primary roles are supervision and standard-setting for its implementing partners, policy coordination, overall administration, and facilitating or securing the international protection of refugees. The presence of NGOs in camps – for the most part international humanitarian agencies – could prima facie be seen as a check and balance on the exercise of power by UNHCR. But NGOs are actually part and parcel of the power structure of refugee camps, since they are normally subcontracted by UNHCR for the provision of particular services. Their financial dependence on UNHCR makes criticism very unlikely.[176] Far from the rhetoric of civil society as selfless champion of the underdogs and the downtrodden, the reality of NGOs in refugee camps rather brings to mind the Gramscian idea of civil society as the 'private hegemonic apparatus' of the constituted authority.[177]

A key feature of the administration of camps is the marginalisation of the host state's law and law enforcement. There is often a presence of national police forces in the camp, but, more often than not, the involvement of the police in maintaining public order in the camp is negotiated with UNHCR or with one of its implementing partner NGOs.[178] Neither the private nor the criminal laws of the state are normally applied. Instead, much of the administration of civil and criminal justice is handled informally either by the humanitarian agencies or by the 'customary courts', which apply the customs of particular

[175] G. Verdirame, 'Human Rights and Refugees: The Case of Kenya', 12 J. Ref. St. (1999) 54 at 54–5.

[176] On humanitarian NGOs, see Harrell-Bond, *supra* note 7, and, by the same author, 'Humanitarianism in a Strait-Jacket', 84 (334) *African Affairs* (1985) 3. Also Verdirame and Harrell-Bond, *supra* note 6 at 312ff.

[177] A. Gramsci, *Quaderni del Carcere* (2nd edn., Turin: Einaudi, 1977) (edited by V. Gerratana), Vol. II, at 801.

[178] On the different types of agreements that UNHCR concludes with host states, other international organisations and NGOs, see Zieck, *supra* note 170 at 70ff.

communities as interpreted by those in power. In Kakuma refugee camp in Kenya in the late 1990s and early 2000s, for example, the Sudan People's Liberation Army (SPLA) was effectively in charge of the Dinka sector of the camp.[179] The 'customary courts' administered by the SPLA were given some jurisdiction over criminal matters, although under Kenyan law state courts have exclusive criminal jurisdiction and the jurisdiction of customary courts is limited to divorce, dowry and inheritance.[180] The extent of criminal jurisdiction of these 'courts', or indeed that they should exercise any such jurisdiction at all, was not specified in any document. It was thus a *de facto* exercise of jurisdiction, not simply endorsed, but also actively encouraged and funded by the UNHCR.

During my first visit to Kakuma refugee camp in April 1997, a woman with mental problems and two children were detained in the prison facilities that UNHCR had built for the Dinka community. During a later visit to Kakuma in April 1998, Barbara Harrell-Bond found out that plans for a new, bigger and 'better' prison were underway.

In March 2006 the Bench Court ordered a female victim of domestic violence to forgive her husband and return to the community to live with him. When the woman refused, she was incarcerated. She was released at the instance of the gender unit and placed under protection for fear of further attack; her husband fled back to Sudan for fear of arrest, but was said to have later come back to the community.

After international human rights NGOs documented the widespread occurrence of rapes and sexual assaults in Dadaab in the early 1990s,[181] the Kenya Chapter of the International Federation of Women Lawyers (FIDA) initiated an advocacy project which led to the establishment of a 'Mobile Court', funded by UNHCR, to hear cases in the camps, particularly cases of rape and sexual violence. The Mobile Court began to operate in 1998 and dealt with a handful of cases involving both refugees and locals. From January 2005 to March 2006 there were in total fifteen sittings of the Mobile Court. The court heard sixty-seven complaints of sex or gender-based violence (SGBV). Eleven perpetrators of sexual offences were apprehended; the accused was found guilty

[179] Verdirame and Harrell-Bond, *supra* note 6 at 191ff.

[180] R. Kuloba, *Courts of Justice in Kenya* (Nairobi: Oxford University Press, 1997) 38 and T. Jackson, *The Law of Kenya: An Introduction* (2nd edn., Nairobi: Kenya Literature Bureau, 1986) 23.

[181] Human Rights Watch, 'Seeking Refuge, Finding Terror – The Widespread Rape of Somali Women Refugees in North Eastern Kenya' (New York, 1993); African Rights, 'The Nightmare Continues … Abuses Against Somali Refugees in Kenya' (London, 1993). See also Verdirame and Harrell-Bond, *supra* note 6 at 144ff.

on seven occasions and jail terms ranging from four to twenty-seven years were imposed in four of the heard cases. In the remaining cases, fines and suspended sentences were ordered. In addition to SGBV, complaints during this period related to perpetrators being drunk and disorderly, creating disturbance in a manner likely to cause a breach of the peace, assault, handling stolen property and robbery. There was also one case of manslaughter. Despite the limited number of cases it considered, the Mobile Court constitutes an example of how humanitarian assistance to refugees can be used to develop local institutions rather than to create separate systems that engender resentment in the local population and undermine the possibility of integrating refugees in the host society.[182]

A practical obstacle to the effective application of national law and to the integration of refugee camps in the administrative structure of the host state is their physical location. Camps are normally established close to the border, more often than not in areas of the host country that are less well-developed economically, less densely populated and less well-served by the government. For example, the closest Kenyan court to the above-mentioned Kakuma refugee camp was a magistrate court in Lodwar, some 100 kilometres away. The local magistrate, like the police, also depended on UNHCR or on NGOs for transport, and tended to deal only with the cases of refugees 'caught' in Lodwar. Judicial access to the refugee camps in Dadaab, some 200 kilometres from Garissa where the closest magistrates court is situated, was compounded by poor roads and by the activities of bandit groups present in the area.

The establishment of a viable administration, at least in part reliant on the cooptation of refugee leaders, is normally regarded as a strategic priority by the administering agencies. In the above example of Kakuma refugee camp in Kenya, the 'gentlemen's agreement' with the SPLA leaders doubtless facilitated the administration of the camp, but had a cost in terms of human rights: diversion of food aid and forced recruitment were tolerated, as were the abuses of fair trial guarantees and of the right to liberty and security of the person resulting from the customary administration of justice.[183]

One of the most interesting case studies in the administration of camps is the introduction of 'self-management' in the Dadaab camps after 1995. Self-management went hand in hand with the

[182] B. E. Harrell-Bond, 'The Experience of Refugees as Recipients of Aid', in A. Ager (ed.), *Refugees: Perspectives on the Experience of Forced Migration* (London, Pinter, 1998) 136 at 146–9 and 155–7.

[183] On forced recruitment in refugee camps, see Verdirame and Harrell-Bond, *supra* note 6 at 173ff.

idea of empowerment, one of the most popular terms in humanitarian and development circles. In Dadaab, CARE International, the principal administering NGO, devised a system aimed at redistributing 'decision-making power by increasing refugee participation and decreasing the role of agencies in determining priorities and projects in the camps'.[184] As noted by Hyndmann, this approach was conceptually flawed as it was based on the misconception that a 'refugee camp can, or does, operate as a village or civil society, and employs community development principles – such as self-governance and democratic decision-making'.[185] In addition, Hyndmann pointed out that the proposed transfer of power from administering agencies to community leaders would necessarily leave out the management of economic resources and would marginalise certain groups of refugees, especially women.

Developments after Hyndmann's departure from Dadaab proved that her criticism was correct. According to CARE and UNHCR, refugees had 'wrongly' assumed that self-management would involve a 'progressive phasing out of the agencies' and a transfer of power to refugees and their communities.[186] When it became clear that power was not actually being transferred, tension between refugees and the agencies began to soar. Furthermore, as a result of budget cuts in 1997–8, refugees employed by UNHCR and by other agencies had to be persuaded to continue working on a voluntary basis without receiving so-called 'incentives'.[187] At a time when such difficult decisions had to be taken, the agencies reclaimed all the power that had apparently been transferred to refugee communities for themselves, and 'self-management' was redefined in a way that no longer threatened them. Relying on the Foucaultian concept of governmentality to analyse power in refugee camps, Hyndmann observes that 'UNHCR meticulously orders the field through exercises of counting, calculating, and coding refugees', and often represents refugees 'as statistical and moral deviations' in its official reports.[188]

[184] Hyndman, PhD thesis, *supra* note 174 at 86. See also Hyndman, *Managing Displacement*, *supra* note 174 and Verdirame and Harrell-Bond, *supra* note 6 at 151–2.

[185] Hyndman, PhD thesis, *supra* note 174 at 87.

[186] Interview with Mr Hussain, Focal Point for the Implementation of Community Self-Management for CARE International, Dadaab, 29 April 1998.

[187] On incentives, see Verdirame and Harrell-Bond, *supra* note 6 at 218–21.

[188] Hyndman, *Managing Displacement*, *supra* note 174, at Chapter VII 'Reporting the Field'. See also Verdirame and Harrell-Bond, *supra* note 6 at 299ff.

Although Foucault never included refugee camps in his analyses of space and power, few institutions lend themselves to a Foucaultian analysis as aptly as refugee camps. Governmentality is the capacity of power to order 'across the boundaries of family and economy, public sector and private sector'.[189] Governmentality is closely linked to the emergence of bio-power, 'a technology of power that does not exclude surveillance, but incorporates it and integrates it'.[190] Bio-politics is principally concerned with population 'as a scientific and political question, as a biological question, and as a question of power'; at the outset, its 'objects of knowledge and its objectives of control ... were ... birth, mortality and longevity'.[191] Such common practices of modern states as social security, individual and collective insurance, environmental regulation and the various forms of assistance are considered by Foucault to be offspring of bio-politics.

Foucault's study of the prison and his observations on the 'plagued city' provide a helpful framework of analysis for understanding refugee camps. Foucault noted that the camp model is the basis for such apparently diverse social spaces as industrial towns, hospitals, hospices, prisons, re-educational centres, and that the underlying principle of the camp is the 'spatial concatenation of hierarchical surveillances'.[192]

One of Foucault's most interesting writings is 'Of Other Spaces', a lecture which he delivered in 1967 but did not publish until 1984. There he distinguished between two main types of space – utopias and heteropias – and then further distinguished 'heteropias of crisis' from 'heteropias of deviance'.[193] Both utopias and heteropias are useful paradigms for analysing refugee camps.

In refugee camps, control over refugees is often achieved through such archetypical means of social control as head-counts. The controllability of refugees, and their powerlessness, is enhanced by their almost complete dependence for survival on the food distributed by the administering agencies.[194] In most refugee camps, the humanitarian

[189] T. L. Dumm, *Michel Foucault and the Politics of Freedom* (London: Sage, 1996) 133.
[190] M. Foucault, *Bisogna Difendere la Societá* (Milan: Feltrinelli, 1998) 208.
[191] *Ibid.* at 209 and 212.
[192] M. Foucault, *Sorvegliare e punire* (Turin: Einaudi, 1976) 188.
[193] M. Foucault, *Archivio Foucault: Interventi, colloqui, interviste*, Vol. III 1978–1985 (Turin: Einaudi, A. Pandolfi (ed.), 1998) 307. See also Dumm, *supra* note 189 at 34–46.
[194] Harrell-Bond, *supra* note 182.

agencies corroborate this complete dependency by sanctioning the sale of food rations or their exchange for other commodities. These sanctions are also a way of preserving the fundamental 'separateness' of refugee camps and their institutionalisation as administrative spaces forcibly isolated from the host community.

Food rations do not normally include fundamental items like milk. Refugees decide to trade part of their ration for other commodities that are not distributed. Recounting his experiences after the Red Army liberated Auschwitz in *La Tregua* (*The Truce*), Primo Levi recollected that one of the first decisions he took after liberation was to sell bread in order to buy shoes: since without shoes he would not have been able to walk and look for food, he realised that sacrificing the little food he had was necessary for his survival. Refugees have to make these sort of decisions in camps, but sanctions are imposed on them if they trade or barter food rations, in some cases their ration cards can be even withdrawn. UNHCR, and other humanitarian agencies, argue that they cannot allow the creation of a trade in goods that are distributed for humanitarian reasons.

Representations of camps by the administering agencies are important – as is the case with any 'self-representation' of power – for comprehending how camps are administered. In strident contrast to the painful reality of encampment, there is an almost joyful representation of the camp 'as the utopia of the perfectly governed city … permeated with hierarchies, surveillances, controls, delegations, and immobilised by the functioning of a pervasive power which operates differentially on individual bodies'.[195] Representations of the camp as utopia, as the perfectly administered city, feature in various ways in much of the official literature of UNHCR and other UN agencies: in some cases, life in camps is represented as an idyll;[196] and, in nearly all cases, the life of refugees and events in camps 'are reduced to a compilation of statistics'[197] in order to convey the scientific perfection of the administration. Most poignantly, visitors in camps are also regularly

[195] Foucault, *supra* note 192 at 216. Foucault referred these remarks to the plagued city.

[196] See, for example, UNICEF, *Children of War: Wandering Alone in Southern Sudan* (1994) written by J. Zutt, where it is also claimed that since they arrived in Kakuma camp the thousands of Sudanese unaccompanied minors could resume 'normalcy' again (at 21–2).

[197] N. Farah, *Gifts* (New York: Arcade Publishing, 1999) 194. Taariq, one of the characters in this novel, writes an essay on aid to Africa in which he employs this expression.

treated to these utopian representations. As part of this induction and briefing upon arrival, they are usually driven around the camp in an air-conditioned four-wheel drive vehicle, with a UNHCR staff member as guide contentedly pointing to the well-ordered components of the camp-mosaic and outlining its perfectly tessellated social structure. Such utopian representations could not be more distant from the perceptions of refugees – and of those visitors, and UNHCR and NGO workers prepared to lift the veil of utopia – for whom camps are probably closer to dystopias.[198]

I was often offered briefing and induction tours of this kind. Controlling outsiders' access to camps is an essential part of UNHCR's rule. I was often told that I needed 'authorisation' from UNHCR to visit camps even when my research had been cleared by the national authorities. Expressions like 'authorisation', 'seeking clearance from UNHCR', 'detailed programme and purpose of the visit' were commonly used. In Kakuma in July 1997, I borrowed a bicycle for transport so that I could be independent of UNHCR or NGO 'lifts'. I was told that I had to inform UNHCR about my movements every day and give them a programme of my intended visits and interviews. On another occasion in the same camp together with other researchers, we were denied 'permission' to visit the camp at night 'for our own security'.

Even the visits of the High Commissioner are carefully planned and imbued with utopian representations. They are carefully staged events, which resemble the visits of heads of states: a show is organised with refugee dances and music, and the Commissioner receives little presents from refugees.

The misrepresentation of camps is a powerful lie that serves many purposes: it causes any criticism of camps directed at UNHCR to rebound, and helps explain certain attitudes among UNHCR personnel towards refugees, in particular the tendency to 'de-humanise' refugees and reduce them to statistical entities. In fact, UNHCR and NGO personnel will normally be prepared to acknowledge that there are some tesserae in the 'perfect' mosaic that still need improvement, they were striving towards realising the ideal of the 'perfect refugee camp'. Bio-political techniques of control provide UNHCR and NGO officials with a precise and detailed list of minimum measurements in health, nutrition, shelter, etc. that should be satisfied and by which the success of their

[198] See James Appe's short story 'A Visit to Kala Settlement' (*Flight and Other Stories* (London: Akira, 1987)) – at the end of the visit 'you will breathe a sigh of relief or pity'.

operation will be measured. The camp administrators, however, will seldom question the underlying assumption of camps (after all, who would not like to live in the 'perfect city'?), and they will be unlikely to accept that there is something irremediably wrong about forcing individuals to live like inmates in segregated, isolated and highly regulated spaces, depriving them of basic freedoms.

In this respect, the attempts in humanitarian circles to improve refugee camps by devising minimum standards miss the main point, i.e. that encampment is a human rights violation in itself, and creates the conditions for other systematic violations of the rights of refugees. The reason for adopting humanitarian charters and minimum standards, such as the Sphere Project, is purportedly 'to improve the quality of assistance provided to people affected by disasters, and to enhance the accountability of the humanitarian system in disaster response'.[199] One of the proposed methods for improving camps is site planning and selection. UNHCR has already adopted guidelines on space requirement and planning, but the guidelines of the Sphere Project contain a wide array of even more precise and always measurable criteria that, according to its authors, will make a 'good camp' or settlement. Such guidelines stress the fact that 'the social structure and gender roles of the affected population and the requirements of vulnerable groups should be reflected in the planning and provision of services' and 'cluster planning should be guided by existing social practices'.[200]

These proposals are generally treated with approval in NGO circles – as the way towards the establishment of a better humanitarian regime. But they are for the most part futile and dangerous. Indeed, international law already knows of long and detailed regulations of spaces. In particular, the Geneva Convention III on prisoners of war contains an exhaustive regulation of the confinement of a human group in a restricted space. The Convention makes meticulous provision for every aspect of the life of prisoners of war in a camp, including registration, hygienic standards, provision of food, clothing, underwear and footwear, frequency of health inspections, types and standards of shelter, religious, intellectual and physical activities, the

[199] Sphere Project, *Humanitarian Charter and Minimum Standards in Disaster Response* (2004), available www.sphereproject.org/component/option,com_docman/task,cat_view/gid,17/Itemid,203/lang,english at preface.

[200] *Ibid.* at 216–17.

wearing of badges, correspondence, etc.[201] The results of the Sphere Project bear a striking similarity to the legal regulation of camps for prisoners of war, and to this extent such endeavours are pointlessly replicative.

They are also dangerous because they end up promoting a treatment of refugees – and of other beneficiaries of humanitarian assistance – that is *au par* with the treatment reserved to prisoners of war and that is essentially based on their encampment in controllable and accurately disciplined spaces.[202] Since these approaches are believed to represent 'good practice' and the 'way forward', the obvious needs to be reiterated: refugees, but also other beneficiaries of humanitarian assistance such as internally displaced persons, are legally entitled to a treatment that has nothing to do with that of prisoners of war. If an encampment-based treatment is proposed for refugees that is in all respects similar to the international legal regulation of camps for prisoners of war, something has clearly gone wrong, not in the implementation phase of humanitarian work but in the thinking behind it.

This regressive soft law of codes of conduct, of regulation and control, of measurements and discipline – often originating from NGOs – constitutes a serious threat to the international legal regime of refugee protection. Deaf to the perceptions of refugees and to the overwhelming evidence against camps,[203] these endeavours aim at putting the finishing touches to the ideal model of refugee camp, which should resemble a Platonic form of eternal perfection for real camps in the perceptible world. They also encapsulate the tendency to reduce human rights to statistical figures, measurable – and thus *controllable* – entities. Glaucon's polemical outburst in Plato's *Republic* should be heeded: after hearing Socrates explain which staples would be part of the diet of the dwellers in Plato's ideal city, Glaucon remarks that the same approach and measurements could be used 'if you were founding a city for pigs'.[204]

[201] Articles 21–76, Geneva Convention III Relative to the Treatment of Prisoners of War (1949) 75 UNTS 135.

[202] On the similarities between refugee camps and prisons, see Harrell-Bond and Verdirame, *supra* note 6 at 149.

[203] Some of the relevant academic literature is discussed in Harrell-Bond, *supra* note 182.

[204] Plato, *Republic II* in J. M. Cooper (ed.), *Complete Works* (Indianapolis: Hackett, 1997) 1011.

Human rights in refugee camps[205]

Freedom of movement

On their face refugee camps constitute a violation of one human right: freedom of movement.[206] Indeed, both the 1951 Refugee Convention (Article 26) and the International Covenant on Civil and Political Rights (ICCPR) (Article 12) protect freedom of movement, defined as encompassing the right to choose one's place of residence and the right to move freely within the territory of the state.[207] Under human rights law, freedom of movement is not a right of 'citizens', but a right of 'every individual' (Article 12, African Charter on Human and Peoples' Rights) or of 'everyone lawfully within the territory of the State' (Article 12, ICCPR).

Freedom of movement can be subject to limitations and to derogations in times of emergency. For example, under Article 12(3) of the ICCPR, restrictions to freedom of movement which are 'provided by law, necessary to protect national security, public order, public health or morals or the rights or freedoms or others' are allowed. Article 26 of the 1951 Refugee Convention contains a similar limitation clause.

The confinement of refugees in camps is often justified with arguments about scarce resources, a ground that cannot be easily subsumed under the permissible grounds for limitation under Article 12(3) of the ICCPR – not to mention the fact that, in any event, the establishment of camps has been shown to be uneconomical[208] and to undermine local health and social welfare structures.[209] Although national security is sometimes invoked for justifying the confinement of refugees in

[205] The violations of human rights suffered by refugees in and outside refugee camps are examined in detail in Verdirame and Harrell-Bond, *supra* note 6.

[206] Verdirame and Harrell-Bond, *supra* note 6 at 179–82. See C. Beyani, *Human Rights Standards and the Movement of People Within States* (Oxford University Press, 2000).

[207] See also Human Rights Committee, General Comment 15 ('The Position of Aliens under the Covenant') at para. 8; and Art. 12, African Charter on Human and Peoples' Rights (1981), 21 ILM 58 (hereinafter African Charter). The ICCPR provisions are normally referred to in this chapter, although some human rights feature in other human rights treaties, too. On freedom of movement under the 1951 Refugee Convention, see J. Hathaway, *The Rights of Refugees Under International Law* (Cambridge University Press, 2005) 695ff.

[208] T. Isherwood 'Camps: at what price?' (2005) available at www.refugees.org, documents the problems encountered in attempting to calculate the cost of Kakuma and Dadaab refugee camps, concluding that no accurate calculation was possible. Irrespective of the cost, Isherwood notes that the apparently common practice of bulldozing the extensive camp infrastructure when the refugees leave, is unlikely to be efficient.

[209] B. E. Harrell-Bond, 'Camps: Literature Review', 2 FMR (1998) 22.

camps,[210] the threshold set under Article 12(3) is high, requiring a particularly serious threat to the security of the state. Nevertheless, even if the limitation or derogation clauses could in theory provide a justification for some cases of encampment, neither host states nor UNHCR articulate this restriction on the free movements of refugees within the framework of those clauses or, more generally, within the framework of international law. In this respect, a remarkable document is UNHCR's Policy on Refugee Protection and Solutions in Urban Areas, published in September 2009.[211] While better on the question of camps than its predecessor, it still fails to develop a policy on camps and urban areas within a clear legal framework; the rights to free movement is mentioned, but the analysis is still essentially conducted in a legal vacuum.

The derogability of freedom of movement can perhaps explain why human rights organisations have not denounced the policy of encampment. While probably recognising that camps represent an infringement of freedom of movement, they tend to justify confinement in camps because of difficult circumstances in host states (mass influx, problems of public order, scarcity of resources).

In any event, the belief that the only human rights issue raised by the encampment of refugees is freedom of movement is misplaced. Analyses of the human rights consequences of encampment have indeed revealed a much more complicated and more troubling picture.

Understanding the context

Spotting human rights violations in camps requires empirical observations and contextualisation. Practices that would not prima facie appear to violate human rights are, on close analysis, an affront to the liberty and dignity of refugees and may constitute forms of cruel and degarding treatment. This is illustrated by head-counts and the case of a Sudanese refugee in Kakuma camp.

Head-counts are periodically conducted by UNHCR as a 'revalidation exercise' to reissue ration cards.[212] Another reason for this practice is

[210] See Human Rights Watch, 'Tanzania – In the Name of Security. Forced Round-ups of Refugees in Tanzania' (New York, 1999). The same argument to justify encampment was given to me during interviews with government officials in Kenya (1997) and Tanzania (August 2000).

[211] Available at http://www.unhcr.org/refworld/docid/4ab8e7f72.html. UNHCR's previous urban policy is in 'UNHCR Comprehensive Policy on Urban Refugees', 25 March 1997.

[212] B. E. Harrell-Bond, E. Voutira and M. Leopold, 'Counting the Refugees: Gifts, Givers, Patrons and Clients', 5 J. Ref. St. (1992) 205; Verdirame and Harrell-Bond, *supra* note 6 at 139–41.

that 'maintaining reliable and accurate population figures and demographic data is to assure continuation of donors' funding for the Programme'.[213] The practice of head-counts is almost universally perceived as debasing and humiliating by refugees who have often protested, at times violently, against it. In order to count them, UNHCR places refugees in enclosures surrounded by barbed wire, where they are normally left to wait for many hours (this is to ensure that nobody is counted twice and receives two ration cards). UNHCR uses special ink to mark a part of the body, normally the arm, to identify those refugees who have already been counted. The sign is only visible under fluorescent light and is indelible for twenty-four hours.

UNHCR maintains that refugees protest against head-counts because they are trying to ensure that those carrying two or more ration cards will not be discovered. This is not a plausible explanation of social behaviour. Indeed, it is hardly conceivable that a mass protest would take place to protect the privileged few who have managed to obtain more than one ration card. On the contrary, unfairness in rationing would be more likely to engender resentment or even revolt among the unprivileged ones. Why would refugees be prepared to protest in order to ensure extra rations for *a few* among them, whereas they seldom stage similar protests about the poor quality and the insufficient quantity of food that is distributed to *all*? In Kakuma refugee camp in 1996–7, refugees often complained that rations were grossly inadequate, but no organised protest took place, although malnutrition had reached preoccupying levels.[214] The harsh measures taken by UNHCR on previous occasions to suppress refugee protest may have deterred the organisation of a protest or a revolt. But another reason may need to be sought in the sociology of obedience and revolt. It has been argued that in different societal contexts revolts occur when there is a clear perception that a certain punishment or treatment is essentially inhuman, and that 'the punishments that are rejected vary in accord with varying conceptions of humanity'.[215]

The proposition that conceptions of humanity are historically determined and culturally variable does not entail an acceptance of cultural relativist pos-

[213] Presentation of Mr Malik in preparation for the head-count, Dadaab, 29 April 1998; Mr Malik is UNHCR's senior regional registration officer, or 'head of the head-counts'.

[214] See Letter submitted by Dr Guluma to *The Lancet*, 4 October 1997, unknown whether published or not, on file with the author.

[215] B. Moore Jr., *Injustice: The Social Bases of Obedience and Revolt* (London: Macmillan, 1978) 29.

itions. On the contrary, the existence of notions of 'cruelty', 'inhumanity' and 'pain' that are to some extent variable can contribute to fleshing out human rights norms when applied to different cultural contexts. For example, Talal Asad has observed that, in order to apply the prohibition of torture to different contexts, 'we need ethnographies of pain and cruelty which can provide us with a better understanding of how relevant practices are actually conducted in different traditions'.[216]

In order to understand why it is expressly against head-counts that refugees decide to revolt, it is necessary to examine the significance of this practice in its socio-cultural context. First, there is a strong cultural resistance among different groups to censuses.[217] Secondly, the way in which 'head-counts' in refugee camps are conducted is particularly debasing: the fact that refugees are forced in enclosures 'like cattle',[218] often have to wait in the scorching sun for many hours, and that the whole process is managed in a cold, impersonal and bureaucratic manner, creates a feeling of humiliation. Thirdly, the use of markings on the body, albeit not permanent, adds to the feeling of aggravation and debasement. For individuals who have already suffered a loss of social status and whom aid has made 'powerless', an imprinted symbol of humiliation can feel unbearable, as a definite stigma. It is certainly no coincidence that the Geneva Convention IV explicitly prohibits 'identification by tattooing or imprinting signs or markings on the body' (Article 100).[219] Placed in its social and cultural context, the practice of head-counts constitutes 'a conduct of a certain level of severity which lowers the victim in rank, position, reputation or character in his own eyes or in the eyes of his people',[220] or one in which an individual is 'treated as an object in the power of the authorities'.[221]

The other example that illustrates the importance of contextualising the acts of UNHCR is the case of Sarah Aruol, a Sudanese refugee woman in Kakuma refugee camp.[222] To punish her for opposing

[216] T. Asad, 'On Torture, or Cruel, Inhuman or Degrading Treatment', in R. A. Wilson (ed.), *Human Rights, Culture and Context: Anthropological Perspectives* (London: Pluto Press, 1997) 111 at 128.

[217] Such opposition to the idea of being counted is particularly strong among pastoralists (E. E. Evans-Pritchard, *The Nuer* (Oxford University Press, 1969) 20), but it is not foreign to Western societies. Censuses are also prohibited under the Jewish Torah (*Exodus*, 30, 11–13).

[218] Refugees interviewed both in Kakuma and in Dadaab used this expression.

[219] Geneva Convention (IV) Relative to the Protection of Civilian Persons in Time of War (1949) 75 UNTS 287.

[220] *East African Asians v. UK* (1973) 3 EHRR 76 at para. 189.

[221] *Tyrer v. UK* (1978) 2 EHRR 1 at para. 33.

[222] Interviews with Sarah Aruol (*not her real name*), Kakuma, July 1997.

the forced recruitment of her child in the SPLA, the local community leaders – who, as has been mentioned, are SPLA officers – condemned her to social ostracism: her friends and other Sudanese refugees in the camp were not to speak to her, alleviate her daily hardships, or give her any form of social recognition or acceptance;[223] at times she would also be pushed to the end of the food distribution queue. Her attempts to bring her situation to the attention of the camp authorities did not yield any results. After camping outside the UNHCR compound, she decided to leave the camp and risk the journey to Nairobi. When I discussed this case with the UNHCR field officer in Kakuma, I was told that nobody could be forced to help, or to be 'nice' to anybody else. It would be hard to argue that social ostracism amounts to cruel, inhuman or degrading treatment in most social situations, but in refugee camps reliance on social networks and family ties is often indispensable for survival.

Other examples of human rights violations in camps

Among the most blatant breach of human rights standards in the Kenyan refugee camps was the punitive suspension of food distribution on two separate occasions in Kakuma, and, on one occasion, in Dadaab. The suspension followed protest of refugees against 'head-counts', and, on one of these occasions, against the introduction of a new method for distributing food. In Kakuma, UNHCR sent a memorandum to the leaders of the refugee communities, explaining that salaries for refugees employed by UNHCR and NGOs – referred to as 'incentives' because these refugees were considered 'volunteers' rather than employees – would also be suspended and that their resumption would depend 'on the co-operation on the part of refugees during the re-construction of the destroyed facilities, recovering all the looted properties and providing the names of the culprits responsible for the damages. This will be evaluated by my office and our implementing partners shortly after this reconstruction starts … anyone whose performance proves to be unsatisfactory will be dismissed without prior warning.'[224]

[223] Martha Nussbaum refers to an example of gender ostracism in Bangladesh: M. C. Nussbaum, *Sex and Social Justice* (Oxford University Press, 1999) 82. On the use of psychological sanctions in traditional dispute settlement, see, for example, A. J. F. Köbben, 'The Cottica Dyuka of Surinam', in L. Nader (ed.), *Law in Culture and Society* (Berkeley: University of California Press, 1969) 117 at 130.

[224] UNHCR Sub-Office in Kakuma, Memorandum from the Officer In-Charge to Refugees Working for NGOs in Kakuma, 4 April 1996 (on file with the author).

In the same incident, an Ethiopian refugee, who had started a human rights education programme in Kakuma, was forcibly relocated to one of the Dadaab camps. UNHCR justified this decision in these terms:

> 'UNHCR has taken the decision to transfer you to the Dadaab area. UNHCR has noted your unwillingness to be transferred … but regrets to inform you that there are no viable options at the moment. Once in Dadaab, you will be expected to refrain from any conduct likely to disrupt public order in the camp, including the organisation of such lectures as you conducted in Kakuma Refugee Camp. *It is the view of UNHCR that the series of human rights lecture was a direct cause for the wave of tension and disruption of public order in the camp.*'[225]

His series of lectures had actually begun a week after the 'disruption of public order' in Kakuma had taken place. In writing to justify its decision, UNHCR referred to 'Art. III of the 1969 OAU Convention and to the Geneva Convention', under which refugees are required 'to conform with laws and regulations as well as with measures taken for the maintenance of public order' in the host country. The forcible transfer of this refugee to another refugee camp, away from his network of family and friends, was carried out shortly after this letter was sent. This decision was in breach of this refugee's freedom of expression and right to a fair trial.[226]

In places like Kakuma, located in one of the most arid regions in Kenya with virtually no arable land, the refugee population was entirely dependent on food distribution for its survival. In Dadaab, the situation was only slightly better because refugees were at least allowed to keep poultry. Neither in Dadaab nor in Kakuma were there any real prospects for local employment, and the 'incentives' paid to a few hundred refugees working for the UNHCR and the NGOs constituted one of the principal ways of integrating the meagre food rations.[227] Given that confinement in camps is involuntary, there can be little doubt that suspending food distribution and 'incentives' in these circumstances amounted to a violation of the rights to an adequate standard of living,

[225] Emphasis added. Letter from the Senior Protection Officer, James Lynch, to Assefa Teferi Woldekidan, 19 July 1994 (on file with the author, and UNHCR ref. KEN/NRB/PT/94/IC/0794).

[226] On violations of the refugees' freedom of expression in refugee camps in Tanzania and Kenya camps see Article 19, 'Voices in Exile: African Refugees and Freedom of Expression' (London: Article 19, 2001) (a report written by R. Carver and G. Verdirame).

[227] See T. Boudreau, M. Lawrence and A. King, 'Household Food Economy Assessment of Kakuma Refugee Camp, Turkana District, North West Kenya. Undertaken on Behalf of WFP and UNHCR' (London: Save the Children Fund, 1996).

including adequate food under Article 11 of the International Covenant on Economic, Social and Cultural Rights (ICESCR), to the enjoyment of the highest attainable standard of physical health (Article 12, ICESCR), and, probably, the right to be free from cruel, inhuman and degrading treatment (Article 7, ICCPR).[228] Furthermore, trying to extort the names of the 'culprits' under conditions of unequivocal duress was a violation of fair trial guarantees (Article 14, ICCPR). It is noteworthy that, under Article 26 of the Geneva Convention III, 'collective disciplinary measures affecting food are prohibited' even in camps for prisoners of war.[229] The conditions for the application of the Geneva Conventions to refugee camps in Kenya were not present, but the fact that collective punishments are proscribed under humanitarian law only underscores the unacceptability of these acts in times of peace.

The example of collective punishment also illustrates the extent of the power assumed by the humanitarian agencies. Deportations, the extortion of confessions under threat, and the imposition of collective punishments are archetypical manifestations of unfettered power. Furthermore, the exercise of punitive rights and the reference to the maintenance of public order, normally a prerogative of states, reveal that the administering agencies are in many respects replacing the state.

The 1951 Convention contains a provision on food rationing that shows the extent to which the reality of assistance to refugees has departed from the legal standards. Under Article 20 of the 1951 Convention, 'where a rationing system exists, which applies to the population at large and regulates the general distribution of products in short supply, refugees shall be accorded the same treatment as nationals'.[230] The preoccupation of the drafters was thus that refugees may be excluded from food distribution in situations of generalised hardships and this provision was meant to ensure the integration, in the sense equal treatment, of refugees in any rationing measure.

The system of 'incentives' denotes the violation of another fundamental right, the right to work. Under this system, refugees, employed by the agencies – as drivers, teachers, administrators, doctors, nurses or security guards – received less remuneration than nationals for the same work. This practice was in breach of 'the right of everyone to the

[228] A. Cassese, 'Can the Notion of Inhuman and Degrading Treatment Be Applied to Socio-Economic Conditions?' 2 EJIL (1991) 141. See also in the UK House of Lords *R (Limbuela) v. Secretary of State for the Home Department* [2006] 1 AC 106, which makes a similar point.

[229] See also Art. 100, Geneva Convention IV, which prohibits the reduction of food rations for internees.

[230] Hathaway, *supra* note 207 at 464.

enjoyment of just and favourable conditions of work, which ensure, in particular ... fair wages and equal remuneration for work of equal value without distinction of any kind' (Article 7, ICESCR). Violations of the prohibition on forced labour may also occur. For example, in Dadaab in 1997–8 the administering agencies decided to phase out 'incentives' and to replace them with a system of non-remunerated work; in Kakuma, they dismissed large numbers of individuals who had been receiving 'incentives' for some time, often for years. In April 1998, UNHCR and CARE International, estimating that at least *some* refugees would refuse to continue to work without remuneration, were considering the imposition of sanctions, including the individualised suspension of food distribution.[231]

Rights of refugees in camps are also violated by acts of private security officers employed by the agencies in the field. Security officers comprise both locals and refugees and, at times, personnel from private security companies. The chief security officer normally works under UNHCR supervision, although he may be an employee of the NGO subcontracted by UNHCR as lead administering agency. Security guards in practice act as an interface between refugees, on the one hand, and UNHCR and NGO staff, on the other, filtering the claims of refugees who, for various reasons, try to see a UNHCR or NGO official. Refugees normally struggle to gain access to the offices of UNHCR and of NGOs, which are located in safe compounds, surrounded by barbed wire, with security guards at the entrance gate. Refugees often complain that the behaviour of these guards and their decisions are completely arbitrary. The support of a security officer can often make the difference between a prompt response to a refugee complaint, and complete lack of action or swift dismissal of the case. Given that security officers are chosen by UNHCR in conjunction with community leaders, they tend to support the claims of refugees who are close or at least not inimical to the leaders of the community, whereas at best they neglect others. As a result of the role assigned to community leaders and security guards as a springboard for protection cases, many – not least women and minors, members of minority clans and groups, opponents, and in general individuals with feeble social networks – are often excluded from protection.

One refugee, for example, wrote: 'With the current system of work by the protection service of UNHCR, which consists in visiting delegates or chairmen

[231] Interviews with UNHCR officials and CARE International Manager, Dadaab, 27 April–1 May 1998). Verdirame and Harrell-Bond, *supra* note 6 at 218–21.

of each community every Wednesday, and notice that only chairmen of community are called to submit different cases settled in their communities, I AM FALLING in THE TOTAL HOPELESS MARGINALISATION BECAUSE MINE WILL NOT GET CHANCE TO BE read one day [sic].'[232]

As discussed above, the customary settlement of disputes in refugee camps, in particular settlement through adjudication in customary courts,[233] can also give rise to violations of rights. The customary norms that are normally applied by these courts are the result of a complex process of transformation, reflecting in part the experience of exile, and in part power relations in camps, including relations between community leaders and the *de facto* authorities, i.e. UNHCR and NGOs. As a result of these transformations, customary law in exile often loses any 'subtle, adaptable and situational' characteristics it may have previously possessed.[234] In Kakuma, the SPLA leaders assumed control of the process of dispute settlement, and as a result individuals like Sarah Aruol[235] whose dispute is *against* the SPLA were basically defenceless. Nor, as has been seen, could she – and others in her position – rely on those kinship and social ties that often act as a shield protecting individuals against abuses in the process of dispute settlement. Had her case arisen in her home town in southern Sudan, it is reasonable to hypothesise that her kinship and social ties would have played an important role and the outcome of the case could have been more favourable to her.[236] But the breakdown of social structures and the fact that for most refugees these ties are not so extensive as in their countries of origin mean that, in this respect too, the application of customary law in camps is not subject to the necessary limitations.

The imprisonment of individuals found 'guilty' by a customary court in cells, which are built by UNHCR and NGOs,[237] was a breach of the

[232] Written testimony of B. D., Burundi refugee in Kakuma, April 1998.

[233] Negotiation is another important way of solving disputes (P. H. Gulliver, 'Case-Studies of Law in non-Western Societies', in Nader, *supra* note 222, 11 at 17), but this section deals predominantly with adjudication in the customary courts.

[234] O. Harris (ed.), *Inside and Outside the Law* (London: Routledge, 1996) 3. On 'mandatory traditional customs' in camps, see Harrell-Bond, *supra* note 7 at 293ff. On the adaptability of Nuer custom and its historical evolution, see S. Hutchinson, *Nuer Dilemmas: Coping with Money, War and the State* (Berkeley: University of California Press, 1996) 217ff.

[235] See *supra* note 221.

[236] For example, see P. H. Gulliver, 'Dispute Settlement Without Courts: The Ndendeuli of Southern Tanzania', in Nader, *supra* note 222, 24 at 59ff.

[237] On these cells, see *supra* note 179.

right to liberty and security of person (Article 9, ICCPR) and of the right to a fair trial (Article 14, ICCPR). Moreover, contrary to the notion that subjecting refugees to the application of customary norms in the manner described is respectful of their cultural rights, this practice is actually in breach of cultural rights, defined in international human rights law principally as the right of an individual to 'freely take part in the cultural life of his community'.[238] In addition, whereas non-state courts in Kenya were under an obligation to respect the principle of non-discrimination, a similar obligation was not imposed on customary courts dispensing 'justice' in refugee camps. Finally, the exercise of jurisdiction by these 'courts' in refugee camps cannot be reconciled with the 1951 Refugee Convention. Indeed, the establishment of parallel dispute settlement systems in camps, including the exercise of criminal jurisdiction, undermines the access of refugees to national courts, although Article 16 of the 1951 Convention accords significant protection to the refugees' right to 'free access to the courts of law'. This right occupies a special position in the system of the Convention, as, together with only a handful of other provisions, it cannot be the object of a reservation by state parties.[239]

In addition to access to courts (Article 16), other provisions to which no reservation is permissible under Article 42 of the 1951 Convention include the refugee definition (Article 1), the principle of non-discrimination in the application of the Convention (Article 3), freedom of religion (Article 4), the principle of non-refoulement (Article 33) and the dispute settlement clause (Article 38). Under this last provision, disputes 'relating to the interpretation or application' of the Convention shall be referred to the ICJ. However, to date no case under the 1951 Convention has been brought to the ICJ.

In both Kakuma and Dadaab the incidence of sexual violence was dramatic.[240] In Dadaab UNHCR had come under considerable pressure following reports of human rights organisations on the plight of Somali women. A lawyer from FIDA (Federation of Women Lawyers, Kenya) was hired in 1994 for a short period to initiate proceedings against those responsible for the violence. The FIDA lawyer also started the Mobile Court programme, which was described above. Unfortunately, once her short-term contract terminated, these initiatives foundered.

[238] Article 17, 2, African Charter. See also: Art. 27, Universal Declaration of Human Rights; Art. 15, ICESCR.

[239] Hathaway, *supra* note 207 at 905ff.

[240] Verdirame and Harrell-Bond, *supra* note 6 at 142–51 and 251–2.

In yet another example of grotesque operationalisation of an originally progressive idea, UNHCR maintained that 'gender issues' had been 'mainstreamed' and that there was no need for a separate programme. In 1998, a newly appointed Senior Protection Officer revived the Mobile Court programme and insisted that those accused of committing sexual violence be brought to justice. However, there was still little acknowledgement of the fact that forcing refugee women to reside in camps like Kakuma and Dadaab was in itself exposing them to the risk of becoming victims of sexual violence:[241] the high proportion of former combatants, the inactivity of the entire population, the complete isolation, the oppressive and inescapable intimacy, the absence of law enforcement and the presence of armed bandits in the region, and, for many women, the absence of male relatives were key factors behind the sexual violence.

Malnutrition, especially among children, was particularly high in the Kenyen camps.[242] The fact that refugees are confined against their will in camps where they cannot achieve self-reliance means that those responsible for the confinement – host states and UNHCR – are obliged to provide them with essential necessities, including food, shelter and water. Keeping refugees on low rations is thus a breach of Article 11 of the ICESCR – the right to an adequate standard of living for himself and his family, including adequate food, clothing and housing, and to the continuous improvement of living conditions – and, when loss of life ensues from malnutrition, of the right to life. In practice, refugees would normally receive food rations well short of the standard applicable to prisoners of war under Article 26 of Geneva Convention III, which provides that 'rations shall be sufficient in quantity, quality and variety to keep prisoners of war in good health and to prevent loss of weight or the development of nutritional deficiencies. Account shall also be taken of the habitual diet of the prisoners'.

241 As noted by Hyndman, in spite of so much rhetoric to the contrary, 'a refugee camp is not a community … (it) is an institution organized as a temporary solution to displacement', and in which refugees 'are the subjects of a tacit and unsatisfactory policy of containment by which camps are enforced "colonies", not communities defined by voluntary association … In exchange for temporary asylum and the provision of basic needs, refugees forfeit a number of entitlements' (Hyndman, *supra* note 174, at 'Simulating Community: Refugee Self-Management').

242 Boudreau *et al.*, *supra* note 226; Verdirame, *supra* note 175; Letter of Dr Guluma, *supra* note 213. On malnutrition in refugee camps outside Kenya, see Harrell-Bond, *supra* note 7 at 276ff.

UNHCR's defence that sufficient resources are not available echoes the argument of states that scarcity of resources would prevent them from implementing economic and social rights, including the right to food. However, this argument does not reflect the nature of the obligations of state parties to the ICESCR. The Committee on Economic, Social and Cultural Rights, established under the ICESCR, has distinguished three different levels of obligations vis-à-vis the right to food: the obligations *to respect*, *to protect*, and *to fulfil* – the latter comprising both an obligation *to facilitate* and an obligation *to provide*. In refugee camps, UNHCR is responsible for a violation of the first of these obligations – the obligation to respect. Indeed, the obligation to respect imposes a negative duty, requiring states '*not* to take any measures that result in preventing' access to food.[243] Confining refugees to camps, depriving them of the possibility to seek employment and to secure livelihood through their own means are measures that prevent, or at least significantly reduce, access to any food other than food aid. As discussed, not all camps are the same: in some, like Dadaab, refugees were allowed to keep poultry; in others, they may even be allowed to cultivate some land; in the worst cases, like Kakuma, refugees have access to no food other than what is distributed by the agencies fortnightly. But, in general, refugees' own ability to gain access to food is at least severely hindered as a result of encampment.

The Committee on Economic, Social and Cultural Rights explains that 'food aid should, as far as possible, be provided in ways which do not adversely affect local producers and local markets, and should be organized in ways that facilitate the return to food self-reliance of the beneficiaries'.[244] Furthermore, according to the Committee, the right to food 'shall therefore not be interpreted in a narrow or restrictive sense which equates it with a minimum package of calories, proteins and other specific nutrients'.[245] However, these 'narrow and restrictive' interpretations of the right to food are predominant not only in the practice of UNHCR and NGOs in camps, but also in the conceptualisation that precedes this practice. Methodical and accurate measurements of the nutrients that need to be in-taken to keep the body of the refugee healthy are in fact part and parcel of the 'utopia of the perfectly governed city', and of the reduction of refugees and their human

[243] Committee on Economic, Social and Cultural Rights, General Comment 12 on Art. 12 ('The Right to Adequate Food'), UN Doc. E/C.12/1999/5, para. 14–15 (emphasis added).

[244] *Ibid.* at para. 39. [245] *Ibid.* at para. 6.

rights to statistical entities. And, to make matters even worse, even these measurements – which would still fall short of 'measuring' freedom, rights, happiness or welfare – are in practice seldom respected, partly because of WFP's policy of reducing food aid automatically after two years, since, according to its *model*, two years is the maximum duration of the emergency and continuing food aid would discourage self-reliance. Thus, both in Kakuma and in Dadaab, food aid was progressively reduced regardless of the fact that self-reliance was not attainable by refugees in those circumstances.

In addition, the refugees' own coping strategies are often undercut by such UNHCR policies as the prohibition of trade in food rations – another example of a violation of the 'obligation to respect'. As has been observed,[246] rations do not include all necessary nutrients, and refugees trade them for other necessities (including milk for infants, staples when these are not distributed, or non-food necessities like clothing and footwear). Although UNHCR blames donor pressure for this, in most refugee camps it still opposes trade in food rations, and at times sanctions this practice with the confiscation of the food.

Because of scarce resources, most developing countries are not able to fulfil their obligation *to provide* such economic and social rights as the right to food, to health and to shelter. States, and *de facto* authorities like UNHCR in refugee camps, have an obligation at least not to hinder – as part of their obligation *to respect* – but at best *to protect* and *to facilitate* the establishment of independent networks of mutual help by refugees. In fact, social solidarity often acts as a private substitute for state action in the area of food, shelter, education or health, when states are unable or unwilling to intervene. In refugee camps, however, there is far less room for solidarity of this kind, and therefore even this avenue of implementing rights is too often denied to the refugees. Harrell-Bond has observed that the process of redefining social responsibility in exile is often painfully slow, and that the extent to which a refugee in a camp can rely on help from others normally continues to depend on the extent of his or her kinship ties.[247] My findings also suggest that, in spite of the availability of only little aid for refugees outside camps, one reason why refugees normally prefer to live outside camps is that they can establish more effective social networks.[248]

[246] See *supra* side note in text after note 194.

[247] Harrell-Bond, *supra* note 7 at 283–4 and 293ff.

[248] At least this is what interviews with refugees in Nairobi have elicited.

This may be a consequence of the 'hard truth' that 'forced intimacy may be an enemy of solidarity and co-operation',[249] but also of the fact that, owing to the lack of prospect of employment or education, camps are places where no one can really 'make it' other than by leaving and where offering help seems often pointless.

Refugee status determination conducted by UNHCR

UNHCR conducts refugee status determination in many Asian and African countries.[250] This practice constitutes an anomaly since states are normally responsible for legal processes within their territory that affect the status and rights of individuals. UNHCR maintains that it embarks upon status determination only in exceptional circumstances, but the number of these 'exceptions', for the most part concentrated in countries in the South, is significant. In most of these situations, UNHCR has determined refugee status for a significant period of time and has normally taken over this process from states once large numbers of refugees arrived. Hence, although there are no definitive statistics of the numbers of asylum-seekers whose applications are considered by UNHCR, it is not far-fetched to hypothesise that the majority of asylum applications in the South, and probably in the whole world, are actually decided by UNHCR rather than states. Most of the refugees recognised by UNHCR are 'requested' to reside in refugee camps.

It has been observed that UNHCR's practice on refugee status determination in Asian countries often failed to comply with international human rights standards – in particular with requirements of procedural fairness – and that its procedure in Kenya fell short 'of the very guarantees and principles set out in its *Handbook on Status*

[249] Barrington Moore Jr., *supra* note 214 at 67.

[250] M. Alexander, 'Refugee Status Determination Conducted by UNHCR', 11 Int. J. Ref. L. (1999) 251 at 251; Verdirame and Harrell-Bond, *supra* note 6 at 78ff. See also M. Kagan, 'Assessment of Refugee Status Determination Procedure at UNHCR's Cairo Office 2001–2002', American University in Cairo Forced Migration and Refugee Studies (CMRS) Working Paper No. 1 (December 2002) and by the same author: 'Refugee credibility assessment and the "religious imposter" problem: A case study of Eritrean Pentecostal claims in Egypt', CMRS Working Paper No. 9 (December 2009), available from www.aucegypt.edu/GAPP/cmrs/Documents/KaganReligiousImposters.pdf; 'Frontier Justice: Legal Aid and UNHCR Refugee Status Determinations in Egypt', 19(1) *Journal of Refugee Studies* (2006) 45; and 'The Beleaguered Gatekeeper: Protection Challenges by UNHCR Refugee Status Determination', 18(1) *International Journal of Refugee Law* (2006) 1. See also the website RDS Watch at http://rsdwatch.wordpress.com.

Determination'.[251] Status determination is a critically important procedure in the life of a refugee. Refugees whose claims have been wrongly assessed and who have been rejected are at risk of being returned to a country where they face persecution. Even if they manage to remain in the country of asylum, they will not enjoy the status of refugees, and the international protection that in principle ensues thereupon. Getting the refugee status determination right is, in other words, the first logical step in a truly rights-based refugee regime.

The view that refugee status determination, as well as immigration decisions, do not constitute a 'suit at law' for the purposes of the right to fair trial might lend some support to UNHCR's position. Australia has explicitly endorsed this position.[252] UNHCR's failure to put in place procedures that comply with minimum standards of fairness could therefore be justified with the argument that these standards do not apply to refugee status determination. It would be a misjudged apology. First, there is ultimately no persuasive reason for excluding refugee status determination from fair trial provisions, particularly since, in many ways, refugee status determination is so unequivocally a 'suit at law' for determining an individual's rights and obligations (Article 14, ICCPR). Secondly, the protection regime for refugees cannot be effective if the underlying determination is improperly conducted thus increasing the probabilities of wrong decisions. Finally, when the practice on a particular aspect of refugee law differs, UNHCR ought to promote the best practice, which is the practice that is most respectful of the rights of refugees and is consistent with the 1951 Convention.

The smokescreen: cultural relativism

The arguments at the end of Chapter 4 (191ff.) on the regressive and instrumental use of anything 'cultural' – identities, processes and rights – by the UN in Afghanistan are germane to refugee camps. Apologetics for culture have actually little to do with the existing positive law on cultural rights.

In Chapter 4 it was argued that one of the justificatory arguments used by the UN in the context of the provision of humanitarian

[251] Verdirame, *supra* note 175 at 58. As has been mentioned, other data pointing to similar findings was collected in Uganda by Barbara Harrell-Bond, Zachary Lomo and Pamela Reynell.

[252] Alexander, *supra* note 249, referring to Australia's submissions before the Human Rights Committee in the case of *A v. Australia*, Communication No. 560/1993.

assistance to Afghanistan hinges on the construction of culture 'as an essentialist and homogenous body of traditions and customs'.[253] Hence the continued involvement of the UN in Afghanistan, and the incorporation of discrimination against women in UN programmes of humanitarian assistance were justified inter alia with an apparently cultural relativist argument. This argument assumes that the Taliban were the true interpreters of Afghani culture, and implicitly removes any cultural representational prerogative from other Afghan groups and individuals, for example the women who constituted 60 per cent of the staff of Kabul University and were dismissed by the Taliban. This regressive construction of culture, and the distortion of the attendant discourse on cultural rights, prejudices the position of those within a culture who challenge dominant interpretations.

In refugee camps, the idea of culture is sub-served to the exigencies of UNHCR and NGOs. The establishment of customary courts, the organisation of refugees in communities, and the concession of wide and arbitrary powers to community leaders are part of the system of indirect rule that is instituted in camps. Far from being neutral and respectful of cultural identities and processes, UNHCR in this way fixates and corroborates one particular interpretation of a given culture, and intervenes in cultural processes siding with one party (normally the strongest one), giving it much-needed legitimacy and funds, and helping in the suppression and marginalisation of other voices and interpretations.

In this respect, the example of the Sudanese Dinka refugees in Kakuma is telling. As has been discussed, SPLA officers were the self-appointed leaders of this 'community'. In the camp, they were tacitly allowed both to forcibly recruit minors and young men in the SPLA, and to divert some food aid to the rebels in southern Sudan. They were treated as the sole legitimate voice of the Dinka community, whereas dissident individuals and groups were not given any recognition. Indeed, when tension arises between the Sudanese leaders and sectors of their community, UNHCR usually espoused the cause of the leaders, at times actively, more often through a failure to intervene. For example, a frequent source of inter-community tension in Kakuma was the presence of thousands of Sudanese boys – for the most part Dinkas – who had spent the better part of their formative years

[253] N. Yuval-Davis, *Gender and Nation* (London: Sage, 1997) 38.

separate from their community of origin, and had developed their own cultural norms during exile. These boys, who have since been resettled mainly in the US, often refused to undergo military training; they rejected much Dinka custom on marriage and sexual relations, and practised homosexuality.[254] UNHCR's policy on the Sudanese boys in Kakuma (whom it referred to as the 'unaccompanied minors' although most of them were no longer minors) was to deny the acceptability, let alone the legality, of the practices that did not conform to Dinka traditional custom as interpreted by the SPLA-controlled leadership in Kakuma, and to encourage their forced assimilation into their 'community' of origin. The (sub)culture developed by these boys was thus considered unworthy of protection, because of its differences with recognised Dinka custom. A consequence of the policy of identifying 'authentic' representatives of certain communities is that UNHCR could at all times claim to be 'in contact with the Sudanese community', or to be 'aware of the claims' of the Sudanese refugees simply by having relations with one group of Sudanese refugees while neglecting the claims of others ('unaccompanied minors', women, draft-dodgers, mixed couples, political or cultural dissidents, etc.).

A misrepresentation of cultural rights and the correspondent obligations of states underlies these UNHCR policies and attitudes. At the field level, UNHCR officers often see themselves as the defenders of endangered cultures.[255] As part of this self-righteous mission to save cultures, they support, encourage and fund practices that are in breach of human rights. In addition, such practices also constitute a violation of the cultural rights they purport to protect as they interfere in a cultural process by giving legitimacy, as well as powers and funding, to the strongest voices. As has been mentioned, human rights law does not recognise the right of groups to exact compliance with cultural practices (or certain interpretations thereof) from individuals; instead, it enshrines the right of the individual 'to opt out' of his or her own culture, or, as so many people choose to do, to embrace its norms and

[254] Particularly unacceptable to the Dinka leaders is the fact that a number of Sudanese boys 'take other boys as their wives' (Interview with Deng Dau, leader of the Sudanese Dinka community, July 1997).

[255] On the institutional ethos of humanitarian workers, see M. Walkup, *Policy and Behavior in Humanitarian Organizations: The Institutional Origins of Operational Dysfunction* (University of Florida, PhD thesis, 1997). See also Susan Sontag's essay on Leni Riefenstahl and the imagery of self-appointed defenders of engendered 'native', in *Under the Sign of Saturn* (New York: Anchor Books Doubleday, 1991) 86.

customs selectively. Finally, the use of mandatory customary practices in refugee camps also relies on the ill-conceived and pre-Freudian belief that individuals are always happy to adhere to the cultural norms of their groups.[256]

The idea of cultural rights as represented in refugee camps, on the other hand, reinforces existing power relations and enhances the oppressive potential of *any* culture over its member individuals. Cultures are open to challenges from within and from outside, they normally accommodate a variety of often conflicting interpretations and voices, and they constantly undergo processes of social transformation and adaptation. These processes can go as far as to overcome a particular custom or even change a whole tradition. Those who are in power naturally perceive this potential for change as a threat. As observed by Pascal,[257] who however saw this as a risk rather than a value, any custom may be overcome from within once its arbitrary nature is unmasked. By promoting the forced membership of individuals in rigidly defined groups and their subjection to the 'cultural' norms of these groups, UNHCR thus suppresses this intrinsic potential for change and reform, and promulgates the immutable authenticity of certain interpretations of a culture.

Conclusion

That human rights are at risk in international administration should come as no surprise: any authority, however constituted, has the potential to violate the rights and liberties of the individual. What is perhaps more surprising is the degree of naivety and even denial about this risk, and the persistence of the notion that an international authority will always protect human rights.

There are also important differences between international administrations – that is exercise of administrative functions *de jure* – and refugee camps – where wide powers are assumed and exercised on a *de facto* basis. Perhaps the most important difference, however, is that international administrations can be improved, refugee camps cannot. By making international institutions accountable and by creating

[256] In *Civilisation and Its Discontents* Freud argued that subjection to social and cultural norms is often a source of discontent (S. Freud, *Il Disagio della Civiltà* in S. Freud *Opere Vol. X* (Turin: Boringhieri, 1978) 557).

[257] B. Pascal, *Pensées* (Paris: Garnier Frères, 1961) 152–3 (pensée n. 294).

a clear legal framework for their operation, international administrations can play an important role in phases of post-conflict reconstruction and transition to a new political and constitutional order. UNHCR's administration of refugee camps, on the other hand, is not simply tainted by the lack of a legal basis. Its 'original sin' is the restriction of the freedom of movement of refugees, whence violations of the other human rights flow. A rights-based refugee regime is simply incompatible with it.

7 Implementation of UN sanctions

Introduction

The term sanction suffers from imprecision.[1] Sanctions are normally understood as a subset of countermeasures, but it is not exactly clear how the ones are distinguished from the others. Although measures adopted unilaterally by a state against another – such as the suspension of diplomatic relations or restrictions on trade – are sometimes classified as sanctions, the term more commonly describes multilateral measures imposed by a group of states through the UN or another international organisation. The UN Charter contains no definition of sanctions, but the legal basis for their adoption by the Security Council is Article 41, which provides for measures not involving the use of armed force, including the total or partial interruption of economic and diplomatic relations and communication links. In the practice of states and international organisations the content of sanctions has varied – trade embargoes, the suspension of economic assistance, arms embargoes, travel bans and so on. A UN sanction regime will often consist of a combination of these measures.

Sanctions imposed by the UN are traditionally seen as a measure of last resort, harsh but preferable to what is often the next available option – the use of force. In President Wilson's words, the theory behind sanctions is that '[a] nation that is boycotted is a nation that is in sight of surrender. Apply this economic, peaceful, silent, deadly remedy and there will be no need for force. It is a terrible remedy. It does not cost life outside the nation boycotted, but it brings a pressure

[1] See 'Introduction to Countermeasures', in J. Crawford, *The International Law Commission's Articles on State Responsibility: Introduction, Text and Commentaries* (Cambridge University Press, 2002) 282.

upon the nation which, in my judgement, no modern nation could resist.'[2] This theory was put to the test on numerous occasions, and the instrument of sanctions has been honed over the years. Two considerations emerging from the experience of the past decades shape current approaches to sanctions. First, President Wilson's idea that no modern nation can resist sanctions has not always been borne out by the facts. Secondly, growing attention has been given to the humanitarian impact of sanctions, and more generally to the morality of holding nations responsible,[3] particularly since sanctions tend to be imposed on authoritarian countries for which claims about the collective responsibility of the population for the acts of their government are inapposite.

In general, it is difficult to find a solid ethical foundation for sanctions. In Jay Gordon's analysis, just war theory, deontological ethics and utilitarianism each fail to provide a convincing justification for them. She has argued that sanctions are a modern form of siege warfare, as they are intended to influence the political and military leadership of a state or a nation by depriving the entire population of economic resources and even of their livelihood. Like siege warfare, considered to be the oldest form of total war, sanctions are inconsistent with the principle of discrimination under the just war doctrine, as they do not distinguish between combatants and non-combatants. The suffering of civilians is not merely collateral damage; it is the primary objective of sanctions. Sanctions also violate the Kantian categorical imperative of respect for every individual as an end in himself, using instead the suffering of innocents as an instrument for exerting pressure on governments. Finally, sanctions cannot be justified from a utilitarian position: on one side of the utilitarian calculus, there is the low likelihood that the measures will have the desired effect, whether it is to stop military aggression or human rights violations; on the other side, there is the considerable harm that they will certainly inflict on civilians, including – and probably especially – the most vulnerable among them.

Is there a way of restoring the moral credentials of sanctions? This has been one of the key challenges underlying changes in sanction policy over the last decades. Attempts have been made to address this challenge by replacing comprehensive sanctions, which affect an

[2] S. K. Padover, *Wilson's Ideals* (Washington DC: The American Council for Public Affairs, 1942) 108.

[3] D. Miller, 'Holding Nations Responsible', 114 *Ethics* (2004) 240.

entire country, with targeted or 'smart' sanctions, which seek to maximise the impact on the ruling elite and minimise the effect on the innocent population.

The development of UN sanctions over the years

During the cold war the Security Council adopted sanctions only on two occasions: Southern Rhodesia in 1968 and South Africa in 1977.[4] The adoption of the comprehensive sanction regime against Iraq in 1990 marked the emergence of sanctions as a preferred form of collective action.[5] Since then the Council has adopted more than twenty different sanction regimes, of which only two were comprehensive – Yugoslavia in 1991 and Haiti in 1993[6] – and the rest targeted.

The humanitarian consequences of comprehensive sanction regimes attracted widespread criticism, particularly after various reports made dramatic claims about the impact of sanctions on Iraqi civilians.[7] It was argued that the political elites quite often benefit from sanctions, being able to control the black market and using the crisis as a further pretext for crackdowns on the opposition.[8] In an attempt to mitigate these and other unintended consequences of sanctions, humanitarian exemptions were introduced, but were soon shown to be largely ineffective: a UN study on the impact of armed conflict on children found that 'humanitarian exemptions tend to be ambiguous and are interpreted arbitrarily and inconsistently ... Delays, confusion and the denial of requests to import humanitarian goods cause resource shortages. While these effects might seem to be spread evenly across the target populations, they inevitably fall most heavily on the poor.'[9]

The real change was, as mentioned, the shift to targeted (or smart) sanctions. The targets of these more focused measures vary. For example, specific commodities have been targeted, where a link was believed to exist between their trade and the funding of a conflict – most

[4] SC Res. 253 (1968) and SC Res. 421 (1977). [5] SC Res. 661 (1990).

[6] SC Res. 724 (1991) and SC Res. 841 (1993).

[7] See, for example, Human Rights Committee, 'Concluding Observations of the Human Rights Committee: Iraq. 19/11/1997', UN Doc. CCPR/C/79/Add.84 and Committee on the Rights of the Child, 'Concluding Observations of the Committee on the Rights of the Child: Iraq. 26/10/1998', UN Doc. CRC/C/15/Add.94.

[8] Secretary General, Millennium Report, *We the Peoples. The Role of the United Nations in the 21st Century*, 50.

[9] Secretary General, 'Promotion and Protection of the Rights of Children: Impact of armed conflict on children', UN Doc. A/51/306 at para. 128.

notably in the case of 'conflict diamonds'.[10] But the most widely used forms of 'smart' sanctions have been arms embargoes, asset freezes and travel bans.[11] Moreover, the imposition of sanctions on non-state actors, first considered in respect of the Khmer Rouge in Cambodia in 1992, is no longer a rare occurrence – especially in the context of counter-terrorism. The counter-terrorist regime often requires the targeting of non-state groups.[12] Non-state actors targeted by sanctions have included the Union for the Total Independence of Angola; the Bosnian Serb leadership; rebel groups in eastern Congo, Rwanda and Sierra Leone; and the Taliban and al-Qaida.[13]

The implementation of comprehensive sanction regimes requires experts and technocrats who can verify that the export and import of goods and services from and into the country accords with the terms of the sanction regime, which are often very technical and detailed. Much of this work of verification is normally conducted by the implementing authorities of each member state rather than by the UN.[14] The implementation of smart sanctions requires instead procedures for the designation of the legal and natural persons to whom the specific measures will apply. As a rule, in charge of these procedures are committees created by the Security Council pursuant to its powers under Article 29 of the UN Charter 'to establish such subsidiary organs as it deems necessary for the performance of its functions'. Eleven sanctions committees were active in 2009–10 and, as of October 2009, more than 1,000 legal or natural persons had been designated by a sanctions committee.[15]

[10] Embargoes on diamond trade were imposed on Angola (SC Res. 1173 (1998)), Sierra Leone (SC Res. 1306 (2000)) and Liberia (SC Res. 1343 (2001)).

[11] Arms embargoes were imposed, for example, on Somalia (SC Res. 733 (1992)), Liberia (SC Res. 788 (1992)), Rwanda (SC Res. 918 (1994)), the FRY (SC Res. 1160 (1998)), Eritrea and Ethiopia (SC Res. 1298 (2000)) and the Democratic Republic of Congo (SC Res. 1493 (2003)). Travel bans were imposed, for example, on Libya (SC Res. 748 (1992)), Sudan (SC Res. 1054 (1996)), terrorists (SC Res. 1373 (2001)), and al-Qaida and Taliban (SC Res. 1390 (2002)).

[12] On Khmer Rouge in Cambodia, see, for example, SC Res. 792 (1992) (non-Chapter VII resolution). On al-Qaida and Taliban, see, for example, SC Res. 1267 (1999). On funding of terrorism, see, for example, SC Res. 1373 (2001).

[13] See, for example, SC Res. 841 (1993), SC Res. 864 (1993), SC Res. 918 (1994), SC Res. 1132 (1997), SC Res. 1160 (1998), SC Res. 1267 (1999).

[14] See V. Gowlland-Debbas (ed.), *National Implementation of United Sanctions: A Comparative Study* (Leiden: Brill 2004).

[15] The Watson Institute, 'Addressing Challenges to Targeted Sanctions: An Update of the "Watson Report"' (Brown University, October 2009) 4 (available at www.watsoninstitute.org/pub/2009_10_targeted_sanctions.pdf). A list of sanctions

The legality of sanctions

There are two main lines of argument on the legality of a sanction regime. One concerns the legality of the resolution of the Security Council that adopted the sanction regime in the first place. In theory, the Security Council may have acted ultra vires in establishing a sanction regime in a particular case. In practice, however, the question of the abuse of Chapter VII powers by the Security Council is confined to the realm of political argument, given the breadth of the categories in Article 39 and the wide discretion enjoyed by the Council in making those determinations.

The other line of argument focuses on the interplay between the state responsibility regime on countermeasures and the sanction regime under the UN Charter. Article 59 of the Articles on State Responsibility provides that the Articles are 'without prejudice to the Charter of the United Nations'. The effect of this provision is that 'the rules of State responsibility, unless specifically derogated from, or overridden by virtue of the Charter's hierarchical nature, are not displaced as such by the Charter'.[16] The regulation of countermeasures does, therefore, provide a relevant legal framework for assessing sanctions, which can be particularly useful as far as questions concerning conditions, proportionality and limits are concerned – areas on which the Charter is silent. While it is true that the Security Council could override the human rights limit under Article 50(1)(b) of the Articles on State Responsibility – i.e. that obligations for the protection of human rights should not be affected by sanctions – it is notable that the shift from comprehensive to targeted sanctions was prompted by the attempt to reduce the scope for human rights violations resulting from the application of sanctions.

In addition to the general legality of a sanction regime, it is also possible to dispute the legality of a particular instance of implementation as an abuse of process or as a breach of other rules of international law, including human rights. This is explored in the next section, but it is

committees that are still active as well as of those that have terminated their work is at www.un.org/sc/committees.

[16] V. Gowlland-Debbas, 'Responsibility and the United Nations Charter', in J. Crawford, A. Pellet, S. Olleson and K. Parlett (eds.), *The Law of International Responsibility* (Oxford University Press, 2010) 115 at 137. See also J. Crawford, 'The Relationship between Sanctions and Countermeasures', in V. Gowlland-Debbas (ed.), *United Nations Sanctions and International Law* (The Hague: Kluwer, 2001) 57.

important to explain at the outset that the decision to list an individual or entity is taken in one of two possible ways. Generally, the relevant sanctions committee of the Security Council takes the decision acting under information provided by states. This is what happened, for example, in the *Sayadi and Vinck v. Belgium* case, where the Human Rights Committee held that the transmission of information from the Belgian authorities to a UN sanctions committee that eventually led to the designation of two individuals as members of a terrorist organisation constituted a breach of Articles 12 (freedom of movement) and 17 (right to privacy) of the International Covenant on Civil and Political Rights.[17] Alternatively, but more unusually, the sanctions committee supplies a general definition of targeted entities or individuals and it is the member states that, at national or regional level, are responsible for listing those who fall within that definition. This procedure has sometimes been found to be more appropriate for targeted sanctions designed to address general threats, including terrorism and nuclear proliferation. Whether it is responsible for individual designations itself or whether that level of implementation is left to member states and regional organisations, the UN ultimately relies on the member states for the enforcement of decisions concerning designations.

The chosen procedure has an impact upon the applicable legal framework and the issue of responsibility. Listing by a UN sanctions committee is conduct attributable to the UN, whereas listing by the state, albeit pursuant to criteria provided by the UN committee, is attributable to the state. The *Sayadi and Vinck* case cited above does not contradict this proposition, since, as explained, what the Human Rights Committee attributed to Belgium in that case was the transmission of the information to the sanctions committee and not the decision to list the individuals. The problematic aspect with the conclusion of the Human Rights Committee is not attribution, but causation – namely the question whether the transmission of information really caused the breach for which Belgium was found responsible (this is discussed in Chapter 8, 381 ff.).

In the European Union the implementation of listing decisions is no longer a matter of national competence, but is effected through Community regulations.[18] EU procedures for the adoption of sanctions normally begin with a proposal for a Common Position under

[17] Human Rights Committee, 20 October 2008, Communication No. 1472/2006, UN Doc. CCPR/C/94/D/1472/2006.

[18] D. Bethlehem, 'The European Union', in Gowlland-Debbas, *supra* note 14 at 123.

the Common Foreign and Security Policy. This proposal is examined and discussed by the relevant Council groups before being referred to the Council for adoption. If the Common Position calls for Community action to implement some or all of the restrictive measures, the Commission will present a proposal for a Council Regulation in accordance with Article 75 of the Treaty on the Functioning of the European Union (ex Article 60 of the Treaty establishing the European Community). Formally the proposal for a Council Regulation should be presented after the adoption of a Common Position, although this is often not the case. As a result of the responsibilities of the EU in this area, the implementation of listing decisions in EU member states will often involve three international legal persons – the UN, the EU and the member state.

Sanctions and human rights

The potential for human rights abuses depends on the type of sanction regime in operation. Whereas comprehensive sanctions harm an entire population indiscriminately, targeted sanctions affect specific individuals or groups.

Paradoxically, greater remedies are generally available for targeted sanction regimes than for comprehensive ones. Indeed, individuals in respect of whom a travel ban or a freezing order has been adopted pursuant to a UN sanction regime have brought claims in domestic courts, and have at times succeeded. But, where entire countries have been the target of sanctions affecting the lives and well-being of hundreds of thousands or even millions of people, litigation in domestic courts is unlikely to yield concrete results. Courts may be persuaded to quash the decision taken by a sanctions committee or a national implementing authority in respect of a particular individual. But they are unlikely to accede to claimants' requests to declare a sanction regime in its entirety illegal. Even if these claims could override the hurdle of territorial jurisdiction, the weight of such constitutional principles as the separation of powers and doctrines of non-justiciability (or political questions) would be brought to bear on them, almost certainly with fatal consequences.

Comprehensive sanctions

The sanctions adopted by the Security Council in response to the Iraqi invasion of Kuwait in 1990 were the most severe in the history of the UN. They included maritime and air blockades, arms embargoes, and, most notably, a ban on all imports and exports, except for medical supplies and foodstuffs.[19] The main objectives of the sanction regime were to bring the invasion and occupation of Kuwait by Iraq to an end and to restore Kuwait's sovereignty, independence, territorial integrity and legitimate government.[20] After Iraq's acceptance of a ceasefire under resolution 687 on 3 April 1991 the same sanction regime was continued, with only slight modification, for the new purpose of compelling Iraq to fulfil its obligations under that resolution. In an attempt to alleviate human suffering the Security Council authorised the 'Oil for Food programme', described as a 'temporary measure', under which controlled exports of Iraqi petroleum were permitted in order to fund the import of food, medicines and essential supplies.[21] Although the Oil for Food programme was first authorised in 1991,[22] it was not until agreement was reached between the UN and the government of Iraq in 1996 that the programme came into effect.[23] However, only about half of the proceeds from exports of petroleum were directed towards humanitarian goods, the rest funded compensation, reparations and administrative costs.

Although the actual extent to which suffering is attributable to the sanction regime rather than Iraqi governmental policy was debated, it was not in dispute that throughout their duration sanctions had a very severe impact on the livelihood, welfare and health of Iraqis. The Humanitarian Panel established by the Security Council in 1999 explained that '[e]ven if not all suffering in Iraq can be imputed to external factors, especially sanctions, the Iraqi people would not be undergoing such deprivations in the absence of prolonged measures imposed by the Security Council and the effects of the war'.[24] The Panel added that '[i]n marked contrast to the prevailing situation prior to the events of 1990–1991, the infant mortality rates in Iraq today are among

[19] SC Res. 661, 665, 666 and 670 (1990). [20] SC Res. 600 (1990); SC Res. 662 (1990).

[21] SC Res. 986 (1995). [22] SC Res. 706 (1991); SC Res. 712 (1991).

[23] Memorandum of understanding between the Secretariat of the United Nations and the Government of Iraq on the implementation of Security Council resolution 986 (1995) annexed to UN Doc. S/1996/356.

[24] Panel on the Humanitarian Situation in Iraq, 'Report of the Second Panel Established Pursuant to the Note by the President of the Security Council of 30 January 1999 (S/1999/100), Concerning the Current Humanitarian Situation in Iraq', UN Doc. S/1999/356, annex II, at para. 45.

the highest in the world, low infant birth weight affects at least 23 per cent of all births, chronic malnutrition affects every fourth child under five years of age, only 41 per cent of the population have regular access to clean water, 83 per cent of all schools need substantial repairs. The ICRC states that the Iraqi health-care system is today in a decrepit state. UNDP calculates that it would take 7 billion US dollars to rehabilitate the power sector country-wide to its 1990 capacity.'[25] A UNICEF survey found that in the heavily populated southern and central parts of the country the mortality rate for children under five had doubled from 56 per 1,000 live births between 1984–9 to 131 between 1994–9. In the same period the infant mortality rate increased from 47 per 1,000 live births to 108. The then Executive Director of UNICEF, Carol Bellamy, characterised these findings as revealing an 'ongoing humanitarian emergency'.[26] Widespread malnutrition and disease resulted partly from massive deterioration in basic infrastructure such as water supply, treatment and waste disposal, as well as from the wider economic and social collapse. In short, Iraq had experienced 'a shift from relative affluence to massive poverty'.[27]

Human rights bodies reached similar conclusions. The Human Rights Committee in 1997 noted that 'the effect of sanctions and blockades has been to cause suffering and death in Iraq, especially in children'.[28] A year later, the Committee on the Rights of the Child recognised that 'the embargo imposed by the Security Council has adversely affected the economy and many aspects of daily life, thereby impeding the full enjoyment by the State party's population, particularly children, of their rights to survival, health and education'.[29] In August 2000, the UN Sub-Commission on the Promotion and Protection of Human Rights adopted a decision 'considering any embargo that condemned an innocent people to hunger, disease, ignorance and even death to be a flagrant violation of the economic social and cultural rights and the right to life of the people concerned and of international law'.[30]

The humanitarian catastrophe in Iraq attracted much public criticism and prompted the resignation of a number of UN officials

25 Humanitarian Panel, *ibid.* at para. 43.
26 UNICEF press release CF/DOC/PR/1999/29 (12 August 1999).
27 Humanitarian Panel, *supra* note 24, quoted at para. 43.
28 Human Rights Committee, *supra* note 7 at para. 4.
29 Committee on the Rights of the Child, *supra* note 7 at para. 5.
30 UN Sub-Commission on the Promotion and Protection of Human Rights, 'Humanitarian situation of the Iraqi population', UN Doc. E/CN.4/Sub.2/2000/L.32.

including two Humanitarian Coordinators, Denis Halliday and his successor Hans von Sponeck, who objected to the continuation of the sanction regime.[31] Secretary General Kofi Annan observed that 'the humanitarian situation in Iraq poses a serious moral dilemma for this Organization. The United Nations has always been on the side of the vulnerable and the weak, and has always sought to relieve suffering, yet here we are accused of causing suffering to an entire population. We are in danger of losing the argument, or the propaganda war – if we haven't already lost it – about who is responsible for this situation in Iraq – President Saddam Hussein or the United Nations.'[32] He emphasised that 'the Council should seek every opportunity to alleviate the suffering of the population, who after all are not the intended targets of sanctions'.[33]

The Oil for Food programme was designed neither to meet all the needs of the Iraqi people nor to act as a substitute for normal economic activity.[34] At best it may have prevented the situation from getting even worse. But, as explained by the Humanitarian Panel, a significant alleviation of the humanitarian crisis required actions on a different scale.[35] Nevertheless, the Oil for Food programme did not have even the limited positive effects it could have potentially produced, because of extensive and systemic corruption. Following revelations suggesting unethical practices within the senior UN ranks associated with the scheme, the Secretary General requested the Independent Inquiry Committee (IIC) to investigate. Apart from noting the maladministration of the programme by the UN and the manipulation of it by the Iraqi government for its own ends, the IIC reported that there had been 'corrosive corruption' amongst the UN and independent contractors.[36]

[31] See *The Independent*, 'Women Fighting to Stem Disaster in Iraq' where Denis Halliday is reported as saying on resignation: 'We are in the process of destroying an entire society. It is as simple and terrifying as that. It is illegal and immoral.' 15 October 1998; *Reuters*, 'Top UN official leaves Iraq, says programme failed', 17 February 2000.

[32] Secretary General Kofi Annan, speech addressing the Security Council at its 4120th Meeting to deliver his Report (UN Doc. S/2000/208) on the situation between Iraq and Kuwait, 24 March 2000.

[33] Secretary General, Press Release of 24 March 2000, UN Doc. SG/SM/7338.

[34] Secretary General, 'Report of the Secretary-General pursuant to paragraph 5 of resolution 1330 (2000)', UN Doc. S/2001/186 at para. 154.

[35] Humanitarian Panel, *supra* note 24 at paras. 42 and 46.

[36] Independent Inquiry Committee into the United Nations Oil-for-Food Programme, 'Management of the Oil-for-Food Programme', 7 September 2005, Vol. I at 4, available from www.iic-offp.org/Mgmt_Report.htm.

Those factors led to the sale of Iraqi oil and purchase of humanitarian goods at prices inconsistent with market values, resulting in significant financial windfalls not only to private entities, but also members of both the Iraqi government and the UN's Oil for Food programme.

These funds ought to have been spent on humanitarian assistance but were instead illegitimately diverted to those engaged in the scheme. The IIC estimated that during the programme the Iraqi government alone earned approximately US$10.2 billion in illicit income from oil surcharges and humanitarian kickbacks amongst other things.[37] As a result, the Oil for Food programme, which was established to alleviate suffering of members of the community without compromising the effectiveness of the sanctions, strengthened the Iraqi elite.

The human rights abuses resulting from comprehensive economic sanctions and from the ineffectiveness of humanitarian exemptions are also evident in the 1996 sanction regime against Burundi in response to the military coup of 25 July 1996. This sanction regime was imposed by a group of African states independently of the UN, although the Security Council expressed 'strong support for the efforts of regional leaders'.[38] A leading study summarised the deleterious effect of sanctions in the following terms: across the social and economic sphere 'the pattern is consistent: serious problems predating sanctions were exacerbated by the imposition of sanctions, which themselves had numerous effects on civilian populations … The imposition of economic sanctions worsens an already grim situation, raising serious moral and ethical questions'.[39]

Another example of failed comprehensive sanctions from the 1990s is Haiti. Between June 1993 and October 1994 sanctions affected import of petroleum and arms, as well as the general finances.[40] In October 1993 medical and food supplies were exempted from the sanctions but nevertheless, in May 1994, it had become clear that the human rights situation had deteriorated sharply.[41]

[37] *Ibid.* at 103. [38] SC Res. 1072 (1996).

[39] E. Hoskins and S. Nutt, 'The Humanitarian Impacts of Economic Sanctions on Burundi', Occasional Paper No. 29 (Thomas J. Watson Jr. Institute for International Studies, Brown University, 1997) 43.

[40] SC Res. 841 (1993) and 944 (1994).

[41] Harvard Program on Human Security, *Sanctions in Haiti: Crisis in Humanitarian Action* (Cambridge: Harvard University Center for Population and Development Studies, 1993).

Targeted sanctions

Targeted sanctions imposed by the UN are aimed at persons and entities believed to be responsible for a breach of or threat to international peace. Targeted sanctions have been adopted to address both localised conflicts and general threats to international security, principally terrorism[42] and the proliferation of weapons of mass destruction.[43] The measures they typically provide for are travel bans, asset freezes, arms embargoes and trade restrictions. Their objectives are either coercive or preventative, although substantively the distinction between the two can at times be a fine one.

The main sanction regime dedicated to the purpose of fighting terrorism is the one created under resolution 1267. Initially adopted after the attacks on US embassies in Nairobi and Dar es Salaam in 1998, the 1267 sanction regime has been amended and expanded on numerous occasions.[44] It provides, among other things, for asset freezes and travel bans on individuals or entities associated with al-Qaida and/or the Taliban as designated by a Committee established for this purpose.

As of September 2010, targeted sanction regimes with procedures for designation of individuals and entities similar to those under the 1267 system were in force in respect of the following conflict situations: Somalia;[45] Sierra Leone;[46] Liberia;[47] the Democratic Republic of Congo;[48] Sudan;[49] and Côte d'Ivoire.[50] Targeted sanction regimes were also put in place to deal with the threat of proliferation of nuclear weapons arising from North Korea and Iran,[51] with the murder of former Lebanese Prime Minister Rafiq Hariri,[52] and to pursue senior officials of the former Iraqi regime.[53] The Security Council has short-circuited the listing process by directly designating some individuals and entities, most notably a group of individuals suspected of involvement in atrocities in Darfur,[54] and another of Iranian individuals

[42] SC Res. 1373 (2001). [43] SC Res. 1540 (2004).

[44] See: SC Res. 1333 (2000), 1390 (2002), 1455 (2003), 1526 (2004), 1617 (2005), 1735 (2006), 1822 (2008) and 1904 (2009).

[45] SC Res. 1844 (2008). [46] SC Res. 1132 (1997) and 1171 (1998).

[47] SC Res. 1521 (2003). The arms embargo element of the sanction regime was terminated by SC Res. 1903 (2009).

[48] SC Res. 1807 (2008) and 1896 (2009). [49] SC Res. 1591 (2005).

[50] SC Res. 1572 (2004).

[51] SC Res. 1718 (2006) on North Korea and on SC Res. 1737 (2006) and 1929 (2010) on Iran.

[52] SC Res. 1636 (2005). [53] SC Res. 1483 and 1518 (2003). [54] SC Res. 1672 (2006).

and entities involved in nuclear or ballistic missile activities.[55] As illustrated by the history of the 1267 regime, sanction regimes are seldom static: their powers and procedures are routinely modified by the Security Council. Nor is the workload of the committees comparable: some are dealing with live issues and remain very active, others with issues and situations that, while not completely resolved, require far less attention than in the past.

The development of targeted sanctions has given rise to new human rights problems. Even before courts brought their rulings to bear on this topic, the human rights record of targeted sanction regimes had attracted criticism. The Special Rapporteur on the promotion and protection of human rights and fundamental freedoms while countering terrorism has consistently highlighted due process problems with the procedures of the sanctions committees.[56] In 2004 the High Level Panel on Threats, Challenges and Change noted 'the way entities or individuals are added to the terrorist list maintained by the Council and the absence of review or appeal for those listed raise serious accountability issues and possibly violate fundamental human rights norms and conventions'.[57]

Three major studies commissioned by the Council of Europe,[58] the UN Office of Legal Affairs[59] and various governments[60] all found the prevailing situation seriously deficient. The same conclusions were reached by a report commissioned by the Parliamentary Assembly of the Council of Europe. In its resolution 1597, the Assembly noted that the procedural and substantive standards applied by the Security Council and the Council of the European Union in imposing targeted

[55] SC Res. 1929 (2010).

[56] See UN Doc. A 64/211, A/63/223, A/62/263, A/61/267, A/60/370.

[57] Report of the High-Level Panel on Threats, Challenges and Change, 'A More Secure World, Our Shared Responsibility', UN Doc. 1/59/656 at para. 153.

[58] I. Cameron, 'The European Convention on Human Rights, Due Process and UN Security Council Counter-Terrorism Sanctions' (Council of Europe, 6 February 2006), available from www.coe.int/t/e/legal_affairs/legal_co-operation/public_international_law/Texts_&_Documents/Docs%202006/I.%20Cameron%20Report%2006.pdf.

[59] B. Fassbender, 'Targeted Sanctions and Due Process' (Institute of Public International Law at the Humboldt University, Berlin, 20 March 2006).

[60] The Watson Institute, 'Strengthening Targeted Sanctions through Fair and Clear Procedures', White Paper prepared by the Watson Institute Targeted Sanctions Project, Brown University, 30 March 2006 annexed to UN Doc. A/60/887-S/2006/331, available from www.watsoninstitute.org/pub/Strengthening_Targeted_Sanctions.pdf.

sanctions 'in no way fulfil the minimum [procedural] standards … and violate the fundamental principles of human rights and the rule of law'.[61] It then recommended that the Committee of Ministers invite the Security Council and the Council of the European Union to implement substantive improvements to the targeted sanction regimes 'aimed at safeguarding individual human rights and the rule of law' and 'in particular to implement an effective and comprehensive appeal mechanism'.[62]

Indeed, smart sanctions will normally interfere with the human rights of the targeted individuals: financial measures such as freezing of the target's bank accounts may affect the right to property; travel restrictions the rights to free movement, free association and private and family life. Smart sanction regimes often leave room for humanitarian exemptions from a travel ban or a freezing order, for instance on the grounds of religious obligation such as the performance of the hajj or for the payment of basic necessary expenses.[63] The discretion to grant such an exemption by a sanctions committee appears to be almost unfettered.

Much of the argument on human rights and targeted sanctions has focused on fair trial and due process. Normally acting on the basis of information provided by states, the sanctions committees make their decisions behind closed doors. The targeted individuals or entities are neither notified in advance nor offered the opportunity to make representations; and they have no right to appeal against a decision of a sanctions committee. The procedures of sanctions committees also offer no way of upholding the right of a person whose human rights or freedoms are violated to an effective remedy (e.g. Article 2(3) of the International Covenant on Civil and Political Rights; Article 13 of the European Convention on Human Rights).

In truth, the UN and member states have not been entirely indifferent to concerns about human rights, and some progress has been made in respect of due process in the implementation of targeted sanctions. Following a report of the Office of Legal Affairs, the Secretary General produced an informal paper enumerating for the first time minimum standards of procedural fairness that should be respected

61 Council of Europe Resolution 1597 (2008) at para. 6.
62 Council of Europe Recommendation 1824 (2008) at para. 1.1.
63 See, for example, SC Res. 1267 (1999) at para. 4(a) and (b).

by sanctions committees, including the right of the individual to be informed of the measures, the right to know the case against him, the right to be heard within a reasonable time and the right to review by an effective mechanism.[64]

This initiative led the Security Council to adopt a series of resolutions establishing review mechanisms for listing decisions and a de-listing procedure.[65] Resolution 1730 (2006) requested the Secretary General to establish a 'focal point' within the Secretariat to function as a depository for the submission of individual petitions for de-listing. This focal point was operational from 27 March 2007 until 17 December 2009. It provided some avenue to make representations, but resulted in internal consultation only, as it lacked authority to conduct an independent review. Resolution 1735 of 2006 provided a more detailed regulation of the process through which states propose names, and resolution 1822 of 2008 ordered a review of all listing decisions by the 1267 Committee. The first review was due to be completed in two years, with one to follow every three years thereafter. De-listing decisions taken as part of this review have included individuals and entities which had started litigation in various fora, in particular Sayadi and Vinck, and Al Barakaat International.[66] Most recently, resolution 1904 (2009) replaced the focal point with an independent and impartial Ombudsman. However, the Ombudsman's role is limited to the gathering and presentation of information. He has no decision-making authority on de-listing, which is still decided confidentially and by consensus within the sanctions committee.[67] In part prompted by litigation in their domestic courts, a group of 'like-minded states'[68] presented a proposal for the creation of an expert panel to review de-listing petitions.[69] The suggested panel,

[64] Letter dated 15 June 2006 from Secretary General Kofi Annan to the President of the Security Council, 'Targeted Individual Sanctions: Fair and Clear Procedures for Listing and De-listing', Proceedings of 5474th Meeting, S/PV.5474, 22 June 2006.

[65] See in particular SC Res. 1617 (2005); SC Res. 1730 (2006); SC Res. 1735 (2006); SC Res. 1822 (2008).

[66] *Sayaadi and Vinck v. Belgium*, Human Rights Committee, 20 October 2008, Communication No. 1472/2006, UN Doc. CCPR/C/94/D/1472/2006; Case T-306/01, *Yusuf and Al Barakaat International Foundation v. Council and Commission*, Judgment of the Court of First Instance.

[67] SC Res. 1904 (2009) at para. 22.

[68] The 'like-minded states' include Denmark, Germany, Liechtenstein, the Netherlands, Switzerland and Sweden.

[69] 'Improving the Implementation of Sanctions Regimes Through Ensuring "Fair and Clear Procedures"', UN Doc. A/62/861-S2008/428.

inspired by Bothe's analysis of the World Bank inspection panels,[70] is intended to include eminent jurists with experience in dealing with sensitive information. The decisions of the panel, like those of the inspection panels, are to be advisory only.

Despite the improvements, there is still no formal right of appeal or legal challenge. Individuals or entities aggrieved by a decision of a sanctions committee have essentially two options. The first one, but available only in respect of listing decisions taken by the 1267 Committee, is to seek the removal of their names from the list by sending a request to the Office of the Ombudsman created under resolution 1904 of 2009. The Ombudsman has no power to order de-listing but can gather information on the request and present a report to the Committee which will then decide.

The second option is to persuade their state of nationality to exercise diplomatic protection on their behalf by sending a request for review or de-listing to the relevant sanctions committee. This course of action may have greater prospects of success. In practice however this route has proved infrequent, which is not all that surprising if one recalls that it is often the states themselves that in the first place designate individuals who are later placed on a sanctions list by a committee.

Case law

As discussed, targeted sanctions lend themselves more easily to litigation than comprehensive ones. It is therefore not surprising that the shift to targeted sanctions has been accompanied by a significant rise in litigation before domestic, European and international human rights courts.

Acts of the UN are generally immune from judicial review, but it is not clear that internal measures implementing Security Council resolutions should also be. The central tension at the heart of this debate is between the protection of human rights and the need to preserve the uniform implementation of Security Council resolutions. The European Court of First Instance sought to resolve this tension by maintaining, on the one hand, that 'the resolutions of the Security Council ... fall, in principle, outside the ambit of the Court's judicial review and that the Court has no authority to call in question, even indirectly, their

[70] M. Bothe, 'Security Council's Targeted Sanctions against Presumed Terrorists: The Need to Comply with Human Rights Standards', 6(3) *Journal of International Criminal Justice* (2008) 541.

lawfulness in the light of Community law'; and, on the other, that '[n]onetheless the Court is empowered to check, indirectly, the lawfulness of resolutions of the Security Council with regard to *jus cogens*'.[71] The ECJ rejected this approach. In its judgment in *Kadi*, it held that the review of lawfulness by the Community judicature applies 'to the Community act intended to give effect to the international agreement at issue, and not to the latter as such'.[72] Nevertheless, the solution propounded by the European Court of First Instance has left some mark. It was adopted, in particular, by the Swiss Federal Tribunal.[73]

In some cases courts have also considered the effect of Articles 25 and 103 of the UN Charter. The ECJ did not address this question directly in its judgment in *Kadi*, although the corollary of the strictly dualist approach it adopted is that the principle of supremacy of Charter obligations has effect on the international plane, but does not displace Community law as applied by a European Court. The same reasoning would apply to constitutional law.

The position is different in the UK because of the *Al-Jedda* decision of the House of Lords,[74] which essentially gave domestic effect to Article 103 of the UN Charter by holding that a decision of the Security Council under Chapter VII can abridge human rights protected under the Human Rights Act. The UK Supreme Court had to grapple with this precedent in its decision on sanctions in the *Jabar Ahmed* case.[75] The Court was presented with a challenge concerning two Orders in Council made by Her Majesty's Treasury giving effect to the freezing of funds provisions in a targeted sanction regime. These Orders were made under section 1 of the United Nations Act 1946 (UK) which authorises the making of Orders in Council that are 'necessary and expedient' to

71 Case T-306/01, *Yassin Abdullah Kadi v. Council of the European Union and Commission of the European Communities*, Judgment of the Court of First Instance, at paras. 225–6 (and the identical paragraphs in *Yusuf and Al Barakaat*, *supra* note 66 at 276–7).

72 Joined Cases C-402/05 P & C-415/05, *Yassin Abdullah Kadi and Al Barakaat International Foundation v. Council of the European Union and Commission of the European Communities*, Judgment of the European Court of Justice, at para. 286.

73 Case No 1A.48/2007, *Nada v. SECO*, Judgment of 22 April 2008. See also: A. Tzanakopoulos, 'Domestic Court Reactions to UN Security Council Sanctions', *forthcoming* in A. Reinisch (ed.), *Challenging Acts of International Organisations before National Courts* (Oxford University Press, 2010).

74 *R (on the application of Al-Jedda) (FC) (Appellant) v. Secretary of State for Defence (Respondent)* [2007] UKHL 58.

75 *Mohammed Jabar Ahmed and others v. HM Treasury* [2010] UKSC 2. See the discussions of Al-Jedda and Jabar Ahmed in Chapter 8 (372ff.).

give effect to the Security Council resolutions. The Terrorism (United Nations Measures) Order 2006, the first of the two Orders, subjected individuals to freezing orders on the basis of 'reasonable suspicion', while the Al-Qaida and Taliban (United Nations Measures) Order 2006 provided that if a person is named on the consolidated sanctions list their assets would be automatically frozen. The appellants advanced two main arguments against the legality of the Orders. First, they submitted that they violated human rights and, secondly, that they were ultra vires in terms of section 1 of the United Nations Act 1946. They succeeded on the second ground, but failed on the first because of the effect of *Al-Jedda*. The appellants had acknowledged the weight of the *Al-Jedda* precedent against their positions, and invited the Supreme Court to reconsider it in light of the *Kadi* decision of the ECJ.[76]

The leading Canadian decision on targeted sanctions in the area of counter-terrorism is *Abdelrazik*.[77] The applicant, a Canadian national listed by the 1267 Committee, challenged the decision to prevent his return to Canada, taken by the Canadian authorities in order to comply with the travel ban. In allowing the application and declaring that the applicant's right to enter Canada under section 6(1) of the Canadian Charter of Rights and Freedoms had been breached, Mr Justice Zinn of the Federal Court found that 'properly interpreted the UN travel ban presents no impediment to Mr Abdelrazik returning home to Canada' because the purpose of the travel ban 'is to prevent these individuals from travelling from country to country raising funds and arms and spreading terrorism. Mr Abdelrazik will have no more mobility, in that sense of the word, if he is in Canada than in Sudan.'[78]

The aforementioned *Sayadi and Vinck* case concerned a transfer by Belgium of the personal information and details of two individuals – Mr Sayadi and Ms Vinck – to the 1267 Committee. Their names were subsequently placed on a sanctions list which resulted in an immediate travel ban and the freezing of their funds. However, they were not given access to the information which was said to justify their inclusion in the list. The Human Rights Committee held that the supply of information by Belgium to the sanctions committee constituted a breach of

[76] *Ibid.* at paras. 71–4 (*per* Lord Hope) and paras. 89–106 (*per* Lord Phillips).

[77] *Abousfian Abdelrazik v. Minister of Foreign Affairs and Attorney General of Canada* [2009] FC 80.

[78] *Ibid. at* para. 129.

the right to freedom of movement and of the right to privacy under the International Covenant for Civil and Political Rights.[79] The Committee found that even though Belgium was not competent to remove the individuals from the list, it was still responsible for the presence of their names on it and the consequent sanctions being placed upon them.[80] In considering the application of Article 12 (freedom of movement), the Committee weighed the travel restrictions against public interests and held that the imposition of the travel ban was not necessary to protect national security or public order. In grappling with the right to freedom of movement '[t]he Committee concludes that there has been a violation of article 12 of the Covenant' without identifying exactly whether it was the listing or the transfer of information that constituted a breach. In relation to the right to privacy, the Committee found that the accessibility of the personal details of each of the authors of the communication to the whole world via the Internet constituted a breach of Article 17 and that Belgium was responsible for this breach. The Committee reached this conclusion despite Belgium's subsequent attempts to have the authors of the communication de-listed and despite the fact that Belgium itself had no power to de-list them.

What conclusions are to be drawn from this case law? The most important conclusion is that courts – whether national or international – are showing less deference to arguments based on the non-reviewability of acts of the Security Council than might have been surmised until a few years ago. Their readiness to step in and assess the merits of claims brought against national or, in the case of the EU, regional implementing authorities is one of the main factors that has prompted procedural reforms at the UN level. There are still national courts that decline any form of review, direct or indirect, of resolutions of the Security Council, but the trend is towards some form of engagement and some measure of review. More specifically, adopting Tzanakopulos's analysis,[81] in addition to abstention, three other outcomes have emerged: low-intensity review, on the basis for example of consistency with *jus cogens*, as advocated by the European Court of First Instance; interpretations that seek to avoid conflict between the international and the internal plane, as the one developed by the Canadian Federal Court in *Abdelrazik*; and the quashing of the domestic measure that gave effect to the resolution, as ordered by the ECJ in *Kadi* (albeit

[79] See *supra* note 66. [80] *Ibid.* at para. 10.8. [81] Tzanakopoulos, *supra* note 73.

subject to a three-month suspensive clause). The last two outcomes are not necessarily premised on the adoption of different standards of review. On the contrary, even a court that is prepared to quash the implementing measure may – and indeed probably should – in the first place explore the possibility of an interpretation that avoids conflict.

Conclusion

Since the end of the cold war, UN sanctions have evolved from comprehensive regimes to targeted ones. The primary concern with comprehensive regimes was the undue suffering of the civilian populations of the sanctioned states. Even programmes adopted to mitigate the harm suffered by the most vulnerable as a result of comprehensive regimes have been abused and manipulated for private gain including by UN officials. The human rights and humanitarian impact of these sanction regimes was too substantial to be ignored.

The shift to targeted sanctions in the late 1990s and in the early 2000s has brought with it its own human rights issues. Individuals and entities have been placed on sanctions lists and subjected to very restrictive measures affecting their substantive rights to property, privacy, and freedom of movement, as well as their right to a remedy in the event of a breach of one or more human rights. Procedural rights have also been affected, with those subject to restrictive measures not being accorded due process and an effective and transparent appeals process. Domestic as well as international courts have been seized of numerous lawsuits brought by listed individuals and entities. Despite the inevitable differences between various courts, it was clear by the late 2000s that the Security Council and its sanctions committees were not going to be given a carte blanche from courts in a number of jurisdictions. The pressure of domestic and human rights litigation has prompted some procedural reforms. It remains to be seen whether such reforms will survive further judicial scrutiny.

8 Accountability

Introduction

Until only a decade ago the question of the accountability of international organisations was confined almost exclusively to the realm of political and administrative remedies.[1] Things have changed quite dramatically since then. Accountability through the judicial process is no longer a merely theoretical possibility, as the jurisprudence of national and of international human rights courts includes a growing number of cases related to the activities of international institutions.

The curious thing is that such a development took place without a change in the fundamentals of the law of immunity. The prospects of bringing a successful lawsuit in a domestic court, where the UN is respondent, have not improved. But many of the activities of international organisations require implementation by member states, and this is where the potential for litigation has been shown to be the greatest: the public body responsible for the implementation is sued in a domestic court or the state in an international human rights court. As amply discussed throughout this book, this litigation faces difficulties, particularly in relation to issues of attribution and jurisdiction *ratione personae*. Nevertheless, claimants have succeeded in a number of important cases. The result is that, in order to minimise their exposure to these claims, states are more likely now than before to ensure that the activities of international organisations comply with human rights law.

This strategy has, however, one limit. States will have an interest in monitoring compliance by the UN with international human rights law only where they are faced with a risk of litigation – that is only where

[1] On the concept of accountability see Chapter 1 (52ff.).

they have adopted measures which give effect to decisions or recommendations of international organisations and which could form the object of a claim. The main example in this area is sanctions, where, as we have seen in the previous chapter, claimants have maximised the exposure of states to litigation that derives from the activity of implementation. But where the conduct requires no implementation on the part of the state, the prospects of bringing a human rights claim that has, albeit indirectly, the conduct of an international organisation as its object remain minimal. The administration of refugee camps, examined in Chapter 6, is an example. Short of success – unlikely in the present state of the law – in defeating the plea of immunity that would be raised by the international organisation in a domestic court, or short of success – even more unlikely – in establishing jurisdiction *ratione personae* before an international human rights body, one more hopeful avenue open to claimants in these cases is to sue the public authorities, or the state, for breach of a positive obligation under human rights law.

Much of this chapter is devoted to the development of legal accountability and, especially, to the doctrine of equivalent protection which is emerging as one of the principal juridical creations behind this phenomenon. Before considering legal accountability, however, political and administrative means of accountability and the role of member states are examined.

Political and administrative controls

Control and oversight under the Charter

Among the principal organs of the UN, the General Assembly carries primary responsibility for control and oversight. This is evident from Article 10 of the Charter, in terms of which the General Assembly 'may discuss any questions or any matters within the scope of the present Charter or relating to the powers and functions of any organs provided for in the present Charter'. The powers of the General Assembly are subject to the 'abstention clause' in Article 12(1) of the Charter, which obliges the General Assembly not to make any recommendation with regard to a dispute or situation if the Security Council is exercising the functions assigned to it in the Charter, that is in relation to the maintenance of international peace and security. In spite of the primacy of the Security Council in the area of peace and security, the Charter imposes an obligation on the Security Council to report to the General

Assembly, but not vice versa (Articles 15(1) and 24(1) of the Charter). Other organs of the UN are subject to a similar obligation to report to the General Assembly (Article 15(2)). Finally, a power of oversight and control is also implied in the General Assembly's competence in budgetary and financial matters, in particular the obligation to consider and approve the budget of the Organisation (Article 17(1)).

Other organs of the UN also have powers of control and oversight. The Secretary General, who is the 'chief administrative officer' of the Organisation in terms of Article 97, has a general responsibility for administrative control and oversight. As part of this general responsibility he can, for example, appoint commissions of inquiry. The Security Council performs functions of control and oversight over matters principally within the area of peace and security, and especially in respect of the subsidiary organs that it has established pursuant to Article 29 of the Charter – such as sanction committees.

The extent to which political organs of the UN exercise their powers of control and oversight in practice varies; as does the effectiveness of their exercise of these powers. As illustrated at various points in this book, the operational programmes, in particular, have escaped pervasive scrutiny over and accountability for the performance of their functions. The peculiar legal status of these programmes – subsidiary bodies in principle, but autonomous organisations in practice – has undoubtedly been instrumental to their lack of accountability to the parent organs, often the General Assembly. The parent organs in turn acquiesced in this situation failing to exercise powers that they legally possess. Nor has the Secretariat been an effective watchdog. One reason is that the 'feudal' structure[2] of the UN with its relatively weak centre and its various principalities and fiefdoms reflects delicate balances of power within the Organisation. The Secretary General could use some of his powers to promote the accountability of the operational programmes, but he is unlikely to do so within the current intra-institutional equilibrium.

Before looking at some specific forms of political and administrative control that require attention, it is worth returning briefly to the role of the General Assembly. Put quite simply, the General Assembly has proven to be the weakest link in the chain of accountability. It has

[2] The comparison with feudal institutions is Paul Szasz's ('The Role of the UN Secretary General: Some Legal Aspects', 24 *New York University Journal of International Law and Politics* (1991) 161).

seldom, if ever, lived up to its responsibilities both as principal watchdog of the UN and as parent organ of most operational programmes. Why has it failed? It was entrusted with an overall function of political control and oversight probably on the basis of the analogy with the role of parliaments in liberal constitutions. But, even in advanced democracies, parliaments sometimes become apathetic and fail to exercise proper scrutiny over the executive. Their ability to perform their role effectively is a function of the political culture and tradition and, more generally, of the state and quality of politics in a particular country. The General Assembly was always unlikely to succeed where some national parliaments had failed. After all, it does not come under real pressure from public opinion to be more proactive in the exercise of its control functions and has no common tradition of political accountability to tap into.

The reports of the Secretary General

One of the most important tasks of the Secretariat 'which touches upon almost all major aspects of the work of the UN' is the 'collection of information and the preparation of studies and reports'.[3] These reports are crucial both to informed decision-making by other organs and to accountability. They are also the main official channel for keeping the Security Council, and less frequently the General Assembly, informed about the implementation of the mandate by UN missions. Particularly when a Chapter VII operation is concerned, the exercise of delegated powers by the Secretary General is subjected to limitations, including the good faith use of discretionary powers and the preservation of a decision-making process that is independent of UN member states.[4] To these limitations, it is necessary to add the duty to keep the delegating organ, the Security Council, accurately informed about the exercise of the delegated powers as well as about relevant factual developments. The existence of this duty was indirectly recognised by the ICJ in the *Certain Expenses* case. Rejecting the Russian argument that the Secretary General had acted ultra vires in determining the size and composition

[3] W. Fiedler, 'Article 98' in B. Simma (ed.), *The Charter of the United Nations: A Commentary* (2nd edn., Oxford University Press, 2002) 1205 at 1209.

[4] D. Sarooshi, *The United Nations and the Development of Collective Security: the Delegation by the Security Council of its Chapter VII Powers* (Oxford University Press, 2000), at 55–7. See also the dictum of the ICJ on the exercise of discretionary powers by the Secretary General in *Application for Review of Judgment 333 of the United Nations Administrative Tribunal*, Advisory Opinion, ICJ Report (1987) 18 at 57–8.

of ONUC, the Court emphasised that there existed a 'record of reiterated consideration, confirmation, approval and ratification by the Security Council ... of the actions of the Secretary-General', and that it was clear that, under these circumstances, the Secretary-General could not have 'usurped or impinged upon' the prerogatives of the Council.[5] For the 'consideration, confirmation, approval and ratification' of the Security Council to be conducted in an informed way, the Secretary General has to provide detailed and accurate background information.

The Secretary General submits periodic reports to the Security Council on the implementation of each mission. They are normally prepared by the staff at the Secretariat on the basis of information and drafts provided by the field staff. Some resolutions expressly state the number of reports that the Secretary General has to submit every year,[6] while others simply request the Secretary General 'to report to the Council at regular intervals' or 'to provide periodic reports'.[7] In the case of at least one peacekeeping mission – the UN Military Observer Group in India and Pakistan (UNMOGIP) – no regular reporting to the Council or the Assembly has taken place.[8] By contrast, the reports submitted by the Secretary General on the UN Mission in Kosovo (UNMIK) have been detailed and rich with information. One argument against intensifying the submission of these reports is that they require a considerable investment of staff time and resources at the field level.

In earlier practice, 'advisory committees' were established to assist the Secretary General in the implementation of a peacekeeping operation. For example, the General Assembly established an Advisory Committee on the first UN Emergency Force (UNEF I) to be chaired by

[5] *Certain Expenses of the UN*, Advisory Opinion, ICJ Reports (1962) 151 at 175.

[6] After the initial report to be submitted within three months of the deployment of the UN troops, SC Res. 1272 (1999) of 30 November 1999 on East Timor requests the Secretary General to submit one report every six months; SC Res. 1289 (2000) of 7 February 2000 on Sierra Leone requests a report every forty-five days.

[7] SC Res. 1244 (1999) of 10 June 1999 on Kosovo and SC Res. 1312 (2000) of 31 July 2000 establishing the UN Mission in Ethiopia and Eritrea (UNMEE). See also SC Res. 1565 (2004) of 1 October 2004 with regard to MONUC. The Secretary General has, in practice, reported three to five times a year on the operations of MONUC. See www.un.org/Depts/dpko/missions/monuc/monucDrp.htm.

[8] R. Higgins, *United Nations Peace-keeping 1946–1967: Documents and Commentary, Vol. II: Asia* (Oxford University Press, 1970) 352.

the Secretary General.[9] An Advisory Committee for the UN Operation in the Congo (ONUC), comprising representatives of the states that were contributing troops to the mission, was created as a result of the personal initiative of the Secretary General, Dag Hammarskjöld. The ONUC Advisory Committee met regularly and assisted both Dag Hammarskjöld and U Thant in handling the Congo crisis and in the strategic management of ONUC.[10] In the 1990s, these advisory committees reappeared albeit under a different denomination and in a less structured format: now referred to as 'Friends of the Secretary General', informal groups comprising representatives from contributing member states have been 'created on an *ad hoc* basis to support the Secretary-General in the discharge of peacemaking and peace-keeping mandates entrusted to him'.[11] The executive committee that was established by the Secretary General shortly after the inception of UNMIK was more than a merely advisory body. The committee was required 'to assist the Special Representative in fulfilling his responsibilities', and to act as 'the main instrument through which he will control the implementation of UNMIK's objectives'.[12]

The UN operation in the Congo (MONUC) has been the largest UN peacekeeping mission for most of the 2000s, with over 20,000 troops and support officers on the ground in 2010. The Secretary General has been issuing reports to the Security Council on the operations carried out by MONUC since pre-deployment in 1998,[13] detailing the major developments in the political situation, the state of implementation of the mission mandate, issues relating to conduct and discipline of the UN force, and administrative and financial aspects of the mission.[14]

[9] GA Res. 1001 (ES-I) of 7 November 1956.

[10] See R. Higgins, *United Nations Peace-keeping 1946–1967: Documents and Commentary, Vol. III: Africa* (Oxford University Press, 1980) 64 ff.

[11] *Supplement to An Agenda for Peace*, UN Doc. A/50/60, S/1995/1 at paras. 83–4.

[12] Security Council, 'Report of the Secretary-General on the UN Interim Administration Mission to Kosovo', 12 July 1999, UN Doc. S/1999/779.

[13] Links to all Reports are at www.un.org/Depts/dpko/missions/monuc/monucDrp.htm.

[14] See, for example, United Nations Security Council, 'Twentieth report of the Secretary-General on the United Nations Organization Mission in the Democratic Republic of the Congo', 28 December 2005, UN Doc. S/2005/832 and 'Twenty-seventh report of the Secretary-General on the United Nations Organization Mission in the Democratic Republic of the Congo', 27 March 2009, UN Doc. S/2009/160. In addition, there have been various thematic reports, including on the prevention of exploitation of natural resources (UN Doc. S/2007/68) and on children and armed conflict in the DRC (UN Doc. S/2008/693) for example.

At their best, these reports do not shy away from cataloguing the challenges and difficulties encountered by the peacekeeping forces and draw attention to violations of human rights (and of the MONUC mandate) by peacekeepers (as in the report where the Secretary General criticised the peacekeeping forces' involvement in sexual abuses).[15] However, it is not clear how the reports, in practice, enhance accountability. Certainly, they make the activities of the peacekeeping forces more transparent to the general public and to other UN organs, notably the Security Council (which has overall responsibility for the mission). At their worst, however, the reports fail to present a complete and accurate picture of the situation. An example of reports that suffered from critical omissions were those submitted by the Secretary General on the situation in Afghanistan under the Taliban, discussed in Chapter 4 (180ff.).

In order to improve the effectiveness of the Secretary General's reports as instruments for promoting accountability, a committee of the General Assembly and the Security Council could, in principle, subject the Secretary General, and other senior members of staff in the Secretariat, to direct and intense questioning. This is one of the methods used by national parliaments to exercise control over the executive, and there is no reason why it could not be adapted to international institutions. To perform such a function effectively, it would be important to have access to other sources of fact-finding. The submission of reports by NGOs and other interested parties, particularly from the affected area, could be encouraged.[16] Under existing rules, the Council can allow the direct participation of NGOs or experts, for example by means of oral presentations.[17]

Investigations and inquiries

The Security Council often designates a delegation for the purposes of conducting fact-finding missions.[18] In the course of these missions, the Security Council officials are generally briefed by high-ranking

[15] Security Council, S/2005/832 *supra* note 14.

[16] In the practice of the Security Council the participation of non-member states and of representatives of UN subsidiary agencies is well-accepted and has occurred with some frequency (for examples, see UN Department of Political Affairs, *Repertoire of the Practice of the Security Council. Supplement 1981–1984* (1992), UN Doc. ST/PSCA/1/Add. 9 and *Supplement 1985–1988* (2000), UN Doc. ST/DPA/1/Add. 10).

[17] Rule 39 and Appendix A and B, Provisional Rules of Procedure of the Security Council, UN Doc. S/96/Rev.7, also available at www.un.org/Docs/sc/scrules.htm.

[18] Reports are available at www.un.org/Docs/sc/missionreports.html.

officials of other UN agencies and organs working in the state,[19] commanders of any relevant UN Force.[20] and, on occasion, by civil society and domestic NGOs.[21] The missions have, on occasion, addressed the accountability of UN agencies and peacekeeping forces. For example, in 2005, the Security Council Mission to Central Africa was briefed on the accountability measures being taken with regard to sexual abuse and exploitation in which members of MONUC were alleged to have been involved.[22]

In some instances, the Security Council has appointed ad hoc commissions of inquiry. For example, the Council instructed the Secretary General to establish an ad hoc panel of experts to investigate the illegal exploitation of natural resources and other forms of wealth in the Congo.[23] The panel's report to the Council in April 2001 attracted severe criticism from the countries it accused of plundering resources in eastern Congo. The ICJ attached significant evidential value to its findings in the *Armed Activities in Congo* case.[24]

Among the most important *ex post facto* investigations carried out by the UN since the end of the cold war are the inquiries into the actions of the UN in Rwanda,[25] the fall of Srebrenica,[26] and the manipulation of the Oil for Food programme.[27]

[19] See Security Council, 'Report of the Security Council Mission on the Electoral process in the Democratic Republic of the Congo', 22 June 2006, UN Doc. S/2006/434 at para. 4 (noting meetings with representatives of the World Bank and IMF).

[20] Security Council, 'Report of the Security Council Mission to Central Africa, 4 to 11 November 2005', 14 November 2005, UN Doc. S/2005/716 at para. 7.

[21] *Ibid.* at para. 4; 'Report of the Security Council Mission to Djibouti (on Somalia), the Sudan, Chad, the Democratic Republic of the Congo and Côte d'Ivoire, 31 May to 10 June 2008', UN Doc. S/2008/460. at paras. 25–32.

[22] Security Council S/2005/716 *supra* note 20 at para. 48.

[23] Statement by the President of the Security Council, 2 June 2000, UN Doc. S/PRST/2000/20. Security Council, 'Report of the Panel of Experts on the Illegal Exploitation of Natural Resources and Other Forms of Wealth of the Democratic Republic of the Congo', 12 April 2001, UN Doc. S/2001/357; UN OCHA Integrated Regional Information Network for Central and Eastern Africa (IRIN-CEA), Weekly Round-up 68, 20 April 2001.

[24] *Armed Activities in the Territory of the Congo (Democratic Republic of Congo v. Uganda)*, ICJ Reports (2005) 168 at paras. 58ff.

[25] Report of the Independent Inquiry into the Actions of the United Nations during the 1994 Genocide in Rwanda, 15 December 1999, UN Doc. S/1999/1257.

[26] Report of the Secretary General, 'Report on the Fall of Srebrenica', 15 November 1999, UN Doc. A/54/549.

[27] Independent Inquiry Committee into the United Nations Oil-for-Food Programme, 'Report on the Management of the Oil-for-Food Programme', 27 October 2005, available from www.iic-offp.org.

The Rwanda report was the result of an initiative of the Secretary General,[28] which was endorsed by the Security Council.[29] The three members of the Commission of Inquiry were appointed by the Secretary General. The final report of this commission[30] was severely critical of the conduct of the UN in Rwanda during the 1994 genocide. However, although it constitutes an important document for ascertaining numerous key facts on the conduct of the UN in Rwanda, it may not be as efficacious as a means of securing accountability for wrongdoing. The terms of the inquiry were limited to fact-finding and to the formulation of recommendations, and did not include the indication of remedies for victims or sanctions against officials.

Unlike the Rwanda report, the report on the fall of Srebrenica was not prepared by an independent panel of experts, but by the Secretary General following a request of the General Assembly.[31] The report does recognise that there was a failure on the part of the Secretariat 'to fully comprehend the extent of the Serb war aims',[32] but it was overall more hesitant than the Rwanda report to lay the blame with either the political or the operational level of the UN, although it is hardly disputable that in this crisis it was the lack of political will on the part of the key members of the Security Council to intervene that facilitated the fall of Srebrenica. In the case of Rwanda, instead, although the unwillingness of member states to intervene was also a crucial factor, the political leadership of the UN mission was clearly responsible for serious mistakes and omissions, particularly the failure to act on the early warning sent by UNAMIR two months before the genocide,[33] and the refusal to authorise UNAMIR to follow the rules of engagement that were in force and that might have allowed its troops to defend civilians more effectively.[34]

[28] Security Council, 'Letter from the Secretary-General to the President of the Security Council', 18 March 1999, UN Doc. S/1999/339.

[29] Security Council, 'Letter from the President of the Security Council to the Secretary-General', 26 March 1999, UN Doc. S/1999/340.

[30] Security Council, 'Report of the Independent Inquiry into the Actions of the United Nations during the 1994 Genocide in Rwanda', 15 December 1999, UN Doc. S/1999/1257.

[31] General Assembly, 'Report of the Secretary-General pursuant to GA Res. 53/35: The Fall of Srebrenica', 15 November 1999, UN Doc. A/54/549; and GA Res. 53/35 of 30 November 1998.

[32] General Assembly 'Report', *ibid.* at para. 496 and 501. According to former Secretary General Boutros Boutros-Ghali, the US had assigned an impossible task to the UN (B. Boutros-Ghali, *Unvanquished: A U.S.-U.N. Saga* (London: I.B. Tauris, 1999))

[33] Rwanda report *supra* note 30 at 10–12.

[34] *Ibid.* at 35. See also R. Dallaire, *Shake Hands with the Devil: The Failure of Humanity in Rwanda* (Canada: Random House, 2003) 232ff.

There were no resignations in the UN following the Rwanda and Srebrenica reports, although some senior officials, including Secretary General Kofi Annan who headed the Department of Peacekeeping during the Rwanda genocide, came under intense criticism. By contrast, similar findings in a domestic inquiry could have resulted in resignations – one of the main sanctions available to the political process of accountability. Indeed, this is precisely what the entire Dutch government did after the publication of the report it had commissioned on the events of Srebrenica.

The Independent Inquiry Committee that investigated the Oil for Food programme was endowed with the power to make findings on both institutional and individual responsibility. Its findings led to indictments by US courts.[35] The Committee was appointed by the Secretary General and endorsed by the Security Council.[36]

Special evaluations units – sometimes known as 'lessons learned' units – have been established within UN organisations and departments. These units can potentially play an important role in promoting debate and changes within institutional cultures that are often still impervious to scrutiny and assessment. Reports evaluating specific projects and policies have been available in the public domain since the 1990s.[37] While this certainly advances accountability and transparency, it is not clear that such evaluation activity has much impact on the actual conduct of the organisation; and the locution 'lessons learned' may in itself seem an indication of premature self-congratulation.

General administrative oversight

As would be the case in any bureaucracy or large company, UN agencies and departments normally have different bodies with an oversight or performance monitoring function, and sometimes even a smaller section within the organisation may have its own oversight unit.[38] Within

[35] C. Lynch, 'Former UN Oil-for-Food Chief Indicted', *Washington Post*, 17 January 2007.

[36] SC Res. 1538 (2004).

[37] For example, the reports of UNHCR's Evaluation and Policy Analysis Unit can be found at www.unhcr.org/pages/4a1d28526.html; the reports of UNICEF's Division of Evaluation, Policy and Planning are available at www.unicef.org/evaldatabase/index_14651.html; the Lessons Learned Unit of the Division of Peace-keeping Operations are at www.peacekeepingbestpractices.unlb.org/PBPS/Pages/Public/Home.aspx.

[38] A comprehensive review of the oversight mechanisms in the operational agencies was undertaken by the Office of Internal Oversight Services (OIOS) and was submitted to the General Assembly (General Assembly, 'Report of the Secretary-General to the

UNHCR, for example, there is an Inspector General's Office located within the High Commissioner's Executive Office. Inspections are an 'internal oversight and management tool that provide the High Commissioner and her senior managers with a broad review of the functioning of her field representation at all levels. Not less importantly, inspections provide UNHCR's field offices with an independent and objective review of their performance …'[39]

UNHCR's Inspector General is also responsible for investigations in case of wrongdoings, and produces standard inspections ('across-the-board' checks of management of an operation) and ad hoc inspections on specific issues.[40] If the Inspector General finds evidence of individual staff wrongdoing, he or she communicates with human resources. Weaknesses of an administrative nature, of an operational policy, guideline, procedure or practice will, however, be reported to the senior management, including at times to the High Commissioner. The Inspector General may make recommendations for actions to redress the identified weakness.[41] Most of these recommendations concern protection issues,[42] and can thus have an impact on the refugees' enjoyment of their rights.

A separate office is the Evaluation and Policy Analysis Unit (EPAU),[43] which reports to the Assistant High Commissioner, and often relies on external consultants to conduct its evaluations.[44] Since 2003, EPAU has been governed by an Evaluations Policy,[45] which aims to fulfil a number of purposes, including accountability of UNHCR to refugees, partner organisations and its own Executive Committee.[46]

General Assembly on Enhancing the Internal Oversight Mechanisms in Operational Funds and Programmes', 20 February 1997, UN Doc. A/51/801; see also the updated report submitted to the General Assembly by the Secretary General on 8 March 2001, UN Doc. A/55/826).

39 Executive Committee of the High Commissioner's Programme, 'UNHCR's Organization Oversight and Performance Review Framework', 18 September 2000, UNHCR Doc. EC/50/SC/INF.6 at para. 7.

40 M. Pallis, 'The Operation of UNHCR's Accountability Mechanism', 37 *The New York University Journal of International Law and Politics* (2006) 869 at 892ff.

41 See www.unhcr.org/pages/49f0619f6.html.

42 Pallis, *supra* note 40 at 893.

43 See *supra* note 37.

44 The full text of the evaluations is available (back to 1994) at www.unhcr.org/pages/4a1d28526.html.

45 UNHCR Policy Development and Evaluation Service, 'UNHCR's Evaluation Policy', 1 September 2002, available at www.unhcr.org/3d99a0f74.html.

46 *Ibid.* at 3.

Evaluations include inspection, audit, programme monitoring and protection oversight,[47] and are based on the principles of transparency, independence, consultation, relevance and integrity. The evaluations may be conducted by UNHCR staff, or by independent and external persons.[48] The management is required to respond in writing to the recommendations.[49] As the Policy states, 'responsibility for the implementation of those recommendations, however, lies with the manager of the operation or activity under review'.[50] Independent reports by EPAU include an evaluation of UNHCR's attempts to prevent and respond to sexual or gender based violence in situations of forced displacement,[51] and an investigation on the use of cash grants in voluntary repatriation.[52]

The most important central mechanism of internal oversight in the UN is the Office of Internal Oversight Services (OIOS) headed by an Under-Secretary General and established by General Assembly resolution 48/218B in 1994. In this resolution the General Assembly, having expressed its concern 'at the inadequate implementation of General Assembly mandates in some cases and the undertaking of non-mandated measures in other cases', decided to establish 'an additional independent entity ... to enhance oversight functions, in particular with regard to evaluation, audit, investigation and compliance'.[53] The Under-Secretary General who heads OIOS is appointed by the Secretary General subject to the approval of the General Assembly.

Since its inception, OIOS has conducted various investigations on allegations of corruption or mis-handling of funds. Although it is difficult to gauge the overall effectiveness of OIOS and assess the claim that it recuperates far more money than it spends for its activities,[54] it has had some impact on oversight within the UN leading to dismissals and even arrests of staff.[55] Partly as a result of the public attention

[47] *Ibid.* at 2. [48] *Ibid.* at 6. [49] *Ibid.* at 10. [50] *Ibid.* at 12.

[51] UNHCR Policy Development and Evaluation Service, 'Evaluation of UNHCR's Efforts to Prevent and Respond to Sexual and Gender-based Violence in Situations of Forced Displacement', 6 October 2008, PDES/2008/08.

[52] UNHCR Policy Development and Evaluation Service, 'The Use of Cash Grants in UNHCR Voluntary Repatriation Operations: Report of a "Lessons Learned" Workshop', 30 September 2008, PDES/2008/09.

[53] GA Res. 48/218B of 23 December 1993 at paras. I.A.1 and II.9.

[54] See the introductory page of OIOS' website at www.un.org/Depts/oios/pages/id.html.

[55] 'UN Rocked by Flood of Fraud Cases', *The Observer*, 3 September 2000. In the period from July 1999 to June 2000, '22 cases were recommended for criminal prosecution

that some of its reports have received, investigations of the OIOS have been followed by some reform, as was the case, for example, with the International Criminal Tribunal for Rwanda, severely criticised in one of OIOS's early reports.[56] In the audit sector, OIOS has achieved important results not only by conducting audits for some UN programmes and departments, but also by spearheading the establishment of resident and field audit units in peace operations.[57] OIOS, as an accountability mechanism, thus scores well on at least two fronts (impact on the future behaviour of the organisation and sanctions), but it still fails to offer a remedy to aggrieved persons, apart from a likely improvement in the future behaviour of the examined organisation/programme. Moreover, its approach to accountability is mainly premised on a notion of accountability that focuses on financial probity and proper management rather than a rights-based approach from the point of view of the beneficiaries.

Other central bodies with an oversight function are the Joint Inspection Unit and the UN Board of Auditors. Both were established by the General Assembly[58] and are responsible respectively for conducting investigations on the management of funds and on efficiency, and for auditing the accounts of the organisation.

Semi-judicial administrative processes

Ombudsmen and other semi- and quasi-judicial bodies to which individuals have access can be effective mechanisms of accountability. Unlike inspectors' offices, which are often located within the hierarchical structure of the institution,[59] ombudsmen are not normally staff members of international institutions, and can exercise independent and impartial oversight over their activities. Their semi-judicial nature also gives them power to indicate remedies for individuals,

by national law enforcement authorities' (UN OIOS, 'Report of the Office of Internal Oversight Services for the Period from July 1 1999 to June 30 2000', 2 October 2000, UN Doc. A/55/436 at para. 156).

[56] UN OIOS, 'Report of the Office of Internal Oversight Services on Audit and Investigation of the International Criminal Tribunal for Rwanda', 6 February 1997, UN Doc. A/51/789.

[57] OIOS Report, *supra* note 55.

[58] GA Res. 74 (I) of 7 December 1946. An External Board of Auditors was instituted later (GA Res. 1438 (XIV) of 5 December 1959). The Joint Inspection Unit was created by GA Res. 31/192 of 22 December 1976.

[59] For example, UNICEF's Inspector General is under the office of the Executive Director, and UNHCR's Inspector General under that of the High Commissioner.

which internal inspectors normally do not always possess, and can promote a rights-based approach to accountability questions rather than one restricted to financial accountability and accountability to donors.

The Inspection Panel of the World Bank is one of the first examples of such semi-judicial bodies. It was empowered to receive complaints from third parties, whether individuals or groups, affected by a project of the Bank.[60] By September 2010, the Panel had received sixty-nine requests for inspection. The Panel can determine if the Bank has complied with its policies and procedures in managing a particular project, but its reports, while public, are not binding on the Bank. The ability of the Panel to make findings of law is constrained not only by its membership – which does not include lawyers and makes it essentially a fact-finding body – but also by the requirement that the Panel seek the advice of the Bank's legal department.[61]

In part modelled on the experience of the World Bank, proposals to establish ombudsman offices with responsibility over a given area have been made in relation to sanctions, peacekeeping and humanitarian assistance.[62] In the area of peacekeeping these proposals gained momentum following the sex abuse scandals discussed in Chapter 5 (215ff.). Based on the recommendations of a report commissioned by the Secretary General in the aftermath of those scandals,[63] the

[60] Resolutions 93–10 of the International Bank for Reconstruction and Development.

[61] D. D. Bradlow, 'International Organizations and Private Complaints: The Case of the World Bank Inspection Panel', 34 Virg. J. Int.L. (1994) 553 at 594, and by the same author, 'Private Complaints and International Organisations: A Comparative Study of the Independent Inspection Mechanisms in International Financial Institutions', 36 *Georgetown Journal of International Law* (2005) 403. See also I. Shihata, *The World Bank Inspection Panel* (Oxford University Press, 1991).

[62] In the area of peacekeeping, this suggestion was made in the aftermath of the intervention in Somalia – see UN Department of Peacekeeping Operations, 'The Comprehensive Report on Lessons Learned from United Nations Operation in Somalia (UNOSOM), April 1992 – March 1995', March 1993, at para. 57, available at www.peacekeepingbestpractices.unlb.org/PBPS/Library/UNOSOM.pdf. As for the humanitarian ombudsman – see the following papers prepared for the Humanitarian Ombdusman Project: C. Beyani, 'The Legal Framework for an International Humanitarian Ombudsman', October 1999; R. Apthorpe and B. Mayhew, 'A Possible Model for a Humanitarian Ombudsman: Report on Action Research in Kosovo', September 1999. On sanctions see: M. Bothe, 'Security Council's Targeted Sanctions against Presumed Terrorists: The Need to Comply with Human Rights Standards', 6(3) *Journal of International Criminal Justice* (2008) 541.

[63] See General Assembly, 'A Comprehensive Strategy to Eliminate Future Sexual Exploitation and Abuse in United Nations Peacekeeping Operations', 24 March

Conduct and Discipline Team was established in the Department of Peacekeeping Operations. Renamed the Conduct and Discipline Unit (CDU) in 2007, it is responsible for overseeing the level of discipline in peacekeeping operations and in special political missions. Apart from providing high-level guidance by formulating policies, conducting training aimed at preventing sexual exploitation and abuse, as well as engaging in outreach initiatives, the CDU has also been tasked with handling individual allegations of misconduct. Conduct and Discipline Teams are also stationed at the field level to deal with allegations of misconduct by the UN personnel within their missions, as well as to provide the mission leadership with advice on all conduct and disciplinary matters. Confidential reporting mechanisms to encourage the submission of complaints by victims have also been established, most notably through the Sexual Exploitation and Abuse Victim Assistance Mechanism. Once an allegation is received, the OIOS can also investigate (lower priority allegations may be investigated by the Special Investigation Unit (SIU), military police, UN police and ad hoc panels), which may result in repatriation of the responsible military or police personnel concerned and their ban from future peacekeeping operations. But the most interesting practice in this field comes from the experience of international administrations. As discussed in Chapter 6 (244ff.), the web of institutions created in Bosnia under the Dayton Peace Agreement and those created in Kosovo in the aftermath of the 1999 NATO campaign include various human rights bodies and ombudsman offices.

An assessment

The overall performance of political and administrative mechanisms of accountability within the UN gives little cause for congratulation. With the few exceptions and qualifications considered above, the standard *modus operandi* of such mechanisms appears to reflect this sequence: a committee or commission of enquiry is (at times) established to examine a particular problem; a report is published and ceremoniously presented to the Security Council and the General

2005, UN Doc. A/59/710; General Assembly, 'Comprehensive Report Prepared Pursuant to GA Res. 59/296 on Sexual Exploitation and Sexual Abuse, Including Policy Development, Implementation and Full Justification of Proposed Capacity on Personnel Conduct Issues', 24 May 2006, UN Doc. A/60/862.

Assembly, which inexorably 'welcome' the findings of the report and invite the Secretary General to follow up; various committees, groups, and task forces are created to deal with the follow up and produce endless reports, feeding on each other's information; focal points and units (often endowed with a generous consultancy budget) are created at the field level to promote 'awareness' and report to the superiors. This system may have produced some positive results in some areas, but its overall efficacy is dismal. Suffice it to give once again the example of gender discrimination already discussed in Chapters 4 (169ff.) and 5 (215ff.). Notwithstanding the proliferation of gender awareness initiatives, the incidence of rape in the Kenyan refugee camps administered by UNHCR remained scandalously high and the policies adopted in response grotesquely ineffective. Furthermore, a treaty which endorsed discrimination against women was entered into by the UN in Afghanistan.

In order to enhance the effectiveness of their action, administrative and political organs ought to adopt measures that are not simply cosmetic. They should also have a clear mandate to enforce human rights and provide remedies for their violations. Measures should include, when necessary, disciplinary sanctions against staff and redress for victims. Moreover, these organs should enlarge their composition to include truly impartial experts.

The political organs should take on a proactive role. The Security Council, the General Assembly and the Economic and Social Council could make use of parliamentary committees as a model for monitoring the work of the subsidiary programmes on a regular basis. Another model for political control features, after all, in the Charter itself. The Trusteeship Council comprised various members, including a representative for each of the five permanent members of the Security Council, and had extensive powers to supervise the conduct of administering authorities in trust territories. Although the trusteeship system cannot apply to 'territories which have become members of the United Nations' (Article 78), it could still provide a model for the role that political organs ought to be expected to perform in similar circumstances. They have manifestly fallen short of performing anything close to that role. Other Charter-based bodies that could play a more proactive role in monitoring UN operations are the human rights bodies, whose involvement in these matters has so far been minimal.

Control by member states

Member states of an international organisation have a right to ensure that the organisation complies with its constituent instrument. Whether they also have an obligation to do so is a different matter. As discussed in Chapter 3 (130ff.), the International Law Commission rejected the argument that states should normally incur responsibility for the internationally wrongful acts of the international organisations of which they are members, limiting the scope of member state responsibility to very narrow circumstances. Nevertheless, the fact that the member states do not, as a rule, bear responsibility for the wrongful acts of the organisation does not entail that an obligation to ensure, as best as they can, that the organisation comply with its constituent instrument can never arise. On the contrary, even a general primary obligation in these terms could coexist with the principle of no automatic responsibility for member states. Arguably, such an obligation might already exist; at a minimum, acquiescence in a breach of the constituent instrument by the international organisation would contravene *pacta sunt servanda*, but a more positive duty of surveillance may derive from the general obligation to carry out the terms of the treaty in good faith.

Even if not devoid of an obligatory content, control and monitoring of the activities of international organisations by member states is part of good institutional governance. It should not be viewed as an optional element in a system of accountability, but as one of its essential components. The plenary organ of the Organisation – the General Assembly of the UN and variously named organs in the specialised agencies – represents one of the main fora where member states can exercise this function of oversight and control. Plenary organs are in principle endowed with large powers, especially – as is the case for the General Assembly – in the area of control and accountability, but whether they exercise them or not largely depends on the member states.

The executive organs of the specialised agencies and operational programmes exercise significant powers and play an important role in the formulation of the policy of the institution.[64] These organs

[64] For example, UNHCR has an Executive Committee (established under GA Res. 1166(XII) of 26 November 1957, whose membership has been enlarged to fifty-seven states to be elected by the Economic and Social Council (GA Res. 54/143 of 16 February 2000); UNICEF's Executive Board (GA Res. 57 (I) of 11 December 1946) has a membership of thirty-six states, also elected by the Economic and Social

have a more limited state membership, and normally meet only a few times a year. As is the case with the plenary organs, member states could, if they so wished, use the executive organs to monitor institutional performance and promote accountability. Such practice would be entirely consistent with the responsibilities of these organs, which in some cases have been established precisely to exercise oversight. For example, WFP's Executive Board has a duty of 'intergovernmental supervision and direction of the management', and an obligation to ensure that 'the activities and operational strategies are consistent with the overall policy guidance set forth by the General Assembly and the FAO Conference, as well as the Economic and Social Council and the Council of FAO'.[65]

Committees and commissions occasionally also offer member states an opportunity to exercise control and oversight. For the most part, these bodies comprise international civil servants rather than representatives of states, but there are exceptions. The FAO Constitution, for example, provides for the establishment of a number of committees to assist the FAO Council, and representatives of member states have usually sat on them.[66]

States can seek to make an international institution accountable by exercising diplomatic protection on behalf of citizens who claim to have been aggrieved by its conduct. The Articles on Diplomatic Protection of the International Law Commission have limited the definition of diplomatic protection to state-to-state relations, but Special Rapporteur Dugard acknowledged that broader definitions of diplomatic protection include actions of 'subjects of international law' in general,[67] the exercise of functional protection by international organisations on

Council. WFP's organ equivalent to UNICEF's Executive Board and UNHCR's Executive Committee was called Committee on Food Aid Policies and Programmes, it was renamed Executive Board in 1995 (GA Res. 50/8 of 1 November 1995). As for the specialised agencies, these organs are regulated by the constituent instrument: the ILO has a Governing Body (Art. 7, ILO Constitution), FAO has a Council with forty-nine member states (Art. 5, FAO Constitution), WHO has an Executive Board with thirty-two members (Art. 24, WHO Constitution).

65 Article 6, General Regulations of WFP as revised by GA Res. 50/8 of 1 November 1995.

66 Articles 5(6) and 6, FAO Constitution.

67 The Articles on Diplomatic Protection are at ILC Report (2008), UN Doc. A/61/10 at para. 49). See also J. Dugard, 'First Report on Diplomatic Protection by the Special Rapporteur', 52nd Session of the ILC (2000), UN Doc. A/CN.4/506 at paras. 36–38.

behalf of their employees as well as diplomatic action protection by states vis-à-vis an international organisation.

An important example of state practice in this area is the conclusion of the Settlement Agreement between the UN and Belgium for the claims brought by Belgian citizens against ONUC.[68] Belgian citizens had brought claims in Belgian courts with a view to making the UN jointly and severally liable with the Belgian state for damages to their property resulting from the UN intervention in Congo, but with no success.[69] With the settlement agreement Belgian citizens had access to some form of compensation. For Congolese citizens, who suffered the brunt of the conflict, no such fund was created, partly because of the failure of their authorities to advocate their case. The International Law Commission has recognised the right of states to exercise diplomatic protection in respect of refugees lawfully and habitually resident in the state (Article 8 of the Articles on Diplomatic Protection), but this, given the connivance of host states with the policy of encampment, is unlikely to become an effective route for improving the conduct of UNHCR.

There have been instances of member states suspending payments to the UN on the grounds of poor management and lack of accountability. In the 1980s and 1990s congressional leaders in the US made the payment of arrears dependent on reform of the UN system.[70] A compromise was reached in November 1999 which made the continued payment of the arrears dependent upon the UN satisfying certain 'reform criteria' over a period of five years. In particular, the UN agreed to carry out a 'system-wide structural reform, entailing a significant reduction in

[68] Exchange of Letters Constituting an Agreement Between the United Nations and Belgium Relating to the Settlement of Claims Filed Against the United Nations in the Congo by Belgian Nationals, 20 February 1965, *UN Juridical Yearbook* (1965) 39. Similar agreements were concluded with other third party states, such as Italy (18 January 1967, 588 UNTS 197), Greece (20 June 1966, 563 UNTS 3) and Switzerland (3 June 1966, 564 UNTS 193). In 1996, Bosnia Herzegovina submitted a request for compensation for damages allegedly caused by the UN during its operations in its territory (D. Shraga, 'UN Peacekeeping Operations: Applicability of International Humanitarian Law and Responsibility for Operations-Related Damage', 94 *AJIL* (2000) 406 at 410, note 24).

[69] *Manderlier v. Organisation des Nations Unies and Etat Belge* (1969) 45 ILR 446.

[70] S. D. Murphy, 'Contemporary Practice of the United States Relating to International Law', 94 AJIL (2000) 348 at 349; J. E. Alvarez, 'Legal Remedies and the United Nations *á la Carte* Problem', 12 Mich. J. Int. L. (1991) 229; R. W. Nelson and M. A. Roy, 'International Law and the US Withholding of payments to International Organizations', 80 AJIL (1986) 973.

staff, that would eliminate all outdated activities and program duplication and would encompass all relevant United Nations specialized agencies', to open the programmes, offices and activities of the UN 'to auditing by the national auditing and inspecting agencies of its member states' and to 'securing adequate funding for the Office of Internal Oversight'.[71]

The events of 11 September 2001 spurred the US to pay its arrears and lift congress-imposed caps on peacekeeping dues.[72] However, in 2005, Congress again voted to prevent payment of UN dues,[73] unless the UN implemented, within two years, more than thirty-two of thirty-nine requested reforms.[74] The reforms included the call for increased accountability, particularly through the creation of an independent oversight body.[75] The act was placed on the Senate agenda, but never considered by it and lapsed.[76] Importantly, as a matter of state practice, the Administration did not support the Act, as explained by its Ambassador to the UN.[77] It should be noted, however, that this opposition did not necessarily hinge on a view that the US was obligated by international law to pay its dues, but rather on domestic issues regarding the appropriate power of Congress versus the President over foreign affairs. As Murphy has argued, 'it is worth noting how little effort the United States has made to defend or even consider the international legality of its withholding'.[78] Efforts by the elected representatives of the US to reform the UN through withholding of dues continued: in January 2008, the United Nations Transparency, Accountability, and Reform Bill was referred to the House Committee on Foreign Affairs.[79]

[71] Section 2(2)(A) and (E), United Nations Reform Act of 1999.

[72] J. F. Murphy, *The United States and the Rule of Law in International Affairs* (Cambridge University Press, 2004) 129 and B. A. Schnoor, 'International Law, the Power of the Purse, and Speaking with One Voice: The Legal Cacophony Created by Withholding U.S. Dues from the United Nations', 92 *Iowa Law Review* (2007) 1133 at 1144.

[73] Henry J. Hyde United Nations Reform Act of 2005, H.R. 2745, 109th Cong. (2005).

[74] *Ibid*. s. 601(b)(1). [75] *Ibid*. s. 104. [76] Schnoor, *supra* note 72 at 1158.

[77] *Ibid*. at 1159.

[78] Murphy, *supra* note 72 at 130; see also at 132.

[79] United Nations Transparency, Accountability, and Reform Act of 2009 H.R. 557, 111th Cong (2009). See also the Act to prohibit United States contributions to the United Nations for the purpose of paying or reimbursing the legal expenses of United Nations Officers or Employees charged with malfeasance, and for other purposes H.R. 1072 (referred to House Committee on Foreign Relations on 13 February 2009).

The US was not the only state in arrears with its payments to the UN. In 2000, for example, one out of four member states were either unwilling or unable to pay their dues. Notwithstanding this state practice,[80] Article 17 of the Charter unequivocally obliges states to bear the expenses of the Organisation 'as apportioned by the General Assembly'. In terms of Article 19 a state that is in arrears with payments risks losing its voting rights in the General Assembly. An exception may be made when 'failure to pay is due to conditions beyond the control of the Member', which seems to apply only to cases of extreme financial hardship in which a non-compliant state could still be allowed to retain its voting rights. Besides these cases, it has been persuasively argued that 'Member States retain the right to resist assessed contributions when they have a *bona fide* claim that the act or the operation to be financed entails a violation of the Charter or of international law'.[81] In this case, member states would violate a provision of the Charter – the obligation to contribute to the expenses of the Organisation – in order to ensure respect for other Charter provisions or principles of international law and thus avoid becoming accessories in their violation. The state that refuses to contribute to the expenses in order to uphold the Charter is, however, in a different position from the state that refuses to make contributions on more generic grounds of policy or management. Even if the state in question were able to show that the UN breached a rule of international law outside the Charter and that it is injured by such a breach, the suspension of payments would not be available to it as a countermeasure because of the limits set by Article 51 of the Draft Articles on the Responsibility of International Organisations: injured states which are members of the organisation may not take countermeasures against it if the countermeasures are inconsistent with the rules of the organisation and if no other appropriate means for inducing compliance exists.

Were the practice of withholding payments accepted as a way for member states to pursue a generic agenda of institutional reform, the

[80] 'Surprising News on UN Dues', *The Forward*, available at www.unwatch.org/site/c.bdKKISNqEmG/b.1289203/apps/s/content.asp?ct=1715095. See also H. G. Schermers and N. M. Blokker, *International Institutional Law* (4th edn., Dordrecht: Martinus Nijhoff, 2003) 645–9.

[81] See: F. Francioni, 'Multilateralism á la Carte: The Limits to Unilateral Withholdings of Assessed Contributions to the UN Budget', 11 EJIL (2000) 43 at 58; J. E. Alvarez, 'Financial Responsibility', in C. C. Joyner (ed.), *The United Nations and International Law* (Cambridge University Press, 1997) 409 at 424.

main contributing states would be in a position effectively to blackmail the institution, a power that the Charter does not accord to any state, and which would constitute a derogation from the principle of sovereign equality of states. Nevertheless, Article 19 only applies to the financial contributions that are made to meet 'the expenses of the Organisation' (Article 17).[82] It does not cover the system of voluntary contributions on which the semi-autonomous agencies and the specialised agencies alike rely for much of their work.[83] Within these institutions, donor states can use their contributions to influence operational activities, and to promote greater accountability.

The interest taken by national parliaments in international organisations is to be welcome; as is – within some limits – their readiness to exercise scrutiny. The latest treaty reform of the EU is important in this respect, as it assigned a greater control and oversight role to national parliaments under the title of provisions on democratic principles.[84]

Interesting state practice on organisations other than the EU emanates from the Select Committee on International Development of the House of Commons. The Committee examined the institutional performance of UNHCR and of the UN Office for the Co-ordination of Humanitarian Affairs (OCHA) in the emergencies in Kosovo (1999) and Mozambique (1999–2000), crises in which the UK government had a significant stake having committed funds and resources.[85] In addition, in one of its reports, the Committee addressed the questions of democracy and transparency within the World Trade Organisation.[86] Quite

[82] In *Certain Expenses*, the ICJ clarified that the locution 'expenses of the Organisation' does not refer only to the regular expenses and includes expenses for operations for the maintenance of peace decided by the General Assembly (*Certain Expenses of the UN*, Advisory Opinion, ICJ Reports (1962) 151).

[83] For example, on UNHCR, see R. Väyrynen, 'The Dilemma of Voluntary Funding: Political Interests and Institutional Reforms', Paper presented at the International Conference 'Commemorating UNHCR at 50: Past, Present and Future of Refugee Assistance' (New York: Columbia University, 16–18 May 2000).

[84] Article 12, Consolidated Version of the Treaty of the European Union and Protocol (No. 1) on the Role of National Parliaments in the European Union.

[85] International Development Committee (House of Commons), 'Kosovo: The Humanitarian Crisis', 15 May 1999, Third Report – Session 1998–99 (HC 422); International Development Committee (House of Commons), 'Mozambique: Report and Proceedings of the Committee, Minutes of Evidence and Appendices', 3 May 2000, Fifth Report – Session 1999–00 (HC 326).

[86] International Development Committee (House of Commons), 'After Seattle – The World Trade Organisation and Developing Countries', 29 November 2000, Tenth Report – Session 1999–00 (HC 227).

importantly, in the data collection phase, the Committee heard evidence from officials working for the UN and the World Bank, including the heads of UNICEF, UNDP and the World Bank. By the beginning of 2001, the Select Committee could list 'scrutiny into multilateral development agencies' as part of its regular work and explain that '[n]ot only is this the first time that a Committee of this House has considered in such detail the work of these multilateral development agencies, it has also become clear that these bodies are unused to such scrutiny from national parliaments'.[87] Two recent investigations and reports in 2008 have scrutinised the work of the World Bank and the World Food Programme (WFP). The investigation into the WFP, like that into the World Bank, was spurred by the Committee's broader investigations into the relationship between the UK's Department for International Development (DFID) and multilateral agencies.[88] These reports contain important and generally constructive critiques of the UN system.[89]

This practice is not limited to the UK. In the US, for example, the House of Representatives Committee on Foreign Affairs affirms that '[t]he Committee will review all aspects of U.S. funding of and participation in international organizations and assess the extent to which the United Nations is fulfilling its role ... the Committee will conduct thorough, ongoing oversight of UN management ... In addition, the Committee will examine implementation of UN reform legislation, progress of additional international organization reform efforts, and oversight of the effectiveness of the promotion and protection of human rights within the United Nations system.'[90] Despite this broad mission statement, however, the Subcommittee on

[87] International Development Committee (House of Commons), 'First Special Report', 24 January 2001 (HC 82).

[88] International Development Committee (House of Commons), 'The World Food Programme and Global Food Security', 15 July 2008, Tenth Report – Session 2007–08 – Volume I: Report, together with formal minutes (HC 493-I) at 5.

[89] *Ibid.* at 22 and at 35–8. See also International Development Committee (House of Commons), 'DFID and the World Bank', 5 March 2008, Sixth Report – Session 2007–08 – Volume I: Report, together with formal minutes (HC 67–1) at 3. See also at 25–32 on reform measures for accountability and governance.

[90] United States House of Representatives Committee on Foreign Affairs, Committee Oversight Plan, International Security/UN/Peacekeeping/General for the 111th congress (28 January 2009), available at www.internationalrelations.house.gov/about.asp?sec=oversight.

International Organizations, Human Rights and Oversight appears to focus most consistently on US foreign policy. Nevertheless, the Subcommittee makes a practice of conducting hearings as part of its oversight function, and has also heard evidence from heads and high-ranking officials[91] of UN agencies, although not always with a view of assessing their performance but as part to fact-finding on regional conflicts.

Scrutiny by national parliaments over the work of the UN is likely to intensify in the future both because of public pressure on governments to account for taxpayers' money spent through international institutions and because of disenchantment with the UN. The idea of UN officials appearing before parliamentary committees and commissions may generate images of international civil servants 'bullied' by national politicians eager to score points in front of their audiences. However, given that powerful states already attempt to influence the work of international institutions behind the scenes, parliamentary control at least offers the benefit of being public and adversarial in nature. One problem is rather that current practice is essentially limited to UN officials appearing before the parliaments of influential states - and important donors - like the US and the UK. There is no reason, however, why this good practice should not be extended to the national parliaments of the countries where a given operation takes place.

Judicial control

International courts should constitute the avenue of choice for ensuring the compliance of international institutions with international law and for promoting their accountability. Yet, the role of the international judiciary in this area is marginal, and will remain so until the jurisdiction of these courts is expanded to include claims brought against international organisations by states or by individuals.

[91] For example, the Assistant Secretary General for Peacekeeping Operations, UN, was interviewed in a hearing on 'United Nations Peacekeeping Operations: An Underfunded International Mandate - the Role of the United States' (2 April 2008, Serial No. 110-161). The transcript of this interview is available at www.internationalrelations.house.gov/hearing_notice.asp?id=963.

The only international judicial body that has been granted extensive powers to review the legality of legislative and administrative acts of organs of an international organisation is the Court of Justice of the European Union.[92] In terms of Article 263 of the Treaty on the Functioning of the European Union (ex Article 230 of the EC Treaty), actions for annulment can be brought on grounds of lack of competence, infringement of an essential procedural requirement, infringement of the Treaties or of any rule of law relating to their application, or misuse of powers. Breach of fundamental rights does not feature among these grounds, but the European Court of Justice has sought to remedy this omission by making 'the material provisions of the European Convention *de facto* binding on the Community' at least since the *Stauder* case.[93] Natural and legal persons have standing to institute annulment proceedings subject to their being able to show that the act is addressed to them or of direct and individual concern to them, or, if the act is regulatory, that it is of direct concern to them and does not entail implementing measures.

National supreme and international human rights courts have dealt with cases raising issues of international institutional accountability. Their review of the conduct of international organisations is, almost without exception, indirect. Indeed, immunity for national courts and jurisdiction *ratione personae* for international human rights courts preclude direct review in virtually all cases. Nevertheless, the body of domestic and human rights case law in which some measure of indirect review was undertaken is significant.

The analysis that follows does not purport to offer a comprehensive survey of the national and international jurisprudence on international organisations. Others have undertaken such a task.[94] It will rather focus on three critical issues that shape the engagement of courts, national and international, with issues of UN compliance with human rights law: the reviewability of the acts of the Security Council

[92] Articles 263–6, Consolidated version of the Treaty on the Functioning of the European Union (pre-Lisbon these were Arts. 230–3 of the EC Treaty). See A. Albros-Llorens, *Private Parties in European Community Law: Challenging Community Measures* (Oxford: Clarendon Press, 1996).

[93] P. Alston and J. Weiler, 'An Ever-Closer Union in Need of a Human Rights Policy', 9 EJIL (1998) 658 at 700 and Case 29/269, *Stauder* [1969] ECR 419.

[94] See, in particular, A. Reinisch, *International Organizations Before National Courts* (Cambridge University Press, 2000) and K. Wellens, *Remedies Against International Organisations* (Cambridge University Press, 2002).

and the effect of Article 103 of the Charter; the question of immunity; and the doctrine of equivalent protection.

The review of the acts of the Security Council

The question of the reviewability of the acts of the Security Council has arisen in cases before international and domestic courts. Quite aside from reviewability is the question of the effect of Article 103 of the Charter which, as is well known, provides that, in the event of a conflict between obligations under the Charter and obligations under any other international agreement, the former prevail. When combined with Article 25 of the Charter, which obliges member states to accept and carry out the decisions of the Security Council, it has been argued that Article 103 obliges member states to give effect to certain decisions of the Security Council notwithstanding conflict with other rules of international or even, according to some, constitutional law.

The reviewability of the acts of the Security Council by the International Court of Justice attracted considerable attention in the context of the *Lockerbie* case.[95] As a general rule, the Court has affirmed that it does not have unlimited powers of judicial review of the resolutions of the Security Council,[96] but has also asserted that it is not hierarchically inferior to the Security Council and is not precluded from adjudicating

[95] See: *Questions of Interpretation and Application of the 1971 Montreal Convention Arising from the Aerial Incident at Lockerbie (Libyan Arab Jamahiriya v. United Kingdom)*, Judgment (Preliminary Objections), ICJ Report (1998) 9 (a substantially identical judgment was delivered in the homonymous case between Libya and the US, ICJ Report (1998) 115. See also the Order of 14 April 1992, ICJ Reports (1992) 3.

Secondary literature on this topic is vast. The main contributions relied upon here include: J. E. Alvarez, 'Judging the Security Council', 90 AJIL (1996) 1; T. M. Franck, 'The "Powers of Appreciation": Who Is the Ultimate Guardian of UN Legality?' 86 AJIL (1992) 519; V. Gowlland-Debbas, 'The Relationship Between the International Court of Justice and the Security Council in the Light of the Lockerbie Case', 88 AJIL (1994) 643; B. Martenczuk, 'The Security Council, the International Court and Judicial Review: What Lessons from Lockerbie', 10 EJIL (1999) 517; N. White, 'To Review or not to Review? The Lockerbie Cases before the World Court', 12 *Leiden J. Int. L.* (1999) 401.

[96] *Legal Consequences for States of the Continued Presence of South Africa in Namibia (South West Africa) notwithstanding Security Council Resolution 276 (1970)*, Advisory Opinion, ICJ Reports (1971) 16 at 45. See also *Lockerbie* Order *supra* note 95 diss. op. of Judge Weearamanthry at 50. Judge El-Kosheri, however, dissenting from the majority, found that SC Res. 748 (1992) of 31 March 1992 was ultra vires (*Lockerbie* Order, diss. op. of Judge El-Kosheri, *supra* note 95 at 105 ff.).

on matters which form the object of resolutions of the Council.[97] The possibility of a conflict between resolutions of the Security Council and obligations arising under human rights law was briefly touched upon in the Bosnia case. In his separate opinion, Judge Lauterpacht wrote that the arms embargo imposed on Bosnia by the Security Council could make members of the UN 'accessories to genocide'.[98]

The Charter did not intend to create a Security Council that is above any law. As the Appeals Chamber of the International Criminal Tribunal for the Former Yugoslavia put it in the *Tadic* case, 'neither the text nor the spirit of the Charter conceives the Security Council as *legibus solutus*'.[99] After conferring 'primary responsibility for the maintenance of international peace and security' (Article 24(1)) – thereby making the Council the most powerful UN organ – the Charter provides that in the discharge of its duties the Council 'shall act in accordance with the Principles and Purposes of the United Nations' (Article 24(2)).[100] The Charter does not contain a similar provision for the General Assembly, and it is reasonable to conclude that the specific mention of the duties of the Council is not casual, especially since it comes immediately before the provision that obliges member states 'to accept and carry out the decisions of the Security Council' (Article 25).

The conferral on the Security Council of wide powers was thus balanced with its express subjection to the principles of international law. It is not correct, however, to infer from the Article 24(2) qualification that the ICJ has unfettered powers of judicial review.[101] Indeed, it is difficult to believe that such a radical power could have been merely implied in the Charter or in the Statute of the Court.

[97] This is well-established, e.g.: *United States Diplomatic and Consular Staff in Tehran (United States v. Iran)*, Judgment, ICJ Reports (1980) 3; *Military and Paramilitary Activities in and Against Nicaragua (Nicaragua v. United States)*, Judgment (Jurisdiction and Admissibility), ICJ Reports (1984) 391 esp. at 432; *Application of the Convention on the Prevention and Punishment of the Crime of Genocide (Bosnia and Herzegovina v. Yugoslavia)*, Judgment (Preliminary Objections), ICJ Reports (1996) 595. See also *Prosecutor v. Tadic* (IT-94-1), Decision on the Defence Motion for Interlocutory Appeal on Jurisdiction (Appeals Chamber) at paras. 23–5.

[98] Bosnia Order, *Application of the Convention on the Prevention and Punishment of the Crime of Genocide (Bosnia and Herzegovina v. Yugoslavia)*, Order of 8 April 1993, ICJ Reports (1993) 325 at 441.

[99] In the *Tadic* case, *supra* note 97 at 28.

[100] On Art. 24 see Judge Lauterpacht's separate opinion in the Bosnia Order, *supra* note 98 at para. 101.

[101] According to Judge Schwebel, Art. 24(2) cannot imply the conferral of a power of judicial review on the ICJ, and 'the subjection of the acts' of the Security Council to

Approaching this question from a policy angle does not lead to a clear answer. The argument that it would strengthen the rule of law and erode the sphere of self-interested political decisions fails to take into account unintended consequences. Indeed, the success of the Security Council in the most difficult task with which it is entrusted, the maintenance of peace and security, hinges upon the fact that it reflects the balance of power among states. A Security Council whose resolutions were subjected to judicial review by an international judicial organ could gain in legitimacy, but judicial review might also act as an incentive for states to revert to unilateralism. Both the fear that a judgment of the ICJ declaring the illegality of an act of the Security Council might undermine the system of collective security and the consideration of the impact that such a hypothetical ruling would have on future UN action were prominent in *Lockerbie*.[102]

The ICJ can review the legality of institutional acts when it is expressly requested to do so by the organ from which the act in question emanated, provided that the organ has the capacity to request an advisory opinion. When the Assembly of the Inter-governmental Maritime Consultative Organisation (IMCO) requested an opinion from the ICJ on the validity of the constitution of the Maritime Safety Committee, the Court held that, by excluding Liberia and Panama from the Maritime Safety Committee, the Assembly had violated the provision in its constitutive Statute that prescribed that the eight countries with the largest commercial fleet be represented in the Committee.[103] The Court did not indicate what the consequences of the invalid constitution of the Committee ought to be.[104] The IMCO Assembly decided to reconstitute the Committee without declaring the nullity of the acts of the irregularly constituted Committee.

The key differences between *Lockerbie* and the *Maritime Safety Committee* are that in *Lockerbie* the Court's judicial review would have

the law 'relies not upon judicial review, but on self-censorship' (*Lockerbie* Judgment, *supra* note 95 diss. op. of Judge Schwebel 64 at 76).

102 See *Lockerbie* Order, *supra* note 95, diss. op. of Judge Bedjaoui at para. 7, and sep. op. of Judge Lachs; and *Lockerbie* Judgment, *supra* note 95, diss. op. of Judge Jennings 99 at 113). See also *Aegean Sea Continental Shelf (Greece v. Turkey)*, Judgment, ICJ Reports (1976) 3 at 33 (sep. op. of Judge Tarazi): 'The Court, if the circumstances so require, ought to collaborate in the accomplishment of this fundamental mission' of the Security Council in the maintenance of world peace and security.

103 *Constitution of the Maritime Safety Committee of the Intergovernmental Maritime Consultative Organisation*, Advisory Opinion, ICJ Report (1960) 150.

104 As a general rule courts pronounce on the *thema decidendum* that has been brought to them by the parties (*ne eat judex extra petita partium*).

been incidental to the resolution of an inter-state dispute, and that the Security Council had not expressed an intention to subject the legality of its acts to the jurisdiction of the Court. On these bases, it is difficult to see how the advisory opinion in the *Maritime Safety Committee* case can have any precedential value for the question of the review of acts of the Security Council. But various authors insist that the Court has powers of incidental judicial review,[105] suggesting that, as in the decision in *Maritime Safety Committee*, this power could be attenuated by excluding the nullity *ab initio* of the ultra vires act.[106]

Of greater relevance to the powers of review of the ICJ than the *Maritime Safety Committee* are cases where, as observed by August Reinisch, the Court has already affirmed the lawfulness of acts of organs of the UN – a finding that is premised on reviewability.[107] In at least one instance, the advisory opinion on the *Legality of Nuclear Weapons (WHO request)*,[108] the Court found that the act of an organ of an international organisation was ultra vires. These precedents may be invoked to justify the reviewability of some resolutions of the Security Council, but it is more difficult to rely on them persuasively to argue in favour of the reviewability of resolutions in the area of peace and security and, especially, of decisions under Chapter VII.

Given this complex and problematic debate on judicial review of Security Council acts by the ICJ, Alvarez is right in observing that 'it is ironic that the first international judicial body actually to do so [to review the legality of an act of the Security Council], in a binding context, is an *ad hoc* war crimes tribunal established by the Council itself'.[109] In the early stages of the proceedings of the *Tadic* case, the defendant challenged, inter alia, the legality of the establishment of the International Criminal Tribunal for the Former Yugoslavia by the Security Council. The Trial Chamber stated that 'it is not for this Chamber to judge the reasonableness of the acts of the Security Council', but then appeared to contradict this statement when it added

105 For example, Martenczuk, *supra* note 95 at 525–8; Gowlland-Debbas, *supra* note 95 at 670–1; E. Lauterpacht, 'The Legal Effect of Illegal Acts of International Organisations', in R. Y. Jennings (ed.), *Cambridge Essays in International Law: Essays in Honour of Lord McNair* (London: Stevens, 1965) 88 at 95–6 (and see Judge Lauterpacht's sep. op. in the Bosnia case, *supra* note 100).

106 Gowlland-Debbas, *supra* note 95 at 673.

107 A. Reinisch, 'Should Judges Second-Guess the UN Security Council?', 6 *International Organisations Law Review* (2009) 257 at 259.

108 'Legality of the Use by a State of Nuclear Weapons in Armed Conflict' (World Health Organization Request), Advisory Opinion, ICJ Reports (1996) 66.

109 J. E. Alvarez, 'Nuremberg Re-visited: The *Tadic* Case', 7 EJIL (1996) 245 at 249.

that 'it is without doubt that, with respect to the Former Yugoslavia, the Security Council did not act arbitrarily'.[110] The Trial Chamber proceeded to examine in some detail the arguments on the unlawfulness of the Tribunal that the defence had submitted. The Appeals Chamber also concluded that the Tribunal had been properly established, and contained an even more detailed refutation of these arguments. The Appeals Chamber reasoned that 'a narrow concept may, perhaps, be warranted in a national context but not in international law', which 'lacks a centralized structure' and 'does not provide for an integrated judicial system operating an orderly division of labour among a number of tribunals, where certain aspects or components of jurisdiction as a power could be centralized or vested in one of them but not the others'; as a result, 'in international law, every tribunal is a self-contained system'.[111] Persuasive as these arguments might be, the self-validation of the Tribunal remains problematic especially given that, once it had decided to pronounce on the matter, its conclusion was foregone. It might have been more appropriate for the Tribunal to dismiss this part of the motion.[112]

The question of the reviewability of acts of the Security Council has moved to the regional and domestic terrain, and was at the heart of the *Kadi* litigation.[113] The European Court of First Instance reached the improbable conclusion that, while the resolutions of the Security Council fell outside the ambit of its judicial review, it was empowered to check their lawfulness with regard to *jus cogens*.[114] The ECJ, instead, held that it could review 'the Community act intended to give effect to the international agreement at issue', thus essentially accepting that there was no bar to indirect review.[115]

The other critical question in the *Kadi* cases was the effect of Articles 25 and 103 of the Charter. The Court of First Instance accepted the

110 *Prosecutor v. Tadic* (IT-94-1), Decision on the Defence Motion on Jurisdiction (Trial Chamber) at para. 16.

111 *Tadic* (Appeals Chamber), *supra* note 97 at para. 11.

112 This was Judge Li's position. *Ibid.*, sep. op. of Judge Li at paras. 2–4.

113 Case T-306/01, *Yassin Abdullah Kadi v. Council of the European Union and Commission of the European Communities*, Judgment of the Court of First Instance and Case T-306/01, *Yusuf and Al Barakaat International Foundation v. Council and Commission*, Judgment of the Court of First Instance; Joined Cases C-402/05 P & C-415/05, *Yassin Abdullah Kadi and Al Barakaat International Foundation v. Council of the European Union and Commission of the European Communities*, Judgment of the European Court of Justice. See Chapter 7 (315ff.) and below in this chapter at 372ff.

114 CFI decision at paras. 225–6 in *Kadi* (and paras. 276–7 in *Yusuf*).

115 ECJ decision at para. 286.

primacy of these provisions of the Charter, holding that 'Member States may, and indeed must, leave unapplied any provision of Community law, whether a provision of primary law or a general principle of that law, that raises any impediment to the proper performance of their obligations under the Charter of the United Nations'.[116] By contrast, the ECJ studiously avoided tackling this question too directly.

But the most unambiguous acceptance of the principle of international and constitutional primacy of obligations arising under Articles 25 and 103 of the Charter is found in the jurisprudence of the English House of Lords and its successor, the UK Supreme Court. In the *Al-Jedda* case, concerning the compatibility of detention without trial by British forces in Iraq with Article 5(1) of the ECHR, the House of Lords concluded that the detention of the appellant was attributable to the UK and that, although it was prima facie in breach of his rights under Article 5(1) of the ECHR, the effect of Security Council resolution 1546 (2004) and Article 103 of the Charter was to empower the UK to exercise, in certain exceptional circumstances, a power of detention in breach of that right *lawfully*.[117] Lord Bingham sought to alleviate the consequences of this finding by explaining that the clash between the power to detain on the express authority of the Security Council, on the one hand, and Article 5 of the ECHR, on the other, could be reconciled as long as the UK ensures that 'the detainee's rights under article 5 are not infringed to any greater extent than is inherent in such detention'.[118] But, despite this qualification, the principle of supremacy of the decisions of the Security Council was accepted in this case and upheld by the Supreme Court in *Jabar Ahmed and others*.[119] Article 103 will require further consideration in the discussion of the doctrine of equivalent protection below.

116 CFI decision para. 190 in *Kadi* (and para. 240 in *Yusuf*).

117 *R. (Al-Jedda) v. Secretary of State for Defence* [2008] 1 AC 332 at para. 39 (*per* Lord Bingham). See F. Messineo, 'The House of Lords in *Al-Jedda* and Public International Law: Attribution of Conduct to UN-Authorised Forces and the Power of the Security Council to Displace Human Rights', LVI *Netherlands International Law Review* (2009) 35 and A. Perreau-Saussine, *British Acts of State in English Courts*, 78 BYBIL (2008) 179, at 214–18.

118 *Ibid., Al-Jedda*. As pointed out by Milanović (Marko Milanović, 'Norm Conflict in International Law: Whither Human Rights?', 20 *Duke Journal of Comparative and International Law* (2009) 69, the speeches of Lady Hale and Lord Carswell contain similar qualifications (respectively at para. 126, and at paras. 130 and 136).

119 This decision arose from different appeals: *Her Majesty's Treasury v. Mohammed Jabar Ahmed and others, Her Majesty's Treasury v. Mohammed al-Ghabra, R (on the application of Hani El Sayed Sabaei Youssef) v. Her Majesty's Treasury* [2010] UKSC 2. See Chapter 7 (315ff.) and below in this chapter 372ff.

The problem of immunity

The main obstacle to the promotion of the accountability of the UN and other international organisations through national courts is the law of immunity. Clearly, immunity 'does not free the organization from any obligation', but it 'may frustrate the enforcement of the law'.[120]

The wording of Article 105 of the UN Charter supports the functional approach to the immunity of the UN and its officials. In terms of Article 105, the privileges and immunities of the UN are those 'necessary for the fulfilment of its purposes'; the privileges and immunities of its officials are those that 'are necessary for the independent exercise of their functions in connection with the Organisation'.[121] But this qualification appears only in the preamble of the General Convention on Privileges and Immunities of the UN.[122] Section 2 of that Convention provides that the UN, its property and assets 'shall enjoy immunity from every form of legal process except insofar as in any particular case it has expressly waived its immunity. It is, however, understood that no waiver of immunity shall extend to any measure of execution'. The General Convention thus signalled a shift to absolute immunity.

In addition to the Organisation's immunity, personal immunity is conferred on three categories of individuals connected with the Organisation: representatives of member states, officials of the UN and experts on missions. In particular, under the General Convention, UN officials are 'immune from legal process in respect of words spoken or written and all acts performed by them in their official capacity' (Section 18). This immunity is, however, subject to an important qualification. Section 20 provides that '[p]rivileges and immunities are granted to officials in the interests of the United Nations and not for the personal benefit of the individuals themselves. The Secretary General shall have the right and the duty to waive the immunity of any official in any case where, in his opinion, the immunity would

120 Schermers and Blokker, *supra* note 80 at 1026.

121 The functional approach is adopted in the constituent instruments of other international organisations as well, see Reinisch *supra* note 94 at 140 and fn. 542.

122 UN Convention on the Privileges and Immunities of the United Nations (1946) 1 UNTS 15 and *corrigendum* 90 UNTS 327. See also UN Convention on the Privileges and Immunities of the Specialised Agencies (1947) 33 UNTS 261, which contains broadly similar provisions. See A. J. Miller, 'Privileges and Immunities of United Nations Officials', 4 *International Organisations Law Review* (2007) 169 and, by the same author, 'The Privileges and Immunities of the United Nations', 6 *International Organisations Law Review* (2009) 7.

impede the course of justice and can be waived without prejudice to the interests of the United Nations'. The power to waive the immunity is vested in the Secretary General, whereas 'executive directors of semi-independent programmes have no such power'.[123] The power to waive the immunity of the Secretary General himself rests with the Security Council.

The general view has been for a long time that courts generally uphold the principle that 'under the [UN] Convention the United Nations' immunity is absolute, subject only to the organization's express waiver thereof in particular cases', and that, as a result, the distinction between *acta jure gestionis* and *acta jure imperii* does not apply to the immunities of international organisations.[124] However, the comprehensive review of judicial practice undertaken by Reinisch suggests that 'national courts, on the whole, do not appear to be convinced that international organisations should enjoy absolute immunity from suit',[125] although techniques for restricting immunity developed by domestic courts have often lacked cogency. In particular, the Italian Court of Cassation has maintained that the application of the doctrine of restrictive immunity should be extended to international organisations, and that, as a result, they should not enjoy immunity for acts *jure gestionis*.[126] In the US courts have often been careful not to exclude, as a matter of principle, the applicability of restrictive immunity to international organisations,[127] and there have been pronouncements contrary to the prevailing trend which favour absolute immunity. For

[123] *UN Juridical Yearbook* (1969) 225.

[124] For example, *Boimah v. UN General Assembly*, 664 F. Supp. 69 at 71; *Ashkir et al. v. United Nations*, Civ. No. 97-2266 (TFH).

[125] Reinisch, *supra* note 94 at 391.

[126] *Food and Agricultural Organisation v. Istituto Nazionale di Previdenza per i Dirigenti d' Azienda Industriali (INPDAI)*, Corte di Cassazione, Case No. 5399 (1982), 87 ILR 1, (1982) *United Nations Juridical Yearbook* 234, but in *FAO v. Colagrossi* 101 ILR 386, the Court of Cassation appears to have departed from its own precedents. On the dispute between FAO and Italy, see Reinisch, *supra* note 94 at 131–4. Morgenstern sees the Italian reservation to the General Convention as the starting point of the dispute (F. Morgenstern, *Legal Problems of International Organizations* (Cambridge: Grotius, 1986) 6 ff.).

[127] See *Askir v. Boutros Ghali et al.*, 933 F. Supp. 368, in which the District Court for the Southern District of New York did not find it necessary to pronounce in favour of absolute or restrictive immunity 'because even if the more limited restrictive immunity doctrine applied, the claims in this case do not arise out of commercial activity by the United Nations'. See also *De Luca v. UN*, 841 F. Supp. 531; *Boimah*, *supra* note 124.

example, a court in New York held that a driver employed by the UN who had exceeded the speed limit was not entitled to immunity because 'to recognize the existence of a general and unrestricted immunity from suit or prosecution on the part of the personnel of the United Nations ... even though the individual's function has no relation to the importance or the success of the Organization's deliberations, is carrying the principle of immunity completely out of bounds'.[128]

The judge added:

> 'To establish such a principle would in effect create a large preferred class within our borders who would be immune to punishment on identical facts for which the average American would be subject to punishment. Any such theory does violence to and is repugnant to the American sense of fairness and justice and flouts the very basic principle of the United Nations itself, which in its preamble to its Charter affirms that it is created to give substance to the principle that the rights of all men and women are equal.'[129]

In another case, originating from a lawsuit brought by a private company against the Organisation of American States, the distinction between *acta jure gestionis* and *acta jure imperii* was applied by a US Court.[130]

In the US, the argument for restrictive immunity gains some traction from the terms of the immunity statutes. Under the International Organizations Immunities Act, international organisations are granted 'the same immunity from suit and every form of judicial process as is enjoyed by foreign governments',[131] and it could thus be argued that the exceptions under the Foreign Sovereign Immunities Act to the general jurisdictional immunity of foreign states ought to apply to international organisations too.[132] However, as observed by Reinisch, US courts 'have been very careful to avoid deciding' the question of the 'same immunity ... as foreign governments' qualification in the Act.[133]

In some cases the plea of immunity was rejected because it fell outside the scope of the General Convention. For example, in *Kadic v. Karadic*, the defendant's argument that, as an invitee of the UN, he was entitled to immunity under the Headquarters Agreement was dismissed.[134] In another case, *Mushikiwabo et al. v. Barayagwiza*, the plaintiffs sought

[128] *Westchester County on Complaint of Donnelly v. Ranollo*, 67 N.Y.S. 2d 31 at 34.
[129] *Ibid.*
[130] *Dupree Associates Inc. v. Organization of American States and the General Secretariat of the Organization*, US District Court for the District of Columbia, 63 ILR 92.
[131] 22 USCS §288a. [132] 28 USCS §1605. [133] Reinisch, *supra* note 94 at 179–80.
[134] *Kadic v. Karadic*, 70 F.3d 232.

damages for the defendant's involvement in the genocide in Rwanda and for the key role he allegedly played in the murder of some of their relatives.[135] The defendant maintained that he enjoyed immunity because he was attending a session of the UN when he was served with the summons. The government of Rwanda sent a note officially to waive immunity, although this was not probably necessary. Neither *Kadic* nor *Mushikiwabo* concerned cases brought directly against either the UN or UN officials. However, Louise Mushikiwabo later unsuccessfully attempted to bring a case against the Organisation for its failure to protect the persons, including many of her relatives, who had sought refuge in the Ecole Technique Officielle in Kigali in the early days of the genocide.

Human rights arguments to limit the scope of immunity of international organisations have been used only sporadically, and generally unsuccessfully. Absolute immunity of the UN was upheld by the District Court in the Hague in a case brought by victims of the massacre of Srebrenica,[136] and by the Second Circuit of the US Court of Appeals in a case of sexual harassment.[137] The Belgian Civil Tribunal upheld the immunity of the UN in *Manderlier v. UN*, despite the plaintiff's argument that his rights under the Universal Declaration of Human Rights, in particular his right to an effective remedy under Article 8, had been infringed upon.[138] The Court of Appeal in Brussels reached the same conclusion but admitted that the fact that there was no court to which the appellant could submit his dispute within the UN 'may be deplored', and 'does not appear to conform to the principles proclaimed in the Universal Declaration of Human Rights'.[139] The *Manderlier* decisions, which date back to the 1960s, arose out of a dispute between a Belgian citizen and UN troops in Congo during ONUC. Even if the Belgian courts had accepted Manderlier's arguments, it would have still been impossible to give execution to their judgment because of the UN's absolute immunity from execution.

135 *Mushikiwabo et al. v. Barayagwiza*, US District Court of the Southern District of New York, 94 Civ. 3627 (JSM).

136 *Foundation Mothers of Srebrenica v. The Netherlands and the UN*, Case No. 295247/HA ZA 07-2973, Judgment in the incidental proceedings of 10 July 2008, available through the search engine of www.rechtspraak.nl. See O. Spijkers, 'The Immunity of the United Nations in Relation to the Genocide in Srebrenica in the Eyes of a Dutch District Court', 13 *Journal of International Peacekeeping* (2009) 197.

137 *Brzak v. United Nations*, No. 08-2799, 597 F.3d 107 (2010).

138 45 ILR 446 and 69 ILR 139 (respectively first instance and appeal decision). The Universal Declaration is GA Res. 217A (III) of 10 December 1948.

139 69 ILR 139 at 143.

Absolute immunity is rooted in concerns about the interference of member states with the work of international organisations. Such concerns cannot be easily brushed aside. Cases such as *Mazilu* and *Cumaraswamy* certainly bespeak the importance of maintaining a regime of immunity for the UN.[140] The *Mazilu* case concerned a Romanian member of the Sub-Commission on Prevention of Discrimination and Protection of Minorities who had been requested to prepare a report on human rights and youth. Mr Mazilu later complained that the Romanian government forced him to retire, and prevented him from submitting his report or otherwise participating in the works of the Sub-Commission. The *Cumaraswamy* case arose from an interview given to the press by the Special Rapporteur on the Independence of Judges and Lawyers, in which he commented on commercial litigation in Malaysian courts. Two Malaysian companies argued that the article was defamatory and filed a lawsuit for damages. In both cases the position of the UN was supported by the ICJ. However, while the *Mazilu* case had to do with the unacceptable interference of a government with an expert on mission, the *Cumaraswamy* case dealt with third parties who considered themselves aggrieved by the words of the Special Rapporteur. The conclusion of the Court was correct in *Cumaraswamy*, too, since it would have been excessive to qualify his statements as 'unofficial' simply by virtue of their being rather incautious or inopportune.

The fact that, notwithstanding the provisions on immunity, UN personnel are still arrested is another indication that immunity serves an important function.[141] International organisations also need to be protected from other types of governmental interference, as the screening of UN employees by some countries of nationality shows (discussed in Chapter 1). In this sense, it is difficult to disagree with the European Court of Human Rights when it states that 'the attribution of privileges and immunities to international organisations is an essential means of ensuring the proper functioning of such organisations free from unilateral interference by individual governments'.[142]

The General Convention seeks to moderate absolute immunity in two ways. First, Section 29 of the General Convention obliges the UN

[140] See *infra* note 147.

[141] C. H. Brower, 'International Immunities: Some Dissident Views on the Role of Municipal Courts', 41 Virg. J. Int. L. (2000) 146 at 38 ff.

[142] *Waite and Kennedy v. Germany*, Judgment, 18 February 1999, Application No. 26083/94 at para. 63. See also *Beer and Regan v. Germany*, Judgment, 18 February 1999, Application No. 28934/95.

'to make provision for appropriate modes of settlement of' disputes of a private law character to which the UN is a party, and disputes involving any official of the UN in respect of whom immunity has not been waived.[143] Such modes of settlement of disputes are normally made available to employees on a permanent basis, but to third parties on ad hoc basis especially for the purposes of settling claims arising in peacekeeping operations. Some courts have taken the view, albeit by way of *obiter dicta*, that a breach of this obligation by the UN could result in the assumption of jurisdiction by the national court.[144] The importance of the existence of an alternative method of dispute settlement was also emphasised by the ECtHR.[145]

Secondly, as mentioned, the General Convention contains provisions on immunity waivers. According to some, these provisions refute the thesis that the General Convention is in contradiction with the Charter, and demonstrate that the Convention subscribes to the functional necessity approach.[146] However, clear criteria for the waiver of immunity are set out only for the immunity of officials but not for the immunity of the Organisation. Moreover, under the Convention, there is no adequate remedial mechanism for all those cases in which the Secretary General wrongly denies the waiver of immunity. In practice, the Secretary General enjoys complete discretion in the exercise of this power as his decision to refuse to waive immunity cannot be appealed to another organ. Such discretion seems incompatible with the fact that, at least as far as the immunity of officials is concerned, the Secretary General has a duty to waive it in certain circumstances. The conduct of the Secretary General can be reviewed only if a request is put to the ICJ by a competent organ of the UN or of a specialised agency under Sections 29–30 of the General Convention. In the two cases arising out of a dispute under the General Convention that the ICJ has so far considered,[147] the requests were submitted by the Economic and Social Council.

[143] Miller (2009), *supra* note 122 at 95ff.

[144] *Ibid.* at 99.

[145] *Waite and Kennedy*, *supra* note 142 at para. 68.

[146] Brower, *supra* note 141 at 27.

[147] *Applicability of Article 6, 22 of the Convention on the Privileges and Immunities of the United Nations* (hereinafter '*Mazilu* case'), Advisory Opinion, ICJ Reports (1989) 177; *Difference Relating to Immunity from Legal Process of a Special Rapporteur of the UN Commission on Human Rights* (hereinafter '*Cumaraswamy* case'), Advisory Opinion, ICJ Reports (1999) 62.

Both cases concerned the immunity of experts on mission, but the question of the exercise of the Secretary General's duty to grant a waiver of immunity in some circumstances has not yet formed the object of an advisory opinion of the Court. In the *Cumaraswamy* case, Judge Koroma did note the Court's reluctance to examine the consistency of the conduct of the Special Rapporteur with the terms of his mandate.[148] But that case dealt, at most, with incautious utterances by an expert on mission, and not with violations of human rights; such reluctance as was observed by Judge Koroma might well be set aside in other cases involving more serious conduct.

Consistently with the terms of Section 2 of the General Convention, domestic courts have not normally agreed to lift the immunity of an international organisation on the basis of an implied waiver.[149] In *Mendaro v. World Bank*, the appellant argued that a provision in the Articles of Agreement of the World Bank amounted to an implied waiver of immunity.[150] However, the US Court of Appeals for the District of Columbia Circuit, affirming the decision of the District Court to reject the claim, added that immunity must be 'narrowly read in light of both national and international law governing the immunity of international organizations'.[151]

The practice on immunity waivers suggests that this power is very seldom exercised.[152] Immunity tends to be waived when an investigation conducted by OIOS gathers evidence of theft of UN property committed by an official.[153] OIOS also seeks the prosecution of individuals

[148] *Cumaraswamy* case, *supra* note 147 at 121 (diss. op. of Judge Koroma).

[149] But see *Lutcher SA Cellulose e Papel v. Inter-American Development Bank*, US Court of Appeals, DC Circuit, 382 F.2d 454.

[150] *Mendaro v. World Bank*, 717 F.2d 610. A comment on *Mendaro* is in M. Singer, 'Jurisdictional Immunity of International Organizations: Human Rights and Functional Necessity Concerns', 36 *Virg. J. Int. L.* (1995) 53. For a discussion of sexual harassment cases brought by women employed by international institutions, see H. Charlesworth and C. Chinkin, *The Boundaries of International Law: A Feminist Analysis* (Manchester University Press, 2000) 187–9.

[151] *Ibid.*, *Mendaro v. World Bank* at 611. Waivers of immunity are traditionally interpreted narrowly in the context of state immunity too, e.g. *A Company Ltd v. Republic of* X, High Court, Queen's Bench Division (Commercial Court), 87 ILR 412, [1990] 2 Lloyd's Rep 520.

[152] On the practice on immunity waivers in respect of the organisation see Miller (2009), *supra* note 122 at 88ff.; on the practice on immunity waivers in respect of officials see Miller (2007), *supra* note 122 at 236ff.

[153] UN OIOS, 'Report of the Office of Internal Oversight Services on the Investigation into Allegations of Theft of Funds by a Staff Member of the United Nations

external to the Organisation who have committed a crime – fraud or theft for the most part – of which the UN has been a victim. In cases of corruption and forgery, the sanction against UN staff is often only a disciplinary one, or consists simply of the dismissal of the officials in question; prosecution by national authorities is seldom sought in such cases.[154] In cases brought by individuals, including former staff, against the UN, there is still enormous reluctance to waive immunity. The UN does not generally waive immunity even for traffic violations, although these are usually insurable.[155]

Brower has argued that 'the expansion of municipal court jurisdiction is unlikely to make international organizations significantly more accountable because international law already requires international organizations to minimize their reliance on immunity and to provide claimants with alternatives to municipal court litigation'.[156] In his view, the current system already adheres 'to the functional necessity doctrine, but give international officials the primary authority for making immunity determinations'.[157] This position may be doctrinally correct, but in practice accountability of both the organisation and the officials is very low under the current system. Clearly, a balance needs to be struck between the needs of the Organisation and the rights of individuals who are directly affected by it. The shield of absolute immunity is one that the UN cannot keep for too long, particularly if it intends to maintain and increase its operational role. Absolute immunity jars with the evolution of the law of immunity in other areas. In a world where in most jurisdictions states have ceased to enjoy immunity for commercial acts and where former head of states have been put on trial, it is difficult not to think of the UN as enjoying absolute immunity on borrowed time. Interestingly, whereas in the past the authoritative scholarship in the

Conference on Trade and Development', 28 January 1999, UN Doc. A/53/811; UN OIOS, 'Report of the Office of Internal Oversight Services for the Period between 1 July 1997 and 30 June 1998', 23 September 1998, UN Doc. A/53/428 at paras. 151 ff.; Report 1999–2000, *supra* note 55 at para. 49. OIOS' rules do not specify when an investigation would result in criminal prosecution by national authorities (see Secretary General, 'Report of the Secretary-General on the Rules and Procedures to be applied for the investigation functions performed by the Office of Internal Oversight Services', 11 October 2000, UN Doc. A/55/469 at paras. 21–2).

[154] *Ibid.*, UN OIOS Report 1997–98 at paras. 75 and 143–4.

[155] Schermers and Blokkers, *supra* note 80 at 378. [156] *Ibid.*

[157] Brower, *supra* note 141 at 8.

field defended absolute immunity,[158] more recent scholarship tends to favour a shift to restrictive immunity.[159]

A restrictive approach to immunity would have to be tailored to the terms of the General Convention. But there are at least two bases for restrictions of immunity that would not conflict with the provisions of the Convention, not least in light of the fact that those provisions must be interpreted against the background of the functional approach in the Charter. First, courts could reject the plea of immunity where the denial of a waiver by the Secretary General is arbitrary or manifestly unfounded. Given that the Secretary General has a right-duty to grant a waiver when it comes to officials, the standard of review could be lower than in the respect of waivers for the organisation for which the discretion of the Secretary General is wider. Secondly, courts should deny immunity to the UN where it has failed to provide alternative means of dispute settlement.

The doctrine of equivalent protection

The origins: the *Solange* decisions

Developed originally by the German Constitutional Court and later adopted by the European Court of Human Rights, the doctrine of equivalent protection offers a basis for the exercise of judicial control over the acts of international organisations. This control, however, is not exhaustive. Judicial scrutiny on the basis of equivalent protection is normally *mediated* rather than *direct*: what comes under examination is the act of the state transferring powers to the international organisation, not the act of the international organisation that caused the breach. The content of the doctrine also appears to vary depending on the nature of the court: treaty-based judicial bodies apply it differently from constitutional or supreme courts. Despite their differences, national and international courts are moving in a similar direction and the doctrine of equivalent protection now enjoys a considerable degree of conceptual coherence.

The German Constitutional Court developed the doctrine of equivalent protection in response to the expansion of the powers and functions of the European Communities. In its well-known *Solange I* decision in 1974 the German Court asserted its entitlement to review

[158] For example, W.C. Jenks, *International Immunities* (London: Stevens, 1961) at 41.
[159] Reinisch, *supra* note 94 at 317ff. and 391ff.; Wellens, *supra* note 94 at 208ff.

the consistency of EC law with fundamental rights protected under the German Constitution, resisting the argument of the European Court of Justice that such constitutional review by national courts could undermine the unity and efficacy of Community law.[160] The Constitutional Court held that, while permitting the transfer of 'sovereign rights' to 'inter-state institutions' (Article 24(1)), the German Constitution does not 'open the way to amending the basic structure of the Constitution, which forms the basis of its identity, without a formal amendment of the Constitution, that is, it does not open any such way through the legislation of the inter-state institution'.[161] In the event of conflict between Community law and the fundamental rights guaranteed under the Constitution, the latter must prevail, with the only qualification that they will do so 'as long as the integration process has not progressed so far that Community law also receives a catalogue of fundamental rights decided on by a parliament and of settled validity, which is adequate in comparison with the catalogue of fundamental rights contained in the Constitution'.[162] The Court rejected the charge that it was ruling on the validity of a rule of Community law, adding, however, that it is open to it to 'come to the conclusion that such a rule cannot be applied by the authorities or courts of the Federal Republic of Germany in so far as it conflicts with a rule of the Constitution relating to fundamental rights'.[163]

The philosophy of international law and human rights that undergirds these findings is elucidated in this passage:

'Fundamental rights can be guaranteed by law in numerous ways and may accordingly enjoy numerous types of judicial protection. As its previous decisions show, the European Court also considers that it has jurisdiction by its decisions to protect fundamental rights in accordance with Community law. On the other hand, only the Bundesverfassungsgericht is entitled, within the framework of the powers granted to it by the Constitution, to protect the fundamental rights guaranteed in the Constitution. No other court can deprive it of this duty imposed by constitutional law. Thus, accordingly, in so far as citizens of the Federal Republic of Germany have a claim to judicial protection of their fundamental rights guaranteed in the Constitution, their status cannot suffer any impairment merely because they are directly affected by legal acts of authorities or courts of the Federal Republic of Germany which are based

[160] *Internationale Handelsgesselschaft mBh. v. Einfuhr- and Vorratstelle für Getreide und Futtermittel* ('*Solange I*'), Case No 2 BvL 52/71, 93 ILR 362 (all reference henceforth to ILR).

[161] *Ibid.* at 390. [162] *Ibid.* at 395. [163] *Ibid.* at 392.

on Community law. Otherwise, a perceptible gap in judicial protection might arise precisely for the most elementary status rights of the citizen. Moreover, no different considerations apply to the constitution of a community of States with a constitution based on freedom and democracy which is called in question than apply to a federal State with a constitution based on freedom and democracy: it does not harm the Community and its constitution based on freedom (and democracy) if and in so far as its members in their constitutions give stronger guarantees of the liberties of their citizens than does the Community.'[164]

Central to the philosophy of equivalent protection are two ideas. First, the liberty of the individual, entrenched in the Bill of Rights of the German Constitution, is inalienable and its judicial protection unrenounceable. Secondly, the 'community of states' created by virtue of the transfer of sovereign rights to international institutions, as expressly contemplated by the German Constitution, is one based on freedom and democracy, and can only be strengthened by the effective guarantee of individual liberty.

This approach to constitutional and international law, typical of German liberalism, can be traced back to the Kantian notion that the principle of liberty founds and overarches both the domestic and the international orders.[165] The Constitutional Court acknowledges at the outset that fundamental rights can be guaranteed 'in numerous ways', preparing the ground for one of the salient features of equivalent protection, namely the notion that the equivalence has to be substantive rather than formal or procedural.

The European Court of Justice responded to the stance of the German Constitutional Court by moving in the only direction that could prevent a deepening of the conflict between these two institutions. In its decision in the *Nold* case, the European Court stated that it would give effect to fundamental rights recognised and protected by the constitutions of member states and that, in doing so, it is 'bound to draw inspiration from constitutional traditions common to' those member states.[166]

[164] *Ibid.* at 392–3.

[165] For a sophisticated history of the idea of individual rights in German constitutional theory, with particular reference to the concept of *Rechtstaat*, see G. Gozzi, '*Rechtstaat* and Individual Rights in German Constitutional History', in P. Costa and D. Zolo (eds.), *The Rule of Law: History, Theory and Criticism* (Dordrecht: Springer, 2007) 237.

[166] Case 4/73, *J. Nold v. Commission* [1974] ECR 491 at 507. See also *Wachauf* case discussed below. For a full discussion of this line of cases of the European Court of Justice, see A. Clapham, *Human Rights Obligations of Non-State Actors* (Oxford University Press, 2006) 180–5.

The effort of the European Court of Justice paid off when, over ten years after its *Solange I* decision, the German Constitutional Court, referring to the *Nold* case, held that:

'Compared with the standard of fundamental rights under the Constitution it may be that the guarantees for the protection of such rights established thus far by the decisions of the European Court, since they have naturally been developed case by case, still contain gaps in so far as specific legal principles recognised by the Constitution or the nature, content or extent of a fundamental right have not individually been the object of a judgment delivered by the Court. What is decisive nevertheless is the attitude of principle which the Court maintains at this stage towards the Community's obligations in respect of fundamental rights, to the incorporation of fundamental rights in Community law under legal rules and the legal connection of that law (to that extent) with the constitutions of member-states and with the European Human Rights Convention …

… so long ["*solange*"] as the European Communities and particularly the case law of the European Court generally ensure an effective protection of fundamental rights as against the sovereign powers of the Community which is to be regarded as substantially similar to the protection required unconditionally by the German Constitution, and in so far as they generally safeguard the essential content of fundamental rights, the German Federal Constitutional Court will no longer exercise its jurisdiction to decide on the applicability of secondary Community law.'[167]

Although the German Constitutional Court never renounced its prerogative of constitutional review with this decision, its 1994 ruling in the *Brunner* case on the Maastricht Treaty was widely regarded as a return to the more aggressive stance in *Solange I*,[168] attracting considerable criticism including the charge that it was inspired by a Schmittian and nationalistic conception of law.[169] In the following years lower courts in Germany relied on *Brunner* in various cases brought by German banana importers, until the German Constitutional Court brought this stream of litigation to an end by declining to exercise

[167] *Wünsche Handelsgesellschaft ('Solange II')*, Case No 2 BvR 197/83, 93 ILR 403 at 433 and 436.

[168] *Brunner v. European Union Treaty*, 2 BvR 2134/92 & 2159/92), [1994] 1 CMLR 57 at 79 and 81. See G. H. Crossland, 'Three Major Decisions Given by the Bundesverfassungsgericht (Federal Constitutional Court)', 19 ELR (1994) 202 at 205.

[169] M. Zuleeg, 'The European Constitution under Constitutional Constraints: The German Scenario', 22 ELR (1997) 19.

its reserved jurisdiction on the grounds that the European legal order afforded equivalent protection.[170]

The German Constitutional Court returned to the doctrine of equivalent protection in its decision on the Lisbon Treaty of 30 June 2009.[171] In a judgment that in places reads like a treatise on political philosophy, the Court elaborated its approach to the phenomenon of the transfer of sovereign powers, of which the doctrine of equivalent protection is one central aspect. According to the petitioners, '[t]he transfer of sovereign powers to the European Union that is effected in the Act approving the Treaty of Lisbon encroaches upon' their right to participate in the election of the German Bundestag, guaranteed under Article 38 of Germany's Constitution (the *Grundgesetz*), 'because the legitimation and the exercise of state authority is withdrawn from their influence'.[172]

The Constitutional Court rejected the complaint but only after a detailed discussion of the limits set by the German Constitution on the transfer of sovereign powers to international institutions. Those limits derive chiefly from the so-called eternity guarantee at Article 79.3 of the *Grundgesetz* which makes the first twenty articles of the *Grundgesetz* unamendable. For the German Constitutional Court this means that the German Constitution 'not only assumes sovereign statehood but guarantees it'.[173] Consequently, when powers are transferred to international organisations, they 'are granted under the condition that the sovereign statehood of a constitutional state is maintained on the basis of an integration programme according to the principle of conferral and respecting the Member States' constitutional identity, and that at the same time the Member States do not lose their ability to politically and socially shape the living conditions on their own responsibility'.[174]

In this decision the German Constitutional Court does not discuss the doctrine of equivalent protection, but its analysis complements the doctrine. Under German constitutional law the doctrine only operates

170 *Bananas*, BVerfG, 2 BvL 1/97 of 7 June 2000, English translation at 21 *Human Rights Law Journal* (2000) 251. On the banana litigation in lower German courts before the ruling of the Constitutional Court, see N. Reich, 'Judge-made "Europe à la carte": Some Remarks on Recent Conflicts between European and German Constitutional Law Provoked by the Banana Litigation', 7 EJIL (1996) 103.

171 2 BvE 2/08, 2 BvE 5/08, 2 BvR 1010/08, 2 BvR 1022/08, 2 BvR 1259/08 and 2 BvR 182/09 of 30 June 2009, available at www.bundesverfassungsgericht.de/entscheidungen/es20090630_2bve000208en.html (hereinafter the 'Lisbon Decision').

172 *Ibid.* at para. 100. 173 *Ibid.* at para. 216. 174 *Ibid.* at para. 226.

in relation to sovereign powers that can be constitutionally transferred to an international institution. If an international institution were to exercise functions that pertain to what the Court characterises as non-transferable core sovereignty – the 'inviolable core content of the Basic Law's constitutional identity'[175] – the Court would not embark upon an assessment of the measure of protection available under the rules of the international institution, but instead strike down the act of transfer as unconstitutional.

The German Constitutional Court has not been the only court in Europe taking a firm stance on the relationship between EU law and constitutionally protected fundamental rights. The Italian Constitutional Court was one of the first constitutional courts in Europe to express apprehension about the effects of the transfer of sovereign powers to the EEC, and in general to international organisations, on the liberty of the individual, holding in 1965 that, while such transfer of powers normally accords with the Italian Constitution, it cannot produce the 'suppression or restriction of the fundamental rights granted to them [Italian citizens] by the Constitution, for these are guarantees that pertain to the relationship between the state and the subject, and cannot as such be disposed of, and most importantly cannot be left at the mercy of international institutions extraneous to the legal system of our country'.[176] Later on, in an *obiter dictum* in its 1973 judgment in the *Frontini* case, the Italian Constitutional Court ruled out limitations on sovereignty resulting from the transfer of powers to organs of the EEC that would confer on such organs the power to violate fundamental constitutional principles or the inalienable rights of the person, and reserved its right to exercise constitutional scrutiny in such unlikely circumstances.[177]

Other constitutional and supreme courts in Europe have reached conclusions similar to those of the Italian and German Constitutional Courts.[178] Far from representing an anachronistic attachment to

[175] *Ibid.* at para. 240.

[176] Judgment no. 98 of 1965. On the Italian constitutional jurisprudence, see M. Cartabia, *Principi inviolabili e integrazione europea* (Milan: Giuffré, 1995).

[177] Judgment no. 183 of 1973 (*Frontini v. Ministro delle Finanze* [1974] 2 CMLR 372). See also Judgment no. 170 of 1984 (*SpA Granital v. Amministrazione delle Finanze* [1984] 21 CML Rev 756 (ICC 1984)).

[178] A thorough analysis of their jurisprudence is found in K. J. Alter, *Establishing the Supremacy of European Law: The Making of an International Rule of Law in Europe* (Oxford University Press, 2003).

national values, these decisions epitomise the dilemmas faced by national judges entrusted with the protection of fundamental rights when they have to deal with the transfer of powers to international subjects. Behind them is a common sentiment of liberal constitutionalism. The merit of the German Constitutional Court is to have articulated this sentiment in the original terms of the doctrine of equivalent protection.

This doctrine can be seen as the attempt of the constitutional plane to shape the international one according to its founding liberal values, and an invitation to international institutions to embrace human rights. On the face of it, in Europe at least, such an invitation seems to have been replied to affirmatively, judging from the post-*Solange I* line of cases. Nevertheless, tensions and unresolved contradictions may continue to simmer beneath the surface. In the *Wachauf* case,[179] the European Court of Justice provided a thorough statement of its new position. While still recognising the importance of the constitutional traditions of member states, it chose language that may reveal an understanding of human rights which continues to stand in contrast with that of some national constitutional courts. The key passage is the following:

> 'The fundamental rights recognised by the Court are not absolute, however, but must be considered in relation to their social function. Consequently, restrictions may be imposed on the exercise of those rights, in particular in the context of the common organisation of a market, provided that those restrictions in fact correspond to the objectives of general interest pursued by the Community, and do not constitute, with regard to the aim pursued, a disproportionate and intolerable interference, impairing the very substance of those rights.'[180]

At the risk of reading too much into the assumptions behind this passage, it is difficult not to note a marked difference from the Kantian idea of liberty that animated the *Solange* jurisprudence of the German Constitutional Court on the doctrine of equivalent protection. It can hardly be doubted that the German Constitutional Court would not discuss fundamental human rights and liberties in the terms used in *Wachauf*. The various socio-economic considerations cited above ('social function', 'common organisation of the market'), that the European Court of Justice is too ready to invoke to justify restrictions

[179] Case 5/88, *Hubert Wachauf v. FRG* [1989] ECR 2609 at para. 18.
[180] *Ibid.*

on human rights, reflect an attitude of 'economism' – the subordination of political issues to economic ones – considered by Siedentop central to the process of European integration as presently conceived, and which is ultimately antithetical to the liberal constitutionalism that pervades the jurisprudence of the German Constitutional Court.[181]

Equivalent protection in the ECtHR and ECJ

A considerable number of ECtHR decisions relate to the conduct of international organisations, although the applications were brought against a state party rather than the international organisation itself for reasons of jurisdiction *ratione personae*. The Strasbourg Court has seized the opportunity offered by these complaints to develop its own doctrine of equivalent protection.

In the first of these cases, *M & Co. v. Federal Republic of Germany*, it was alleged that a judgment of the ECJ to which German authorities had given effect violated the presumption of innocence under Article 6 of the ECHR.[182] The Court found that its jurisdiction *ratione personae* was engaged by the decision of the German authorities to grant executory power to the ECJ ruling, rejecting the argument that the German authorities were acting 'quasi as Community organs and … to that extent beyond the scope of control exercised by the Convention organs'.[183] The Court held the application inadmissible, ostensibly because it was 'incompatible with the provisions of the Convention *ratione materiae*', but the specific factors with which it justified this conclusion – such as the capacity of the European legal system to secure fundamental rights and the transfer of powers to international organisations – do not appear to have anything to do with jurisdiction *ratione materiae* properly understood.

The Strasbourg Court did a better job at developing its own doctrine of equivalent protection in two subsequent decisions: *Matthews v. UK* and *Bosphorus v. Ireland*. In *Matthews v. UK*, the object of the complaint was EC legislation that excluded residents of Gibraltar from participating in the elections to the European Parliament.[184] The Court held that the UK was responsible for the disenfranchisement of residents

[181] L. Siedentop, *Democracy in Europe* (London: Penguin, 2001) 33–4, 145–6, 190–1.
[182] Decision on Admissibility, Application No. 13258/87, 9 February 1990.
[183] *Ibid*. at 6.
[184] Judgment, 18 February 1999, Application No. 24833/94.

of Gibraltar in elections to the European Parliament, and that such conduct constituted a breach of the appellant's right to participate in free elections under Article 3 of Protocol I to the European Convention. The Court reiterated the propositions that the 'Convention does not exclude the transfer of competences to international organisations provided that Convention rights continue to be "secured"',[185] and that 'the Convention is intended to guarantee rights that are not theoretical or illusory, but practical and effective'.[186] But the factor that tilted the balance in favour of a different outcome from *M & Co.* was the consideration that the EC legislation in question 'cannot be challenged before the European Court of Justice for the very reason that it is not a "normal" act of the Community, but is a treaty within the Community legal order'.[187]

With *Bosphorus v. Ireland* the doctrine of equivalent protection under the ECHR assumed greater conceptual coherence.[188] The applicant was a Turkish airline which had leased aircraft from the Yugoslav airlines after the entry into force of the UN sanctions against the Federal Republic of Yugoslavia. Invoking the Security Council resolutions that had imposed the sanctions and the EC legislation that had given effect to them, the Irish authorities impounded one of the leased aircraft at Dublin airport – an act which, according to the applicant, breached its right to property under Article 1 of Protocol I. While finding that there was no violation in the present case, the Court fleshed out the doctrine of equivalent protection.

According to the decision in *Bosphorus*, the application of the doctrine of equivalent protection comprises up to three separate elements. First, it is necessary to determine if the act of the respondent state giving effect to the act of the international organisation was discretionary; if it was, then the complaint will be considered on its merits as any other complaint. Secondly, if the act was necessary, rather than discretionary, the general level of human rights protection afforded by the international organisation must be assessed. If it is held not to be equivalent to what would have been available domestically, the breach by the international institution is established. If, instead, the general level of human rights protection is found to be equivalent to that of the state, the presumption arises that the Convention was not breached. That presumption may however be rebutted – and this is the

[185] *Ibid.* at para. 32. [186] *Ibid.* at para. 34. [187] *Ibid.* at para. 33.
[188] Judgment, 30 June 2005, Application No. 45036/98.

third element in the application of the doctrine – if it is shown that the protection of Convention rights was 'manifestly deficient' in the particular case.

As explained by the Court in its later decision *Boivin v. France and Belgium (and 32 other states)*, the examination of manifest deficiency 'would only be meaningful if the Court were to consider that there was a presumption of an "equivalent" protection of Convention rights and then ascertain whether or not that presumption had been rebutted in the circumstances of the case'.[189] An example of an assessment of manifest deficiency is the case *Cooperatieve Producentenorganisatie van de Nederlandse Kokkelvisserij U.A. v. Netherlands*, where the applicants complained against the refusal of the ECJ to allow a response to the Opinion of the Advocate General in proceedings before it.[190] Having examined the procedures before the ECJ, the Court concluded that the applicant had failed to rebut the presumption that equivalent protection was provided for in this specific case, though it did not offer any guidance as to what exactly would be required for a finding of 'manifest deficiency'.

The third element in the analysis of the ECtHR in the *Bosphorus* judgment marks a difference between the German Constitutional Court and the European Court's approach to equivalent protection. In the *Solange* decisions, the German Court appeared to indicate that, in the event of the level of protection being found to be equivalent, it would not exercise any review. In *Bosphorus*, instead, the European Court reserves the possibility of a review *in extremis* even where the level of protection is generally equivalent. This is an important analytical difference, although practical outcomes are not likely to differ. It is reasonable to assume that the German Court would not find a level of protection to be generally equivalent where there is evidence to show that protection in a particular case was manifestly deficient if compared with what is provided for under the Bill of Rights in the German Constitution.

The analytical clarity achieved with the *Bosphorus* decision unravelled with the decision of the Grand Chamber in *Behrami and Saramati v. France and others*.[191] As explained in Chapter 3 (108ff.), this case

[189] Judgment, 9 September 2008, Application No. 73250/01 at 6.
[190] Decision on Admissibility, 20 January 2009, Application No.13645/05.
[191] Judgment, 2 May 2007, Application No. 71412/01 and Application No. 78166.

confuses the law on attribution, and conflates issues pertaining to attribution with those relating to territorial jurisdiction and to equivalent protection. In the final sections of its judgment the Court unpersuasively attempts to distinguish *Behrami* from *Bosphorus* with an argument on jurisdiction *ratione materiae* that has repercussions on the doctrine of equivalent protection. The relevant passages read as follows:

'The applicants argued that the substantive and procedural protection of fundamental rights provided by KFOR was in any event not "equivalent" to that under the Convention within the meaning of the Court's *Bosphorus* judgment, with the consequence that the presumption of Convention compliance on the part of the respondent State was rebutted.

... the circumstances of the present cases are essentially different from those with which the Court was concerned in the *Bosphorus* case. In its judgment in that case, the Court noted that the impugned act (seizure of the applicant's leased aircraft) had been carried out by the respondent State authorities, on its territory and following a decision by one of its Ministers (para. 135 of that judgment). The Court did not therefore consider that any question arose as to its competence, notably *ratione personae*, vis-à-vis the respondent State despite the fact that the source of the impugned seizure was an EC Council Regulation which, in turn, applied a UN Security Council Resolution. In the present cases, the impugned acts and omissions of KFOR and UNMIK cannot be attributed to the respondent States and, moreover, did not take place on the territory of those States or by virtue of a decision of their authorities.'[192]

The main effect of *Behrami* on equivalent protection is to narrow down the category of acts to which the doctrine applies. The basis for such narrowing down is ostensibly attribution, in itself an entirely proper boundary to the doctrine given the limits in the Court's jurisdiction *ratione personae*: there is simply no getting around the fact that the ECtHR has no jurisdiction over the UN or the EU.[193] However, what gives rise to difficulty is the Court's muddled analysis of attribution examined before, and its confusion about the role of territory.

[192] Judgment, 2 May 2007, *supra* note 190 at paras. 150–1.

[193] Attribution was an important factor in a number of post-*Behrami* decisions. See, for example, the case of *Boivin v. France and Belgium (and 32 other states)* discussed below. In *Cooperatieve Producentenorganisatie van de Nederlandse Kokkelvisserij U.A. v. Netherlands*, the Court distinguished the position on attribution from that in *Boivin* on the grounds that the applicant's complaint was based on an intervention of the ECJ sought by a domestic court, and it could not therefore be found 'that the respondent Party is in no way involved'.

Indeed, as discussed in Chapter 3, reading *Behrami* one is left with the distinct impression that the crucial factor was the extraterritorial nature of the acts, distinguishing this case from *Matthews* and *Bosphorus*. In the passages cited above, for example, the Court refers to territory, although the geographic location of the act is immaterial to its attribution. Until *Behrami* the doctrine of equivalent protection had been considered, whether by the German Constitutional Court or the Strasbourg Court, only in relation to acts that had a clear link with the territory of the respondent state. In *Behrami*, instead, the acts in question took place outside the territory of the respondent states. The jurisdiction *ratione loci* of the Court was probably engaged, as these acts came under one of the *Bankovic* exceptions,[194] but the references to territory in passages that have nothing to do with jurisdiction *ratione loci* indicate that the extraterritoriality of the acts resonated beyond the determination of the Court's jurisdiction *ratione loci*. This may be explained as a policy-based reaction to the prospect of a significant expansion in the jurisdiction of the Court over the conduct of international organisations as would have resulted from the combined effect of extraterritoriality and equivalent protection.

The doctrine of equivalent protection was also invoked by the Court in cases concerning the jurisdictional immunities of international organisations. Faced with a claim that the immunity of the European Space Agency (ESA) breached a former employee's right to fair trial, the Court held that 'a material factor in determining whether granting ESA immunity from German jurisdiction is permissible under the Convention is whether the applicants had available to them reasonable alternative means to protect effectively their rights under the Convention'.[195] The Court concluded that such reasonable alternative means of protection were available under the ESA regulations, and that '[t]o read Article 6 para. 1 of the Convention and its guarantee of access to court as necessarily requiring the application of national legislation in such matters would, in the Court's view, thwart the proper functioning of international organisations and run counter to the current trend towards extending and strengthening international cooperation'.[196] In a subsequent decision, *Boivin v. France and Belgium*, the Court declared

[194] *Bankovic and others v. Belgium and others*, Decision on admissibility, 12 December 2001, Application No. 52207/99.

[195] Judgment, 18 February 1999, Application No. 26083/94 at para. 68.

[196] *Ibid.* at para. 72.

the application inadmissible because the impugned decision – a judgment of the International Labour Organisation Administrative Tribunal (ILOAT) – emanated from a body outside the jurisdiction of the respondent states.[197] The Court distinguished this case from *Matthews* and *Waite and Kennedy* because the respondent states in *Boivin* had not been involved 'directly or indirectly' in the impugned decision.[198] It must be noted however that the applicant in *Boivin* appears to have pleaded his case differently from the *Waite and Kennedy* applicants, choosing not to challenge the decision of the respondent states to transfer functions to the international organisation, but only the ruling of ILOAT.

It is difficult to draw firm conclusions on the approach of the ECtHR to equivalent protection. It is not clear which authorities still stand and which have been overruled, but it is clear that there is no single account which can comprehend the *ratio decidendi* of *M & Co*, *Matthews*, *Bosphorus* and *Behrami*. The confusion arises in no small part from the failure to address certain doctrinal issues by the Court with the necessary rigour. The Strasbourg Court may also be attempting to backtrack from earlier decisions on equivalent protection and territorial jurisdiction which had the combined effect of extending its jurisdiction to situations which, for policy reasons, it prefers to keep outside its purview. In particular, the Court is reluctant to review the conduct of peacekeeping operations, and, where its jurisdiction *ratione loci* is engaged, it has found no better alternative than the wholly unsatisfactory *Behrami* solution to decline jurisdiction (on *ratione personae* grounds).

With the *Kadi* decision of the ECJ the doctrine of equivalent protection has gone full circle: it has been adopted by the very organ against which it had been developed by the German Constitutional Court in the first place.[199] True, the *Kadi* decision contains no clear and express espousal of the doctrine by the ECJ, and the locution 'adequate protection' appears only once in the judgment, in a passage that summarises the applicant's submissions.[200] Nevertheless, the *ratio* of the judgment is imbued with elements of equivalent protection. First, the Court examines in some detail the mechanism of review available under the UN system of sanctions, and finds it inadequate.[201] The Court embarks upon this examination in response to an argument of the Commission clearly framed in *Solange* terms: 'so long as under

[197] *Boivin*, *supra* note 188. [198] *Ibid*.

[199] Case No C-402/05 P and C-415/05 P, *Kadi v. Council of the European Union*.

[200] *Ibid*. at para. 256. [201] *Ibid*. at paras. 320–5.

that system of sanctions the individuals or entities concerned have an acceptable opportunity to be heard through a mechanism of administrative review forming part of the United Nations legal system, the Court must not intervene in any way whatsoever'.[202] Secondly, the consequence that arises from such inadequacy is, in the reasoning of the Court, the obligation to review 'Community measures which, like the contested regulation, are designed to give effect to the resolutions' of the Security Council.[203] Thirdly, the Court devotes much attention to the *Behrami* decision, which it distinguishes on the grounds of attribution.[204]

Equivalent protection in England

The House of Lords missed an opportunity to apply the doctrine of equivalent protection in the *Al-Jedda*, discussed above in the context of the review of acts of the Security Council. The appellants had relied on the *Bosphorus* doctrine, but all references to *Bosphorus* in the judgment of the House of Lords are in the context of attribution. In Lord Bingham's analysis *Al-Jedda* raised three issues: whether the detention was attributable to the UK or the UN; whether Article 5(1) was qualified by Security Council Resolution 1546; and whether English common law or Iraqi law applied to the detention (and, if the former, whether it provided any legal basis for it).

Equivalent protection could have been the fourth issue in *Al-Jedda*, and formulated in the following terms: if it is true that, as a matter of international law, Security Council resolution 1546, combined with Article 103 of the Charter, has the effect of empowering British public authorities to act in contravention of fundamental human rights, was the UK constitutionally allowed to empower the UN to qualify the fundamental human rights of individuals within the jurisdiction of the UK? Since the UK, unlike Germany or Italy, does not have a written Constitution *stricto sensu*, the only framework for this argument was the Human Rights Act. There is no way of knowing how the House of Lords would have approached this issue, but what is certain is

[202] *Ibid.* at para. 319. [203] *Ibid.* at para. 326.

[204] *Ibid.* at para. 314. With such telling elements, it is difficult to see how the contention that *Kadi* contains aspects of equivalent protection can be dismissed as 'beauty that comes from the eye of the beholder' (J. H. H. Weiler, 'Editorial', 19 EJIL (2008) 896 at 897).

that the judgment in *Al-Jedda* separates the House of Lords from courts in the Western world which have consistently rejected the principle that the transfer of sovereign functions to an international organisation – under whichever guise and for whichever purpose – includes the power to violate fundamental rights within the national jurisdiction.[205] The decision in *Al-Jedda* would be viewed as constitutionally aberrant by courts in other liberal democracies founded on the rule of law: 'executive-mindedness' is no less dangerous if the executive is an international one.[206]

Courts that resisted the principle of normative supremacy of Security Council resolutions include the Federal Court of Canada and the Bosnian Constitutional Court. In *Abousfian Abdelrazik v. The Minister of Foreign Affairs and the Attorney General of Canada*, the Federal Court of Canada ruled that the sanctions regime under Security Council resolution 1267 constitutes 'a denial of basic legal remedies' and is also 'untenable under the principles of international human rights'. The Bosnian decision was discussed in Chapter 6.

The Supreme Court, as the House of Lords had been renamed in the meantime, returned to the question of the compatibility of Security Council resolutions with fundamental human rights in the case of *Jabar Ahmed and others.*[207] The Court quashed various orders which had been adopted pursuant to Section 1 of the United Nations Act 1946 to impose certain measures on individuals who had been designated under the anti-terrorism sanctions system. Without overruling *Al-Jedda*, the Supreme Court justified this conclusion on rule-of-law grounds, in particular the argument that 'fundamental rights may not be overridden by general words' and that Section 1 of the United Nations Act does not 'give authority for overriding the fundamental rights … either expressly or by necessary implication'.[208] 'Parliament' – Lord Phillips

[205] *Abousfian Abdelrazik v. The Minister of Foreign Affairs and the Attorney General of Canada*, 2009 FC 580 at para. 51 (See A. Tzanakopoulos, *An Effective Remedy for Josef K: Canadian Judge Defies Security Council Sanctions through Interpretation*, at www.ejiltalk.org/an-effective-remedy-for-josef-k-canadian-judge-defies-security-council-sanctions-through-interpretation). The Bosnian case on the effect of Security Council resolutions is *Milorad Bilbija et al*, Case no. AP-953/05, Constitutional Court of Bosnia, 8 July 2006.

[206] In one of the best-known dissenting judgments in British constitutional history, Lord Atkin famously criticised his colleagues for being 'more executive-minded than the executive' in a case concerning the liberty of the subject in times of emergency (*Liversidge v. Anderson* [1942] AC 206).

[207] *Supra* note 119. [208] *Ibid.* at para. 76 (*per* Lord Hope).

explained – 'would not have foreseen this possibility'.[209] This decision is an improvement on the executive-mindedness of *Al-Jedda*, although it does leave many important questions unanswered.

How did the Supreme Court avoid overruling *Al-Jedda*? Did *Al-Jedda* not decide that a Convention right could be lawfully breached if a Security Council decision adopted under Chapter VII of the UN Charter so required? Unlike *Al-Jedda*, however, *Jabar Ahmed* engaged Section 1 of the United Nations Act 1946, which refers to Security Council resolutions under Article 41. The Supreme Court justified its conclusion on the construction of that Section on the basis of what Lord Rodger called the *Simms* principle, that is that courts must presume that Parliament never intended to legislate contrary to human rights when the words are general or ambiguous (at para. 193 (*per* Lord Rodger). To understand such a principle, one needs to be bear in mind that, under the British Constitution centred on the principle of parliamentary sovereignty, it is not open to any court to declare an act of Parliament unconstitutional, although under the Human Rights Act it is possible to adopt a declaration of incompatibility. Faced with 'outrageous' legislation, the traditional English solution until the Human Rights Act was to say 'Parliament cannot have possibly meant this' rather than 'Parliament was wrong'.

Nevertheless, the reconciliation of *Al-Jedda* with *Jabar Ahmed* remains difficult. The reason why Section 1 of the United Nations Act refers to Article 41 and not to Article 42 measures is that, since the latter are measures involving the use of force, they come under the prerogative of the Crown. There was no constitutional need for the United Nations Act to make provision for them. Thus, Article 41 measures required a statutory transformer, but Article 42 ones did not. The detention of *Al-Jedda* however falls in a grey area: it was based on a resolution adopted under Article 42, but it does not follow from this that the detention was an act within the prerogative of the Crown in a constitutional sense. Whether an act is within the prerogative or not is a constitutional question, which cannot be resolved on the basis of the classification of the measure under the UN Charter. *Jabar Ahmed* highlights the problematic nature of the domestic legal basis of the detention of Al-Jedda: it was not pursuant to an order in terms of Section 1 of

[209] *Ibid*. at para. 154 (*per* Lord Phillips).

the United Nations Act, nor was it an exercise of prerogative powers. If not a logical contradiction, there is at least some tension between *Jabar Ahmed* and *Al-Jedda*: the former says that the UK cannot violate human rights in giving effect to a Security Council decision adopted under Chapter VII; the latter says the opposite.

The Human Rights Committee also avoided embracing the doctrine of equivalent protection, particularly in the case of *Sayadi and Vinck v. Belgium*[210] (see chapter 7, 315ff.).

Untangling equivalent protection

With its success in the ECtHR and ECJ the doctrine of equivalent protection has lost some of the juridical and intellectual coherence that it enjoyed in its original statement in the *Solange* decisions. As understood by the ECtHR, the doctrine is sufficiently clear to allow the identification of a large category of acts to which it would apply, but not sufficiently clear to exclude its application from a similarly large, and potentially more important, category of acts – namely those having an extraterritorial character and originating from peacekeeping and other international operations.

A challenge faced by every court applying equivalent protection is to identify the philosophical and juridical basis of this doctrine. As discussed, the German Constitutional Court seems to have been inspired by a form of Kantian liberalism. It traditionally approved of the transfer of sovereignty to international organisations with two qualifications, to which the Lisbon decision added a third. The first qualification is the essence of the doctrine of equivalent protection, namely that international organisations must protect fundamental liberties and human rights on an equivalent basis to that guaranteed under the domestic order. The second qualification is that the power of a supreme court to protect liberty is a core sovereign function, which can never be transferred or in any way disposed of. The inalienability of this sovereign function is a corollary of the inalienability of the liberty of the individual; no cosmopolitan plan, no matter how worthwhile, can sever this umbilical cord which links the sovereignty of the state with the liberty

[210] *Sayadi and Vinck v. Belgium*, Communication No. 1472/2006, 20 October 2008, UN Doc. CCPR/C/94/D/1472/2006.

of the individual. Considered from another point of view, this qualification reflects the notion that a coherent legal system should not permit a transfer of competences that would result in its self-destruction.[211] The third qualification is an expansion of the second one: there exists a core set of sovereign functions – associated in the German case with three principles, liberty, democracy and federalism – which cannot be transferred to an international organisation.

Clearly, as the doctrine is applied by different courts, it cannot have a uniform juridical basis. The bodies of law which these courts apply vary considerably and the limits to which they are subject, as well as the powers with which they are endowed, are also different. Constitutional courts operate under national laws, while the ECtHR or the ECJ are treaty-based judicial bodies. Issues of sovereignty, which are the backcloth of the doctrine of equivalent protection, will be approached differently by constitutional courts – and rightly so since they are the custodians and guarantors of popular and democratic sovereignty. While the juridical basis, and the range and depth of relevant legal issues will vary from one court to the other, a liberal philosophical inspiration should accompany the application of this doctrine in every setting. Its ultimate rationale is in fact the protection of liberty vis-à-vis the different permutations that sovereign power can assume.

Another challenge for courts applying the doctrine of equivalent protection is to decide its scope and effects. Again, no uniform answer may be possible or even advisable, but it may help to identify the key doctrinal issues that any application of the doctrine of equivalent protection must resolve.

(1) The scope of the doctrine of equivalent protection must not be confused with attribution to the state of the conduct allegedly breaching the fundamental human right.

A sound analytical approach should begin with setting out the different types of conduct that form the object of the claim, followed by an examination of the attribution of each conduct to the right legal person. The *Behrami and Saramati* decision would have greatly benefitted from such an analytical approach.[212]

[211] This question bears some similarity to the constitutional puzzle of rules for the amendment of the constitution analysed by Alf Ross in 'On Self-Reference and a Puzzle in Constitutional Law', 78 *Mind* (1969) 1.

[212] The judgment of Laws LJ in *The Queen on the Application of Faisal Attiyah Nassar Al-Saadoon, Khalaf Hussain Mufdhi v. The Secretary of State for Defence* [2007] EWCA Civ 7, would have also benefited from a similar analysis.

One of the issues in *Bosphorus* and *Behrami* was whether the binding act of an international organisation that left no discretion to the implementing state should have been attributable exclusively to the international organisation. Exclusive attribution to the international organisation is the approach advocated by the European Union and has found favour with a panel established under the World Trade Organisation, which took the view that the organs of a state implementing the binding act of the European Union 'act *de facto* as organs of the Community, for which the Community would be responsible under WTO law and international law in general'.[213] Special Rapporteur Giorgio Gaja, relying on a more substantial body of judicial authority, preferred the view that state conduct implementing a binding act of an international organisation is still in principle attributable to the state.[214] This is surely the correct position: states never agree to be demoted to the status of '*de facto* organs' of international organisations, even when they are giving effect to binding acts of international organisations – such as a decision of the Security Council adopted under Chapter VII of the UN Charter or a regulation of the European Union.

In most of the recent decisions on attribution of conduct to international organisations, courts appear to have proceeded on the assumption that attribution to an international organisation excludes attribution to a state, and vice versa. As discussed extensively in Chapter 3 (103ff.) this assumption is incorrect.[215]

A separate issue within the realm of attribution is complicity. An international human rights court may lack jurisdiction *ratione personae* over the main acts that caused the violation because those acts are entirely attributable to an international organisation, but still have jurisdiction over acts through which the state aided or assisted the international organisation in that violation, as long as it can be

[213] WTO, 'European Communities – Protection of Trademarks and Geographical Indication for Agricultural Products and Foodstuffs', Report of 15 March 2005 (WT/DS174/R) at para. 7.725.

[214] G. Gaja, 'Seventh Report of the Special Rapporteur on Responsibility of International Organisations by the Special Rapporteur', 61st Session of the ILC, 2009, UN Doc. A/CN.4/610 at paras. 31–3.

[215] For example, G. Gaja, 'Second Report on Responsibility of International Organisations by the Special Rapporteur', 56th Session of the ILC, UN Doc. A/CN.4/541 at para. 6. See also S. Talmon, 'Responsibility of International Organisations: Does the European Community Require Special Treatment?', M. Ragazzi, (ed.) in *International Responsibility Today: Essays in Memory of Oscar Schachter* (Leiden: Martinus Nijhoff, 2005) 413.

shown that the state acted with knowledge of the circumstances of the internationally wrongful act and that the act would be internationally wrongful if committed by that state.[216]

The jurisdiction *ratione personae* of a constitutional court is a matter of constitutional law. This is the reason why the question of attribution has arisen in the ECtHR and ECJ cases, but not in the *Solange* decisions of the German Constitutional Court. In general, it would be rather odd for a constitutional court to decline jurisdiction over acts that have full legal force and directly affect the position of individuals within the jurisdiction of the state as constitutionally defined, simply on the basis that those acts do not emanate from national institutions. Nevertheless, in the constitutional and administrative jurisprudence of some countries arguments of act of state and non-justiciability may arise in relation to the review of acts of international organisations. Moreover, certain remedies may not be available against international organisations on grounds of immunity. Constitutional adjudication would also greatly benefit from a careful dissection of all conduct involved in the case and a proper analysis of attribution.

The ECtHR, on the other hand, is established under a treaty to which the EU and the UN are not parties; it consequently lacks jurisdiction *ratione personae* over acts of those legal persons. It is entirely proper that such an international court should address the question of attribution, for its jurisdiction may depend on it. In many of the cases decided by the ECtHR, a series of acts were involved: the act of the international organisation giving rise to the alleged breach; the internal measure giving effect to that act; the decision of the respondent state to transfer powers to the international organisation. Jurisdiction *ratione personae* may exist in relation to some but not all of these acts. The primary determination – whether a breach was committed – is necessarily confined to acts in respect of which jurisdiction can be established. It is therefore possible that, while the entire series of acts violated a particular right, the particular act in respect of which the court or tribunal has jurisdiction did not effect a breach.

(2) The scope of the doctrine of equivalent protection must not be confused with the territorial application of the bill of rights (jurisdiction *ratione loci*), be it the ECtHR or a constitution.

[216] Article 57 of the draft articles discussed in Chapter 3 (135ff.).

One of the factors which in the judgment of the ECtHR distinguished *Behrami and Saramati* from *Bosphorus* was the place of the conduct. Yet, whether a particular conduct is within the geographic scope of the ECtHR – or of a national constitution or domestic legislation – is a discrete preliminary determination that should have nothing to do with the scope and application of equivalent protection. In the case of the ECtHR, the outcome of that determination depends on the interpretation of the terms 'within the jurisdiction' in Article 1. The ICCPR, on the other hand, uses different terms ('within the territory and subject to the jurisdiction'), while the ICESCR is silent. Whichever the legal basis for that determination, once a particular conduct is found to be within the geographic scope of the human rights treaty, the place of the conduct is immaterial to other jurisdictional and preliminary determinations.

(3) The particular act, i.e. the measure which gives rise to the breach directly, must be distinguished from the general act, i.e. the decision to transfer sovereignty to the international organisation.

In a typical case of equivalent protection, two international legal persons are involved – a state and an international organisation. Three international legal persons are involved in cases arising from the implementation of UN sanctions in a member state of the EU given the competence of the EU in this area, as well as in cases arising from UN-mandated peace operations in which states intervene through another international organisation like NATO. In these circumstances the allegation that an international or constitutional human rights norm has been breached may in actual fact relate to different acts. As far as the responsibility of the state is concerned, the following acts may be relevant:

(i) the transfer *ab origine* of certain powers to the international organisation (e.g. the ratification of the constituent instrument of the organisation);
(ii) the endorsement of an operation or mission of the international organisation (e.g. the vote of the state representative in favour of a particular resolution);
(iii) the specific contributions made to that operation or mission (e.g. the supply of troops or funds);
(iv) the secondary legislation implementing a decision of the international organisation (e.g. EU regulations implementing UNSC sanctions); and
(v) specific actions of officials of the state (e.g. an arrest carried out by national troops as part of a UN operation).

One of the main causes of confusion in the doctrine of equivalent protection is the lack of clarity about the acts to which it applies. From the case law two scenarios emerge. In the first scenario (*Solange I and II*; *Matthews*; *Bosphorus*; *Kadi*) an international organisation adopts certain measures (for example Security Council resolution or an EU regulation) to which a state gives effect by means of domestic legislation. This scenario involves one general and two particular acts: the particular acts are the measure of the international organisation and its implementation by the respondent state; the general act is the original transfer of such powers by the state to the international organisation as to enable it to adopt the disputed measure.

In the second scenario an international organisation puts in place the conduct alleged to violate the fundamental right, and the state has no involvement in its implementation. This is what happened in *Behrami and Saramati* according to the ECtHR, although, as discussed, there were problems with the Court's analysis. This scenario involves one particular act and one general act: the particular act is the conduct of the international organisation that gives rise to the alleged breach; the general act is the original transfer of powers by the state to the international organisation. How and when those powers were actually transferred may be a matter for argument. In some cases, the transfer will have occurred at the time of the ratification or accession of the multilateral treaty establishing the international organisation. In other cases, the act effecting the transfer of the powers on which the contested conduct rested will have occurred subsequently – for example the decision to vote in favour of a particular resolution, or the decision to assign troops to a UN mission.

A key question affecting the scope of the doctrine of equivalent protection is the determination of the category of acts to which it applies. A court may take the view that it will not scrutinise general acts, that is the original decisions to transfer powers to an international organisation, but only the particular acts alleged to have caused the breach, and, in so doing, effectively limit its review and the application of the doctrine of equivalent protection to the first scenario. In constitutional adjudication this approach may find some support in doctrines that limit the power of courts to review foreign affairs, such as non-justiciability and act of state. If one looks at this question from the point of view of ensuring a purposive protection of human rights, it is preferable to avoid the outright exclusion of general acts from the scope of equivalent protection.

(4) Causation requires separate consideration.

The decisions on equivalent protection devote hardly any attention to causation. Yet, causation should be a central factor in cases involving multiple acts by a variety of international actors. As discussed, courts may have jurisdiction *ratione personae* in respect of only some of those acts, and need to ask themselves whether it is those particular acts that caused the alleged breach. In *Behrami and Saramati*, for example, the ECtHR might have had jurisdiction over the decision of the French and German authorities to contribute troops to the UN mission in Kosovo. The question is whether, on the facts, the breach alleged by the applicants was caused by that decision, or by acts or omissions in respect of which the ECtHR had no jurisdiction *ratione personae*. The case of *Sayadi and Vinck* also turned on causation. The Belgian government's transmission of information to the Security Council was clearly an act attributable to Belgium, but the question was whether that act caused the inclusion of the authors of the communication in the Security Council list, and thus the breach.

The analysis of causation can obviate some of the difficulties posed by the distinction between particular and general acts outlined above. A court would first determine over which acts it has jurisdiction on the basis of the particular rules governing its personal and territorial jurisdiction, and then proceed to consider whether it can be shown on the facts that those acts caused the alleged breach. It is conceivable, for example, that a court may hold that the decision to contribute to an international mission caused the violation where the mission lacked adequate safeguards for the protection of human rights, but reach a different conclusion where adequate safeguards were in place or where the nature of the mission, its scope and powers in particular, was such that the commission of human rights violations was not foreseeable.

(5) There needs to be clarity on the nature of the presumption that results from a finding of equivalent protection.

From the case law two approaches emerge to the nature of the presumption resulting from a finding that the international organisation to which the state transferred powers generally provides a measure of protection that is equivalent to that available under the domestic constitution or under the ECtHR. First, the presumption can be treated as absolute, leaving no scope for review of the particular acts alleged to have caused the violation of human rights. The German Constitutional Court seems to prefer this solution. Secondly, the presumption can be treated as rebuttable, if it is shown that the level of protection in the particular case was manifestly deficient, notwithstanding the general finding of equivalent and adequate protection. The ECtHR in *Bosphorus* opted for this approach, which results in a deeper measure of human rights protection.

The *Bosphorus* approach is still premised on attribution of the act to the state, but – in substance if not in name – the assessment of manifest deficiency entails a review of the conduct of the international organisation. In fact, it will be remembered that under the *Bosphorus* doctrine the question of equivalent protection arises only in relation to necessary acts, that is non-discretionary acts through which a state is mandated to implement the act of an international organisation. The state may be the agent of the violation, but to determine if the protection was manifestly deficient in the particular case it will be necessary to look at the international institutional act which the state was implementing and assess its impact.

(6) Claims of external normative superiority need to be resolved in a constitutionally principled manner.

Various claims of external normative superiority have been canvassed to trump the human rights arguments. In some cases (*Al-Jedda, Behrami and Saramati, Kadi*) it was argued that international or constitutional human rights norms should give way to Article 103 of the Charter and, via that, to decisions of the Security Council adopted under Chapter VII; in others (the *Solange* cases) that they should give way to EU legislation. In dealing with such claims, courts have generally exhibited 'a tendency to do what they can to avoid norm conflicts'.[217] Moreover, with the exception of the decision of the House of Lords in *Al-Jedda* and of the European Court of First Instance in *Kadi*, courts have been extremely reluctant to accept arguments of external normative superiority at face value. And so they should be.

The reason for this reluctance varies from constitutional to human rights treaty adjudication. Even constitutions which include provisions that automatically import rules of international law into the domestic legal order do not offer a credible legal basis for the proposition that the effect of those provisions is that Article 103 or EU legislation are the highest norms in the domestic order – higher than the constitution itself.[218] Testimony to this is the considerably qualified, and still

[217] Milanović, *supra* note 118 at 71.

[218] For example, Art. 25 of the German Constitution; Art. 11 of the Italian Constitution; Arts. 231–3 of the South African Constitution.

far from settled, acceptance by constitutional courts in Europe of the superiority of EU law – a principle that stands on more solid ground as a matter of domestic law than the principle granting normative superiority to all decisions of the Security Council under Chapter VII by virtue of Article 103.

The position is different in human rights treaty adjudication, because an argument about the superiority of Article 103 of the UN Charter is an argument about the hierarchy of sources in international law, and it will have, understandably, a different standing before courts or tribunals constituted under international law. The question is whether those courts and tribunals must give effect to the hierarchy of sources that Article 103 is traditionally understood to have created.[219] The predominant view among international lawyers is that they should, because 'something that is created by treaty, no matter how self-contained, cannot but be part of a unified, universal international legal order'.[220] On another view, however, it does not suffice that, as a matter of general international law, Article 103 may prevail, for a court established by treaty must apply the treaty in accordance with its terms: if this results in a ruling that puts the country potentially in breach of the UN Charter, this is, in principle, a problem for the state and not for the court. There are principles and rules of international law – on state responsibility, treaty interpretation or the formation of customary law for example – that, while not expressly provided for under every treaty, can be relied upon in adjudication under that treaty, but is Article 103 one such rule? Ultimately, there is no clear analytical way of dealing with this question, and the answer will depend on the assumptions that we make about the nature of the international legal system and the sources of international law.[221]

The ICCPR might be an exception because it expressly provides that '[n]othing in the present Covenant shall be interpreted as impairing the provisions of the Charter of the United Nations' (Article 46). In

[219] Questions of Interpretation and Application of the 1971 Montreal Convention arising from the Aerial Incident at Lockerbie (*Libya v. UK*) para. 37 (Order of 14 April 1992), available at www.icj-cij.org/docket/files/88/7085.pdf. See also Sir Michael Wood, 'The Sir Hersch Lauterpacht Memorial Lectures: The UN Security Council and International Law', available from www.lcil.cam.ac.uk/lectures/2006_sir_michael_wood.php.

[220] Milanović, *supra* note 118 at 108. In the cited passage, Milanović is referring to EU law, but his remark applies, *a fortiori*, to human rights treaty adjudication.

[221] This is also Milanović's view, although he argues for a different position on the effect of decisions of the Security Council (*ibid.* at 109).

Sayadi and Vinck, the Human Rights Committee considered the Article 46 point even though no party had pleaded it, but concluded, its logic perhaps a bit tenuous, that the case concerned 'the compatibility with the Covenant of national measures taken by the State party in implementation of a Security Council resolution. Consequently, the Committee finds that article 46 is not relevant in this case.'[222]

By contrast, the ECHR does not contain any such reference to the Charter, and an interpretation of its provisions that has the effect of impairing the Charter is not, in principle, precluded. In the jurisprudence of the American Commission of Human Rights, Article 29(b) of the American Convention on Human Rights, which precludes interpretations of the Convention as 'restricting the enjoyment or exercise of any right or freedom recognized by virtue of the laws of any State Party or by virtue of another convention to which one of the said states is a party', has been interpreted as a sort of valve through which other rules of international law, for example international humanitarian law, can be imported into the applicable law.[223] The purpose of Article 29(b) is, however, to ensure that the higher human rights standard is applied, and this provision could not be credibly relied upon to justify a restriction of human rights guaranteed under the American Convention on the basis of another treaty.

Both in constitutional and in human rights treaty adjudication, thus, the argument that norms external to the constitutional or treaty system – such as Article 103 or EU legislation – should enjoy superiority must be approached with the greatest caution, even with a healthy measure of scepticism. The result of such caution and scepticism will sometimes be conflicting statements by different courts – a state of affairs that is far from unusual and certainly not unmanageable, judging by the experience of the EU which has coexisted with conflicts on the question of normative superiority for some time.

The function of equivalent protection

The doctrine of equivalent protection has a curious history. It was developed by a constitutional court as a way of resisting the expansion in the powers of a supra-national organisation, the EEC, and its main

[222] *Sayadi and Vinck*, *supra* note 211 at para. 10.3.

[223] See C. McCarthy, 'Human Rights and the Laws of War under the American Convention on Human Rights', 6 EHRLR (2008) 762.

judicial body, the ECJ. It was then discovered by a treaty-based body, the ECtHR, to defeat the argument of respondent states that it lacked jurisdiction to entertain certain claims. More recently, the ECJ, against whose forays into domestic constitutional sovereignty the doctrine was first developed, adopted it in all but name.

The thread that unites this history is the relationship between courts mandated to protect the fundamental rights of individuals and international institutions which acquired or otherwise developed a power to interfere with those rights. Courts, whether domestic or international, need to decide on the proper terms of engagement with claims against the conduct of an international organisation, and to develop a principled approach for dealing with the objection that such conduct falls outside their remit. Such a principled approach requires clarity on the scope of the court's jurisdiction, which, in the case of an international court, will be related to the rules governing its jurisdiction *ratione personae*, and, in the case of a constitutional court, to constitutional principles such as non-justiciability or political questions doctrine as may apply under that particular constitutional order.

Not every case which raises questions about the conduct of an international organisation is one to which it will be appropriate to apply the doctrine of equivalent protection. Much depends on how the case is pleaded. In the case of *D v. Turkey*, for example, no discussion of equivalent protection appears to have taken place.[224] The applicants were an Iranian couple sentenced to one hundred lashes each for premarital sex. Having fled to Turkey, they applied for refugee status at the local offices of the United Nations High Commissioner for Refugees (UNHCR), as Turkey is one of many countries in the world where refugee status determination, normally a state-run administrative procedure, is entirely handled by the UNHCR.[225] In November 2006 their application for refugee status was rejected with a 'barely reasoned decision by UNHCR',[226] which also produced a statement dismissing the severity of the sentence inflicted by Iran and alleging that

[224] Judgment, 22 June 2006, Application No. 24245/03.

[225] See G. Verdirame and B. E. Harrell-Bond, *Rights in Exile: Janus-Faced Humanitarianism* (Oxford: Berghahn Books, 2005); M. Alexander, 'Refugee Status Determination Conducted by UNHCR', 11 Int. J. Ref. L. (1999) 251; and the website www.rsdwatch.org. On *D v. Turkey*, see G. Verdirame, 'Breaches of the European Convention on Human Rights Resulting from the Conduct of International Organisations', 2 EHRLR (2008) 209.

[226] *D v. Turkey*, *supra* note 227 at para. 21.

it would have in practice involved 'the symbolic application of the sentence bearing in mind the individual's state of health'.[227] With a very short judgment the ECtHR found in favour of the applicants on the basis of the serious risk to their Article 3 rights.[228] The applicants had not complained of a violation of their Article 6 rights by the UNHCR-administered refugee status determination procedures, although, if they had couched it in terms of equivalent protection, they would have potentially had a good case.

Equivalent protection is becoming one of the key doctrines for ensuring judicial oversight over the exercise of executive powers transferred from the entity long regarded as their sole depository – the sovereign state – to international organisations. As we have seen, it is not a doctrine for the exclusive use of national courts. In its applications to date, it has been invoked to justify control over the acts of states, the EU, the UN, the ILO and the European Space Agency.

Viewed from the standpoint of its systemic function of control and oversight to promote respect for the human rights and liberty of the individual, the main obstacle to the effectiveness of the doctrine of equivalent protection is the jurisdictional limits in relation to acts of international organisations. As discussed, these jurisdictional limits will vary depending on which court is seized of the matter, but, where they do apply, the consequence will be to preclude the court from reviewing what can be rightly regarded as the source of the problem, that is the act of the international organisation from which the violation originates.

A role for NGOs?

According to Charnovitz, it was before the First World War and during the interwar period that NGOs exercised the most significant influence at the international level.[229] He reaches this conclusion measuring the impact of NGOs on international life on the basis of two criteria: their 'degree of penetration' into intergovernmental meetings and international organisations, and the degree of influence that they exerted on the agenda of governments. Applying these criteria nowadays can perhaps allay some of the precipitate enthusiasm that characterises

[227] *Ibid.* at para. 28. [228] *Ibid.* at para. 28.

[229] S. Charnovitz, 'Two Centuries of Participation: NGOs and International Governance', 18 *Mich. J. Int. L.* (1997) 183.

much debate on NGOs. Indeed, although we may have entered a cycle in which the influence of NGOs is in the ascendant,[230] their 'degree of penetration' in international organisations remains limited and their powers within the organisations are still based on the constitutional arrangements negotiated in the 1940s and 1950s.

In theory, NGOs could act as 'watchdogs' of multilateral institutions by spearheading international public interest litigation; in practice, the rules on *locus standi* and on the submission of *amicus curiae* briefs curb NGO participation in international judicial proceedings.[231] Interestingly, the Permanent Court of Justice had a more liberal approach to the submission of briefs on the part of NGOs than its successor.[232] In fact, there is only a very small number of cases of the International Court of Justice (ICJ) in which non-governmental actors played some role, namely the 1950 *South West Africa* case,[233] the two advisory opinions on *Nuclear Weapons*,[234] and *Gabcikovo-Nagymaros*,[235] although much of their participation had to remain 'behind the scenes'. Even so, their indirect involvement was not unanimously welcomed. In the *Nuclear Weapons* opinion, Judge Guillaume questioned whether the requests could really be regarded as 'emanating from the Assemblies that had adopted them' and whether it would not have been appropriate for the Court to declare the requests 'inadmissible'.[236]

NGOs have submitted requests for inspection to bodies such as World Bank Inspection Panel, which will accept such requests provided that the NGOs can show they are 'an affected party in the territory of the borrower which is not a single individual (i.e., a community of persons such as an organization, association, society or other grouping of

[230] Charnovitz claims that the impact of NGOs on international life is 'cyclical'.

[231] This is mainly true of the ICJ. NGOs have been involved in cases before the European Court of Justice, the Inter-American Court of Human Rights, and, subject to more restrictions, before the European Court of Human Rights. D. Shelton, 'The Participation of Non-governmental Organisations in International Judicial Proceedings', 88 AJIL (1994) 611.

[232] Charnovitz, *supra* note 238 at 216–17 (especially fn. 294) and at 279; Shelton, *supra* note 240 at 623.

[233] *International Status of South-West Africa*, ICJ Reports (1950) 128.

[234] *Legality of the Use by a State of Nuclear Weapons in Armed Conflict* (WHO Request), Advisory Opinion, ICJ Reports (1996) 66 and *Legality of the Threat or Use of Nuclear Weapons* (GA Request), Advisory Opinion, ICJ Reports (1996) 226.

[235] *Gabcikovo-Nagymaros Project (Hungary v. Slovakia)*, Judgment, ICJ Reports (1997) 7.

[236] *Nuclear Weapons* (GA Request), sep. op. of Judge Guillaume at para. 2. Judge Oda also appeared to frown upon the involvement of NGOs (*ibid.* diss. op. of Judge Oda at para. 8).

individuals)'.[237] The Inspection Panel provides an 'unusual window for members of the public to access quasi-legal processes and norms'[238] vis-à-vis an international institution, but it is not a judicial organ.

NGO presence in UN organs is overall trifling. The Charter simply concedes that 'the Economic and Social Council may make suitable arrangements with non-governmental organisations which are concerned with matters within its competence' (Article 71).[239] By 2008 such arrangements had been made with over 3,000 NGOs. ECOSOC resolution 1996/31, which contains a detailed regulation of this status, fails even to protect an NGO's basic freedom from state interference by providing that an organisation which engages 'in a pattern of acts contrary to the purposes and principles of the Charter of the United Nations including unsubstantiated or politically motivated acts against Member States of the United Nations incompatible with those purposes and principles' shall have its consultative status withdrawn or suspended.[240] States use these provisions to have the status of NGOs hostile to their policies suspended or withdrawn. For example, Cuba successfully lobbied for the suspension of an NGO of Cuban exiles, and Russia secured a majority of votes in the Committee on Non-Governmental Organizations in favour of its proposal to suspend the Transnational Radical Party, which had been critical of Russian policy in Chechnya.[241] Cuba was also involved in instigating the suspension of a French NGO – Reporters Without Borders – in 2003.[242] Algeria lobbied for the suspension of the Arab Commission for Human Rights, alleging

[237] IBRD Res. 93–10 and IDA Res. 93–6, 'The World Bank Inspection Panel', at para. 12.

[238] R. E. Bissell, 'Recent Practice of the Inspection Panel of the World Bank', 91 AJIL (1997) 741 at 744.

[239] The provisions applying to NGOs contained in the statutes of specialised UN agencies normally replicate Art. 71. See R. Lagoni and E. Chaitidou, 'Article 71', in Simma, *supra* note at 2 at 1077–8. UNHCR's Statute mandates the High Commissioner to keep 'in close touch with … inter-governmental organisations concerned, establishing contacts in such manner as he may think best with private organisations dealing with refugee questions, facilitating the co-ordination of the efforts of private organisations concerned with the welfare of refugees'.

[240] ECOSOC Res. 1996/31 of 25 July 1996 at 57(a).

[241] ECOSOC, 'Report of the Committee on Non-Governmental Organizations on the first and second parts of its 2000 session', 13 July 2000, UN Doc. E/2000/88 (Part II). The final decision on the suspension is taken by the Council, but a recommendation of the Committee normally anticipates a decision to suspend.

[242] Committee on NGOs, 'NGO Committee Recommends Suspension of Consultative Status for "Reporters Without Borders"', Press Release, 20 May 2009, available at www.un.org/News/Press/docs/2003/ngo509.doc.htm.

that its Permanent Representative to ECOSOC was linked to a terrorist organisation and subject to an arrest warrant issued by Interpol. The discussion of the suspension released by the relevant ECOSOC committee suggests that ECOSOC was prepared to make the decision to suspend the NGO despite the concerns of various state representatives that not enough information had been provided to substantiate the complaint.[243]

Not only is the status of NGOs precarious within the ECOSOC – the UN organ in which they are more 'visible' – but their rights are also limited. NGOs can make written submissions to the members of the ECOSOC via the Secretary General, and can make oral presentations only upon a recommendation of the Committee on Non-Governmental Organisations and with the approval of the Council.[244] The new UN Human Rights Council (HRC) provides for some NGO participation. The HRC states that 'the participation of NGOs in the regular and special sessions of the HRC ... is a prerogative of NGOs enjoying consultative status with ECOSOC'.[245] NGOs are virtually absent from UN organs other than the ECOSOC. However, practice is cautiously evolving and NGOs may be allowed to make submissions to other organs in some circumstances; for example some NGOs 'made a presentation to the Security Council on the crisis in Africa's Great Lakes region'.[246] But there is still a long way to go before the rhetoric about UN civil society partnership becomes reality.[247]

A fundamental problem with viewing NGOs as promoters of the accountability of international institutions is that 'NGOs themselves need to be subjected to standards of accountability and good governance'.[248] In many situations, NGOs' vested interests coincide with those of the very international institutions or states which they

[243] See ECOSOC/6379 NGO/662, Press Release, 23 January 2009. The suspension proceedings are detailed in ECOSOC/6380 NGO/663, Press Release, 26 January 2009.

[244] ECOSOC Res. 1996/31 of 25 July 1996 at paras. 30–2.

[245] GA Res. A/Res/60/25 of 3 April 2006 at para. 11. ECOSOC Res. 1996/31 governs this relationship.

[246] Charnovitz, *supra* note 238 at 278.

[247] Gramsci is credited with coining the term 'civil society' or, at least, with its diffusion. However, the Gramscian dismal analysis of civil society, in particular the emphasis on its hegemonic nature and on the social interests that civil society represents, seem to have been entirely forgotten. Gramsci can be a good anti-body to the current pandemic excitement about the role of NGOs.

[248] N. Woods, 'Good Governance in International Organizations', 5 *Global Governance* (1999) 39 at 45.

ought to monitor. In the humanitarian field, for example, NGOs are often 'implementing partners' or subcontractors of international institutions.[249] If competition exists, it is normally over funds rather than over standards. The case of refugee camps, examined in Chapter 6, demonstrates that, far from attempting to make UNHCR accountable for violations of human rights, NGOs too often decided at best to acquiesce in them, and for the most part to be zealous executors. In other words, NGOs have often been co-opted into the power structure of which the UN is a part, especially in the context of the provision of humanitarian assistance and the administration of refugee camps.

Although the general picture on the role of NGOs as 'watchdogs' of international organisations is not encouraging, some interesting practice is emerging. First of all, there are examples of humanitarian NGOs that defend their independence and integrity fiercely and have not hesitated to part company with international organisations and challenge their actions.[250] Secondly, beginning in the 1990s human rights NGOs have published reports in which they criticise the conduct of various UN organisations and of peacekeeping operations, certainly contributing to pressure for accountability.[251]

[249] Verdirame and Harrell-Bond, *supra* note 228 at 312ff.

[250] Médecins sans Frontières has often been critical of the way particular humanitarian operations have been conducted. On at least four occasions (Ethiopia 1984–6, Eastern Congo 1994–6, Afghanistan 1996–7, Sudan 1998), it broke ranks with other humanitarian agencies even deciding to suspend its operations because it believed that fundamental principles were neglected. More recently, Human Rights Watch has criticised the UN's failure to protect civilians in areas its MONUC peacekeepers had identified as priority protection zones (Human Rights Watch, 'Killings in Kiwanja' (New York, 2008), available at www.hrw.org/en/reports/2008/12/11/killings-kiwanja-0). Amnesty International has also reported on the disappointing performance of the UN and its agencies and peacekeeping forces. See, for example, Amnesty International, 'Empty Promises on Darfur: International Community Fails to Deliver' (London, 2009) available at www.amnesty.org/en/library/info/AFR54/001/2009/en.

[251] On UNHCR, Human Rights Watch, 'Uncertain Refuge' (New York, 1997) available at www.hrw.org/en/reports/1997/04/01/uncertain-refuge; on UNDP, Human Rights Watch, 'Failing the Internally Displaced: The UNDP Displaced Persons Program in Kenya' (New York, 1997), available at www.hrw.org/en/reports/1997/06/01/failing-internally-displaced; on peacekeeping operations, African Rights, 'Somalia: Human Rights Abuses by the United Nations Forces' (London, 1993), available at www.hartford-hwp.com/archives/27c/423.html, and Amnesty International, 'Peacekeeping and Human Rights' (London, 1994) available at www.amnesty.org/en/library/asset/IOR40/001/1994/en/d9675696-ec2b-11dd-8d9d-a7825928c0bf/ior400011994en.html.

Conclusion

The last two decades have witnessed important developments in the area of accountability. Although the extent and quality of administrative controls is patchy at best, institutional practice, especially in relation to *de jure* international administrations and peacekeeping has shown signs of progress. The development of a credible system of administrative justice for third parties affected by the UN, especially for those who have suffered violations of their human rights, remains the only viable alternative to greater involvement on the part of domestic courts.

Political controls remain generally weak. The main organ with overall responsibility for control and oversight within the UN, the General Assembly, barely performs this function at all. Successive Secretaries General have not done much better, although they have from time to time appointed commissions of inquiry on UN failures and wrongdoings that have attracted considerable publicity and prompted some policy reassessment. Member states may be willing to bring their political power to bear on the UN for all sorts of purposes, but control, oversight and accountability are seldom among them. The exception is the US which has however focused almost exclusively on questions of management and financial probity rather than on accountability more broadly understood, but then larger revolutions often begin with a focus on finances. Moreover, mainly as a result of pressure from domestic political constituencies, some national parliaments are becoming quite assertive.

The judicial review of acts of the Security Council could undoubtedly enhance the rule of law in respect of the UN, and offer safeguards against the ultra vires acts of the Council.[252] However, as long as the existing rules on *locus standi* before the World Court remain in place, these safeguards would be of limited benefit, and available only to states. In addition, an entire category of international acts – those 'of a kind which could also be committed by states' including 'denial of justice, misuse of territory'[253] – could not form the object of judicial

[252] The Court could thus act as a 'restraining factor in tracing the limits of Security Council action in terms of both the Charter and of international law', Gowlland-Debbas, *supra* note 95 at 662.

[253] Lauterpacht, 'The Legal Effect', *supra* note 105 at 89. The 'other class of unlawful acts … which can arise only in the context of international organisation', includes, for example, the consistency of certain acts with the constituent instrument. These acts are more likely to form the object of a request of judicial review or of incidental judicial review.

review. As a mechanism for ensuring the accountability of the UN for violations of human rights, judicial review as presently construed and applied is of very limited impact.

The role that international courts should play to ensure UN compliance with international law is not, however, limited to the judicial review of the legality of the acts of political organs. For example, international judicial bodies should play a role in the UN administration of territory. The 'silence' of the ICJ on international administrations is surprising if compared with the experience of its predecessor. The Permanent Court of International Justice delivered five advisory opinions on various legal questions inherent to the administration of the Free City of Danzig, ranging from the capacity of the City to join the International Labour Organisation (ILO),[254] to the constitutionality of legislation in criminal law and criminal procedure,[255] to administrative questions including appeals against decisions of the High Commissioner of the League of Nations.[256] Although the Permanent Court had been assigned a specific role under the Versailles Treaty, the ICJ could still play an active role in international administrations within the constraints of the Charter and of its Statute if, for example, the General Assembly empowered, under Article 96(2) of the Charter, UN organs involved with the administration to request advisory opinions.

But the most significant development has been the emergence of a national and international jurisprudence that addresses issues of international institutional accountability, including compliance with human rights. This jurisprudence generally does so in an indirect manner, that is by reviewing the conduct of states. Nevertheless, in some jurisdictions, mainly through the application of the doctrine of equivalent protection, the pressure exerted by courts is so significant that states have had to prompt the UN (and the EU) to change course. This was the case, most notably, in the area of sanctions. The absolute

[254] *Free City of Danzig and International Labour Organisation*, Advisory Opinion (1930) PCIJ Reports Series B, No. 18.

[255] *Consistency of Certain Danzig Legislative Decrees with the Constitution of the Free City* (1935) PCIJ Reports Series A/B, No. 65. On the other hand, the Permanent Court itself did not deal with the Saarland where the League exercised wider administrative powers than in Danzig.

[256] *Polish Postal Services in Danzig*, Advisory Opinion (1925) PCIJ Reports Series B, No. 11; *Jurisdiction of the Courts of Danzig*, Advisory Opinion (1928) PCIJ Reports Series B, No. 15; *Treatment of Polish Nations and Other Persons of Polish Origin or Speech in the Danzig Territory* (1932) PCIJ Reports Series A/B, No. 44.

immunity of the UN has not been dismantled by national courts, although many are clearly very uneasy about it. The greater engagement of courts with international institutional law has also led to some unwelcome results, in particular the idea that decisions of the Security Council adopted under Chapter VII should be accorded primacy as a matter of both international and constitutional law. Overall, however, the greater control by national courts and international human rights courts over the conduct of international organisations is a positive development, insofar as it remains subject to certain principles and conditions.

Conclusions

The critical analysis of the UN developed in this book neither rests on, nor entails an outright rejection of international organisations as such. The fact that international organisations violate human rights and that existing mechanisms for dealing with these violations are inadequate does not refute the idea that international organisations might be, and in many ways are, a good thing. One could be a cosmopolitan and still accept much of what I have argued in this book.

Nevertheless, the systemic liberty deficit of the UN – and of international organisations in general – does raise troubling questions. The transfer of power from states to international organisations is seen as an essential aspect of globalisation. For many, especially in the field of international law, it is a desirable inevitability. But is it really inevitable? And is it really desirable? The consolidation of a novel form of power, vested in international organisations, but also in NGOs, may conceal the emergence of a new leviathan – bigger and in some situations perhaps more powerful, but also more mercurial and less accountable than the state. Think about how the most politically ambitious of all international organisations, the EU, is often perceived and you will realise that for much of public opinion the new leviathan is already here.

The tension between human rights and international organisations is – it could be argued – simply another manifestation of the omnipresent tension between liberty and power, but it is not, in and of itself, an argument against international organisations and in favour of the state, for states are, after all, still responsible for many more human rights violations than international organisations. This is true, but only up to a point.

When an international organisation takes over functions that pertain to governments and, with those, the capacity to interfere with human rights, all of the limits that derive from it not being a state become evident. To begin with, while international organisations promote important values, like the maintenance of peace or international cooperation, they do not embody an idea of collective liberty as the state does. *The institutional expression of self-determination remains the state.* It may be so, as Immanuel Kant would have argued, because our ethical development is still highly imperfect. But the fact that it is so, Kant himself would have added, is crucial. Moreover, *the state enables the exercise of individual liberty and the enjoyment of human rights.* Liberty and human rights do not exist in a political vacuum; the state provides a political space which no international organisation has been able to match. International organisations can seek to emulate the achievements of the state by creating institutions, mechanisms and procedures that imitate domestic ones. And they will often do so with some success. But the political achievements of the state do not lend themselves to copy-cat solutions.

This discussion may seem abstract, but it is the kind of reflection on which we need to embark to design the future of the international system. The power of international organisations is a phenomenon that is here to stay. But as for its inevitable growth, and as for the ensuing inevitability of the demise of the state, we should not proceed on the basis of unreflecting assumptions. The same applies to the desirability of the power of international organisations. Kant, generally regarded as one of the fathers of cosmopolitanism, did believe that his federation of peoples should involve 'no sovereign authority'[1] and that 'the separation of many neighbouring states independent of one another … is nevertheless better than the fusion of them by one power overgrowing the rest and passing into a universal monarchy, since as the range of government expands laws progressively lose their vigour, and a soulless despotism, after it has destroyed the seed of good, finally deteriorates into anarchy'.[2]

Does this mean that international organisations should never exercise functions of government and that, if they do so, they are doomed to be 'soulless' and 'despotic'? Not quite. In some cases, an international

[1] I. Kant, 'Metaphysics of Morals', in M. J. McGregor (ed.) *The Cambridge Edition of the Works of Immanuel Kant in Translation: Practical Philosophy* (Cambridge University Press, 1999) 311 at 483.

[2] I. Kant, 'Toward Perpetual Peace', in McGregor *supra* note 1 at 336.

protectorate is the lesser evil. But it is one thing to regard the *power* of international organisations as a necessary evil, quite another to consider it as a more advanced form of political power and authority than the state. Similarly, to mention two other international institutional activities that have come under scrutiny in this book, it is clearly true that refugees need an international organisation that makes up for the lack of diplomatic protection of their state of nationality or origin, and advocates their rights in a principled and efficient manner; and it is equally true that humanitarian assistance can secure the survival of millions of persons affected by armed conflict or natural disaster.

As for the question in the title of this book – who guards the guardians? – the short answer is that some purport to do so, but hardly anyone does so effectively. But an important development is that courts, both national supreme courts, and international human rights ones, are venturing into this area with increasing frequency, sometimes even with zeal. The doctrine of equivalent protection has proven to be a powerful juridical invention in this respect. The UN and other international organisations have not been completely indifferent to the greater scrutiny, including judicial, that their activities have attracted. In the case of both international administrations and peacekeeping operations, as we have seen, more institutions and rules are in place today than ten or fifteen years ago to ensure some measure of accountability in the event of human rights violations. The shift from comprehensive to targeted sanction regimes is encouraging for human rights; as is the progress in promoting standards of due process in the implementation of targeted sanctions.

But there are also areas where progress has been minimal or nonexistent. The 'warehousing' of refugees in UN-administered camps is an example. And not all the colours of the growing domestic and international jurisprudence that deals, albeit indirectly, with the human rights performance of international institutions are bright. If, within this jurisprudence, equivalent protection is the flagship of liberalism in this field, the notion of Article 103 of the UN Charter as trump card is a standard bearer of illiberalism.

International organisations have not been fully in the line of judicial fire so far, because immunity has often protected them. Cases have normally proceeded against the states that implemented, or were otherwise connected to, their conduct. But international organisations would be ill-advised to assume that this will continue to be the case.

Abandoning the idea that 'international institutions, and international culture [are] necessarily emancipatory';[3] becoming less starry-eyed about the UN; and subjecting every international institution to the kind of intense and relentless scrutiny to which governments in the most advanced liberal democracies are already exposed will do a service not only to the people whose lives are affected by them, but also to the institutions themselves. Far from undermining the cause of international organisation and cooperation, it might help restore its original idealism. The struggle for the accountability of the UN[4] will need a concerted effort of academics and practitioners to succeed. The first stage must be to dismantle the hubris that comes with blind faith in international organisations and multilateralism, to admit and then explore the possibility that these organisations may do wrong as well as good, and, for lawyers especially, to develop the arguments for enhancing the framework of accountability. It would be unimaginably damaging for many the world over, as well as for international law itself, if international institutions, entrusted as they are with ever more powers, were to remain 'unbound'.

[3] A. Orford, 'Locating the International: Military and Monetary Interventions after the Cold War', 38 Harv. Int. L. J. (1997) 443 at 444.

[4] The expression is taken from J. A. Fox and L. D. Brown (eds.) *The Struggle for Accountability: The World Bank, NGOs and Grassroots Movements* (Cambridge, MA: MIT Press, 1998).

Bibliography

In some cases, I have used Italian translations for books not originally written in English. Whenever possible, in this bibliography I have also referred to the English translation. The references for publications of international organisations are for the most part treated as primary sources. I have, however, treated publications like UNHCR's *State of the World's Refugees* as secondary sources and they are therefore listed here.

Abi-Saab, G. (1978), *The United Nations Operation in the Congo 1960–1964*. Oxford University Press.

African Rights (1993), 'Somalia: Human Rights Abuses by the United Nations Forces'. London.

(1993), 'The Nightmare Continues ... Abuses Against Somali Refugees in Kenya'. London.

(1994), 'Humanitarianism Unbound?' Discussion Paper No. 5. London.

(1995), *Rwanda: Death, Despair and Defiance* (2nd edn.). London.

The Age (2000), 'The UN Faces Genocide Suit', 10 January.

Ager, A. (ed.) (1998), *Refugees: Perspectives on the Experience of Forced Migration*. London: Pinter.

Ajayi, J. F. Ade (ed.) (1989), *General History of Africa. Africa in the XIX Century Until the 1880s*. Oxford: Heinemann.

Akande, D. (1998), 'The Competence of International Organisations and the Advisory Jurisdiction of the International Court of Justice', 9 *EJIL* 437.

Albros-Llorens, A. (1996), *Private Parties in European Community Law: Challenging Community Measures*. Oxford: Clarendon Press.

Alexander, M. (1999), 'Refugee Status Determination Conducted by UNHCR', 11 *IJRL* 251.

Allot, A. (1924), *Le Bassin de la Sarre. Organisation politique et administrative*. Paris: Berger-Levrault.

Allott, P. (2001), *Eunomia* (2nd edn.). Oxford University Press.

(2005), *Towards the International Rule of Law: Essays in Integrated Constitutional Theory*. London: Cameron May.
Alston, P. (1992), 'The Security Council and Human Rights: Lessons to be Learned from the Iraq-Kuwait Crisis and its Aftermath', 13 *Austral. YBIL* 107.
Alston, P. (ed.) (1992), *The United Nations and Human Rights*. Oxford: Clarendon Press.
Alston, P. and Simma, B. (1992), 'The Sources of Human Rights Law: Custom, Jus Cogens and General Principles', 12 *Austral. YBIL* 82.
Alston, P. and Weiler, J. (1998), 'An Ever-Closer Union in Need of a Human Rights Policy', 9 *EJIL* 658.
Alter, K. J. (2003), *Establishing the Supremacy of European Law: The Making of an International Rule of Law in Europe*. Oxford University Press.
Alvarez, J. E. (1991), 'Legal Remedies and the United Nations *á la Carte* Problem', 12 *Mich. J. Int. L.* 229.
(1996), 'Judging the Security Council', 90 *AJIL* 1.
(1996), 'Nuremberg Re-visited: The *Tadic* Case', 7 *EJIL* 245.
(1997), 'Financial Responsibility', in Joyner, C. C. (ed.), *The United Nations and International Law*. Cambridge University Press.
(2005), *International Organisations as Law-Makers*. Oxford University Press.
Amerasinghe, C. F. (1991), 'Liability to Third Parties of Member States of International Organizations: Practice, Principle and Judicial Precedent', 85 *AJIL* 259.
(1994), *The Law of the International Civil Service* (2nd edn.). Oxford: Clarendon Press.
(2005), *Principles of the Institutional Law of International Organizations* (2nd edn.). Cambridge University Press.
Amnesty International (1994), 'Peacekeeping and Human Rights'. London.
(1997), 'Human Rights Overlooked in Mass-repatriation'. London.
(1997), 'Rwanda Ending the Silence'. London.
(2000), 'East Timor: UNTAET, Justice and Refugees One Year after the Ballot'. London.
(2000), 'Federal Republic of Yugoslavia (FRY)/Kosovo: Risk of Serious Miscarriage of Justice in Trial of Serbs', Press release of 20 April. London.
(2000), 'Setting the Standard? UNMIK and KFOR's response to the violence in Mitrovica'. London.
(2001), 'Amnesty International Protests the Unlawful Detention of Afrim Zeqiri', Press release of 12 February. London.
(2009), 'Empty Promises on Darfur: International Community Fails to Deliver'. London.
Aoi, C., de Coning, C. and Thakur, R. (eds.) (2007), *Unintended Consequences of Peacekeeping Operations*. New York: United Nations University Press.
Appe, J. (1987), *Flight and Other Stories*. London: Akira.
Apthorpe, R. and Mayhew, B. (1999), 'A Possible Model for a Humanitarian Ombudsman: Report on Action Research in Kosovo'. London: Humanitarian Accountability Project.

Araujo, R. J. (2005), 'Objective Meaning of Constituent Instruments and Responsibility of International Organisations', in Ragazzi, M., *International Responsibility Today: Essays in Memory of Oscar Schachter.* Leiden: Martinus Nijhoff.

Archer, C. (1992), *International Organizations* (2nd edn.). London: Routledge.

Armstrong, D. (1982), *The Rise of International Organisation: A Short History.* London: Macmillan.

Arnull, A., Dashwood, A., Dougan, M., Ross, M., Spaventa, E. and Wyatt, D. (eds.) (2006), *Wyatt and Dashwood's European Union Law* (5th ed.). London: Thomson Sweet & Maxwell.

Arnull, A. and Wincott, D. (eds.) (2002), *Accountability and Legitimacy in the European Union.* Oxford University Press.

Arsanjani, M. H. (1981), 'Claims against International Organizations: quis custodiet ipsos custodes', 7 *Yale Journal of World Public Order* 131.

Article 19 (2001), 'Voices in Exile: African Refugees and Freedom of Expression' (A Report written by Carver, R. and Verdirame, G.). London: Article 19.

Asad, T. (1997), 'On Torture, or Cruel, Inhuman or Degrading Treatment', in Wilson, R. A. (ed.), *Human Rights, Culture and Context: Anthropological Perspectives.* London: Pluto Press.

Ashworth, A. (2009), *Principles of Criminal Law* (6th edn.). Oxford University Press.

Aust, A. (1986), 'The Theory and Practice of Informal International Instruments', 35 *ICLQ* 787.

(2007), *Modern Treaty Law and Practice* (2nd edn.). Cambridge University Press.

Bagshaw, S. (2005), *Developing a Normative Framework for the Protection of Internally Displaced Persons.* New York: Transnational Publishers.

Bailey, S. D. (1992), 'The Security Council', in Alston, P. (ed.), *The United Nations and Human Rights.* Oxford: Clarendon Press.

Bakunin, M. A. (2000), *Statism and Anarchy*, in Shatz, M. (ed.), *Cambridge Texts in the History of Political Thought.* Cambridge University Press.

Bar Human Rights Committee of England and Wales (2000), 'Kosova 2000: Justice, not Revenge'. London.

Barnett, M. and Duvall, R. (eds.) (2005), *Power in Global Governance.* Cambridge University Press.

Barnett, M. and Finnemore, M. (1999), 'The Politics, Power and Pathologies of International Organizations', 53 *Int. Org.* 699.

(2004), *Rules for the World: International Organisations in Global Politics.* New York: Cornell University Press.

(2005), 'The Power of Liberal International Organizations' in Barnett, M. and Duvall, R. (eds.), *Power in Global Governance.* Cambridge University Press.

Bass, G. J. (2008), *Freedom's Battle: The Origins of Humanitarian Intervention.* New York: Vintage.

Baylis, E. A., (1997), 'Parallel Courts in Post-Conflict Kosovo', 32 *Yale J. Int. L.*1.

Bekker, P. H. F. (1994), *The Legal Position of Intergovernmental Organizations.* Dordrecht: Martinus Nijhoff.

Bender, T. (ed.) (1992), *The Anti-slavery Debate. Capitalism and Abolitionism as a Problem in Historical Interpretation.* Berkeley: University of California Press.

Bensman, J. (1988), 'The Aesthetics and Politics of Footnoting', 1(3) *Politics, Culture and Society* 443.

Bentham, J. (1843), 'Anarchical Fallacies', in Bowring, J. (ed.), *The Works of Jeremy Bentham*, Vol. 2, 489.

Besson, S. and Tasioulas, J. (eds.) (2010), *The Philosophy of International Law.* Oxford University Press.

Bethlehem, D. (2004) 'The European Union', in Gowlland-Debbas, V. (ed.), *National Implementation of United Sanctions: A Comparative Study.* Leiden: Brill.

Bettati, M. (1991), 'Un Droit d'Ingérence?' 95 *RGDIP* 639.

(1998), 'Création et Personalité Juridique des Organisations Internationales', in Dupuy, R. J., *A Handbook of International Organizations* (2nd edn.). Dordrecht: Martinus Nijhoff.

Bettati, M. Domestici-Met, M.-J. and Tanja, G. J. (eds.) (1995), *Law in Humanitarian Crises. Vol. II: Access to Victims: Right to Intervene or Right to Receive Humanitarian Assistance?* Luxembourg: Office for Official Publications of the European Union.

Bettelheim, B. (1986), *The Informed Heart.* Harmondsworth: Penguin.

Beyani, C. (1999), 'The Legal Framework for an International Humanitarian Ombudsman'. London: Humanitarian Accountability Project.

(2000), *Human Rights Standards and the Movement of People Within States.* Oxford University Press.

Bissell, R. E. (1997), 'Recent Practice of the Inspection Panel of the World Bank', 91 *AJIL* 741.

Black, R. (1998), 'Putting Refugees in Camps, 2 *FMR* 4.

Bobbio, N. (1990), *L'età dei diritti.* Turin: Einaudi. English edn. (1996) *The Age of Rights.* Cambridge: Polity.

Boisson de Chazournes, L. (2010), 'Responsibility to Protect: Reflecting Solidarity' in Wolfrum, R. and Kojima, C. (eds.), *Solidarity; A Structural Principle of International Law.* Heidelberg: Springer.

Boisson de Chazournes, L. and Sands, P. (eds.) (1999), *International Law, the International Court of Justice and Nuclear Weapons.* Cambridge University Press.

Born, H. and Hänggi, H. (eds.) (2004), *The 'Double Democratic Deficit': Parliamentary Accountability and the Use of Force under International Auspices.* Aldershot: Ashgate.

Borsi, U. (1912), 'Carattere ed oggetto del diritto amministrativo internazionale', 12 *Riv. It. Dir. Int.* 368.

Bothe, M. (1989), 'Relief Actions: The Position of the Recipient State' in Kalshoven, F. (ed.), *Assisting the Victims of Armed Conflict and Other Disasters.* Dordrecht: Martinus Nijhoff.

(1999), 'The Who Request', in Boisson de Chazournes, L. and Sands, P. (eds.), *International Law, the International Court of Justice and Nuclear Weapons.* Cambridge University Press.

(2008), 'Security Council's Targeted Sanctions against Presumed Terrorists: The Need to Comply with Human Rights Standards', 6(3) *Journal of International Criminal Justice* 541.

Boudreau, D. G. (1997), 'Creating a United Nations Sanctions Agency', 4 *International Peace-keeping* 115.

Boudreau, T., Lawrence, M. and King, A. (1996), 'Household Food Economy Assessment of Kakuma Refugee Camp, Turkana District, North-West Kenya. Undertaken on Behalf of WFP and UNHCR', London: Save the Children Fund.

Bourloyannis-Vrailas, C. (1995), 'The Convention on the Safety of United Nations and Associated Personnel', 44 *ICLQ* 560.

Boutros-Ghali, B. (1999), *Unvanquished: A U.S.–U.N. Saga*. London: I.B. Tauris.

Bowett, D. W. (1966), *UN Forces: A Legal Study of United Nations Practice*. London: Stevens.

(1982), *The Law of International Institutions* (4th edn.). London: Sweet and Maxwell.

Bowles, E. (1998), 'From Village to Camp: Refugee Camp Life in Transition on the Thailand–Burma Border', 2 *FMR* 11.

Bowring, B. (2008), *The Degradation of the International Legal Order*. New York: Routledge-Cavendish.

Boyle, A. and Chinkin, C. M. (2006), *The Making of International Law*. Oxford University Press.

Bradlow, D. D. (1994), 'International Organizations and Private Complaints: The Case of the World Bank Inspection Panel', 34 *Virg. J. Int. L.* 553.

(2005) 'Private Complaints and International Organisations: A Comparative Study of the Independent Inspection Mechanisms in International Financial Institutions', 36 *Georgetown Journal of International Law* 403.

Brandtner, B. and Rosas, A. (1998), 'Human Rights and the External Relations of the European Community: An Analysis of Doctrine and Practice', 9 *EJIL* 468.

Bretton, P. (1979), 'La transformation de l' ONUDI en institution spécialisée', 25 *AFDI* 567.

Brölmann, C. (2007), *The Institutional Veil in Public International Law: International Organisations and the Law of Treaties*. Oxford and Portland, Oregon: Hart Publishing.

Brower, C. H. (2000), 'International Immunities: Some Dissident Views on the Role of Municipal Courts', 41 *Virg. J. Int. L.* 1.

Brownlie, I. (2008), *Principles of Public International Law* (7th edn.). Oxford University Press.

Burke. E. (1986), *Reflections on the Revolution in France [1790]*. London: Penguin Classics.

Cain, K. L. (1999), 'The Rape of Dinah: Human Rights, Civil War in Liberia and Evil Triumphant', 21 *Hum. Rts. Q.* 265.

Cameron, I. (2006), 'The European Convention on Human Rights, Due Process and UN Security Council Counter-Terrorism Sanctions', Council of

Europe, 6 February (available from www.coe.int/t/e/legal_affairs/legal_co-operation/public_international_law/Texts_&_Documents/Docs%202006/I.%20Cameron%20Report%2006.pdf).

Cammack, D. (1999), 'Gender Relief and Politics During the Afghan War', in Indra, D. (ed.), *Engendering Forced Migration*. Oxford: Berghahn Books.

Cannizzaro, E. (ed.) (2002), *The European Union as an Actor in International Relations*. The Hague: Kluwer Law International.

Canor, I. (2000), '*Primus Inter Pares*: Who is the Ultimate Guardian of Fundamental Rights in Europe', 25 *ELR* 3.

Caplan, R. (2005), 'Who Guards the Guardians? International Accountability in Bosnia', 12 *International Peacekeeping* 463.

Carlevaris, A. (1998), 'Recenti Sviluppi nella Prassi degli Status of Force Agreements per le Operazioni di Peace-Keeping delle Nazioni Unite', 53 *Com. Int.* 667.

Cartabia, M. (1995), *Principi inviolabili e integrazione europea*. Milan: Giuffré.

Cassese, A. (1991), 'Can the Notion of Inhuman and Degrading Treatment Be Applied to Socio-Economic Conditions?' 2 *EJIL* 141.

(1996), *Inhuman States*. Cambridge: Polity Press.

(1999), '*Ex Iniuria Ius Oritur*: Are we Moving towards the International Legitimation of Forcible Humanitarian Counter-measures in the World Community?' 10 *EJIL* 23.

Cassirer, E. (1946), *The Myth of the State*. New Haven: Yale University Press.

Cerone, J. (2000), 'Outlining KFOR Accountability in Post-Conflict Kosovo', American Society of International Law Insights (available from www.asil.org/insigh54.cfm).

Chandler, D. (2000), *Bosnia: Faking Democracy After Dayton* (2nd edn.). London: Pluto Press.

(2006), *Empire in Denial: The Politics of State-Building*. London: Pluto Press.

Charlesworth, H. and Chinkin, C. M. (1993), 'The Gender of Jus Cogens', 15 *Hum. Rts. Q.* 63.

(2000), *The Boundaries of International Law. A Feminist Analysis*. Manchester University Press.

Charlesworth, H., Chinkin, C. M. and Wright, S. (1991), 'Feminist Approaches to International Law', 85 *AJIL* 613.

Charney, R. and Goldsmith, J. (2008), 'Terrorism and the Convergence of Criminal and Military Detention Models', 60 *Stanford Law Review* 1079.

Charnovitz, S. (1997), 'Two Centuries of Participation: NGOs and International Governance', 18 *Mich. J. Int. L.* 183.

Chimni, B. S. (1995), 'The Incarceration of Victims: Deconstructing Safety Zones', in Al-Nauimi, N. and Meese, R. (eds.), *International Legal Issues Arising under the United Nations Decade of International Law: Proceedings of the Qatar International Law Conference 1994*. The Hague: Martinus Nijhoff.

Chinkin, C. M. (1989), 'The Challenge of Soft Law: Development and Change in International Law', 38 *ICLQ* 850.

(1993), *Third Parties in International Law*. Oxford University Press.

(1997), 'A Mirage in the Sand? Distinguishing between Binding and Non-Binding Relations between States', 10 *Leiden J. Int. L.* 223.

(1999), 'A Critique of the Public/Private Dimension', 10 *EJIL* 387.

(2000), 'The Legality of NATO's Action in the Former Republic of Yugoslavia under International Law', 49 *ICLQ* 910.

CIA, 'Ethiopia: Political and Security Impact of the Drought', 4 January 1985 (available from www.foia.cia.gov).

Clapham, A. (2006), *Human Rights Obligations of Non-State Actors*. Oxford University Press.

Cohen, A. (1968), *Belle du Seigneur*. Paris: Gallimard.

Cohen, M. (1955), 'The United Nations Secretariat – Some Constitutional and Administrative Developments', 49 *AJIL* 295.

Cohen, R. (2004), 'The Guiding Principles on Internal Displacement: An Innovation in International Standard Setting', 10 *Global Governance* 459.

Cohen, R. and Deng, F. (1998), *Masses in Flight: The Global Crisis of Internal Displacement*. Washington DC: The Brookings Institution.

(2009), 'Mass Displacement Caused by Conflicts and One-Sided Violence: National and International Responses', 40 *Stockholm International Peace Research Institute Yearbook* 15.

Collier, J. and Lowe, V. (1999), *The Settlement of Disputes in International Law*. Oxford University Press.

Committee on NGOs (2009), 'NGO Committee Recommends Suspension of Consultative Status for "Reporters Without Borders"', Press Release, 20 May.

Conforti, B. (1994), *Le Nazioni Unite* (5th edn.). Padova: Cedam.

(2005), *The Law and Practice of the United Nations* (3rd edn.). Leiden: Martinus Nijhoff.

Cook, R. (1994), 'State Responsibility for Violations of Women's Human Rights', 7 *Harv. HRJ.* 125.

(1995), 'The Elimination of Sexual Apartheid: Prospects for the Fourth World Conference on Women', Issue Paper on World Conferences No. 5, American Society of International Law.

Costa, P. and Zolo D. (eds.) (2007), *The Rule of Law: History, Theory and Criticism*. Dordrecht: Springer.

Cox, D. M. (1998), 'The Dayton Peace Agreement in Bosnia and Herzegovina: A Study of Implementation Strategies', *LXIX BYBIL* 201.

Crawford, J. (1998), 'First Report (and Addenda) on State Responsibility by the Special Rapporteur', 50th Session of the ILC, UN Doc. A/CN.4/490.

(1999), 'Revising the Draft Articles on State Responsibility', 10 *EJIL* 435.

(2001) 'The Relationship between Sanctions and Countermeasures' in Gowlland-Debbas, V. (ed.), *United Nations Sanctions and International Law*. The Hague: Kluwer.

(2002), *The International Law Commission's Articles on State Responsibility: Introduction, Text and Commentaries*. Cambridge University Press.

(2006), *The Creation of States in International Law* (2nd edn.). Oxford University Press.
(2007), 'Holding International Organisations and their Members to Account', Fifth Steinkraus-Cohen International Law Lecture, School of Oriental and African Studies, University of London, 15 March.
Crawford, J., Pellet, A. and Olleson, S. (eds.), assisted by Parlett, K. (2010), *The Law of International Responsibility.* Oxford University Press.
Crawford, J. and Watkins, K. (2010), 'International Responsibility', in Besson, S. and Tasioulas, J. (eds.), *The Philosophy of International Law.* Oxford University Press.
Crossland, G. H. (1994), 'Three Major Decisions Given by the Bunderverfassungsgericht (Federal Constitutional Court)', 19 *ELR* 202.
Curtin, D. and Nollkaemer, A. (2005), 'Conceptualising Accountability in International and European Law', *XXXVI Netherlands Yearbook of International Law* 3.
Curtis, M. (1998), *The Great Deception. Anglo-American Power and World Order.* London: Pluto Press.
Daget, S. (1989), 'The Abolition of the Slave Trade', in Ajayi, J. F. Ade (ed.), *General History of Africa. Africa in the XIX Century Until the 1880s.* Oxford: Heinemann.
Dagory, J. (1969), 'Les rapports entre les institutions spécialisées et l' organisation des Nations Unies', 73 *RGDIP* 286.
Daillier, P., Forteau, M., Dinh, N. Q., Pellet, A. (2009), *Droit International Public* (8th edn.). Librairie Générale de Droit et de Jurisprudence.
Dale, Sir W. (1974), 'UNRWA – A Subsidiary Organ of the United Nations', 23 *ICLQ* 576.
Dallaire, R. (2003), *Shake Hands with the Devil: the Failure of Humanity in Rwanda.* Canada: Random House.
Dashwood, A. (1998), 'Implied External Competence of the EC', in Koskenniemi, M (ed.), *International Law Aspects of the European Union.* The Hague: Kluwer Law International.
Darrow, M. and Arbour, L. (2009), 'The Pillar of Glass: Human Rights in the Development Operations of the United Nations', 103 *AJIL* 446.
D'Aspremont, J. (2007), 'The Abuse of Legal Personality of International Organisations and the Responsibility of Member States', 4 *International Organisations Law Review* 91.
David, E. (1997), 'Aspects juridiques de la responsabilité des différents acteurs dans les évènements du Rwanda (avril-juillet 1994)', Commission d'enquête parlementaire du Sénat concernant les évènements du Rwanda, in Belgian Parliamentary Documents, Sénat, 1997–98, 1–611/13, 6 December, Annexe 6.
Davis, D. B. (1975), *The Problem of Slavery in the Age of Revolution: 1770–1823.* Ithaca NY: Cornell University Press.
Dawson, W. H. (1934), *The Saar Territory: Its History, Population, Industry and Government by the League of Nations.* Publisher not indicated.

Dekker, I. F. (2006), 'Making Sense of Accountability in International Institutional Law', *XXXVI Netherlands Yearbook of International Law* 83.
Dennis, M. J. and Surena, A. M. (2008), 'Application of the International Covenant on Civil and Political Rights in Times of Armed Conflict and Military Occupation: The Gap Between Legal Theory and State Practice', 6 *EHRLR* 714.
De Ruggiero, G. (1959), *Storia del Liberalismo Europeo*. Milan: Feltrinelli.
De Vareilles Sommières, P. (2007), 'The Mandatory Nature of Article 2 of the Brussels Convention and Derogation from the Rule it Lays Down', in De Vareilles Sommières, P. (ed.), *Forum Shopping in the European Judicial Area*. Oxford: Hart Publishing.
De Waal, A. (1997), *Famine Crimes. Politics and the Disaster Relief Industry in Africa*. Oxford: James Currey.
Dewey, J. (1926), 'The Historic Background of Corporate Legal Personality', *XXXV Yale L. J.* 655.
Dickinson, E. D. (1929), *A Selection of Cases and Other Readings on the Law of Nations*. New York: McGraw-Hill.
Dinh, N. Q., Daillier, P. and Pellet, A. (1999), *Droit International Public* (6th edn.). Paris: LGDJ.
Dinstein, Y. (ed.) (1989), *International Law at a Time of Perplexity. Essays in Honour of Shabtai Rosenne*. Dordrecht: Martinus Nijhoff.
Domestici-Met, M. J. (1989), 'Aspects Juridiques Récents de l'Assistance Humanitaire', 35 *AFDI* 117.
(1995), 'Propos sur le droit à l' assistance', in Bettati, M., Domestici-Met, M.-J. and Tanja, G. J. (eds.), *Law in Humanitarian Crises. Vol. II: Access to Victims: Right to Intervene or Right to Receive Humanitarian Assistance?* Luxembourg: Office for Official Publications of the European Union.
Donini, A. (1998), 'Asserting Humanitarianism in Peace-Maintenance', 4 *Global Governance* 81.
Doyal, L. and Gough, I. (1991), *A Theory of Human Need*. Basingstoke: Macmillan Education.
Doyle, M. W. (1995), *UN Peace-Keeping in Cambodia: UNTAC's Civil Mandate*. London: Lynne Rienner Publishers.
Dubin, M. D. (1983), 'Transgovernmental Processes in the League of Nations', 37 *Int. Org.* 469.
Dugard, J. (2000), 'First Report on Diplomatic Protection by the Special Rapporteur', 52nd Session of the ILC, UN Doc. A/CN.4/506.
Dumm, T. L. (1996), *Michel Foucault and the Politics of Freedom*. London: Sage.
Dupree, N. (1998), 'Afghan Women under the Taliban', in Maley, W. (ed.), *Fundamentalism Re-born? Afghanistan and the Taliban*. London: Hurst and Company.
Dupuy, R. J. (1989), 'L'assistance humanitaire comme droit de l'homme contre la souveraineté de l'Etat', in Kalshoven, F. (ed.), *Assisting the Victims of Armed Conflict and Other Disasters*. Dordrecht: Martinus Nijhoff.
Dupuy, R. J. (ed.) (1998), *A Handbook of International Organizations* (2nd edn.). Dordrecht: Martinus Nijhoff.

Eagleton, C. (1950), 'International Organisation and the Law of Responsibility', 76(I) *RC* 323.
Easterly, W. (2006), *The White Man's Burden: Why the West's Efforts to Aid the Rest Have Done So Much Harm and So Little Good*. Oxford University Press.
The Economist (1997), 'Somalia: Good Intentions Turned to Shame', 5 July.
(2001), 'The Dangers of Trying to Help', 10 March.
Eeckhout, P. (2004), *External Relations of the European Union: Legal and Constitutional Foundations*. Oxford University Press.
Eide, A. (1992), 'The Sub-Commission on Prevention of Discrimination and Protection of Minorities', in Alston, P. (ed.), *The United Nations and Human Rights*. Oxford: Clarendon Press.
Engdahl, O. (2007), *Protection of Personnel in Peace Operations: The Role of the 'Safety Convention' against the Background of General International Law* (2007). Leiden: Martinus Nijhoff.
Erb, N. E. (1998), 'Gender-based Crimes Under the Draft Statute for the Permanent International Criminal Court', 29 *Columbia Human Rights Law Review* 401.
European Stability Initiative (2007), 'On Mount Olympus: How the UN Violated Human Rights in Bosnia and Herzegovina, and Why Nothing Has Been Done to Correct it', 10 February.
Evans-Pritchard, E. E. (1969), *The Nuer*. Oxford University Press.
Faite, A. (2007), 'Multinational Forces Acting Pursuant to a Mandate of the United Nations: Specific Issues on the Applicability of International Humanitarian Law', 11 *Journal of International Peacekeeping* 143.
Farah, N. (1999), *Gifts*. New York: Arcade Publishing.
Fassbender, B. (2006), 'Targeted Sanctions and Due Process', Institute of Public International Law at the University of Hamboldt in Berlin.
Fiedler, W. (2002) 'Article 98' in Simma, B. (ed.), *The Charter of the United Nations: A Commentary* (2nd edn.). Oxford University Press.
Financial Times (1997), 'Italy to Probe Torture Claims', 14 June.
(1998), 'Refugees' Agency Lost in Wilderness of Bungling and Waste', 29 July.
(2001), 'UN Probe Raises Concern over Drug Programme', 26 April.
Fischer, H. (1950), 'The Suppression of Slavery in International Law', 3 *ICLQ* 28.
Fitzmaurice, G. (1956), *The Law and Procedure of the International Court of Justice*. Cambridge: Grotius.
(1959), 'The Law and Procedure of the International Court of Justice 1954–9 – General Principles and Sources of International Law', 35 *BYBIL* 183.
Fitzmaurice, M. (2009), 'Dynamic (Evolutive) Interpretation of Treaties: Part I', 21 *Hague Yearbook of International Law* 101.
Fleck, D. (ed.) (1995), *The Handbook of Humanitarian Law in Armed Conflict*. Oxford University Press.
(2008), *The Handbook of International Humanitarian Law* (2nd edn.). Oxford University Press.
Focsaneanu, L. (1957), 'Le droit interne de l' Organisation des Nations Unies', 3 *AFDI*.

FOI Swedish Defence Research Agency (2009), 'Managing Unintended Consequences of Peace Support Operations' (available from www2.foi.se/rapp/foir2916.pdf).

Forsythe, D. P. (2005), *The Humanitarians: The International Committee of the Red Cross*. Cambridge University Press.

The Forward (2000), 'Surprising News on UN Dues', 11 February 2001 (available from www.unwatch.org/site/c.bdKKISNqEmG/b.1289203/apps/s/content.asp?ct=1715095).

Foucault, M. (1979), *Discipline and Punish: The Birth of the Prison*. Harmondsworth: Penguin. Italian edn. (1976) *Sorvegliare e Punire*. Turin: Einaudi.

(1998), *Archivio Foucault: Interventi, colloqui, interviste* Vol. III 1978–1985, Pandolfi, A. (ed.). Turin: Einaudi.

(1998), *Bisogna Difendere la Societá*. Milan: Feltrinelli. French edn. (1997) *Il faut défendre la société: cours au Collège de France*. Paris: Gallimard.

Fox, J. A. and Brown, L. D. (eds.) (1998), *The Struggle for Accountability: The World Bank, NGOs and Grassroots Movements*. Cambridge MA: MIT Press.

Francioni, F. (2000), 'Multilateralism á la Carte: The Limits to Unilateral Withholdings of Assessed Contributions to the UN Budget', 11 *EJIL* 43.

Franck, T. M. (1992), 'The "Powers of Appreciation": Who Is the Ultimate Guardian of UN Legality?' 86 *AJIL* 519.

(1995), *Fairness in International Law and Institutions*. Oxford University Press.

Franck, T. M. and Rodley, N. (1973), 'After Bangladesh: Humanitarian Intervention by Military Force', 67 *AJIL* 275.

Freud, S. (1978), *Il Disagio della Civiltà*, in *Opere Vol. X*. Turin: Boringhieri. English edn. (1994) *Civilisation and its Discontents*. New York: Dover.

Friedrich, J. (2005), 'UNMIK in Kosovo: Struggling with Uncertainty' 9 *Max Planck Yearbook of United Nations Law* 225.

Fukuyama, F. (2006), 'After Neo-Conservatism', *New York Times (Magazine)*, 19 February.

(2006), *After the Neocons: America at the Crossroads*. London: Profile Books.

Fusinato, G. (1914), *Avis sur les questions touchants la personalité juridique de l' Institut International d' Agriculture*. Rome: Imprimerie de l' Institut Internationale de l' Agriculture.

Gadamer, H. G. (1989), *Truth and Method* (2nd edn.). London: Sheed and Ward.

Gaja, G. (1987), 'A "New" Vienna Convention on Treaties between States and International Organisations and between International Organisations: A Critical Commentary', 58 *BYBIL* 235.

(1996), 'Opinion 2/94, Accession by the Community to the European Convention for the Protection of Human Rights and Fundamental Freedoms' 33 *Common Market Law Review* 973.

(2003), 'First Report on Responsibility of International Organisations by the Special Rapporteur', 55th Session of the ILC, UN Doc. A/CN.4/532.

(2004), 'Second Report on Responsibility of International Organisations by the Special Rapporteur', 56th Session of the ILC, UN Doc. A/CN.4/541.

(2005), 'Third Report on Responsibility of International Organisations by the Special Rapporteur', 57th Session of the ILC, UN Doc. A/CN.4/553.

(2006), 'Fourth Report on Responsibility of International Organisations by the Special Rapporteur', 58th Session of the ILC, UN Doc. A/CN.4/564.
(2007), 'Fifth Report on Responsibility of International Organisations by the Special Rapporteur', 59th Session of the ILC, UN Doc. A/CN.4/583.
(2008), 'Sixth Report on Responsibility of International Organisations by the Special Rapporteur', 60th Session of the ILC, UN Doc. A/CN.4/597.
(2009), 'Seventh Report on Responsibility of International Organisations by the Special Rapporteur', 61st Session of the ILC, UN Doc. A/CN.4/610.
Garcia-Amador, F. V. (1956), 'First Report on State Responsibility by the Special Rapporteur', 8th Session of the ILC, UN Doc. A/CN.4/96, and in (1956, II) YBILC 173.
Gasser, H. P. (1994), 'Die Anwendbarkeit des humanitären Völkerrechts auf militärische Operationen der Vereinten Nationen', 5 *Revue Suisse de Droit International et de Droit Européen* 443.
George, S. (1995), 'The World Bank and its Concept of Good Governance', in Hippler, J. (ed.), *The Democratisation of Disempowerment*. London, Boulder: Pluto Press with Transnational Institute.
Ghebali, V. Y. (1988), *The International Labour Organisation: A Case-Study on the Evolution of UN Specialised Agencies*. Dordrecht: Martinus Nijhoff.
Giorgetti, C. (2010), *A Principled Approach to State Failure*. Leiden and Boston: Brill.
Goffman, E. (1961), *Asylums: Essay on the Social Situation of Mental Patients and Other Inmates*. New York: Doubleday Anchor.
Goldstein, J., Kahler, M., Keohane, R. K. and Slaughter, A. M. (2000), 'Introduction: Legalization and World Politics', 54 *Int. Org.* 385.
Goodwin-Gill, G. S. (1999), 'Refugee Identity and Protection's Fading Prospect' in Nicholson, F. and Twomey, P. (eds.), *Refugee Rights and Realities*. Cambridge University Press.
(2007), *The Refugee in International Law* (3rd edn.). Oxford: Clarendon Press.
Gordon, J. (1999), 'A Peaceful, Silent, Deadly Remedy: The Ethics of Economic Sanctions', 13(1) *Ethics and International Affairs* 123.
Gowlland-Debbas, V. (1994), 'The Relationship Between the International Court of Justice and the Security Council in the Light of the Lockerbie Case', 88 *AJIL* 643.
(1994), 'Security Council Enforcement Action and Issues of State Responsibility', 43 *ICLQ* 55.
(ed.) (2004) *National Implementation of United Sanctions: A Comparative Study*. Leiden: Brill.
(2010), 'Responsibility and the United Nations Charter', in Crawford, J., Pellet, A. and Olleson, S. (eds.), *The Law of International Responsibility*. Oxford University Press.
Gozzi, G., (2007), '*Rechtstaat* and Individual Rights in German Constitutional History', in Costa, P. and Zolo D. (eds.), *The Rule of Law: History, Theory and Criticism*. Dordrecht: Springer.
Gramsci, A. (1975–1977), *Quaderni dal Carcere* (2nd edn., V. Gerrantana (ed.)). Turin: Einaudi.

Gray, C. D. (2001), 'Peacekeeping after the *Brahimi Report*: Is there a Crisis of Credibility for the UN', 6 *Journal of Conflict and Security Law* 267.
(2008), *International Law and the Use of Force (3rd edn.)*. Oxford University Press.
Green, L. C. (2000), *The Contemporary Law of Armed Conflict* (2nd edn.). Manchester University Press.
Greenwood, C. (1993), 'Is There a Right of Humanitarian Intervention?' 49(2) *World Today* 34.
(1995), 'Historical Development and Legal Basis', in Fleck, D. (ed.), *The Handbook of Humanitarian Law in Armed Conflict*. Oxford University Press.
(1995), 'Scope of Application of Humanitarian Law', in Fleck, D. (ed.), *The Handbook of Humanitarian Law in Armed Conflict*. Oxford University Press.
(1998), 'International Humanitarian Law and United Nations Military Operations', 1 *YB Int. Humanit. L.* 3.
(1999), 'Humanitarian Intervention: The Case of Kosovo', 10 *Finnish Yearbook of International Law* 141
(2000), 'International Law and the NATO Intervention in Kosovo', 49 *ICLQ* 926.
Grewe, W. G. (ed.) (1992), *Fontes Historiae Juris Gentium*. Berlin: Walter de Gruyter.
Griffin, J. (2008), *On Human Rights*. Oxford University Press.
The Guardian (1993), 'UN Forces Deny Somali Detainees Legal Rights', 25 September.
(2000), 'Genocide Lawsuit Against the UN', 11 January.
(2001), 'Amnesty and UN Staff Accuse Kosovo War Crimes Tribunal of Ethnic Bias', 20 June.
(2005), 'Report reveals shame of UN peacekeepers: Sexual abuse by soldiers "must be punished"', 25 March.
Gulliver, P. H. (1969), 'Case-Studies of Law in non-Western Societies', in Nader, L. (ed.), *Law in Culture and Society*. Berkeley: University of California Press.
(1969), 'Dispute Settlement Without Courts: The Ndendeuli of Southern Tanzania', in Nader, L. (ed.), *Law in Culture and Society*. Berkeley: University of California Press.
Guluma, W. (1997), Letter to *The Lancet*, submitted on 4 October, unknown whether published or not, on file with the author.
Gutman, R. (1999), 'United Nations and the Geneva Conventions', in Gutman, R. and Rieff, D. (eds.), *Crimes of War: What the Public Should Know*. London: W. W. Norton.
Gutman, R. and Rieff, D. (eds.) (1999), *Crimes of War: What the Public Should Know*. London: W. W. Norton.
Halpin, A. (1996), 'The Concept of a Legal Power', 16 *Oxford Journal of Legal Studies* 129.
Hampson, F. J. and Kihara-Hunt, A. (2007), 'The Accountability of Personnel Associated with Peacekeeping Operations', in Aoi, C., de Coning, C. and Thakur, R. (eds.), *Unintended Consequences of Peacekeeping Operations*. New York: United Nations University Press.
Hancock, J. (1989), *Lords of Poverty*. London: Macmillan.

Hardcastle, R. J. and Chua, A. T. L. (1998), 'Humanitarian Assistance: towards a Right of Access to Victims of Natural Disasters', 325 *Int. Rev. R.C.* 589.
Harlow, C. (2002), *Accountability in the European Union*. Oxford University Press.
Harrell-Bond, B. E. (1985), 'Humanitarianism in a Strait-Jacket', 84(334) *African Affairs* 3.
(1986), *Imposing Aid*. Oxford University Press.
(1998), 'Camps: Literature Review', 2 *FMR* 22.
(1998), 'The Experience of Refugees as Recipients of Aid', in Ager, A. (ed.), *Refugees: Perspectives on the Experience of Forced Migration*. London: Pinter.
(2002), 'Can Humanitarian Work with Refugees Be Humane?' 24 *Hum. Rts. Q.* 51.
Harrell-Bond, B. E., Voutira, E. and Leopold, M. (1992), 'Counting the Refugees: Gifts, Givers, Patrons and Clients', 5 *J. Ref. St.* 205.
Harrington, A. R. (2008), 'Prostituting Peace: The Impact of Sending State's Legal Regimes on U.N. Peacekeeper Behavior and Suggestions to Protect the Populations Peacekeepers Guard', (available from http://works.bepress.com/cgi/viewcontent.cgi?article=1011&context=alexandra_harrington).
Harris, O. (ed.) (1996), *Inside and Outside the Law*. London: Routledge.
Hart, H. L. A. (1968), *Punishment and Responsibility: Essays in the Philosophy of Law*. Oxford: Clarendon Press.
(1977), 'American Jurisprudence through English Eyes: The Nightmare and the Noble Dream', 11 *Georgia Law Review* 969.
(1982), *Essays on Bentham*. Oxford University Press.
Harvard Program on Human Security (1993), *Sanctions in Haiti: Crisis in Humanitarian Action*. Cambridge: Harvard University Center for Population and Development Studies.
Harwig, M. (1993), *Die Haftung der Mitgliedstaaten für Internationale Organisationen*. Berlin: Springer.
Haskell, T. L. (1992), 'Capitalism and the Origin of Humanitarian Sensibility', in Bender, T. (ed.), *The Anti-slavery Debate. Capitalism and Abolitionism as a Problem in Historical Interpretation*. Berkeley: University of California Press.
Hathaway, J. (2005), *The Rights of Refugees Under International Law*. Cambridge University Press.
Hazzard, S. (1989), 'Reflections. Breaking Faith-I', *The New Yorker*, 25 September.
Helsinki Committee for Human Rights (2007), 'Report on the Status of Human Rights in Bosnia and Herzegovina: Analysis for the period January – December 2007', Br: 02A-02/2008 (available from www.bh-hchr.org/Reports/reportHR2006.htm).
Higgins, R. (1963), *The Development of International Law through the Political organs of the United Nations*. London: Oxford University Press for the Royal Institute of International Affairs.
(1969–1981), *United Nations Peace-keeping 1946–1967: Documents and Commentary*. Vol. I: Middle East; Vol. II: Asia; Vol. III: Africa; Vol. IV: Europe. Oxford University Press.

(1994), *Problems and Process: International Law and How We Use it*. Oxford: Clarendon Press.
(1995), 'The Legal Consequences for Member States of Non-Fulfilment by International Organisations of their Obligations toward Third Parties: Provisional Report', 66-I *Annuaire de l' Institut de Droit International* 373.
Hilf, M. and Khan, D.-E. (2002), 'Article 22', in Simma, B. (ed.), *The Charter of the United Nations: A Commentary* (2nd edn.). Oxford University Press.
Hilhorst, D. and Van Leeuwen, M. (2000), 'Emergency and Development: the Case of *Imidugudu*, Villagization in Rwanda', 13 *J. Ref. St.* 264.
Hill, N. L. (1931), *International Administration*. London: McGraw-Hill.
Hippler, J. (ed.) (1995), *The Democratisation of Disempowerment*. London, Boulder: Pluto Press with Transnational Institute.
Hirsch, M. (1995), *The Responsibility of International Organizations Toward Third Parties: Some Basic Principles*. Dordrecht: Martinus Nijhoff.
Hochschild, A. (1999), *King Leopold's Ghost*. London: Macmillan.
Holborn, L. (1975), *Refugees: A Problem of Our Time*. Metuchen NJ: Scarecrow Press.
Hoskins, E. and Nutt, S. (1997), 'The Humanitarian Impacts of Economic Sanctions on Burundi', Occasional Paper No. 29, Thomas J. Watson Jr. Institute for International Studies, Brown University.
Howell, R. (1987), *The Royal Navy and the Slave Trade*. London: Croom Helm.
Human Rights Watch (1993), 'Seeking Refuge, Finding Terror – The Widespread Rape of Somali Women Refugees in North Eastern Kenya'. Vol. 17(1A), 7 March. New York (available from www.hrw.org/en/reports/2005/03/06/seeking-justice-0).
(1997), 'Failing the Internally Displaced: The UNDP Displaced Persons Program in Kenya'. New York.
(1997), 'Uncertain Refuge'. New York.
(1999), 'Federal Republic of Yugoslavia: Abuses against Serbs and Roma in the New Kosovo'. New York.
(1999), 'Tanzania – In the Name of Security. Forced Round-ups of Refugees in Tanzania'. New York.
(1999), *World Report 1999*. New York.
(2001), *World Report 2001*. New York.
(2005), 'Seeking Justice: The Prosecution of Sexual Violence in the Congo'. New York.
(2008), 'Killings in Kiwanja'. New York.
Human Rights Watch/Federation Internationale des Ligues des Droits de l' Homme (1999), *Leave None to Tell the Story: Genocide in Rwanda*. New York.
Hunt, L. (2007), *Inventing Human Rights*. New York: W. W. Norman & Company Inc.
Hutchinson, S. (1996), *Nuer Dilemmas: Coping with Money, War and the State*. Berkeley: University of California Press.
Hyndman, J. (1996), *Geographies of Displacement: Gender, Power and Culture in UNHCR Refugee Camps*. University of British Columbia: PhD Thesis.

(2000), *Managing Displacement: Refugees and the Politics of Humanitarianism*. Minneapolis: University of Minnesota Press.
Ignatieff, M. (2004), 'Democratic Providentialism', *New York Times (Magazine)*, 12 December.
The Independent (1998), 'Women Fighting to Stem Disaster in Iraq', 15 October.
(2001), 'Sudan's Child Soldiers Go Hungry in Unicef's Filthy Demob Camps', 23 April.
(2004), 'Cover Story: Sex and Death in the heart of Africa', 25 May.
(2004), 'Will Congo's Women Ever Have Justice?' 12 July.
(2005), 'Annan backs tough action to stop Congo Sex abuse', 11 February.
Institut de Droit International, Preliminary Report of Rapporteur Higgins, R. (1995), 'The Legal Consequences for Member States of the Non-Fulfilment by International Organizations of Their Obligations Towards Third Parties', 66-I *Annuaire de l' Institut de Droit International* 373.
(2003), *Resolution on Humanitarian Assistance*, adopted by the Sixteenth Commission in Bruges, 2 September 2003.
International Commission on Intervention and State Sovereignty (2001), *The Responsibility to Protect: Report of the International Commission on Intervention and Sovereignty*. Ottawa: International Development Centre.
International Law Association – Committee on the Accountability of International Organisations (2000), 'Second Report presented at the London Conference, July 2000' (available from www.ila-hq.org/en/committees/index.cfm/cid/9).
(2002), 'Report of the Seventh Conference', New Delhi.
(2004), 'Final Report', Berlin.
Isherwood, T. (2005), 'Camps: at what price?' (available from www.refugees.org).
Jackson, T. (1986), *The Law of Kenya: An Introduction* (2nd edn.). Nairobi: Kenya Literature Bureau.
Janis, M. W. (ed.) (1991), *The Influence of Religion on the Development of International Law*. Dordrecht: Martinus Nijhoff.
Jenks, W. C. (1961), *International Immunities*. London: Stevens.
Jennings, R. Y. (ed.) (1965), *Cambridge Essays in International Law: Essays in Honour of Lord McNair*. London: Stevens.
Jennings, R. Y. and Watts, A. (eds.), (1992) *Oppenheim's International Law* (9th edn.). London: Longman.
Jones, R. and Sherman, S. S. (1927), *The League of Nations: From Idea to Reality*. London: I. Pitman.
Jonsen, A. R. and Toulmin, S. (1988), *The Abuse of Casuistry*. Berkeley: University of California Press.
Joyner, C. C. (ed.) (1997), *The United Nations and International Law*. Cambridge University Press.
Kagan, M. (2002), 'Assessment of Refugee Status Determination Procedure at UNHCR's Cairo Office 2001–2002', American University in Cairo Forced Migration and Refugee Studies (CMRS) Working Paper No. 1.

(2006), 'Frontier Justice: Legal Aid and UNHCR Refugee Status Determinations in Egypt', 19(1) *Journal of Refugee Studies* 45.

(2006), 'The Beleaguered Gatekeeper: Protection Challenges by UNHCR Refugee Status Determination', 18(1) *International Journal of Refugee Law* 1.

(2009), 'Refugee Credibility Assessment and the "Religious Imposter" Problem: A Case Study of Eritrean Pentecostal Claims in Egypt', CMRS Working Paper No. 9 (available from www.aucegypt.edu/GAPP/cmrs/Documents/KaganReligiousImposters.pdf).

Kälin, W. (2008), 'Guiding Principles on Internal Displacement: Annotations' (revised edn.), 38 *Studies in Transnational Legal Policy* 1.

Kalshoven, F. (ed.) (1989), *Assisting the Victims of Armed Conflict and Other Disasters*. Dordrecht: Martinus Nijhoff.

Kaminski, M. (1999), 'UN Struggles with a Legal Vacuum in Kosovo; Team Improvises in Effort to Build a Civil Structure', *Wall Street Journal*, 4 August, A14.

Kant, I. (1999), 'On the Common Saying: 'This May be True in Theory but it does not Apply in Practice', in Gregor, M. J. (ed.), *The Cambridge Edition of the Works of Immanuel Kant in Translation: Practical Philosophy*. Cambridge University Press, 273.

(1999) 'The Metaphysics of Morals' in McGregor, M. J. (ed.), *The Cambridge Edition of the Works of Immanuel Kant in Translation: Practical Philosophy*. Cambridge University Press, 311.

(1999) 'Toward Perpetual Peace' in McGregor, M. J. (ed.) *The Cambridge Edition of the Works of Immanuel Kant in Translation: Practical Philosophy*. Cambridge University Press, 311.

Kaufmann, C. D. and Pape, R. A. (1999), 'Explaining Costly International Moral Action: Britain's Sixty-year Campaign Against the Atlantic Slave Trade', 53 *Int. Org.* 631.

Kaufmann, J. (1980), *United Nations Decision-Making*. Alphen aan den Rijn: Sijthoff & Noordhoff.

Keen, D. and Wilson, K. (1994), 'Engaging with Violence: A Re-assessment of Relief in Wartime', in Macrae, J. and Zwi, A. (eds.), *War and Hunger: Rethinking International Responses to Complex Emergencies*. London: Zed Books.

Kelly, M. (2001), 'Transitional Justice in peace Operations: Shaping the Twilight Zone in Somalia and East Timor', 4 *YB Int. Humanit. Law* 213.

Kelsen, H. (1950), *The Law of the United Nations: A Critical Analysis of its Fundamental Problems*. London: Stevens and Sons.

Kennedy, D. (2001), 'The International Human Rights Movement: Part of the Problem?' 15 *Harvard Human Rights Journal* 99.

(2004), *The Dark Sides of Virtue: Re-assessing International Humanitarianism*. New Jersey: Princeton University Press.

Kent, V. (2007), 'Protecting Civilians from UN Peacekeepers and Humanitarian Workers: Sexual Exploitation and Abuse', in Aoi, C.,

de Coning, C. and Thakur, R. (eds.), *Unintended Consequences of Peacekeeping Operations*. New York: United Nations University Press.
Keohane, R. O., Moravcsik, A. and Slaughter, A. M. (2000), 'Legalized Dispute Resolution: Interstate and Transnational', 54 *Int. Org.* 457.
Keynes, J. M. (1936), *The General Theory of Employment, Interest and Money*. London: Palgrave Macmillan.
Kirby, J., Kleist, T., Frerks, G., Flikkema, W. and O'Keefe, P. (1997), 'UNHCR's Cross Border Operation in Somalia: The Value of Quick Impact Projects for Refugee Settlement', 10 *J. Ref. St.* 181.
Klabbers, J. (2002), *An Introduction to International Institutional Law*. Cambridge University Press.
(2005), 'Two Concepts of International Organisations', 2 *International Organisations Law Review* 277.
Klappe, B. E. (2008), 'International Peace Operations', in Fleck, D. (ed.), *The Handbook of International Humanitarian Law* (2nd edn.). Oxford University Press.
Klein, P. (2007), 'Responsabilité pour les faits commis dans le cadre d' operations de paix et étendue du pouvoir de contrôle de la Court européenne de droits de l' homme: quelques considerations critiques sur l' arrêt *Behrami et Saramati*', 53 *AFDI* 43.
(2010), 'The Attribution of Acts to International Organizations', in Crawford, J., Pellet, A. and Olleson, S. (eds.), *The Law of International Responsibility*. Oxford University Press.
Kleine-Ahlbrandt, S. T. E. (2004), *The Protection Gap in the International Protection of Internally Displaced Persons: The Case of Rwanda* (2nd edn.). Geneva: Graduate Institute of International Studies.
Klotz, A. (1995), *Norms in International Relations: The Struggle against Apartheid*. Ithaca NY: Cornell University Press.
Knoll, B. (2005), 'From Benchmarking to Final Status? Kosovo and the Problem of an International Administration's Open-Ended Mandate', 16 *EJIL* 637.
(2008), *The Legal Status of Territories Subject to Administration by International Organisations*. New York: Cambridge University Press.
Knoll, B. and Uhl, R. J. (2007), 'Too Little, Too Late: the Human Rights Advisory Panel in Kosovo', 7 *EHRLR* 534.
Köbben, A. J. F. (1969), 'The Cottica Dyuka of Surinam', in Nader, L. (ed.), *Law in Culture and Society*. Berkeley: University of California Press.
Koskenniemi, M. (ed.) (1998), *International Law Aspects of the European Union*. The Hague: Kluwer Law International.
(2005), *From Apology to Utopia: The Structure of International Legal Argument* (re-issued with new Epilogue). Cambridge University Press.
Kuloba, R. (1997), *Courts of Justice in Kenya*. Nairobi: Oxford University Press.
Kunz, J. L. (1947), 'Privileges and Immunities of International Organisations', 41 *AJIL* 828.

Lagoni, R. and Chaitidou E. (2002), 'Article 71', in Simma, B. (ed.), *The Charter of the United Nations: A Commentary* (2nd edn.). Oxford University Press.
Lapidoth, R. and Hirsch, M. (eds.) (1994), *The Jerusalem Question and Its Resolution: Selected Documents*. Dordrecht: Martinus Nijhoff.
Larsen, K.M. (2008), 'Attribution of Conduct in Peace Operations: The "Ultimate Authority and Control" Test', 19 *EJIL* 509.
Lassall, H. D. and McDougal, M. S. (1992), *Jurisprudence for a Free Society: Studies in Law, Science and Policy*. New Haven Press.
Lauterpacht, E. (1956), 'The Contemporary Practice of the UK in the Field of International Law: Survey and Comment', 5 *ICLQ* 405.
(1965), 'The Legal Effect of Illegal Acts of International Organisations', in Jennings, R. Y. (ed.), *Cambridge Essays in International Law: Essays in Honour of Lord McNair*. London: Stevens.
(1976), 'The Development of the Law of International Organization by the Decisions of International Tribunals', in 152(IV) *RC* 381.
(1999), 'Judicial Review of the Acts of International Organisations' in Boisson de Chazournes, L. and Sands, P. (eds.), *International Law, the International Court of Justice and Nuclear Weapons*. Cambridge University Press.
Lawyers Committee for Human Rights (1999), 'A Fragile Peace: Laying the Foundations for Justice in Kosovo'. New York.
(1999), 'Kosovo: Protection and Peace-Building. Protection of Refugees, Returnees, Internally Displaced Persons, and Minorities'. New York.
(2000), 'Safeguarding the Rights of Refugees under the Exclusion Clauses: Summary Findings of the Project and a Lawyers Committee for Human Rights Perspective' in the Special Supplementary Issue, 12 Int. J. Ref. L.
Leach, P. (2008), 'The Chechen Conflict: Analysing the Oversight of the European Court of Human Rights', 6 *EHRLR* 732.
Leary, V. (1999), 'The WHO Case: Implications for Specialised Agencies', in Boisson de Chazournes, L. and Sands, P. (eds.), *International Law, the International Court of Justice and Nuclear Weapons*. Cambridge University Press.
Leckow, R. (2005), 'Conditionality in the Developments in the International Monetary Fund', 3 *Current Developments in Monetary and Financial Law* 53.
Levi, P. (1971), *La Tregua*. Turin: Einaudi. English trans. (1996) *The Truce*. London: Vintage.
(1986), *Se Questo e' un Uomo*. Turin: Einaudi. English trans. (1979) *If This is a Man*. Harmondsworth: Penguin.
Lillich, R. B. (ed.) (1973), *Humanitarian Intervention and the United Nations*. Charlottesville: University Press of Virginia.
Lindblom, A.-K. (2010), 'The Responsibility of Other Entities: Non-Governmental Organisations', in Crawford, J., Pellet, A. and Olleson, S. (eds.), *The Law of International Responsibility*. Oxford University Press.
Linderfalk, U. (2007), *On the Interpretation of Treaties*. Dordrecht: Springer.
Loescher, G (2001), *UNHCR and World Politics: A Perilous Path*. Oxford University Press.

Lowe, V. (2000), 'International Legal Issues Arising in the Kosovo Crisis', 49 *ICLQ* 934.

(2007), *International Law*. Oxford: Clarendon Law Series.

Lowe, V. and Warbrick, C. (eds.) (1994), *The United Nations and the Principles of International Law. Essays in Memory of Michael Akehurst*. London: Routledge.

Lupi, N. (1998), 'Report by the Enquiry Commission on the Behaviour of Italian Peace-Keeping Troops in Somalia', 1 *YB Int. Humanit. L.* 375.

Lynch, C. (2007) 'Former UN Oil-for-Food Chief Indicted', *Washington Post*, 17 January.

Macalister-Smith, P. (1989), 'Rights and Duties of the Agencies Involved in Providing Humanitarian Assistance and their Personnel in Armed Conflict', in Kalshoven, F. (ed.), *Assisting the Victims of Armed Conflict and Other Disasters*. Dordrecht: Martinus Nijhoff.

Macdonald, R. St. J. (ed.) (1994), *Essays in Honour of Wang Tieya*. Dordrecht: Kluwer.

Macdonald, R. St. J. and Johnston, D. M. (1983), *The Structure and Process of International Law: Essays in Legal Philosophy, Doctrine and Theory*. The Hague: Martinus Nijhoff.

Macintyre, A. C. (1988), *Whose Justice? Whose Rationality?* London: Duckworth.

Macrae, J. and Zwi, A. (eds.) (1994), *War and Hunger: Rethinking International Responses to Complex Emergencies*. London: Zed Books.

Malanczuk, P. (1993), *Humanitarian Intervention and the Legitimacy of the Use of Force*. Amsterdam: Martinus Nijhoff International.

Maley, W. (ed.) (1998), *Fundamentalism Re-born? Afghanistan and the Taliban*. London: Hurst and Company.

Mamdani, M. (1996), *Citizen and Subject: Contemporary Africa and the Legacy of Late Colonialism*. Kampala: Fountain; London: James Currey.

Marks, S. and Clapham, A. (2005), *International Human Rights Lexicon* (2nd edn.). Oxford University Press.

Marsden, P. (1998), *The Taliban: War, Religion and the New Order in Afghanistan*. Oxford University Press.

Martenczuk, B. (1999), 'The Security Council, the International Court and Judicial Review: What Lessons from Lockerbie', 10 *EJIL* 517.

Martinez, J. (2007–2008), 'Anti-Slavery Courts and the Dawn of International Human Rights Law', 117 *Yale L. J.* 550.

Marx, K. (1846), 'The German Ideology', in O'Malley, J. (ed.) (1994), *Marx: Early Political Writings*. Cambridge University Press.

Masumbuko, M. (1997), 'Implementing Protection', Unpublished manuscript by the UNHCR Protection Assistant in Kakuma refugee camp.

Matheson, M. J. (2001), 'United Nations Governance of Postconflict Societies', 95 *AJIL* 76.

Mathews, J. (1997), 'Power Shift', 76 *Foreign Affairs* 50.

McCarthy, C. (2008), 'Human Rights and the Laws of War under the American Convention on Human Rights', 6 *EHRLR* 762.

McDougal, M. S. and Reisman, M. (1983), 'International Law in Policy-Oriented Perspective', in Macdonald, R. St. J. and Johnston, D. M. (eds.), *The Structure and Process of International Law: Essays in Legal Philosophy, Doctrine and Theory*. The Hague: Martinus Nijhoff.
McNair, Lord A. (1961), *The Law of Treaties*. Oxford: Clarendon Press.
McNamara, D. (2000), 'UN Human Rights Activities in Cambodia: An Evaluation', in Henkin, A. (ed.), *Honouring Human Rights*. The Hague: Kluwer Law International.
McRae, P. (2002), 'The Search for Meaning: Continuing Problems with the Interpretation of Treaties', 33(2) *Victoria University of Wellington Law Review* 209.
Mégret, F. and Hoffmann, F. (2003), 'The UN as a Human Rights Violator?' 25 *Human Rts. Q.* 314.
Meng, W. (2002), 'Article 57', in Simma, B. (ed.), *The Charter of the United Nations: A Commentary* (2nd edn.). Oxford University Press.
Merrills, J. G. (2005), *International Dispute Settlement* (4th edn.). Cambridge University Press.
Messineo, F. (2009), 'The House of Lords in Al-Jedda and Public International Law: Attribution of Conduct to UN-Authorised Forces and the Power of the Security Council to Displace Human Rights', *LVI Netherlands International Law Review* 35.
Milano, E. (2006), *Unlawful Territorial Situations in International Law: Reconciling Effectiveness, Legality and Legitimacy*. Leiden: Brill.
(2008), 'Il trasferimento di funzioni da UNMIK a EULEX in Kosovo', 91 *Riv. It. Dir. Int.* 967.
Milanović, M. (2009), 'Norm Conflict in International Law: Whither Human Rights?' 20 *Duke Journal of Comparative and International Law* 69.
Milanović, M. and Papić, T. (2009) 'As Bad As It Gets: The European Court of Human Rights' Behrami and Saramati Decision and General International Law', 58 *ICLQ* 267.
Mill, J. S. (1991), *On Liberty*, Oxford University Press.
Miller, A. J. (2007), 'Privileges and Immunities of United Nations Officials', 4 *International Organisations Law Review* 169.
(2009), 'The Privileges and Immunities of the United Nations', 6 *International Organisations Law Review* 7.
Miller, D. (2004), 'Holding Nations Responsible', 114 *Ethics* 240.
Molier, G. (2006), 'Humanitarian Intervention and the Responsibility to Protect After 9/11', 53 *Netherlands Journal of International Law* 37.
Moore Jr., B. (1978), *Injustice: The Social Bases of Obedience and Revolt*. London: Macmillan.
Moorehead, C. (1998), *Dunant's Dream: War, Switzerland and the History of the Red Cross*. London: Harper Collins.
Morgenstern, F. (1976–77), 'Legality in International Organizations', XLVIII *BYBIL* 241.
(1986), *Legal Problems of International Organisations*. Cambridge: Grotius.

(1989), 'The Convention on the Law of Treaties between States and International Organisations or between International Organisations', in Dinstein, Y. (ed.), *International Law at a Time of Perplexity. Essays in Honour of Shabtai Rosenne*. Dordrecht: Martinus Nijhoff.

Morris, N. (1997), 'Protection Dilemmas and UNHCR's Response: A Personal View from within UNHCR', 9 *IJRL* 492.

Münch, W. and Göttelmann, W. (2002), 'Article 101', in Simma, B. (ed.), *The Charter of the United Nations: A Commentary* (2nd edn.). Oxford University Press.

Muravshik, J. (1991), *Exporting Democracy: Fulfilling America's Destiny*. Washington DC: American Enterprise Institute Press.

Murphy, C. N. (1994), *International Organisation and Industrial Change. Global Governance Since 1850*. Cambridge: Polity Press.

Murphy, J. F. (2004), *The United States and the Rule of Law in International Affairs*. Cambridge University Press.

Murphy, L. (2010), 'International Responsibility', in Besson, S. and Tasioulas, J. (eds.), *The Philosophy of International Law*. Oxford University Press.

Murphy, S. D. (1995), 'Nation-Building: A Look at Somalia', 3 *Tulane Journal of International and Comparative Law* 19.

(1996), *Humanitarian Interventions: The UN in an Evolving World Order*. Philadelphia: University of Pennsylvania Press.

(1999), 'Contemporary Practice of the United States Relating to International Law', 93 *AJIL* 628.

(2000), 'Contemporary Practice of the United States Relating to International Law', 94 *AJIL* 348.

Nabulsi, K. (1999), *Traditions of War: Occupation, Resistance and the Law*. Oxford University Press.

Nader, L. (ed.) (1969), *Law in Culture and Society*. Berkeley: University of California Press.

Nagel, T. (2010), 'What Peter Singer Wants of You', LVII(5) *New York Review of Books* 24, 25 March 2010.

Nelson, R. W. and Roy, M. A. (1986), 'International Law and the US Withholding of payments to International Organizations', 80 *AJIL* 973.

Ni Aolain, F. (1998), 'The Fractured Soul of the Dayton Peace Agreement: A Legal Analysis', 19 *Mich. J. Int. L.* 957.

Nicholson, F. and Twomey, P. (ed.), (1999) *Refugee Rights and Realities*. Cambridge University Press.

Nijman, J. E. (2004), *The Concept of International Legal Personality: An Inquiry into the History and Theory of International Law*. The Hague: T. M. C. Asser Press.

Nordic Africa Institute Policy Notes (2009), 'Sexual Exploitation and Abuse by Peacekeeping Operations in Contemporary Africa'. Upsala (available from www.nai.uu.se/publications/series/notes/policy_notes2009-2.pdf).

Noyes, J. (1991), 'Christianity and Late XIX Century British Theories of International Law', in Janis, M. W. (ed.), *The Influence of Religion on the Development of International Law*. Dordrecht: Martinus Nijhoff.

Nozick, R. (1974), *Anarchy, State and Utopia*. Oxford: Basil Blackwell.

Nussbaum, M. C. (1999), *Sex and Social Justice*. Oxford University Press.

N'zatioula Grovogui, S. (1996), *Sovereigns, Quasi Sovereigns, and Africans. Race and Self- Determination Under International Law*. Minneapolis: University of Minnesota Press.

The Observer (1997), 'Military Disgrace: Child Roasted on the Peacekeepers' Pyre', 22 June.

(2000), 'UN Rocked by Flood of Fraud Cases', 3 September.

O'Connell, M. (1999), 'New International Legal Process', 93 *AJIL* 334.

(2000), 'The Role of Soft Law in a Global Order', in Shelton, D. (ed.), *Commitment and Compliance*. Oxford University Press.

Oliver, D (1991), *Government in the United Kingdom: The Search for Accountability, Effectiveness and Citizenship*. Milton Keynes: Open University Press.

O'Neill, W., Rutinwa, B. and Verdirame, G. (2000), 'The Application of the Exclusion Procedure in the Great Lakes', 12 *IJRL* 135.

Oppenheim, L. F. L. (1905), *International Law*. London: Longmans, Green and Co.

(1912), *International Law* (2nd edn.). London: Longmans, Green and Co.

Orford, A. (1997), 'Locating the International: Military and Monetary Interventions after the Cold War', 38 *Harv. Int. L. J.* 443.

OSCE Mission in Kosovo (2003), *Parallel Structures in Kosovo* (available from www.osce.org/documents/mik/2003/10/698_en.pdf).

Oswald, B., Durham, H. and Bates, A. (2010), *Documents on the Law of UN Peace Operations*. Oxford University Press.

Paasivirta, E and Kuijper, P. J. (2005), 'Does One Size Fit All? The European Community and the Responsibility of International Organisations', 36 *Netherlands Yearbook of International Law* 169.

Padover, S. K. (1942), *Wilson's Ideals*. Washington DC: The American Council for Public Affairs.

Palchetti, P. (2002), 'Reactions by the European Union to Breaches of Erga Omnes Obligations', in Cannizzaro, E. (ed.), *The European Union as an Actor in International Relations*. The Hague: Kluwer Law International.

(2007), 'Azioni di forza istituite o autorizzate dalle Nazioni Unite davanti alla Corte europea dei diritti dell' uomo: i casi *Behrami* e *Saramati*', 90 *Riv. It. Dir. Int.* 681.

Pallis, M. (2006) 'The Operation of UNHCR's Accountability Mechanism', 37 *The New York University Journal of International Law and Politics* 869.

Pascal, B. (1961), *Pensées*. Paris: Garnier Frères.

Perlmutter, A. (1971). 'Patrons in the Babylonian Captivity of Clients: UNRWA and World Politics', 25 *Int. Org.* 306.

Perreau-Saussine, A. (2008), 'British Acts of State in English Courts', 78 *BYBIL* 179.

Philipp, C. E. (2005), 'Somalia – A Very Special Case', 9 *Max Planck Yearbook of UN Law* 518.

Phillimore, R. (1879), *Commentaries upon International Law* (3rd edn.). London: Butterworths.

Phuong, C. (2004), *The International Protection of Internally Displaced Persons.* Cambridge University Press.
Physicians for Human Rights (1998), *Report on Afghanistan.* Boston.
Picone, P. (ed.) (1995), *Interventi delle Nazioni Unite e Diritto Internazionale.* Padova: Cedam.
Pictet, J. (1984), 'Les principes fondamentaux de la Croix-Rouge et la Paix', 746 *Int. Rev. R. C.* 79.
Pisillo Mazzeschi, R. (2004), *Esaurimento dei ricorsi interni e diritti umani.* Turin: Giappichelli Editore.
Plato (1997), in Cooper, J. M. (ed.), *Complete Works.* Indianapolis: Hackett.
Plattner, D. (1996), 'ICRC Neutrality and Neutrality in Humanitarian Assistance', 311 *Int. Rev. R.C.* 161.
Plaut, M. (2010), 'Ethiopia Famine Aid "Spent on Weapons"', editor of BBC World Service, broadcast on 3 March 2010 (available from http://news.bbc.co.uk/1/hi/world/africa/8535189.stm).
Pogany, I. (1986), 'Humanitarian Intervention in International Law: The French Intervention in Syria Re-Examined', 35 *ICLQ* 182.
Polman, L. (2010), *War Games: The Story of Aid and War in Modern Times.* London: Viking.
Pontecorvo, C. M. (1995), 'Somalia e Nazioni Unite' in Picone, P. (ed.), *Interventi delle Nazioni Unite e Diritto Internazionale.* Padova: Cedam.
Quinn, G. (1992), 'The General Assembly into the 1990s', in Alston, P. *The United Nations and Human Rights: A Critical Appraisal.* Oxford: Clarendon Press.
Ragazzi, M. (ed.) (2005), *International Responsibility Today: Essays in Memory of Oscar Schachter.* Leiden: Martinus Nijhoff.
Rama-Montaldo, M. (1970), 'International Legal Personality and Implied Powers of International Organisations', in XLIV *BYBIL* 111.
Ramcharan, B. G. (ed.) (1985), *The Right to Life in International Law.* Dordrecht: Martinus Nijhoff.
(1985), 'The Concept and Dimension of the Right to Life', in Ramacharan, B. G. (ed.), *The Right to Life in International Law.* Dordrecht: Martinus Nijhoff.
(1991), 'The Security Council and Humanitarian Emergencies', 9 *Netherlands Quarterly of Human Rights* 19.
Randelzhofer, A. (2002), 'Introduction to Article 2' in Simma, B. (ed.), *The Charter of the United Nations: A Commentary* (2nd edn.). Oxford University Press.
Ratner, S. (1993), 'The Cambodia Settlement Agreements', 87 *AJIL* 1.
Rauschning, D. (2002), 'Article 81' in Simma, B. (ed.), *The Charter of the United Nations: A Commentary* (2nd edn.). Oxford University Press.
Raz, J. (2010), 'Human Rights Without Foundations', in Besson, S. and Tasioulas, J. (eds.), *The Philosophy of International Law.* Oxford University Press.
Reich, N. (1996), 'Judge-made "Europe à la carte": Some Remarks on Recent Conflicts between European and German Constitutional Law Provoked by the Banana Litigation', 7 *EJIL* 103.
Reinisch, A. (1999), Case Note on *Beer and Regan* and *Waite and Kennedy*, 93 *AJIL* 933.

(2000), *International Organizations Before National Courts*. Cambridge University Press.
(2001), 'Securing the Accountability of International Organisations', 7 *Global Governance* 131.
(2009) 'Should Judges Second-Guess the UN Security Council?', 6 *International Organisations Law Review* 257.
(2010), 'Aid or Assistance and Direction and Control between States and International Organisations in the Commission of Internationally Wrongful Acts' (unpublished paper).
Reinsch, P. S. (1909), 'International Administrative Law and National Sovereignty', 3 *AJIL* 1.
(1911), *Public International Unions: Their Work and Organisation. A Study in International Administrative Law*. London: Publication for the World Peace Foundation.
Reka, B. (2003), *UNMIK as International Governance in Post-war Kosova: NATO's Intervention, UN Administration and Kosovar Aspirations*. Skopje: Lagos A.
Reuters (2000), 'Top UN official leaves Iraq, says programme failed', 17 February.
Rieff, D. (2002), *A Bed for the Night: Humanitarianism in Crisis*. New York: Simon & Schuster.
Riphagen, W. (1987), 'From Soft Law to Jus Cogens and Back', 17 *Victoria University of Wellington Law Review* 81.
Risse, T., Ropp, S. C. and Sikkink, K. (eds.) (1999), *The Power of Human Rights: International Norms and Domestic Change*. Cambridge University Press.
Roberts, A. (1993), 'Intervention and Human Rights', 69 *Int. Aff.* 429.
Ross, A. (1969), 'On Self-Reference and a Puzzle in Constitutional Law', 78 *Mind* 1.
Rousseau, J. J. (1997), 'Discourse on the Origin and Foundations of Inequality Among Men', in Gourevitch, V. (ed.), *Rousseau: The Discourses and other early political writings*. Cambridge University Press.
Roy, M. A. (1986), 'US Loyalty Program for Certain UN Employees Declared Unconstitutional', 80 *AJIL* 984.
Russell, F. M. (1926), *The International Government of the Saar*. University of California Press.
Sadurska, R. and Chinkin, C. (1989–1990), 'The Collapse of the International Tin Council: A Case of State Responsibility?' 30 *Virg. J. Int. L.* 845.
Said, E. (2001), *Reflections on Exile*. Cambridge MA: Harvard University Press.
Sands, P. and Klein, P. (2009), *Bowett's Law of International Institutions* (6th edn.). London: Sweet and Maxwell.
Sari, A. (2008), 'Jurisdiction and International Responsibility in Peace Support Operations: The *Behrami* and *Saramati* Cases', 8 *Human Rights Law Review* 151.
Sarooshi, D. (1996), 'The Legal Framework Governing United Nations Subsidiary Organs', LXVII *BYBIL* 413.
(2000), *The United Nations and the Development of Collective Security: the Delegation by the Security Council of its Chapter VII Powers*. Oxford University Press.

Schade, E. (1995), 'Report on experiences with regard to the United Nations peace-keeping forces in Mozambique'. Redd Barna, Norway.
Schermers, H. G. (1988), 'Liability of International Organisations', 1 *Leiden Journal of International Law* 3.
Schermers, H. G. and Blokker, N. M. (2003), *International Institutional Law* (4th edn.). Dordrecht: Martinus Nijhoff.
Schindler, D. (1994), 'Humanitarian Assistance, Humanitarian Interference and International Law', in Macdonald, R. St. J. (ed.), *Essays in Honour of Wang Tieya*. Dordrecht: Kluwer.
Schmalenbach, K. (2006), 'Third Party Liability of International organisations: A Study on Claim Settlement in the Course of Military Operations and International Administrations', 10 *International Peacekeeping: The Yearbook of International Peace Operations* 33.
Schmidt, A. (2003), 'Camps versus Settlements', Forced Migration Online Thematic Guide (available from www.forcedmigration.org/guides/fmo021).
Schnoor, B. A. (2007), 'International Law, the Power of the Purse, and Speaking with One Voice: The Legal Cacophony Created by Withholding U.S. Dues from the United Nations', 92 *Iowa Law Review* 1133.
Schrijver, N. J. (1994), 'Introducing Second Generation Peace-keeping: The Case of Namibia', 6 *African Journal of International and Comparative Law* 1.
Schucking, W. (1908), 'L'organisation internationale', 15 *RGDIP* 15.
Scobbie, I. (1998), 'International Organizations and International Relations', in Dupuy, R. J. (ed.), *A Handbook of International Organizations* (2nd edn.). Dordrecht: Martinus Nijhoff.
Scott, C. (ed.), (2001), *Torture as Tort: Comparative Perspectives on the Development of Transnational Human Rights Litigation*. Oxford: Hart Publishing.
Seidl-Hohenveldern, I. and Rudolph, K. (2002), 'Article 104', in Simma, B. (ed.), *The Charter of the United Nations: A Commentary* (2nd edn.). Oxford University Press.
Sen, A. (1981), *Poverty and Famines: An Essay on Entitlement and Deprivation*. Oxford: Clarendon Press.
Seyersted, F. (1963), *Objective International Personality of Intergovernmental Organisations: Do Their Capacities Really Depend upon the Conventions Establishing Them?* Copenhagen.
(1964), 'International Personality of Intergovernmental Organizations: Do Their Capacities Really Depend upon Their Constitutions?' 4 *Indian J. Int. L.* 1.
(2008), *Common Law of International Organisations*. Leiden-Boston: Martinus Nijhoff.
Shaw, M. N. (1997), *International Law* (4th edn.). Cambridge University Press.
Shawcross, W. (1984), *The Quality of Mercy: Cambodia, Holocaust and Modern Conscience*. London: André Deutsch.
Shelton, D. (1994), 'The Participation of Non-governmental Organisations in International Judicial Proceedings', 88 *AJIL* 611.
(ed.) (2000), *Commitment and Compliance*. Oxford University Press.

(2005), *Remedies in International Human Rights Law* (2nd edn.). Oxford University Press.

Shihata, I. (1991), *The World Bank in a Changing World*. Vol. I. Dordrecht: Martinus Nijhoff.

(1994), *The World Bank Inspection Panel*. Oxford University Press.

Shraga, D. (2000), 'UN Peacekeeping Operations: Applicability of International Humanitarian Law and Responsibility for Operations-Related Damage', 94 *AJIL* 406.

Shyla, V. (1996) 'Impartiality in United Nations Peace-Keeping', 9 *Leiden Journal of International Law* 63.

Siedentop, L. (2001), *Democracy in Europe*. London: Penguin.

Simes. D. K. (2003), 'America's Imperial Dilemma', 82 *Foreign Affairs* (Nov/Dec) 91.

Simma, B. (ed.) (2002), *The Charter of the United Nations: A Commentary* (2nd edn.). Oxford University Press.

Singer, M. (1995), 'Jurisdictional Immunity of International Organizations: Human Rights and Functional Necessity Concerns', 36 Virg. J. Int. L. 53.

Singer, P. (2009), *The Life You Can Save: Acting Now to End World Poverty*. New York: Random House.

Skran, C. (1995), *Refugees in Inter-War Europe*. Oxford: Clarendon Press.

Lord Slynn of Hadley (1993), 'What is a European Community Judge?' 52 *Cambridge Law Journal* 234.

Skubiszewski, K. (1989), 'Implied Powers of International Organisations', in Dinstein, Y. and Tabory, M. (eds.), *International Law at a Time of Perplexity: Essays in Honour of Shabtai Rosenne*. Dordrecht: Martinus Nijhoff.

Smith, M. (2004), 'Warehousing Refugees: A Denial of Rights, a Waste of Humanity' (available from www.refugees.org/data/wrs/04/pdf/38–56.pdf).

Sontag, S. (1991), *Under the Sign of Saturn*. New York: Anchor Books Doubleday.

Sorel, J. M. (1992), 'La Somalie et les Nations Unies', 38 *AFDI* 61.

Sphere Project (2004), *Humanitarian Charter and Minimum Standards in Disaster Response*. London (available from www.sphereproject.org).

Spijkers, O. (2009), 'The Immunity of the United Nations in Relation to the Genocide in Srebenica in the Eyes of a Dutch District Court', 13 *Journal of International Peacekeeping* 197.

Spiry, E. (1998), 'Interventions Humanitaires et Interventions d'Humanité: La Pratique Francaise face au Droit International', 102 *RGDIP* 407.

Stahn, C. (2007), 'Responsibility to Protect: Political Rhetoric or Emerging Legal Norm', 101(1) *AJIL* 99.

(2008), *The Law and Practice of International Territorial Administration*. Cambridge University Press.

Stoppard, T. (2002), *The Coast of Utopia Part III: Salvage*. London: Faber and Faber.

Strange, S. (1996), *The Retreat of the State. The Diffusion of Power in the World Economy*. Cambridge University Press.

Szasz, P. (1991), 'The Role of the UN Secretary General: Some Legal Aspects', 24 *New York University Journal of International Law and Politics* 161.
Szurek, S. (2010), 'Circumstances Precluding Wrongfulness in the ILC Articles on State Responsibility: Distress', in Crawford, J., Pellet, A. and Olleson, S. (eds.), *The Law of International Responsibility*. Oxford University Press.
Takkenberg, L. (1998), *The Status of Palestinian Refugees in International Law*. Oxford: Clarendon Press.
Talmon, S. (2005), 'Responsibility of International Organisations: Does the European Community Require Special Treatment?' in Ragazzi, M. (ed.), *International Responsibility Today: Essays in Memory of Oscar Schachter*. Leiden: Martinus Nijhoff.
Temple Lang, J. (1997), 'The Duties of National Courts under Community Constitutional Law', 22 *ELR* 3.
Teson, F. R. (1988), *Humanitarian Intervention: An Inquiry into Law and Morality*. Dobbs Ferry: Transnational Publishers.
Thirlway, H. (1991), 'The Law and Procedure of the International Court of Justice 1960–1989', 62(III) *BYBIL*.
The Times (2004), 'Sex scandal in Congo threatens to engulf UN's peacekeepers', December.
Tocqueville, A. de (2003), *Democracy in America* Vol. II, in Kramnick, I. (ed.), *Democracy in America and Two Essays on America*. London: Penguin.
Tomuschat, C. (2010), 'The Responsibility of Other Entities: Private Individuals', in Crawford, J., Pellet, A., Olleson, S. (eds.), *The Law of International Responsibility* (Oxford University Press, 2010).
Trebilcock, A. M. (1985), 'Slavery', in Bernhardt, R. (ed.), *Encyclopaedia of Public International Law* Vol. VIII. Amsterdam: North-Holland Pub. Co.
Tuitt, P. (1996), *False Images: The Law's Construction of the Refugee*. London: Pluto Press.
Tunkin, G. I. (1966), 'The Legal Nature of the United Nations', 119(III) *RC* 1.
Tzanakopoulos, A. (2009), 'An Effective Remedy for Josef K: Canadian Judge Defies Security Council Sanctions through Interpretations', 19 June (available from www.ejiltalk.org/an-effective-remedy-for-josef-k-canadian-judge-defies-security-council-sanctions-through-interpretation).
(2010) 'Domestic Court Reactions to UN Security Council Sanctions', to appear in Reinisch, A. (ed.), *Challenging Acts of International Organisations before National Courts*. Oxford University Press.
UK Ministry of Defence (2004), *The Manual of the Law of Armed Conflict*. Oxford University Press.
UN Department of Humanitarian Affairs (1996), *Afghanistan Weekly Update No. 191*, 6 November.
UNHCR (2000), *The State of the World's Refugees*. Oxford University Press.
UNHCR and Save the Children-UK (2002), 'Sexual Violence and Exploitation: The Experience of Refugee Children in Guinea, Liberia and

Sierra Leone' (available from www.savethechildren.org.uk/en/docs/sexual_violence_and_exploitation.pdf).
UNICEF (1994), *Children of War: Wandering Alone in Southern Sudan*.
UN News Centre (2005), 'Peacekeepers' sexual abuse of local girls continuing in DR of Congo, UN finds', 7 January.
UN Office of Legal Affairs (1972), 'Possible Accession of Intergovernmental Organisations to the Geneva Conventions for the Protection of War Victims', *UN Juridical Yearbook* 153.
US Committee for Refugees and Migrants (2009), 'Statement Calling for Solutions to End the Warehousing of Refugees' (available from www.refugees.org/uploadedFiles/Investigate/Anti_Warehousing/statement.pdf).
Valticos, N. (1998) 'Contrôle', in Dupuy, R. J. (ed.), *A Handbook on International Organizations* (2nd edn.). Dordrecht: Martinus Nijhoff.
Van Damme, W. (1995), 'Do Refugees Belong in Camps? Experiences from Goma and Guinea', 346 *The Lancet* 360.
(1999), 'How Liberian and Sierra Leonean Refugees Settled in the Forest Region of Guinea (1990–1996)', 12 *J. Ref. St.* 36.
Van der Veur, P. W. (1964), 'The United Nations in West Irian: A Critique', 18 *Int. Org.* 53.
Väyrynen, R. (2000), 'The Dilemma of Voluntary Funding: Political Interests and Institutional Reforms', Paper presented at the International Conference 'Commemorating UNHCR at 50: Past, Present and Future of Refugee Assistance', Columbia University, New York, 16–18 May.
Verdirame, G. (1999), 'Human Rights and Refugees: The Case of Kenya', 12 *Journal of Refugee Studies* 54.
(2001), 'Testing the Effectiveness of International Norms: UN Humanitarian Assistance and Sexual Apartheid in Afghanistan', 23(3) *Hum. Rts. Q.* 733.
(2007), '"The Divided West": International Lawyers in Europe and America', 18(3) *European Journal of International Law* 553.
(2008), 'Breaches of the European Convention on Human Rights Resulting from the Conduct of International Organisations', 2 *EHRLR* 209.
(2008), 'Human Rights in Wartime: A Framework for Analysis', 6 *EHRLR* 689.
Verdirame, G. and Harrell-Bond, B. E. (2005), *Rights in Exile: Janus-Faced Humanitarianism*. Oxford: Berghahn Books.
Verdirame, G. and Wickremasinghe, C. (2001), 'Responsibility and Liability for Violations of Human Rights in the Course of UN Field Operations', in Scott, C. (ed.), *Torture as Tort*. Oxford: Hart Publishing.
Verdross, A. and Simma, B. (1984), *Universelles Völkerrecht: Theorie und Praxis* (3rd edn.). Berlin: Duncker und Humblot.
Verhoeven, J. (2000) *Droit International Public*. Brussels: De Boek & Larcier.
Viano, C. A. (1990), *Teorie etiche contemporanee*. Turin: Bollati Boringhieri.
Waldock, H. (1964), 'Third Report on the Law of Treaties', ILC Yearbook Vol. 2.
Walkup, M. (1997), *Policy and Behavior in Humanitarian Organizations: The Institutional Origins of Operational Dysfunction*. PhD Thesis, University of Florida.

The Washington Post (1993), 'Somalis' Imprisonment Poses Questions about UN Role', 7 November.

(1997), 'Canadian Panel Blames Brass For Army Misdeeds in Somalia; Violence linked to "Leadership Failures"', 3 July.

Watson, G. R. (1993), 'Constitutionalism, Judicial Review, and the World Court', 34 *Harv. Int. L. J.* 1.

The Watson Institute (2006), 'Strengthening Targeted Sanctions through Fair and Clear Procedures', Brown University, annexed to UN Doc. A/60/887-S/2006/331 (available from www.watsoninstitute.org/pub/Strengthening_Targeted_Sanctions.pdf).

(2009), 'Addressing Challenges to Targeted Sanctions: An Update of the "Watson Report"', Brown University (available from www.watsoninstitute.org/pub/2009_10_targeted_sanctions.pdf).

Weatherill, S. and Beaumont, P. (1995), *EC Law* (3rd edn.). London: Penguin.

Weber, M. (1922), *Wirtschaft und Gesellschaft*. Tübingen: Verlag Von J.C.B. Mohr (Paul Siebeck).

(1999), *Economia e Società*. Turin: Edizioni di Comunità.

Weiler, J. H. H. (2008), 'Editorial', 19 *EJIL* 896.

Weiner, M. (1998), 'The Clash of Norms: Dilemmas in Refugee Policies', Paper presented at the Conference on the Growth of Forced Migration, hosted by the Refugee Studies Programme at Wadham College, Oxford, 25–27 March.

Weiss, T. and Korn, D. (2006), *Internal Displacement – Conceptualization and its consequences*. New York: Routledge.

Wellens, K. (2002), *Remedies against International Organisations*. Cambridge University Press.

Weller, M. (1997), 'The Relativity of Humanitarian Neutrality and Impartiality', *American Society of International Law – Proceedings of the 91st Annual Conference* 441.

(2009), *Contested Statehood: Kosovo's Struggle for Independence*. Oxford University Press

Westlake, J. (1904–1907), *International Law*. Cambridge University Press.

White, N. (1996), 'The UN Charter and Peacekeeping Forces: Constitutional Issues', 3 *International Peacekeeping* 43.

(1997), *Keeping the Peace: The United Nations and the Maintenance of International Peace and Security*. Manchester University Press.

(1999), 'To Review or not to Review? The Lockerbie Cases before the World Court', 12 *Leiden J. Int. L.* 401.

(2005), *The Law of International Organisations* (2nd edn.). Manchester University Press.

White, N. and MacLeod, S. (2008), 'EU Operations and Private Military Contractors: Issues of Corporate and Institutional Responsibility', 19 *EJIL* 965.

Wiessner, S. and Willard, A. R. (1999), 'Policy-Oriented Jurisprudence and Human Rights Abuses in Internal Conflict: Toward a World Public Order of Human Dignity', 93 *AJIL* 316.

Wilde, R. (1998), '*Quis Custodiet Ipsos Custodes?* Why and How UNHCR Governance of "Development" Refugee Camps Should be Subject to International Human Rights Law', 1 *Yale H. R. Dev. L. J.* 5.

(2001), 'The Complex Role of the Legal Adviser when International Organizations Administer Territory', *American Society of International Law – Proceedings of the 95th Annual Meeting.*

(2008), *International Territorial Administration: How Trusteeship and the Civilizing Mission Never Went Away.* Oxford University Press.

Williams, D. (1987), *The Specialised Agencies and the UN: The System in Crisis.* London: C. Hurst.

Williams, E. (1944), *Capitalism and Slavery.* Chapel Hill: University of North Carolina Press.

Wilson, R. A. (ed.) (1997), *Human Rights, Culture and Context: Anthropological Perspectives.* London: Pluto Press.

Wolfrum, R. and Kojima, C. (eds.) (2010), *Solidarity; A Structural Principle of International Law.* Heidelberg: Springer.

Wood, Sir M. (2006), 'The Sir Hersch Lauterpacht Memorial Lectures: The UN Security Council and International Law' (available from www.lcil.cam.ac.uk/lectures/2006_sir_michael_wood.php).

Woods, N. (1999), 'Good Governance in International Organizations', 5 *Global Governance* 39.

Yuval-Davis, N. (1997), *Gender and Nation.* London: Sage.

Zacklin, R. (2002), 'United Nations Management of Legal Issues', in Howard, J. and Oswald, B. (eds.), *The Rule of Law on Peace Operations: A: 'Challenges of Peace Operations' Project Conference.* Melbourne: Asia-Pacific Centre for Military Law.

Zieck, M. (2006), *UNHCR's Worldwide Presence in the Field.* Nijmegen: Wolf Legal Publishers.

Zuleeg, M. (1997), 'The European Constitution under Constitutional Constraints: The German Scenario', 22 *ELR* 19.

Zwanenburg, M. (2005), *Accountability of Peace Support Operations.* Leiden: Martinus Nijhoff.

Index

CAMBRIDGE STUDIES IN INTERNATIONAL AND COMPARATIVE LAW

Books in the series

The UN and Human Rights: Who Guards the Guardians?
Guglielmo Verdirame

Sovereign Defaults before International Courts and Tribunals
Michael Waibel

Making the Law of the Sea: A Study in the Development of International Law
James Harrison

'Fair and Equitable Treatment' in International Investment Law
Roland Kläger

Legal Aspects of Transition from Illegal Territorial Regimes in International Law
Yaël Ronen

Access to Asylum: International Refugee Law and the Globalisation of Migration Control
Thomas Gammeltoft-Hansen

Trading Fish, Saving Fish: The Interaction between Regimes in International Law
Margaret Young

The Individual in the International Legal System: State-Centrism, History and Change in International Law
Kate Parlett

The Participation of States in International Organisations: The Role of Human Rights and Democracy
Alison Duxbury

Theatre of the Rule of Law: The Theory, History and Practice of Transnational Legal Intervention
Stephen Humphreys

'Armed Attack' and Article 51 of the UN Charter: Evolutions in Customary Law and Practice
Tom Ruys

Science and Risk Regulation in International Law: The Role of Science, Uncertainty and Values
Jacqueline Peel

The Public International Law Theory of Hans Kelsen: Believing in Universal Law
Jochen von Bernstorff

Vicarious Liability in Tort: A Comparative Perspective
Paula Giliker

Legal Personality in International Law
Roland Portmann

Legitimacy and Legality in International Law: An Interactional Account
Jutta Brunnée and Stephen J. Toope

The Concept of Non-International Armed Conflict in International Humanitarian Law
Anthony Cullen

The Challenge of Child Labour in International Law
Franziska Humbert

Shipping Interdiction and the Law of the Sea
Douglas Guilfoyle

International Courts and Environmental Protection
Tim Stephens

Legal Principles in WTO Disputes
Andrew D. Mitchell

War Crimes in Internal Armed Conflicts
Eve La Haye

Humanitarian Occupation
Gregory H. Fox

The International Law of Environmental Impact Assessment: Process, Substance and Integration
Neil Craik

The Law and Practice of International Territorial Administration: Versailles, Iraq and Beyond
Carsten Stahn

Cultural Products and the World Trade Organization
Tania Voon

United Nations Sanctions and the Rule of Law
Jeremy Farrall

National Law in WTO Law: Effectiveness and Good Governance in the World Trading System
Sharif Bhuiyan

The Threat of Force in International Law
Nikolas Stürchler

Indigenous Rights and United Nations Standards
Alexandra Xanthaki

International Refugee Law and Socio-Economic Rights
Michelle Foster

The Protection of Cultural Property in Armed Conflict
Roger O'Keefe

Interpretation and Revision of International Boundary Decisions
Kaiyan Homi Kaikobad

Multinationals and Corporate Social Responsibility: Limitations and Opportunities in International Law
Jennifer A. Zerk

Judiciaries within Europe: A Comparative Review
John Bell

Law in Times of Crisis: Emergency Powers in Theory and Practice
Oren Gross and Fionnuala Ní Aoláin

Vessel-Source Marine Pollution: The Law and Politics of International Regulation
Alan Tan

Enforcing Obligations *Erga Omnes* in International Law
Christian J. Tams

Non-Governmental Organisations in International Law
Anna-Karin Lindblom

Democracy, Minorities and International Law
Steven Wheatley

Prosecuting International Crimes: Selectivity and the International Law Regime
Robert Cryer

Compensation for Personal Injury in English, German and Italian Law: A Comparative Outline
Basil Markesinis, Michael Coester, Guido Alpa, Augustus Ullstein

Dispute Settlement in the UN Convention on the Law of the Sea
Natalie Klein

The International Protection of Internally Displaced Persons
Catherine Phuong

Imperialism, Sovereignty and the Making of International Law
Antony Anghie

Necessity, Proportionality and the Use of Force by States
Judith Gardam

International Legal Argument in the Permanent Court of International Justice: The Rise of the International Judiciary
Ole Spiermann

Great Powers and Outlaw States: Unequal Sovereigns in the International Legal Order
Gerry Simpson

Local Remedies in International Law
C. F. Amerasinghe

Reading Humanitarian Intervention: Human Rights and the Use of Force in International Law
Anne Orford

Conflict of Norms in Public International Law: How WTO Law Relates to Other Rules of Law
Joost Pauwelyn

Transboundary Damage in International Law
Hanqin Xue

European Criminal Procedures
Edited by Mireille Delmas-Marty and John Spencer

The Accountability of Armed Opposition Groups in International Law
Liesbeth Zegveld

Sharing Transboundary Resources: International Law and Optimal Resource Use
Eyal Benvenisti

International Human Rights and Humanitarian Law
René Provost

Remedies Against International Organisations
Karel Wellens

Diversity and Self-Determination in International Law
Karen Knop

The Law of Internal Armed Conflict
Lindsay Moir

International Commercial Arbitration and African States: Practice, Participation and Institutional Development
Amazu A. Asouzu

The Enforceability of Promises in European Contract Law
James Gordley

International Law in Antiquity
David J. Bederman

Money Laundering: A New International Law Enforcement Model
Guy Stessens

On Civil Procedure
J. A. Jolowicz

Trusts: A Comparative Study
Maurizio Lupoi

The Right to Property in Commonwealth Constitutions
Tom Allen

International Organizations Before National Courts
August Reinisch

The Changing International Law of High Seas Fisheries
Francisco Orrego Vicuña

Trade and the Environment: A Comparative Study of EC and US Law
Damien Geradin

Unjust Enrichment: A Study of Private Law and Public Values
Hanoch Dagan

Religious Liberty and International Law in Europe
Malcolm D. Evans

Ethics and Authority in International Law
Alfred P. Rubin

Sovereignty Over Natural Resources: Balancing Rights and Duties
Nico Schrijver

The Polar Regions and the Development of International Law
Donald R. Rothwell

Fragmentation and the International Relations of Micro-States: Self-determination and Statehood
Jorri Duursma

Principles of the Institutional Law of International Organizations
C. F. Amerasinghe

www.ingramcontent.com/pod-product-compliance
Ingram Content Group UK Ltd.
Pitfield, Milton Keynes, MK11 3LW, UK
UKHW032346160225
455049UK00011BA/318

9 781107 617476